DATE DUE

ILL 2/09		

Demco, Inc. 38-293

Grenada
A History of its People

Beverley A. Steele

MACMILLAN
CARIBBEAN

Macmillan Education
Between Towns Road, Oxford OX4 3PP
A division of Macmillan Publishers Limited
Companies and representatives throughout the world

www.macmillan-caribbean.com

ISBN 0 333 93053 3

First published 2003

Designed by Sue Clarke
Typeset by EXPO Holdings, Malaysia
Illustrated by Tek–Art
Cover design by Gary Fielder at AC Design
Cover illustration:
View of the town and harbour of St George's, Grenada, by Captain
H.A. Turner, Royal Artillery, 1851. First published by Ackerman
& Co., London, 1852. Courtesy of the Grenada National Museum.

Printed and bound in Malaysia

2007   2006   2005   2004   2003
10   9   8   7   6   5   4   3   2   1

Contents

List of Illustrations

French – as well as the British – used this form of capital punishment until the guillotine became popular in France in the 1790s.

17 The Right Hon. George Macartney, who was Governor of Grenada when the French retook the island in 1779

18 Paraclete Estate, the Home family estate, where Lieutenant-Governor Ninian Home first received news of the outbreak of the Fédon Revolution.

19 A contemporary aerial view of Gouyave, the town where Governor Ninian Home landed and was taken prisoner by Fédon in 1795

20 Artist's impression of Julien Fédon with his white stallion. No likeness survives of Fédon, nor is there a contemporary description of this famous French Grenadian.

21 George Bain was born forty years after Fédon of a white father and a black mother. Did Fédon look like him?

22 York House, which has been the seat of the Grenadian legislature from the early nineteenth century. The previous House of Assembly is believed to have been on the site of the present Knox House, near Fort George.

23 The National Museum of Grenada occupies one of the oldest structures in Grenada. In the seventeenth century it served as a prison. The building exhibits many interesting architectural features, including French iron balconies and an indoor courtyard.

24 The Georgian buildings of St George's and the schooners which link Grenada and other islands form an interesting backdrop for this portrait of Jennifer Hosten, the Miss Grenada who became Miss World in 1972.

25 A cocoa plantation owner's house

26 A cocoa-drying house

27 Cocoa beans drying in the sun

28 An old waterwheel – a reminder of the days of 'King Sugar' in Grenada

29 Washerwomen at St John's river, around the end of the nineteenth century. Peasant huts can be seen in the background.

30 A view of the Carenage and St George's town, c.1900

31 A basket maker, around the end of the nineteenth century

32 Governor Walter Sendall, Governor of Grenada between 1885 and 1889, who was acclaimed by Grenadians as 'the Prince of West Indian Governors'. It was at his direction that the Sendall Tunnel was built to ease the passage of porters going from 'Bay Town' to St George's proper.

33 Workers collecting nutmegs, around 1880

34 The Didier family, about 1897. The grandparents are surrounded by their grandchildren who were left in their care when their parents – the couple to the right of the picture – emigrated to work on the Panama Canal. They never returned. The senior Mr Didier was a

master carpenter who had migrated to Grenada from Barbados. The smallest child, Ruby Didier, later lived a quietly distinguished life on Tyrrel Street, St George's

76 The memorial erected in St George's Cemetery by friends of Maurice Bishop. The remains of Maurice Bishop and those killed with him at fort George have never been recovered.

77 An armed soldier of the US Army on guard over some of the ammunition discovered at Frequente after the fall of the People's Revolutionary Government

78 A US Army tank travels around Lagoon Road, St George's

79 Herbert Blaize, the first Prime Minister of Grenada after the People's Revolution, greets Queen Elizabeth II and Prince Philip during their visit to Grenada in 1986

80 Sir Paul Scoon remained the Governor General and representative of the Queen throughout the revolution. He retired from the post in 1992. He is seen here with George Bush, Vice President of the United States, on his visit to Grenada in March 1985.

81 Keith Mitchell, Prime Minister of Grenada since 1995, and the Vice Chancellor of the University of the West Indies, the Hon. Rex Nettleford, at the Grenada Campus, UWI, during the university's Fiftieth Anniversary celebrations in 1998

List of Maps

Acknowledgements

The author wishes to thank her employers, the University of the West Indies, for facilitating this research, particularly through the provision of periods of leave of absence that enabled uninterrupted blocks of time for writing, and permitted research to be carried out in the United Kingdom and in Jamaica. I am particularly indebted to the Vice Chancellor, the Hon. Rex Nettleford, and Pro Vice Chancellor Lawrence D. Carrington for their encouragement and support, Professor Emeritus Woodville K. Marshall for his invaluable comments on the draft manuscript, and to the many others who provided extremely useful comments, especially William Steele, Savitri and Leslie St John, Curtis Jacobs, Norma Sinclair, Margaret Payne, Claudia Halley, Lennox Honychurch, Peter Harris and Joseph Palacio.

My thanks also go to those who provided me with first-hand accounts of contemporary events, chief of whom were Nellie Payne, Alice McIntyre, Ruby Didier, Barry Renwick, Patrick Compton and Josephine Davis.

For the photographs and illustrations I am very grateful to Jim Rudln, Government House, the Grenada National Museum, Nellie Payne, Paul Slinger, Joan Sylvester, Esmai Scoon, Trish Bethany, Elinor Lashley, Leo Cromwell, Rosa Hughes and Alec and Colina Bain.

It would be remiss of me to neglect to thank all those who maintained a keen interest in this project, especially the staff of the Grenada Centre of the University of the West Indies, Nick Gillard and Diana Meadowcroft of Macmillan, copy-editor Anstice Hughes, Jean Baptiste of Sea Change Bookshop, St George's, and, last but no means least, Percy and Gloria Phillips who opened their home to me on my research trip to London.

Beverley A. Steele

A Note to Readers

This book is primarily written for the people of Grenada who longed for an easy-to-read overview of the history of their island which would help them to understand the events of the past that have shaped the Grenada of today, and also for a younger generation of Grenadians who need to be introduced to their historical heritage. It was written to be enjoyed as a story of Grenada and its resilient people. It is my hope that this book will succeed in informing, delighting and enriching all who delve into its pages to discover more about themselves and their country. I also hope that this book will be used as a springboard for future detailed research by Grenadians into aspects of their history. There is so much more to learn, and so much more to discover!

To assist the reader, and to avoid interrupting the text, notes have been placed at the ends of chapters, and sources have been cited as briefly as possible. Books and articles are referred to by the author's name, date of publication where there is more than one by that author, and page reference. Full publication details may be found in the Bibliography. Other documents, reports, letters, and unpublished sources are cited in full in the notes. The Bibliography gives details of where such sources, or copies of them, may be found.

This book is dedicated to all Grenadians, but particularly to those who have contributed to the building of our homeland: the proud Kalinago and Galibi, the nameless slaves and workers who cleared the forests and established our agriculture, the French-speaking Grenadians such as Julien Fédon and Roumé de St Laurent, those of English extraction such as William Wells, and the builders of our modern nation – Galwey Donovan, T. Albert Marryshow, Eric Gairy and Maurice Bishop.

Finally I would like this book to be a tribute to the historians who have previously written of Grenada, and especially to pay tribute to the pioneering and fine scholarship of Father Raymond P. Devas OP, and the seminal works of George Brizan, Edward Cox and Pat Emmanuel. Many other authors whose books, memorials, newspaper articles and letters give us glimpses of the quality of life and details of events of yesteryear also enriched the literature on Grenada.

Prelude: Grenada – Land we Love

The story of Grenada is about an island so beautiful that it inspires poets like Grenadian Paul Keens-Douglas to write love songs to it.[1] This island is so desirable that nations and peoples have fought each other for it. It is so fickle that one day it provides abundance, and at other times people starve. Many fortunes have been made in Grenada, but as many fortunes have also been lost.

The story of the people, settlements, battles, insurgencies and colourful culture that is part of Grenada's past is also the foundation of Grenada's present culture and society. We cannot properly understand one without sufficient knowledge of the other. However, the land is the backdrop to the drama, and geography has played its part in the shaping of events. Before the story begins, then, let the scene be set with a look at this land of heart-break and happiness.

The state of Grenada is not a single island, but several islands of exceptional beauty. The three largest are known today as Grenada, Carriacou and Petit Martinique, although these have been called other names by other peoples at other times. The state of Grenada is the second southernmost of the island group known as the Lesser Antilles, the twin-island Republic of Trinidad and Tobago being south of Grenada. With St Vincent, St Lucia and Dominica, Grenada belongs to a yet smaller grouping called the Windward Islands.

Grenada is situated between latitude 12.3 and 11.5 degrees north and longitude 61.2 and 61.3 degrees west. The islands lie 90 miles north of both Trinidad and Venezuela, and 70 miles south of St Vincent. Between Grenada and St Vincent are the Grenadines – a chain of tiny islands and cays. These offshore islands are dissimilar geologically – some are volcanic and craggy, covered with trees and scrub, while others are coral cays. A few are inhabited, while some of the beautiful coral cays simply provide occasional anchorage for small craft and their occupants. Only three of the Grenada Grenadine Islands are inhabited – Carriacou is the largest. It is two and a half miles wide, and seven and half miles long with approximately 6000 inhabitants. Petit Martinique is a little less than two square miles, with a population of approximately 800 people. The Isle de Ronde is

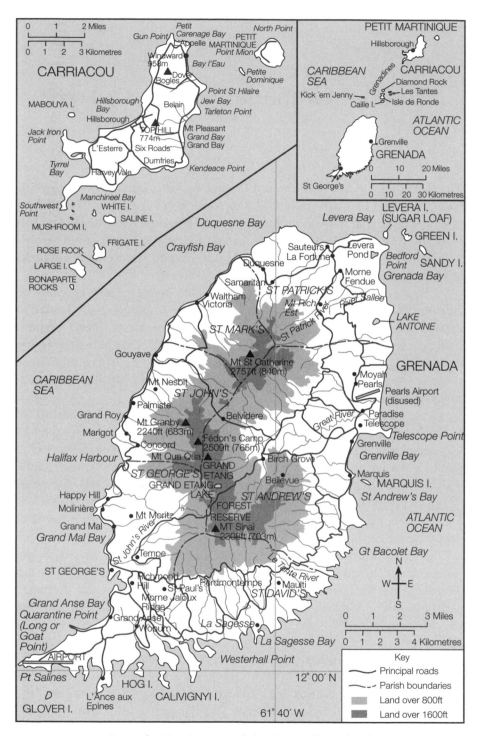

Grenada, Carriacou and the Grenadine Islands

inhabited by about twenty fisher folk, which is eighteen more than in 1817 when one white man called David Young, and his 50-year-old slave called Catherine, lived on that island.[2] Carriacou is 27 miles by sea from Grenada, as far as Britain is from France.

Throughout the early history of Grenada and up to 1783,[3] the entire string of Grenadine Islands was counted as a unit with Grenada. The division of the Grenadines by Great Britain in 1783 artificially divided an island people accustomed to roam up and down the chain without restrictions. Even though Carriacou, Petit Martinique, Isle de Ronde and all the rocks and cays in between were allocated to Grenada, and Union, Canouan, Mustique, Bequa and all the others between Petit Martinique and St Vincent allocated to St Vincent, the people all still regard themselves as Grenadine Islanders, ignoring at times the necessities for passports and immigration controls. It is nothing unusual for a group of Carriacouans to set off by boat for a wedding in Union, and return without ever having encountered immigration authorities. Inhabitants of the Grenadines from pre-Columbus days to the present have used the sea as a highway, and have maintained close contact with each other and with the larger islands. Besides being neighbours and kinsfolk, they have served as traders, fishermen, ship builders and sailors.

The sea between Grenada and St Vincent abounds with coral reefs. These may circle the islands and cays or not be associated with an island at all, lying just submerged by the waves. These reefs teem with many varieties of tropical fish, and the importance of the Grenadines as a lucrative fishing ground has always been recognized. The area is also very beautiful and pleasurable to sail though, and it is not surprising that it is has become one of the most famous yachting areas in this hemisphere, where the craft of the rich and famous are seen regularly, along with the local boats and vessels which are really the sea-going taxis and trucks of the Caribbean Sea. Approximately halfway between Grenada and Carriacou is the Kick 'em Jenny submarine volcano. This volcano is highly active and is constantly monitored by the Seismic Research Centre of the University of the West Indies.

The main island of the state of Grenada, which is also called Grenada, is about 21 miles long and 12 miles across at its greatest width, an area of 120 square miles. To differentiate between the state, comprising Grenada, Carriacou and Petit Martinique, and Grenada Island, the main island will be called Grenada, and the other islands given their names when they are specifically referred to. This will be important in this narrative because the histories of Grenada Island and Carriacou are slightly different.

The shape of the main island of Grenada is roughly oval, if we exclude the Point Salines Peninsula that juts towards the southwest. Grenada has almost no flat land. The mountains dominate all other physical features. The main mountain ridge runs through Grenada slightly more to the west than the centre. Thus, the slopes are gentler to the east and the coastal plains a little wider on that side. From this main ridge of mountains, cross-ridges run out to the sea on both sides. Between these lie sheltered valleys of great beauty and fertility. Because they rise so steeply, the mountains seem taller than they are. Only five of the peaks are over 2000 feet, with Mount St Catherine being the tallest at 2749 feet (ft), followed by Fédon's Camp[4] (2512 ft), Mount Qua Qua (2412 ft) Mount Sinai (2359 ft) and Southeast Mountain (2359 ft).[5] Carriacou and Petit Martinique also exhibit very rugged terrain.

All the major towns of Grenada except one are on the coast. St George's is the capital, with Grenville and Sauteurs being the next largest population centres. Hillsborough is the main population centre of Carriacou. These and the other towns of Grenada began as seaports, for until the beginning of this century sea transportation between the parts of Grenada was often the only means of travelling from one place to another, and for transporting produce, mail and other commodities. The roads that did exist were unpaved and were very soon churned into mud whenever rain fell. Grenada's roads were and are precipitous, both along the coast and in the interior. They wind themselves around the edge of mountains and hang off the edge of sea cliffs. However cautiously some of the roads need to be traversed, they form an excellent road system. As the road network developed, ribbon development took place. Houses have been built along the roads that traverse Grenada, usually one-deep once the urban area has been left behind. Housing clusters form villages at the crossroads.

Fifty-two main rivers water Grenada, along with their tributaries and smaller streams. The largest river is the Great River, which has at least three sources. It meanders diagonally through St Andrew's and empties into the Atlantic Ocean near Grenville. Several rivers drop over cliffs into spectacular waterfalls. Of these falls the best known are Concord Falls in St John's, Annandale Falls in St George's, and Mount Carmel and St Margaret Falls in St Andrew's.

Grenada's coastline is rugged, although there are some long bays with excellent beaches. In the south and west, the northeast trade winds have driven the sea between the ridges, eroding the alluvial earth and producing narrow bays between narrow fingers of land. This has given the southeast side of Grenada's coast the appearance of mini-fjords. Several of these bays are protected by offshore islands, three of the largest being Hog Island, Glover Island, and Calivigny Island. Three other offshore islands are situated just off the north coast of Grenada. These are Sandy Island, Green

Island and Sugar Loaf Island. The first two are important nesting grounds for turtles.

The geographical position of Grenada and its mountainous terrain has influenced every aspect of its history. Its position in the southern Caribbean explains why the island was one of the first to be inhabited by Amerindians from South America who were seeking new homelands. Its mountainous nature explains why it was one of the last to be colonized by Europeans, even though it was such a convenient stopping place on the journey to South America. Once the aboriginal population was no longer a threat to European settlement, Grenada became a valued possession of whichever European nation occupied it, and a coveted prize of those who did not. Its desirability decreed that it was well bastioned, and garrisoned by soldiers who would defend it in turn from the Kalinago and Black Caribs from the other Windward Islands, the Spanish, the English, the French, the Dutch, the Germans, the Americans, and the Cubans together with their Russian allies. The names of the towns, villages, rivers and mountains also reflect Grenada's multi-cultural heritage. Some are called after those who conquered or settled the island – Duquesne, Marquis, Darbeau, Laborie, Melville, Young, Scott. Others describe, as they always did, the characteristics of the terrain – Beausejour, Beaulieu, Morne Rouge, Perdmontemps, Grand Anse, River Sallee, Apres Tout.

Grenada's Geology

Grenada and the Grenadines are remnants of a larger island that was above water during the Miocene Period when the sea was between 50 and 150 fathoms lower than it is today. This submerged island is known today as the Grenada Bank. Almost all of the Eastern Caribbean island chain was formed by volcanic action and the movement of the sections of the earth's crust, called tectonic plates, which float on the molten rock of the earth's core. Throughout the history of the earth, these plates have rubbed against each other, buckled and otherwise competed for space. During the Miocene Period, about 26 million years ago, the Atlantic Plate was forced under the Caribbean Plate into the hot mantle of the earth. The Atlantic Plate melted, and the liquid rock under pressure was forced through weak spots in the Caribbean Plate. The result produced a string of volcanoes. As the volcanoes broke the surface of the sea, they built up land through lava flows and ash. As the tectonic plates continued their restless activity and pressed into each other, sections of the seabed limestone were forced so high above their usual level that they become the caps of some of the mountains.

Grenada is one of the islands formed partly by volcanic activity. The rest of the island was built up by coral formation, and sedimentary rocks. As a result of the upheavals of the earth, limestone caps several of its mountains, and limestone outcrops appear in other unexpected places. There are other interesting geological features in Grenada's landscape, such as Grenada's white and black sand beaches, and features that show the tremendous power of the natural forces that contributed to the formation of the island.

At least forty craters of dormant volcanoes form a crescent across Grenada, starting from the southwest and running north to end with Kick-'em-Jenny, the Caribbean's most active submarine volcano. St George's Harbour, Radix, Grand Etang Lake, Mount St Catherine, Plaisance, Lake Antoine, Levera Pond and the Punch Bowl at Mount Rich are all known to be dormant volcanic craters. These craters once spouted ash, lava and stones, which, with time, have been transformed into the shales, basalt, andesite, volcanic sandstone and graywake rocks of Grenada. These craters are all extinct, and will never erupt again, but the gigantic stones that were thrown from the craters still litter the fields and the mountainsides, some buried or half-buried in the soil. They remain ever-present reminders of the violent creative forces that formed the island. They are also the bane of every farmer and builder, and often have to be dynamited and hauled away in pieces to permit the use of the land.

Today Grenada exhibits little of its violent geological past. Although volcanic activity was reported in St George's Harbour in 1867, 1902 and 1929, it is now known that what was reported as volcanic activity was activity due to small tsunami or earthquakes, some originating as far away as the British Virgin Islands. Kick-'em-Jenny is recognized as the only active volcano in Grenada. Kick-'em-Jenny, reputedly named because the sea action in the area makes the boats behave like a kicking donkey, is situated five miles north of Sauteurs and three miles west of Isle de Ronde. It erupts frequently, and there is an exclusion zone around it, forbidden to air and sea traffic.

Hot springs which are to be found in areas of past and present volcanic activity were noted on one of the earliest topographical maps of the island, drawn in 1763. At the time it was felt that the hot springs could be 'of great Service in many different disorders, in Case their Qualities and Virtues were sufficiently known'.[6] No one has ever done the necessary analysis of the waters. The most spectacular hot spring is the Hapsack hot spring on Mount St Catherine. Other notable hot springs are located in Belvidere, Samaritan, Chambourd and River Sallee, all in the north of the island.

Vegetation and Flora

The lush tropical forests of Grenada have been commented on ever since the first letters and chronicles were sent back to Europe by the European explorers. These forests comprise several distinct types, related to the levels of elevation. Dwarfed forests known as 'elfin woodlands' with palm brake and scattered tree fern still cover most mountaintops and upper slopes. These blend into the montane thicket. Rainforests cover the lower slopes and dry evergreen forest is a feature of the lowlands and, in the driest areas, cactus and thorn trees are to be found naturally. Vegetation still covers the earth right down to the sea in some places, where mangroves grow in thick profusion.

The forests and attendant vegetation flourish, given the heavy annual rainfall. This varies between 50 inches and 160 inches in the interior. The rainfall is heavier in the second half of the year. The climate also contributes to the ease with which plants grow. There is only a slight variation in temperature between seasons and between elevations. Generally, the temperature does not get much cooler than 70 degrees Fahrenheit or rise above 90 degrees Fahrenheit.

Four centuries of habitation have left a mark on the land use of Grenada. Some forests remain, and there are extensive areas of forest reserve. Even in these areas, however, some of the original flora has been replaced due to the need for speedy reforestation after hurricanes, and the need for commercial woods. In the lower areas, farming has supplanted the native vegetation. Domestic, commercial and urban structures have also claimed a part of the land.

In the cultivated gardens of Grenada or growing in the wild are to be found almost any plant that can grow in the tropics. In addition, many plants found in the temperate regions also flourish. Apart from the plants that provide food, many decorative trees and shrubs were imported into Grenada to provide both shade and beauty. Among these are the flamboyant or poinciana, the Flame of the Forest or spathodia, the yellow and the pink poui, oleander, alamanda and bougainvillea.

Grenada is extremely fertile. There is a saying that if you throw a few seeds away, you will get an instant forest. Many householders can give testament to this, if you can interpret instant forest to mean tangled pumpkin and watermelon vines and young mango plants!

Wild Life and Fauna

Few mammals and terrestrial animals found in Grenada are indigenous, because Grenada has always been geologically separated from other land by deep trenches of water. Animals arrived in Grenada by swimming, flying, catching a ride on debris floating on the sea currents, or being carried here by settlers. The first Amerindian settlers found non-poisonous snakes, turtles, iguana and other reptiles here, as well as very many varieties of birds, fish and sea mammals such as the manatee. Unfortunately, the manatee and some of the other indigenous animals have now disappeared from Grenada, and others are endangered. Several species of turtle and iguana are on the verge of extinction because of over-hunting by man. No Grenadian snakes are poisonous, but some grow to six feet, with bodies that are wrist-thick. Nevertheless, Grenadians have a traditional fear of snakes, and kill them on sight. The continued existence of these beautiful creatures is thus endangered. The tatou and manicou, which are usually reported as indigenous to Grenada, were brought here by Grenada's first settlers from the South American mainland, and later seamen brought monkeys from Africa as pets. These multiplied and now are common in the forests. Farm and domestic animals, introduced from many different parts of the world, fit easily into the Grenadian scene.

Apart from useful animals and pets, many pests have also been introduced, some of which have no natural enemy. The mongoose, which preys on chickens, birds and lizards, was brought into Grenada in the 1870s by a planter who hoped that this animal would end his prolonged problems with the rats that ate his crops. However, the mongoose preferred more elegant dining than the rats, preferring chickens, birds and other small animals. The mongoose also became a primary carrier of rabies, transferring this disease to dogs, cats, farm animals and man through bites. Nematodes that destroy the coconut and banana trees were also brought into Grenada, as was the more recently introduced pink mealy bug, which has been a serious concern to farmers, foresters and horticulturists alike, and which has almost removed plants of the hibiscus family from the list of flora in Grenada.

Agriculture

Although there has been a gradual shift to tourism as a pillar of Grenada's economy, agriculture remains extremely important. Grenada's soils are generally clayey and rich in minerals. Grenada's cash crops are bananas, some varieties of which are indigenous to the region, nutmeg, which was introduced from Indonesia, and cocoa, native to South America. Several other plants were introduced to provide food for Grenada's population over the centuries. Breadfruit trees were brought in from Polynesia; mango, tamarind, coconut, sorrel, ginger, black pepper, and turmeric from

India; beetroot, carrots, watercress, peppermint and cabbage from England; and thyme from Italy. These joined plantains, annatto, sweet potatoes, manioc, guava, mammee apples, pineapples and the other food crops and fruit which were either indigenous or which were introduced by the Amerindians – Grenada's first inhabitants. In addition to all of this, other spices such as cinnamon, cloves, vanilla, turmeric, sapote, pimento and bay leaf are grown, some of which are exported. Nutmeg alone has not earned Grenada the title of 'The Isle of Spice'! Grenada also produces a small amount of sugar cane – used mainly to make rum – some citrus, a profusion of fruits, vegetables and root crops.

Grenadians have always been fishermen, and today the fish caught in Grenadian waters are sold both abroad and locally for cash, and provide food for the fisherman's family. Fish is the most important source of protein in the Grenadian diet. Some farmers raise cattle, sheep, goats, pigs and chickens for home consumption or local sale. The forests also produce valuable timber for building and for a small furniture industry. Grenadian furniture made from mahogany, samaan and blue mahoe is greatly prized locally and by others who are lucky enough to be owners of these pieces.

Camerhogne

From its fiery birth and violent upheaval of its land, time and nature between them laid gentling hands on Grenada, quietening the movement of the earth, and almost completely dousing the fires inside the mountains. Now this volcanic island has beautiful and fertile land, in which flora and fauna flourish, a land that provided adequate shelter, food and the other basic needs of its first human inhabitants. This is the point at which we will begin to look at the history of Grenada and to trace the events leading up to the island we know today, which is home to approximately 91,000 people with a unique and colourful culture derived from many ethnic origins.

Notes
1 Paul Keens-Douglas, 'Ah Love Yu Island' in *Tell Me Again*, Keensdee, Trinidad, 1979.
2 Slave Register for St Andrew's and Carriacou, 1817, Public Records Office (PRO), London.
3 The division of the Grenadine island chain by Britain came into effect in 1783, but was first applied in 1791. When Governor Edward Matthew was appointed Governor of Grenada, his appointment was to Grenada including all the Grenadine islands south of Carriacou.
4 The summit of this mountain has a spectacular view of almost the entire west coast, which was a factor in its choice as the headquarters for the leader of Grenada's most

romantic revolutionary. On the site there is a concrete slab with a brief description of the importance of this site in Grenadian history. The significance of Fédon's Camp and the lookout will become clear in Chapter 6.

5 Government of Grenada, *The Grenada Handbook*, p. 18.
6 Paterson, Daniel, p. 1.

1

Grenada's First People

Grenada remained in pristine splendour for thousands of years after its creation by the action of volcanoes and violent upheavals of the earth. This green and well-watered island fostered abundant animal and plant life, and was a highly attractive place for human settlement.

Grenada was first discovered by groups of people from the Orinoco region of South America. Archaeological evidence found at East Dry river, Trinidad, suggests the arrival in that island of the first people to settle the Lesser Antilles from the Orinoco delta in South America about the year 2000 BC.[1] These people are sometimes erroneously called Ciboneys. The Ciboneys were, however, a different people who entered the Greater Antilles by a different route at a later date.

After settling Trinidad it was only a matter of time before these pre-ceramic people began to explore what lay to the north. The strong Orinoco Current meets the Equatorial Current off Trinidad, and then shifts north into the Caribbean Current, assisting the northward passage of expert canoeists. Perhaps these people visited Grenada as a stopping-off point on their way up the chain of islands in search of the larger, flatter islands, which they preferred. There is no archaeological evidence of permanent settlement of pre-ceramic people in Grenada. However, until recently, there was no evidence of permanent settlements in Barbados by these people either. To the great surprise of archaeologists, Ronald Taylor of the Barbados Museum discovered such a site in 1966.[2] It is still possible that a site will be found providing evidence of a similar settlement in Grenada, and therefore identifying these people as Grenada's first inhabitants.

These early people were Stone Age hunter-gatherers who lived near the sea in caves or simple shelters. They did not make pottery, use metals, or engage in cultivation. They had simple tools and utensils, including axes, implements for making canoes, sinkers for their fishing nets, hammers, and conical stone pestles for grinding food. These utensils were made out of stone, bone, wood and shell. Their food consisted of fish, shellfish and wild plants.

The Arrival of the Arawakan People

If the pre-ceramic people are believed to be the discoverers of Grenada, the Arawakan people are undeniably Grenada's first settlers. After thousands of years of a simple existence in the Caribbean, the pre-ceramic peoples were joined by newcomers who made their appearance in long, flat-bottomed canoes, similar to the canoes that brought the original settlers to this region. The newcomers spoke an Arawakan language, and are commonly referred to as Arawaks,[3] although the people who were to displace them, commonly referred to as Caribs, also belonged to the same group of Arawakan people.

The Arawakan-speaking people probably made their appearance in Grenada before AD 700[4] because an archaeological dig at Mill Reef, Antigua, indicates that these people had reached Antigua by AD 400.[5] If they found pre-ceramic people in Grenada, they absorbed them, drove them away, or killed them. This was the fate of all the pre-ceramic people in the Caribbean as, after AD 700, there is no further archaeological evidence of the existence of the simpler people in the Eastern Caribbean sub-region. Somewhere between AD 900 and AD 1300, and 100 to 250 years before Columbus sailed into the Caribbean,[6] a third major wave of migration of peoples from South America occurred. These new migrants were more developed and more aggressive than the people already in the islands.

There are many difficulties in being precise about the date on which the first Grenadians made Grenada their home, and the date they were joined by other groups. The people from South America were not a literate people, and knowledge of their history and society has to be reconstructed mainly from archaeology. As archaeological work in the Caribbean progresses, more and more details are revealed about Grenada's first inhabitants, and much of what was previously believed has to be revised in the light of new evidence.

Warriors from the Amazon

The second and subsequent waves of migration were of more aggressive people who were also Arawakan speakers, and so technically could be called 'Arawaks'. New research has proved that it is a myth that the 'Arawaks', 'Caribs', 'Island Caribs' or the 'Caraibe' were separate ethnic units, and that the 'Caribs' conquered the 'Arawaks'. Instead, recent archaeological research substantiates that the Caribbean received group after group of migrants of different origins. Sometimes they lived in peace, making treaties among themselves, and intermarried as means of establishing political links. Sometimes they brought old animosities with them from the mainland of South America, and sought to annihilate their enemies by raiding their settlements, and by taking away whatever they chose, including the men to make their slaves, and the women to be their wives. It is thought that Grenada's population density was greater than the islands to the north, because of the quantity of pottery and other remains discovered in Grenada. Grenada, only 90 miles from Venezuela, was very convenient both as a place to live and as a transit point for indigenous people[7] travelling up and down the island chain. For the same reason, Grenada also probably had the most advanced culture, as the people here received innovations first-hand from visitors from the mainland. The culture became more sophisticated over time as better ways were found of doing things and managing the environment.

The second, more aggressive, group of migrants who settled the Eastern Caribbean called themselves the *Kalinago*.[8] They had first tried to invade the islands of Trinidad and Margarita, which were both closer to the South American mainland, but had been firmly repelled by the inhabitants of those islands. They thereafter avoided these two islands, always sailing north to Grenada, St Vincent and further up the archipelago. The Eastern Caribbean became their homeland.

Sometimes the Kalinago made treaties with the more settled people already in the islands. However, invasion and capture of previous settlements was more common than making treaties. Settlements were invaded and subdued. Some were burnt, and others taken over and used as bases from which to raid and progressively colonize settlements further and further north. Forays to new territories took place typically after the hurricane season, when bands of warriors from neighbouring islands would organize war parties up to 900 strong. Armed with bows, arrows and huge wooden swords, male and female warriors would sweep down on unsuspecting settlements, plundering, killing and taking both men and women captive. The women would become wives, secondary wives or concubines of their captors. The most attractive were reserved to be used as prizes for warriors who performed extremely well in battle. Children and, surprisingly, some men were taken back to the base camps and integrated into the community to replace the men killed in battle.

There are several reasons offered as to why the Kalinago ventured into the Caribbean at this time. Perhaps they were being pushed out of their lands by peoples more developed and aggressive than they. Perhaps they had to travel afield in search of food due to a population explosion, a drought, or both. It may even be that they came in search of women, as it is forbidden by the culture of the indigenous peoples from the Amazon for a man to marry within his tribe, and the only way of obtaining a wife, or wives, was by capture. Not even the Kalinago remembered. In the words of Father Breton:[9] 'if you ask why they separated from the mainlanders and moved to the islands, they can give no reason'.[10] Time hides the exact truth, but the most likely reason of all is that the Kalinago were in search of new lands and new peoples into which they could expand their trading activities. The new people gave Grenada the name 'Camerhogne',[11] and called the smaller island to the north, 'Kayryoüacou'.[12]

A United People of the Sea

The new people were a united people and did not set up political units with territorial boundaries. They had a philosophy of brotherhood and co-operation among people of their own group, and this philosophy was to play an important part in their history, and to be a unique aspect of their strength as a people. Typically the Kalinago were nomads, moving their place of abode from island to island and to the mainland of South America as they saw fit, constantly on the move, travelling up and down the Caribbean in their large canoes. The entire island chain was their habitation, and each island belonged to everyone.

Their seamanship and constant communication with each other allowed them to hold their society together. The location of each of the islands was known so well that they could navigate at night assisted by their knowledge of the position of the stars. They could quickly respond to distress calls, coming to each other's assistance with great speed. A system of message relay enabled messages to be sent all the way along the archipelago with remarkable speed. In addition to the need to keep a diffusely settled population mobile, seamanship and adequate vessels were also important because the new people were both raiders and traders. Very soon after their entry into the Caribbean, they set up a proficient trading system between the islands and the South American mainland.

The sea-going craft of the newly arrived people were of three types. First, there was a simple raft used for fishing in the shallows. Next there was a small vessel called a *couliana,* about 20 feet long, used for fishing. The largest vessel, a magnificent craft, was known as the *canoua.* It is from this vessel that we get the word 'canoe'. The *canoua* could be up to 50 feet long, and could carry up to fifty people. This was the canoe used for long journeys and raids.

The *couliana* and *canoua* were made from trunks of hardwood trees such as the gommier (*Dacryodes excelsa*), which is still to be found in the forests of Grenada. After felling, the tree trunks were cut longitudinally, and the soft interior was carefully burned out. The charcoal was then dug out with stone axes and shell implements. The process of burning and scraping was repeated until the trunk was sufficiently hollowed out. The trunk was then stretched open by putting water and stones on the inside of the trunk, and heating the outside with fire, thus producing steam, which expanded the wood. The canoe was finished with wooden ribs to keep the hull open, and the construction of narrow, shovel-shaped paddles for propulsion. A long pole, usually made of mahoe, assisted in the navigation of reefs and shallow water. The canoe was also fitted out with rope made from the bark or fibre of trees, and a stone anchor. Planks were lashed to the hull to give it additional freeboard in heavy weather. A large vessel took years to make.

Some of these sea-going craft have been preserved. The remnants of one are on display in the Grenada National Museum. On the mainland of Central America, the Miskito Indians still make craft in almost the same manner. In Dominica the type of craft used by these people 500 years ago is still made in the traditional way, and used for fishing in the open sea, or for travelling to Martinique and Guadeloupe.

When Europeans first came to Grenada, the Kalinago inhabited the north of the island, and a different ethnic group, the Galibi, inhabited the south of the island. The Galibi were Cariban-speakers,[13] but they lived in relative peace with the Arawakan-speaking people, and could speak their language. Most of the other islands of the Lesser Antilles were still inhabited by the Arawakan-speakers, and most identified themselves as Kalinago. By the time of the first European settlements in the Lesser Antilles, all the Arawakan people, together with the Galibi, had bonded together for mutual protection against the Europeans.

The Kalinago Way of Life

Much more is known about the Arawakan-speaking people than is known about their predecessors, especially towards the end of their existence as a people. Archaeology and the writings of European chroniclers contain observations on the people they met when they arrived in the Caribbean. Christopher Columbus,[14] as well as writers such as Bartolemé de las Casas[15] detailed aspects of the life of the native peoples. The French, especially French clerics between 1630 and 1700, and later Père Labat,[16] wrote accounts of the indigenous people and their life. Further information on the native people of the Caribbean can also be extrapolated from later generations of the people who came to the Caribbean who survive today in isolated regions in Guyana and Venezuela. There are many similarities in way of life and belief systems between these contemporary people and the people who ventured into the Caribbean so long ago, although the political organization and status of the remnants of the indigenous people of the region have been severely and detrimentally affected.

Settlement Patterns

The Arawakan-speaking Kalinago made their homes all over Grenada, but most of the settlements in Grenada were on the south coast of the island, on bluffs facing the sea, or near rivers. There are at least fifteen important archaeological sites in Grenada. The seven most important are at Pearls, Westerhall Point and Calivigny Island, Point Salines, Savanna Suazy near River Sallee, and Grand Bay in Carriacou. The largest and most important site is at Pearls on the northeast coast, which covers 25 acres.[17] Bullen calls Pearls 'a large and important centre during the early part of the Christian era'.[18] First settled by agricultural people, it later became a trade and manufacturing centre for jewellery and beads made out of semi-precious stones such as amethyst, quartz crystal, chalcedony and an unidentified rock resembling marble.[19] A drill bit for the manufacture of jewellery and ornaments was uncovered at a 'dig' at Pearls.[20] This was made out of hard stone and used to manufacture beads by setting it in the end of a wooden shaft that was turned between the hands. Quantities of the beautiful pottery have also been unearthed, many being handles wonderfully fashioned in the form of animals or *zemi*.[21] Other artefacts include stone axe heads, bone needles, *zemi* and shell knives.

Despite the later importance of Pearls, the earliest Arawakan settlement site on Grenada is most possibly Black Point.[22] Black Point is a small peninsula jutting out from Point Salines. The International Airport now covers this site.

Islands were deemed very special places in Amerindian mythology, which explains why they chose to settle islands as small as Calivigny Island, situated off the coast of St David's, or the smaller islands of the Grenadines. Carriacou and Petit Martinique were very heavily settled by Kalinago, and Carriacou abounds with Kalinago artefacts. Mabouya Island[23] near Carriacou carries the name of the evil spirit of the Kalinago religion. The name 'Carriacou' is derived from the Kalinago word *Kayryoüacou* or *Cariouwacou*, which is said to mean, 'Island surrounded by reefs'.

Villages, or *carbets*, as they were called, consisted of a number of women's houses, round in shape and thatched with palm fronds. Children of both sexes would live with their mothers in huts surrounding a central house where the men slept. The smaller houses were built of a circle of poles fixed into the ground, drawn into a point at the top and lashed together with strong vines. The walls were made of reeds, the roof of thatch, and the floor of hard-packed earth. The men's house was an oval structure 60 to 90 feet long, with room for about 120 men. It was cleverly designed so that central beams both supported the roof and provided a place to which the hammocks in which people slept could be tied. From this, beams were placed in a circular pattern to meet the poles placed in a large circle to mark the diameter of the house. The roof sloped to let the rain run off quickly. In the roof, people stored their few belongings, together with the bones of their ancestors, which ensured their protective power over the house and its inhabitants. The houses were so sturdily built that they could stand up to strong gales.

Arawakan Features

There are several descriptions of the Kalinago. Abbé Raynal says that they were:

> Of moderate stature, thickset and strong, and such as seemed adapted to form men of superior strength, if their manner of life and exercises had seconded their natural appearances. Their legs thick and muscular were well made; their eyes black, large and somewhat prominent. Their whole figure would have been pleasing, had they not spoiled their natural beauty by fancied and artificial ornaments, which could only be agreeable among themselves. The eyebrows and head were the only parts of the body on which they suffered any hair to grow. They wore no garment, nor had this any influence on their chastity. In order to guard against the bite of insects, they painted all their body over with the juice of the rocou of arnotto, which gave them the appearance of a boiled lobster.[24]

Brian Edwards adds:

> The men cut deep incisions in their cheeks and painted the scars black. They painted white and black circles around their eyes. Some of them perforated the cartilage of the nostrils, inserting fish bone, a parrot's feather or fragment of tortoise shell.[25]

As is evident from the above quotation, a certain amount of body mutilation was common, and done in the name of beauty. Perhaps the most drastic was the flattening of the skull of babies to produce a high forehead believed to be beautiful. While the skull bones were still soft, mothers bound the head tightly between two pieces of wood. This exerted pressure on the *os frontis* and *occiput* bones of the skull, and elevated the forehead and back of the skull to produce a squared head.[26] The Kalinago pierced their ears and lips as well as their nostrils in order to wear ornaments of shell and bone in them. At puberty women began to wear very tight cotton bands below the knee and above the ankle. These acted to constrict the passage of fluids in the leg, and eventually produced large calves, which were thought to be attractive.

Ornamentation

The Kalinago also wore bracelets called *rasada*, and on festive occasions both men and women wore panels of cloth around the waist. The most prized possession of an Arawakan male was the ornamental necklace called a *caracoli*. This crescent-shaped ornament was a pendant hung around the neck and resting on the chest. It was made from gold, copper, silver or tin, or of alloys of these metals, and framed in wood. It was almost certainly a traded object, as the indigenous people in the Caribbean had no knowledge of metal work.[27] This ornament was rare and so valued that the men passed it on to their sons as a part of their heritage. *Caracoli* of any enemies killed in battle were acquired by the victorious warriors and worn as permanent trophies.

Smaller *caracoli* and types of ornaments were similarly made, or made out of semi-precious stones, shell, stone or bone. These were used as ear or nose pendants, or as hair decorations. During excavations at Grand Anse and at Pearls, as described earlier, exotic rocks and semi-precious stones have been found, some in a semi-worked state.[28] These materials may have been discovered in Grenada, or imported in quantities for the manufacture of ornaments for local use and export. Fragments of *caracoli* have been found at the Savanna Suazy site.

The Kalinago were very proud of their shining, black, straight, coarse hair, and only Kalinago were allowed to wear their hair long. The hair of the men was often adorned with ornaments and feathers, and it was part of a wife's duty to comb and decorate the man's hair. Kalinago cut their hair short as a sign of mourning. Brian Edwards also mentions 'They strung together the teeth of the enemies they had slain in battle, and wore them on their legs and arms.'[29]

Gender Relations

In a society that featured raiding and trading, and continual danger of attack, a great premium was put on strength, and the ability to protect the lives of the community. Although it is recorded that women went along with the men on raiding parties, it was the men who were the warriors, and important, while the women had little status. Raynal accuses the Kalinago of being:

> Little acquainted with the strongest passions of the soul, not even that of love. This passion was with them merely a sensual appetite. They never showed the least marks of attention or tenderness for that sex, so much courted in other countries. They considered their wives rather in the light of slaves than companions; they did not even suffer them to eat with them, and had usurped the right of divorcing them, without granting them the indulgence of marrying again. The women felt themselves born to obey, and submitted patiently to their fate.[30]

Language

The status of the men and the status of the women were reflected in a unique gender difference in language. Both men and women had separate customs of speech that they used in addressing those of their own gender. The language was Arawakan, but the speech of the men contained loan words from Cariban and from the Kalina people of the South American mainland, and words specifically pertaining to war and trade.[31] On the other hand, the women spoke the language of everyday life, and everyday things. Both men and women understood each other, but women were not permitted to utter the words and expressions exclusive to the men's language, and men would not use words unique to women. Boys used the women's speech until they were initiated into manhood. In Belize today, the two speech patterns are still used by the Garifuna (or 'Black Caribs') who were removed there from St Vincent in 1798.[32]

The use of two languages and constant accretions from trading activities and from culture contact soon produced regional differences in speech. These, however, were never so great that branches of the extensive family of Arawakan-speaking peoples could not understand each other. After the Spanish arrived in the Caribbean, the language underwent further change. The indigenous people of the northern Caribbean began to flee south into the Windward Islands, trying to escape the brutality of the Spanish occupation in those islands. They added yet another dimension to the speech patterns of Eastern Caribbean people.

Skills and Technology

Before contact with the Europeans, the indigenous people had their own sophisticated hunting and fishing techniques. They fashioned bows out of pliable saplings from such trees as *Bois Verde* or *Bois de Lette*, using bark or fibre from plants for bowstrings. Arrows, about three feet in length, were tipped differently for war or hunting. Sometimes the arrow would be tipped with a wooden plug instead of a pointed arrowhead, if the hunter wanted to stun the animal rather than to kill it. The arrowheads used for hunting were of wood. The indigenous people also hunted on land with spears and traps. War arrowheads were made of sharp fish bone, and the tips poisoned by the application of sap from the manchineel tree (*Hippomane mancinella*).

The men were expert fishermen and hunters. They made harpoons, spears, traps, hooks, lines and nets out of wood, stone, shell, vine and available material. With these, they harpooned turtles and manatees. They tied suckerfish to thin lines to locate submerged turtles. They ensured their supply of fresh fish by driving fish into seaside enclosures to keep them alive until they needed them.

Excellent potters and woodworkers, the men of the indigenous people designed appropriate tools for these tasks. For work around the village they made axes, awls, needles, mortar and pestles, all sorts of bowls and clay implements including clay baking trays, graters and presses called *matapis* to extract the poisonous juices from manioc, grindstones, basic spinning equipment and other tools to effect domestic chores.

From the superb cotton they grew and from wild plants such as agave, rope, cord and thread were made. Cloth was woven from the thread that they spun. They dyed some of the cloth red. They grew the calabash tree for its gourds, which they used as containers. As a bonus, they cut the tendrils of the epiphytes that liked to grow on the calabash plant when they needed to tie or to fasten items. These they used as we would use twine. They made baskets out of the fibres of palm trees. Also cultivated were coconuts and annatto. Annatto and the fruit of the *Genepa* tree provided body paint for the people. The manzanilla fruit was used for its laxative properties.

There was a strict division of labour between the sexes. The men fished, hunted, trained the boys and went into battle, while the women planted, ground maize, prepared cassava, gathered cotton, made cloth, cord, hammocks, baskets and pottery, prepared meals and looked after the children and cooked. Archaeological literature often states that pottery styles of the 'Caribs' are crude in comparison to the delicate pottery of the 'Arawak' people they conquered, and that the vessels in the 'Carib' style are characterized by being larger, flat bottomed, straight sided with finger-indented rims. Instead of being decorated and coloured, the surface of 'Carib' pottery is scratched, as if it had been brushed with stiff bristles.[33] Recent research seems to indicate that the indigenous people had two types of pottery. The pottery for everyday use was of the cruder form, and the pottery for decorative or ceremonial use was refined and artistically decorated. This answers the difficulty of the archaeologists who found the two types mixed in the same archaeological levels. More of the cruder forms were found, because nobody uses their 'good' things every day!

The skills and technology of the people underwent a process of development with time. New and improved methods of doing things were shared among the peoples living in the area, and more efficient techniques were readily adopted from any instances of culture contact. Originally ignorant of metal, the Arawakan people soon found out its uses from the Europeans. Nails, hatchets and other metal tools were soon items of importance for barter and trade between the Europeans and the people of the Eastern Caribbean.

Fishing Techniques

The men, with their superb seamanship and propensity to use it, fished far away from their settlements. They would travel from Grenada and the other Windward Islands to the Leeward Islands in search of lobster and conch, and make trips to Marie Galante, a small island just south of Guadeloupe, to catch the best crabs. They also fished in the rivers and near the shores, using bow and arrow to shoot fish near the surface, and poison from the manioc root to stun fish in pools. They made baskets to gather *titiwe*, a tiny fish,[34] from the river mouth, and used fish pots, nets and spears as appropriate. The birds, such as Pecheur and Grand Gosier, were trained to help locate schools of fish in the sea.

Farming Technology

The indigenous people had both farming and fishing communities. Private property was unknown, and cultivation was carried out by joint labour, and the harvest collected in communal granaries. Many of their agricultural methods were remarkably inventive and appropriate. They introduced slash-and-burn agriculture into the Caribbean, first clearing the land, and then setting fire to the debris. They grew some of their crops on little mounds, which reduced erosion and retained moisture. The mounds were fertilized with wood ash and plant waste. Around AD 700, the people learnt the fertilizing value of urine, and began using this on the mounds as well. In dryer areas, they brought in water to the fields through a system of canals and irrigation ditches. For planting, they had a special type of pole with which to dig holes, and a sort of wooden machete called a *macana*, which they used both for digging and as a bush knife.

The indigenous people brought many of the plants they cultivated from their original homeland. Others were introduced later into the islands by the Amerindian traders who made regular visits up and down the islands, and from the mainland of South America. Manioc root had multiple uses. They extracted the poison from this root, and used it for tipping arrows and stunning fish. When the poison was extracted from the juice of the root, the residue was used as a preservative, called *casareep*. The solid part of the root was called *cassava*, and this was moulded into cakes, and baked. Cassava was a dietary staple. The people also cultivated maize, beans, sweet potatoes, yams, arrowroot, peanuts, peppers and squash. Many fruit popular in Grenada today, such as pineapples, guava, mammee apple and paw-paw, were introduced, grown and enjoyed. Peppers were very important for seasoning and preserving meat, and were an essential ingredient of the pepper-pot.

The indigenous people put all their rubbish on middens outside their villages, away from the wind. The discovery of a midden is the first clue to locating a site of an Amerindian village.

Diet

The earlier inhabitants of the Eastern Caribbean ate turtle, manatees, pigs and eels. These meats were later strictly shunned as the value of avoiding meat rich in fat was learned. The leaner meats of the agouti, fish and shellfish, waterfowl, pigeons, doves, iguanas and crabs replaced the meat richer in fat. Salt was also excluded from the later dietary habits. The people were particularly fond of crabs. After gathering them at night by the light of flambeaux, the men would turn the crabs over to the women who would then make a stew adding cassava and *tamaulin,* which was a sauce made of lemon juice, manioc juice, fish bones, red pepper and the meat of the crab nearest the shell. Although the Kalinago and the Galibi who came to Grenada later did not eat turtle, they were still hunted for their shells, out of which sharp implements could be made.

Food preparation included baking, stewing and roasting. The pepper-pot[35] was a delicious means of preserving meat. This is a dish of highly seasoned meat, slowly cooked, usually in an earthenware vessel. It contains every kind of meat, except fish. *Casareep* and red pepper are added as preservatives. The pot may never become empty, as meat and other ingredients are constantly added. Pepper-pot is one of the lasting gifts of the indigenous people to contemporary Caribbean people. It is a favourite item in the cuisine of many Caribbean countries. Beer, called *ouicou,* was made from manioc. It was drunk at festivals, and before raids.

Spirituality

Daily life among the Arawakan-speaking people was infused and influenced by spiritual beliefs. The religion involved both ancestor worship and animism, and their body ornaments and the use of tobacco had religious significance. Tobacco was extremely important to the indigenous people, and was one of the ways in which they enhanced their spirituality. They rolled it into cigars and used it as snuff. The priests used the juice as the potent narcotic substance in it induced altered states of consciousness during which they communed with the gods, sometimes seeking advice for their clients. Priests also offered manioc to the spirits. Several vessels that could either have been used for inhaling narcotic substances or pouring narcotic liquids, such as tobacco juice, into the nostrils have been found in the Grenadine islands, though not on Grenada itself. An object found at Grand Bay in Carriacou was almost certainly a pipe for tobacco smoking, as the tubular part of the object was smoke-blackened.[36]

The Kalinago accepted that the earth was a bountiful parent, which provided them with the things necessary to life. They believed in an invisible supreme being of absolute and irresistible power who they called Icherire. Subordinate to this power were other spirits. Everyone had a special spirit whose duty it was to protect and instruct. Mabouya was the evil one, the spirit of the underworld. All misfortune, whether sickness, accident or death, was blamed on a spell invoking Mabouya. It was part of the job of the priest or *boyez* to counteract these spells, undo the evil deeds, and placate Mabouya. Offerings of appeasement to Mabouya were made through the hands of the *boyez,* and the Kalinago were sometimes called upon to wound themselves with instruments made with the teeth of the agouti at ceremonies meant to placate Mabouya.

In the practice of their religion, people prayed directly to the spirits, asking them to provide a good harvest, good weather, or other favours. They offered fruits and food to images of the spirits, and each hut had an altar for this purpose. The zemi, which were symbolic representations of spirits or their attributes, were used as aids to their worship. Kalinago also decorated their pottery vessels with religious symbols.

The *boyez* were also healers. To perform in this area, they had both a repertoire of *piai* (spells), and a wide knowledge of medicinal herbs. A few of the youth were selected to be trained as priests. The rest were trained as warriors. In addition, every object, animate and inanimate, and the forces of nature had a spirit. People had spirits too, and on death these spirits would go to another place, similar to the Christian heaven if the deceased were virtuous and brave. Cowardly persons were doomed to everlasting banishment beyond the mountains, and unremitting labour in demeaning employment. The dead ancestors of the indigenous people were honoured, and were implored to provide protection and other favours. The Kalinago believed that the spirits of their ancestors were secret spectators to their conduct, sympathizing with their suffering, and overseeing their welfare.

The inhabitants of Grenada made carvings called petroglyphs on large boulders near rivers. Most of the petroglyphs feature a human face surrounded by rings or arcs. Rock carvings are to be seen at Duquesne Bay, at Victoria and in the La Fortune river on the Mount Rich Estate.[37] Bullen is of the opinion that the petroglyph at Mount Rich was carved by the pre-ceramic people.[38] All the petroglyphs were possibly of religious significance.

The indigenous people loved dancing and music, which were also related to their spiritual life. They fashioned trumpets, whistles, flutes and shack-shacks (maracas), castanets and other sorts of rattles from wood, shell and bone.

Education

Brian Edwards quotes Rochefort's[39] observation on the education of the Kalinago boys. Rochefort says that the education of a boy was to make him:

> Skilful with the bow, dexterous with a club, to catch fish and to build a cottage. One method to make the boys skilful was to tie their food unto the branch of a tree, compelling them to shoot it through with an arrow before they could obtain permission to eat.[40]

Edwards further observes that children were 'Instructed in patience and fortitude, and courage in war, contempt of danger and death and above all a heredity of hatred and thirst for revenge against the Arawaks'.[41]

Rituals and Festivals

Both important events for the community, and the rites of passage for the individual, were marked by rituals and festivals. When a wife was about to give birth, the father would go into a period of fasting, called *couvade*. The sympathetic and supportive action of her partner gave the woman courage. As soon as a male child was born, he was sprinkled with his father's blood, which was supposed to transmit his father's courage to the son. The father would retire to his bed, and engage in a period of fasting, which was supposed to protect the newborn from hereditary guilt. The fasting was succeeded by a feast of rejoicing and triumph at the birth, at which the men would drink to excess.

Brian Edwards[42] collected stories of the initiation rites for boys and men. He recounts that the initiation rites for boys were designed to prove that the youths could withstand pain. Fathers were asked to inflict pain on their sons, who were threatened by taunting and aggressive behaviour from the men. The more the youths stood up to the ordeals of the initiation with endurance and composure, the more they were applauded. When the young men emerged from their ordeal, they were given new names, and their manhood was celebrated with a festival involving much eating, drinking, dancing and merrymaking. After initiation, the boys would leave their mothers' huts and go to live with the other men in the men's central house, and speak the men's language.

A man was not chosen to lead others into battle unless he had successfully undergone a second initiation rite. This initiation involved excruciating torture, flogging, burning and partial suffocation. If he passed all the tests, a great feast was held for him. His name was changed for a second time to the name of the most formidable warrior that he had slain in battle. The man was then presented with captives, and some of the most beautiful daughters of the Kalinago who were to be his wives.

Kalinago funeral rites involved the mourners cutting off their hair. The corpse would be buried in the central large men's house, which was then abandoned. Another house would be built to serve as the men's dwelling and meeting house. Captives were sacrificed at the funeral of deceased heroes.

The principal sport among the indigenous people was a ball game, which involved keeping a ball in the air without using the hands or feet.

This game was played by two teams of thirty players each, and was played on a ball court in the village. Sometimes the players wore a stone belt to assist in keeping the ball in the air. The stone belt was a device made out of stone and fastened to the waist of the ball player, enabling him to use his midriff to hit the ball and keep it in the air. This game appears to be similar to a game played by the indigenous people of Central America. A well-preserved ball court, lined with large stones, and fragments of the stone belts, were found at the Mill Reef dig in Antigua.[43] A ball court is a ubiquitous feature in Mayan ruins of any size in Belize and Central America.

Political Organization

The chief or *ubutu* controlled large areas and had absolute power. The *ubutu* could be deposed if he did not lead well, especially in raids and battles. In times of war, the warriors fro n several islands would select a war chief from their number at a solemn general assembly. During periods of hostilities, it was recognized that subordination to the leadership of the war chief was essential. However, the power of the war chief ended when the fighting was over. Brian Edwards states that in peacetime the old men were allowed some authority, but otherwise there was no subjugation of one man to another. The value the Kalinago placed on equality between persons was so great that Père Labat observed: 'At any time they are witness to the respect and deference which the natives of Europe observe towards their superiors, they despise us as abject slaves, wondering how any man can be so base as to crouch before his equal'.[44]

Headmen, *tuibutuli hauthe*, were in charge of village organization. It was their responsibility to oversee the fishing, farming, distribution and storage of food. The *ubutu* was not a hereditary post. When the *ubutu* died, the men elected another for life. The *ubutu* presided over feasts and festivals, and they dispensed justice. Apart from the *ubutu* and the *tuibutuli hauthe* there was no aristocracy and the society was virtually classless. Justice was also kept very simple. Those who were wronged were permitted to exact revenge.

Although most men had only one wife, the *ubutu* had several. Having more than one wife allowed him to create kinship networks. To further strengthen these networks, only the sons of the chief were allowed to live in the community. When other men married, they had to live with their wives' families. This arrangement cemented the power of the chief, and dispersed potential rivals.

A Way of Life Ends

In 1700 Labat observed that 'There is not a nation on earth more jealous of their independence than the Caribs. They are impatient under the least infringement of it'.[45] These people had enjoyed several hundreds of years of settled, healthy living in Grenada and the rest of the Caribbean, with a sophisticated and complex culture. This culture was in harmony with the island environment, encouraging the people to live close to and in communion with nature. The Kalinago and Galibi were who were so passionate about maintaining their independence and freedom, were soon to have to defend their very existence as they encountered a people armed with superior weapons, carrying diseases for which they had no immunity, and bent on subjecting them and occupying their territory.

The arrival of Europeans and the Africans they enslaved heralded a new age during which the land would be wrest from the control of the indigenous peoples of the Caribbean, and they would be exterminated because their continued existence was an impediment to European colonization. The people in Grenada and the Lesser Antilles would lose even the right to their correct name. They would be called 'Caribs' by European conquerors for propaganda purposes.

Notes

1 Cody Holdren (1998) and others give this date, but various other arrival dates are given. Desmond Nicholson (Olsen, *Indian Creek*, p. v) gives the dates of artefacts associated with these people found in Venezuela as 12,000 BC, and those found in Hispaniola as early as 5000 BC. Some others quote much later dates. Honychurch (p. 15) states that carbon dating of artefacts at Mill Reef, Antigua, gives a date of about 3100 BC for the occupation of that island by aboriginal people. Bullen puts the earliest occupation of Grenada between before AD 120 (p. 60) and the arrival of the 'Arawak' at AD 700 (p. 62).
2 Hoyos, p. 1.
3 Bullbrook gives a detailed description of the life and culture of the people of the first wave of Arawakan migrants to the Caribbean.
4 Bullen, p. 62
5 Olsen, *Indian Creek*, p. 52.
6 As with other dates in Grenada's pre-history, estimates differ.
7 Although the word 'indigenous' refers to a people born in a country, the people who came to Grenada were indigenous to the Greater Caribbean region, and did not share our modern territorial concept of 'nation'. I believe that the Arawakan-speaking people and the Galibi who made Grenada their home are rightfully called 'indigenous people'.
8 This is also spelt Kallinago or Callinaga; I have used the same spelling as Lennox Honychurch.
9 In 1642 Father Raymond Breton, a Dominican Priest, was sent to Dominica to minister to the aboriginal people. Even before he arrived in Dominica, he had been teaching himself the Kalinago language. Treated well by the aboriginal people, he remained on the island for many years, during which time he wrote a dictionary of the Kalinago language, and recorded some of their oral history and myths.

Knowledge of the Kalinago names of the islands and other items is mainly due to the painstaking research of this Catholic priest. Only a few words – canoe, hammock, hurricane, boucan, manicou, tatou, titiwe and mabouya – remain in the lexicon of Grenada today.

10 Quoted in Davis and Goodwin, p. 39.
11 I am told this means 'Land of Abundance'.
12 There are many different spellings of this name.
13 Cody Holdren, p. 2.
14 Christopher Columbus was an assiduous chronicler of his own travels. Although the original of his journal is lost, it was abstracted by las Casas (see note 15).
15 Bartolomé de las Casas accompanied Columbus on his second voyage to the New World. He became a Dominican priest in Hispaniola in 1522, and devoted six years to writing the *Historia de las Indias* – an account of Columbus's third voyage. This history was not published until 1875. Since then it has been republished, edited and extracted. It is perhaps the main source of information about changes in the region at this time.
16 Père Labat was also a Dominican priest who visited the region around 1700 and wrote extensively on what he saw and did. His eight-volume *Nouveau Voyage aux Isles de l'Amérique* was published in Paris in 1743. Extracts from this work, together with a summary of the voyages made by Père Labat between 1694 and 1705 are to be found in *The Memoirs of Père Labat*, edited and translated by John Eaden, Frank Cass, 1970.
17 Bullen, p. 18 and pp. 53–61.
18 Bullen, p. 22.
19 Cody (1989), p. 9.
20 *Ibid.*
21 These were small images of stone, wood, rock, shell or pottery. Many were made in the likeness of animals, although obvious fertility symbols are by no means rare. In addition there are some more abstract *zemis* that might symbolize volcanoes, islands or heaven.
22 Bullen, p. 51.
23 'Mabouya' is one of the word survivals in Grenadian parlance. It carries the conno- tation of a dark, little understood and underworld spirit. One of the lizards found in Grenada, a 'wood-slave', has been given this name. The *Hemidactylus mabouya* is believed to be impossible to remove from the human skin unless hot irons or lighted cigarette ends are used to burn it off. If it is not removed, it is believed that the person will die within twenty-four hours. This lizard also makes a chattering noise that alarms the superstitious. There is also a village in St Mark's called Mabouya.
24 Raynal, Book x, p. 404.
25 Edwards, p. 35. See note 22 on p. 48.
26 Edwards, p. 43.
27 Bullen, p. 58.
28 Cody (1989), pp. 1–5.
29 Edwards, p. 35.
30 Raynal, Book x, p. 405.
31 See Davis and Goodwin, p. 44.
32 My colleague, Dr Joseph Palacio, a Garifuna, told me that he uses one language to speak to other male Garifuna, and his wife speaks to him in the language of the women.
33 Bullen, p. 56.
34 This fish is still called *titiwe*, and is the same one also called 'millions'.
35 See Allsopp, p. 436.
36 Sutty, p. 24.

37 For a discussion on these petroglyphs see Cody (1990).
38 Bullen, p. 25.
39 César de Rochefort was a Protestant minister and author of the book *Histoire Naturelle et Morale des Isles Antilles de l'Amerique*, which was published in 1658 and translated into English in 1666. Rochefort gives sketches of the West Indian islands as they were at the time, but is best known for his description of the indigenous people. See Goveia, pp. 23–6.
40 Edwards, p. 37.
41 *Ibid.*
42 Edwards, pp. 39–40.
43 Olsen, *Indian Creek*, p. 30.
44 Quoted in Edwards, p. 34.
45 Quoted in Edwards, p. 34.

2

Struggle for a Homeland

On his first voyage, Columbus heard from the Tainos, the indigenous people of some of the islands of the Greater Antilles, of woman-stealing cannibals to the south. Thinking he was near the Orient, he believed that these were the advance warriors of the ferocious Kublai Khan, who had been sent to destroy him. Later he learnt that these were simply a more aggressive group of indigenous people, feared by their northern neighbours for their expansionist ambitions. The inclination to think of the Kalinago as the savage enemy, however, never left Columbus, or any Europeans venturing into the Eastern Caribbean in the next century and a half. The few exceptions were members of the clergy, who wished to make friends with the Kalinago, and to convert them to Christianity.

A New Name for an Ancient People

Columbus began to call the more aggressive Kalinago 'cariba' which was the Spanish word for cannibal. Even when he was presented with evidence that the cannibalism of the indigenous people was a myth, he continued to perpetuate that myth because it suited his purposes. He needed an excuse to enslave the people and take possession of their homeland because, before 1520, the Spanish Crown had forbidden the enslavement of the indigenous people, provided that they were friendly. All others were defined legally as 'barbaric enemies of the Christians, those who refused conversion, and those who eat human flesh'.[1] These could be captured and enslaved.

On one occasion, he sent a shipload of indigenes who were definitely not Kalinago back to Spain, claiming that they were the cannibals. He suggested that they should be made slaves in Spain, because in a Catholic country they could be baptized and thus have a better chance of giving up cannibalism. In exchange for the slaves, however, he wanted cattle and other supplies sent to the colonies.

On his second voyage, Columbus found Taino women in Guadeloupe, and had them sent back to their homes in the Greater

Antilles. This he took as proof of the rumours of the women-stealing habits of the Kalinago. In Guadeloupe, too, the Kalinago tradition of keeping the bones of their ancestors in their houses was taken as evidence that they ate human flesh, the bones supposedly being the leftovers of cannibal meals. This convenient assumption was never supported by eyewitnesses of cannibal feasts, or any other hard evidence. Missionaries such as Père de la Borde, Père Jean Baptiste Labat and César de Rochefort described the Kalinago practice of preserving the bones of their ancestors in their houses in the belief that the ancestral spirits would look after the bones and protect their descendants. Today a practice similar to this is still to be found among contemporary tribes in the Amazon. It was also the practice of the Kalinago to sever a limb of each adversary killed, and take that limb home as a trophy. Finally, although the Kalinago would chew and spit out one mouthful of the flesh of a very brave warrior, so that his bravery would accrue to them, there is no evidence that they ate humans to satisfy their hunger.[2] A comparison can be made with the thousands of human bones found in the catacombs in Rome, Italy. The existence of the bones did not prove that the inhabitants of Rome were cannibals! Further evidence in support of the theory that the bones were preserved for ritualistic reason is that human bones are not found in middens, as are the remains of meals and domestic waste.

The reported sensationalism of cannibalistic practices overshadowed the more positive reports about the life of the indigenous inhabitants of the Caribbean. For example, the surgeon of Columbus's fleet[3] commented that the indigenes of the Caribbean seemed more civilized than the others he had seen. He observed that their houses were better constructed, they had larger stocks of food, and cloth woven from the thread they had spun was in no way inferior to European cloth.

Nevertheless, the reputation for fierceness of the inhabitants of Grenada, St Vincent and Dominica is not in dispute. They protected with such vigour the last of the islands of their archipelic homeland that these islands were also known as 'the Cannibal Islands', and were deemed to be islands that should be avoided at all costs by the Europeans because of the aggressiveness of their inhabitants.

The Kalinago had no reason to treat the Europeans gently. The Spanish, who had frustrated their expansionist drive into the northern islands, now began to disturb their southern homelands. In colonizing the Greater Antilles, the Spanish had been so brutal that the inhabitants fled, bringing to the Kalinago and Galibi accounts of the genocide inflicted on their people. The people in the Windward Islands were determined that what had happened to these refugees would not happen to them. They therefore ferociously resisted every effort at colonization and all that went with it. This determined action prevented European colonization of the Windward Islands for one hundred years. During this time the members of the indigenous societies in the Windward Islands offered sanctuary to those fleeing the horrors of the Spanish, and integrated them into the Kalinago and Galibi way of life.

In spite of this, early in the era of European penetration into the region, Spanish ships often used Dominica as a 'wood and watering' stop, even after it became clear that the Kalinago attitudes towards the Europeans had changed. On most occasions the Spanish were permitted to take on these supplies unmolested.[4] Survivors of shipwrecks were recovered alive on Dominica in spite of the fact that the Kalinago, with their hunting and tracking skills, could easily have found and killed them.[5] On several occasions Europeans who got lost in the forests on the islands returned to their vessel safely, although the Kalinago could have easily caught and eaten them if they had cared to.[6] There are many accounts of the indigenous inhabitants offering genuine hospitality to Europeans who did not threaten their security. English and French vessels calling at the islands found the Kalinago willing to trade agricultural produce for coloured beads, trinkets, glass, hatchets and knives, saws and other tools. When European prisoners taken by the Kalinago were enslaved[7] rather than killed, they were made to live like the servants of their captors, but lived to tell the tale.

The Kalinago became belligerent only to those who meant them no good. They also became very angry if visitors to whom they offered their hospitality attempted to seduce their women. It was only later when they could no longer take the chance of letting any Europeans who reached their shores remain alive that any Europeans who dared to venture to land, by adventure or by misadventure, were driven off or slaughtered. Nevertheless, sensationalist and grisly 'hearsay' accounts decorate narratives of the time.

In 1645 a Spanish ship, bound for Venezuela, found itself in need of provisions and, braving the reputation of the inhabitants of Grenada, put in to the island for wood, water and other supplies. As the indigenes realized that the vessel only wanted to take on supplies, they treated the Spanish kindly and hospitably. A young Spaniard, Don Tiburcio Radin, was a passenger on this vessel, and witnessed the kindness and hospitality with which the indigenes treated the Spanish. This belied their cannibalistic and hostile reputation, and was in contrast to the treatment of those who had come to try to settle Grenada. The young Spaniard, who was on his way to South America to enter the religious life, vowed to return to Grenada to Christianize these kind people.[8]

Proof that the Kalinago would help those in distress is to be had by the experience of the refuge given to Africans who chanced upon Kalinago territory. Some time towards the end of the sixteenth century two slave ships were wrecked off Bequia, a Grenadine island near St Vincent. The Kalinago welcomed all of the Africans who survived. Some were invited to St Vincent, as Bequia was too small to provide sustenance for all the new-comers. The Africans were integrated into Kalinago society, and became Kalinago, speaking the language, adopting the customs, and taking wives from the society into which they were welcomed. They certainly were not eaten. Later, news that in St Vincent the runaway slave would find a welcoming refuge travelled to the plantations. Slaves joined the Kalinago in St Vincent and added to the growing population of Kalinago of mixed race. Europeans began to refer to these as the 'Black Caribs'. The history of the Kalinago of mixed race made this group even more suspicious of Europeans and their promises. They refused to parley with them, and warned the Kalinago who had no African blood, called by Europeans the 'Red Caribs', to have no dealings with white men from any country.

Resistance to Spanish Settlement

In an effort to discourage Spanish settlement, the Kalinago raided the Spanish settlements on a regular basis, causing much damage and blood-shed. They captured as well as killed, and there are records of slave women being captured and taken to live with the Kalinago. The Spanish would dearly have loved to engage in a war aimed at the extermination of the indigenous peoples of the Eastern Caribbean, but the Spanish Crown pro-tected indigenous people from slaughter. Queen Isabella's response to the continued harassment of Spanish settlements was to decree that the efforts to Christianize the Kalinago should increase.

This pacifist policy towards indigenous people stopped in 1511 after the Kalinago had attacked a settlement on Puerto Rico, killing Don Cristobal de Sotomayor, a Lieutenant of the Captain in that island, his nephew Don Diego de Sotomayor, and several other people. Isabella had died, and her husband, Ferdinand, was in control, acting as regent for their daughter Queen Juana. Incensed by the incident in Puerto Rico, Ferdinand issued a new *cédula* on 23 December 1511, permitting just warfare on the indigenous people, and the taking and selling of those taken in war as slaves.

In spite of this *cédula*, the Spanish Crown remained reluctant to permit an all out aggressive war against the indigenes, regardless of their constant harassment, and the constant pleas of the Spanish settlers. It was not until nearly a century later, in 1608, that Phillip III sanctioned armed offensives against the indigenous people. By this time, Spanish domination in the Caribbean had been broken. Later, at the end of the Thirty Years War in Europe, by the Treaty of Westphalia, Spain had to concede to the other European nations that effective occupation, and not just discovery, gave the right of ownership to lands in the Caribbean. Weakened by war, and challenged by the ascendancy of the French, English and Dutch, Spain would eventually lose all the islands but Cuba, Hispaniola and Puerto Rico. One by one, the islands were occupied by the European nations, and the indigenous people killed, enslaved, or driven to seek refuge in dwindling island sanctuaries.

Columbus Sights Grenada

On his third voyage, five years after the first, Columbus steered a more southerly course, and first came upon Trinidad, which he gave that name because the three peaks of Trinidad was a symbol to him of the Holy Trinity, to whom he had dedicated the voyage before he left Spain. Having entered the Gulf of Paria by its southernmost approach, he sailed out through the Dragon's Mouth, and sailed far enough northwards before turning to the west so that Tobago came into view, and then Grenada. Columbus sighted Grenada on 15 August 1498, but he did not land. From the deck of his ship, Columbus called the island Concepción.

The smaller islands of the Caribbean did not really interest Spain for several reasons. Experience with the islands of the Greater Antilles led Columbus to doubt that he would find silver or gold on them. They were also too hilly for cattle rearing. Moreover, they were not in a favourable position for the best winds to take heavily laden vessels back to Spain, and therefore were unsuitable as rendezvous points for convoys that sailed once a year from South America to Spain. Finally, there was the drawback of the inhabitants of these islands, who would fight fiercely to prevent occupation of their land. Therefore, it took nearly one hundred years for the Europeans to attempt a settlement.

In 1500, the European mapmakers, Alonso de Hojeda, Amerigo Vespucci and Juan de la Cosa sailed through the Caribbean, mapping all the islands they saw. They changed the name Columbus had given the island from Concepción to Mayo[9] meaning *fortunate to have*. However, it was Ribero's Chart of 1529 that listed Grenada as La Granada, and it is this name in various versions that has been used ever since.

Who Owned Grenada?

In a bull[10] issued in 1493, the Pope had confirmed the existing rights of Portugal in the New World and also established the rights of Spain by drawing an imaginary line from north to south, 100 leagues (about 300 miles) west of the Azores and the Cape Verde Islands. The Portuguese were to have exclusive rights over the lands to the east of the line, and the Spanish over lands to the west. Subsequently, adjustments were made to this bull at the request of both Spain and Portugal, but this bull gave the Spanish the right to claim as its own all the territories in the Caribbean Sea, as well as other, richer territories in South America. When Spain became too weak to protect all her territories against other European nations by the beginning of the seventeenth century, a swarm of eager adventurers from Europe, anxious to procure land in the New World, descended on Spain's empire in the West Indies, eager to claim them in the name of France, England and the United Netherlands. During the second half of the seventeenth century the history of the West Indies, and therefore that of Grenada, was determined by the struggle for territory and power between these nations.

Merchants in European countries who had funds to invest were approached by adventurers and persuaded to finance expeditions and settlements. The promise of great returns on successful completion of such ventures was held out to these merchants. Occupation and colonization were at first left to private enterprise, although any territory occupied was listed as a possession of the mother country. In claiming an island as their private property, Europeans took no cognisance of the fact that a territory was already owned and had been inhabited by other human beings for thousands of years.

The First European Attempts to Settle Grenada

According to documents written much later, in the reign of the English King, Charles II, by Major John Scott, a group of London merchants had backed an expedition in 1609 to make the first attempt at acquiring and settling Grenada. The merchants provided equipment and provisions for the expedition and recruited 204 adventurers. The leaders of the expedition were Messrs Godfrey, Hall, Lull and Robinson. The supplies and men left England in three ships, the *Diana*, the *Penelope*, and the *Endeavour*.

When the ships arrived in Grenada at a place called Great Bay,[11] the company of men disembarked, and the ships departed for Trinidad. Almost as soon as they began to establish a settlement, they were attacked by the indigenous inhabitants, many were killed and the settlement destroyed. Others were killed in subsequent attacks, or became ill with tropical fevers. There were only a few survivors who rejoiced when the ships returned from Trinidad on 15 December 1609, eight months later. The first attempt at settlement was a complete failure.

In 1627 Grenada, on which no European had yet successfully established a settlement, was given as a land grant by Charles I of England to his cousin the Earl of Carlisle.[12]

The French Colonization of Grenada

In 1624 France established a colony on St Christophe, known today as St Kitts. The island was shared with England, the English occupying the central portion, while the French occupied the northern and southern sections. In 1625 a French adventurer called Belain d'Esnambuc and the company of men whom he led took refuge in St Kitts after a Spanish galleon attacked his ship. There he met an English adventurer called Warner who had also suffered at the hands of the Spaniards, and had previously taken refuge in that island with his company of men. For a while the French and English lived peaceably with the Kalinago who inhabited the island, but eventually distrust bred skirmishes, and this developed into the complete annihilation of the local population by the French and English. Satisfied that the Kalinago would give them no more trouble, both Warner and d'Esnambuc set out for Europe to obtain the approval and help of their respective kings and governments in the permanent settlement of St Christophe. St Kitts was to become the base from which both French and English would set forth in search of other lands that might be occupied and claimed, and on which first tobacco farms and later sugar plantations could be established and made profitable. To manage their possessions in the West Indies, several companies were set up by France.

The first was the Company of St Christopher, set up in 1626. This was replaced after nine years by the Company of the Isles of America. D'Esnambuc and his friend du Rossey were appointed the agents of this Company for the Eastern Caribbean area and were authorized to establish settlements not only in St Kitts, but also in Barbados, St Lucia and the neighbouring islands. Any islands that were settled were claimed for France, but were for all practical purposes owned by the Company and could act autonomously. The Company also had the monopoly of trade between these islands and France. Among the islands settled was Martinique, on which d'Esnambuc established a settlement in 1635.

Among the shareholders of this Company were three gentlemen, du Parquet, Houel and de Cerrilac. Du Parquet was a nephew of the pioneering d'Esnambuc, and had been sent by his uncle to take charge of the settlement in Martinique in 1637. He proved to be a capable administrator with a penchant for acquiring more territory. One of du Parquet's ambitions was to acquire Grenada:

> Notwithstanding that the French establishment in Martinico was itself of recent date, and that a great part of that island still remained uncultivated; and although another establishment was, at the same time, begun by the same nation, in the large and fertile island of Guadeloupe.[13]

Under the umbrella of the Company of the Isles of America, du Parquet organized several attempts to settle Grenada, but all were abandoned before even setting sail. Eventually, in 1638, twelve years after the Company was formed, a successful expedition under du Parquet landed on Grenada using Martinique as a base, and established a settlement. The story[14] is that he sent a ship's captain called La Rivière, who was accustomed to fish near Grenada, to build a house near one of the indigenous villages. The plan was that arms and ammunition would be stored in this house in readiness for the landing of others, and for the building of a fort.

La Rivière chose a spot on what is now St George's Harbour to land, and built the house at the foot of a hill. He seemed to have been trusted by the indigenes, and spoke their language. He was left undisturbed by them for a while, but eventually they came to investigate. He began to talk to them on the advantages of forming an alliance with the French against the English. Sensing that his listeners were receptive, he returned to Martinique where he reported on his adventures.[15]

Kairouane Agrees to French Settlement

In 1649 du Parquet recruited 203 able-bodied men from Martinique and hired two ships, one of which belonged to La Rivière. Wells states that among this company were 'some of the most distinguished inhabitants of Martinique'.[16] Du Parquet appointed Jean Le Pelletier, also known as Captain Le Pas, and Captain Lorimer as captains and commanders of these ships, and packed them with sufficient supplies of cassava bread, salt meat, pork, peas and beans to last several months. He sent with the ships prefabricated sections for building a house. The ships also carried arms, munitions and agricultural implements. Finally, three kegs of whisky and two pipes of Madeira wine were put on board. Crouse remarks: 'Never before had an expedition for the colonization of a West Indian Island been so well fitted out; even its personnel was carefully considered for it numbered several masons, carpenters, locksmiths, and artisans of various kinds'.[17]

Du Parquet and his personal chaplain sailed with the ships on
14 March 1649 from Fort St Pierre, Martinique, and entered St George's
Harbour three days later. Today we wonder why a person like du Parquet
would bother to take a priest on an expedition designed to trick, subdue
and defraud people of their land. In those times neither du Parquet nor
his chaplain saw any inconsistency in his actions. Many Europeans at this
time regarded non-Europeans, especially if they were also not of the
Christian faith, as lesser human beings than themselves. The lack of a
Christian baptism made them 'heathen' or 'pagan', not children of God,
and for ever barred from the Christian heaven. As lesser mortals, their
welfare was to be subjugated and even sacrificed for the betterment of the
Christian Europeans.

On landing, du Parquet took the cross that was being carried by his
chaplain, planted it in the ground, and had all bend low in a prayer of
thanksgiving, asking God to bless the expedition. Immediately after these
prayers, du Parquet had his company of men unload the arms and cannon
he had brought. They immediately set about building a palisade fort on a
strip of land[18] that bordered a deep lake of brackish water (today's
Lagoon). The site of the first settlement was chosen for the ease of defence.
It was bordered by water on two sides, and all that was necessary was to
guard against attacks coming from either side of the narrow strip of land
on which the fort would be built.

The ramparts of the fort were built with the trees cut from this spit of
land. Two cannon were placed on these ramparts, and a musket-proof
blockhouse was built in the middle. The pre-fabricated building that had
been brought from Martinique was erected in the centre of the compound.
Du Tertre, who visited Grenada around 1656, several years after the
French arrived, describes this as a large pavilion.[19] Several smaller buildings to be used for living quarters were also built inside the compound.
There was also a structure used as a church for the resident Dominican
missionary. These buildings were surrounded by a stockade. As soon as
the stockade and living quarters for the men were completed, du Parquet
set his men to cutting more trees and clearing the land around the lake in
the area that is today's Tanteen. This fortified settlement was called Fort
Annunciation.

The inhabitants, most likely Galibi, who by this time were living in
the southern part of Grenada, had been watching the progress of construction from the surrounding hills. Filled with misgivings as to why the
French would need a fort and ammunition if they were friends, fifty of
them arrived on the scene in a war canoe, splendidly adorned with feathers, but otherwise, in *puris naturalibis,* as a shocked missionary observed.
They were armed with bows and war clubs and led by their chief,

Kairouane.[20] Captain La Rivière, the first one to sight the canoe, rushed down to greet them, and he persuaded them to come ashore.[21]

Brian Edwards[22] says that du Parquet was received and entertained with the utmost 'kindness and cordiality', contrary to his expectations, and perhaps his wishes.[23] During this reception a parley was held between du Parquet and Kairouane, with La Rivière as interpreter.[24] Kairouane insisted that, if the French wanted to settle on Grenada, he must be given a real treaty.[25] Edwards says that du Parquet '[T]hought it necessary to affect some little regard to moderation, by pretending to open a treaty with the Chief of the Charibs for the purchase of the country'.[26]

A treaty was drawn up and presented, along with gifts of billhooks, glass beads, crystals, knives, axes, scythes and other goods requested by Kairouane for his community, as well as two quarts of brandy, a red cloak strewn with silver and a grey hat ornamented with feathers, which were a personal gift to Kairouane. The island was not 'Fairly ceded by the natives themselves to the French nation in lawful purchase'[27] for trinkets. This is a persistent error in most histories of Grenada. The treaty between Kairouane and the French allowed French settlement in return for French protection, agricultural development and trade. As Europeans occupied more and more islands, Kairouane, and those who thought like him, realized that if they did not try negotiation, their fate would be the same as that of their brothers in St Kitts and in the Greater Antilles. It was because of this understanding that du Parquet met no resistance in landing in Grenada.

The agreement between Kairouane and the Frenchmen was for peaceful co-existence between the settlers and the native inhabitants of Grenada. There was agreement on the division of the island into two unequal parts. Basseterre included the south and the western part of the island, and was to be settled by the French. This side of the island had calmer waters, and good harbours. Cabesterre to the east comprised about three-quarters of the island. There was coastal plain on this side, and it enjoyed the trade winds. It was the part of the island that was more heavily populated by the indigenous people. This part of the island, and the north, would remain in the possession of the indigenous inhabitants, and the agreement was that they would be left undisturbed.

The agreement du Parquet made with Kairouane was simply a ruse to ensure the acceptance of the French until the settlement was well established and made secure, and Grenada could be taken over completely. Du Parquet's objective was to colonize Grenada, establish plantations, and use the natives to provide the workforce. He never had any intention of keeping to the agreements made.

Grenada Sold

On 27 September 1650, du Parquet bought Martinique, St Lucia and Grenada and the Grenadines from the Company of the Isles of America for 41,500 livres, which Jesse says is equal to £1660.[28] The next year the king of France named du Parquet Lieutenant-Governor over the islands he had purchased.

With the purchase and governorship acquired, du Parquet set about establishing settlements in the islands he had newly acquired. In Grenada houses were erected on the shores of the lagoon near the fort, and the lands that had been cleared were planted with tobacco. Du Parquet was well aware of the profits to be made from tobacco. Tobacco was one of the first crops planted by the colonists in St Kitts and Barbados, and the export of the tobacco crop had brought the tobacco planters an excellent return on their investment. Richard Sheridan[29] points out that a single tobacco crop brought investors in these colonies to an early state of prosperity. Lands were given out to many all over Grenada, including to members of the Dominican Order, who were given a property that they called *Le Fonds du Grand Pauvre.*

After supervising the planting and then reaping of the first tobacco crop, du Parquet returned to Martinique in La Rivière's ship, while Le Pas sailed away for Santo Domingo. Du Parquet left his cousin, Jean Le Comte,[30] a man of 55, as the first Governor of Grenada. Governor du Parquet wrote a brief character sketch of Le Comte. He was described as a man of martial bearing, good and affable and possessing all the qualities necessary for a governor. He would soon need all of his personal resources to deal with the situation that would develop in Grenada.

Trouble Brews

The Kalinago in St Vincent greeted the news that Kairouane had made a treaty with the French with great anger and consternation. A conference of the chiefs of Grenada, St Vincent and Dominica was called in Grenada, and one of the actions considered appropriate was to punish Kairouane by passing a death sentence on him for making a treaty allowing Europeans to enter one of the last remaining islands free of European influence, and this without any reference to the other chiefs. In the end the chiefs decided to wait and see if the French would honour the treaty they had signed with Kairouane.

They did not have long to wait to be sure that the French were not to be trusted. Early historians John Scott and Abbe Raynal[31] both agree that the people of Grenada soon felt that the French had duped them, and that their hospitality and friendship had been betrayed. An incident in which three fishermen from Martinique looted a Kalinago canoe was the trigger. An expedition was organized from St Vincent with the help and participation of warriors from Dominica to attack the French in Grenada and drive them out. In November 1649, eleven war canoes containing 500 men attacked Fort Annunciation. For reasons of his own, the French were warned of the plan by a chief in Grenada called Duquesne. The French were therefore prepared for the attack.

The French stored provisions inside the fort and ordered all inhabitants inside. Discovering this situation, some of the warriors laid siege to the fort, while others roamed around the settlement, destroying everything. They did not attack the fort directly, but tried to set it alight by burning the dry vegetation on the windward side of the fort, in the expectation that the fire would spread to the palisade. After eight days the French had run out of water. What looked like disaster for the French turned into good fortune when a heavy downpour of rain put out the flames, provided those inside the fort with water, and dampened the spirits of the warriors. A few days later, the warriors gave up and sailed away.

The French Break Trust

This visitation from a large and hostile force of indigenous people immediately made Le Comte wary. He had further reasons to be on guard, as the agreements made with the indigenes were steadily eroded. As the French population grew, the French built fortified settlements all over Grenada to accommodate the increasing population. The indigenous inhabitants became increasingly alarmed as they witnessed the rapid settlement and fortification of their island in contravention of the agreement and attendent understanding that the French were simply to establish a trading post. Fort Du Marquis was built in Beausejour in 1649 to accommodate twenty persons, as well as Fort St Jean at Darbeau Hill to accommodate seventy people. Construction on the Monckton Hill Redoubt overlooking St George's Harbour began the next year for the further protection of Fort Annunciation, now referred to as 'The Great Fort'. Fort D'Esnambuc was built later – in 1654. These types of forts, built as refuges for the protection of the inhabitants and for defence against attack, fit the definition of a deodand.[32] In addition to contravening the spirit of the treaty signed with Kairouane, the French also began to abuse other aspects of hospitality. Short of European women,[33] the French courted the local women. These liaisons added to the growing animosity between the indigenous inhabitants and the French. The Kalinago and Galibi men historically did not tolerate interference with their women. Such interference had occasioned attacks on the sailors of several vessels in the past, who had initially been treated with hospitality. The Kalinago and Galibi men began to retaliate against the French breach of trust by attacking Frenchmen who wandered outside their fortified settlements. The French were obliged never to go out alone, to work always in groups and always to be heavily armed. Nevertheless, clever ruses got the Frenchmen to come out of the forts.

The Indigenous People Attacked

The French had always intended either to encourage the original inhabitants to leave Grenada, or to enslave them and use them as labour. Now the French began in earnest to make things very uncomfortable for them to remain. Offensives were made on the *carbets*. In one instance, Le Comte mounted an attack against the largest *carbet*, somewhere on the slopes of Mount St Catherine. The offensive was a complete failure, and ended with many French lives being lost. Reinforcements were requested, and du Parquet sent 300 more men to Grenada in 1652.

Le Comte was ordered by du Parquet to chase the indigenes to the north of the island, and annihilate them if possible. On hearing that French reinforcements were coming in, the Kalinago and Galibi sent a call for help to Dominica and St Vincent. A fighting force of about 800 was assembled, and a plan made to attack the Great Fort and the settlement around it. Again, the French learned of these plans, and made a counter plan. They waited until the attackers were only a few yards away from the fort, and then opened fire. The surprise and the terror at the thunder of the cannon routed the warriors and they fled through the forest towards Cabesterre in complete disarray. The French followed on their heels, and for several days the French pursued and killed all they caught.

A reduced force of 300 warriors reached a mountain top *carbet* in Cabesterre. The French attacked this *carbet*, killing about eighty more warriors. The remainder got away down the mountain to the sea, where they escaped by canoe.

Relentlessly the French pursued the warriors to the very north of the island where the remnants of the fighting force had sequestered themselves in a *carbet* on a high cliff approached by a narrow, secret pathway. The French could not discover the way to this camp. Then the French got help from an unlikely quarter. A young indigene called Thomas[34] sought the daughter of Chief Duquesne in marriage, but was refused. In a fit of pique and disappointment, he killed the girl's brother, and then fled to Martinique. There he met with du Parquet, telling him that he had fled because he had always been friendly to the French. He further told him that he could lead the French soldiers to the spot where the warriors had ensconced themselves. Du Parquet, Thomas, and 300 fighting Frenchmen sailed from Martinique on 20 May 1651, arriving in Grenada six days later.

With the help of Thomas, the French discovered the way up to the camp and surprised about forty warriors, who were sleeping with a very false sense of security. They fought bravely, but they were surrounded. Rather than face capture or death, the forty warriors threw themselves onto the rocks beneath the cliff. The place where this dramatic event took place became known as *Le Morne de Sauteurs*.

The traditionally identified of site of Le Morne de Sauteurs is the cliff at the rear of the present Roman Catholic Church. Recently the view has been expressed that the site of the camp was the present site of Helvellen House across the bay from Sauteurs town.

After the massacre at Le Morne de Sauteurs, du Parquet ordered the indigenous people's huts destroyed, as well as their gardens. He then returned to the fort, and instructed that another fort should be built a quarter of a league from the first. This fort was called Fort St Jean, and was occupied by a garrison of seventy men.

It is often thought that this marked the extinction of Grenada's indigenous people. This belief is romantic myth. In fact, there were quite a few remaining who continued to live in the mountains in Cabesterre. They waged guerrilla warfare in reprisal against the massacre of their people, killing every Frenchman they found hunting in the woods or away from the forts, and in addition raided isolated villages, killing the inhabitants.

The Kalinago from other islands also continually harassed the French in Grenada. On one such occasion,[35] a fleet of canoes from St Vincent travelled to Grenada, landing unseen near Fort Du Marquis, near today's Happy Hill. The Kalinago hid themselves in the bushes with a captive pig. They then released the pig, which ran along the beach. Three Frenchmen came out of the fort, running after the pig, and were ambushed and killed. This particular fort had to be abandoned several times, due to attacks by warriors. After being resettled in 1653, it was attacked in 1654 and was ransacked and burnt by a force of about 500 Kalinago.

During 1653 and the following year, the indigenous chiefs in the Windward Islands met and determined that, if they did not get rid of the Europeans in their remaining homelands, they would soon all face extinction. It was now or never to mount a final attempt to get rid of the intruders who had destroyed their way of life and killed so many of their people, and restore control over their homelands. This was the message distilled in the war cry sent through the islands – death to all white men! This would be the final effort and it would be a fight to the finish. The warriors in Grenada needed no persuasion to join in this final war, for they were still smarting from the massacres of 1652.

The Massacres of 1654

In April of 1654, Sieur Imbaut, one of the French planters, was killed. One story is that Imbaut, heedless of danger, accepted the invitation of some local people to visit them. During the visit, he was set upon and murdered. The other version is more likely. Angered at the extreme cruelty shown by a sea captain[36] to one of their number, Kalinago came down from St Vincent and joined those in Grenada in taking vengeance. They carried out several attacks including the murder of Imbaut, and one on the house of a man called de la Mare where a number of people had taken refuge. They set fire to the roof with flaming arrows, and though the occupants escaped, they were later caught in an ambush and many of them killed.

News of the attacks spread quickly, and the French inhabitants sought refuge in the forts. The warriors were right behind them, burning the houses and laying waste to the plantations. A month later, in May 1654, Kalinago landed at Beausejour, scattering the population and causing them to take refuge in the forests, where many died of starvation. A ship from Cayenne saved the white population of Grenada from extinction. It arrived carrying 300 Dutch mercenaries. These soldiers remained behind, occupying the newly built Fort d'Esnambuc near Le Morne de Sauteurs, and making frequent sorties against the indigenous inhabitants. In order to try to neutralize this fort, about 1000 indigenous warriors laid siege to it, causing the Dutch mercenaries there to flee temporarily to Fort Annunciation.

By the end of 1654, Le Comte, hearing that the Kalinago, including 'fugitive negroes' from St Vincent who were encouraging them to further hostilities, were actually present in the island, decided that there had to be a final solution to the harassment of the French. Du Parquet approved Le Comte's plan to take a force northwards into the territory of the indigenous people, but gave instructions that the French should only kill the Kalinago from St Vincent.

Le Comte knew that it was impossible to hunt down and exterminate the Kalinago from St Vincent without touching those who normally lived in Grenada. Nevertheless, Le Comte set out with about a hundred men from Beausejour, sending another fifty men under Sieur Le Marquis by another route. The French travelled quickly and unnoticed through

Cabesterre, and effected a pincer movement on the area where Le Comte believed most of the Kalinago and 'Black Caribs' from St Vincent were to be found.

The raid was carried out at daybreak, and the usually canny people were caught absolutely and completely by surprise, and were unprepared to defend themselves. The largest *carbets* were attacked first. The houses were set alight, and, as the unfortunate people tried to escape, the French cut them to pieces without regard to age or sex. Du Tertre, a French priest who was stationed in the Caribbean around this time, records a story of a quarrel between two French soldiers over a beautiful Amerindian girl of about twelve or thirteen years of age who was captured during this massacre. As the tale goes, a third soldier witnessing the scene shot the girl in the head to settle the argument.[37]

As part of the same operation, the French went down to the beaches, and burnt all the canoes to prevent escape by those who were away from the villages at the time of the massacre. The French also combed the forests and areas near the rivers, killing the indigenous people as they were found. About eighty people, both from St Vincent and Grenada, were found and killed.

After the attack on Fort d'Esnambuc in 1654, Le Comte decided to pay a visit to this fort, which was situated on the present site of the Anglican Church in Sauteurs, to boost the morale of Dutch mercenaries who were stationed there. He tried to come ashore in rough weather. Some say he drowned in an attempt to save a soldier who went overboard and could not swim. Some say the rowboat in which he was coming ashore capsized, and all drowned. Le Comte, therefore, did not live to achieve his ambition of the final extinction of the indigenous people of Grenada.

Their Spirit Broken

These massacres of 1654 did not go without reprisal from the Kalinago in the other islands. They set out from St Vincent on a regular basis, carrying out surreptitious raids on several settlements in Grenada, and causing much loss of life and property. On one occasion twenty-four war canoes proceeded down the western side of the island to Grande Anse, where they landed and began to lay waste the countryside. A month later they returned and attacked the fortified dwelling of a planter called Sieur Mariage.[38] This was too well fortified for them to take. Du Parquet had again and again to send additional military assistance to Grenada. However, despite the support from the Kalinago in St Vincent, the spirit of the Kalinago and Galibi in Grenada had been finally broken by the massacres of 1654.

The massacres of 1654 marked the end of an era. The original inhabitants of Grenada had lived here for at least 2000, possibly 6000, years. Now their numbers had been so decimated that they could no longer control any part of their ancestral homeland. In comparison all the people – the Africans, Europeans, East Indians and others – whose ancestors crossed the Atlantic to live in Grenada or the Caribbean can trace their arrival no further than 400 years.

Many of the remaining Kalinago and Galibi left the island, taking refuge in Guiana, St Vincent and Dominica. Those who chose to stay secreted themselves in the most inaccessible regions, living as quietly as possible. In 1709 some were still in Grenada. This is verified by pottery remains and by Père Labat who visited the island in 1700, and found some of them living on lands belonging to the Dominican Order.[39] Seventy years later the descendants of the indigenous people are mentioned as a group in a population report of 1778, when 256 'Mulattos or Mestizos' are counted.[40] Finally, and most curiously, the seventeenth item of the capitulation terms Governor Macartney would demand of d'Estaing, the commander of the French forces, in 1779, was that 'no Caribs be allowed to remain in the island'.[41]

Eventually those who remained were absorbed into the already polyglot colonial society of the seventeenth century. As late as 1879, a European visitor to Grenada lodging at the Grand Etang Rest House, reported: 'From a woman who came up from the village of Delphi I bought a Carib basket; this art of basket weaving having survived the Indians who practised and taught it.'[42]

Maybe that woman from Delphi was a survivor of a proud race of people. There are people in Grenada today who are proud of the certain knowledge that the blood of Kalinago or Galibi ancestors runs in their veins.[43]

Kalinago and Galibi heritage remains a part of the Grenadian culture. Many words such as *hurricane, ajupa* (a hut), *titiwe* (the name for little fish), *mabouya* (evil spirit or the much-feared little lizard) are part of the Grenadian's vocabulary. Grenadians plait both the African and 'Carib' baskets, and enjoy the other skills and items passed on to the Africans in Grenada by the indigenous people, including fishing and hunting techniques, canoe building, knowledge of the sea and of nature, the art of pottery making, cassava manufacture, and useful items of everyday life such as hammocks and cassava strainers, the knowledge of the goodness of some food such as peanuts, fish and cassava, and the less good, such as the fatty meats and too much salt. Grenada's aborigines left more of a stamp on everyday Caribbean living than is traditionally presented.

We should pause a moment to mourn the genocide of the entire indigenous people of the Caribbean by the Europeans. When Columbus sailed into the Caribbean, there were an estimated one million people living in the islands. In twenty years, only 60,000 remained, and that number rapidly declined. Today only about 2500 Kalinago live on the Carib Reserve in Dominica, together with a few people of mixed race in that island, in Grenada, St Vincent, Belize and Honduras, and in some of the other islands of the Caribbean – these are all that remain of a people who were independent, intelligent, inventive, proud and brave. Their determined resistance to political and cultural domination has relevance to the people of the Caribbean today, in their struggles for self-determination and survival as a viable group of nations.

Notes

1 Davis and Goodwin, p. 38.
2 One of the contemporary writers who believed that the 'Caribs' chewed human flesh only for ritualistic purposes was John Scott, who wrote his 'History of Grenada' around this time. See Honychurch, p. 22.
3 See Honychurch, p. 22.
4 Barome, p. 33.
5 *Ibid.*
6 See Honychurch, p. 22.
7 Barome, p. 35.
8 In the midst of the activity of the French settlement of Grenada, Tiburcio Radin did return. He had taken his vows as a Capuchin priest and had brought with him several other missionaries full of zeal. They hoped to stay in Grenada and work with the indigenes. The French received the missionaries with hospitality, but explained to them that they could not be invited to stay because just then the French and Spanish were not on good terms as nations. Comforted by seeing a Dominican priest in the settlement, Radin and his travelling companions, disappointed though they were, re-embarked and went to Cumana in Venezuela instead, to save souls there.
9 Devas (1974), p. 24.
10 A Papal bull was an edict or decision by the Pope invested with all his authority as head of the Roman Catholic Church.
11 Most possibly this is today's Grand Anse, although there is a Grand Bay on the Point Salines peninsula.
12 Govt of Grenada, *Grenada Handbook*, p. 19.
13 Edwards, p. 353.
14 There are several books and documents written in times contemporary to the first settlement of Grenada that describe the events that would end in the eventual loss of Grenada as a homeland of native peoples. Two of the writers were Dominican priests. Père Jean Baptiste du Tertre was a contemporary, and sometimes an eye-witness to what he recorded. He wrote a four-volume *General History of the Antilles* in French, which was published in France in 1667–71. The other Dominican was Père Jean Baptiste Labat who wrote forty or fifty years later. His manuscript was a two-volume description of his voyages to the Caribbean, again in French, and was published in France in 1724. In addition, there is a handwritten manuscript by John Scott, compiled in the reign of Charles II, and an anonymous history *L'Historie de l'Isle de Grenade en Amerique*, which appeared in 1659.

These documents do not always agree, but they are all useful in that they provide accounts of events that throw light on a very important part of Grenada's history, and the history of Grenada's indigenous people.

15 Père Labat gives a different version of the settlement of Grenada by the French. His account, reported in Devas (1974), p. 42, is that du Parquet had previously been approached by the chief of Grenada, Kairouane, who begged du Parquet to assume control of the island to protect them from the Spanish and the British. Spanish cruelty to indigenous people was well known, and the British had just effected a terrible massacre of the indigenous people in St Kitts.

16 Wells, p. 6.

17 Crouse (1977), p. 195.

18 This bit of land is now submerged. The outline of it can be clearly seen under the water. This piece of land once joined the present yacht club to the area known locally as 'The Ballast Ground', enclosing a freshwater lagoon.

19 Du Tertre, reported in Devas (1932), p. 7.

20 Kairouane has been identified as the Galibi chief of the southern section of Grenada.

21 Crouse, p. 196.

22 Brian Edwards was an Englishman by birth, but is said to have produced a history seen through the eyes of a Creole planter. His book, *History Civil and Commercial of the British West Indies*, provides a comprehensive view of the British islands. See Goveia, pp. 80–9, for a fuller appraisal of Brian Edwards's contribution to the historiography of the Caribbean.

23 Edwards, p. 354.

24 La Rivière met an unfortunate end in St Lucia some years later. As far as the indigenous people of St Lucia were concerned, he was a bad choice to succeed M. de Roseland, the Governor of that island, when he died. De Roseland was married to an indigenous woman, and had excellent relations with them. This was not the case with La Rivière. It may be that the indigenous people in St Lucia needed to pay back La Rivière for duping their brothers in Grenada, or maybe La Rivière had indulged in new deceit. In any event, to please them, he began to invite a few to his home in St Lucia, which was a little distance from the fort. On one occasion while they were all drinking together, the warriors pounced on him, killing him and ten men who were with him.

25 This account is based on du Tertre's account reported in Devas (1932) and on Crouse's.

26 Edwards, p. 354.

27 Stark, p. 161.

28 Jesse, p. 45.

29 Sheridan (1974), p. 394.

30 This name is spelt Compte in the *Grenada Handbook*, and in all the accounts that have used the *Handbook* as their main source book for this period.

31 Devas (1974), p. 46.

32 David Buisseret reserves this classification only for Fort Royal and does not mention the smaller forts. For a discussion on the early fortifications of Grenada see David Buisseret, 'The Elusive Deodand: A Study of Fortified Refuges of the Lesser Antilles', *Journal of Caribbean History*, vols 6 and 7, 1973.

33 In 1702 the Governor, M. Bouloc, wrote to the Minister in Paris that: 'We have a real need of 20 or so young women. I would undertake to get them married as soon as they arrived.' Devas (1974), p. 66.

34 After the European settlement of the Windward Islands, many indigenous people adopted Christian names, or answered to Europeanized versions of their Kalinago or Galibi name. Two examples of the latter are said to be Chiefs Duquesne and Marquis, who have given their Europeanized names to areas in Grenada.

35 Jessamy, p. 11.
36 Crouse gives this tale: 'A Sea Captain, labouring under the impression ... that a Carib of St Vincent whom he had on board his vessel was responsible for the death of one of his men, caused him to be lashed to the mast and given a fearful flogging. The fellow managed to escape and rejoined his tribe where he displayed his wounds, demanding vengeance for the suffering he had undergone and for the insult offered the tribal honour by this assault on his person.' (p. 214).
37 Stark, p. 162.
38 Crouse, p. 216.
39 Devas (1974), p. 63.
40 CO 101/21, Macartney to Germain 'State of Grenada on 31st Day of May, 1778', Colonial Office papers, Public Records Office (PRO), London.
41 CO 101/23, 'Terms of Capitulation', Macartney to D'Estaing, 4 July 1779, PRO, London.
42 Ober, p. 271.
43 See Franklyn (1992), author's note (frontispiece).

3

French Grenada

Several years of fighting had left the French settlers in Grenada weary and traumatized. Although the indigenous people in Grenada were decimated in number and those that remained had escaped to inaccessible mountain dwellings, Kalinago from St Vincent and Dominica still harassed French shipping in the waters of the Windward Islands. No French vessel was safe from the possibility of being spotted and pursued by the very fast Amerindian canoes, and sometimes captured. Coastal settlements remained vulnerable to raids, the inhabitants being taken to St Vincent as slaves.

The Consolidation of French Settlement under de Valmenière

In 1654 du Parquet appointed Louis Cacquery, Sieur de Valmenière,[1] as successor to Le Comte. De Valmenière was faced with a mutiny as soon as he arrived. An officer named Lefont, who was First Captain and Major of the French garrison in Grenada, thought that the Governor's position should have been his. Du Parquet would have named him Governor, except that Lefont was known to be a man of haughty manners and brutal tendencies. With seventy followers Lefont took over Fort St Jean and refused to accept the new Governor.

Learning of the crisis, du Parquet sent orders to Lefont to accept de Valmenière as Governor, and at the same time bolstered his forces with 100 Walloons. (The Walloons were European mercenaries, natives of a country that is today both part of of France and part of Belgium. This group of Walloons had previously been employed by the Dutch in Brazil, but were evicted by the Portuguese in 1654. They were therefore available to join du Parquet's attempt to restore order in Grenada at this time. Throughout the history of Grenada, mercenaries originating from different nations played a significant role in the outcome of wars and internal conflicts.) Lefont refused to receive the Captain of the Walloons who had come to reason with him. A gun battle ensued, with casualties on both sides.

Lefont ended up in prison. Rather than wait for trial and an ignominious death, he committed suicide, allegedly by drinking poison provided by his black – or some say 'Carib' – woman servant. His main supporter, Le Marquis, was at first sentenced to death, but du Parquet subsequently commuted this to banishment along with Lefont's other supporters.

After this incident, de Valmenière established a government that is recorded as being characterized by tact, moderation and good judgement. He suggested that the inhabitants no longer sleep on their scattered plantations, but stay together in the forts, which had been built at strategic points around the island,[2] at least one to serve every six plantations. De Valmenière not only restored settlements abandoned during the period of resistance by the Kalinago and Galibi people, but established several new settlements and plantations, increasing the population by inducing settlers from the other islands to come to Grenada with their slaves. Under his leadership, the colony began to prosper. It produced timber, rich fruits, gums, dyewoods, resins, balsam, ground provisions, river and sea fish, turtles, fowl, game and cattle. The sugar was said to be fine and more valuable than that of Martinique or Guadeloupe, and the indigo the finest in the West Indies. At this time tobacco was still the staple commodity, and one or two pounds of Grenada tobacco were said to be worth two or three that grew in any of the other islands. Cacao and cotton were also grown.[3]

Grenada is Sold to Comte de Cérillac

The prosperity that de Valmenière brought to Grenada came too late for du Parquet. Grenada had been a financial nightmare for him, with the continual resistance by the indigenous people, the resulting loss of life and property, and finally Lefont's insurrection. Du Parquet also had other financial troubles, and in 1657, he decided to sell Grenada and some of his other possessions in the West Indies. Comte de Cérillac was immediately interested, but before he jumped to purchase he sought the advice of the wise and experienced cleric, Père du Tertre, who had come out with him to the West Indies to survey several of the French islands that were for sale. After visiting all the islands and making enquiries of people in each who were in a position to give them sound information, de Cérillac decided to purchase Grenada because it seemed to be the most promising. Although the price was steep, du Tertre advised that the island was well worth its price, and de Cérillac would, in three years, be able to make ten times the amount he had paid for the island. Grenada was twice the size of St Christopher. It had an excellent harbour, large enough to accommodate fifty vessels. There was also the possibility of cutting through the neck of land separating the harbour from the lagoon and opening up additional anchorage for smaller vessels. The fort was strongly built, although the

church was merely a large shack made out of branches and reeds. Fifty
years later Labat would confirm Grenada's potential despite the apparent
poverty of the place:

> [Admitting] the broken conditions of its terrain along the Basseterre
> coast, which was due to the hills and mountains skirting the shore-
> line, it had excellent ground further inland where houses and
> wagons would be able to go as soon as it was opened up. Numerous
> rivers gave an ample supply of water, while a large number of sturdy
> trees proclaimed the fertility of the soil. There was plenty of game
> on land and swarms of fish in the surrounding waters. After taking
> soundings, they found that St George's harbour had enough depth
> and was sufficiently large to shelter a fleet of fifty sail.[4]

In 1657, de Cérillac bought Grenada and the Grenadines for approximately £1890.[5] For this he got not only normal rights and ownership but
also everything on Grenada and in it: the slaves, cannons, muskets, and
munitions of war, buildings and equipment. The workmen and indentured
servants on Grenada would also labour for the new owner's benefit. Du
Parquet's position as ruler of the island also passed to de Cérillac, subject
to the king's approval. It was de Cérillac's intention to sail for Grenada
from France with a well-provisioned ship and 400 men. After several
drawbacks and misfortunes, he abandoned his plan, appointed his
lieutenant, a man called du Buc,[6] as Governor and as his personal representative, and sent him ahead to Grenada until he could arrive accompanied
by the men and provisions. Governor du Buc arrived in Grenada during
the year 1658.

A Tyrant for Governor

De Cerrillac had made a very unwise choice in making du Buc Governor
of Grenada. Du Buc was a tyrant, described by Raynal as a 'rapacious,
violent and inflexible governor'.[7] His manner of government was so
extreme, arbitrary, haughty, severe and intolerable that many colonists,
including the island's Dominican priest, Father Bresson, pulled up stakes
and migrated to Martinique. The two Capuchin priests sent as replace-
ments for the departing cleric also came to detest the Governor. Du Tertre
records that they met very hard times, had not sufficient food, and survived only by hunting game.[8] Instead of modifying his manner when he
observed the exodus to Martinique, du Buc became worse than ever,
exercising his bad temper and overbearing behaviour on the remaining

population, and effecting many injustices and tyrannies. Eventually the people could stand him no longer. They rose up against him, and dragged him before what today would be called a 'People's Court'.

Only one of the persons involved in the apprehension and trial of the Governor could write. His name was Archangeli, and he was made the clerk. The role of prosecutor was taken by a farrier called de la Brie, who signed his name by the impress of a horseshoe. At the end of the proceedings, the Governor was found guilty of all his crimes, and sentenced to hang. Du Buc, haughty to the last, demanded to be beheaded, as he was a nobleman. Since no one in Grenada knew how to behead a person, a compromise was agreed, and the Governor was run through with a sword.[9]

De Tracy Investigates

Upon hearing of the execution of the Governor, the French Court sent a warship with the Governor-General of all the French islands, de Tracy, as a Special Commissioner to inquire into the events leading up to the execution of the Governor. De Tracy landed in Grenada on 22 November 1664. Not surprisingly, he found that all the persons who had been involved in the trial of the Governor had disappeared, except Archangeli, and there was no one else who could be held accountable for what had happened. De Tracy banished Archangeli to the island of Marie Galante, where he lived until 1692.[10] He also found the entire society was in a miserable state. Not only was the population demoralized, but also they were almost starving.

De Tracy made a valiant effort to attend to the grievances of the colonists, and settle the society. He did not have an easy time. Right up to the last day of his stay in Grenada he was faced with problems. On that day he heard that a group of individuals had begun a church of their own, challenging the supremacy of the Catholic Church. De Tracy warned them that if they continued in their heresy, they would be fined and possibly apprehended and tried as felons.

The most important recommendation that de Tracy made to the French government towards re-establishing stability was to request that de Cérillac sell his shares in the Company of the Isles of America, and be relieved of his responsibility for Grenada. De Cérillac received his allotted payment of 10,000 crowns and severed his connections with Grenada.

De Tracy appointed M. Vincent, a captain, as Governor before he left the island. In that same year, 1664, Louis XIV, the king of France, created the French West India Company. It was the king's intention, and that of his Minister, Colbert, to arrange things so that the islands would bring

direct profit to the king and to France. The king offered to buy out the
interest holders in the former Company of the Isles of America, and,
although the owners of the various islands were not pleased, they eventually had to acquiesce. For a while, it appeared that Grenada under the new
Company would prosper. The Directors of the Company sent in people to
resettle and work the old plantations. Very soon, however, Louis XIV and
his government levied such heavy taxation on the produce that many
planters found it impossible to stay in Grenada. They sold their holdings
and left.

Ten years later, in 1674, the French West India Company was also
dissolved by the king of France due to growing abuses and corruption in
the Company. In 1674, Grenada became a French Colony rather than a
piece of private property in the hands of Companies of Frenchmen.

And What of the Ordinary Man?

Since the main interests of the writers of the time were ownership and
control of territory, very little is written about Grenadian society, and the
conditions of life of the population. The date of the introduction of
African slaves into the colony is not known, but the first slaves were
almost certainly purchased from the Dutch, who were slave traders selling
slaves to Barbados and the other islands in this region.

Great was the trauma in the lives of Africans who had the misfortune to be taken as a prisoners-of-war in Africa or kidnapped, and sold
to the Europeans by other Africans as slaves. While awaiting shipment
to the New World, they were herded into baracoons, where many died
from the diseases spread by the appalling conditions in those awful
places. Prospective purchasers had the slaves inspected for sicknesses
and deformity before they were packed away as tightly as sardines in a
can in the dark, stinking, hot holds of the slave ships. The 'Middle
Passage', as the voyage of the slaves to the New World is often called,
occasioned very high mortality of the persons on board ship, due to the
lack of proper food, adequate water, ventilation, sanitation and medical
attention. This did not unduly upset the captains, as the minimum conditions had been determined by which sufficient slaves would survive to
produce the greatest profit. When the slaves arrived at their destination,
they were sold to the planters by auction. In Grenada they were sold in
the Market Square.

Grenada was a thickly forested island, and in order to establish plantations, these trees had to be cut down by the slaves, the ground cleared of
boulders and stones, and prepared for the first planting. This hard work

fell to people who were unaccustomed to this much physical labour, and their suffering was great.

Under the French, the slaves were governed according to a code called the 'Code Noir'. Although this provided guidelines for the treatment of slaves, many planters did not adhere to either the letter or the spirit of the code. The treatment of slaves on the estates differed according to the disposition and attitudes of the estate owner or, in the case of owners who lived in Europe and hired managers to run their estates, these managers.

The State of the Island

All did not go smoothly at the beginning of French colonial rule. John Campbell[11] tells us that in 1674 the suppression of the colony by Louis XIV '[R]evived further disturbances, which, though they were very soon quelled, yet were followed from an ill impression of the new administration, by the desertion of some of the more opulent planters.'[13]

The movement of planters and resources out of Grenada impeded its development. Grenada remained underdeveloped in comparison to other islands such as Barbados and Martinique. The statistics for the year 1700 given by the *Encyclopaedia Britannica* of 1777–84 put the population at this time at 835 people – 257 whites, 53 coloureds and 525 blacks. Interestingly, there is no mention of the remainder of the Kalinago and Galibi people who lived in the mountains. There were three sugar estates and fifty-two indigo plantations on the island, and a stock of sixty-four horses and 569 head of cattle.[12] In spite of the fact that Grenada was underdeveloped, the island supplied livestock and poultry to Martinique. Grenadian tobacco continued to be of the highest quality. Grenada also produced salt at the salt ponds at Point Salines.

Under French rule, the name of the Great Fort was changed from Fort Annunciation to Fort Louis. The permanent military garrison varied between thirty-five to forty soldiers of the Compagnie Detachie de la Marine. The soldiers lived in miserable little huts built using the wall of the fort as the rear wall. The officers' quarters were not much better. We can only imagine the housing conditions of the rest of the population, and especially that of the slaves. Travel around Grenada was mainly by sea in small craft, or on horseback.

In 1675 Dutch privateers captured the island. Luckily for the French, a French man-of-war arrived unexpectedly, and the island was recaptured. After this incident, French occupation of Grenada was to remain unchallenged for eighty-seven years.

The Development of Carriacou

Very soon after the Lesser Antilles were settled by the French, Carriacou became known to them as a place where a living could be made. Frenchmen from Guadeloupe began to frequent the island in search of turtles. An early edition of the *Encyclopaedia Britannica* reported that these turtle hunters:

> [I]n the leisure afforded them by so easy an occupation, employed themselves in clearing the ground. In process of time, their small number was increased by the accession of some of the inhabitants of Guadeloupe, who, finding that their plantations were destroyed by a particular sort of ant, removed to Carriacou. The islands flourished from the liberty enjoyed there. The inhabitants collected about 1,200 slaves, by whose labour they made themselves revenue ... in cotton.[13]

Nothing is said of the fate of the native people who lived in Carriacou, but we can assume that some left as the French came in, possibly taking refuge in St Vincent and Dominica which were the last refuges of the native peoples. There is some evidence that some remained in Carriacou, finding a niche in the new society.

Grenada with the Grenadines became the private property of Houel and du Parquet in 1650, and the alienation of Carriacou from the native people came shortly after that. The earliest mention of Carriacou in historical records is in the writings of the Dominican missionary Jean Baptiste du Tertre. Carriacou is mentioned three times in his *Histoire des Antilles*, published in 1656. In one place he provides the name of the island as it was known by the native people. This was 'Kayryoüacou'. In this and the other places du Tertre calls the island beautiful and good, 'with the advantage of having a very good harbour, and is capable of supporting a proper colony',[14] and describes the features of the island that would interest the European settler, or European naturalists. He describes the soil as dark, appearing to be fertile. He mentions the abundance of wildlife on Carriacou including guinea fowls, which he calls 'a kind of pheasant'. He seems especially fascinated with the large pool near Harvey Vale of:

> *Chomache* water, that is to say, half salt, which cannot come from anything else than a river or spring of fresh water that loses itself in the salt water close to the seashore. The colour of this water is as red as blood, and even the crabs there take on this colour; but the bottom of the pond is white sand covered with red slime, which makes me believe that this water passes over some deposit of ochre.[15]

Forty years later, Père Labat sailed up to the Grenadine Islands from Grenada, but did not land, and left inaccurate records of these islands based on hearsay.

A hundred years after its 'purchase' by the French, Carriacou was well organized as an agricultural extension of France, designed to produce profit for the enrichment of the estate owners. In that year the French Governor of Grenada, de Poincey, ordered that a census of Carriacou should be carried out by the commandant of Carriacou, Lieutenant de la Bourgerie du Sabon. This was done in meticulous detail, except that the arithmetic concerning the number of people on the island is inaccurate. The census document was discovered in the Archives of Paris by Francis Grant of Philadelphia, who was a friend of Frances Brinkley, a North American who lived almost all her adult life in Carriacou and who had a passion for Carriacou history. To Miss Brinkley we owe a most detailed and interesting analysis of this document.[16]

The census of 1750 reveals that at that time there were 199 to 202 people living in Carriacou. Of th's number there were 44 white men, 15 white women and 33 white children, making a total of 92 whites. There were also 29 negro men, 25 negro women, and 20 negro children, making a total of 74 negroes, plus 18 more who could not work, making 92 in all. There were 15 mulattoes, one man, one woman and 12 children. Interestingly, there are no statistics of who was slave and who was free, only the word 'libre' appended to the name.

The tribal origins of some of the negroes are also appended to the names. The naming of the slaves by the census document ensures their remembrance across the centuries:

> Agate Armada, Angelique Anan, Marie Anne Arrada, Marie Negresse Arrada, Madelaine Aura, Francois Bambara, Tite Bambara, Michele Negre Bambara, Antoine Congo, Hector Congo, Louis Negre Congo, L'Eveille Congo, Luce Congo, Mathieu Congo, Phillipes Congo, Son Negre Congo, Therese Congo, Angelique Negresse Ibo, Elizabeth Ibo, Jeannot Mogue son Negre, Jerome Mondong (Mandig).

Later slaves would also come from the Cromanti-Akan, Tenmé Moko, Chamba and Banda peoples.[17]

Carriacou was divided into nine districts or *quartiers*:

> Some districts can be easily identified today: La Baye des Juifs – Limlair-Tibeau; La Baye L'eau – Windward; La Grande Bay – Grand Bay; La Breteche – Sabazan. The others are not so

simple: La Grande Anse, L'ance Noire Joignant Le Carenage, La Machenilliers Joignant Le Grand Carenage, Le Grand Carenage, and Raiemut; even the spelling of the last named is uncertain, due to de la Bourgerie's handwriting. It is not possible to identify them by assuming each *quartier* adjoins the next named around the island, as the four that can be identified are not in that order.[18]

Brinkley goes on to say that she believes Harvey Vale was La Grande Anse, Hillsborough or L'Esterre Bay was Le Grande Carenage, and to speculate on the likely boundaries of the 'lost' *quartiers*.

A Portrait of Grenada at the End of the Seventeenth Century

The description of Grenada in 1700 comes from the pen of Père Labat, who had come to Grenada in that year to inspect the Dominican property in Grand Pauvre. The ruins of the Dominican estate are still to be seen in St Mark's on Diamond Estate, as this estate is now called.

In his *Memoirs* Père Labat bemoans the state of underdevelopment of Grenada and says, that had this island been British, it would have been flourishing.

> Instead of which we have not put to use a single advantage, as we could have done, and for so many years now the country has been unexploited, sparsely inhabited, lacking amenities as well as trade, remaining poor; while the houses, or rather the huts, are badly built and even more badly furnished: in a word, the island is much the same as it was when M. Du Parquet bought it from the savages.[19]

Père Labat further observed that the land in Grenada was fertile, and watered by many rivers. The meat was very good, the fowl fat, tender and delicate and the game plentiful. He notes the abundance of fish, turtles, and sea cows. On the Dominican estate he found pigeons, ramiers and ground-doves, grieves, parrots and *perriques* (possibly parakeets) in abundance, as well as tatous,[20] and agouti. In the river on the estate he noted that fish, eels, mullets and crayfish were plentiful. With regard to the terrain, he found that:

> It is less broken up and more beautiful the further one gets from the fort. The roads were passable, and would be very good and suitable for every kind of vehicle, if it were possible to work on them a little … [21]

Père Labat reached the Dominican estate following a road that is almost the same as the coastal road used today. In 1700, however, the journey from the fort to the estate in Grand Pauvre took him three hours.[22]

By 1700, Fort Louis stood on land that had become hardly habitable. It was marshy, and rapidly subsiding, partly due to the removal of the original vegetation to create a space to build the fort and ancillary buildings, and partly due to earth movement in the area. Moreover, the marshy nature of the place encouraged mosquitoes, which made life very uncomfortable, even if one was lucky enough not to succumb to the debilitating and often fatal mosquito-borne diseases. No one at the time knew that mosquitoes carried the organisms that caused the terrible fevers that were the main drawback to the well-being of the colony.

The main population centre of the island had by this time spread out on the lands surrounding the fort, and also across the bay. In 1690 a new church had been built on the ridge across the water from Fort Louis, on the site of where the Anglican Church stands today, and a house for the Capuchin Friars beside it on the site now occupied by the Anglican rectory. Père Labat described it as 'not large, nor beautiful, nor well built, nor clean'.[23] A town was developing across the water from Fort Louis, on a hill that is now traversed by Church Street. A new fort was started on that side of the bay, and was called Fort Royale. The new settlement was also called Fort Royale.

Père Labat did his job assiduously, writing a detailed account not only of the state of the property, as well as everything he saw and did. It was during this visit that he discovered the continued existence of Grenada's indigenous people, some of whom had built a *carbet* on the lands owned by his Order. Another unauthorized occupant on the church's lands gave him a meal of venison, fish and cassava, and *ouicou*, the Kalinago beer.

The population of Grenada in 1700 consisted of 251 whites, 53 'free savages or mulattoes' and 525 slaves. Père Labat thought that an increase in population would profit Grenada, and regretted that the French refugees from St Christopher had not been sent to Grenada, where they would quickly have regained their losses, and at the same time would have made Grenada an even more profitable island.[24] France and Britain, once happy with the division of St Kitts, began to fight for total possession of these islands in 1666. The battle for full possession of St Kitts did not cease until 1782 when Britain took control of the whole island. Many inhabitants migrated to get away from the constant fighting.

John Campbell was also of the opinion that Grenada's development would be assisted by an influx of people. Campbell observed that settlers in Grenada were well aware of this, and constantly insisted to the French

Ministry that Grenada could become very valuable if it did not remain 'the weakest and the worst settled of all their colonies'.[25] The eventual prosperity of Grenada would act as a pull factor for migration to this island from other colonies, but this was not to be for a while yet.

A Prosperous Country with a Prosperous Church

In 1705 de Bellair, the Governor of Grenada, formally established a town on the western side of the harbour. Fort Royale was started under the supervision of a French engineer, de Caillus. This fort was completed the next year, 1706, and the new town was also given the same name as the fort. Fort Louis was gradually abandoned. During this time, also, Grenada was divided into six parishes of unequal size: Basseterre, Gouyave, Grand Pauvre, Sauteurs, Mégrin and Marquis. The rivers, streams and mountains were used to demarcate the boundaries of each parish.

After 1714, ships travelling between Martinique and South America began to call at Grenada for water and supplies. The travellers on the visiting vessels opened a window to the wider world for Grenadians, and provided a much needed impetus for increased production and export trade, for from them the Grenadians learned that their produce could be sold with profit. Although the records show that Grenada had three sugar estates in 1700,[26] through this increased communication they were introduced to the most modern methods of sugar cultivation, and were sold the essential tools and equipment for building and erecting new and more efficient sugar works. Contact with the travellers and traders on these ships also persuaded the Grenadian planters that cocoa, coffee and cotton were also profitable. The cultivation of these crops began immediately, and Grenada started to prosper. An open account was established between Grenada and Martinique, providing advances and credit to the planters in Grenada, and allowing them to pay through the sale of its produce. This maritime link was to remain important to Grenada up until the early twentieth century. It provided a cultural link with the French colony after the island became British, and provided a means of transport for French creoles to visit or settle in Grenada.

The Roman Catholic Church, represented in Grenada since the first Frenchmen landed in 1650, continued to play an important role in the colony. Franciscan Capuchin monks not only looked after the spiritual needs of the people, but were planters as well. While M. Pradine was Governor of Grenada, he set aside about 14 acres of land in each parish to be worked to produce income for the Roman Catholic Church. Thus was the church able to sustain itself. These lands, called glebe lands, were also provided in Grand Pauvre where the Dominicans had their estate, but no church was ever built, as the Dominicans continued to minister to the people from their mission dedicated to St Rose. The General and Intendant[27] of the French Windward Islands approved this appropriation of lands for the church in 1721. By this year also, the Roman Catholic Church had acquired several pieces of property in Basseterre, most near to the town. These properties also earned income for the church. Thirty years later the possession of this real estate by the church became one of the causes of resentment and complaint on the part of the Protestant British citizens of the island.[28]

Under the governorship of Pradine, also, Dominican priests were allowed to return to Grenada. They reoccupied their estate in Grand Pauvre in 1721 or 1722, and ran it as a working estate. They also looked after the spiritual welfare of the people of the area, and established a mission, which they dedicated to St Rose. By 1747 six parish churches had been built in addition to the Dominican mission on their estate.

In 1736 a hospital was built by the French government on one of the ridges above St George's near where the present Presentation Brothers College is now situated. It was managed by Roman Catholic Fathers of Charity of the Order of St John of God from 1742 to 1760. A spate of transfers, illnesses and deaths of the Brothers resulted in the unavailability of any further Brothers to manage the hospital. In 1760 the French government took over the management. The hospital was supported by charity, and the profits from a sugar estate in St George's, which had been purchased with hospital funds, with the objective of providing a steady income for the hospital and those that ran it.

Grenada's economy grew in spite of very heavy taxes on Grenadian produce, and the sense the planters had of being abandoned by their mother country. Taxes on tobacco were so heavy that a point was reached where the cultivation of this crop allowed only the slightest of profits to the farmer, insufficient to import the slaves they required to expand the production of sugar. In the end planters resorted to indulging in a flourishing but illegal trade with the Dutch. This illegal trading changed their circumstances for the better, increased the population, and facilitated the further settlement of Grenada.

In 1744 France joined the War of the Austrian Succession which was fought in Europe between 1740 and 1748. By this time, almost all of the debt owed by investors in Grenada was paid off. The war was to halt Grenada's new economic prosperity. The sugar industry was particularly affected, and the planters turned heavily to coffee to try to counter the decline in the profits they had made from sugar. Peace in 1748 revived the economy, restored the trade and the growing sugar industry.

By 1753 the population had grown to 13,432 people, of whom 262 were white, 179 coloured and 11,991 were slaves.[29] Sugar was grown on eighty-three sugar plantations, and coffee, cocoa, cotton, cassava, bananas, sweet potatoes and yams produced for home consumption as well as sale. Numerous small settlements had grown up, including the population centres that would become Sauteurs town and Marquis village, as well as settlements still known today as Grand Bacolet, La Baye, Le Requin, Beausejour, Marigot and LeGrand Roy. Around this time, the French allowed some 'Carib' families to settle in Grenada. These came chiefly from Dominica, and were useful to the colonists in that through their trade with the mainland of South America they could procure cochineal, balsam of tutu and capachu oil, used by the colonists.[30]

With this wave of development and influx of planters came an extremely interesting character by the name of Charles Alexandre Cazaud, alias Marquis de Casaux. Cazaud arrived in Grenada between 1752 and 1753. He had been born in 1727 in France to a middle-class family of some means and good connections. His family had property in Guadeloupe and, after a brief career in the army, he married and came to Grenada to establish himself as a planter. He planned to set up a model plantation which would be characterized by the humane treatment of slaves and which would produce cocoa, coffee, cotton and sugar. In December 1753 he signed contracts with various workmen to build his estate house on land near Levera, St Patrick's. Cazaud would play an interesting part on the fringes of the Grenada government as Grenada changed hands twice in two decades.[31]

The Outbreak of the Seven Years' War

As before, the economy of Grenada was to suffer with the outbreak of the Seven Years' War in 1756. This war involved most of the nations in Europe. By entering into hostilities, Austria hoped to recover Silesia, a territory lost to Prussia in the War of the Austrian Succession, and to crush the power of Prussia. The war was used as an excuse by Britain and France to fight for colonial possessions, and therefore was extended to the Americas. As soon as the war broke out, the British began capturing the French ships plying between the Caribbean and Europe, seizing the produce they carried. They also captured the smaller vessels that serviced the islands. Fourteen of the fifteen vessels involved in inter-island trade between Grenada and Martinique were captured after only one year of the war.

As the war progressed, the British convincingly established supremacy of the sea. Towards the end of 1761 Admiral Rodney arrived in the Caribbean with eighteen ships of the line, and 10,000 men under the command of General Monckton. Their strategy was directed to the capture of the French islands instead of simply capturing French ships. Guadeloupe was the first to be captured, followed by Martinique in January 1762 and, on 25 February 1762, St Lucia. Then it was Grenada's turn.

Grenada Falls into British Hands

A squadron under the command of Commodore Swanton arrived in Grenada on 3 March 1762. Unlike the citizens of Martinique who had defended their island honourably, the English met absolutely no resistance from the Grenadians. Not a single shot was fired, in spite of the heavy fortifications guarding the harbour. The date of the French capitulation of Grenada to the British is 4 March 1762. Grenada had been in French hands for 112 years.

Why did the Grenadians not defend themselves against the British? Abbé Raynal says the colonists were fed up with French rule. They had suffered greatly from the burdensome taxation that had made tobacco cultivation unprofitable, and the island had been neglected in favour of Martinique. 'A concurrence of long succeeding evils has thrown Granada into the hands of Great Britain'.[32] It is possible also that, like Père Labat, comparisons had been made between the development of the British territories and the underdevelopment of Grenada. Under the Treaty of Paris, which was signed on 10 February 1763, Martinique and St Lucia were returned to France, but Grenada, the Grenadines, St Vincent, Dominica and Tobago were to remain in British hands, except for minimal amounts of time during wars to come.

The Treaty of Paris allowed the French to remove from Grenada what records they wanted. Many of the remaining records were lost in the fire of 1771. This makes research on the early history of Grenada difficult. However, it is unlikely that these records would have told any story other than military and economic events, as those that controlled the island were not particularly concerned about anything else, and certainly not about the conditions of the slaves and the poor on the island.

Records are unnecessary to reach the conclusion that when the British took over the island of Grenada, they found a country which might not have been as well developed or as populous as Martinique and Guadeloupe, but one full of potential, in which there were over 300 estates and farms varying in size from 1363 acres to 20 acres.[33] Some of the larger estates were planted in sugar cane, but there were several large coffee plantations, and many smaller ones. Cotton and indigo were also grown. There were 30,021 slaves, most of them on the sugar estates. The larger estates had watermills. A road system had been established, although the roads were very bad, and as a consequence small harbours had been developed whereby people and goods could be transported to all part of the islands. The island had been divided into six parishes, and all the amenities of the civilized world were to be found in small and less sophisticated quantity and quality. The town had a substantial fort, a building to hold the courts, and a residence for the Governor, several warehouses, shops, dwelling houses, and a parade ground for soldiers. The slaves also used this as a Sunday market. In this parade ground stood a permanently and prominently placed gallows. Several other population centres had spaces that were set aside for parade grounds *cum* markets and there was a series of lesser forts scattered around the island, including a large one on the heights over Gouyave.

Apart from the buildings, estates, roads, forts and towns, Grenada had a well-developed culture based on French culture. The love of all that was French was deep-rooted not only among the French and coloured citizens, but among the slaves as well. The slaves adopted much that was French, but changed the original culture to a unique form in which were to be found both French and African elements. They spoke a version of French referred to in later times as French creole. Both slave and free were Roman Catholics, and there had been Roman Catholic priests and chapels on the island since the first settlement was established in 1650. The influence of the French on the culture of Grenada proved to be so enduring that after more than 200 years fragments of French creole culture still survive.

Notes

1 Devas (1932) spells this name Vauminier, but uses Valmenière in his *History* of 1974.
2 Many of these forts were the ones that had been built previously to protect the inhabitants against attacks from indigenous people.
3 See [John Campbell], pp. 173 and 176.
4 Crouse, p. 232.
5 Govt of Grenada, *Grenada Handbook*, p. 21.
6 This name is also spelt Du Buc or sometimes Du Bu as in the *Histoire de l'Isle de Grenade ...*, edited by Roget. In 1750 a woman called Perine Dubucq was living in Carriacou (Brinkley (1978), p. 52). Was she a relative of the one of the most notorious inhabitants of Grenada's early history?
7 Raynal, Book XIV, p. 69.
8 Devas (1932), p. 7.
9 Some accounts say he was shot.
10 Archangeli met with an unfortunate end. In 1692 the British invaded Marie Galante. Archangeli approached the British, offering to reveal the whereabouts of

the French Governor, M. Augier, who was in hiding. He was later hanged at the church door with his two children by the British, perhaps because they felt that he could never be trusted if he had betrayed his own Governor.

11 [John Campbell], p.187. John Campbell was a Scottish lawyer who wrote his history and description of the West Indies with the purpose of publicizing the value of Britain's colonies acquired in 1763. It is said that his history may have been commissioned for the purpose of garnering support for the expansion of the British sugar empire in the West Indies. See Goveia, p. 73.

12 Devas (1974, p. 61) says that these figures were culled from a census done by Abbé Raynal about 1700.

13 *Ibid.*, p. 181. The report of 1200 slaves was probably exaggerated. The 1750 census reports only 92.

14 Devas (1974), p. 178.

15 *Ibid.*, p. 179.

16 Brinkley (1978).

17 McDaniel, p. 60.

18 Brinkley (1978), p. 44.

19 Père Labat quoted in Devas (1974), p. 63.

20 'Tatou' is the Kalinago word for armadillo. It is commonly used by Grenadians to refer to this animal. See Allsopp, p. 549.

21 *Ibid.*, p. 65.

22 See Devas (1932), p. 13.

23 Père Labat, *Memoirs of Père Labat*, quoted in Devas (1974), p. 65.

24 See [John Campbell], p. 187.

25 See [John Campbell], p. 173.

26 Govt of Grenada, *Grenada Handbook*, p. 22.

27 An Intendant was a person who had authority over business and financial matters. Thus this person was in charge of both the religious and the financial affairs of the Dominican Order.

28 Devas (1931), p. 22.

29 *Encyclopaedia Britannica*, quoted by Devas (1974), p. 68.

30 See [John Campbell], p. 185.

31 See Roux, Phillipe de (1951).

32 Raynal, Book XIV, p. 71.

33 Paterson, Daniel, pp. 3–10. An acre is about 0.4 hectares.

4

The Making of an English Colony

Grenada was formally ceded to Great Britain on 10 February 1763 by the Treaty of Paris, which ended the Seven Years' War. Under the terms of this treaty, all the lands in Grenada were declared Crown property. Arrangements were immediately made to survey the entire island, and to advertise the land for sale. The survey was done by M. Pinel in 1763 on the instructions of Lieutenant Daniel Paterson. Lieutenant-Governor George Scott, who had previously been appointed Governor of Dominica, was temporarily put in charge of the administration of Grenada after the capture of the island.

The question now for Great Britain was how best to govern her new possessions in the West Indies, referred to as the 'Ceded Islands'. The solution was to set up one government for all these tiny but valuable islands. Thus, on 7 October 1764 George III, king of England, issued a Royal Proclamation, creating the Government of Grenada and Councils and Assemblies for the representation of the people for

> [t]he island of that name, together with the Grenadines, and the islands of Dominica, St Vincent and Tobago and providing councils and assemblies of the representatives of the people therein in such a manner and form as is used and directed in those colonies and provinces in America; the legislatures created are empowered to pass laws as may be agreeable to the laws of England, and the governor shall create courts of justice with the rights of appeal to the Privy Council.[1]

Robert Melvill[2] was appointed the first British Governor of Grenada and the other territories. Before he left England to take up his post in Grenada, he received instructions to give the French Roman Catholics in Grenada and the other territories 'free exercise of their religion, as far as the laws of England permit'.[3] He was commissioned to report on the condition and numbers of the religious communities on the island, being careful not to acknowledge any rights by Rome over the Catholics. It was hoped that 'the conversion of the inhabitants to Protestantism was gradually to be effected'.[4] This was in keeping with the policy of both George III and his Ministers to allow French settlers in their newly acquired territories religious freedom. The French Roman Catholics in Grenada were also to enjoy civil rights, including the right to vote for members of the Assembly, and to elect two of their Members to the Assembly.

Melvill arrived in Grenada on 13 December 1764, and immediately set about establishing British rule in Grenada, within the policy laid down by the Crown. Creating a Government of Grenada, which included the Grenadines, St Vincent, Dominica and Tobago, had its problems. The nearest islands were at least one day's sail away from Grenada and, although there was communication between planters and merchants who knew and did business with each other, it could not be said that there was much unity of purpose. In order to make the governing of the colonies easier, and also to placate the colonists, especially those in Dominica, who were not pleased to be under a Government of Grenada, Melvill immediately established a House of Assembly for each island, in addition to the overall General Council.

The Sale of Estates

When the land survey of Grenada had been completed and the necessary regulations passed, arrangements for the sale of land began. However, lands that had been owned by the French settlers would be leased back to them, if they wished, for a period of forty years, provided that they swore allegiance to the king of England. If they did not want to live under British rule, they were allowed eighteen months to sell them to British subjects. All other land available was to be sold only to British subjects, with no one person being allowed to purchase more than 500 acres.[5] The sale of lands in Grenada was advertised in Britain and in Barbados.

Some of the French-speaking planters felt uncomfortable under a 'foreign' government and the lease arrangement offered to them, and took the option of selling their property and taking the proceeds and their slaves away with them to settle elsewhere. Most others took the second option of leasing back their own estates from the government and remaining in Grenada. One of the French planters who remained was Alexandre Cazaud. He was happy to live under British rule and British citizenship, welcoming the opportunity to learn new agricultural techniques and explore new political ideas.

Among the estates sold was the estate belonging to the French Dominican friars in St Mark's. This sale caused a great deal of confusion and letter writing between the Governor of Grenada, Lieutenant-Colonel

George Scott, the Dominicans and the Secretary of State for the Colonies, because the Governor was under the impression that the Dominicans could not sell their land. The quarrel was so contentious that the Governor imprisoned a friar, Père Vidal. Finally, the Secretary of State allowed the sale, and it was the Governor who had to explain himself to the Secretary of State for the manner in which he had dealt with the matter.

The Dominican Order also sold all the other land they had in Grenada, including an estate called La Potrie, also situated in St Mark's. The French Dominicans then withdrew from the island completely, leaving Grenada in the hands of English clergy, some of whom were also of the Dominican Order.

On the other hand, the advertisement of lands for sale in Grenada caused great excitement among investors in Britain, for in the eighteenth century no property was deemed as valuable to European nations as the sugar islands of the West Indies. There was a rush to buy estates, so much so that the demand caused many estates in Grenada to be sold for much more than they were worth. Among those who purchased estates as soon as they came available were William Lucas, and two brothers Ninian and George Home. These were some of the wise investors, and the estates they purchased were among the most desirable real estate in Grenada.

The Anglicizing of Grenada

While the sale of lands proceeded, alongside the movement of planters and slaves in and out of Grenada, Melvill began the work of creating a British colony out of a French one. The majority of people in Grenada spoke French, and for any official business transacted by persons who were not bilingual, interpreters had to be supplied. All government notices had to be posted in French and English. Melvill now set out to change all that and more.

All the parishes, capitals and major streets in Grenada were renamed on 10 February 1764. The former French *quartiers* became parishes in the English tradition. Basseterre became St George's, Grand Pauvre became St Mark's, L'Ance Gouyave became St John's, Grand Marquis became St Andrew's, and Mégrin became St David's. The Fort Royale was renamed Fort George, after King George III, and the capital became the Town of St George. Melville Street, Scott Street, and Monckton Street were named for the heroes of the day. The capital of L'Ance Gouyave was called Charlotte Town. The change of names upset the 'New Subjects' as the French-speaking Grenadians were now called, but there was nothing they could do, except to use the old names in defiance. This is why

Gouyave remains the capital of St John's, although 'Charlotte Town' is recorded doggedly on the maps of Grenada.

The Administration of the Roman Catholic Church

Not only were the names of places changed to English names, but also the British institutions and connections were introduced to replace French ones. The Roman Catholic Church was no longer supervised by the church authorities in the nearby French islands, but was now placed under the jurisdiction of Bishop Challoner, the Roman Catholic Bishop of London, who was 3000 miles away.

Management of the church in Grenada from such a distance was difficult enough, but the problems Bishop Challoner had to face made the management of the church in Grenada 'a burden which is beyond my strength'.[6] He describes a situation where 'divers French priests have thrust themselves into different parishes without approval'[7] and would not accept his jurisdiction. He had a good aide in a French Capuchin, Father Benjamin, who served as Bishop Challoner's Vicar General and who shared with the bishop the administration of the church in Grenada. When Father Benjamin died, Bishop Challoner was at his wits' end because the person needed to replace him 'must be a Frenchman, and yet acceptable to the English Government, and I confess that I cannot find anyone like that'.[8] This and the other problems of the church in British Grenada made the Bishop plead that a superior for Grenada and the other former French islands be appointed.

A letter from Bishop Challoner to his priests in the West Indies dated 17 December 1770 survives. He urges them to be guardians of the faith, to warn their parishioners against vice, and to practise charity. This is one of the few documents that mention the welfare of the slaves. In his pastoral letter, Bishop Challoner says, 'The salvation of the poor Negro slaves is not to be forgotten.'[9]

Protests over the Four-and-a-Half per cent Tax

Another instruction Melvill was given even before he took up office in Grenada was to institute, under the authority of the Royal Letters Patent, a four-and-a-half per cent duty on the value of exports from Grenada to be paid to the British government. This duty was to replace the duty formerly paid to the king of France. This tax was vigorously opposed in Grenada. A colonist called Campbell brought a legal case against the Crown, contending that the duty was illegal, as it had been imposed by the king, but after the king had granted lawmaking authority to the Grenadian House of Assembly. Legislation such as this could only now be legal if it was made by the Assembly with the consent of the Governor in Council. It took ten years, but the Grenadian planters eventually had cause for rejoicing as Lord Mansfield, the Chief Justice of the Privy Council in England, ruled in their favour in 1774.

In the meantime, while the case was slowly wending its way through the English law courts, the merchants and planters took more immediate retaliation for this four-and-a-half per cent duty by borrowing large amounts of money from Britain.[10] They then refused to repay their creditors at the appointed time. When the creditors attempted to seize the estates, the House of Assembly passed a bill on 6 June 1774, effectively postponing payment of the debts for thirty-two months. There was uproar in Britain. Creditors who had interest in the matter were incensed that 'a very small part of the empire should arrogate to itself a right of annihilating engagements contracted under the sanction of a law universally established, in the good faith of trade',[11] and asked the English Parliament to 'repair without delay this great breach made in the important and imprescriptible right of property'.[12] Parliament, however, upheld the decree of the Grenada Assembly to make their laws, and the creditors in Britain had to wait for their money.

Slave Discontent and Revolt

Problems of a different sort arose over the treatment of slaves. The recently arrived English and Scottish planters and merchants in Grenada were unlikely to take advice from the French planters who remained on how to handle the slaves they had bought along with the plantations, as the British looked upon the French-speaking planters as inferior to His Majesty's subjects, especially as some of them were coloured. The newly arrived, instead of looking to see how this slave society had survived in relative peace for over one hundred years under French rule, immediately began to substitute the harsher British mode of handling the slaves for the gentler, more humane conditions practised by the French planters.

In 1700 Père Labat observed that in Barbados:

> The English do not look after their slaves well, and feed them very badly ... the overseers get every ounce of work out of them, beat them without mercy for the least fault, and appear to care far less for the life of a Negro than for a horse.[13]

Père Labat goes on to say:

> The poor wretches pushed to extremes more often by their drunken, ignorant and cruel overseer than by their masters at last lose patience. They will then throw themselves on the man who has ill-used them and tear him to pieces, and although they are certain to receive terrible punishment, they rejoice that they took vengeance on these pitiless brutes. On these occasions, the English take up arms and there are massacres. The slaves who are captured are sent to prison and condemned to be passed through the cane mill, or be burnt alive, or be put into iron cages that prevent any movement and in which they are hung up to branches of trees and left to die of hunger and despair.[14]

How much of this kind of cruelty was meted out on the slaves in Grenada is not recorded, but there is no reason to believe that the British estate owners and their managers and overseers behaved any differently in Grenada as compared with Barbados or any of the other British West Indian islands.

There had also been an unfortunate incident involving a member of the French Fathers of Charity of the Order of St John of God in August of 1765. The Brothers had run the Hospital in St George's before the British took over Grenada. One of the Brothers, a Father Cleophas, was sent from Martinique to Grenada with a Power of Attorney for his religious order to reclaim the eleven slaves who had worked at the hospital, and to take them back to Martinique. He left, unsuccessful in getting the slaves. Determined to repossess the slaves, he hired a mulatto slave and sent him to Grenada with instructions to round up the eleven slaves, and take them to the bay at Petit Havre (now Halifax Harbour) where a waiting boat would to take them to Martinique. The plot to sneak the slaves out of Grenada was discovered, and troops were dispatched in pursuit of the slaves. The troops prevented their departure from the island, and arrested the mulatto slave. At an inquiry into the incident, the slaves pleaded that they were led to believe by the mulatto that he had the government's permission to take them to Martinique. The mulatto was the only one hanged, protesting to the end that he had done what was the duty of a slave, namely, to obey his masters.[15]

The decision to execute the unfortunate slave was not popular, and added to the discontent and hostility of the slaves and former French towards the British. As the months passed, concern grew among free people in the island that there would be trouble with the slave population. In an attempt to avert an uprising, a bill was introduced and passed by the House of Assembly on 25 April 1766 'For the Better Government of the Slaves etc.' It was hoped that this bill would institute among the planters a more humanitarian approach to slave handling. Although passed by the Assembly, the bill failed to pass the Council. Conflict in the Assembly ensued, resulting in the House adjourning itself without the Governor's permission, as required by royal instructions. Governor Melvill then dissolved the House on 21 May 1766. A new House of Assembly was convened on 15 October 1766.

The very next year, 1767, the slaves revolted. The uprising was put down by the troops from the garrison. Several slaves were killed and, although a semblance of peace was restored, Abbé Raynal recorded that the estate owners lived in terror of being burnt or massacred, especially, no doubt, 'those who had laid themselves under the necessity of using violent methods'.[16]

As a measure for their own protection in the future, the British planters avoided some excesses of treatment and punishment, and as a result had fewer problems with slave labour, but the harm was done. Not only had the uprising cost them money due to the cessation of production and some destruction of property, but also the execution of the ringleaders of the uprising further increased the hostility to the British among the free French population and the slaves.

The Maroons

During the confused times following the capture of Grenada by the British, when so many estates changed hands in rapid sequence, and subsequently when the slaves were subjected to conditions harsher than they had experienced under their French masters, some of the slaves escaped from the plantations and made settlements in the mountains. Bayley notes that between 600 and 700 slaves deserted,[17] but there were probably many more than this number. From their settlements in the mountains, the escaped slaves, who were called Maroons, periodically raided the plantations. The raids were a nuisance, and the opportunity of the slave rebellion presented an excuse to deploy the troops against these Maroons. So many Maroons were caught that the prison could not hold those captured. Therefore, construction of a new prison began in 1767.

Attempts to escape the yoke of slavery continued. Some slaves left the islands, instead of hiding in the mountains. There are records of slaves escaping from the island by canoe. The *St George's Chronicle and New Grenada Gazette* of 19 August 1790 offers a reward for two male slaves from Carriacou. These were identified as Jack, a house servant of the Congo nation and Jame, of yellow complexion and a carpenter of the Ibo nation. A reward of five Joes[18] was offered in the same paper on 14 September 1798 for the capture of Jean Françoise and Sylvester, both creoles from Hermitage Estate in Carriacou, and Janga, also a creole from Union Estate,[19] also in Carriacou. There were possibly many others who braved the waters rather than be a slave, even on an island as beautiful as Carriacou. Maroons would be the first to join the revolution led by Julien Fédon at the end of the eighteenth century.

Further Disasters

Further disasters temporarily slowed the development of the colony. In 1766 a severe earthquake destroyed several sugar works, and caused enormous landslips blocking many roads. In 1768 Grenada experienced the fringes of the most disastrous hurricane ever recorded for the Caribbean.[20] In 1770 a plague of red ants (*Formica omnivera*), sometimes called sugar ants, appeared in Grenada, probably brought to Grenada from Barbados or from Martinique by smugglers. The ants first appeared at Petit Havre, which is today called Woodford Estate in St George's. From there, they spread all over the island, crippling the production of sugar cane and citrus. This account by an unnamed 'eyewitness' was left for posterity:

> Their numbers were incredible. I have seen the roads coloured by them for miles together: and so crowded were they in many places that the print of the horses' feet would appear for a moment or two, until filled up by the surrounding multitude.[21]

In 1771, and then again in 1775, the town of St George's burnt to the ground, almost all of the buildings being of wood. The damage in 1771 was estimated at £200,000 sterling, and in 1775 even more disastrously, at £500,000 sterling.[22] In order to prevent repetition of such disasters, an Act was passed by the legislature ordering that all rebuilding was to be in either brick or stone, and tiles used for roofs. Bricks and tiles were brought to Grenada for reconstruction as ballast in the ships coming to collect sugar. Some of these red-brick buildings with the distinctive fish-scale tiles can still be seen around the town of St George and in Grenville.

A Society Divided

The slave uprising, the earthquake, the plague of ants and the fires notwithstanding, by far the greatest problem in Grenadian society at the time was the non-acceptance by the English and Scottish planters of the French-speaking Roman Catholic population, for many of whom Grenada had been their birthplace. The French Roman Catholic population were accepted as 'New Subjects' by the king of England and given full civil and religious privileges. This did not make it any easier for the British-born subjects to accept them. England and France were traditional enemies, and there was also great antipathy between members of the Church of England and Presbyterians on the one hand, and Roman Catholics on the other. French was the language of the majority of persons in Grenada, and the English and Scottish felt foreign in a colony that was British. The resentment and hostility was such that there was the view that all the French-speaking planters should have been turned out of Grenada, leaving lands completely empty and available to His Majesty's British-born English-speaking subjects.

One of the new Protestant settlers in Grenada, a Scot called William Lucas, became a spokesman for those who disapproved of the British policy of tolerance towards the French-speaking Roman Catholic Grenadians. He further insinuated that Melvill was a friend of the New Subjects because Melvill upheld the wishes of the king, and not the wishes of those like himself. Lucas and his supporters felt so strongly about the rights given to the New Subjects that he got together with other like-minded members of the Grenada Council, including Ninian Home, to try to thwart every attempt of the Governor to implement the religious toleration and civil rights the king wanted to see implemented in Grenada. Lucas and Home wrote a petition to Melvill, calling the New Subjects for whom Grenada had been home for decades 'aliens', and protesting that they had been given the right to vote, which would put too great power into the hands of the New Subjects, as they were in the majority.

Not all the English and Scot planters shared the views of Lucas and his group. As soon as others in Grenada heard that this protest had been made, another petition in support of the right to vote for the New Subjects was written and sent to the Governor, signed by twenty-three Englishmen. This was backed by yet a third petition signed by thirty-five Frenchmen.

Melvill's Dilemma

What was Melvill to do? He had his orders from the king, but he was now caught between two opposing groups, one of which was making him out to be a French sympathizer. He offered a compromise which allowed the French Roman Catholics the right to vote, but would not allow French-speaking Grenadians to be elected to serve in the Assembly as representatives of the French section of the population. As with most compromises, this pleased no one. The faction led by Home and Lucas continued to say that Melvill was a friend of the Roman Catholics, while the Catholics accused Melvill of duplicity. How could he agree that they had the right to vote, but not to sit in the Assembly? They wrote off to England towards the end of 1767, asking not only for the right to sit in the legislature, but also specifically for exemption from 'The Test', which was a declaration against the Roman Catholic doctrine of transubstantiation, and had become standard for all English subjects serving the Crown after 1673,[23] although they would willingly swear allegiance to the king.

Lucas continued to agitate against civil rights for the New Subjects. In a letter written to England on 15 April 1768, Lucas stated that all the difficulties would end if the law were changed to allow only natural-born subjects and Protestants to vote at elections.[24] However, the impression had been given in England that Grenada was in turmoil, and that this would get worse if the New Subjects were kept out of the legislature. Regardless of the orders to allow votes to Roman Catholics, the non-Catholics refused to observe the instructions from Britain.

The Roman Catholic Reaction

The New Subjects put up several candidates for elections to sit in the Assembly, and in this a faction of the British planters supported them. However, the Returning Officer refused to accept the candidates put forward by the French, and there was an immediate protest. Among those protesting was Alexandre Cazaud. When the Returning Officer rejected the candidate he proposed, he made a disturbance at the place of nomination, insisting that he was being denied his rights, and was taken into custody and sent to gaol. A protest of 'breach of privilege' was brought to a Justice of the Peace by the members of the French-speaking community against the Returning Officer, supported by some of the English citizens. The Justice of the Peace was asked to release the protestors in custody and, when this was refused, was asked to state the condition of release. No information was forthcoming. Cazaud was eventually released on bail when he agreed to write an apology for his behaviour. Shortly after this incident, Cazaud travelled to England, where he availed himself of the opportunity of pleading the case of the New Subjects in Grenada to the authorities there.

On 7 September 1768 Ulysses Fitzmaurice, who was the Acting Governor, received instructions that five French Roman Catholics would be allowed to sit in the legislature: two Catholics in the Council and three in the House, 'without having to take the Test, and they were also to be admitted to positions of trust in the island' provided that they took an oath of allegiance to the king. The number of members in the House of Assembly was increased from twenty-one to twenty-four. Two New Subjects, Chanteloupe and Devoconnue, were elected to serve as Assemblymen.

When Fitzmaurice tried to introduce these French-speaking Assemblymen into the Assembly, and to appoint a Roman Catholic Puisne Judge, he was told that the Assembly had the requisite number of members, and that he would have to get an order from the king to change the number. The Acting Governor did write, and the Secretary of State, Lord Hillsborough, wrote back on 12 October 1768 that the New Subjects were to be admitted to the legislature without the Test. He was told that the instructions to do so had been 'the most precise ordered ... in conformity to the Treaty of Paris'.[25] However, the Acting Governor was advised to begin to promote the establishment of the Church of England in Grenada, in the expectation that some of the New Subjects would be converted, and the influence of the Roman Catholic Church would gradually diminish. To enable this to be done, the king would not demand payment of the Capitation Tax, on condition that a law was passed as soon as possible for a stipend for a minister of the Church of England in each parish of the island, and for the building of new churches in each parish.

When, on 16 February 1769, Fitzmaurice introduced the two Roman Catholic members to the Assembly for the second time, six members of the Assembly walked out, preventing the Assembly from meeting. The Acting Governor then suspended the six members who had walked out of the Assembly. His action was protested, so the Governor repeated the suspension by an instrument in writing. The suspension of the members and the continual opposition to everything he tried to do made the conduct of public affairs difficult and complicated.

On 2 January 1769 Fitzmaurice published the proclamation that gave the Roman Catholics the right to vote, the right to sit in the legislature and exemption from the Test. The Roman Catholics rejoiced as much at the granting of the provisions as Lucas and his supporters showed their resentment. Nor did they appreciate the diplomatic moves by the colonial government. Yet another petition was sent to the king saying that Roman Catholics were not meeting the provisions of British law in Grenada on the matter of the taking of the Test. But this proclamation was in keeping with the wishes of the king and his government to protect the rights of the New Subjects as British subjects, under the 1763 Treaty of Paris. There were legal grounds for saying that the guarantee of these rights whilst the Test Act was in force was a contradiction in terms. The Test was required of all Roman Catholics who wished to take public office as British subjects. Only another law would exempt Roman Catholics from this requirement. Nevertheless, the king refused to rescind the provision.

The appointments by the Acting Governor of the two new members and the Catholic Puisne Judge were confirmed the Secretary of State. The Secretary of State said in the letter of confirmation that it would give him great satisfaction to hear that 'all the other matters contained in the instructions upon that subject were carried into execution without difficulty or opposition'.[26] The six members who had staged the walkout never accepted the decision to allow the New Subjects to take their place in the Assembly. Fitzmaurice took this action as their resignation, and settled the original objection that the number of the Council was complete by asking the two Roman Catholics to take two of the places vacated by the objectors.

Roman Catholics Further Distressed

In addition to the difficulties the Catholics had in exercising their civic rights, the Roman Catholic Church authorities faced problems collecting rents from some of the tenants on church lands. Some of the tenants who rented church lands in St George's said that the laws of Britain did not oblige them to give anything to the curés of the Roman Catholic Church. A protest from the church in 1774, supported by about fifty parishioners, brought a request to Governor Leybourne for an investigation into the matter which, if the complaint was justified, would occasion 'the necessary orders for redress'.[27] Because of the problems and contentions over church lands, the Capuchins, from their headquarters in Martinique, began to consider the advantages of selling the properties they held in Grenada.

Between 1763 and 1779 the French Catholics fought for, and succeeded in maintaining, religious freedom. The legal and religious rights of the New Subjects were safeguarded by the terms of the Treaty of Paris, obliging every British Governor to defend the Roman Catholics' cause, whatever may have been their personal feelings. Obviously, members of the non-Catholic population thought something else should be done. For example, a handful of Scottish planters wanted to destroy the six churches the French had built around Grenada, but this was not permitted, nor was the suggestion that the churches be appropriated, or even shared, by the British. Instead both Governor Leybourne and, after him, Lord Macartney reminded the legislature on several occasions that it was their duty and the king's wish that they provide for the building of new Protestant churches and for the upkeep of clergy of the Church of

England. A bill had been introduced to this effect in 1769. They were to leave the Roman Catholic churches alone.

The Catholic priests continued their ministry, administering the sacraments and performing marriages. The British government recognized these marriages as valid and legal contracts. There were also processions through the streets to celebrate traditional Roman Catholic feast days, for funerals and for other special occasions. All of this did not please the bigoted, but there was little they could do about it.[28]

Efforts to Get Rid of Melvill

Melvill was an unpopular Governor. Fitzmaurice did not like him and both the English and Scottish planters did not like him, and accused him of being a friend of the Catholics. The Catholics did not like him or trust him. While he was in England, strenuous efforts were made to prevent him from returning to Grenada. Towards the end of 1769 a number of British planters presented a petition against Melvill,[29] but the charges laid against him were all answered satisfactorily, and could not prevent his return to Grenada. On his return, he wrote to Hillsborough, the Secretary of State, that he found the relations between the colonists a little better, and that it was his ambition to remove all ill will. He also indicated that 'inflammatory people in England' were stirring up the colonists in Grenada.[30] Perhaps it was that he tried to please everybody, and so pleased nobody.

In spite of Melvill's initial feeling that acrimony in the society had abated during his absence, this must have only been a temporary respite, for the opposition of influential planters to admitting Roman Catholics to the Council and to the judiciary continued. The appointments of two Catholic Justices, Philippe-Rose Roumé de St Laurent and Mony de Bordes, were thwarted on a technicality of the law that bore no relation to the king's wish for religious tolerance. Yet another petition signed by Ninian Home and a number of others was sent by the Grand Jury in Grenada to the king on the subject of allowing rights to Roman Catholics. The constant opposition to a legislature in which the New Subjects would be allowed to participate, the struggle to legislate against the exemption of the New Subjects from the Test, and other confusions eventually threw into jeopardy the very legality of the legislature. The British and French each issued their own petition to the colonial government asking that the legality of the Grenada legislature be cleared up. Before this happened, Melvill's term of office ended, and William Leybourne was sent to Grenada as his successor.

Roman Catholics Vindicated

In February 1771 the right of two Roman Catholic councillors to take their places in the House and be exempted from the Test was confirmed by Letters Patent, making those in the opposition very angry. They renewed their efforts at causing disruption. Strategies used included the sudden resignation of Ninian Home and another member the night before the May Sessions. Leybourne sensed that these men were setting a trap for him, hoping he would fill the vacancies with the wrong type of person. He sidestepped the trap, filling the void with another non-French official rather than asking a Roman Catholic to act.

Leybourne died in 1775, and William Young, Governor of Tobago, was appointed to act as Governor. During the short time he was Governor, another attempt was made to prevent the appointment of a French Roman Catholic Assistant Judge. On this occasion, a respected French Grenadian, Roumé de St Laurent, led the formal counter-protest.

Lord Macartney Becomes Governor

On 4 May 1776, a new Governor, George, Lord (afterwards Earl) Macartney arrived in Grenada. He had already distinguished himself, having previously been a Member of Parliament, Chief Secretary for Ireland and envoy to the Court at St Petersburg. He had recently been raised to the peerage. Macartney was educated and cultured, and a man of much tact. At the time of his arrival in Grenada, he was about forty years old.[31] He was the first Governor-in-Chief of Grenada, the Grenadines and Tobago. In 1770 Dominica had been granted its own Constitution, and in 1776 a separate government was created for St Vincent.

From Bracey we learn that Macartney lived in St George's, possibly within the precincts of the Fort. He was a great sightseer and journal keeper. He was: '[c]harmed with the scenery, the climate and the tropical vegetables, and with the hospitality and good humour of the planters. He revelled in the "fish of the finest" the "beef, mutton and kids excellent as a proverb".'[32]

Governor Macartney was appointed Governor of Grenada one year after the War of American Independence broke out. Although the planters were polite to him, he soon discovered the division, discord, discontent, conflict and feuds that raged within the population, and between sections of it. Grenada's white inhabitants were divided into three groups – the French, the English, and the Scottish – disliking each other, and the Scottish in particular exhibiting 'rancorous hatred of the Catholic religion'.[33] In addition to the white section of the population, there was a strong group of coloured

French-speaking Roman Catholics who were particularly resented and despised by the bigots among the English and Scottish.

A Modicum of Prosperity

Despite the wrangling over export duties, the religious intolerance, slave revolts and natural disasters, Grenada was economically prosperous, and was looked on by some as being 'the second best of the English islands'.[34] The 1771 census put Grenada's white population at 1661, the free coloured population at 415, and counted 26,211 slaves.[35] Raynal reported that, under British rule, the number of slaves increased to at least 40,000 and 'the value of produce trebled'.[36] Grenada was at this time was producing goods annually to the value of £528,750, of which £300,000 was from sugar, £68,750 was from rum, £62,500 from coffee, £81,250 from cotton, £10,000 from indigo and £6,250 from cacao.[37]

There were other positive developments. A road to link St George's with Grenville via the Grand Etang was begun in 1774. Also of some excitement was the capture of a French smuggling vessel sporting 120 guns and eighteen men by an armed schooner of the Grenada Customs.

Cazaud was one of the planters who began to enjoy the fruits of his investments in Grenada. In spite of his arrest and gaol term, Cazaud seemed to bear no grudges. He developed a fast friendship with the Acting Governor. Over the years he became an expert agronomist. As a planter, he did not share the growing view in Europe that slavery should be abolished, but, like Ninian Home and a few others, his estate was run on the theory of 'enlightened paternalism' as regards treatment of the slaves.

An interchange of ideas took place between Cazaud and the Governor, particularly on the merits of small plantations, and methods of improving cane cultivation, including the best time of year and the least labour-intensive methods for cane planting. In 1777, after spending twenty-five years in the West Indies, Cazaud returned to Europe, a rich man. In Europe he was recognized as an expert on sugar cultivation. In London and Paris he met with other agronomists, and became an adviser and a speaker on the cultivation of cane. He was elected to the Royal Society in 1780, and wrote a manual on sugar cultivation in 1781.[38]

The British in Carriacou

The development of Carriacou under the British as was rapid as that of the island of Grenada. A document entitled *The State of Carriacou and the other Grenadine Islands in 1776* gives us an idea of what Carriacou was like in that year. It lists over fifty proprietors in Carriacou and eight in Petit Martinique. The population of the island was 86 whites, and 3153 negroes. There was no count of the free people of colour.[39] One of these, however, was 'Jeanette, a Free Negro Woman' who owned 160 acres of land near Tyrell Bay, and the entire island of Petit Martinique. A map of 1793 shows that this estate passed to her daughter, identified in several places as 'Mrs. Judith Phillip'.

The products of Carriacou and Petit Martinique were sugar, rum, coffee, cocoa and indigo. The document mentions the presence on the island of a Roman Catholic priest called Maisonneuvre, resident at least from 1771. This man, who might have been the first resident priest, owned ten slaves, and had ten acres of land on which cotton was grown.[40] The first church was a Catholic church built by Father Guis, who arrived in Carriacou in 1780, and served continuously for forty years, until about 1820.

In 1778 the population was 107 whites, a few coloured people and 3046 slaves. Of the estates, twenty-two estates with a total of 2027 slaves were British owned; twenty-one estates with 866 slaves were French owned; four estates and 138 slaves belonged to free negroes or mulattoes. There were also five sharecroppers with 82 slaves. That year Carriacou produced 133,495 pounds of sugar, 71 puncheons of rum, 772,765 pounds of cotton, 4832 pounds of coffee, 1100 pounds of cocoa and 8332 pounds of indigo.[41]

Pirates and Privateers

Before discipline was put on sea traffic through the mutual agreement of all nations, the islands of the Caribbean were vulnerable to attacks from free-roaming and lawless privateers and pirates of all nations. Sometimes the pirate leader and his crew began their career as people setting out to make their fortune through plunder. Sometimes they had been crew of vessels bent on legitimate business, who commandeered the vessel by disposing of the captain and anyone else who would not join them in their mutinous behaviour. When their vessel became unserviceable, they would simply attack a seaworthy vessel, and take it over, disposing of the crew, and commandeering the goods carried as spoil.

The outlying coastal plantations and towns of Grenada and the Grenadines, as well as shipping bringing goods to the islands and taking away the produce were very vulnerable to attack by such privateers and pirates. 'Men would land on a moonlight [*sic*] night, or unexpectedly make a raid, carry off what they could, especially slaves, and be gone'.[42] Whereas the strategic points in Grenada were guarded by forts and the soldiers garrisoned there, and the British erected cannon on strategic points such as Gun Point, Pegus Point and Belair in Carriacou, many outlying areas in Grenada and Carriacou had to protect themselves. Thus even the priest in Carriacou owned two muskets and two pistols for his personal protection.

In 1774 four persons – Thomas Sawyer, Samuel Brown, Charles Ingersoll and Henry Lenard – were arrested in Grenada for piracy. In his deposition Sawyer said that the crew of the sloop *Hannah* had been harshly treated and kept on short rations by the captain, William B. Master. When the crew could no longer stand this treatment, they threw the captain and first mate Samuel Henoly overboard and sailed to the Caribbean meaning to dispose of the cargo and the belongings of the ship's captain and first mate, and share the proceeds of the sale among themselves. Three or four days after they had disposed of the captain and first mate, they arrived at Trinidad, where they procured a pilot to take them into Grenada. As soon as they arrived, they were immediately suspected of piracy, and arrested on 24 August 1774. Samuel Brown refused to confess to his misdeeds, but the others gave evidence implicating him and themselves. They were all put on a ship bound for England, where they were subsequently tried for murder, one of them being persuaded to turn King's Evidence against the rest.[43]

On 1 September 1778 a vessel from Martinique carried away between 30 and 40 negroes from the islands of Petit Martinique, Prune and Canouan, and the next day a schooner came into L'Ance Aux Epines, Grenada, and captured a mulatto family and several negroes.[44]

Throughout the history of Grenada there are instances of pirate attack. This was one of the many things that beset the inhabitants of Grenada. It was a scourge to the planter freedman and slave alike, as one of the commodities taken by the pirates was people, and they cared nothing for their legal status.

The War of American Independence

No one liked war. War meant a disruption of commerce and shipping that was essential for the prosperity of the plantations in Grenada and elsewhere. The War of American Independence was different to all other wars, as the main theatre was so close to home, and an immediate effect of the war was that the planters and merchants in Grenada could no longer trade with the American colonies. In addition there were fewer vessels trading in the area, insurance on goods went up, and privateers once more roamed the seas, seeing what they could carry away from unprotected settlements.

Those with vested interest in the Eastern Caribbean islands, including Grenada, had another reason to be nervous when France joined the war in 1778. They feared that France would seek to recapture its former colonies, and sensed correctly that the French citizens would welcome this. There was also a conflict of interest among many of the planters, who sympathized with the American cause. All British colonies were dissatisfied by British trading practices. The policy of Britain was to make the colonies return profit to Britain, while putting back as little as possible into the development of the colonies. A regulation particularly resented by the thirteen colonies in America was the fact that produce from America could only be shipped in British ships, and goods imported only from Britain. Resentment of these policies started to grow among the colonists, along with a desire to assert their rights. Eventually things spilled over in a demonstration called the Boston Tea Party. Many of the same dissatisfactions were shared by the West Indian planters, who felt that Britain was anxious to receive West Indian sugar, but was not anxious to allow the colonies to trade with those who could provide them with the most satisfactory goods, and otherwise to act as they saw fit.

In June 1775 the Grenada Assembly passed an Address of Support for the thirteen rebel American Colonies, expressing horror at the bloodshed of the American colonists. The prime mover of this resolution was the Speaker of the Assembly, Alexander Winniett, who had Boston connections. He had considerable support for his resolution. Among those supporting it was George Leonard Staunton, the Attorney General, and friend of the Governor.

Lieutenant-Governor Young, who was Acting Governor of Grenada at the time, had been on a visit to St Vincent when the Address was passed. As soon as he learnt of it, and that copies of the Address had been sent to England by members of the Assembly, the Governor sent a message back to Grenada asking the Assembly to rescind the Address and Minutes which ought to have come through the Commander-in-Chief to be laid before the throne according to custom. This they could not do because the Address had already been sent to England. Later some members of the Assembly declared that they have been led astray by 'a mischievous few'.[45] To punish the Grenada Assembly, and as an object lesson to the other islands under his jurisdiction, Governor Young dissolved the Grenada Assembly.[46]

The punitive action on the part of the Lieutenant-Governor spurred the planters to rethink their earlier enthusiasms. Regardless of their feelings towards the trade policies of Great Britain, most planters preferred, in the end, to remain loyal to the Crown, rather than make themselves vulnerable to capture by France or other European nations active in the

Caribbean on account of the war. In this attitude they were joined by the other British colonies in the Caribbean. Not one island in the Caribbean decided to declare their independence along with the thirteen American colonies, in spite of their sympathies.

The war brought tense times to Grenada. Food and other goods imported from Britain or the American colonies became scarce. The slaves particularly felt the deprivation, as salt fish, flour, and biscuits, which were part of their food provision, were among the imported items. Another item that became scarce was rope. To counter these shortages, extra land was planted in provisions. In Dominica the planters obtained wood and thick vines from the forest to make their own barrels for sugar.[47] They probably did the same thing in Grenada.

The Threat of Invasion

Macartney was never under any illusions about the danger Grenada was in from French capture. A French attack on Grenada was expected at any time, and there were several false alarms of the French having landed, or being sighted. Macartney did what he could. He established a Militia:

> [c]omposed of the very parties who, previous to his arrival, had been endeavouring to tear each other to pieces. The invidious distinction of English, Scotch, and French was no longer kept up, but was happily buried in the general desire for the protection and preservation of the island.[48]

But reactions to the false alarms of French attacks made it clear that Macartney could not depend on the French to be loyal, neither could he depend on the Militia, which was made up exclusively of whites – overseers, clerks, tradesmen and some of the planters. Macartney described this section of the white population as 'mere banditti, averse to all order, discipline and obedience, turbulent, mutinous, and impatient of all restraint'.[49] In the face of attack, he could depend on the loyalty of some British planters alone, and the few regular soldiers of the garrison.

One of the measures proposed for the protection of Grenada was the establishment of a naval dockyard to be situated at the excellent twin harbours of St George's. An Act of Legislature was passed in 1778 suggesting this. The British colonists promised to subscribe material and slave labour for the project. Nothing came of their request. However, some cannon, ammunition and stores arrived on 4 June 1778 on the vessel *Adventure*. This was all the help Macartney was to get from the mother country.

1 Lake Antoine is one of the many volcanic explosion craters
in Grenada (Photo: Jim Rudin)

2 Large volcanic boulders at the end of L'Ance aux Epines, typical of
Grenada, illustrate the island's volcanic origins (Photo: Jim Rudin)

3 The Mona monkey, brought to Grenada by Europeans, now abounds in the forests (Photo: Jim Rudin)

4 A canoe under construction by the Black Caribs of Dominica, showing how stones are placed inside to widen it (From *LIAT* magazine. Photo: Macmillan Caribbean/Oliver Benn)

5 Early inhabitants of Grenada carved pictures believed to be of religious significance on large volcanic boulders. One of the most elaborate of these petroglyphs is at Mount Rich. (Photo: Jim Rudin)

1 Lake Antoine is one of the many volcanic explosion craters in Grenada (Photo: Jim Rudin)

2 Large volcanic boulders at the end of L'Ance aux Epines, typical of Grenada, illustrate the island's volcanic origins (Photo: Jim Rudin)

3 The Mona monkey, brought
to Grenada by Europeans, now
abounds in the forests (Photo: Jim Rudin)

4 A canoe under construction by
the Black Caribs of Dominica,
showing how stones are placed
inside to widen it (From *LIAT* magazine.
Photo: Macmillan Caribbean/Oliver Benn)

5 Early inhabitants of Grenada carved pictures believed to be of
religious significance on large volcanic boulders. One of the most
elaborate of these petroglyphs is at Mount Rich. (Photo: Jim Rudin)

21 George Bain was born forty years after Fédon of a white father and a black mother. Did Fédon look like him?
(Photo courtesy Colina Bain)

22 York House, which has been the seat of the Grenadian legislature from the early nineteenth century. The previous House of Assembly is believed to have been on the site of the present Knox House, near Fort George.
(Photo: Jim Rudin)

23 The National Museum of Grenada occupies one of the oldest structures in Grenada. In the seventeenth century it served as a prison. The building exhibits many interesting architectural features, including French iron balconies and an indoor courtyard.

(Photo: James Davis Travel Photography)

24 The Georgian buildings of St George's and the schooners which link Grenada and other islands form an interesting backdrop for this portrait of Jennifer Hosten, the Miss Grenada who became Miss World in 1972.

(Photo: Jim Rudin)

6 The Kalinago regarded small islands such as Calivigny Island as religious sanctuaries (Photo: Jim Rudin)

7 Kevin Keens-Douglas claims to be one-quarter Kalinago
(Photo: Jim Rudin)

8 Grand Anse Bay, the possible site of the ill-fated British expedition
to settle Grenada in 1609 (Photo: Jim Rudin)

9 Christopher Columbus, who was the first European to set eyes
on Grenada, named it Conceptión (Photo: Hulton)

10 Aerial view of St George's, with its twin harbours. The ledge of land, now submerged, on which the 'ancient town' was established, can be faintly seen under the water at the mouth of the smaller harbour. (Photo: Jim Rudin)

CARTE DE L'ISLE DE LA GRENADE,
Pour servir à l'Histoire Générale des Voyages. Par M. B. Ing.ᵉ de la M.ᵉ 1758.
Echelle de 3 Lieues communes de France.

1   2   3

Ance David
Cap David
Grande Ance des Sauteurs
Bourg et Paroisse des Sauteurs
Levera
Saline de Levera
Cap de la Grenade

Ance du Quesnel

Ance aux Ecrevisses

PAROISSE DES SAUTEURS

Islet d'Antoine

Bourg et Paroisse du Grand Pauvre

Ravine Gauter

Par.ᵉ DU

Islet de la Conference

la Grosse Pointe

R. de Maran

GRAND PAUVRE

Bourg et Paroisse de l'Ance Goyave

Ic Alaboya

R. Simon

PAROISSE DU Gᵈᵉ Riviere

Gᵈᵉ Ance de la Conference

Ance des Palmistes

PAROISSE DE

le Grand Roy

le Marigot
l'Ance Noire
Pointe de l'Ance Noire

L'ANCE GOYAVE

GRAND

P.ᵗᵉ de la Gᵈᵉ Riviere

Petit Havre

MARQUIS

La Baye

Beau Sejour

I. du Marquis

Pointe de la Citerne ou de Bois Maurice

PAROISSE

Paroisse du Grand Marquis

Ance Grand Male
Pointe S. Eloy
R. St Jean

DE LA

PAROISSE DU

Grand Bacolet

Ville et F.ᵗ Royal

MAIGRIN

R.ᵉ Menevet
le Crochet

Rade
Banc
Grande Ance

BASSE

Ance des Galibis

Banc

le Requiem

TERRE

le Petit Trou
Bourg et Paroisse du Maigrin

Salines

Bacolet

Petit Marquis
Cul de Sac de la R.ᵉ du Chemin

Points des Salines

Ance Carienne

Pointe du Fort Jeudi

Isle à Ronde

Blie Ilet Marigalan

I. Calaveny
les Pirogues

Longitude Occidentale du Méridien de Paris.

38   37   36   35   34   33   32   3ᵗ 64ᵈ 30ᵐ 29   28   27   26   25

11 French map of Grenada, 1758

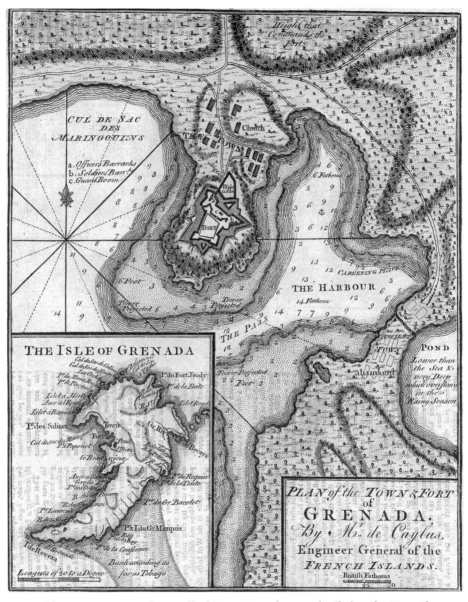

12 Fort George, then called Fort Royale, was built by the French
to replace Fort Annunciation, and has remained a citadel and historic
landmark up to the present day. This map of the fort and surrounding areas
by M. de Caylus shows the site of the abandoned 'ancient town'.

13 This is a modern photograph of Leapers' Hill (Morne de Sauteurs) from which it is traditionally believed that some forty Kalinago leapt to their deaths rather than be captured by the French in 1651 (Photo: Jim Rudin)

14 The battle between the British and the French for Grenada, 6 July 1779
(Redrawn from an old print by Michael Steele)

D'Estaing Assaults Hospital Hill, July 4th, 1779
Original painting by G. Michael Steele from an Historical print.   Grenada National Museum/Organization of American States

15 The French take Grenada, 1779

(Photo: Mary Evans Picture Library)

16 The Market Square in 1780, illustrating the dress worn by the gentry and slave vendors at the time. Careful examination of this painting shows the gallows in the further right-hand corner of the square: the French – as well as the British – used this form of capital punishment until the guillotine became popular in France in the 1790s.

17 The Right Hon. George Macartney, who was Governor of Grenada when the French retook the island in 1779

(Courtesy Government House)

18 Paraclete Estate, the Home family estate, where Lieutenant-Governor Ninian Home first received news of the outbreak of the Fédon Revolution.

(Photo: The Paxton Trust)

19 A contemporary aerial view of Gouyave, the town where Governor Ninian Home landed and was taken prisoner by Fédon in 1795 (Photo: Jim Rudin)

20 Artist's impression of Julien Fédon with his white stallion. No likeness survives of Fédon, nor is there a contemporary description of this famous French Grenadian. (Drawing by Trish Bethany)

During the early months of 1779, the presence in the Caribbean of a powerful British fleet under the command of Vice-Admiral Sir John Byron was a comfort to the people of Grenada. However, Byron received orders to convoy a fleet of merchant ships part of the way back to Britain, until they were out of danger from attack by the French. He was to bring his fleet to Grenada to meet the fifty-six merchant ships carrying produce from Grenada on 6 June 1799, and then sail to St Kitts to meet ships assembled there from St Kitts, Antigua and the Virgin Islands. Altogether, it was estimated that the convoy would comprise 200 ships, staffed by 4000 seamen, and carrying produce valued at £2 million.

The planned departure date was 15 July, but the convoy set out early. As soon as it left, escorted by the fleet, Count d'Estaing, who had a fleet almost as large and only a little less inferior to Lord Byron's fleet tucked away in the harbour at Martinique, ventured forth to see which islands could be captured for France. D'Estaing is supposed to have had the ambition to make a 'short breakfast of the English fleet and army, and of taking possession of all the British Colonies in that part of the world'.[50] Choosing between an attack on St Lucia and St Vincent, d'Estaing decided on St Vincent, and captured that island on 18 June 1779 and returned to Martinique.

Strengthened with the reinforcement of five ships of the line and five frigates which had just returned from convoying merchant ships to Brest, France, d'Estaing set out for Barbados which, if captured, would have surely been the greatest prize of the war. However, he met particularly strong and adverse winds, and changed his plans because he needed to make a quick capture before Byron and his fleet returned from England. Thus was Barbados spared, and Grenada decided upon.

News of the capture of St Vincent was brought to Grenada by a vessel that managed to escape from that island. With it came the further information that d'Estaing intended to attack Grenada. On hearing this news, Macartney dispatched letters to St Kitts, Antigua, Barbados and St Lucia, to try to stop Byron leaving the Caribbean with his fleet. On 2 July, the very same day that the French fleet was sighted off Grenada, he got news that none of these dispatches had arrived in time to stop the departure of the fleet, which had left earlier than scheduled.

Macartney knew that his position was almost indefensible, and that it would be quite impossible for him to stop a French landing. Nevertheless, he did what he could, hoping that he would be able to hold out until Byron, with the fleet, came to his relief. He declared martial law, and fortified Hospital Hill overlooking St George's. The slopes of the hill were very steep. The hill was fortified with large quantities of piled-up stones and a palisade at the bottom. Three lines of entrenchments were made, one above the other, on its sides. Here he placed what cannon and guns he had, and sent all his regular troops. The regulars comprised 101 rank and file of the 48th Regiment and 24 artillery recruits. These were joined by sections of the Militia from St George's, St David's, St Andrew's, St Patrick's and St John's, numbering between 300 and 400. The regulars and the Militia would man the emplacements and defend the hill. In addition, a few sailors from vessels in the harbour joined in the defence, and a troop of 24 cavaliers was stationed at the foot of Hospital Hill to patrol, reconnoitre and bring intelligence.[51]

Macartney chose to fortify Hospital Hill rather than Fort George because the fort was too exposed and was dominated by higher ground. 'From the heights', he said, 'the very buckles on one's shoes could plainly be seen on the parade'.[52] However, he left two companies and some sailors in the fort where the magazine was, and established means to communicate between Hospital Hill and the fort. On the south side of the Carenage, Monckton's redoubt was manned by the seamen from the *Adventure* under the command of their Lieutenant.

The Battle for Grenada

D'Estaing's fleet dropped anchor at Moleniere Bay on 2 July 1779. His fleet consisted of 25 ships of the line and 10 frigates with 10,000 troops. D'Estaing was in a hurry. He did not want Byron to return before he had secured Grenada. To save time, he did not unload any cannon or guns, but immediately ordered between 1300 and 2000 Irish soldiers under the command of Count Arthur Dillon and Edward Dillon, and who were in the employ of the French, to disembark. Their instructions were to march inland, and then make a turning movement towards St George's. This would surprise the British, as they would be attacked from the north. When they got near to Hospital Hill, they were to surround it and occupy the heights around it, including Mount St Eloi.

As the soldiers marched, they met no resistance from the people whom they met along the way. The majority of Grenadians had never been reconciled to British rule, and harboured simmering hostility towards the British. They now anticipated a victory of the French, and rejoiced in the arrival of the troops.[53]

That evening, one of the French battleships sailed to St George's and fired several shots on shore. Finding that the fort guns did not reach her, the ship sailed up and down, flaunting the French presence, until one of the shots from a 24-pound cannon on the fort scored a near miss, sending the ship scurrying back to the protection of the rest of the fleet at Moleniere.

When the invading troops reached Hospital Hill, they were divided into three columns.[54] The column on the right, furthest to the north, and which faced Hospital Hill, comprised 300 men, the column in the centre comprised 310 men, and the column on the left and the furthest one south would approach the hill by following the road, possibly the one now called Lucas Street, to the Carenage, and from there climb the entrenchments on the hill. The left column was led by d'Estaing himself, and comprised 300 men. The left column would, during the main attack, be preceded by an advance guard of 180 men led by Count de Durat, who would be the French Governor after the capitulation.

D'Estaing set up his headquarters in a little hut on top of one of the hills near the hospital. On the afternoon of the next day, 3 July, d'Estaing sent one of his aides-de-camp towards the British lines under a flag of truce. Observing the messenger, Macartney dispatched an officer to intercept him and receive the message. The message was 'a peremptory summons to surrender',[55] pointing out 'the superior force with which he is attacked and against which he presumes to resist'. The note went on to say that if Macartney did not surrender 'he must be personally responsible for all the consequences which his obstinacy may occasion'. In addition, if he did not surrender, the merchants and planters taking up arms against the French would lose their estates and properties, and the free coloured would be reduced to slavery.[56] Macartney replied that 'He did not know the strength of Count d'Estaing's forces, but he knew his own, and would do all that rested with him to defend the island'.[57]

About eleven o'clock that night, the troops under French command started to climb Hospital Hill, and by midnight they were in the positions they had selected. At 2 a.m. the French made a feint or an opening skirmish designed to confuse the enemy below Hospital Hill, possibly on the road along the river, outside the palisade. At the same time, and by accident, one of the ships having dragged its anchor found itself under the battery of the fort, and took the opportunity to cannonade the fort and town of St George's. As it passed near the entrenchments on Hospital Hill, it also opened fire on them. This and the planned diversion drew attention away from the fact that the columns that had previously taken up position had begun to move on Hospital Hill.

The left column was fired on by a small ship, the *York*, which carried about eight guns. Sailors on board fired muskets as well. In spite of this, shortly before daybreak the advance guard, followed by the left and centre columns, reached the entrenchments, and the soldiers placed there were driven from each position in succession. Shortly after, the third column arrived and broke through almost simultaneously with the arrival of the other two at the British placements on top of the hill.

Surprised and outnumbered, the British held on for about an hour and a half, during which over 300 men, mostly white, were either killed or injured. Macartney reported that the enemy came so fast that it was impossible to 'nail up all our cannon [i.e. spike the guns], the gunners on the Great Battery being killed with the matches in their hands'.[58] Almost all of the coloured people and the greatest part of the New Subjects deserted during the night. Apart from assessing the situation and feeling that d'Estaing's forces made a French victory a foregone conclusion, the coloured people may also have feared their fate after a French victory if they were taken in arms.

The remnants of Macartney's forces, faced with the surprise attack, rushed to the fort, leaving the guns on the emplacement at Hospital Hill unspiked.[59] The French used these guns later in the morning against Fort George. At the first shot, a British officer appeared with a white flag of truce, indicating that Macartney was ready to surrender. When Macartney met with d'Estaing, he was given an hour and a half to make his proposals for the surrender.

Terms of Capitulation

Macartney drafted seventeen Articles of Capitulation, which were completely and immediately rejected by d'Estaing. D'Estaing drafted his own twenty-eight Articles of Capitulation. These were delivered to Macartney, with the message that the British were immediately to comply with them without the smallest deviation. Macartney reports that these:

> I rejected in turn; and, there being no possibility of obtaining any other, all the principal inhabitants to whom I communicated it thought it better to trust the law and the custom of nations, and to the justice of one Court and to the interposition of any other by surrendering at discretion.[60]

The terms of capitulation gave hint as to what would happen to the British in the four years of French occupation, and are also important to an understanding of the retribution that would occur when Britain regained possession of Grenada at the end of the war.

Apart from surrender, the Articles of Capitulation[61] decreed that all slaves were to be taken as lawful prize of war and were to be delivered up to a person appointed. All negroes and mulattos taken in arms were to be deemed as slaves, and transferred to the ownership of the king of France. Ships and vessels in the harbour were also prizes of war, as was all money in the Treasury and customhouse. Four vessels named by Lord Macartney and Count d'Estaing would be allowed to leave Grenada with produce in the next six months, and would be provided with passports, and 'they shall sail as flags of truce'. There were to be six months of irrevocable neutrality, and the French would ensure the neutrality was observed by all British vessels calling at Grenada for purposes of trading. These would be allowed free access, and not be seized as prizes of war, but no British ship of war was to come and interfere during the six months of neutrality.

With regard to the treatment of people of the captured island, 'The inhabitants, French and English, shall continue to enjoy the public exercise of their religion, and the priests and ministers the exercise of their functions, with the enjoyment of their prerogatives, privileges and immunities.' Citizens of Grenada were released from their oath to His Britannic Majesty, and were now to take the oath to His Most Christian Majesty. No money was to be paid to the British in Martinique, including debt payment, taxes, or for anything else. Twelve Englishmen were to be selected to serve as hostages.

The French had been angered at the custom of calling the French-speaking Grenadians 'New Subjects', and had heard of the difficulties they had faced in Grenada at the hands of some of the British colonists. The Terms of Capitulation reflected this:

> As we are informed of the oppression exercised by the English Government, particularly against the French inhabitants of Grenada distinguished by the appellation of New Subjects in contempt of the Capitulation of the colony on 4th March, 1762; the Peace Treaty of Versailles in 1763, of the Treaty of Utrecht in 1713, and others confirmed and re-enacted in the said treaty of 1763; in contempt of the natural right and the right of nations, even of the laws of England; these vexations have done an injury which has extended to all members of the colony (which will be the object of a special memorandum to be sent to our respective courts) – We have suspended from henceforth for a limited time which shall be determined by the exigencies of the cases, or perhaps forever, and the inhabitants of Grenada are discharged of all moneys and debts of all kinds contracted with the city of London and all other places of commerce under the dominion of His Britannic Majesty, without any exception, reserving to the French nation to enforce all the just and well-founded claims incidental to the present Article.[62]

With Grenada, all the little islands belonging to her were understood to be included.

The capture of Grenada was costly in terms of human life. There are varying accounts of the amount of casualties from each side. Macartney admitted to losing over 300 men, and claims that the French lost 400 men, while the French admitted to losing only 107. In addition, the French took 700 prisoners, including a lieutenant-colonel, two captains and three captains of the regular troops, as well as five colonels, and six majors of the Militia.

The Sacking of St George's[63]

D'Estaing showed no leniency for the people of St George's. One writer, Beaton, says that d'Estaing was annoyed at Macartney for offering any resistance at all. He had hoped to take Grenada without a shot having been fired, and thereby be in line to collect a huge ransom. Beaton further says that when Macartney refused to accept his Articles of Surrender, d'Estaing was even more annoyed at Macartney. Further, it would seem d'Estaing was motivated by a desire to get revenge against the British. During a previous war, the British had accused d'Estaing of breaking parole, and thrown him into the dungeon at Portsmouth in England. The claim was that he was treated so severely that from that time he swore eternal hatred of the British.[64]

D'Estaing ordered St George's to be sacked, and carried off an immense booty from the town. He also took possession of the *York*, and thirty merchant ships in the harbour and roadsteads, loaded with large cargoes of rum and cotton and other goods. Bayley states that £40,000 worth of shipping fell into French hands.[65] The French also captured 100 pieces of cannon, twenty-four mortars, and a great quantity of all sorts of military stores and provisions.[66] It is reported that excesses were prevented by Count Dillon, an Irish officer serving under the French, who despised brutality and grossness.[67]

Macartney lost everything he owned. He lost all his plate, silver, jewels and most precious possessions which he had carried up to the fortifications on Hospital Hill, believing this to be the safest place for them.[68] He had the indignity of having his clothes sold in the market place.[69] He wrote in his report that: 'The Count d'Estaing was present in the affair [i.e. the battle], and in order to animate his troops to the attack promised them the Pillage of our Quarters...Among the sufferers I am the Principal.'[70]

Admiral Byron Arrives too Late

In response to Macartney's desperate pleas for help, Admiral Byron, now returned to the Caribbean region, arrived at Grenada on 6 July with a squadron. A monumental sea battle ensued within full view of St George's, during which both the British and French suffered heavy casualties. The reported French casualties were 1200 killed and 2000 wounded. Several of the British ships were battered by the French including Admiral Byron's. He remained near Grenada overnight, but determined that recapture of the island was impossible at that time. He retreated with what was left of his fleet to St Kitts.

Macartney Made Prisoner

In due course Macartney was taken to France as a prisoner-of-war. Before he left, he received from the members of the Grenada House of Assembly a vote of thanks for his zeal and energy in the preparation for the defence of the island, and for his brilliant defence despite his forces being so greatly outnumbered. The document had thirty-two signatories, all of them British. Included among those who signed were Ninian Home, Alexander Campbell and Alexander Winniett.[71] As expected, not one French Grenadian signed the document. The document concluded: 'We wish Your Excellency a safe passage to Europe…and all happiness in the future'.[72] On board the ship bound for France, Macartney, the indefatigable journal-keeper, spent his time writing a long and detailed report of the events leading up to the capture of Grenada.[73] This he managed to dispatch when the ship put into La Rochelle.

In France, the *Te Deum*, a Roman Catholic Celebration of Thanksgiving, was sung in Paris as well as in other cities. Macartney was treated well, in a manner befitting a noble prisoner. He was invited to dine with the Bishop of Paris, and spent some time with him. This bishop had sought and was granted permission from the Court for the postponement for a few days of the singing of the *Te Deum*. This ceremony had been scheduled for the same day on which the boat carrying Macartney arrived in port. This was to spare Macartney's feelings. Nothing, however, would completely assuage the terrible feeling of humiliation that the loss of Grenada brought Macartney. While in Paris, he might even have seen the British flags, called 'colours', taken at Grenada, suspended over the high altar in the Cathedral of Notre Dame.[74] Macartney was paroled and allowed to return to England after about two months.

Four and a Half Years of French Reconstruction

The French king made Jean-Francois, Comte de Durat, Governor of Grenada. The day after the naval battle, 7 July 1779, he issued a lengthy Proclamation, much of it repeating the terms of the Articles of Capitulation, which set the context for the re-establishment of French rule in Grenada, and for the retribution of the wrongs done to the French inhabitants of Grenada under the British.

The Proclamation began by recognizing these wrongs, including the humiliation of the French in contempt of the terms of the capitulation of the colony on 4 March 1762, and the Treaty of Versailles in 1763, and other treaties, including the laws of Britain. The absolving or at least delaying of the payment of mortgages and debts to Britain or other places under the control of Britain was repeated, and it was declared that any appeals based on this announcement had to be taken to the Court of France.

De Durat also let the British inhabitants know that, if Macartney had surrendered instead of defending Grenada 'on an apparent point of honour', those who fought with him would not have had all their possessions confiscated, and the inhabitants of Grenada would have enjoyed the same privileges that had been enjoyed by the inhabitants of St Lucia. Therefore, it would now be punishable under penalty of death to pay those who had fought in defence of Grenada any money owed to them.

The terms of surrender demanded that all slaves, free mulattoes and free negroes who had carried arms against the French were to be handed over to the French. The free coloured and blacks were to revert to slavery. On the estates confiscated from British absentee landowners, the managers were allowed to continue to manage them, once they had been proved efficient managers and had taken an oath of allegiance to France. The government would nominate custodians called 'conservators' to receive and sell the goods of the absentees, to pay the managers for their services, and put the rest of the funds into the public Treasury. However Brian Edwards reports that some of the British planters lost their estates temporarily, if a French claimant came forward professing ownership:

> The shameful facility with which every French claimant was put into possession of estates to which they had the slightest pretension was set up, gave resident planters reason to apprehend that the only indulgence that they were to expect was that ... of being devoured last.[75]

Dispossessing the British of their estates was most likely only one of the hardships the British in Grenada are said to have suffered from the action of Governor de Durat, whom the *Grenada Handbook* calls 'despotic'.[76] The *Handbook* says: 'the Government of France had to intervene on several occasions to cause justice to be done'.[77] Devas,[78] on the contrary, doubts that the British inhabitants were that harshly treated. Perhaps being ruled by the French was not very comfortable for the English and Scot inhabitants, but there is no record of any religious persecution such as they had tried to inflict on the French inhabitants when England became the colonial master. Although they might have found the French haughty and even domineering, they could find no real fault. If they had, they certainly would have listed all the wrongs for the British government as soon as they were in a position to do so.

Alexander Cazaud, who had taken up residence before the capture of Grenada, now became a champion for the British planters, and successfully appealed to the king of France not to confiscate the properties of the absentee landlords, as de Durat wanted to do. He did not, however, choose to return to Grenada. He stayed in England, started to spell his name 'Casaux' and began to use the title 'Marquis'. In 1788 he went home to France, where he published several pamphlets on social and economic issues, and became a great friend of Mirabeau who admired his understanding of British systems and government. He travelled for the rest of his life between England and France. His long and varied career ended when he died in London in 1796.[79]

Ironically, it was during the period of the French interregnum that the gentleman planter and public figure, Roumé de St Laurent, began negotiating with the Spanish Governor of Trinidad to allow foreign immigration into Trinidad. Many French citizens of Grenada had been discussing the possibilities of migration to the united provinces of Georgia, Carolina and Florida. Now St Laurent began persuading the planters to give up this idea for the possibility of migration to Trinidad. The prohibition on immigration was lifted in 1783, just in time to permit a massive migration of planters of French extraction with their slaves to Trinidad after the return of Grenada to Britain in that year. The successful negotiations of St Laurent also benefited planters from the other French islands who decided that they would be better off in Trinidad, which at the time was very sparsely populated by the Spanish. Fifty-seven families migrated to Trinidad from Grenada with 4965 slaves.[80]

This period is also remembered for the commencement of the fortifications on Richmond Hill. De Durat realized that it was the lack of fortifications on Richmond Hill and on the other high hills surrounding Hospital Hill that had allowed the French to advance on St George's and

Hospital Hill without being detected and surprise the British. De Durat appropriated the Mount George Estate from the Honourable William Lucas, and began to build Fort Adolphus, Fort Lucas, Fort Frederick and Fort Matthew, which would provide a formidable ring of defence for the capital.

During the French occupation, Grenada was hit by a storm on 10 October 1780. Nineteen Dutch ships were caught by this storm in Grenada, and were destroyed. There was a hidden blessing in this disaster, however, as the hurricane also destroyed the cane ant, which had been a plague to crops and to inhabitants for ten years.[81]

The War of American Independence ended in 1783, and Grenada was returned to Britain under the Treaty of Versailles on 3 September 1783. For Grenadians of both British and French origin, however, the internal affairs of the country were far from peaceful. Resentments based on the treatment of the British under the French occupation, and old feuds concerned with religion and ethnic plurality would flare up again, and in the new period got completely out of control.

Notes

1 Govt of Grenada, *Grenada Handbook*, p. 23.
2 Almost all the documents, as well as Devas, spell this name 'Melvill', and this is the correct spelling. However, the contemporary spelling adds an 'e'. Brizan also spells the name this way. There is a street in St George's – Melville Street – named after Grenada's first British Governor.
3 Act, Privy Council, vol. V, 1766–83, pp. 6–10. See Devas (1974), p. 81. It was also an article of the Treaty of Paris.
4 Devas (1932), p. 38.
5 See Ragatz, p. 113.
6 Bishop Challoner, quoted in Devas (1931), p. 34.
7 *Ibid.*
8 *Ibid.*
9 *Ibid.*
10 The amount was put at £2,082,333 6s. 8d. Figure from Raynal, quoted in Devas (1974), p. 77.
11 Raynal, quoted in Devas (1974), p. 77.
12 *Ibid.*
13 Père Labat, quoted in Devas (1974), p. 75.
14 *Ibid.*
15 Devas (1974), p. 79.
16 Abbé Raynal in the 1788–97 *Encyclopaedia*, quoted in Devas (1974), p. 74.
17 Bayley, p. 643.
18 Allsopp, p.314, describes a Joe (short for Johannes) as a gold coin and later a note of Portuguese and Dutch origin, the value of which was twenty-two guilders. In the mid-nineteenth century, a guilder was worth sixteen British pence, and was divided into one hundred cents. A bit was equal to eight cents. A Joe was a considerable sum of money, hence the expression 'To cost a Joe and a crown' which today survives as 'To cost a pound and a crown'.
19 The reports are from McDaniel, p. 40.
20 Govt of Grenada, *Grenada Handbook*, p. 25.

21 *Ibid.*
22 *Ibid.* pp. 24, 25.
23 Two Acts were passed in the English Parliament in 1673 and 1685 to prevent the English throne from ever again being held by a Roman Catholic. The Acts, among other provisions, called on all government officials and heirs to the throne to renounce any belief in transubstantiation, which was a doctrine central to the beliefs of the Roman Catholic Church. The act of renunciation became known as 'The Test'.
24 CO 102/4, Colonial Office papers, Public Record Office (PRO), London.
25 CO 101/12, PRO.
26 CO 102/1, PRO.
27 CO 101/17, PRO.
28 For a fuller discussion see Devas (1932), chs 6 and 7.
29 *A Narrative of the Proceedings upon the Complaint Against Governor Melvill*, printed for T. Becket and P.A. de Hondt in the Strand, London, 1770.
30 CO 101/14, PRO.
31 After his short and traumatic stint in Grenada, he was appointed Governor of Madras, and still later would figure prominently as England's first Ambassador to China. See Bracey, p. 103.
32 Bracey, p. 104.
33 John Barrow, *The Earl of Macartney*, London, 1807, vol. I, p. 51, quoted in Devas (1974), p. 83.
34 See Devas (1974), p. 77.
35 Raynal quoted in Devas (1974), p. 76.
36 *Ibid.*
37 *Ibid.*
38 Roux, ch. 2.
39 Brinkley (1971), p. 9.
40 Devas (1974), p. 182.
41 Brinkley (1971), p. 9.
42 Devas (1974), p. 182.
43 ADM 1/5117/5, PRO.
44 Jessamy, p. 48.
45 CO 102/7, p. 1, PRO.
46 *Ibid.*
47 See Honychurch, p. 84.
48 Barrow, *The Earl of Macartney*, quoted in Devas (1974), p. 83.
49 CO 101/23, Macartney to Lord George Germain, 10 Jan. 1779, PRO.
50 Bracey, p. 105.
51 Devas (1974), p. 88.
52 CO 101/23 (PRO), Macartney's dispatch dated 5 July describing the capture of Grenada, quoted in Devas (1974), p. 88.
53 See Devas (1932), p. 53.
54 The account of this battle is based on the account given by Devas (1974), ch. 7.
55 Paper no. 1, accompanying the 5 July dispatch, Egerton MS 2135, f 54, quoted by Devas (1974), p. 92.
56 *Ibid.*
57 Paper no 2, as above, quoted in Devas (1974), p. 92.
58 Quoted by Devas (1974), p. 96.
59 *Spiking the cannon* is a term indicating that a metal spike had been driven down into the chamber of the cannon where the fuse and the powder were laid, making the cannon unusable. Since soldiers could not withdraw hastily with heavy cannon, part of the exercise of retreat was to disable them, so that the enemy could not use them. In this case this did not happen.

60　Quoted in Devas (1974), p. 103.
61　A detailed list of the Articles of Capitulation are to be found in Devas (1974), p. 101; earlier pages contain a blow-by-blow account of the battle preceding the surrender.
62　Devas (1974), p. 101.
63　The opportunity for plunder was one of the fringe benefits for soldiers and sailors signing up for duty in the West Indies in the eighteenth century. The sacking of St George's took place as a matter of course. That it was an expected result of defeat did not make it any easier for those who lost produce and possessions.
64　*Biographie Universelle*, Paris, 1848, quoted by Devas (1974), p. 104.
65　Bayley, p. 644. This was £40,000 at the 1830 value, which would be much, much more today.
66　See Devas (1974), p. 105.
67　Bracey, p. 106. Bracey records that both d'Estaing and Dillon were guillotined during the French Reign of Terror.
68　*Ibid.*
69　Bracey, p. 106.
70　Devas (1974), p. 103.
71　This surname is variously spelt in different accounts and documents.
72　CO 101/ 23, PRO.
73　Devas (1974), p. 113.
74　*Ibid.*
75　Edwards, p. 379.
76　Govt of Grenada, *Grenada Handbook*, p. 26.
77　*Ibid.*
78　Devas (1932), p. 57.
79　Roux, chs 3–6.
80　Gomes, p. 39.
81　Govt of Grenada, *Grenada Handbook*, p. 26.

5

An Era of Oppression

When Grenada was restored to Britain in 1783, Lieutenant-General Edward Matthew was appointed as Captain General and Commander-in-Chief of Grenada. His commission read that he was Captain General and Governor-in-Chief 'In and over the island of Grenada, and such of the islands commonly called the Grenadines to the southwards of the island of Carriacou, including that island, and lying between the same and Grenada.'[1] This was the first time the Grenadine Islands were divided between the Government of Grenada and the Government of St Vincent.

Governor Matthew arrived in Grenada on 6 January 1784, with instructions to revive the legislature and the courts of justice on the same lines laid down for Lieutenant-Governor Melvill in 1768. Therefore, the rights and privileges of the French Grenadians professing the Roman Catholic faith were also to be restored.

Although Governor Matthew carried out these instructions, it was common knowledge that he identified with those who wished to loosen the grip of French-speaking Roman Catholics in Grenada. The general animosity towards the former French settlers had increased under the brief French rule, in spite of the French allowing the English and Scottish planters to keep their estates. In addition, the French-speaking Grenadians who departed Grenada when the island was returned to Britain took slaves with them that had been used as collateral for advances from British creditors. Some had stolen their neighbours' slaves, or 'substituted' their neighbours' slaves for those they could not find at the moment of departure.[2]

The English and Scottish planters would have preferred that the former French inhabitants be forced to sell their assets and leave Grenada. When all efforts to make them leave failed, the British planters once more began their agitation to remove the rights and privileges of the French-speaking Roman Catholics.

A map of Carriacou[3] drawn in 1784 shows Carriacou divided into fifty-one estates, of varying sizes. Some of the estates in Carriacou owned by the French were leased back to the original owners, and others were sold to new owners from Great Britain. The Roman Catholic priest,

Father Guis, unlike the priests in Grenada, was allowed to keep his lands and his slaves for the time being, and therefore had enough to live on. He built the first church in Hillsborough in 1784.

One of the first things that Governor Matthew did was to complete the ring of forts and barracks at Richmond Hill that the French had started. The Grenada government purchased the Mount George estate from William Lucas. This estate had been acquired by the French for the erection of fortifications. The government also made grants of slave labour and materials to finish the fortifications. A pledge was given by Britain that two regiments would always be stationed in Grenada. The forts served the island until the manner of warfare made them obsolete, and they were turned to other uses. The ruins of these forts today still give testament to their original grandeur.

Governor Matthew spent most of the time of his appointment as Governor away from the island. He left Grenada in 1788, and only returned for a brief period until 1793 when he was replaced. During his prolonged absence, the President of the Council acted as Governor. At various times this position was held by William Lucas, James Campbell and Samuel Williams. All of these were English and Scottish planters who had made their homes in Grenada, and who had by 1767 established a firm opposition to the French-speaking Roman Catholics. Lucas, Campbell and Williams were men of influence, and had the support of many others in the Colony, including Ninian Home.

The Slave Society

Under British rule, thousands of slaves were imported into Grenada each year. In 1784 alone, 1688 slaves were imported.[4] At this time the value of a male slave was £40, and a female two pounds less. The famous Methodist missionary, Coke, reported around 1790 that the slaves in Grenada were treated with less severity than in the other British colonies,[5] but this hardly meant that the slaves lived a happy life.

When the slaves were bought at auction after arriving in Grenada, they were taken to the estate for 'seasoning'. Once, a man called Castles of Grenada was asked by a Committee of the House of Commons in England what he meant by 'seasoning'. He replied:

> When a new Negro has been two or three years in the country, and acquainted with the language and manner of it, and has got his provision ground in such a situation as to provide himself with food, we consider him a seasoned Negro.[6]

When questioned further regarding adjustment to the labour they were subjected to, Castles said: 'I fancy Negroes in their own country do very little work, and therefore they must be habituated to it by degrees.'[7]

Not every person in charge of an estate believed that the slave needed to be gradually accustomed to hard work in a broiling tropical sun by being given the easier tasks such as turning cane trash. Some new slaves were put immediately to hard work, often with fatal consequences. The slaves' workloads, diet, housing, clothing, punishments and provision of medical services also differed from estate to estate. In every case the slave's life was one of hardship, deprivation and oppression. Bernard Marshall observes that in the Windward Islands, where the economy was based on the work of the field slaves, they were subjected to a life of degradation and misery.

> On the plantation the field slave was forced to work for long hours under the whip. Because he had fewer opportunities for earning a cash income than those slaves working in the towns, he became heavily dependent upon his master for most of the basic necessities of life. But because of the need to keep profit margins as high as possible, and also because of the low rate of and sometimes the absence of profit in the sugar industry, the quantities of food, clothing and other necessities made available to him were exceedingly small.[8]

Very early in Grenada it was decided to allot each slave – man, woman and child – a piece of land on which it was expected that the slave would raise food to feed him or herself. What was raised would be supplemented by rations of imported grain, meat or salted fish. This practice suited the estate owners because feeding the slaves entirely from imported foodstuffs was costly. In addition, the very hard work on the plantation was seasonal, and there were some months of the year when the demand for slave labour was not as great. The slaves could then be released to work on their own account to grow more food at these times. Moreover, cultivation of plots by slaves was a hedge against starvation of the population in times of war. The slaves were given provision grounds in the hills and on the boundaries of the plantation, and often had to walk as much as ten miles to get there. The land was very fertile, but access was difficult. The slaves were also given time to work the ground, and could keep anything they realized in sales of surplus. Sundays and Saturdays out of crop time were given as time off for the cultivation of provision grounds and sale of the goods. In addition, the slaves were allowed to have kitchen gardens around their dwellings, and to raise poultry and small stock as well.

The slaves worked assiduously at cultivation of their plots, in addition to providing for themselves, and soon supplied all of Grenada with fresh vegetables, fruit and ground provisions as well. They peddled these from door to door, but also sold produce in markets that quickly grew up in the main population centres of the parishes. At these markets the slaves could buy the goods they required, including little luxuries for themselves.

The practice of providing slaves with provision grounds was subjected to legal regulation in 1775. In 1788 Alexander Campbell observed that it was the custom among planters in Grenada to give the slaves as much land as they could work because it was: 'universally considered the greatest benefit to a planter that his Negroes should have a sufficient quantity of provisions, and the more money the Negroes got for themselves, the more they were attached to their property.'[9]

In 1788 the Slave Amelioration Act instituted several measures designed to improve the conditions of the slaves. Now slaves were to be given time for rest and for meals, and could not be compelled to work during specified free time. The sanctity of marriage was extended to slaves, in that there was a fine of £165 for 'debauching' a married slave. Further laws were passed in 1789 to provide guardians for the protection of negroes, who would investigate cases of abuse. Some slaves had the satisfaction of seeing people punished for cruelty against their brothers and sisters. A case is reported of a woman being fined £500 for cruelty to a slave. Nevertheless, the planters were wary of the slaves, and as news of the effect of the French Revolution on other countries in the Caribbean became known, they became even more worried.

The Effect of the French Revolution on Grenada

Although French-speaking Grenadians undeniably supported the French against the British when Grenada was captured by d'Estaing, the world scene had changed in a few years, and they were now quite willing to live under British protection. Grenada got all the European news, and the news of the French Revolution and the atrocities committed in France struck fear into the hearts of Grenadian planters.[10] Among the French-speaking planters in Grenada were minor members of the nobility, and they were stunned to hear about the events of the French Revolution, including the massacre of those identified as aristocrats. Moreover, the French Revolutionary government, the National Assembly, had freed the slaves in 1794. The slaves in any country falling to Revolutionary France would also be free. How would they survive in the West Indies? Even the merchants depended on slaves for the manual work concerned with their business of shipping produce and importing plantation goods. And what about those slaves on whom the smooth running of their homes depended?

As early as 10 August 1789, less than one month after the Fall of the Bastille, there were rumours that the planters in St Domingue, St Lucia and Tobago wanted to secede from France. They were terrified as to what would be their fate at the hands of the Republicans. The French-speaking Grenadians shared the worries of the French planters, especially after war broke out between France and Britain in 1793. Should Republican France retake Grenada, the lives and property of the French Grenadians would be in serious jeopardy, as French Republicans in Guadeloupe had made it known that they would kill all who had lived under British rule, and allow their slaves to pillage their property. Alarmed at this prospect, thirty of the most prominent French-speaking Grenadians made a proclamation of allegiance to Britain in 1790, at the same time asking Britain to protect Grenada against French attack. One of the signatories to this proclamation was a coloured planter by the name of Julien Fédon.

In 1793 the abolition of slavery was announced in St. Dominigue, and was ratified by the French National Convention in February 1794. By the Decree of Pluviose, slavery was abolished in all the French colonies. By April 1794 the French islands of Martinique, Guadeloupe and St Lucia were occupied by Britain, helped by the French planters in those territories who would rather live under Britain than under the French Republican government. In November of that year Britain ordered the soldiers from the garrisons in the Windward Islands to assemble in Barbados.

Immediately, the French Republican government dispatched Victor Hugues, a member of the Republican Party called the Jacobins, and a mulatto, to retake the islands, and to implement the Decree of Pluviose. Hugues arrived off Guadeloupe in June 1794. He was successful in being able to retake Guadeloupe and St Lucia for Republican France. There was much bloodshed, with several French planters and their families being guillotined. Hugues declared the immediate emancipation of the slaves, and encouraged them to take whatever actions they wished against their former masters.

Hugues planned to restore all the former French colonies to Republican France not through direct military attack alone, but through internal revolt among the Francophone community in the British islands. As soon as possible, he began to use undercover methods to spread revolutionary propaganda and ideas of rebellion among the slaves and free coloureds in Grenada, Martinique and St Vincent.

Instead of working with the French inhabitants to effect the integration of people of different heritages, religious beliefs and language, to ensure the solidarity of Grenadian society and the well-being of Grenada, the Government of Grenada devoted itself instead to alienating the French-speaking citizens and their slaves as well. The Grenadian legislature was temporarily unhampered by any restraining influence that might have been exerted by a wise diplomatic Governor, as Governor Matthew was absent from Grenada for lengthy periods of time. The legislature was now both dominated by British members and temporarily led by one of their number. The legislature now had a free hand to carry out the suggestions they had made in the previous era to Governor Macartney who, in his wisdom, had gently admonished them and turned them away from their mischief. In quick succession the legislature passed several laws intended to weaken and humble the French Roman Catholics in Grenada, and put pressure on them to abandon their religion if they wished to prosper in Grenadian society. Britain would only object to legislation passed by the Grenadian legislature in very special circumstances, after some debate, and the occasional referral to lawyers. The non-Catholics in Grenada were correct in their assumption that they could pass the discriminatory measures against the Roman Catholics without opposition from Britain.

The Establishment of Methodism

Protestant clergy were welcomed to set up churches in Grenada. On 28 November 1790 Dr Thomas Coke, the famous Wesleyan missionary, arrived in Grenada with the intention of establishing Methodism in this country. Three years later he built the first Methodist Chapel in St George's. The Methodists would remain a small religious group, but would have some impact on the thinking of the population, and diversify religious affiliations, especially in St George's, and in particular the areas of Woburn, St Paul's and Annandale. The Methodists were instrumental in converting a number of slaves to Christianity.

Acquisition of the Roman Catholic Churches

In contrast to the welcome and encouragement given to other religions in Grenada, a concerted effort began to suppress the Roman Catholic religion. The government passed a series of discriminatory laws, the first decreeing that the Roman Catholics had to share their churches with those of other faiths who wanted to use them. As far as the Roman Catholics were concerned, this was preposterous. No other religion could use a

Roman Catholic church without special permission from Rome. The church authorities tried to use diplomacy to deal with any requests for the use of the Catholic churches by Protestant ministers, but there came a time when the government took the churches by force.

The test case was a request by Governor Matthew that the Roman Catholic church in St George's be made available for the use of the Reverend John Wingate, a Church of England minister. On 18 January 1784 the priest, Father Gasquet, sent the minister away, buying time with a diplomatic answer. He himself had no objection, but they had to get the permission of the churchwardens. When Wingate and his interpreter went to the warden, a man named St Bernard, they were told that he had to consult the church in St John's Parish. The 'run-around' given to Wingate angered the Governor. He sent a firm message to the priest that he expected the church to be opened at 11 a.m. on Sunday for the Protestant service.

When the priest and his warden informed Governor Matthew that a Protestant service could not take place in a Catholic church without the permission of the Pope, they were warned that the doors would be forced open. Still they refused to give up the keys or open the church. At the appointed time, a detachment of Grenadiers arrived at the church, broke the doors, and the service took place.[11] Some days after the Grenadiers forced the doors, the holy water stoup and baptismal font were destroyed and thrown away with some other furniture into the yard outside the church. A wall was built around the church, and the access door in the wall locked. Thus were the Roman Catholics denied access to their church.

Similar incidents took place at all the Roman Catholic churches. Not only was the use of the buildings forced for Protestant services, but they were also desecrated in a similar manner to the church in St George's. The Catholics, instead of risking further confrontation, saved what they could of their sacred vessels and other holy objects, and used other buildings for Mass and other services, including the priests' houses.

Governor Matthew knew full well that this would happen, for he wrote to the Secretary of State for the Colonies that Catholics were 'not permitted by the tenets of their religion to use the churches alternatively with us'.[12] It is evident that the Established Church did not have a pressing need for the Roman Catholic buildings. Except for the church in St George's, the Catholic churches throughout Grenada were seldom used, and, as will happen in Grenada, were soon overgrown by bush. The motive, then, for requesting that the Roman Catholics share their churches was not to obtain a place of worship for Protestants, but was simply to find an excuse to confiscate the Roman Catholic churches, thus preventing Roman Catholic services from being held in them.

Appropriation of the Glebe Lands

Not satisfied with turning the Catholics out of their churches, the government then moved to appropriate the revenue of the church, and to confiscate all church lands, called glebe lands. The revenue from the church lands was very small, about £371 14s. 10d.[13] but, with subscriptions and gifts, the revenue was an important means of livelihood to the Roman Catholic priests. The lands, which included the land on which the churches stood, were purchases or gifts willed to the church. Most had been in the possession of the Roman Catholic Church since Grenada had been under French rule, and remained church property when the island became British. Now the lands were confiscated. It is instructive that neither the revenue nor the lands were turned to the use of the Anglican Church.

New Regulations for the Registration of Births, Marriages and Deaths

A third piece of legislation entitled 'An Act to Supply the Defects of former Parish Registers' was passed on 21 October 1785. This Act had little to do with the way in which the registration of baptisms, marriages and deaths were recorded, for the Roman Catholic clergy were meticulous in this respect. This piece of legislation was another attempt to break the power and control Roman Catholicism had on its followers by making adherence to this religion a burden. The Act decreed that the only legal marriages, and the only baptisms or funerals recognized for legal purposes, would be those performed by Protestant clergymen. If the Catholic population chose, their priests could perform these rites, but the records kept by the Roman Catholic priest had to be copied for a fee into the parish records of the Church of England. Besides being a nuisance and an affront to Roman Catholics, this new regulation was a financial liability for Roman Catholics, especially for the poor. A Roman Catholic who wished to have a baptism, marriage or funeral performed according to Roman Catholic rites had now to provide two stipends: one to the Roman Catholic priest and another to the Minister of the Established Church for recording the event in the register of the Established Church, thus giving legal sanction to the desired action.

Imposition of the Test

The Roman Catholics were angered and dismayed at these measures. The freedom of religion guaranteed to the Roman Catholics in Grenada by the Treaty of Paris and the Treaty of Versailles had been contravened. But worse was to come. In 1789 the 1768 Royal Order exempting Grenadians from the Test was revoked, with effect from 1792. From now on, the Test was imposed as a condition for sitting in the legislature and for holding positions of trust, excluding Roman Catholics from serving in the government unless they renounced their religion. Before 1792 the small number of French Roman Catholic Grenadians in the Grenadian legislature could not prevent anti-Roman Catholic laws from being passed, although they tirelessly protested against the proposed measures. But, after 1792, French Roman Catholic Grenadians lost almost all the legal and socially acceptable ways of airing and addressing the grievances of the large section of the population that they represented in the legislature. Their only avenues of protest were petition and Memorials[14] to the king. Thus the ultimate dream of the British settlers to deprive the French Roman Catholics of all their civic and religious privileges, and to set them apart as second-class citizens, was realized.

After each piece of legislation, Memorials were written to the Acting Governor, William Lucas, seeking redress, but they were ignored. The Memorial regarding the right to vote and the right to sit in the legislature without taking the Test was sent to the Colonial Office by Lucas, with a long covering letter of justification for all the actions complained of by the French Grenadians. His attitude was that the French Grenadians should be weaned away from adherence to their religion by conforming to laws set down, rather than be encouraged to ask for special privileges under the law.

The Home Office entertained the complaints of their New Subjects. Toleration for Catholics in Britain was growing, and Britain was about to pass a second Catholic Relief Act. The Home Office sent the complaints of the New Subjects to the Crown lawyers for an opinion. The Secretary of State acted on the opinions of the Crown lawyers. It was the advice of the Crown lawyers that influenced the Home Office not to disallow those laws that contravened the Treaties of Paris and Versailles. Very likely, Lucas, Campbell and their supporters had friends in high places who could influence the Crown lawyers. Otherwise it is difficult to understand why these pieces of discriminatory legislation were allowed to pass into law. There were many non-Catholics who felt that the Government of Grenada was being unjust. Among these were James Farquhar and another prominent non-Catholic, Strachan.

Ninian Home Appointed as Lieutenant-Governor

The post of Lieutenant-Governor of Grenada fell vacant. Ninian Home, who had been on an extended visit to Britain from about 1788, applied for the post while he was there. Although he resided most of the year in Grenada, Ninian Home was the owner of his family's ancestral home in Scotland, called Paxton House, and his upbringing was staunchly Protestant. Ninian Home had expensive tastes, and had a penchant for nice furniture and paintings. Like so many others of his countrymen, Home saw investment in Grenada as the means to satisfy his material desires and to acquire even greater wealth. The position of Governor would not only enhance his personal prestige, but the income from the post would assist him in the acquisition of the material things that he loved.

Home looked after his two estates in Waltham and Paraclete, and also took an interest in the property of his brother and his friends. Ninian Home's brother George, and his friend Alexander Campbell, owned property in Grenada and the Grenadines. Ninian was therefore very interested in any threat to the Grenadines. On 25 October 1793 he wrote to his friend Matthew Munro that:

> French Privateers have been very troublesome between this island [Grenada] and St Vincent; several vessels have been captured about Carriacou, and one loaded with corn, cut out of Hillsborough Road, which was a very great loss for they have been in great distress in that Island for the want of Provisions.[15]

Ninian Home was determined, therefore, that nothing would be allowed to happen in Grenada that would prevent its development and continued prosperity. This included any actions by the remaining inhabitants of a French colony that had been twice captured by Britain.

While a member of the Assembly, Home had worked on the drafting of the Acts that had disenfranchised the French Roman Catholics. He was not completely bigoted, as he believed that the Roman Catholics should be allowed freedom of worship, and supported the idea that the Roman Catholic clergy who had been deprived of their livelihood after the Government of Grenada took the church's glebe lands should be granted a small annuity during their lifetime. But it was his ambition to replace the primacy, power and influence of the Roman Catholic Church with that of the Established Church.

In 1792 Home was offered the post of Lieutenant-Governor of Grenada. This he accepted and was appointed on 29 January 1793, on his return to Grenada. The French-speaking Roman Catholic Grenadians, already bristling with indignation at the discriminatory legislation, sorely disappointed at the British government for having apparently reneged on the promises enshrined in the treaties, were now completely chagrined that Britain should appoint as their Lieutenant-Governor a man who had actively sought to deprive them of their civic and religious rights and who had drafted much of the discriminatory legislation. Was this person to now preside over their humiliation as a people? Discontent was palpable. Home became a symbol of oppression. Julien Fédon, soon to be the leader of the French Roman Catholic community, would later refer to him as 'the Tyrant Home'.

Storm Signals

The receipt of the ruling from the Privy Council in London stating that Roman Catholics in Grenada should be treated as Roman Catholics in Britain, and not as in Canada, almost coincided with the revolution in St Domingue that overthrew the traditional French government in that country. Ill-treated by the Grenada government and abandoned by the British government, some of the French-speaking citizens of Grenada begun to feel that, if they wanted to stay in Grenada, which had been their homeland for 150 years, the only way to improve their situation and recover their rights was to espouse French republicanism and engage in a revolution as the free coloureds and the slaves in St Domingue had done. The ideology of the French Revolution with its slogan 'Liberty, Fraternity and Equality' promised all that they had been denied.

French republican ideas were already being discussed among the French-speaking population in Grenada. Since the outbreak of the war, Grenada had become a refuge for Frenchmen fleeing the terrors in St Domingue and Guadeloupe. In one six-month period, 1200 foreigners arrived seeking asylum in Grenada.[16] Among the genuine refugees were others posing as displaced persons, who were really emissaries of the French Revolution, spreading its doctrines. Discovering the means by which infiltration of republican ideas into the population were taking place, Lieutenant-Governor Home stopped all refugees entering Grenada. Although he was sympathetic to the plight of the genuine cases, the spread of revolutionary ideas in Grenada was very dangerous to the status quo, based as it was on plantation slavery and a society that was still essentially French in culture, with French speakers outnumbering English speakers. If Grenada were to be attacked by France, the loyalty of the French-speaking inhabitants to Britain was doubtful, because of their old allegiance, but also because they were dissatisfied with having to conform to the laws passed by the Grenadian legislature that forced them to recognize the primacy of Britain, and the Established Church.

The Lieutenant-Governor shut the gate too late. Revolutionary ideas had already taken root among Grenadians, particularly among the free coloureds of French heritage. Rumours came back to the Lieutenant-Governor of the holding of clandestine meetings in the colony, mainly involving free coloured French Grenadians.

To increase the Lieutenant-Governor's concern, and in spite of their promise always to keep two regiments in Grenada, Britain withdrew more than half the soldiers stationed in Grenada to help to retake and hold Martinique and St Lucia. Grenada was left with only 293 men, of whom only 103 were fit for duty, and a Militia of about 900, 500 of whom were British, about 70 to100 of whom were French and 300 of whom were coloured and mainly of French extraction. In 1793 the bulam or blackwater fever (a type of malaria) had been brought to Grenada from West Africa on a ship called the *Hankey*. It ravaged the people of Grenada, including the foreign troops stationed there with consistence and severity for the next five years. It would take a heavy toll of the population, and be a serious handicap to the military.

Several people urged the Lieutenant-Governor to issue a proclamation calling in all arms on the island. Then, in case of hostilities, the French and free coloured population would have no weapons, and he could then arm those loyal to Britain. Home refused this option, because he said that to take it would be to show weakness and apprehension.

Ninian Home wrote to his brother George Home in Scotland of his anxieties and worries about the situation in Grenada. As early as 18 July 1793, he wrote that he feared the minds of the slaves in Grenada would be poisoned by the immigrants from the French islands, promoting ideas of liberty, equality and fraternity.[17] To his friend Matthew Munro, living in England, he wrote about the suspicious activities of some of the Roman Catholic priests, 'especially the one[18] who lives on the road to Belmont. I have the best reason to think…[he] is the most dangerous in the whole island; and before it is long, I may be able to prove it.'[19]

The Lieutenant-Governor was right to be worried. Not only were the majority of French Grenadians ready for action, but also they were no longer leaderless. From among the free coloured French several men of great leadership ability and military acumen emerged to take the lead in a revolution against the status quo and a revolt against the British.

Julien Fédon

There is a substantial collection of old French records in the vaults of the Registry at the Supreme Court, York House, in St George's. A search of these reveals that Julien Fédon was the son of a Frenchman, Pierre Fédon, and a free black woman, Brigitte, a native of Martinique.[20] Fédon had a brother called Jean, and the names of both Julien and Jean Fédon appear on the list of property owners for 1794. Fédon was married to Marie Rose Cavelan, reputed to be a person of mulatto and Amerindian ancestry. Hay says that Fédon was educated in England,[21] but there is no other evidence to substantiate this. As was common among the West Indian French, Fédon was baptized a Roman Catholic, and was raised in his father's house. Fédon had two daughters.

Fédon and his wife owned Lancer Estate up to 1791, when they sold it. Belvidere Estate was purchased by Fédon from James Campbell in May 1791. It was an estate of 450 acres and eighty slaves. Fédon also bought a house in Gouyave from Charles Nogues and his wife, Marie Louise Fédon Nogues, Julien's sister. Jean Fédon owned a coffee plantation of 139 acres in St John. Charles Nogues, Fédon's brother-in-law, was a tailor in St George's, and previously a landowner there. At the time of the Revolution, he owned a cotton plantation in Sauteurs. Joachim[22] Philip came from one of the oldest coloured landowning families in Grenada. His family owned land in St George's and cotton estates in Carriacou and Petit Martinique. Jean-Pierre La Valette was a tailor in Sauteurs and Stanislaus Besson a silversmith in Grenville.[23]

Fédon, Nogues and Philip, together with Jean Pierre La Valette and Stanislaus Besson, were known as leaders of the coloured French Grenadians by 1790. Fédon, his brother Jean, and most of his close associates signed the Declaration of Allegiance to the British government. Eventually Fédon emerged as the leader of the group. All his associates appreciated his charismatic personality, his attitudes, his leadership qualities and military ability.

Fédon and his group met regularly to discuss affairs in the country, and particularly the options open to them to right the wrongs suffered by the French Roman Catholic Grenadians. By the end of 1793 Fédon and his group had decided that, given the attitude of the Grenada legislature and the ratification of their laws by the British over the protests of the French-speaking citizens, their only option was armed insurrection. They began to lay their preparations towards this end. Soon after the arrival of Victor Hugues in Guadeloupe, the group established contact with him because they realized that a successful revolution needed help from outside Grenada. Hugues encouraged the group in their revolutionary ideas. The group came to a firm conviction that a revolution was necessary and desirable in Grenada. This revolution would stand for religious and civil rights for all who accepted it, would stand for the end of slavery, and would stand for the overthrow of the British government, which had abandoned its New Subjects to those who despised the Roman Catholic religion.

Preparations for the Revolution

About September or October 1793, the planning and preparations for an armed revolution against the British in Grenada began in earnest. Fédon planted plantains and root crops at Belvidere to provide food for his revolutionary army, which would be headquartered there. The many streams that ran through the estate would supply all the fresh water needed. Belvidere also was ideally located, remote from St George's, but with several points which provided commanding views of the east and west coasts. Construction of four camps began on the estate. One, later to be known as Camp Liberty, was on the lower reaches of Belvidere Estate, another on much higher ground called Fédon's Camp, Camp Equality was on Mount Qua Qua and the Camp of Death, the highest of all, on Mount Vauclain.[24] The Camp of Death was almost impregnable, and served as Fédon's headquarters and command centre.

Meetings with the general population increased in frequency and fervour. At these meetings, the oppression of the French-speaking Roman Catholics was discussed, and revolution proposed as the only way to break the oppression, as all other means had already been tried, to no avail. Meetings also undoubtedly took place among the slaves, who were well aware of the fact that the slaves had been freed in Guadeloupe.

Early in 1795 two revolutionaries from Grenada, Charles Nogues and Jean-Pierre La Valette were sent to Victor Hugues in Guadeloupe, requesting his support for the Revolution planned for the island. He not only gave his blessing to the plans but also arranged for military training and commissions in the French military for some of Fédon's key supporters. He promised Fédon and his group speedy and effectual support in their revolutionary efforts, and sent Fédon's emissaries home with some ammunition, flags and other symbols of the Revolution, and with commissions from the French Republic signed by himself and two other French Commissioners in Guadeloupe, Goyrand and Le Bas. Julien Fédon was made the Commandant-General of the French Republican forces in Grenada, with Stanislaus Besson his second-in-command. Charles Nogues and Jean-Pierre La Valette were appointed Captains.

Fédon had a great rapport among the French-speaking slaves, and used them as an information-gathering network. Fédon was particularly supported by the domestics, drivers, tradesmen and other principal slaves on the estates, in particular those on the estates of his friends. This was unusual, because these categories of slaves were relatively privileged, and were more likely to betray a rebellion than to join one. The close affinity between these slaves and the free coloured at this point in Grenada's history made for solidarity between these two groups, and this solidarity was strengthened by the religious persecution that many of them suffered due to their espousal of the Roman Catholic religion. Fédon used this network of slaves as his informers. Whatever was planned by the British, the revolutionaries knew beforehand. Garraway later observed, 'The rebels were in possession of all the Lieutenant-Governor's movements.'[25] An interesting theory[26] has been put forward in contemporary times by Curtis Jacobs, a young Trinidadian researcher. Jacobs believes that Fédon either believed in, or used, Congo and Yoruba religious rituals and symbolism throughout the Revolution as an aid (or tool) to ensure that the Africans would believe that Fédon and the Revolution would be successful because the gods of the African people were on his side.

The Distress of Ninian Home

Perhaps Home realized that his situation in Grenada was untenable. Records show that he was also under enormous mental distress as his wife was ill. He had applied for leave to take her back to Britain in the summer of 1795,[27] but she died on 30 September 1794, and he buried her on his Paraclete Estate, high in the mountains in the north of Grenada, and about twenty miles from St George's. Ninian Home loved his wife dearly. Every letter he wrote to his brother, friends and even business acquaintances during 1794 gave news of her,[28] and expressed the hope that she would recover from her chronic illness. The news of her eventual death had to be conveyed to George Home by Ninian Home's closest friend, Alexander Campbell:

> Ninian … was in very great distress and not able to write himself. What effect this might have on his intentions of returning, I know not. Mr Campbell says he <u>must not</u> remain longer in that country. I wish most earnestly he may himself be of that opinion, and we must persist in endeavouring to obtain his leave if it can be done without great impropriety, not being a military man there is not the same delicacy attached to his requesting it.[29]

All efforts to get leave for the Lieutenant-Governor approved were futile up to the point at which the turn of events would make this leave inconsequential.[30]

Personal distress did not hinder Lieutenant-Governor Home from doing all he could for Grenada even though he was without the garrison that he needed for the protection of Grenada. His best defence was in early warning, so he had alarm posts set up and manned by members of the St George's Militia, and arranged a system of alarm signals to be sent off from the most windward point of the island along the coast on both sides of St George's on the appearance of any fleet.

On 1 March 1795 a Mr Ross of Calivigny visited Lieutenant-Governor Home at Government House, bringing with him the information that a woman on the estate had told him that a French force was to land at Calivigny 'at the full of the moon', and that he, Ross, should keep out of the way and so save his life. Home asked Ross to bring the woman to him so that she could be questioned further, but Ross refused. The refusal of Ross to produce the informant weakened the information in Lieutenant-Governor's view, and he therefore made no mention of it in a letter he drafted to Lieutenant-General Sir John Vaughan the next day, which stated the deficient situation of the island in case of any attempt against it. This same letter communicated information Home had received that a French fleet had arrived at the island of St Bartholomew.[31]

When Ninian Home completed drafting the letter to Vaughan, Alexander Campbell prevailed on him to dine early, and then travel to Paraclete to spend the night on a place he had recently acquired in that area.[32] Some accounts of the events in Grenada are very unkind to Lieutenant-Governor Ninian Home. Many falsify events and motives in an attempt to make Home seem incompetent. One misrepresentation that has been repeated by subsequent scholars is the account that describes Home's visit to Paraclete on 2 March as a 'hunting party'.[33] This could hardly have been the case as Home was in no frame of mind to engage in recreational pursuits. More likely, Campbell thought that Home needed a break from the pressures of office, given his continuing state of grief over the death of his wife and his worry over the vulnerability of Grenada to attack. Campbell arranged to take the Governor to his own estate, which was also at Paraclete, and for the letter to Vaughan and others that needed to be signed to be sent there later for the Lieutenant-Governor's signature. All objections met, Home gave in to the entreaties of his well-meaning friend and set out with Campbell and James Farquhar, his aide-de-camp, despite his reluctance to leave St George's. Farquhar stayed the night at Hervey's Plantation, for which he was attorney, and Campbell and the Lieutenant-Governor went on to Campbell's estate. Had Campbell not prevailed on his friend to take a respite from the pressures of office, events would have taken a slightly different course.

The Storm Breaks

Governor Home and his party arrived at Paraclete safely. However, at about midnight between 2 and 3 March 1795, while Home and his party slept, all Home's fears for the security of Grenada came to a head, though not exactly as he imagined. Home had expected a French invasion, and had prepared for it. Instead, the French attacked from within, in alliance with citizens of Grenada whom they had groomed for revolution, and who had their own grievances and their own agenda.

Notes

1 Govt of Grenada, *Grenada Handbook*, p.27.
2 'Presentation on the Propriety of Permitting the French Inhabitants to Remain in Grenada', 1784, papers in the Supreme Court Registry, St George's.
3 This map shows that the modern spelling of Carriacou had been established by 1784.
4 Bayley, p.645.
5 *Ibid.*
6 Reported in Sheridan (1990), p.138.
7 *Ibid.*
8 Marshall, Bernard (thesis), pp.385–6.
9 Quoted in Marshall, Woodville (1993), p.50.
10 See Williams, ch. 15, for a discussion of how the French Revolution affected the various sectors of the population of the French colony of St Domingue.
11 Devas (1932), p.62.
12 CO 101/26, Matthew to Lord Sydney, 27 Dec. 1784, Public Record Office (PRO), London.
13 Devas (1931), p.65.
14 These were lengthy, reasoned position papers designed to prove the rightness or wrongness of a situation using fact and reason.
15 Ninian Home to Matthew Munro, esq., 25 Oct. 1793, quoted in Devas (1974), p.183.
16 CO 101/36, President Samuel Williams to Dundas, 4 July 1792, PRO.
17 Letter to George Home dated 18 July 1793, quoted by Devas (1974), p.124.
18 This priest is elsewhere identified as Father La Pointe.
19 Home to Matthew Munro, dated 1 September 1793, quoted in Devas (1974) p.125.
20 Old French records: 'Births, Deaths and Record of Property', July 1772–Aug. 1809, Supreme Court Registry, St George's.
21 Hay, p.76. Not all the details Hay's short biography of Fédon match with the public records.
22 This name is spelt Joachin in some of the literature.
23 Old French records: 'Births, Deaths and Record of Property', July 1772–Aug.1809, Supreme Court Registry, St George's.
24 Jacobs, Curtis (2000), p. 11.
25 Garraway, p. 5.
26 Jacobs, Curtis (2000), p. 21.
27 CO 101/8, Ninian Home, private dispatch.
28 GD 267/7/3, Ninian Home's letter book, June–October 1794, Scottish Record Office (SRO), Edinburgh.
29 GD 267/3/11/37, Letter from George Home to Patrick Home, 12 Nov. 1794, SRO.
30 See GD 267/1/18/12, Letter from George Home to Patrick Home, 15 March 1795, and GD 267/1/18/14, Letter from George Home to Patrick Home, 23 March 1795, SRO.
31 GD 267/5/19/1, Letter from Mather Byles to George Home, 26 March 1795, SRO.
32 *Ibid.*

33 The *Grenada Handbook* says: 'Lieutenant-Governor Home, instead of being at
    headquarters at such a time of danger, was spending some days with a party of
    gentlemen at his estate, Paraclete' (p. 31). Brizan says that Home was with a
    'hunting party at Paraclete' (p. 65). Home was at Paraclete, but not at his own
    estate, and definitely not enjoying himself.

6

The Fédon Revolution

Various words are used by commentators to refer to the events that began at midnight between 2 and 3 March 1795. Fédon's Revolution is variously called an 'insurgency', an 'uprising', a 'rebellion', a 'revolt', and a 'slave rebellion'. When it is referred to as 'the Brigands' War', it includes the uprisings in Grenada, St Vincent, St Lucia, and to some extent in Dominica and Guadeloupe. Notwithstanding Chatoyer and Duvalle and the colourful Caribs' War in St Vincent, the events in Grenada were by far the most spectacular.

This unforgettable and fascinating period of Grenadian history is very difficult to label, as several distinct elements operated together to produce an enormous social conflagration. I have chosen to identify the period as a revolution because the intention was to change things for the French-speaking Roman Catholics and to create a new type of society in Grenada, for both the free and the slave. Although some of the revolutionaries spouted the rhetoric of the French Revolution, and dressed in the uniforms of the French Republican Army, the French Roman Catholics in Grenada had greivances long before the French Revolution broke out. Although the French Grenadians under Fédon also had some resources, they were glad to have these supplemented by Revolutionary France. It is arguable that had they had all the resources they needed, they would have preferred to fight their own war. Fédon saw himself as the leader who would bring about true freedom for all in Grenada who would join him in overthrowing the old regime. How could a movement like this be looked on as a simple rebellion?

The Revolution Begins

There are numerous accounts of the Revolution led by Fédon. The contemporary accounts were written by John Hay, D.G. Garraway, Francis McMahon ('a Grenada planter'), 'An eyewitness'(Gordon Turnbull), Henry Thornhill and Thomas Wise. This account draws from all of them, as well as subsequent narratives and commentaries.

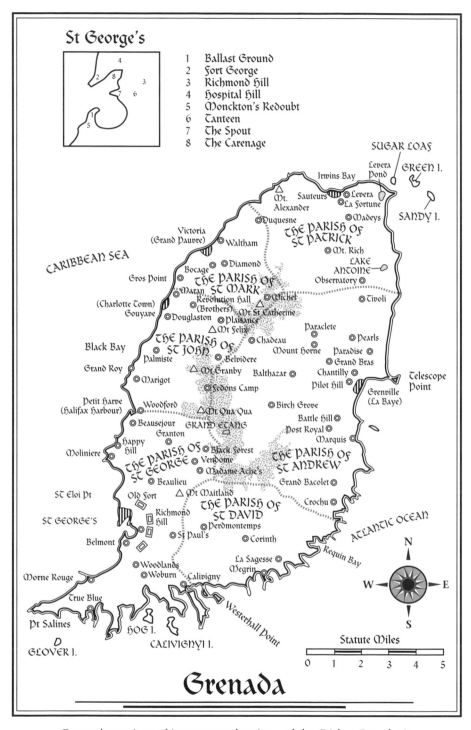

St George's

1 Ballast Ground
2 Fort George
3 Richmond Hill
4 Hospital Hill
5 Monckton's Redoubt
6 Tanteen
7 The Spout
8 The Carenage

Grenada: points of interest at the time of the Fédon Revolution

At about midnight between 2 and 3 March 1795, Julien Fédon, supported by free people of colour and slaves, about 100 in number, marched to the hamlet of Grenville.[1] The population was taken completely by surprise, as they never expected an attack without the French first landing by sea. The British planters and their families were taken from their beds into the street, and were shot, and then their bodies were mangled with cutlasses. Their houses were plundered before the revolutionaries departed for Fédon's estate at Belvidere. Only three of the fourteen British inhabitants of the hamlet escaped. On the way to Belvidere, the revolutionaries stopped at Balthazar Estate and took Mr Ross, the planter, prisoner. Abbé Peissonier was shot dead by La Valette. He excused the execution by saying that the Abbé was 'an aristocrat'.[2]

Simultaneous with the attack on Grenville, Gouyave was captured by a detachment of revolutionaries led by Etienne Ventour and Joachim Philip. This assault was more controlled, perhaps because those accompanying Ventour and Philip were mainly planters and tradesmen who had undergone some military training. They were also well equipped, and some of them, including Philip, were wearing regulation French Republican Army uniforms.

A number of prisoners were taken, including the doctor, John Hay, and the Anglican priest, McMahon, both of whom later wrote eyewitness accounts. No one was killed, but the prisoners were marched up to Belvidere Estate, which was owned by Fédon. On the way, several other estate owners and managers were captured and made prisoner. When the prisoners arrived, they were first lodged in a boucan, which is a hut used to dry cocoa beans.[3] Later they were taken to another spot higher up into the mountains. Hay was sent back to Gouyave to fetch medical supplies, principally to attend to Etienne Ventour who had been wounded in the capture of that town. He found the town, including his own house, plundered.

The Capture of the Lieutenant-Governor and his Party

At Paraclete, Lieutenant-Governor Home was awakened by the arrival of a distraught group of people who came to give him a confused account of the happenings in Grenville. Alexander Campbell offered to ride to Grenville, and was joined by several members of the Militia whom he met at Paradise Estate. When they reached Grenville, they found the place in great distress. Campbell hurriedly returned to confirm the massacre, and to say that it was believed that the French had invaded.

On receipt of this confirmation from Campbell, Home immediately got ready to try to return to St George's. First he sent a letter to a senior member of the Council and the Attorney General, Kenneth Francis Mackenzie, with a messenger, who was sent by the shortest route over the mountains to St George's. In the letter he set out what he thought had happened at Grenville, and news of the massacre that had taken place. Home, wary of ambush, did not want to use the road over the mountain to St George's. Instead, he thought it more prudent to ride to Sauteurs, accompanied by Campbell, Farquhar and James Kerr, and to get a boat from there to St George's. By the time Home arrived in Sauteurs, he had found out that the massacre in Grenville had not been carried out by French invaders, but by French-speaking coloured inhabitants of Grenada who were part of an uprising.

Ninian Home and his party located a sloop called *New Diamond* owned by a man called Lepelly, which was moored at Irwin's Bay near Sauteurs. They embarked on this vessel later on the morning of 3 March, giving instructions to sail around the north point of Grenada and down the west coast of the island to St George's. Nearing Gouyave, this voyage was cut short.

There are two versions of what happened when the *New Diamond* reached Gouyave. The more usual account[4] is that a boat was seen approaching the town from the south. Fearing that they were about to be captured on the high seas, Home and some of his party decided to try to land at Gouyave by using the sloop's boat. As soon as the small boat pushed off, the *New Diamond* was fired on from the battery at Gouyave. Armed canoes and a sloop set out from Gouyave while the *New Diamond* raced away, abandoning the Lieutenant-Governor and his party to their fate.

Mather Byles, the Lieutenant-Governor's secretary, recounted a more likely scenario in a letter to George Home. Byles says:

> They were near to the shore, and the captain observing the Flag Staff at the Bakery cried out that the colours were French. The Lieutenant-Governor saw it was so, and immediately ordered him to bear away from the land. He attempted to do this, but the wind failed him; a fire from the Battery commenced and some armed canoes put off from the land. In this moment the Lieutenant-Governor appears to have given up any idea of escaping and have adopted the desperate solution of trying how far his presence would awe a band of Ruffians and bring them back to a sense of their duty. He ordered out the boat, and together with Mr Campbell, Mr Farquhar and two other gentlemen, made towards the shore. The canoes met and conducted them in.[5]

One way or the other, Lieutenant-Governor Home was made captive, and marched to Belvidere to join those taken prisoner in Gouyave and elsewhere.

Home's letter and news of his capture arrived in St George's almost simultaneously. A council of war was summoned. Mackenzie assumed the role of Acting Lieutenant-Governor and chief commander of the forces. His first action was to put the small garrison and the Militia in St George's on full alert. He then sent urgent appeals to Martinique, the headquarters of the British forces in the Caribbean, addressed to Lieutenant-General Sir John Vaughan and to Admiral Sir John Jervis, joint commanders of the British forces. Mackenzie also wrote to Don José Maria Chacon, Governor of Trinidad, and to Lieutenant-Governor Seton of St Vincent saying that Grenada had been invaded, possibly by French privateers. He appealed to Chacon to send a frigate or sloop of war, as this might deter those in Grenada sympathetic to the French Republican cause from joining this force. Chacon responded immediately, sending forty Spanish soldiers in two armed brigs and a schooner. The St Vincent government was unable to render any assistance, as they were coping with a similar uprising led by the Black Caribs assisted by Victor Hugues. Sir John Vaughan responded immediately by sending Brigadier John Lindsay to Grenada with a small detachment of soldiers.

Fédon Proposes British Surrender

As soon as the Revolution was confirmed:

> The Negroes flocked to Fédon's standard in hundreds, no fewer than four thousand joining him in the month of March alone. Moreover, not only Negroes, but also Frenchmen of all classes and colours in Grenada.[6]

It soon became obvious to the prisoners that Belvidere had been prepared as the headquarters for an armed uprising against the British.

On Wednesday 4 March, Fédon asked Home to surrender Grenada to him. Home replied that he had no power to do this, as he was a prisoner, and thus deprived of all the power and authority of office. Fédon then prepared documents demanding the surrender of the British, and dispatched these with two officers, accompanied by a drummer, to St George's, to present the documents to the Acting Governor.

Later that morning, the inhabitants of St George's heard the beating of drums coming along the road from the north. The inhabitants, nervous and panicky, believed that that French invasion was imminent. The Militia took up defensive positions, but soon it was clear that the drumming heralded not the expected arrival of a French fighting force, but the arrival of the solitary drummer and the two rebel officers dressed in uniforms of the French Republican Army, bearing a flag of truce. The rebel officers were blindfolded by troopers of the St George's Light Calvary and taken to the Grenada Council Chamber. Here they presented the Council with the documents from Fédon.

One document was written in French, and demanded that the island be surrendered within two hours. Fédon signed it as the 'General of the French Republican Forces'. The document said that, if the island did not surrender, Grenada would suffer the scourges of war, and any person taking up arms against Fédon would have their estates burnt, and be put to death if captured. The document also warned that, if any 'brothers or friends' of the republic were ill treated by the British, such ill treatment would be retaliated doubly upon each prisoner in the hands of the revolutionaries.

The second document was written in English, was addressed to the Commanders-in-Chief of the British forces, and was signed by three French Republicans – Victor Hugues, Goyrand and Le Bas – who described themselves as 'Commissioners delegated by the National Convention of France'. After a preamble which made reference to the 'heinous crimes' perpetrated against the French in the West Indies by the British, and referring to the Commanders-in-Chief as 'cannibals', the document went on to promise that any republican killed in Grenada would occasion the death by guillotine of two English officers who were prisoners of the French. It further stated that any Frenchman who did not join the republican cause would be outlawed, and his property forfeited to the republic. Furthermore, any Frenchmen who accepted employment under the British were traitors to France.

Fédon's officers were sent back with a message that the Council was aware that evil-minded persons had led a number of British citizens astray. They should immediately return to their former occupations. If they persisted in rebelling, hurt any persons who fell into their hands, or destroyed any property, they would have only themselves to blame for the severe consequences resulting from their actions. When the two officers returned with the reply from the Council, Fédon interviewed the prisoners, and told them that they would be put to death if they made any noise, or attempted to escape or if the camp came under attack.

French-speaking Grenadians continued to arrive at Belvidere to join the Revolution. Most came because the revolutionary spirit had belatedly reached them, and they were reacting to the accumulated effect of thirty-two years of grievances, and the hope that they could be free of them. Others came more reluctantly, spurred on by the threats made to any Frenchman who did not support the Revolution. Hay recognized many of them, and carefully noted the names of all whom he saw at the camp, reporting these people by name in his notes of the events at Belvidere. At the end of the Revolution, his notes would be used as evidence against those who had participated in it.

To feed the growing crowd of people at Belvidere and to ensure that little sustenance would be available to the people of St George's, men were sent out to bring in cattle, horses and food of any kind from the nearby English estates. The numbers at Belvidere would eventually reach 7000, and it would take eight to ten cattle a day to feed the assemblage.

The next day, 5 March, Fédon again approached Lieutenant-Governor Home, asking him to write an order to Mackenzie in St George's to deliver up the island to the revolutionary forces. The Lieutenant-Governor replied that he would never sign a 1 order that would disgrace his memory, that his authority ended with his capture and that authority for the island and its defence now lay with Mackenzie and the officer commanding His Majesty's forces on the islands, and that the lives at the prisoners lay now entirely at Fédon's mercy and discretion. Home agreed to write a letter, but not one requesting surrender.

Home had to draft this letter twice and further amend it before Fédon was satisfied with it. It was addressed to the Council, and said that Fédon had informed him of the reply that they had sent to his request for surrender. In response, General Fédon had warned him and all the prisoners at the Camp that the instant an attack was made on the Camp every one of the prisoners would be put to death. The letter asked that the Council take this fact into serious consideration and do all in their power not to put the lives of innocent people at risk. The forty-three prisoners then in captivity all put their signatures to this letter. Fédon also had some of his officers read to the Governor and the prisoners the commissions that they had received from the French Republican Army in Guadeloupe, and which Victor Hugues had signed. The next day, Chevalier DeSuze Cadet and Pierre Alexandre, two of Fédon's supporters, delivered the letter in St George's.

An Unsuccessful Attack on Fédon's Camp

Despite Fédon's warning that the prisoners he held would be killed if his camp were attacked, the Council in St George's decided to mount a three-pronged attack on Belvidere. To this end, at dawn on 5 March, forty regular soldiers and ninety Militia under the command of Captain Gurdon[7] of the 58th Regiment left St George's in small vessels escorted by an armed brig.

Two letters each were also dispatched by a squadron of the St George's Light Infantry to the commanding officers of the St Andrew's and St Patrick's Militia. One ordered them to assemble all the white men who could be spared from the defence of their area, and to proceed with them under cover of night to Fédon's estate at Belvidere. There they were to take up positions as near to the revolutionaries as possible, and be ready for a daylight attack. The other letter, under confidential cover, recognized that the Militia forces were small in number, and advised the arming of 'trusty Negroes', who could be depended upon, to assist in the attack. They were to begin by recruiting the slaves belonging to Alexander Campbell and Ninian Home from Tivoli, Paraclete and Waltham Estates. The plan was that Captain Gurdon's forces would attack from the west, while the St Patrick's and St Andrew's Militia would attack from the north and the east early in the morning.

This plan met with disaster. Gurdon landed with his troops at Champion Bay, and marched through Palmiste and Douglaston to Gouyave. When the troops arrived, they found it abandoned by the revolutionaries, who had gone to Fédon's estate at Belvidere. Gurdon decided to stay in Gouyave for the night, before proceeding to Belvidere. In occupying Gouyave, the soldiers discovered a quantity of rum, wine and port left unsecured. They 'captured' the liquor, indulged unrestrainedly, and got drunk. About 400 revolutionaries attacked the town at 4 a.m. It was the Militia who managed to repulse the attack, as the regular soldiers were still under the influence of alcohol, and quite useless. Twelve revolutionaries were killed, and about twice that number injured, while the British lost four officers. It would appear that one of the strategies of the revolutionaries was to leave quantities of alcohol about or to have their people bring alcohol to the soldiers wherever they were, with the objective of seducing the soldiers into drinking too much, thus becoming useless. Even when the soldiers were on the march, people whom they encountered offered them alcoholic drinks. What happened to Gurdon's troops in Gouyave was the first in a series of instances where events turned with the corks of bottles of spirits.

Meanwhile, both the St Andrew's and St Patrick's Militia were reluctant to take part in the military exercise as they were afraid for the safety of the women, children and elderly. They perceived dangers from the hostile gangs who had begun to roam both the towns and countryside, as well as from whites loyal to the revolutionaries. They only mobilized after

Mackenzie sent them a further very angry letter that promised to hold the Militia commanders responsible for any consequences that resulted from their disobedience. The two branches of the Militia then marched to Gouyave following a northern coastal route, and joined the forces of Captain Gurdon and the sailors from the frigate *Quebec*, on 7 March.

Again rum drinking was their undoing. The forces at Gouyave broke into the rum stores in Gouyave and partook liberally. The plan of attacking Fédon's stronghold that day had to be changed. Instead the Militia was marched up to a neighbouring estate to recover from the effects of too much alcohol. Captain Gurdon was thwarted in his plan to dry out the soldiers because some people brought the soldiers rum, so that very few of the troops were in a fit condition for any military activity the following morning.

Eventually the troops marched out in an assault on Fédon's Camp on Sunday 8 March. Captain Gurdon got his first look at the camp and its defences, and thought that he was too weak to have any success at an assault on the camp without reinforcements. Fédon's troops had improved the fortification of the camp, and now occupied an almost impregnable position on top of a heavily fortified hill. Gurdon decided that it would be better to withdraw to Gouyave. On the return to Gouyave the troops mutinied. They heard that the enemy was marching on St George's and feared for their families and property left undefended in that town. They refused to guard the houses and warehouses in Gouyave, and some of them deserted, and more threatened to do so. In view of this state of affairs, Captain Gurdon decided to abandon any attempt to attack Fédon's headquarters and withdrew to St George's.

As soon as the British troops left, Fédon's men reoccupied Gouyave, letting it be known that the British had been defeated in Gouyave. A further call was sent to the slaves to rise up in a revolt against their masters throughout Grenada. Within a matter of days, all of Grenada, except St George's and a few outlying military posts, was in the hands of Fédon's forces. Shipments of arms and ammunition were supplied for the revolutionaries through the ports of Gouyave and Grenville. All that lay between Fédon and success was the capture of St George's. However, he was unable to mount an all-out attack on the capital, in which was concentrated all the fighting power of his adversaries.

The Arrival and Strange Death of Brigadier-General Colin Lindsay

On 12 March, Brigadier-General Colin Lindsay was sent from Martinique to take command of the military operations in Grenada. At dawn on

15 March, General Lindsay marched north from St George's, leading 400 regular troops and Militia, leaving 200 behind to protect St George's. The revolutionaries abandoned Gouyave at the approach of the British troops, allowing Lindsay to form a defensive beachhead for the safe disembarkation of 140 men of the 9th and 16th Regiments who had been sent as reinforcements from Martinique. Two days later Lindsay set out for Fédon's Camp at Belvidere. Unfortunately, he called a two-hour rest stop for the troops a mile away from the camp. This meant that the attack was carried out at dusk. Although Lindsay captured a minor enemy post, the engagement was largely unsuccessful and quite costly. Two of Lindsay's men were killed and seventeen injured. The onset of night called a halt to any further offensive. Immediately Fédon gave instruction to move the Lieutenant-Governor and the rest of the prisoners from the boucan at Fédon's Camp where they had been lodged to the highest camp, the Camp of Death.

Heavy rain fell during that night and for the next few days. While they were engaging the enemy, the soldiers' haversacks had been stolen, so the troops were wet and uncomfortable without a change of clothing, and without their blankets. Moreover, the troops were almost always drunk. A few of them wandered away, and were caught by the revolutionaries or rebel supporters. Half of the Militia deserted. As a reward for their loyalty and steadfastness, and because he could not proceed with his plans to take Fédon's Camp, Lindsay gave the remainder of the Militia a two-day leave to go back to St George's and refresh themselves. In the meantime, Lindsay asked for reinforcements to bring his force back to the strength it was when he set out, as he considered anything under this inadequate for the task of capturing the camp. Lindsay himself caught a fever, and the records relate that in an acute depression caused by the fever, he shot himself. The news that this had happened was thought by George Home to be most unfortunate but not particularly surprising. He said of Lindsay:

> Lindsay was a madman, but he was a fighting one, and the few men he had along with him had confidence in him. He grew impatient at the bad weather and shot himself not from lowering of spirits, or any resolution about his success, but merely from bad humour because the wind and the rain would not stay at his bidding.[8]

Another quite plausible theory is that a slave loyal to Fédon slipped a dose of manchineel poison to Lindsay, or that he was shot by a poisoned arrow. If George Home knew that Lindsay was not exactly the most stable person in the world, it is likely that many other people knew this, including Fédon. Lindsay's frustration and illness undoubtedly were factors in his suicide, but perhaps his unbalanced frame of mind was helped into insanity.[9] Lindsay was a very able commander, and probably would have succeeded in defeating Fédon quite quickly if he had lived. His death on 22 March dealt a severe blow to the British.

Lieutenant-Colonel Schaw[10] succeeded Lindsay. Schaw's instructions from General Vaughan in Martinique were to play a defensive role until reinforcements arrived. Schaw was to maintain a position at Belvidere Estate in the valley below the rebel stronghold, and to send more men to reinforce and hold Gouyave. Armed vessels were to patrol the sea around Grenada to prevent supplies reaching the revolutionaries. Sometimes they were successful and sometimes the arms and ammunition got through to the revolutionaries. One of the ships that were captured by the British was a ship on its way to Guadeloupe on which travelled a revolutionary, Pierre Alexandre, a former member of the British Militia. Alexandre had previously taken Lussan, a merchant from Gouyave and a prisoner, to Trinidad to use his credit there to procure arms and ammunition. Lussan had temporarily escaped from his captor and reported the movements of the vessel to Governor Chacon. Lussan was sent back to Grenada in time to give evidence against Alexandre at his court martial. Alexandre was hanged in St George's market place on 5 April 1795. In retaliation the town of Grenville was burnt to the ground, as well as the pilot's house overlooking the harbour. Fédon's men set up a post on that spot, which became known as Pilot Hill.

The British Fail to Establish Posts at Grenville and Mitchell's

With the revolutionaries now in control of the port at Grenville, it was imperative that the British mount an offensive against them to prevent the off-loading of arms and ammunition for the camps at Belvidere. On 24 March, Schaw was ordered by the Council to send a detachment of three officers and fifty men and a troop of light cavalry overland to hold a beachhead and await the arrival of the main body of soldiers travelling by sea in two armed vessels under the command of Captain Gurdon who would retake Grenville. When Gurdon reached Grenville Bay, however, he found that the revolutionaries had moored a ship at the mouth of the harbour, blocking the entrance. Gurdon had to disembark the troops at Levera instead, and later march to Observatory Estate near Grenville to meet the troops from St George's that had been sent to support them.

On 2 April, Gurdon marched on Grenville. Just outside Grenville, they encountered a force of about a hundred revolutionaries, which they routed, with the cost of two wounded. As they came nearer to the town, the British came under cannon fire from an emplacement on Pilot Hill. This fire killed a grenadier, and caused Gurdon to take the troops under cover to give him a chance to observe the positions of the revolutionaries.

Reconnaissance stated there were two cannon and 200 men on Pilot Hill under the command of Captain Nogues, and that the heights over Grenville were commanded by men with muskets. This reconnaissance was inaccurate. In fact, it was later discovered, from a piece of correspondence found at Belvidere after the defeat of Fédon, that there were only two companies of revolutionaries on Pilot Hill, and they were very low on ammunition. Supplies of ammunition for the revolutionaries arrived on 7 April from Guadeloupe, demonstrating that the British blockade was ineffective, but too late to supply the revolutionaries for the battle on 8 April. Nevertheless, at this moment in time, it seemed to Gurdon and his fellow officers that even if Grenville could be taken, his forces could not hold it. He therefore ordered a retreat to Observatory Estate.

From Observatory, Gurdon wrote Mackenzie a dismal report. Not only had he failed in establishing a post at Grenville, but also he added notes on the condition of his forces. They had no bread, and so he had sent them in search of plantains. Of these, they had found very few. Nine soldiers were very ill with fever, two were wounded, and a considerable number had sore legs.

Notification of the failure to take Grenville was relayed to Colonel Archibald Campbell, who was in charge of three divisions comprising 900 men being sent from Barbados to bolster the forces at Grenville. The reinforcements were diverted to Gouyave, and Campbell met with Mackenzie to discuss how these troops could be best deployed. It was decided that on 4 April, a detachment of 300 of these men should leave Gouyave by boat for St George's under Major Wright. When they got to St George's, they were to march overland to join Major Gurdon and reinforce his troops. Another attempt was then to be made to take Grenville.

On the march northwards through the island, Wright and his troops did not fare well. Fédon's guerrilla fighters harassed them as they travelled. Twelve soldiers overcome by sickness and fatigue had to be abandoned to their fate. When Wright did link up with Gurdon and his forces at Observatory, the planned attack on Grenville could not take place because Wright, who now assumed command, had to wait for provisions and artillery. In the meantime, information had reached him that arms and ammunition had been supplied to the revolutionaries camped at Pilot Hill, and that the rebel forces there had been strengthened. He wrote to

Lieutenant Colonel Campbell requesting that a detachment of 100 men be sent from the post at Grand Etang, so that he might make an assault with some hope of success.

Another detachment left St George's also on 4 April, a under Major Mallory, with orders to establish a post in the mountains at a place called 'Mitchell's'. The establishment of a post at this position would cut off the enemy supply line from Grenville. Mallory's detachment ran into an ambush at a place called 'Aché's'. A sergeant was killed and another officer and four privates were injured. The next morning Mallory himself was dangerously wounded, and had to return to St George's, where he died of a fever on 22 April.

Another Disastrous Assault on Fédon's Camp

Campbell was promoted to Brigadier-General on 3 April. On 7 April, he was visited by Mackenzie at the camp near Belvidere, to discuss future operations. These discussions ended in a bitter dispute over strategy and tactics. Mackenzie, described by General Vaughan as a 'respectable gentleman, but totally unqualified for the conduct of a military operation',[11] was in favour of an immediate assault on Fédon's Camp, stressing the necessity for immediate action before the revolutionaries received supplies and reinforcements, and before the bulam fever, raging in St George's, decimated the ranks of the British troops. Campbell, on the other hand, was vehemently opposed to an attack on Fédon's heavily fortified stronghold. He estimated that his troops were outnumbered by about ten to one. Although the initial attack on the camp had not resulted in the deaths of any of the hostages, there was still concern that Fédon would keep his threat to execute Lieutenant-Governor Ninian Home and the prisoners taken as hostages, if an attack was made on the camp. He would have preferred to use the troops in hit-and-run tactics against the revolutionaries, and in defence of those parts of the island still held by the British.

Mackenzie over-ruled Campbell, stressing that the military was subservient to the civil government. The troops at Belvidere, reinforced with 150 volunteer seamen from ships lying at Gouyave, made an attack on Belvidere early in the morning of 8 April. On being attacked, Fédon's troops fell back to the ridge of Mount Qua Qua, on which they had established two batteries of nine-pounder cannon, one of which was manned by regular French artillerymen. Campbell managed to seize the lower battery, but later had to withdraw under blistering fire from the revolutionaries. This fire could not be answered because the rain had continued, and the steep slopes of Mount Qua Qua were slippery. The soldiers had a choice either to climb, or use their muskets. They could not do both. Besides, the upper battery was almost inaccessible. It was situated on the crest of a mountain protected by strong *abbatis* [12]of felled trees. The ground was so slippery from the rain that had been almost continuous, that men unaccustomed to the terrain could hardly get a foothold.

Campbell's troops suffered tremendous casualties. Two regular officers and nineteen others were killed, and fifty-two regulars were wounded. One Militia officer was killed, and one-quarter of the volunteer seamen were either killed or wounded. Jean, Fédon's brother, was among those killed during this battle.

The Execution of the Prisoners and the Arrival of La Grange

The news of the death of Fédon's brother had reached the camp before Fédon himself arrived. The prisoners had heard the guards calling to each other in French that the prisoners were to be shot as soon as Fédon arrived. Some of the prisoners, who did not understand French perfectly, asked others if they had heard correctly. John Hay was one of the ones who had been queried but he chose not to answer.

Most of the prisoners had been kept in stocks during their imprisonment, and were accommodated in a small hut near the summit of the mountain. As soon as the sounds of the assault on the camp began, all the prisoners who were not already in the stocks were secured, and those prisoners who could not be secured for the lack of enough stocks, were also locked in the same hut. Everyone was therefore inside the hut when Fédon reached the camp. Fédon had an armed guard of thirty-two men draw up about five paces from the door of the hut. He took up a position on a battery about twenty yards from the hut. He then ordered that all the prisoners not in stocks to come out of the hut first, while he sent men to release those who were restrained. Hay was the first one out. Fédon invited him to come up to the battery with him. As he started to walk to where Fédon was standing, he heard a shot. When he turned around to look, he saw Peter Thompson, the prisoner who had been walking behind him, fall. Hay records:

> I flew to Fédon, in order to try if I could prevail on him to have mercy on the innocent. 'They have none on our people below', he replied. He began the bloody battle in the presence of his wife and daughters, who remained there, unfeeling spectators of this horrid barbarity. He gave the word *Feu* himself to every man who came out; and of fifty one prisoners, only Parson McMahon,

Mr Kerr, and myself were saved. All bore themselves like
Christians, and, except a young boy of twelve years of age, I did
not hear a word from one of them. Doctor Carruthers attempted
to run, and was shot at about fifty yards distance from the prison.
I think it is possible that he counted them as they came out,
because when the last was shot he lighted his segar and walked
with great indifference back to the battery. [13]

McMahon, another eyewitness continues the story:

As it was now getting towards noon and hot, the large flies
began to collect over the heap of dead bodies, attracted to the
blood of those not quite dead, and some of the rebels reported
to Fédon that a few of them were yet alive, and amongst whom
I could plainly see Mr Farquhar, who could move his head and
hands in a supplicating manner. Fédon desired some of his men,
to go and dispatch all those that still gave signs of life, and I saw
a tall, stout fellow I knew well, an inhabitant of Charlotte
Town, one Jean B. Cotton, step over the dead bodies, and strike
with his cutlass over the face and heads of each that had the
least symptoms of life. [14]

The irony of the situation was that arrangements had been made for
the Lieutenant-Governor and the hostages to be taken to Guadeloupe as
prisoners-of-war. A French schooner had arrived in Grenville the previous
day for the purpose of transporting the prisoners to Guadeloupe. On it
was a mulatto officer called La Grange, who had been sent by the French
Commissioners of the National Convention of the Windward Islands to
assume direction of the military operation in Grenada. The conduct of the
Revolution was to be taken out of Fédon's hands as the French were not
happy with Fédon. The French thought that Fédon's leadership was too
individualistic. Furthermore, he would not take orders from the French.
La Grange carried a *Declaration* from Victor Hugues, which mentioned
only Nogues as continuing to have command over the revolutionary
forces in Grenada. Charles Nogues had been trained in Guadeloupe, and
had the approval and trust of Victor Hugues, and may even have been his
personal agent.

La Grange arrived at Fédon's Camp the evening after the battle to find
that all but three of the hostages he had come to escort back to
Guadeloupe had already been executed. The scene witnessed by La Grange
was horrible. There the prisoners lay in the mud, some with their heads
split open. The stench of blood was everywhere for Fédon's men had

walked uncaringly through the mess, and had spread the blood over a wide area. Fédon was in a monumental anger at the death of his brother, so much so that he seemed possessed.

A furious argument ensued between La Grange and Fédon. La Grange was alarmed at what Fédon had done of his own accord. La Grange left the camp with the three remaining prisoners – Hay, Kerr and McMahon. The small party walked all the way to Grenville, stopping at Balthazar, and then at Chantilly Estate where they slept. The next morning they proceeded to Grenville where the four boarded the vessel that should have carried all fifty-five prisoners back to Guadeloupe.[15]

The news of the death of Ninian Home and forty-seven others first appeared in the newspapers in England in June. Shortly afterwards a letter from Mather Byles to George Home advising him of the circumstances of the death of his brother arrived in Scotland. George Home grieved for his brother, Ninian. This grief is palpable across the years in the uncharacteristically short and emotional letter from George Home to Patrick Home in America, telling him of his uncle's death.[16]

The Arrival of Brigadier-General Oliver Nicolls

Following the disastrous attempt to take Fédon's Camp, which culminated in the execution of the hostages, Mackenzie requested Sir John Vaughan, the Commander-in-Chief in Martinique, now in British hands, that he send an officer to Grenada to take full and undisputed control of the regular troops and Militia, and to direct their operations. Vaughan sent Brigadier-General Oliver Nicolls to Grenada on 13 April. This was an excellent choice, as Nicolls had previously served in Grenada as commanding officer of the 45th Regiment, knew Grenada well, and was known by many in Grenada. General Campbell, who had long harboured doubts about Mackenzie's ability to direct military operations, also rejoiced in Nicolls's appointment.

Nicolls assumed command on 16 April. He was scandalized at the lack of discipline among the troops, especially their almost constant state of drunkenness, and set to the task of restoring discipline. He also got the approval of Vaughan and the support of Mackenzie to create the Loyal Black Rangers. The creation of this battalion of 300 blacks, most of them slaves, formalized the use of free coloured people and slaves in military service in Grenada, although they had been of use since the first few days of the hostilities.[17] The Rangers were divided into five companies of sixty men each, with each company under the command of a white officer. The commanding officer was Major John Farquharson.

To the soldiers killed in military engagements were added the casualties of bulam fever. More died from fever during the war than died from wounds sustained in battle. Two serious drawbacks to the campaign in Grenada were the bulam fever and the lack of food. Nicolls himself contracted the fever soon after his arrival, but he made a good recovery. Many of the other white officers were not so fortunate. Three of these casualties were the officers commanding the companies of the Loyal Black Rangers who died of this fever within two weeks of the formation of the battalion. The official report on the garrison on 7 July counted 1280 regulars who were fit for duty, and 168 others who were out of action due to illness. From the ranks of regular soldiers, on average, two died every day.

Food became more and more scarce for both sides as the months passed. Both the revolutionaries and the forces under British command ate mainly from the land. Detachments of soldiers and rebels alike, together with supporting civilians, would be sent out in foraging parties to find whatever food they came across, which was usually plantains. These were the mainstay of their diet. Foraging for food was dangerous. On 22 April, a foraging party of Militia Light Cavalry from Major Wright's post at Observatory Hill was ambushed and two of the Militia killed. On learning of the incident from those who scampered back to the camp, Major Wright dispatched Captain Gurdon with a detachment to seek out the guerrilla fighters. The detachment met and engaged them, causing the revolutionaries to retreat, leaving behind a six-pound cannon. Unfortunately, this engagement was costly – Captain Gurdon was killed, and eight of his men were wounded.

Nicolls's Strategies

As soon as he was able, Nicolls began a new strategic plan against the revolutionaries. On 22 April, Belvidere was evacuated, freeing 900 troops for alternative deployment. The major portion of the troops was earmarked for Grenville, with the specific target of capturing Pilot Hill, which was secured on 27 April. Some of the troops were sent back to St George's. A post was also established at St Patrick's. From the 29th Regiment sixty men were sent to establish and maintain a post at Mégrin in St David's, in the abandoned French church, along with twenty-six men from the St David's Militia. The post was under the command of Captain Scott from 4 May 1795.

On 22 May at about 2 a.m. about 500 revolutionaries, half of them armed with muskets, made a surprise attack on the newly established post at Mégrin. After capturing the two sentries, the revolutionaries sneaked up to the church and fired through the windows. A sergeant called Sully was in virtual command, because the two senior British officers, Captain Scott and Lieutenant Richards, were both ill with fever. A third officer was wounded as he slept. Richards tried to direct from his sickbed, but it was Sully who managed to secure the door of the church and fix a defensive guard. Fortunately for the British, the mulatto leader of the revolutionary forces, called St Bernard, was killed, leaving the attackers leaderless. They retreated, but continued to snipe at the church. During the night of the attack, the two captured British sentries were tortured to death, their screams clearly heard by their comrades barricaded in the church. By the next morning the revolutionaries had completely disappeared, but had left the two unfortunate sentries and twenty of their own dead behind. The British casualties were eleven men dead and twenty-four wounded. Among the wounded were Lieutenant Williams, Sergeant Sully and one other. All three were dead within three weeks.

While the events at Mégrin were being played out, the troops earmarked for the attack on Pilot Hill embarked from Gouyave in twenty small vessels escorted by a frigate and two gunboats. In addition, various troops of the Militia Light Cavalry and the Loyal Black Rangers marched towards Grenville along the southeastern coastal road. Thus Major Wright planned to cut off the rebel retreat from the Grenville area.

On 4 May, the troops travelling by boat from Gouyave landed at Marquis Bay, under cover of the fire of the accompanying frigate and gunboats. The British found and dislodged a small force of revolutionaries from Post Royal Hill near Marquis Bay, but found that the revolutionaries had abandoned Pilot Hill after spiking the cannon and were free to scamper back to Belvidere, as Major Wright had not been in time to cut off their escape route. Pilot Hill was occupied by a strong party of the British under the command of Lieutenant-Colonel the Honourable John Hope.

Grenada in Ruins

By May most of the estates not owned by those supporting Fédon and the Revolution lay in ruins. With the spread of the news of the Revolution came the burning and pillaging of the estates. Every British-owned estate was burned, usually at night, and the white employees and some of the slaves murdered unless they were lucky enough to escape. Gordon Turnbull, the reputed author of an eyewitness account, reports that:

On the night of the 5th [March] several fires were perceived from ships in the direction of Pearls and Carriere areas, which proved to be the trash-houses or buildings for preserving the cane fuel on these estates, and some others. The house of Mr Stuart near De Glapion was also on fire. This was the beginning of a conflagration, which was lighted up every night by the Negroes of different parts and in the end desolated the whole island.[18]

Many of the slaves employed by the British planters remained loyal to their masters, or at least did not join the revolutionaries. They hid in terror the forest and mountains near the estates, and lived as best they could. Some went back to tend the crops on those estates near to the British military posts. A few plantation owners brought their slaves into town, in the hope of having them fed in exchange for labour, but St George's could not accommodate the entire slave population. Many slaves starved.[19] The records show how the slaves from Ninian Home's Waltham Estate fared. The female slaves and children from the Waltham Estate were housed in a disused building at Government House. Eleven male slaves joined the Black Rangers, and the rest of the slaves belonging to the late Governor were left to fend for themselves. This was the fate of slaves who were privileged by accident of ownership. The circumstances of the slaves of other British planters were much more disastrous.

Some of the slaves from the English- and Scottish-owned estates joined the French-speaking slaves in the support of Fédon and the revolutionaries,[20] or joined gangs of slaves in carrying out their own rebellion independent of Fédon. No writer denies that the beginning of the Revolution was also the beginning of a slave revolt.

Samuel Cary, Jr, was a young American who was approximately twenty-two years old at the time of the outbreak of the Fédon Revolution. His father owned Mount Pleasant Estate near Grenville, and was also the manager of Simon Estate. The elder Samuel Cary was not in Grenada when the hostilities broke out, leaving Samuel Cary, Jr, to bear the brunt of the distress. The letters Samuel Cary, Jr, wrote to Joseph Marryat and to his father are preserved in Chelsea, Massachusetts, USA. They give an eyewitness account of events from the perspective of a young man who was not British or Scottish or French, and who did not carry the attitudinal baggage of Grenada's élite. On 6 May, Cary wrote to Joseph Marryat that:

Affairs in this island wear a bad face. The estates are almost every one burned, either wholly or in part. The Negroes are more in awe of the enemy than of us, so much so that they dare not venture amongst us, lest on their return to their estates they should be massacred ... The Rebels had burnt the houses at Mt Pleasant and part of the Caves but the works were still standing a few days ago. I have fortunately saved almost the whole of the Gang, which I brought to town.[21]

The revolutionaries had the run of the countryside, and it was dangerous for whites to travel through it, and dangerous for slaves to be caught by Fédon's men, as by this time it was expected that all slaves would have joined the Revolution, or were to be counted as traitors to the cause. On 12 May Cary wrote to his father that:

The English Negroes of the Estates have almost all gone into the woods being afraid to venture to communicate with their masters, even in the quarters in which we are posted, lest we should go away from the quarter and leave them, in which case they would be exposed to the fury of the rebels who would sacrifice them without mercy and who spread amongst them reports of various kinds to our disadvantage, such as us being upon the point of starving, or intention to evacuate the island, etc. etc ...

I went up the other day with McCarthy and a few Negroes to Mt Pleasant to see if I could save anything. I found the dwelling house and Negro houses burnt. They also burnt your papers. But the works are all standing ... The Negroes came running to us from different Bushes and Cane pieces and informed us that the enemy had been there two days before and had killed four stout men and mangled a fifth shockingly, who, however, will recover. Of Negroes I brought 65 to town, six being hiding about whom I could not find. I am going to place these Negroes on Gahagans's estate at the hospital where they will get fed for their work. Your Negro man Joe behaved steadfastly.[22]

John Hay recounted the sights that met his eyes as he sailed down the western coast of Grenada in July 1795, on his return journey to Grenada after his stint as a prisoner-of-war in Guadeloupe:

What a melancholy prospect! What change and devastation in the short space of five months! Fields of luxuriant canes in the highest state of cultivation, sugar-works, dwelling houses, all reduced to ashes by fire; here and there a stone wall or brick chimney remained, a solitary monument, and served to point out to the wandering eye, the site of some commodious and expensive building: no human creature or animal of any kind was to be seen all along the coast, the whole appeared one vast extended waste, over-run with brush and high weeds.[23]

A short time after his return, Hay went back to his hometown of Gouyave. There he found 'nothing but misery and devastation in every direction, and as far as the eye could reach, shocking to be seen, and too painful to relate'. At this time the Revolution had almost a year to run, but the destruction of rural Grenada was almost complete.

The condition of the population living in St George's was as pitiable. Soldier and citizen, white and black, freeman and slave alike were short of food, and subject to the ravages of bulam fever. The epidemic was made worse by the overcrowded conditions under which the inhabitants lived. There was no time to construct housing for the troops, and they were billeted anywhere, even at Government House.[24]

The Doldrums

Although there were no major engagements between the revolutionaries and the British forces between 4 May and October, several skirmishes and ambushes took place, incurring losses on both sides. One such ambush took place in Gouyave on 6 July. On that day a foraging party of British soldiers and black Grenadians, some of them slaves, went out into the lands near Gouyave. On the return journey, revolutionaries ambushed the party of thirty men of the 68th Regiment and 200 black men and women, wounding some of them. Fifty black people were captured, taken to Fédon's Camp and shot the next day as an example to other slaves who had refused to join the Revolution.

The British could not dislodge the revolutionaries from their mountain strongholds, but the operations of the revolutionaries were gradually curtailed by a more effective naval patrol of the waters around Grenada and by Nicolls's effective command, especially the control of several posts throughout the island. There were rumours that the revolutionaries were also now short of food and necessities, and that there were desertions. After May, forts were built all over Grenada for the protection of the inhabitants that needed to go outside St George's, and to prevent reinforcements from reaching the revolutionaries by sea. The British also began to copy and use with great effect the revolutionaries' guerrilla tactics, especially their 'hit and run' tactics. The British had learned by experience and observation, and had also been taught by deserters from the revolutionaries, whom they allowed to join the Loyal Black Rangers. A British officer, a Major McLean from Gouyave, became very adept at this method of guerrilla warfare.[25]

Increased French Involvement

At this time, Fédon and his supporters were in a state of depression and anxiety at the progress of the war. It was clear that the French Commissioners in Guadeloupe had not forgiven Fédon for the execution of the hostages. Nor had he been able to compensate for his independence of action by achieving a quick victory. All the indications were that the French had intentions of taking over operations in Grenada.

Despite the more effective British blockade, at the beginning of October, a substantial number of regular French troops were landed in Grenada. There were other attempts, some successful, and others not. Then, on 10 October, a French brig was captured in the process of unloading seventy soldiers, fifty seamen and a number of supplies. Shortly after, another ship, *The Republican,* was also captured off Grenada by a British warship. On board were 250 men commanded by General Giraud, who had orders from Goyrand, who was directing the French operations in Grenada from St Lucia, to assume command of the French forces in Grenada. Nevertheless, the French did not cut off the supplies to Fédon. In October, two ships from St Lucia were able to land 200 armed men and supplies for the revolutionaries without discovery. The men and supplies also arrived at Belvidere without being apprehended. These reinforcements allowed Fédon to successfully retake Gouyave.

Fédon Recaptures Gouyave

Gouyave was of great strategic importance to the revolutionaries as it was not only a town but also the main port on the leeward side of the island. Gouyave also controlled the road to Belvidere. The town was fairly well garrisoned with 285 men fit for duty and fifteen officers. Because it was considered a healthy place, many of the sick soldiers were sent there to recuperate. In October these numbered five subalterns and 133 men. The garrisons at Gouyave and Fort St John in the hills above it were under the command of Lieutenant-Colonel Schaw.

During the day of 15 October, a deserter told Schaw that seven companies of Fédon's troops were assembled nearby, ready to attack Fort

St John. Unfortunately, Schaw gave this information no credence what-ever. That night, at about eleven o'clock, under cover of darkness and rain, a force of about 500 revolutionaries attacked and captured Fort St John, which was garrisoned by only forty-two men. On hearing the news, Schaw, considering that the forces in Gouyave were too few to hold the town, ordered a hasty retreat to St George's. Left behind in Gouyave were 177 sick men, and 36 men of the 68th Regiment who were asleep in their barracks. Some of the sick and convalescent tried to leave when the town was evacuated, but could not keep up with the main party.

As soon as Gouyave was evacuated, the revolutionaries, including some white troops from Guadeloupe, moved in, taking prisoner the sick and infirm who had been left behind. Some prisoners died from the lack of medical attention, but there were no executions, as strict instructions had been received from the French in Guadeloupe that any further prisoners taken were to be treated with 'all possible humanity'.[26] The French commanders in Guadeloupe, and the French among the revolu-tionaries saw to it that these orders were carried out. Schaw was subsequently accused of misconduct, but was allowed to resign, as witnesses among the military gave statements of prevailing mitigating circumstances.

French Confidence and British Worries

The loss of Gouyave was a serious setback to the British. As soon as they left, the French occupied Gouyave and its fort. The French renamed Gouyave *Port Libre*, and established a small naval base there, from which vessels were sent out to harass British shipping. More trained French troops were landed, and became so bold that they began to parade where they could be seen from British-held positions, just outside the town of St George's. St George's was fortified as a last line of defence:

> [T]hat part of St George's called Montserrat has been palisaded from the Carenage to the fortifications on the Hospital Hill, immediately above it. The lower and upper barriers, and upper fleche, have been made musket-ball proof. The saddle to the westward of Hospital Hill, immediately above the town, has also been palisaded, and a deep entrenchment dug from thence to join the fortifications at the end with a stone blockhouse, situated in a direction to rake it in case of being possessed by the enemy. The town barrier towards the river is like-wise

musket-ball proof, and defended by six swivels and a nine-pound cannonade. These precautions were judged necessary to preserve the town from insult, and prevent the sudden irruption of the brigands into town, who might set it on fire and profit from the confusion which naturally would ensue among the inhabitants.[27]

On 26 October the British rounded up a number of people at Grand Bacolet whom they suspected were in league with Fédon, took them to St George's and hanged them. With boldness and confidence, Chevalier Charles Sugue, the Commissioner and Administrator-in-Chief for Grenada appointed by Goyand sent two letters to Nicolls under a flag of truce. The first, delivered on 4 November, demanded that all French prisoners should be treated with much solicitation, as the French prisoners were treated by the British in Grenada. The letter also elaborated on the Rights of Man, decried the monarchy and declared that the edifice of slavery had to be torn down.

Nicolls answered this letter, and a reply arrived on 26 November, reminding him that every French citizen that fell into his hands should be treated with humanity according to the laws of war. Nicolls was chided for the execution of certain black citizens who had been captured at Grand Bacolet and who had been hanged at St George's, and asked whether he was operating a double standard with respect to his prisoners – humane treatment for the white French, and brutality towards the black and mulatto citizens. Nicolls was told that the French had a great many British prisoners in Grenada and in Martinique who were being treated with every consideration regardless of their colour.

Another instance of the growing confidence of the French revolutionaries was a daring attempt to steal a ship from St George's Harbour. On 29 November, at about 11 p.m., two or three canoes from Gouyave entered the port of St George's and attempted to cut the moorings of the commercial schooner *Pegasus* that had just arrived from Barbados. Some of the sailors, observing what was happening, jumped overboard and gave the alarm. Armed vessels manned by citizens of St George's came to the assistance of the *Pegasus*, saving the vessel, and chasing off the revolutionaries. However, the revolutionaries made their escape, with the captured master of the ship, a Mr Seymour, as their prisoner.

The British forces, civilians, and slaves loyal to the British were constantly the victims of sniping, and were caught off guard and terrorized by unexpected raids on their camps or the British estates. The situation was so bad that the population were afraid to leave their compounds in search of food. The population of St George's became dependent on food supplied by vessels from Britain and from the neighbouring islands. Eighty men and horses of the 17th Light Dragoons and 200 infantrymen that arrived from Barbados on 21 October did not make a real difference to the deteriorating British military position. For the first time, the British began to feel that the whole of Grenada might be lost.

The French Break with Fédon

By December 1795 the rift between Fédon and the Revolutionary French Command was complete. Fighters loyal to Fédon operated under Fédon's command, while French Republican officers commanded the trained French forces in Grenada. Both acted independently of each other. Fédon continued to have successes, however, dealing several decisive blows to the enemy. In December Fédon's revolutionaries attacked Pilot Hill in St Andrew's. The small garrison under the command of Major Wright defended the post well, and after a few days of struggle to capture the hill, the revolutionaries abandoned the effort, and instead established a post on Post Royal Hill, which gave them control over Marquis and Marquis Bay. Both sides lost men. The British lost the surgeon of one of the black companies and a lieutenant. In addition to losing men, the revolutionaries lost two cannon.

On 18 February 1796 the revolutionaries sent out two canoes from Marquis Bay to surprise and capture the schooner *Mistress Quickly* which was in government service and which was lying off Grenville Bay. Their attempt was successful. The captain and two of his men were killed, and the eight other men on board jumped off the ship and swam to safety. Unfortunately for the British, the ship was carrying four six-pound cannon, other ammunition and supplies, very much needed by the revolutionaries.

Elated by their success, the revolutionaries again launched an attack on Pilot Hill. This time the revolutionaries were successful. Major Wright and his garrison again defended well, but the revolutionaries had erected a battery on Telescope Hill, which prevented His Majesty's ship *Mermaid* from delivering assistance. In fact, the battery sank one of her launches. In addition, of the two gunboats sent by Nicolls to render assistance, one, the *Jack,* ran onto the rocks in Marquis Bay, and was captured by the revolutionaries. Those on board got away in a rowboat. It appears that the other gunboat was also no help. The revolutionaries took possession of the eighteen-pounder cannon, six smaller cannon and a quantity of ammunition from the *Jack.*

Low on ammunition and short of provisions, Major Wright decided to retreat, abandoning Pilot Hill on Monday 29 February, and joining the post at Sauteurs. Both Wright and the commanding officer at Sauteurs decided to abandon that post as well, and return to St George's. Because the population in St George's had heard that all the men at Pilot Hill and Sauteurs were dead, great was the rejoicing when Major Wright and Major O'Meara from Sauteurs with about 300 troops arrived, by way of boats, in St George's.

The posts at Mégrin, Calivigny and Observatory had also to be abandoned, and once again the whole of the island, except St George's, was in the control of the French or Fédon's troops. Apart from Fédon's stronghold on the Belvidere Estate, the French were firmly established at Gouyave, Amboy, Dalincourt, Mount St Margaret above Birchgrove, Black Forest near Vendome, and at the head of the Beausejour Valley. Recent victories had put Pilot Hill, Grenville and Marquis in their full control. Only the capture of St George's stood in the way of victory, and often it seemed as if the capture of St George's was imminent. The revolutionaries got quite close. At one point they set up a post on Mount St Eloi, just outside St George's. From here, however, they were quickly evicted by the British, who established their own post on this mountain.

The general slave revolt continued, and there was hardly a plantation building left standing. The suffering of the British population was acute, and in August 1795 the Grenada legislature sent a petition to the House of Commons requesting a loan of £100,000 of which £40,000 was needed immediately to purchase food for the citizens and loyal slaves of the colony.

The Beginning of the End

Mackenzie had done remarkably well for one not trained for wartime or warfare. However, he could no longer take the strain, and his health broke down. He passed civil command to Samuel Mitchell, and left Grenada. If Mackenzie had held on a little longer, he would have been able to see the events through to the finish.

Shortly after Mackenzie's departure, large reinforcements of both soldiers and horses were sent to Grenada. Thus strengthened, General Nicolls devised a new offensive. On 22 March he set out for Grenville with nearly 1000 men, and captured Post Royal Hill after a bloody battle in which over 300 revolutionaries were killed. On the British side, forty men and five officers were killed and a large number wounded, including six officers. Fédon, who was at this battle, was himself wounded. Sensing defeat, he slipped away to Pilot Hill, after giving orders that the men should abandon the post, and find their way back to the camp at Belvidere through the mountains.

This battle marked the beginning of the end for the French and for Fédon. Still more reinforcements came for the British and on 9 June, Lieutenant-General Sir Ralph Abercromby, who had taken over from Vaughan on his death in Martinique, designed the strategic plan to rout the French and Fédon's revolutionaries, and then left. Before he left Grenada, he gave instructions that there was to be no negotiation with Fédon, and that a price of £500 was to be put on Fédon's head, dead or alive.

Under the relentless offensive of the fortified British forces, one by one the revolutionaries' posts were taken. On 10 June, Captain Jossey, the commander of the French Republican Army in Grenada and the commander of the rebel post at Douglaston, surrendered to Nicolls. General Campbell defeated the revolutionaries at Black Forest and Beausejour. Fédon's stronghold fell to a simultaneous attack launched from both sides of the camp. The attacks were led by Colonel Gledstanes commanding the 57th Regiment, attacking from the head of the Grand Roy Valley via Mount Granby, and Colonel Count d'Heillimer in command of a brigade of Lowenstein's Jagers and a corps of Loyal Black Rangers from the Gouyave side.

The Jagers were skilled in mountain guerrilla warfare. They lit campfires lower down the mountain, as a ruse to let their enemy think they were still encamped. They then silently climbed to Fédon's Camp during the night. At daybreak the revolutionaries were astounded to find the enemy in occupation of the higher camps, and offered little resistance. There were enormous losses on both sides. The British lost nine men and fifty-five were wounded. Fédon and his remaining revolutionaries escaped to the highest camp, but when they were pursued, evaded capture by throwing themselves down the precipitous sides of the mountain. When the unattended Camp of Death was entered, Fédon's parting gift was discovered. All the prisoners held at the camp had been stripped naked, their hands tied behind their backs, killed, and left lying in pools of their own blood. The capture of Fédon's Camp meant the final defeat of Fédon, and an end to the to the Revolution. The Revolution had lasted fifteen months, and these months had been filled with suffering, death, destruction and social devastation.

Fortesque related that after this the war became:

merely a chase. The main body of the insurgents was dispersed and taken piecemeal; the Whites, over eighty in number, surrendered;

and Fédon alone, with a small body of ruffian Negroes, remained at large in spite of all efforts to capture them.[28]

The Price of Failure

The hunt for Fédon and all who had not surrendered voluntarily began immediately. Most of the wanted were rounded up quickly. They were easily identified, as John Hay had carefully listed all the people he had seen at Fédon's Camp, and there were others who were as willing to point fingers. An Act of Attainder was passed, allowing a simple identification to be sufficient proof of involvement with Fédon, and treason.

The manner in which the trial of those identified as part of Fédon's revolutionary band was conducted made many in wonder if the British were any less barbaric than Fédon. A Court of Oyer and Terminer is a special court with unusual powers, which can be constituted in times of dire national emergency when it is imperative that order in the society be restored without delay. This type of court, consisting of six members, was appointed to try the revolutionaries. On 30 June in the afternoon, forty-seven people who had been listed in the Act of Attainder were brought before the court, were convicted and sentenced to death on proof of identity. They were not allowed to say a word in their own defence, and were told that any representations should be made to the Crown. There was no chance of exercising this option, as the date for their execution was the next morning. In an effort to temper the enthusiasm of the Grenada Council for retaliation, Lieutenant-Governor Houston intervened and managed to negotiate a stay of execution for all but fourteen of the convicted.

Those the Lieutenant-Governor could not save were hanged on a specially constructed gallows in the Market Square. When they were dead, their heads were cut off, and hung on pikes as a lesson to all sympathizers, and for the enjoyment of the bloodthirsty. Among those executed were Baptiste, who had shot Lieutenant-Governor Home, Chevalier DeSuze who was an old man of over seventy-five, and Pascal Mardel, the Roman Catholic priest at Gouyave.

The Lieutenant-Governor met with very hostile criticism over his leniency to the convicted revolutionaries, although his action met with the approval of the British government. The feelings in Grenada against the revolutionaries were so strong that he yielded to local pressure, and agreed that twenty-four others should keep their date with the gallows. Houston, however, saved a great many others from a similar fate by having them transported. In 1797, eighty-six free coloureds, 143 slaves and some children were transported to the Honduras Settlement. In June 1797 the Court of Oyer and Terminer convicted three more whites and fifty-one other coloured people. Of these, the Lieutenant-Governor reprieved the whites completely, and pardoned the coloureds on condition that they leave Grenada and never return.

During 1795 an Act had been passed making association with Fédon and the Revolution an act of high treason, and giving the government the right to confiscate the property of the revolutionaries. All the property of the revolutionaries was now appropriated by the state after the claims against the estates were settled. They were then sold, several to members of the Grenada government. One such case was an estate called Plaisance in St John's. This was purchased by Benjamin Webster, Speaker of the Grenada Assembly, and a member of the Court of Oyer and Terminer. Many of the wives of the revolutionaries were left destitute when the properties were confiscated. A lucky few were later given grants. Fortesque observes wryly:

> So the White insurgents paid dearly for their alliance with the Blacks, and the Blacks as dearly for the more pardonable crime of rising against their masters. Men were in no gentle mood just at that period. So ended the revolt.[29]

The Last of the Revolutionaries

Fédon was never captured. From Fortescue we learn that: 'Once indeed his pursuers came upon him by surprise, but he disappeared like a cat over a precipice whither none dared to follow him'.[30]

Some authors say Fédon drowned, attempting to escape to Trinidad, where he had connections, in a canoe. However, there is now some evidence that he hid sometimes in the mountains, and sometimes in Carriacou and in Petit Martinique before making good his escape by rowing out in a canoe to meet a vessel in the open waters off Grenada. This vessel took him to Cuba, where he lived for the rest of his life. Ten years after the Revolution ended the Grenada government put in motion proceedings to extradite him from that country.[31]

Fédon's canoe was found with his compass nailed to the bottom of the boat. Jacobs[32] interprets Fédon's action of nailing a compass to his upturned boat as a sign that the Africans in Grenada would have understood. The canoe stood for an *nkisi,* or a symbol of power in times of trouble. The compass marked the location of the potent power of the *nkisi,* and also symbolized the Congo cosmogram. The message that Fédon left was of: 'The certainty of reincarnation: the especially righteous person will never be destroyed but will come back in the name or progeny, or in the form of an everlasting pool, waterfall, stone or mountain.'[33]

Joachim Philip had successfully lived in hiding on his family's estate on Petit Martinique for eight years. In 1803 bounty hunters finally caught up with him there. When he was delivered up, the Legislative Council passed a resolution that:

> a reward of twenty Joes be given to Alexander Murray, ten Joes to James Tazwell and five Joes to Joseph Barthelemey for their vigilance and activity in taking and securing the noted traitor Joachim Philip lately in the island of Petit Martinique.[34]

Captain Jacques Chadeau successfully avoided capture for some time, living incognito for twelve years. His whereabouts was revealed to the authorities in 1808 by a girlfriend who was jealous of his attentions to another. Chadeau was taken by a detachment of the Loyal Black Rangers. The Lieutenant-Governor and his Council determined that Chadeau was a slave from the Crawfish Estate, and that three magistrates, under the provisions of the Act for the More Effectual Trial and Punishment of Slaves, should try him. [35]

Chadeau was sentenced to be hanged by the three judges, and the sentence was carried out at Mount Eloi Point,[36] which is today called Cherry Hill. His body was left to rot on the gallows, plainly visible to all who used the king's highway. More than a decade after Fédon was defeated, the population got a new, grim reminder of the consequences of supporting the losing side of a revolution.

The Revolution and Carriacou

The *Grenada Handbook* reports that during the Fédon Revolution in 1795–96: 'The slaves in Carriacou were faithful and well behaved during the rebellion, and this too, although there was no garrison there, and that they outnumbered their masters by at least forty to one.'[37]

However, even if there were no disturbances in the Grenadines in sympathy with Fédon, there were some people in these islands who supported the Revolution. There is a story about a slave from Carriacou who joined Fédon and his band of revolutionaries, and is now revered as one of the three most important ancestral spirits in Carriacou:

It is said that Cromanti Cudjoe was a confederate of Fédon, and that upon the collapse of the rebellion he escaped to Sauteurs, Grenada. From there he swam north, through the convergent currents around Kick 'em Jenny rock to Carriacou. In Carriacou the slaves gave him shelter and food. He is said to have dressed as a woman and hid among the slaves for some time, going from estate to estate, trying to lead resistance against the British.[38]

The Grenadine Islands had a strong military presence during the Fédon Revolution. It was necessary for the British to patrol these waters to prevent supplies reaching Fédon from the French islands or from Trinidad. Carriacou was also used as a staging area by the British for the defence of Grenada during the Revolution. And it is said that 700 troops were stationed on Isle de Ronde during 1796.[39] Troops were stationed in Carriacou in preparation for landing in Grenada. Carriacou was visited by General Ralph Abercromby in 1796.

Fédon: Hero or Villain

The Fédon Revolution has been the subject of much discussion, speculation and analysis among scholars and laymen alike. Although the 'what-ifs' provide entertainment, they cannot change the outcome. There is also a real danger in romanticizing Fédon and re-engineering him into a folk hero and liberator of the slaves. He probably had mixed motives, one being his wish to be seen as the champion of the French-speaking Roman Catholics oppressed by the British, and another being to be the first French Governor of Grenada, if the island could be wrested from the British and put under the banner of Revolutionary France. Victor Hugues, who at first was pleased to use Fédon's charisma to marshal support for a revolution he thought was French, probably encouraged these ambitions.

Often hidden from popular view is that a lot of seeming support for Fédon was a response to the threats he made against the free coloureds if they would not join the Revolution, and likewise to the slaves. It was the knowledge of these threats that occasioned some of the people in Grenada and possibly Lieutenant-Governor Houston to be inclined to be lenient with all but the captured ringleaders of the Revolution.

Fédon became notorious for his brutality and atrocities and, for this reason, together with his unwillingness to take direction, the French disassociated themselves from him halfway through the Revolution.

Nevertheless, Fédon was a fearless leader and brilliant strategist. He sacrificed everything he had, and put his family at risk to bring Grenada back under French rule. He showed all people of African blood, whether mixed or not, that they could meet the whites on equal terms and defy a repressive government. If the British forces had not been augmented by mercenaries, Fédon's might have been victorious. But Britain had to do whatever was necessary to put down the Revolution. Britain could not risk defeat in Grenada, for Fédon's success would have given encouragement to revolt to other French-speaking citizens who were bristling under the social disadvantages visited on them by the vagaries of fortune in other colonies.

In retaliation for British losses there would be no accommodation whatsoever to the people of French extraction. The affairs of Grenada would now be run for the benefit of Britain and the British planters, and every effort would be made to wipe out French culture and to impose British ways and customs on the population. Any ameliorative measures for the slave population or free coloured would be hard to win and, if effected, would be a result of prevailing philosophy in Britain, imposed on the local government.

But whatever scholars may say, Fédon passed gloriously into Grenadian folklore. People today remember being told as children to listen out at night for the sound of Fédon's white stallion, as Fedon did the rounds protecting all children from any evil. Fédon is believed by the folk to have extraordinary powers, and to know the secrets of the lake. It is said that one of the reasons why he was never captured was that he had the ability to dive into the Grand Etang Lake, swim through subterranean passages, and emerge in Black Bay. Another story is that on the night after Jacques Chadeau was hanged, Fédon came on his white horse, and took his body down. Cradling him in his arms, he rode away with the body of his friend to lay him to rest somewhere in the mountains that he loved. In spite of the atrocities he committed on people as young as twelve years old, Fédon is unreservedly looked upon a symbol of emancipation and an eternal protector of the oppressed people of Grenada.

Notes

1 This was not the present town, but was a small settlement near the site of the present Marquis.
2 Devas (1974), p. 135.
3 See Allsopp, p. 112.
4 Devas (1974), p. 139.
5 GD 267/5/19/1, Letter from Mather Byles to George Home, 26 March, 1795, Scottish Record Office (SRO), Edinburgh.
6 Fortesque, p.459.

7　This name is spelt by some authors as Guerdon.

8　GD 267/1/18/22, Letter from George Home to Patrick Home, 4 July 1795, SRO.

9　Jacobs, Curtis (2000), p. 11.

10　This spelling is used by John Hay. Some of the accounts spell this name 'Shaw'.

11　Quoted in Ashby, p. 227.

12　*Webster's Third New International Dictionary* defines an *abbatis* as 'a defensive obstacle usually formed by felled trees, whose butts are secured towards the place defended, with the often sharpened branches directed outwards against the enemy; but sometimes made of live small trees bent down and often reinforced with the barbed wires'.

13　Hay, pp. 76–7.

14　Garraway, p. 43.

15　Hay, Kerr and McMahon remained in Guadeloupe and witnessed many distressing sights, including many more prisoners-of-war brought in. Hay was exchanged for a French officer, and freed on 6 July, returning to Grenada via Martinique. He arrived in Grenada on 22 July in a ship of war called the *Montague*.

16　GD 267/1/18/20, Letter from George Home to Patrick Home, 29 June 1795, SRO.

17　This was not the first time black soldiers had been used by the British. The Black Carolina Corps were recruited by the British from slaves to fight on the British side during the War of American Independence. After the war, they were assigned duties in several West Indian islands, including Grenada. See Buckley (1979) and Buckley (1998).

18　[Turnbull], p. 58.

19　See the Letters of Samuel Cary, Jr, 6 May 1795 – 15 Sept. 1795, Cary Papers, copies in the Grenada Centre, University of the West Indies.

20　See Letters from Mather Byles to George Home during 1795: GD 267/5/19/2, 7 July; GD 276/5/19/4, 23 July; GD 276/5/19/7, 10 Aug., SRO.

21　Samuel Cary to Joseph Marryat, 6 May 1795, Cary papers, copies held at Grenada Centre, University of the West Indies (UWI).

22　Samuel Cary, Jr, to Samuel Cary, Snr, 12 May 1795, Cary papers, Grenada Centre, UWI.

23　Hay, p. 126.

24　Fortesque (p. 462) related that when Governor Houston arrived to replace Home and take over from Mackenzie, 'to his disgust he found that Government House was occupied by the Light Dragoons, who were by no means disposed to make room for him'.

25　This term was not yet in use. The term was used first during the Peninsular War in Spain, where some British forces were led by General Sir John Moore, who had been the military governor of St Lucia in 1796. Moore had learned these tactics from the 'Brigands' in the Windward Islands, and now used them against the French forces in Europe. The term was also used by the Duke of Wellington some time during the first decade of the nineteenth century.

26　Garraway, p. 62.

27　Hay, p. 144–5.

28　Fortesque, p. 462.

29　Fortesque, p. 463.

30　Fortesque, p. 462.

31　Minutes of the Board of the Legislative Council, 16 December 1814, Supreme Court Registry, St George's.

32　Jacobs, Curtis (2000), p. 41.

33　*Ibid*.

34　Minutes of the Legislative Council, 1801–17, Minutes for 17 March 1803, Supreme Court Registry, St George's.

35 Minutes of the Board of the Legislative Council, Thursday 28 May 1808 at Government House, Supreme Court Registry, St George's.

36 There is a folk legend that Jacques Chadeau was not hanged, but put into a cage at Mount Eloi Point where food was put out daily just outside of his reach, and so he starved to death. Alister Hughes, in personal communication, related having been to the Point as a small boy, and being shown a rusty cage and told the story. He believes that some credence can be given to the story, as things do not always happen according to the official version.

37 Govt of Grenada, *Grenada Handbook*, p. 35.

38 Donald Hill, quoted by Chris Searle, p. 7.

39 Jessamy, p. 49.

7

Moving Towards Freedom

The Fédon Revolution had rent asunder the social and economic fabric of Grenada. Grenada now had before it the task of rebuilding both a shattered economy and a shattered society. The economy and its supporting infrastructure was completely devastated, with the rum and sugar works and other buildings completely destroyed on sixty-five estates, almost a complete loss of cattle, horses and mules, 7000 (one-fourth) of the slaves killed, run away or dead, some of them from starvation, and the loss of the crops for the years 1794, 1795, 1796 and 1797. To this had to be added the loss of life of the insurgents and of innocent citizens. The total financial loss resulting from the events of the Fédon Revolution was reckoned at £230,000, the equivalent of five years' revenue.[1]

Economic Recovery

The British government made the sum of £100,000[2] available to the planters of Grenada to assist them recover from the devastation of the uprisings. The properties of the Roman Catholic Church that had not yet been acquired were now seized by the government without compensation. Some were put up for sale, along with estates confiscated from those unfortunates convicted under the Act of Attainder. Two such parcels were those owned by the Roman Catholic Church in Hillsborough, Carriacou. One parcel was in Hillsborough and was of approximately 5 acres, and the other was 16 acres on Bay l'Eau.[3] The church building which was situated on the Hillsborough property was handed over to the Anglican Church between 1800 and 1802, despite there being no Church of England minister in Carriacou at this time. The first minister, the Reverend W. Davis, arrived in 1792, but left within a few weeks, and was not replaced for a long time.

The economy also got a slight boost from servicing the ships that assembled at St George's for convoy. Until the end of the French Revolutionary War, Grenada was used as the chief rendezvous point for the vessels bound for England, under the protection of ships of war. The port of St George was also a depot for prisoners of war. In July 1806, for example, there were 200 vessels in or near the harbour, carrying produce worth £3,000,000. There were also 400 French prisoners in custody. In 1799 pipes had been laid to bring water from the spring in Springs to the Spout, for the convenience of ships wishing to take on water.

A valuable trade also developed between Grenada and the Spanish mainland, then in the throes of rebellion against Spain. To encourage this trade, the Governor issued short-term licences to some foreign vessels, giving them British protection while plying between Grenada and South America. The trade was so important to Grenada at this time that in 1815 the Governor expelled Abbé Planquais, the Vicar General, from Grenada for having interdicted two Spanish priests who had been given licences by the Governor to perform religious duties. Although potentially contentious, the expulsion of the Abbé went uncontested by the leading Roman Catholics because good relations with people on the Spanish mainland was of more importance to them. Moreover, the Abbé seemed to have been unpopular, and the Roman Catholic community was glad to see the back of him. The expulsion of the Abbé was also approved by the Home Office.

To take advantage of the increasing trade done by Grenada, Scottish ship-builders were brought to Carriacou by the Scottish estate owners there to build sloops and schooners to carry the produce of Carriacou to Grenada for further shipment to Europe. They settled in Windward and Petit Martinique, and the people of these areas still exhibit the lighter skin tone and surnames associated with their Scottish heritage.[4]

Shattered Peace, and Peace of Mind

While the rebuilding of the economy gradually took place, the old society continued to be destroyed after the end of the Revolution. This destruction was deliberate. Grenada had had a culture, which was largely derived from French culture. Roman Catholicism was the major religion, and French the most commonly spoken language. Now Grenada was to be made an English society, with the Church of England as the state religion, and English the only official language. The people were to be socialized into British ways, and to think of themselves as British, regardless of their ethnic origin. It was seen to be advantageous to adopt the new ways, and retrograde to hold onto the old.

The French-speaking Roman Catholics, still reeling under the loss of so many of their number, therefore had much more to suffer. Any group identity that remained was now demolished. Large hints were given that individual self-respect and status could only be retrieved by renouncing one's French heritage. This would be demonstrated by speaking English instead of French, and attending the Church of England services while forsaking the Roman Catholic Church. The example of Captain Louis La Grenade, the coloured Grenadian who had earned the respect of the British for his loyalty and devotion to duty before and during the Fédon Revolution, was held up to the French population as an example for the French-speaking Grenadians to emulate. He had been so trusted by Ninian Home that only his troops of all the coloured troops were armed when a state of emergency was called just before the Revolution broke out. During the course of the Revolution, he was placed at the head of the mulatto troops, and was involved in several of the battles. After the Revolution, he was given a virtual title by being referred to as La Grenade instead of the name he was born with. Brian Edwards recalls seeing him:

> Louis La Grenade, chief of the Gens de coulieur, and captain of a militia company, came to Government House. He seems a fine spirited athletic fellow, and wears a large gold medal about his neck, being a gift from the colony, in reward for his valiant services and experienced fidelity on all occasions.[5]

The French-speaking Roman Catholic population was further demoralized by emigration. Despondent over their prospects of future happiness and prosperity in Grenada, alienated from the country of their birth, and intensely bitter against the British, many French-speaking Grenadians chose to migrate to Trinidad under the arrangements negotiated by Roumé de St Laurent, and make a new start.

Thankfully, there was a third group of Roman Catholics, including many slaves, who stayed in Grenada, holding fast to their culture and their faith, and gave continuance to the French cultural heritage. Even though Grenada's French heritage was forced to the level of a substratum, it would survive and play a vibrant part along with the substratum of African culture in the rich mix of Grenadian culture.

The movement of French-speaking Grenadians out of the country, and the pressures to adopt English ways, produced a great deal of social and individual tension. These added to the general feelings of insecurity left over from the Revolution. Some of the revolutionaries, including Fédon, it will be remembered, were still at large up to 1808.

Slave revolts in other islands also made the planters nervous, and in January 1802 the Militia was put on alert and an alarm raised because of a report that the slaves in Carriacou were planning a rebellion. This restiveness of the slaves was blamed on the preaching of the new Church of

England minister, the Reverend William Nash, whose sermons and activities, the planters claimed, had put thoughts of insurrection in the heads of the slaves. Lieutenant-Governor George Hobart sailed for Carriacou immediately, and his careful investigation did not substantiate either the allegations made against Nash by the slave owners, or that an insurrection was imminent. The next alarm took place in 1803 when some of the French Grenadians who had fled to Trinidad tried to return. This they were prevented from doing.

Grenada badly needed the sense of security that would have come from having a long-serving capable Governor. But Grenada's Governors changed with regularity, and even so, these Governors were seldom in place as they were more often than not called away for military service. During the absence of the various Governors, the responsibility of the island fell to the Presidents of the Council. Some of the Governors assigned to Grenada were incompetent, dishonest and unworthy. In 1812 the public was shocked when a Governor Adye had to be censored by the House of Assembly for conveying to another person, in trust for his wife, certain slaves who were the property of the Crown.

In 1812 the Souffrière volcano in St Vincent erupted, and the resulting explosion was interpreted in Grenada as distant cannon. The nervous planters called the Militia out. Then in 1816 the news of the Bussa slave rebellion in Barbados brought further alarm to the planters and Government of Grenada. This news caused great excitement among the slaves in Grenada, and the Militia was called out by George Patterson, President of the House of Assembly and Acting Governor. The Militia was instructed to occupy the military posts that had been built throughout Grenada during the Fédon Revolution. Although Bussa's rebellion had no repercussions but this in Grenada, fear of slave uprisings did not cease until after the abolition of slavery.

The next year, 1817, the élite and the growing middle class got a reminder of the personal cost of war when several ships of the Spanish fleet arrived in St George's Harbour. The ships carried the remnants of the garrison and surviving inhabitants from the Angostura settlement in Venezuela. This settlement had just been evacuated after a long siege, and the remaining inhabitants arrived in Grenada in a very sorry state. They were well treated, and left greatly improved in health and appearance.

To the tensions generated by the possibilities of a recurrence of revolution, slave rebellion or capture were added the stresses of natural disasters. Late in 1817, Grenada was struck by a hurricane. Roads and bridges were damaged to the extent of between £20,000 and £30,000. Another natural disaster, this time a flood, took several lives in October 1819.

The society was also plagued by drunkenness and dissolute behaviour among certain sections of the population, including the soldiers in the army garrison. F.W.N. Bayley who visited Grenada around this time was horrified at the effects of rum drinking on the population. Although Grenada was to be praised for instituting and enforcing licences, the imbibing of rum

> [i]s the cause of many, nay of most of those deaths among the army, navy, and merchant ships ... In the garrisons the greatest severity and most unabated vigilance may be employed by the officers of a corps to keep the rum from the soldiers, but to no purpose.[6]

A New Start

Concurrent with the events that maintained a state of worry, stress and tension in Grenada, changes we·e made in the society that signalled a return not only to more normal preoccupations, but also to a determination to establish an effectively run British colony, with all the symbols of the British Empire. In 1800, the two Courts operating in Grenada, the Court of the King's Bench and Grand Sessions of the Peace and the Court of Common Pleas were amalgamated to become the Supreme Court of Judicature. This was occasioned by the imperfections of the old system, and dissatisfaction with some of the judges. The purchase of York House in 1801 as the new seat for the legislature could also be interpreted as a sign of the now undisputed supremacy of British rule, through the Government of Grenada, which was now firmly and exclusively controlled by the English and Scottish planters. Even a new map of Grenada drawn by Garvin Smith was purchased, and became Grenada's official map. Finally the planned reconstruction of Government House at an estimated cost of £14,000, was begun.

Social life of the élite revived, and there were reports in 1828 of balls and dinners at Government House. An Old Year's Night ball and supper there in 1828 featured quadrille dances and 'good old English country dance'.[7] There were also balls and dinners at private homes, such as the residences of Captain Otway, Mrs Rowley, Hon. George Gun-Munroe at Bacolet, Mr Bell at Lower La Tante and William Swap at Clarke's Court. A season of Garrison Balls was held in the ordnance rooms at the Fort, and other 'entertainments' were put on by officers of the regiments at places such as the Royal Hotel in St Andrew's and the Long Room in St George's. The band of the 27th Regiment was imported to play for one such occasion.

On the estates there were 'ploughing matches', in which gangs of labourers vied to see which team could plough regular deep furrows in the shortest time. These matches were witnessed by the estate owner and his friends. At the conclusion of the match, the estate owner would give an appropriate speech of encouragement and praise, and award monetary prizes to the winners, and the lady of the estate house placed a garland around the neck of the leader of the victorious team. Sloop races took place in the harbour, and there was horse racing at Grand Anse. Newspapers and journals were once more published with regularity, including the *Free Press*, the *St Andrew's Journal and La Baye Miscellany*, and *The Star or Occidental Comet.*[8]

By 1830 St George's was once more a charming little town. Bayley quotes an anonymous poet:

> Art worked to build, and built the little town
> The houses all in excellent array
> The streets now rising up, now sloping down
> As the proud hillocks have inclined the way.[9]

By this time several merchants had established business places on the Carenage. The gaol was just off the Carenage, and there was a treadmill in the yard after 1827. The market place was

> Surrounded by houses irregularly built, the lower rooms of which are generally stores of minor importance, and containing a cage for runaway slaves, a few trees, and one or two butcher's stalls: it is also a place of execution, and a parade ground for the Militia troops.[10]

The gaiety of the élite and growth of St George's was soon to be overshadowed by economic collapse brought about by the freeing of the slaves.

Abolition of the Slave Trade

Amidst all the distractions and preoccupations of this era, certainly the concern that was of the most importance to the planters in Grenada and others who had financial interest in this island was the future of the colony in an era when they would not be able to have access to new slaves. In 1807 Britain abolished the slave trade due to mounting pressure at home to disallow the monopoly of West Indian sugar produced by slave labour and allow the importation of sugar from countries such as the East Indies.

Economic arguments were also brought against slavery, and evidence was produced that sugar could be produced more economically with free labour than with forced. Apart from these objective arguments against the monopoly of West Indian sugar, humanitarian thought was becoming popular in Britain, and a distaste for the cruelties of the institution of slavery developed.

The abolition of the slave trade meant that no British colony, including Grenada, could legally import slaves. From now on, planters had to take better care of their slaves. If they did not, they would face an acute labour shortage. The slave owners not only had to care for their adult slaves, but they also had to do what they could to ensure natural replacement of the slave population. One such incentive in Grenada was the Annual Award to three slave mothers who had the healthiest children.

There had always been some slave owners who treated the slaves well, regarding them as human beings. One such slave owner was George Home, the brother of Ninian Home, who had assumed the control of Waltham and Paraclete Estates after the death of his brother. But there were also others who were less enlightened in their attitudes. Even these had to make adjustments to the manner in which they managed their slaves, because the option of replacing slaves through purchase of new ones had been removed.

Slave Registration

The abolition of slavery was the first step in the dismantlement of the institution of slavery itself. In 1819 the British government took a further step with the passing of the Slave Registry Act. This Act ordered that all slaves were to be registered.

The registration of slaves solved many problems. The ownership of a slave became dependent on the slave being registered, and after the first registration, no unregistered person could be held as a slave. It would force the slave owners to take better care of their slaves, as births, deaths, mutilations, runaways and injuries had to be recorded. Registration also prevented the illegal transportation of slaves from one territory to another. Finally, although this might have been fortuitous and not by design, the compensation to the slave owners at Emancipation would be based on the recorded ownership of slaves.

The Slave Registers in which the slaves in Grenada were listed were huge books approximately three inches thick and measuring 24 inches long and 18 inches wide. Each slave was recorded by name, gender and country of origin, supposed age, colour and marks. For example, the Slave Register

for 1817 for St David's and Carriacou listed 232 slaves on the Carriere
Estate as of 11 July 1817. Of these 109 were male and 123 were female. Of
the total, 111 were African-born. There were 24 male and 34 female
children under fifteen years of age.

The physical manifestation of disease among the slaves was
described with horrible frankness. The Slave Register for 1817 for St
George's records that Harriet, a black African slave woman aged fifty-
five, belonging to George Gun Munroe and attached to the Point Salines
Estate, had her 'face nearly eaten up with venereal sores';[11] Nanon, a
male slave on the Douglaston Estate, was a leper;[12] and there was plentiful evidence of others with these diseases, or who had elephantiasis and
smallpox.

The Slave Registers show the extent to which slaves had been injured.
Nellie, a 50-year-old black African woman on the Douglaston Estate had
lost an arm, and 40-year-old American Jim was without half of his left
foot.[13] Some slaves were described as black, while the lighter-skinned
progeny of the female slaves and white men were described as yellow.
Some had tribal marks, like Sally, who belonged to George Agiton of
St George's, who was of the Mandingo nation, and had three stripes on her
cheeks.[14] James, also belonging to George Agiton, was of the Chambo
nation, and was similarly marked. Every scar was recorded meticulously,
whether it was a simple scar on the eyebrow, due perhaps to a fall, or
marks on the belly, which were the probable legacy of a whipping.

If slaves were not present when the Registrar of Slaves visited the
estates to which they were attached, their whereabouts had to be verified.
For example, Roseanne, a black creole slave of twenty-eight years belonging to Marie Angelique de Goubault, was not on the estate at the time of
registration, because she was in England with her mistress.[15]

Amelioration of the Conditions of the Slaves

Apart from slave registration, there were other signs of the concern of the
British government for the spiritual and temporal welfare of the slaves in
Grenada and about the future creation of a free citizenry from a population of slaves. One of these signs was the suggestion by Britain to the
Grenada government that they establish schools and provide for pastors
and churches for the education and conversion of the slaves. In 1823 there
were only two Anglican and two Roman Catholic priests in Grenada, and
eleven schools, six of which were in St George's.

In response to the suggestion that the slaves be Christianized, the
Anglican Church in St George's was rebuilt in 1825, and in 1830 Anglican

churches in St David's and St Patrick's were begun with funds from the British government. However, most of the pleas for the education of the slaves fell for the time being on deaf ears. In 1827 the Bishop of Barbados visited Grenada, and after inspecting the schools set up by the Society for the Education of the Poor, expressed

> a wish that some arrangement might be made for admitting young slaves, without restriction; and added that if the Committee could allow the admissions to be without reserve, he would have it in his power to assist them to a greater extent.[16]

The Committee, it is reported, while wishing to agree with the bishop's views, could not oblige immediately, because, they said 'the original object of the institution is the education of poor free children'.[17]

However the Grenadian élite might wish to hold back the inevitable, they could not stop a movement that had its impetus in Britain. In 1823 Lord Bathurst, the Colonial Secretary, instructed the legislatures in the British West Indies to pass laws improving the conditions of the slaves. In 1825 the Grenada legislature responded by passing a Consolidated Slave Law, bringing together all the laws regulating the slaves, the laws that restricted the owners, and measures that ameliorated the lot of the slaves. Unfortunately, the Grenada Consolidated Slave Law did not contain many of the ameliorative measures suggested by Bathurst, and the opportunity was used by the Grenada legislature to tighten the controls on the individual slave.

Previous regulatory measures for slaves incorporated into this Consolidated Slave Law were: Slaves had to have written permission, called a pass, to be off the plantation on which they were residing. Slaves who were stopped, and did not have a pass, were taken into custody, and returned to the plantation where they belonged. The owner was compelled to pay a fee for the return of such slaves. If a slave were found in St George's between 9 p.m. and 4 a.m. without a pass, he or she would be kept for the night in a cage in St George's. Any slave caught dancing in a public place in St George's at night would be arrested and kept overnight.

Slaves who were absent from the estate for forty-eight hours without a pass were deemed to be runaways. Harsh punishment was the penalty for being absent without permission. After the first conviction, the runaway was sentenced to a whipping or to hard labour, but if a slave was a habitual runaway, or if a slave remained at large for longer than six months, the sentence could involve transportation. Anyone who hid a runaway slave or carried off a slave was liable to corporal punishment, or (if white) face a very heavy fine.

The practice of obeah, any practices associated with it, or possession by a slave of any items connected with the practice of witchcraft such as poisons, powdered glass, parrots' beaks, dogs' or alligators' teeth, would be punishable by death or transportation. It was illegal to sell arms to or give arms to slaves. Murder, manslaughter, armed robbery, rebellion, arson and burglary were all punishable by death or transportation. Slaves could not beat drums or 'hand instruments' after 10 p.m. Swearing, using obscene language, drunkenness, committing indecent acts, cruelty to animals, fast or careless driving of carts within the town, were all punishable with twenty-five lashes.

The ameliorative measures included permission for slaves to receive instruction in the Christian religion and to be baptized. The workday of the slave was limited to the hours of 5 a.m. to 7 p.m., with a half-hour break for breakfast, and a two-hour break for lunch. It became illegal for masters to abandon old slaves on account of illness and, if a slave owner was caught doing this, he was fined £50. If the slave was to be whipped, no more than fifteen lashes could be administered without a free person witnessing the whipping, and more than twenty-five lashes could not be administered in one day. Violation of both these restrictions cost the owner a fine of £10. Women slaves with five or more children were given fifty-two days every year to cultivate their own grounds, and were not to be separated from their children. Nor was it any longer permissible to separate married slaves from each other.

The slave owners in Grenada were conscious that the attitude towards slavery in Britain had changed. They knew it was useless to protest against the abolition of the trade, slave registration, or ameliorative measures, but they did what they could to let the British government know what they thought of the suggestions for the abolition of slavery itself. The correspondence of George Home[18] is full of intimations that Emancipation would be the harbinger of ruin for the planters. In 1823 James Baillie, a member of the Assembly representing the combined parishes of St George's and St John's, wrote a 48-page tract[19] defending slavery in Grenada.

On the estates, the slaves were, as often as not, managed the traditional way, despite the ameliorative measures advised by Britain. This was deeply resented by the slaves, who knew of and appreciated the new status given to them by Britain. A case in point was a stoppage of work in 1824 by the slaves on Duquesne Estate. A driver, in contravention of the laws protecting slaves, had brought a whip into the fields and struck two slaves, and threatened to do likewise to others. The slaves protested to the Receiver who should have sought their interest. But, when the protest was heard, the judgment went against the slaves, and many of them were whipped as punishment for standing up for their rights. Neither was any sympathy forthcoming from the Governor who reported the incident to the Colonial Office as the 'Riot of Slaves on the Duquesne Estate'.

The recalcitrance of the élite regarding amelioration was again manifested in 1827, when the Act was passed to erect the treadmill at the prison in town. The treadmill could either be a form of hard labour, or an instrument of torture, depending on how fast it was operated. This became a popular way of punishing slaves.

The planters chose to continue the repressive plantation order as long as possible and to ignore all the measures that were meant to bring change to Grenada. However, the time was at hand when the choice of changing or not changing would no longer be within the planters' power. Britain, which had built the institution of the West Indian sugar plantation based on slavery and the slave trade, was now responding to other voices seeking to dismantle it. Sugar was being allowed into Britain from other British colonies at the same rate of duty as West Indian sugar, and the sugar from the other sources was cheaper. Thus the prices for West Indian sugar were depressed to a level that did not allow the West Indian planter to cover his costs. All but the most efficiently run and productive estates went bankrupt. By 1830, out of 342 estates, 86 went bankrupt, were abandoned, and allowed to go into bush. Of these, 18 were in St George's, 22 in St Andrew's, and 31 in St David's, which was more than half the number of estates in that parish. In Britain many of the financial houses that provided credit to the plantations and estates in the West Indies went into liquidation. The plantation era was about to end.

A Race to Create a Free Christian population

As the end of the plantation era approached, the race began to create a free Christian population, loyal to the Church of England, out of the population of slaves. Some of the slaves were already devout Roman Catholics, and it was hoped that they could be converted to the Church of England. Many of the slaves that had been imported after 1767 had not had the same opportunity for Christianization under their English masters, and these especially were targeted for religious instruction. Whereas, before, some slave owners had believed that the slaves had no souls, and therefore did not need to be taught religion, with the prospect of freedom they now thought that if the slaves were taught to obey the dictates of Christianity, this would be a means of creating a more docile and obedient free population.

Three organizations aimed at giving slaves and free coloureds religious education, reading skills sufficient to allow them to read their Bibles, and useful crafts, were established in Grenada, including, in 1824, the Society for the Education of the Poor, mentioned earlier. This was a society under the auspices of the Church of England, with the Governor as its patron. It counted among its members the Church of England's ministers in Grenada, prominent Assemblymen and some planters. This Society started the Central School in St George's for the children of the free black and coloured population, where the children received religious instruction and were taught reading, writing and useful crafts.

The second society to be established for the Christianizing of the slaves was the Society for the Promotion of Christian Knowledge, founded in 1826. This Society drew its membership from prominent members of the ruling and propertied class. The Grenada District Committee for the Conversion and Religious Instruction and Education of Negro Slaves was also formed in 1826, with the Governor as its chief patron.

At the same time membership of the Church of England was made more accessible to the slaves. Two new rectors of the Church of England were appointed, and the parishes of the Church of England regrouped, providing benefices for St George's and St John's as one, and then St David's, St Patrick's and St Andrew's. In addition, the catechist of the Church of England together with the headmasters and four monitors of the Central School gave religious instruction to 150 of the slaves in the town of St George's. Catechists were appointed to assist the clergy in visiting the estates in St George's to instruct the slave children. Catechists in Gouyave ran another Church of England school three days a week for fifty children. On the other days the catechist visited the children on the estates in St John's and St Mark's. If the catechist was not available, the manager or members of their families took over the job of instruction.

However, the faithfulness of the free coloureds and the slaves to the Roman Catholic religion proved a barrier to the recruitment of members for the Church of England. Their Sunday School was attended by twice as many as the Sunday instruction offered by the Church of England. The stability of the Roman Catholic Church and the loyalty of the population to it was eventually recognized, as this church was now seen as an ally in providing a religious discipline for the guidance of the behaviour of the Grenadian population. Salaries were granted to Roman Catholic priests in 1818. New Roman Catholic schools were built. Any traditional religion was in fact seen as an instrument in establishing a peaceful society, and in September 1830 the government gave the old Court House lot to the Presbyterian Church for the erection of a kirk. Erection of this church was begun, financed by public subscriptions, especially the Freemasons Lodge. In 1832 salaries were granted to Presbyterian ministers. In return for these salaries, the Roman Catholic and Presbyterian clergy had to visit the estates each week to instruct the slaves.

Towards a Free Society

The winds of change, once they started to blow, blew in all directions. Before 1828, the slaves could sell their produce in the towns on any day of the week. In 1828 an Act was passed prohibiting Sunday markets, and decreeing Thursdays and Saturdays as public market days, in order to encourage the slaves to go to church on Sundays. In that year, too, the testimony of slaves was admitted in the courts of justice without any restriction. Before this the testimony of a slave against a white man was not allowed.

Manumission, or the freeing of slaves by the masters, or the purchase by the slave of his own freedom, became more common. Between 1817 and 1831 there was the manumission of 1226 slaves, more than half of whom were women. The price of manumission could be as much as £300, or as little as £26, but the usual price was between £56 and £100. In addition to the actual fee for manumission, there were other fees amounting to about £5 that had to be paid to the registrar and judge handling the manumission. Before 1818 an additional £100 had to be paid into the Treasury to provide the person being manumitted with an annuity of £10 for ten years, but this was now discontinued.

Not only the slaves enjoyed amelioration in their conditions. This period saw the lifting of some of the restrictions on the free coloured and free black population. At this time this sector of the population was rapidly growing. In 1821 there were 3456 free coloured people in Grenada, in 1828 there were 3748, and by 1840 about 4000. Legal distinctions operated to ensure that the free coloureds would not enjoy the same privileges as the white population. Now these legal distinctions began to be repealed. In 1823 legislation was passed equating the penalty for the unlicensed practice of surgery for people of colour and whites. Different sentences to those for slaves were now prescribed for the free coloured and black population for arson and theft. In addition, the free coloured and black population were allowed to serve summons on the members of the Assembly and also members of the Council. They were also given the right to vote, but not to stand for election, and the valid evidence of two capable free coloured and black persons was enough to secure the conviction of a person of any colour in a court of law.

These measures were not sufficient to wipe out the bitterness still felt by the free coloured at their status as second-class citizens, especially as they were aware that many of their number surpassed the whites in education and fine manners. The better educated among the free coloured group would continue to agitate for equality under the law until all legal discrimination was removed. This would take many decades, but by 1830 some of the free coloureds were assertive enough to send a letter to the Colonial Office complaining against the injustice of stigmatizing men of colour by making them inferior in local law and customs. They complained against their exclusion from civil rank and honour, from being appointed magistrates, and from serving in the legislature.

In the same year, the free coloureds addressed a letter to the House of Commons complaining that, although they owned two-thirds of the properties in the town of St George's, and formed the greatest number in the rank and file of the Militia, they could not hold rank in the Militia, were excluded from service on the Grand Jury, and from all other positions of honour. They also felt that the recent concessions, which allowed them to serve as petty jurors and constables, would be a benefit to the whites rather that a boon to them, as the whites would be relieved of duties seen as onerous. Most importantly, they were still barred from service in the legislature.

Tired of waiting to be noticed, the free coloureds, led by Frances Danglade, a free coloured woman, demonstrated in the streets of St George's against the inequities of their class. Frances Danglade was imprisoned for ten days, and the incident reported to the Secretary of State. Victory was hers, for as a result the legislature was advised to pass laws abolishing discrimination against the free coloureds and free blacks. In 1832 the government removed all civil disabilities from free coloured and black inhabitants, giving them the right to sit in the legislature. After sixty-nine years and a bloody civil war, a woman had forced the Government of Grenada to redress the wrongs that had been a major cause of Fédon's Revolution.

Planter Attitudes to Change

The ruling class was far from comfortable with the changes in society, which would enhance the status position of the slaves, free coloureds and free blacks. The ruling class – the judges, public officers and politicians – all owned slaves. Even members of the clergy had domestic slaves. All whites, no matter how kindly they viewed the blacks, believed them to be inferior. They did all in their power to maintain the system, and came down heavily upon any white person who was not of like mind. This attitude operated in later action taken against the Chief Justice, J.H. Bent, and three priests of the Roman Catholic Church.

In 1829 Bent summoned before him the Vicar General, Father LeGoff, and two other priests under the Vagabond Act. These clerics had been sent from Trinidad by Bishop O'Donnell to replace a priest by the name of Father O'Hannan, who had angered the ruling class by his sermons, which condemned the injustices committed by the ruling class against the free people of colour. For this action, but really for his friendship with Father O'Hannan and the sympathy for the masses which he shared with this priest, Bent was suspended from office without his being given an opportunity to defend himself by the President in Council. Bent was reinstated by the Secretary of State for the Colonies, Lord Goderich, but was again suspended, this time on a series of charges. The matter was eventually referred to the Privy Council, which again reinstated him, but the Secretary of State transferred him from Grenada, requiring him to accept a position as Puisne Judge in Trinidad. Writing to Lord Goderich on 25 January 1831, the Governor indicated that Bent had disturbed the peace and tranquility of a happy and united colony, and this could not be restored so long as he was allowed to preside on the bench of justice.[20]

The Colonial Office was greatly disappointed that none of the West Indian islands, including Grenada, used the amelioration measures to make significant changes for improving the conditions of the slaves. When it was evident that, left to the planter-dominated legislatures, any attempt at change would be thwarted, the matter of slavery and its continuation became a subject for debate in the House of Commons. The prevailing opinion there was that slavery should be abolished throughout the British Empire.

The news of this decision threw the West Indian planters into panic. The governments of Barbados, St Kitts, Nevis, the Virgin Islands, Dominica, Demerara and Essequibo, St Vincent, Grenada and Tobago were asked to send representatives to a congress in Barbados in February 1831. Grenada was represented by Robert Stronach and John Hoyes. Hoyes chaired the drafting committee for the memorandum that the congress decided to send to the British government setting out their position.

The petition outlined the hardships the planters were facing. The petition said that: after fifteen years, they were still paying war tax; other countries which had not abolished the slave trade now had the advantage in producing sugar; the end of slavery would bring ruin and destruction on the planters; that by supporting the abolition of slavery the anti-slavery movement was interfering with the planters' property and advocating their ruin; that it was the planters who had had the job of civilizing and bringing comfort to the slaves who had been brought into the islands in a state of barbarism; and finally that the plantation system, which was dependent on slavery, had been created and approved by the laws of Great Britain, and that any attempt now to injure or destroy property previously sanctioned was a gross violation of every principle of law and justice. If slavery were to be abolished by Great Britain, the planters would expect that the government in Britain would provide them with full and complete indemnification of all the losses that might arise, and all injuries that might be sustained by changes in their property.

After the regional meeting in Barbados, local meetings of planters were subsequently held, at which the planters were urged to resist any attempts by the British government to deprive them of the ownership of the slaves without compensation. At one such meeting in June 1831, three resolutions were passed. The first resolution agreed that slavery could be abolished. The second resolution called for full compensation to slave proprietors and all others who depended on slaves for their livelihood. The third suggested secession from Great Britain, freeing the planters to look for other protectors who would appreciate the value of a possession such as Grenada, which contributed so much to Britain's wealth and power.

A meeting of merchants and planters in July 1831 took the suggestion of secession to another level. At this meeting it was resolved that, since Britain had driven Grenada to the verge of desperation by gradual encroachments on the island's institutions and domestic privileges, the planters now had to look after their own interests. As Britain had abandoned them, they were no longer obligated to show further allegiance to Britain. One of the most ardent advocates of secession was James McQueen. He accused the anti-slavery movement in Britain of making the British electorate political slaves and deliberately planning the destruction of the West Indian planters.

Despite these outcries and threats, it become clear that it was just a matter of time before full emancipation of the slaves would be granted. The House of Commons considered several plans to effect the transition of the slaves to free men. The plan that was deemed to be most suitable was drafted by Lord Stanley, the Colonial Secretary, and became the basis for the Imperial Emancipation Act.

A major political change was effected in 1833, in preparation for Emancipation, and to make the government of the islands easier for Great Britain. A Windward Islands government was formed comprising Grenada, Tobago, Barbados and St Vincent and the Grenadines. This meant that Grenada would no longer have its own Governor, but would have a Lieutenant-Governor, who reported to the Governor in Barbados. The first Governor-in-Chief appointed was Sir Lionel Smith.

Major-General George Middlemore was appointed Grenada's Lieutenant-Governor.

Emancipation

On 28 August 1833, the British government passed the Imperial Emancipation Act, and sent it to all the West Indian colonies, instructing each colony to use it as the basis for drafting their own Acts without deviating from the principles embodied in the Imperial Act. The Imperial Act declared all the slaves in the British colonies to be free from 1 August 1834. However, in order to prepare them for this freedom, there would be a period of apprenticeship during which they were required to remain assigned to their former masters for another six years, or four years if they were domestic servants.

Further provisions said that all slave children aged six and under were to be freed immediately. All male children would be apprenticed until they were twenty-four and female children until they were twenty, or until the end of the apprenticeship period, whichever came first. Special Magistrates would be appointed to oversee the apprenticeship system. These would visit the estates at the behest of either the planter or the apprentice, to investigate complaints. Finally, an amount of £20,000,000 was granted as compensation to the slave owners in the West Indies for the economic loss that they would face as a result of freeing the slaves. As instructed, the legislature passed a local Emancipation Act on 11 March 1834, under the title 'An Act for Carrying into Effect the Provisions of an Act of the Imperial Parliament of Great Britain for the Abolition of Slavery'. Some of the provisions in this Act were amended, and the final version took effect on 1 August 1834. The Grenada planters received an amount of £616,255 in compensation for their 23,638 slaves who had been registered on 31 July 1834.

Emancipation Day was greeted by the slaves and free coloured population with great jubilation. The Proclamation was read to the slaves on each estate after a religious service. Some of the planters had anticipated trouble, but there was none, only a few incidents of insubordination on two of the estates. However, it would soon become evident that the law that ended slavery did not emancipate the slave.

The Operation of the Apprenticeship System

The historian, W.L. Burn, writing about apprenticeship, observed that the fatal flaw in the apprenticeship system was that the system had been devised by one set of men motivated by one type of philosophy, while the implementation of the scheme was left in the hands of men who had no such humanitarian views.[21] The management of apprenticeship was simply too dependent on the planters and the judiciary that it controlled for the checks and balances of the system to operate effectively. Therefore the apprenticeship period, which was designed to be a time for both the former slaves and the planters to adjust to each other and socio-economically to the changes that a free society would bring, was interpreted by the planters as a grace period during which they should get as much compulsory labour from the ex-slaves as possible.

The legislation to establish apprenticeship divided Grenada into three districts for the purpose of administering the apprenticeship scheme. Each district was provided with a police force consisting of a Special Magistrate, one sergeant and ten privates. The Special Magistrates received their appointments from England and were to be the guardians of freedom, ensuring that the provisions of the Emancipation Act were fulfilled. Their duties included mediating the disputes between the apprentices and the masters, investigating complaints within twenty-four hours of receiving them, handing down fines or sentences, and generally helping to create a smooth transition between slavery and freedom. Special Justices of the Peace appointed by the Governor assisted the magistrates in these duties. The Special Magistrates prepared weekly reports to the Governor, who forwarded them to the Secretary of State. The Secretary of State would use them in a report to the House of Commons. The Act also provided for Inspectors, who would visit the estates to ensure that the tasks set the apprentices were reasonable. If the Inspectors found that the tasks were excessive, they had the authority to reduce them.

At Emancipation 18,316 apprentices were created in Grenada: 8826 males and 9490 females. Apprentices were divided into three categories: praedial attached, praedial unattached and non-praedials. Each apprentice was to be registered in the appropriate category. Every year each apprentice was to receive from the estate six yards of the type of cloth called *pennistoun*, eight yards of the type of cloth called *osnaburg*, and one hat or cap, and every three years one blanket. Each apprentice was to receive a weekly allowance of two pounds of salted, dried or pickled fish, and either ground provisions, eight pints of flour or six quarts of meal or grain, or the money equivalent. Negligence or refusal to provide these goods to the apprentice incurred a fine of £5, plus the value of the allowances.

The hours of work for apprentices were controlled by the Act. Sundays were guaranteed work-free, except in the case of a disaster or dire emergency. When it was required that an apprentice work at night, the apprentice was not to work more than nine hours at a stretch. Provision was also made for the health of the apprentices. At the risk of a fine of £50, each estate was to have a hospital, a medical practitioner and appropriate medicines. Moreover, all sick, aged and infirm apprentices were to be cared for by the masters. Special food had to be provided for the sick, or a fine of £5 would be levied.

However, the rest of the Act showed the preoccupation of the planters' desire to confine the apprentices to the places of their former enslavement, and rigidly confine their movements. The punishments decreed for infringements of articles of the legislation were also grossly unfair. Punishments for infringements by apprentices ensured that the apprentices would continue to be ruled by fear of physical punishment. On the other hand, the penalty for planters who were caught in infringing the laws governing the apprenticeship system was a fine, which benefited public coffers.

Of primary concern were measures to keep the labour on the estates. Gaols and cages were readied in each district to receive apprentices that fell foul of the vagrancy laws, for if an apprentice was found wandering beyond the limits of the plantation without a permit, any free person could detain that apprentice. Without extenuating circumstances, that apprentice would be judged a vagabond. Any apprentice absent from work without cause was to work an extra two hours for every hour absent, provided this did not exceed fifteen hours weekly. Those who absented themselves for nine hours in one week were deemed deserters, and those who were absent for two days without permission were deemed vagabonds. Those who were absent without permission for five days were deemed runaways. Deserters were imprisoned for one week, vagabonds for not more than two weeks, and runaways for not more than one month, with the addition of not more than thirty lashes. Those absent for more than seven days were deemed notorious runaways, and were sentenced to three months' hard labour, and, in addition, males received a flogging of not more than thirty-nine lashes.

Other provisions were written into the legislation with the objective of maintaining maximum control over the former slaves. To counter the tendency of the apprentices to establish themselves as a community, the community would be dislodged and the houses destroyed if the persons who lived there habitually neglected to perform their estate duties. If an apprentice worked indolently, carelessly or negligently, he or she could be called upon to give his employer up to fifteen hours' free labour, or be imprisoned for one month's hard labour. Wanton destruction of the master's property, such as the ill-use of cattle or livestock, the careless use of fire, or wilful disobedience to the master's orders also carried the sentence of fifteen hours of extra work or one month's imprisonment with hard labour. Hard labour could either be working the treadmill, fixing the public roads, or work designated as punishment on the plantation.

If there was a need for apprentices to appeal to the Special Magistrate, they could not leave the plantation to seek out the magistrate. Instead they were to appoint up to three persons to represent their case to the magistrate. They then had to apply for a pass from the master. If the master refused the pass, they could then leave the estate without one. The master could be fined £5 for refusing a pass or preventing the apprentices from going to summon the magistrate.

There were also checks against wasting the Special Magistrate's time. If the magistrate went to investigate a complaint, and found it frivolous, vexatious or malicious, an apprentice would be whipped or imprisoned. A guilty employer would be liable for a fine not exceeding £4. A master could confine an apprentice for up to 20 hours before being brought before the magistrate, but if the magistrate found that the apprentice was maliciously detained the master was fined £1. The fine for beating, whipping, imprisoning or putting an apprentice into stocks without the permission of the magistrate brought a fine of £5 or one month's imprisonment for the guilty.

An effort to quell any thought of group resistance by apprentices was made in the provisions against conspiracy. If three or more apprentices combined to resist the lawful instructions of the master, they could be accused of conspiracy, and receive a sentence of six months' solitary confinement in prison, or a flogging of not more than thirty-nine lashes. Drunkenness, fighting, insolence and insubordination were all punishable crimes, each carrying a sentence of one week's imprisonment or a flogging of not more than fifteen lashes. As the Emancipation Act forbade the flogging of women: women were sentenced to either imprisonment or being confined in the stocks for up to eight hours during the daytime.

Separate laws against larceny were passed two days after apprenticeship began. Every act of larceny, regardless of the value of the property stolen, was called simple larceny. The punishment for larceny was two years' imprisonment or seven years' transportation. In addition, males were to receive up to three whippings, which could be in public. A person convicted of, or proved to have the intention of, committing burglary was to be executed.

The Operation of Apprenticeship

Two weeks after the commencement of apprenticeship, the Grenada government appointed a committee comprising Louis La Grenade, John

Wells and Alexander Baillie to investigate how the apprenticeship system was working. In their report, they found nothing good to say about the apprentices. They reported that the apprentices showed less and less inclination to fulfil their religious obligations, had absented themselves from Mass and services on Sunday, and had discouraged their children from attending religious instruction given by the catechists. Many had withdrawn their children from the free schools, and seemed to have lost control of their children. Further, the laws in force had not effected any improvement in the moral fibre of the apprentices. They were less industrious and preferred to spend their time in idleness, indulging their passion for rum, or in robbing and plundering their master's property. It was also the opinion of the committee that the apprentices had been granted too much land.

Some of this might well have been true. The apprentices were coming out of an oppressive system, and more and more prized whatever opportunities they had to take their rest. The masters had introduced them to the pleasures of alcohol, and had hardly set them good examples as Christians. Why then should they go to church or let their children be instructed in the Christian faith? Generally, though, the population were peaceful, law abiding and very religious. This committee and the report it submitted may have been used as an excuse to continue the drafting of repressive legislation.

In June 1835 a piece of legislation was passed that regulated the amount of work for the apprentices. The objective of this piece of legislation was to attempt to standardize tasks to create a clear basis for the payment of wages and to provide clear guidelines for the planters and magistrates. At the same time, it would not permit planters to increase the amount of work for each field worker's daily task, and allow the unscrupulous to overwork submissive workers.

The élite lived in mortal fear of the rest of the population through the entire period of apprenticeship. Laws were made to shore up the power of the élite and their control over the rest of the population. Such law was passed by the legislature on 2 June 1836. This was the Act to Create a Local Police Force. A force of 53 constables and officers was created to assist the 826 non-commissioned officers and 97 commissioned officers of the Militia. All members of the police force and Militia were to be either white or coloured.

On 8 May 1838 an 'Act To Provide for the More Effectual Suppression of Vagrancy and for the Punishment of Idle and Disorderly Persons' was passed. Any apprentice who deliberately refused to work, and did not have any means of maintenance, was deemed a vagrant. Any apprentice who engaged in peddling, huckstering or hawking without a licence was also deemed a vagrant, as were prostitutes, and any healthy person begging alms, or encouraging children to beg. The penalty for vagrancy was one month's hard labour. Persons suspected of theft or who were repeatedly caught thieving were deemed vagrants, and tried as such. Persons deemed to be incorrigible rogues were sentenced to one year's hard labour. Many of the particularly repressive pieces of legislation were disallowed by Britain, and sent back to the legislature for revision.

The planters also objected to the way in which the Special Magistrates conducted themselves. In September 1835, a Special Magistrate by the name of T.A. Sinclair was transferred to Carriacou after difference of opinion with a planter called Harford. The planters in Carriacou were known for their harsh treatment of apprentices, and here Sinclair met further opposition to his impartial judgments, which ran counter to planter interests. Sinclair, exemplary in the performance of his duties, was defended by the Governor.

Not every magistrate was like Sinclair. Some treated the apprentices with severity, passing very heavy sentences for slight misdemeanours. One magistrate's hand was so heavy that the abundance of sentences for solitary confinement was noticed in the reports by the Secretary of State, who asked the Governor to conduct an investigation into the matter. Abuses of the apprentices also were frequent by those managers and overseers who saw the apprenticeship period as their last chance to make profit from the labour of their former slaves, or who were simply exceptionally cruel.

One of the worst examples of planter behaviour at this time was to be found in the wickedness of Dr John Brown, the manager of Clarke's Court Estate. Dr Brown, a medical practitioner, continued to put slaves in stocks even after the practice was discontinued by law. He confined slaves to hospital and administered seawater to them, claiming that it was medicine, when in fact it was punishment. His cruelty was such that he was taken to court. As often happened in cases of this kind when a white was accused of harming members of the black population, the jury acquitted Dr Brown although overwhelming evidence was heard against him. The publicity and public outcry surrounding this case, however, served to check the worst abuses.

The End of Apprenticeship

The House of Commons and the Anti-Slavery Society in Britain had both been monitoring apprenticeship very carefully. As early as 1836, it was evident that the system was not serving the purpose it had been designed to serve. The Anti-Slavery Society began to agitate for the system's premature end, holding meetings and publicizing pamphlets highlighting the abuses of the system. Eventually Parliament set up a committee to evaluate apprenticeship.

The committee found multiple abuses in the system, including excessive amounts of punishment meted out to the apprentices, the constant flogging of women although forbidden, abuse of the apprentices' free time and unjust valuation of the worth of the apprentices for the purpose of manumission. In addition, there was no protection for the Special Magistrates against lawsuits, and the practice remained to accept as legal only marriages celebrated or annotated by ministers of the Church of England. The committee also noted that the education of the children was sadly neglected.

Apprenticeship had failed not because the provisions for it were seriously flawed, but because the planters in the West Indies were not able to adjust to the idea of Emancipation. They would not accept that the apprentices needed different treatment from slaves. There was mistrust between the managers or overseers and the apprentices, and the leaders of society did not seek to create such trust. The upper classes felt threatened by the ex-slaves, and feared an uprising that would see them all slaughtered. Their reaction was to pass draconian laws and effect coercive measures. On the other hand, the apprentices did not trust the planters, to the extent that they would not accept medicines or food for their free children, in fear that such offers were traps to force them to sell the children into slavery.

The system of apprenticeship was brought to a premature end on 1 August 1838. On that date all persons living in Grenada and the other West Indian islands became free in the eyes of the law.

Notes

1 Fortesque, p. 463.
2 *Ibid.*
3 Devas (1932), p. 26.
4 Donald Hill, 'England I Want to Go: The Impact of Migration on a Caribbean Community', PhD dissertation, Indiana University, 1973, quoted in McDaniel, p. 60.
5 Edwards, p. 261.
6 Bayley, p. 351.
7 *St Andrew's Journal and La Baye Miscellany*, 1828, p. 33, British Library (BL), London.
8 See reports in the *St Andrew's Journal and La Baye Miscellany*, 1828 and 1829, BL.
9 *Ibid.*, p. 354.
10 *Ibid.*, p. 360.
11 Slave Register for St George's, Grenada, 1817, Public Records Office (PRO), London.
12 *Ibid.*
13 Slave Register for St Andrew's, Grenada, 1817, PRO.

14 Slave Register for St George's, Grenada, 1817, PRO.
15 Slave Register for St George's, Grenada, 1817, PRO.
16 *Third Annual Report of the Society for the Education of the Poor*, printed by W.E. Baker, 1827, p. 8, BL.
17 *Ibid.*, p. 9.
18 George Home, Letters held by the Scottish Record Office (SRO), Edinburgh.
19 *A Few Remarks on Colonial Legislation as connected with the Late Communications for the Noble Secretary of State for the Colonies by a Member of the Assembly of Grenada*, printed by John Sphan, 1823, BL.
20 *Grenada Free Press*, no. 226, 25 May 1831, quoted in Brizan, p. 111.
21 Burn (1970), p. 162.

8

Accommodating Free Labour

The first day of August 1838, which was the day on which the ex-slaves received their total freedom, came and went quietly in Grenada. There were no acts of violence or disorder, such as some of the élite feared. At first the freed slaves had little choice but to remain on the estates and accept the wages offered to them. Later some of the former slaves left the estates to pursue alternative ways of earning a livelihood. Thus, the decrease in labour at the beginning was marginal, and the movement away from the estates a drift rather than a rush.

The freed slaves who had a skill other than farming were the best placed to move off the estates. The census returns of 1844 showed over 8000 people working outside agriculture, mostly self-employed. Of these, 300 worked as hucksters, 308 as fishermen, 1036 as house servants, 661 as washerwomen and 1409 as seamstresses. In addition 4498 persons were employed in other trades such as porters, carpenters, masons, blacksmiths and wheelwrights. By 1881 the percentage of people in trades rose to 12 per cent of the population.

There were some estate owners who firmly believed that sugar could not be produced without slave labour, and that there was no future in sugar cultivation after Emancipation. Those who felt like this simply took their losses, shut down the estates, and went to reside in Britain, if they did not already live there. The first claim on the compensation money paid at Emancipation for the slaves was for the liquidation of long-outstanding debts to British merchants, and therefore few planters in Grenada actually received even a portion of it. Other planters looked to see how they could continue to grow sugar, or to earn money from the land in the changed economic circumstances.

In spite of the careful enumeration of slaves, after Emancipation there was much legal confusion. The authorities received many petitions insisting that persons who had their freedom before 1834 were now counted as slaves for the purpose of compensation, and on the other hand, slave owners claimed that the registrars of slaves had not enumerated slaves absent from the plantations at the time of their visit. There was confusion over which slave had belonged to which master, slaves passed over to

wives without a legal will or document, and claims for runaway slaves.
Some people claimed for 'Slaves that had been absent for many years, and
were probably dead'.[1]Slaves in the United Kingdom became free on
1 August 1833. There were petitions asking compensation for these. The
value of a slave was reckoned at £59. 6s.

The way in which the compensation money was awarded was set up
without consideration for the poorer person. Compensation money could
only be claimed in England, and it was not within everyone's means to
present their claims in person. A letter from M. Mair to Henry Hill in
London exclaims:

> If the report ... is correct; we apprehend that many poor persons
> who have only one or two apprentices and are unable either to read
> and write, and who have no friends in England will be put to great
> inconvenience and may subject themselves to complete forfeiture of
> the monies to which they may be entitled unless arrangements are
> made for the payment of their small portions of the Compensation
> in this Colony ... The blank forms of Power [of Attorney] are
> nearly exhausted and if all the compensation monies are to be paid
> in England, we shall require a large additional supply.[2]

The Special Magistrates appointed during the apprenticeship period
were retained and renamed Stipendiary Magistrates. Theirs was the task of
overseeing the transition of the economy from one based on forced labour
to one based on the wages paid to a free labour force.

To ease the transition to a society with a free labour force, several laws
to regulate the relationship between employers and free labour were
passed. In 1838 an 'Act to Better Adjust and More Easily Recover the
wages of Domestic Servants in Industry, and Other Labourers on Estates'
was passed. By the provisions of this Act, all disputes between employers
and wage earners were to be heard by two justices. Awards were limited to
three times the existing wage rate. Absence from work, misdemeanours or
misconduct by workers could bring deductions from their wages,
or imprisonment. It became another duty of the Stipendiary Magistrates to
adjudicate disputes between the worker and employers.

In the next year 'An Act for Regulating the Duties of Masters and
Servants' was passed, setting out the conditions for work contracts.
Contracts between the planters and workers were to be valid for one year,
all contracts had to be signed, or made in the presence of a Stipendiary
Magistrate. Children between ten and sixteen years could be apprenticed
for five years by their parents in a trade, or apprenticed as labourers on the
estates.

The Birth of the Grenadian Peasantry

During slavery, it was customary for the slaves to be allowed to work provision grounds, so this type of agriculture was already established in Grenada. Several estates now chose to rent or sell small plots of land for provision grounds to those who could afford it. The hope was that those who went off to farm their own pieces of land might be available for occasional work on the estates. The sale of lands also profited the owner as it brought in funds to be set against the losses of a declining sugar industry. The sale of lands did not interfere with the continuing production of sugar, as the lands sold were the marginal and more inaccessible. The willingness of the planters to sell land was welcomed by the ex-slaves. Buying land was their heart's desire, as having a plot of their own signified the real transition from slavery to independence. Renting land was much less preferred, especially after an Act was passed allowing the eviction of a tenant of less than seven years from the piece of rented land.

Those who did not have the money to rent or to buy land had to be content with yet another sort of accommodation by the estate owners, whereby labourers were allowed to remain in their houses on the estates, and to work on the estates for a reduced wage, while cultivating provision grounds which were part of the estate rent free. This arrangement provided the estate with a guaranteed supply of labour, while not alienating any land that could be devoted to sugar cultivation. The 1844 census showed that roughly 33 per cent of those who had been apprentices in 1838 still lived on the estates.

Some estates came to be worked on the metayage system. This was a system of sharecropping introduced into Grenada in 1848 when the situation of the sugar estates worsened after the passing of the Sugar Duties Act. Money was scarce at the very time when wages needed to be more attractive to retain labour, which was more and more unwilling to work on the sugar estates. Under the metayage system, the estate provided the worker with an allotment of land and the machines, stock and carts to work it. When the canes were harvested, and the sugar produced, the sugar was equally divided between the estate owner and the metayer. Usually the estate owner would purchase the metayer's share of the sugar.

In a letter dated 16 March 1854, Lieutenant-Governor Keate of Grenada remarked to Governor Colebroke of the Windward Islands that: 'The cocoa and coffee estates throughout the island are managed without exception upon the Metairie system and with success.'[3]

This was a romantic view, for this system pleased nobody. Woodville K. Marshall states that:

The use of the metayage in sugar production was limited to the attitude of many of the planters to the system. Stipendiary Magistrate Hutcheson reported in June 1850 that five out of every seven planters had opposed the introduction of the system ... Presumably the planters were opposed to any innovation which seemed likely to lessen their profits and to weaken their control over the disposal of land and allocation of Negroes' labour. The depression in the sugar industry did force some of them to adopt the system in 1850, but by the late 'fifties it seemed as though it was the coffee and, particularly, the cocoa estates rather than the sugar estates that provided a stimulus for the survival and extension of this system. The new and expanding cocoa estates which enjoyed little if any of the small-scale boom in the sugar industry needed the system and used it extensively. By 1854, nearly all the estates were being cultivated exclusively on some sort of metayage system.[4]

The metayage also suffered from the conviction of the planters that the labourers did not work hard enough, while the metayer was dissatisfied that he had to wait too long to realize the product of his labour. Despite all the problems, the metayer system continued, as planters could do no better under the economic circumstances, when labourers were unwilling to work simply as paid labour.

Up to 1855, most of the sugar estates managed to keep in production through employing wage labour or working on the metayer system, but relations between tenant, metayers and paid labour were always fraught with contention. Most of the cases brought before the courts during this period concerned disputes between labour and employers, and involved the use of abusive and obscene language, the destruction of property, disputes over wages and the breaking of contracts.

If an ex-slave wanted to leave the estate, could not rent or buy land, and was disinclined to become a sharecropper, he or she simply found a piece of Crown Land or a piece of land belonging to an estate but far away from the workings of the estates, and farmed illegally. In reaction to this practice, an Act was passed to discourage squatting. This was 'An Act to Prevent Persons Taking Illegal Possession of Planters' or of Ungranted Land' and provided for the eviction of any squatter by a Justice of the Peace. If a person was found squatting twice, that person was deemed a vagrant, and was punished.

Own-account farming and metayage were the means by which a peasantry gradually established itself. The peasantry that came into existence was quite unique. Woodville K. Marshall has pointed out the differences between this peasantry and the traditional type of peasant found elsewhere in the world.[5] Unlike other peasants, the West Indian peasant had no ties of tradition and sentiment to the land, and could not be seen as the 'rural dimension of old civilizations'.[6] It is true that white yeoman farmers worked in some islands before slavery, but none of these survived the establishment of the plantation and slave-based sugar industry. Small settlers were soon bought out by the large estates, and went to seek their fortunes elsewhere, often in the United States. Neither could the Maroons who established settlements in the bush be called peasants, as they were fugitives, always in danger of being captured and their gardens destroyed. The only antecedent of the West Indian peasantry, therefore, was

> the activity of the slaves as producers of their own food, and even of surpluses, on land granted to them by their owners. In this role the slaves were partly peasant cultivator or, as Mintz [7]calls them, 'proto-peasants'.[8]

The West Indian peasantry began in 1838 with the end of apprentice-ship, when the opportunity was provided for an independent existence for the ex-slave outside the boundaries of the estate. The peasantry would also grow to become a new and important dimension to the economic and social history of Grenada, as well as in the other Caribbean islands.

The Creation of Beggars

By the provisions of the Act of Emancipation the aged and infirm were allowed to remain on the estates until August 1839. After that they were legally no longer the responsibility of the estate owner and there was absolutely no provision for their maintenance. With the closing of some estates, and the new regulations concerning free labour, Lieutenant-Governor Doyle became very concerned at the lack of provisions of any sort to care for the aged and infirm. As early as 1838 he wrote to the Governor-in-Chief, Lionel Smith, advising that it was necessary to consider how these people would live. However, nothing was done.

After they ceased to be the legal responsibility of the estates on which they had worked, the aged and the sick who had given their youth and fitness to make money for the estate, were for the most part neglected and discarded without a thought as to how they would survive. Many became dependent on hand-outs from the charitable. In the 1840s a few almshouses were established by private funds to meet the needs of the destitute. Just as the Governor had feared, the number and extent of the misery of these unfortunate people increased.

Labour Unrest on the Estates

On account of the continuing hard times besetting the Grenadian economy and the increasing inability of the planters to meet the wage bills for workers, in December 1847 the planters in St Patrick's tried to get the workers to accept lower wages. The worker, who was currently paid between 10d. and one shilling a day, was asked to take a cut of between 2d. and 4d. per day. In 1847 one shilling could buy 3 lbs (about 1.3kg) of rice, or 4 to 5 lbs (2kg) of flour or the same of muscovado sugar or 1 lb. (about 0.5kg) of beef. A yard of unbleached calico (about 1 metre) cost 4d., and a gallon (about 4.5 litres) of kerosene oil cost 2 shillings.[9] This request for a reduction in wages was supported by the Governor, who appealed to the workers, by means of a circular, to be content with the new wage. The Governor reminded them that they occupied estate accommodation free of charge, and were allowed to farm lands on the estates.

The workers did not believe that the Governor had written the circular, as they did not believe he would have asked this of them. They thought it was a conspiracy between their employers and the Stipendiary Magistrates to get them to accept lower wages. The workers went on strike.

On 11 January 1848 several hundred labourers marched to the St Patrick's Courthouse where the Stipendiary Magistrates were meeting to discuss the strike. They attacked the constables on duty, and stormed inside the courthouse, bringing an end to the meeting of the magistrates. More constables arrived and eventually the labourers dispersed, but not without threatening to return with more supporters the next day.

Fearing an insurrection, the Chief Stipendiary Magistrate, Romney, appealed for assistance to the Lieutenant-Governor. Fifty military men were dispatched by boat to Sauteurs. They arrived to find all quiet. Assessing that the situation had the potential to become seriously disruptive, the Governor requested that a meeting of the headmen of each estate be called on the 13 January 1848. He personally addressed them in the company of a Roman Catholic priest, and explained the dire financial situation that had occasioned the decision to reduce the wages. After this meeting, most of the labourers returned to work, but others stuck to their decision to withdraw their labour.

The Causes of the Depression

The economy of Grenada had to decline further before it got better. When sugar could be sold at protected prices in Britain, the estates could survive, even though the cost of production of sugar made Grenadian sugar expensive. The costs of many sugar estates began to creep up beyond the profit margin, and estates fell into debt. One of the reasons for this was that many of the estates had absentee landlords, and were run by attorneys and managers. Some of these absentee landlords followed the financial matters of their estates very closely, but others did not. In 1844, of 152 estate owners in Grenada, only 39 resided in Grenada.[10] If more of the absentee landowners had known the true position of their business in Grenada, they might have taken some measures to try to save their estates. As it was, they continued to mortgage the estates to sustain the lavish lifestyle exemplified by the West Indian planters, whether they lived in Grenada or Britain.

To compound the effect of careless absentee ownership the estate managers who ran the estates for the disinterested absentee landlords were often quite unaware of the financial condition of the estate. All the accounting was done in Britain, and the managers simply carried out instructions. Even if they were of the disposition to warn the absentee owner of increasing debt, they could not, because they had no knowledge of it themselves, not being allowed to see the total financial condition of the estate. Douglas Hall describes such a situation for the Westerhall Plantation.[11] In many cases, too, owners put too much trust in the managers and attorneys who also spent the resources of the estates extravagantly, demanded a high salary to maintain their own comforts, and were not unknown to take as little interest as possible in their duties.

Grenadian estates also suffered as a result of British mercantile policy. This policy required that all British colonies buy goods from Britain, and discouraged import substitution. Therefore, estates in Grenada had to purchase supplies for the estates from Britain, when these could have bought at a lower cost from other countries. During slavery, when the estate was obliged to feed the slaves, food was purchased in Britain, when it could have easily been grown on the estates.

Whereas a few owners kept firm control over their managers and their estates, the lack of personal interest and the absolute trust they put in the managers, attorneys and agents in Grenada led in many cases to bad management by the untrustworthy, who were only interested in their salaries. As a consequence, no stop was put to wastages in the grinding and boiling operations, which reduced the amount of sugar produced. These managers also did not seek to introduce any cost- or labour-saving new technology on the estates. In any case, they could make no major investment decision without the permission of the owners, who might not know too much about sugar production. Some of the estates became unproductive in relation to those that were being modernized in other parts of the region. By then it was too late to think of modernization, as there were no savings and no credit for investment in new technology. As late as 1876 there were only six ploughs and seven steam engines on the seventy-nine estates in operation in Grenada. Again, agents in England made their money from sales to the estates. Thus they were not keen on economies.

Before the Sugar Equalization Act Grenada used to sell sugar to Britain at 41 shillings per hundredweight. The prices fell to 21 shillings per hundredweight by 1854, and 13 shillings per hundredweight by 1884–90.[12] It was clear to all concerned with the production of sugar in Grenada that Grenada's sugar was totally uncompetitive due both to the price of sugar on the British market and to the planter's costs of production. Grenada could no longer sell sugar even to cover the cost of running the estates, and the estates were deeply in debt.

One by one the estates ceased production and were offered for sale. Some were divided into small lots and sold to the newly emerging peasantry. Others were converted to cocoa production. But the days of sugar production were done. Between 1852 and 1882 the production of sugar declined 72 per cent. In 1833 Grenada produced 10,203 tons of muscovado sugar for export. By 1873 the amount decreased to 3168 tons. By 1878, the number of estates completely abandoned and lying fallow was thirty-two, and by 1883 Grenada was producing very little if any sugar.[13]

The Encumbered Estates Act

Recognizing the desperate situation regarding the sugar estates in the West Indies, Britain passed the 'Encumbered Estates Act' in 1854 to assist the debt-burdened and financially ruined owners of West Indian estates to sell their properties to others who had funds to invest in the estates and the economic development of the colonies. This Act was adopted in Grenada in 1866, and operated until 1885, when the Act was repealed. A court in Britain heard all claims against estates offered for sale in the West Indies, negotiated sale of the estates, ensured the new proprietor got an unimpeachable title for the estate, settled any of the proven claims against the estate, and then paid the old proprietor the balance. To facilitate the process, subsidiary courts were set up in each island under the Act. Under the Encumbered Estates Act, and between 1866 and 1885, twenty-eight estates were sold in Grenada. One gentleman, Theophilus Law, sold his four estates – Bocage, Pearls, Boulogne and Madeys – in January 1867 under the provisions of the Act.[14]

Although the Encumbered Estates Act facilitated the transfer of estates into the hands of those who might be able to bring them back into production, the strictly legal manner in which the court acted brought disaster for many small, new landowners. Many peasants had purchased lands on the outskirts of the estates. When these estates were put up for sale under the Act, their Grenada deeds to their land had to be presented to the court in London by a specified date. This they were unable to do, and the boundaries of the estates were deemed to include their plots, thereby dispossessing them without compensation and with no recourse. The provisions of the Encumbered Estates Act also meant bankruptcy for many owners of lands in Grenada. When the estates were sold, the agents in London, called consignees, who had previously sold the sugar and procured the machinery and stores and generally acted as financial brokers for the estates were given the first claim on the funds. The funds realized from the sale of the estate were often insufficient to pay even the claims of the consignee, and all others having claim on the estate, including the previous owner, were rendered bankrupt.

Land Hunger in Carriacou and Petit Martinique

Carriacou had always suffered from lack of water, and the natural dryness of the island was exacerbated by a rapid deforestation of the islands during the period of expansion of sugar, and to provide wood for building houses and boats, and for domestic use. In 1797 a spring was discovered in Carriacou, which was then kept locked by the owner of the land on which it was discovered, as it was deemed very valuable. Devas comments wryly that if this spring is still locked 'it might as well be left unlocked,'[15] since this spring was usually dry in the dry season, when water is most needed. During droughts Carriacou had to depend on supplies of water from Grenada.

Many people believed that the lack of water was due to deforestation. As early as 1829 there were campaigns to replant trees. A society called the Tree Planting Society issued a description of intense and protracted droughts in Carriacou in an article in the *Grenada Free Press and Public Gazette* of 13 May 1829. They commented that it was 'in the recollection of many of the elder inhabitants, that in former times, Carriacou was seasonable and productive'.[16]

In spite of known occurrences of slave escapes and restiveness, Carriacou was pictured as a model slave colony. In 1833 the following description was published in England:

> The model of all slave islands seems to be Carriacou. Mr McLean
> is their principal proprietor there...The total population is about

4000, of whom, 3200 are slaves. The principal production by which the Negroes make money is poultry, which they breed and send down by small vessels, which are constantly running up and down between [Carriacou] and Grenada. They cultivate provision grounds for themselves, but as the island suffers much from dry weather, they have a weekly issue of Grenada corn – six quarts each – continued from six to ten months of the year according to the produce of their grounds.[17]

When the slaves were emancipated, there was no land to which they could escape as in Grenada, as all of Carriacou was divided into estates. Many of the ex-slaves continued to work on the estates, but this work would disappear when many of the large sugar and cotton estates failed after Emancipation. When this happened, some of the estates turned to alternative crops such as limes, and some were left idle. Some of the ex-slaves got the use of idle land, and became subsistence farmers, small livestock tenders, fishermen and sailors. Carriacou soon became a land where:

A chain of ruined windmills and the remains of a number of immense and massive buildings, the fine stonework of which can only have been cut and squared under the supervision of master-masons ... bear eloquent testimony today to the sure tradition that Carriacou was once an exceedingly prosperous island, thriving on the cultivation of sugar.[18]

To compound the problem, Carriacou seemed to get even less rain. When Bishop Smith, the Roman Catholic bishop visited Carriacou in 1841, he found: 'A general crisis and extreme want unfortunately existed everywhere on the island. For an extraordinary, continual drought had, during two or three successive years, destroyed all the crops.'[19]

Bishop Smith commiserated with the people who were very poor and began a novena[20] to ask God for rain. Throughout the novena the sky remained cloudless and bright, and many laughed at the prayers, but, the bishop relates with some humour:

Soon we saw clouds appear, accompanied by loud, distant thunder; a storm was brewing and it did not delay long before breaking over Carriacou; the sky became dark, the heavens were obscured, and the rain poured down in torrents. This sudden salutary change struck us all deeply; and the Protestants believed a real miracle was taking place! Yet some of the ladies were dissatisfied that the rain had fallen so soon! One of them indeed expressed her chagrin at the sudden heavy downpour...'These Catholic Gentlemen, while begging for rain, ought to have also begged that it would not fall until we had time to get home'[21]!

Petit Martinique is a volcanic cone. It was first settled by French fishermen. Later these were joined by some of the Scottish ship-builders from the village of Windward in Carriacou, which faces Petit Martinique from across the bay. Later this community of white skinned people was joined by pirates and their descendants, who sailed into Windward to collect supplies and to repair their ships.[22] Soon two distinct communities were flourishing, the two separated by a gully running down the side of a hill. The community on the windward side was called Madam Pierre after the first owner of the island, and was populated by poor whites. Descendants of the African slaves who worked on the cotton estate in Petit Martinique populated the other community, which came to be made up of three villages – Paradise, Ceten and Kendace.

The people survived by living for and off of the sea. They were boat-builders, traders and fishermen. Very little could be grown on the tiny, dry island. Petit Martinique with its capital Sanchez was the 'last outpost' of Grenada. Its population, like that of Carriacou and Grenada, struggled for existence in an environment of fertile soil and seas teeming with fish. The knowledge, overall mechanisms and capital to grow rich off the land were missing from the equation of hardworking labour and a land that could be made productive.

Notes

1 Governor to Henry Hill esq., 7 April 1835, Colonial Office Dispatches, Grenada, 1837 Public Record Office (PRO), London.
2 M. Mair to Henry Hill esq, 21 July 1835, Colonial Office Dispatches, Grenada, 1837, PRO.
3 Letter book 1854, Lieutenant-Governor Robert Keate to Governor Colebroke, 16 March 1854, quoted by Brizan, p. 193.
4 Marshall, Woodville K. (1965), p. 31.
5 Marshall, Woodville K. (1968) p. 252.
6 *Ibid.*, quoting Robert Redfield, *Peasant Societies and Culture*, Chicago, 1956, pp. 27–9.
7 Sydney Mintz, 'The Question of Caribbean Peasantries: A Comment', *Caribbean Studies* , vol. 1, no. 3, pp. 32–4.
8 Marshall, Woodville K. (1968), p. 252.
9 Brizan, pp. 145–6.
10 Brizan, p. 147.
11 Hall, Douglas (1961).
12 Brizan, p. 147.
13 Noel Deer, *History of Sugar*, quoted in Brizan, p. 191.
14 Brizan, p. 149.

15 Devas (1974), p. 183.
16 McDaniel, p. 47.
17 From the *Bristol Mirror*, 15 June 1833, quoted in Smith (1962), p. 22.
18 Devas (1926), p. 60.
19 Devas (1932), p. 371.
20 A novena is a Roman Catholic devotion involving nine days of prayer.
21 Devas (1932), p. 371.
22 Sinclair, p. 64.

9

The Importation of Labour

Planters in Grenada longed for the former opulent times. They were convinced that their economic problems would disappear if only an adequate replacement for slave labour was found. But the return to slavery was impossible, and there was now a continual drift of workers away from the estates. Thus various schemes to recruit labour became a preoccupation of the planters. The planters in Grenada were delighted to discover a new source of labour in Africans liberated from slavers going to South America.

The Indenture of Liberated Africans

After the end of the British slave trade, Britain elicited from Spain and Portugal assurances that they also would cease the importation of slaves. After 1815 this was done officially, but nationals of these countries continued to conduct a fairly large illegal trade in slaves, especially to Cuba and Brazil. If discovered, the British would capture the ships and free the Africans being transported. In 1836 three such ships, the *Negrinha*, the *Phoenix* and another, carrying a total of 1250 Africans, were captured off Grenada. The Africans were landed and were allowed to stay as indentured workers on the plantations. A total of 3072 Africans came to Grenada in this manner between 1834 and 1865. A number of Africans were also recruited in Africa as indentured labour.

The conditions of these indentures were regulated by an Act passed in Grenada in April 1837. The provisions of the Act were that the costs incurred by landing the Africans were to be met from the local Treasury, but the planters who wanted the Africans to work for them had to pay the Treasury £1 for every African employed on their estate. The planters also had to promise that fit and proper persons would supervise the Africans; Stipendiary Magistrates were to oversee their welfare. If an African was ill-treated, the planter would forfeit the indenture, and pay the African £5 in recompense. The Africans would receive religious instruction, and their health would be attended to. The Africans were indentured for three years, and these indentures could be renewed by mutual consent. They were to be paid 5d. per day for the first year, 10d. a day for the second year, and 1s. 3d. for the third and subsequent years.

In addition to the Africans who were freed from the illicit slavers, a scheme to import labour from Sierra Leone was approved by the Colonial Office for the Caribbean from 1840. Needless to say, there was objection in Britain to this scheme by the Anti-Slavery Society, which thought that it would approximate the slave trade. The Colonial Office, under pressure from the powerful West India interest lobby, nevertheless approved the scheme in 1840. Grenada received the first indentures under this scheme in 1849 when 1057 workers arrived from Sierra Leone in four batches carried in the ships *Ceres*, *Clarendon*, *Brandon* and *Atlantic*. These Africans were indentured with three-year contracts. Later importees were indentured for five years, but after 1869 no indenture of more than three years was allowed.

Maltese and Madeira Indentures

In 1839 the Government of Grenada approved a scheme to import workers from Malta and Madeira to work on the plantations. A loan of £6000 was raised to provide for the transportation of workers from Malta and Madeira to Grenada, to give them advances by way of inducement, to pay Maltese clergymen as interpreters and to meet other expenses connected with the scheme. The ship *Inglist Naprin* brought 164 Maltese immigrants in 1839. These immigrants were distributed among fifteen estates, but it quickly became apparent that the immigrants were totally unsuitable for the work they were expected to do. The *Grenada Handbook* reports that the Maltese labourers 'were a complete failure, and in 1841 their contracts were dissolved by mutual consent, and the greater number of them went to Trinidad, some few remaining in the island becoming hucksters and porters.'[1]

The only permanent reminder of these Maltese workers is a village in St David's, called after these people, Maulti. A touching plaque paying tribute to a Maltese woman also adorns a wall in the old Roman Catholic church in Grenville.

Portuguese workers from Madeira were also tried as estate labour, and between 1846 and 1850 about 601 Portuguese[2] were indentured to estates in Grenada. An exact number cannot be given because a substantial number of these immigrants came at their own expense, and were not recorded.

Although Madeira belonged to Portugal, there was a British settlement there, composed of Jacobites seeking refuge from religious persecution in Britain. Madeira had been prosperous and famous for its wines but, as Donald Wood recounts:

By 1840 Madeira was no longer thriving; one of those unpre-
dictable changes in taste had taken place, which puzzle historians
of wine drinking; the fortified Madeirans were no longer in
fashion. Wine prices fell, and by 1845 the vineyards were
neglected. Distress grew in the countryside that proved to be a
mild foreshadowing of the disaster of 1852 when 'oideum', the
cholera of nineteenth century viticulture, appeared in the island
and wiped out the ancient grape vines.[3]

He goes on: 'In Madeira, then, were people used to agricultural labour
under a hot sun, who were known to British mercantile interests and who,
moreover were not averse to emigrating to escape from poverty.'[4]

The health of the workers from Madeira was not good. The sickness and
mortality rates of the immigrants to the Caribbean were high, especially in
the first few months. This might have been due to the conditions of famine
and poverty in Madeira, which may have reduced the capacity of the immigrant to withstand the impact of the hard field work demanded. Malaria fever
also struck down all newcomers. The workers from Madeira eventually acclimatized, but were never deemed suitable for plantation work. Within three
years of taking up field labour, most left the estates to become shopkeepers,
or had become assistants in the sugar mills. In any case, as soon as the famine
ended in Madeira, the stream of immigration to the Caribbean stopped.

The Indian Indenture Scheme

The Indenture Scheme using labourers from India[5] was set up mainly to
provide labour for Trinidad and British Guiana, which were undergoing a
period of rapid development. By 1854 news had reached Grenada and the
other Windward Islands of the industry of Indian labour in Trinidad and
British Guiana. The Grenadian planters, along with planters in the other
islands who needed labour and could afford it, became anxious to share in
this scheme. Indian immigration was sanctioned for Grenada in 1856, and
the first boat with immigrants, the *Maidstone*, arrived on 1 May 1857 with
375 workers from Calcutta. Between then and 1885 ten shipments of
workers from India, mainly from Calcutta, but some from Madras, arrived
in Grenada, with a total of 3205 persons. Most of these workers were
indentured to estates in St Patrick and St Andrew's.

Indian immigration was tightly controlled in a joint agreement
between Britain and India. It is noteworthy that the overall Immigration
Act, which permitted immigration to Grenada (Act No. 21 of 1855), contained an important new clause that immigration would only be allowed to

proceed if the laws made in the receiving colonies met with the approval of the Indian government.

Under this Immigration Law[6] there was to be an Immigration Department in each colony headed by a Superintendent or Protector of Immigrants. The Immigration Department was to exercise constant vigilance to ensure the good welfare of the Indian workers, to monitor the conditions under which they worked on the estates, to investigate all complaints and generally enforce all the provisions of the Immigration Act. This they were to do by regular inspection.

The law provided that the period of indenture would be for five years, with a nine-hour workday, and a six-day workweek. Failing to report for work and misconduct were criminal offences punishable with arrest and a fine or imprisonment for the Indian worker, with or without hard labour. The indentured Indian had to reside on the estate to which he/she was indentured, and the estate was required to provide free, good and clean accommodation, with separate apartments for the men and the women. Food was to be provided, for which 4d. weekly was deducted from wages. In addition to their wages, the Indian workers were allotted provision grounds of at least one acre. The indentured Indians were not permitted to wander more than two miles from the estate to which they were indentured without a pass. If they did and were caught, they would be liable to arrest and imprisonment.

By law, also, each estate was required to provide the services of a medical doctor who would pay regular visits to the estate to ensure the health of the workers. For this the estate was to pay the doctor one shilling a day per indentured worker. In addition, each estate was required to have its own hospital, staffed by a resident nurse and stocked with a supply of necessary medicines. If the estate could not maintain its own hospital, adequate alternative arrangements had to be made. The grant to the Colony Hospital was also increased by £200 specifically to provide care to Indian indentured workers who fell seriously ill. The grants to the mental hospital and the almshouse were similarly increased to provide care for the Indian workers who needed the services of these institutions.

Conditions of the Indians

The Governor of Grenada at this time, Kortright, wrote glowingly of the conditions in Grenada that would make it attractive to the Indian worker:

> There are several advantages this island possesses which appear trifling, but which nevertheless tend to the comfort of the labourer, accessibility of markets for the purchase or sale of

provisions, the low price of ground provisions, and the abundance of running water, the free use of which I believe the Coolies[7] consider of great importance.[8]

Again the Governor wrote:

> I am ... under the impression that with the advantages possessed by the Indian labourer in Grenada, among which I do not reckon at the least the proverbial healthiness of the island, in consequence of which very few days are lost the labourer by sickness, he will at the termination of his contract of service have saved more money than in some of the larger colonies. Ground provisions, such as yams, sweet potatoes etc., are easily produced, and it is found that the Cooly soon acquires a taste for this description of food. An arrangement has been made with the employers by which the labourers are supplied with the articles of consumption to which they are accustomed at cost price.[9]

Kortright's letters were encouraging but inaccurate. The conditions under which the Indian workers came to and worked in Grenada proved hazardous to their health. To begin with, insufficient measures were in place to protect the health of the immigrants aboard the immigrant ships. Although every effort was made to recruit only healthy persons, the voyage from India to Grenada involved several climatic changes, and lasted over three months. Disease often broke out on the immigrant ships bound for the Caribbean, and there was insufficient medical provision to deal with such occurrences.

It was estimated that 24 per cent of the people who boarded the *Maidstone* in India bound for Grenada died in transit.[10] Noting the high death rates, the authorities were made to tighten the medical care of the immigrants on board the ships and, as a result, mortality levels instantly dropped. On the *Jalawar* there were only 13 per cent deaths in transit from India, and after 1873 the mortality on board was seldom more than 3 per cent.

Another problem that beset Indian indenture was the gross imbalance in numbers between the men and women recruited for indentures. The paucity of women encouraged immorality among the workers from the moment they were recruited and living at the immigration depots in India awaiting transportation. The immorality continued aboard the immigrant ships and later in the colony. Infidelity among mates encouraged by competition for women occasioned dangerous jealousy. This jealousy led to several cases of wife-beating and wife-murder. In India it was permissible to kill one's wife for adultery. The Indian worker in Grenada could not understand that different laws pertained in Grenada.

It was not easy to effect a better gender balance of immigrants. Many estate owners were only keen to employ men, believing that men worked harder. Moreover, fewer women offered themselves for indenture. In order to ensure a more equal ratio of women to men, an Act of 1860 set a ratio of 25 women to every 100 men. This proportion was altered several times, always with the objective of effecting a compromise between the availability of women, the willingness of the estates to offer them indenture, and the dangers to the morals of the Indian worker if a reasonable gender balance was not kept. On the *Maidstone*[11] 268 males and 68 females embarked. On the *Fulwood* the proportion was a better – 194 males to 124 females.[12] On the *Jalawar* 208 males and 81 females embarked.[13]

When the Indians got to the estates to which they were indentured, they were always subjected to a strict application of the disciplinary regulations, but generally a careless and negligent attitude to the regulations ensuring their well-being. Moreover, the supervision of Indian labour by the Protector of Immigrants was neither as regular nor as thorough as it should have been. Since many of the planters and managers of the estates largely regarded Indian indentures as a replacement for slave labour, slack supervision led to abuses of Indian labour on the estates. Planters and managers had no interest in the well-being of the worker. If the worker got sick, he was cast aside. Some managers even threw sick workers off the estates, thereby sentencing them to die on the road from their illnesses.

The Excuses for Abuses

The Lieutenant-Governor tried to excuse the ill treatment of labour by blaming the decline in the economy and the impoverishment of the estates for the way in which the estates treated their Indian labourers. The financial state of the estates was no secret, and the estates were hard pressed to meet the cost of employing the labour they had indentured. By now the planters and managers should have understood the cause. They still hoped, however, that sugar would revive, because they could not conceive of any other existence. Although the Lieutenant-Governor was sympathetic to the situation, he nevertheless warned the planters and managers that, if the maltreatment of the Indian indentures continued, they would eventually suffer the consequences of their negligence. Laurence puts the cause of the impoverishment of the Grenadian sugar planter succinctly:

The smaller islands employed a labour force so small in absolute numbers as to leave very little margin for fluctuations in the prosperity of the sugar industry, so that the short-term depression was likely to cause unemployment among the indentured workers. In such circumstances in 1866 some Indians were moved from Grenada to British Guiana, and the case for indentured labour in the smaller islands could not thereafter be very strong, although the local planters did not easily accept this.[14]

The Indians were poorly housed. Each one-room house measured 12 feet by 9 feet, and was occupied by two persons. They defecated near their living quarters, no other provision having been made. They washed their sores in a pond from which they also drew drinking water, thus causing infectious diseases to spread quickly. Although the doctor was required to visit twice a week, he did not do so. One Indian with tetanus received no medical attention, and was left to die, and thirteen others who had been put on the sick list remained without medical attention for two weeks. The hospitals were too dilapidated to be of any use, and there was the unacceptable practice of the doctor prescribing medicine, and leaving the overseers and managers to administer it.

The conditions of the hospitals illustrated the extent to which the managers of the estates reneged on their obligations. In 1867 a claim was made by thirty-one estates that they maintained estate hospitals, as law required them to. However, when the Protector of Immigrants inspected these so-called hospitals in that same year, only six hospitals were up to standard. The rest were hospitals in name only. Moreover, the estates often neglected to feed the inmates of the hospitals the legal dietary prescriptions. Only threats of legal proceedings against some estate owners caused the deficiency in mandated health care to be made good.

That the health of the Indians was bad can be seen from the fact that in 1863 forty-five Indians were admitted to the General Hospital in comparison to seven Africans. The average Indian patient remained in hospital 8.74 days, while the average African patient remained in hospital 1.26 days.[15]

In 1867 a scandal broke with regard to the condition of Indian labour on the Mount Alexander Estate. Mortality on this estate was so high that a Commission of Enquiry was appointed consisting of George Gun-Munroe, the Protector of Immigrants in Grenada, George Palmer and the police magistrate for the Western District. The Commissioners condemned what they found. Of the 17 Indians assigned to that estate in February, seven had died by July. All deaths were attributable to the lack of proper health facilities, disregard for the stipulations concerning their diet, and the state of their dwellings.

Mount Alexander was deprived of its Indian labourers on the advice of the Protector of Immigrants, and they were either relocated in Grenada or invited to opt for indenture in British Guiana. It was found that Mount Alexander was not the only estate on which there was an abuse of the indenture regulations. Similar abuses were found on the Calivigny and Clarke's Court Estates in particular. Eight Indians from Calivigny Estate and four from Clarke's Court were also allowed to migrate to British Guiana.[16]

Measures to Protect the Indian Workers

A consequence of the report of the Commission of Enquiry into the conditions on Mount Alexander Estate was that the Lieutenant-Governor asked for quarterly reports from all estates employing Indian labour. The Lieutenant-Governor made it emphatically clear that legal proceedings would be taken against any estate owner who failed to honour the obligations they had taken on when they had signed up indentured labourers.

In 1869, to better protect all indentured workers, all the pieces of legislation passed in Grenada regulating immigration schemes and indentured labour were consolidated into one Act. The 114 clauses of this Act covered every aspect of recruitment: indenture contracts, conditions on the estates, care of the workers and repatriation. Improved conditions consequent on the stemming of abuses concerning indentured labour resulted in the Indian population increasing naturally for the first time. The Indian population in Grenada began to increase at a rate of about 6 per cent per year.

Nevertheless, another scandal arose in 1878 caused by inadequate supervision as laid down in the Immigration Law. On 19 March 1878, 466 immigrants arrived in Grenada on board the *Hermione* and were allotted to various estates. The *Grenada Handbook* records:

> Some of these immigrants had been located on unhealthy places, in buildings that were a disgrace to the owners, and as, through the laxity of the officer charged with their care, their employers did little to assist them with medical comforts and relief when attacked by illness, their condition became pitiable.[17]

When the condition of these immigrants was brought to the attention of the local authorities, they took swift action to alleviate their distress, but the damage had already been done.

Because of the conditions on most of the estates many of the Indians left the estates, and became vagrants. Some of the Indians were arrested. The Governor's report for the year 1863 states:

Convictions from the Provost Marshall show an increase of 64 prisoners over the convictions of the previous year. The increase has been for minor offences adjudicated by the magistrates, the greater portion of which has been for Breach of Contract.[18]

Some estate owners on hard times were glad to see some of their Indian workers leave, and never bothered to look for them to prosecute them. Many of these became destitute vagrants. In 1866 the number of vagrants in St Andrew's came to the Lieutenant-Governor's attention. He wanted to know whether the vagrants who were seen to be wandering about St Andrew's Parish in an emaciated condition had chosen vagrancy, or whether their vagrancy had resulted from the general neglect of the Indians on the estates.

Establishment of Grenada's East Indian Community

In spite of the abuses and harsh conditions, most Indian workers survived and either were able to return to India, or chose a bounty in lieu of the return passage. Of the 3205 Indians who served indenture in Grenada, 302 returned to India using the passages stipulated in their contracts. Most returned with considerable savings, which was a testament to their thrift. Another option for the Indian was to migrate to other countries, especially to Trinidad and British Guiana at the end of their contracts. The majority of Indian workers, however, remained in Grenada, re-indenturing themselves for one or two additional periods, and choosing to accept bounty money, paid to them instead of a passage home, to start bank accounts and to purchase land. Many became prosperous cocoa and nutmeg farmers, building on their experiences during indenture.

Indian indenture officially came to an end in 1893, when the last of the Indians from Grenada who had chosen repatriation shipped out, together with the last of the Indians who were returning to India from St Lucia. About 1889 Hesketh Bell, an Englishman, said of the Indians who stayed in Grenada: 'Nearly all these Coolies now possess houses and plots of land, and are generally ten times as well off as their fellows in India.'[19]

Although said to have gained a reputation of being 'respectful, thoughtful looking, industrious and careful of his means,'[20] it took a while for the Indian to be fully accepted by the rest of the population.

It is amusing to see the disdain and superiority the blacks affect in their dealings with the coolie immigrants from Calcutta and Madras. Most of them are Hindoos or Mohammedans, and as such are very much looked down upon by their black fellow labourers. Sambo's distinction between the human being and the animal creation is that one is a Christian, and the other a beast, so poor coolie, until he is baptized, is only considered to belong to the latter category.[21]

Perhaps due to the fun made of them, perhaps due to isolation from India, and perhaps partly due to the proselytizing of the Christian churches, the Indians who settled in Grenada soon began to adopt the ways of the creole society, hoping for acceptance. The Indian workers adopted creole dress and speech patterns, became fluent in the French creole spoken by the working class up to about 1920, and participated in the folk culture, including the creole dances and folk religion. Bell relates what he found on a visit to a grotto, and what he was told by his guide:

> From the queer looking odds and ends about the place, I made sure that I was in a temple dedicated to some mysterious rites and ceremonies, and, in fact, my guide informed me that frequently Africans, old Creoles, and sometimes coolies, came here to pray and dance.[22]

The Work of the Canadian Presbyterian Mission

Most active in the work of Christianizing the Indian workers was the Presbyterian Church. Kenneth James Grant was a famous Canadian Presbyterian missionary who devoted the greater part of his life to proselytizing and educating the Indians in Trinidad. It was his dream to establish training schools for teachers and preachers in Trinidad to produce men to labour in Grenada, St Lucia and Jamaica.

The Reverend James Muir became the pastor of the Presbyterian Church in Grenada in 1884. He had already seen the work of the Canadian Mission among the Indian workers in Trinidad, and observing that the Indian workers in Grenada were both unbaptized and uneducated, his immediate resolve was 'to do something for the twelve or fifteen hundred East Indians settled in Grenada'.[23] Thus, as soon as Trinidad was in a position to offer native missionaries who could speak both Hindi and English, the Presbyterian Church in Grenada applied to Trinidad for catechists and missionaries to work among the Indian workers in Grenada.

Muir was able to get Lal Beharrysingh, the first Indian from Trinidad ordained as a minister in the Canadian Presbyterian Mission Church, together with two others, to visit Grenada in 1884, to establish a Mission to the Indian workers in Grenada. The Mission was inaugurated at a public meeting in St George's, and soon after began to receive aid in the form of money and personnel.

Muir had hoped to build twelve centres in the areas where the Indian workers had settled. The centres would serve both as schools for the Indian children, and as places where services could be held. However, he was transferred, with only three centres completed. He was succeeded by the Reverend Charles Stephen, who was unable to complete the expansion as the church became plagued with money problems.

Although the Presbyterian Church made the greatest efforts to win converts among the Indian workers and their families, the Anglican and Roman Catholic Churches also made converts. Soon the practice of Hinduism and Islam disappeared completely.

Immigration Fails to Save the Economy

The period of indentured labour into Grenada coincided with very hard times for the island. Between 1855 and 1889 the Government of Grenada spent approximately £133,000 on immigration, which they financed through loans and revenue. This enormous amount of money was spent because the planters erroneously blamed the hard times on the lack of labour. Rather, the economic decline was due to Grenada's technological backwardness, capital shortage, poor management, and the changing market conditions. The money might have been better spent on improving the methods of production of the major crops and seeking methods to diversify the economy. However, the planters were fixated in their idea that more labour was the answer to their economic woes.

Some indentured workers helped in the conversion of some estates from sugar to cocoa. As the success of the cocoa estates became obvious, more and more estates converted to cocoa, so that by 1878 cocoa cultivation had surpassed sugar in its importance to the economy, and there were more acres in cocoa than in sugar. In 1860 the export earnings from sugar were £95,000 and £17,000 from cocoa. In twenty years, by 1880, the earnings from sugar were £25,000, while the earnings from cocoa were to rise to £125,000.

But the main purpose for Indian immigration into Grenada was to try and save the island as a sugar producer. This did not happen. Nevertheless, through the Indian Indenture Scheme Grenada received an injection of persons who would add diversity to the culture, and who would provide a good example to others in the manner in which they improved themselves through industry and thrift.

Immigration of Barbadian 'Poor Whites'

Indian indenture was the largest effort at procuring labour, but not the only one attempted at this time. Grenada also tried to obtain labour from Barbados. Barbados had quickly become the most densely populated of the Caribbean islands, and with the decline of sugar was suffering from overpopulation and attendant unemployment and under-employment. Among the poorest were the descendants of indentured labourers sent to Barbados from Scotland and Ireland in the seventeenth century. During slavery, these 'poor whites' had played a fairly important role in the life of the colony, including serving in the Militia, in which at this time only whites could serve. Emancipation had utterly ruined the poor white segment of the population, as they could no longer rent land at the inflated rates, and lost their holdings. Many were prevented from starving by liberal aid from parishes.

In 1859 Governor Hincks of Barbados outlined a scheme to the Secretary of State whereby 500 to 1000 of the poor white population of Barbados would be resettled in other islands and given land of between 5 and 10 acres. Grenada was the only island that accepted the idea of white Barbadian immigration. The Governor was of the opinion that Barbadian farmers would become an industrious farming community and thus an asset to Grenada. The Executive Committee shared his view, provided the scheme involved the island in no expense. Grenada was prepared to settle the Barbadians on 2000 acres of Crown Land in the vicinity of the Grand Etang, 'at an elevation suitable to "European Constitutions".'[24]

Although this scheme was never officially instituted, unofficial immigration of poor whites from Barbados began around 1861 and continued for ten years. A total of approximately 4600 people migrated from Barbados to Trinidad, Tobago, Grenada, St Vincent and St Lucia, and to Bequia in the Grenadines.[25]

The poor whites migrating to Grenada did not settle in Grand Etang, as had been previously suggested. The original settlers were a small group of about a dozen men and women who were recruited to work on the Mount Moritz cocoa plantation on the west coast, about three miles from the town of St George's. Other poor whites from Barbados came to join those already in Grenada, settling almost exclusively on the west coast. During the 1880s many Barbadian poor whites were living on the Grand Mal and Beausejour Estates. Eventually most of the original settlers and their descendants settled in Mount Moritz, especially after leasehold land became available there.[26] Because of the concentration of poor whites in this area, all poor whites from Barbados became known as 'Mount Moritz Bajans' or disparagingly as 'Mong-Mong'.

Other poor white immigrants from Barbados may have come in under different schemes, such as the scheme of the Victoria Emigration Society in 1897 to assist indigent poor white women to find a better life outside Barbados. However, migration between the islands before independence was not easy to track, as there was little regulation of movement between territories, particularly between the British territories.

In the 1930s the majority of the Mount Moritz Bajans were still poor, hardworking market gardeners, cultivating plots of land seldom bigger than one and a half acres, disregarded and treated with scorn by the rest of the population. H. Gordon Andrews states that the rest of the population of Grenada so looked down on these people that: 'No mulatto or black who may consider himself of good class would inter-marry with one of these whites, so great is the contempt in which these poor unfortunates are held'.[27] When they came to town to sell their produce, children shouted at them, 'Poor Backra' or 'Backra Johnny',[28] or sang a little song:

> Cricket gill and dry barnabis'
> Good enough for poor backra.

Which, in English, means that a diet of cricket wings and dried homemade biscuits was good enough for the poor white.[29]

In the census of 1946 the Mount Moritz Bajans made up 90 per cent of the persons enumerated as white. Slowly, the Mount Moritz Bajans forsook the land for employment in town, where they were valued as hardworking, honest employees. Although still living in Mount Moritz, they have now become absorbed as part of the Grenadian community. The community was greatly reduced during the last years of the Gairy Government and during the People's Revolutionary Government when there was massive migration of this community mainly to Brisbane, Australia. These Grenadian immigrants have formed a distinctive West Indian community in Brisbane.

A Cosmopolitan Society

Very soon, Grenada's society was cosmopolitan in composition. The indentured Africans would soon blend in with those whose ancestors had arrived as slaves, renewing elements of African culture in Grenada. The Indians, although retaining many Indian traditions, would also adopt enough of the local lifestyle to be accepted as part of Grenadian society. The Maltese and poor whites were marginal to the population, and lived slightly removed from the mainstream of culture until the second half of the twentieth century.

Although a sharing of culture took place between the ethnic groups that made up Grenada's population by the end of the nineteenth century, a more serious rift in the culture kept Grenadians apart. Grenadians were to continue to be separated by the twin evils of racial and economic discrimination, which had its roots in slave society, and now flourished in a society on the brink of the modern era.

Notes

1   Govt of Grenada, *Grenada Handbook*, p. 42.
2   Roberts and Byrne.
3   Wood, pp. 101–2.
4   *Ibid.*
5   Much of the information on Indian workers in Grenada first appeared in my article 'East Indian Indenture and the Work of the Presbyterian Church among the Indians in Grenada', *Caribbean Quarterly*, vol. 22, no. 1, March 1976, pp. 28–39.
6   'An Act to Alter the Law of Contracts with regards to Immigrants, and for the Encouragement of Immigration, and for General Regulation of Immigrants', in *British Parliamentary Papers*, Sessions 1856–58, vol. 13, pp. 145–70, Sixteenth General Report of the Emigration Commissioners, Appendix 62.
7   The term 'coolie' was extensively used to identify indentured labourers from India, or their descendants. The term in the modern Caribbean is pejorative and racial, and is not used except to insult.
8   Kortwright to Governor-in-Chief of the West Indies, 7 August 1857, in the Appendix to the 18th Emigration Report, p. 250.
9   *Ibid.*, letter dated 22 Oct. 1857.
10 *British Parliamentary Papers*, 18th General Report of the Emigration Commission. Appendix 17, p. 97.
11 *Ibid.*
12 *Ibid.*
13 *British Parliamentary Papers*, 20th General Report of the Emigration Commission, Appendix 26, p. 112.
14 Laurence, p. 16.
15 *British Parliamentary Papers*, 20th General Report of the Emigration Commission, Appendix 26, p. 112.
16 Govt of Grenada, *Grenada Handbook*, p. 47.
17 *Ibid.*, p. 50.
18 'Reports made for the year 1863 to the Secretary of State from the Governor of the British Colonies', transmitted with the Blue Book for 1863, Part 1, HMSO, 1865, p. 43.
19 Bell, p. 128.
20 Scott, p. 80.
21 Bell, p. 43.
22 Bell, p. 39.
23 Grant, p. 161.
24 Roberts, p. 251.
25 *Ibid.*
26 Sheppard (1977), p. 98.
27 Andrews, p. 49.
28 This is an appellation common in the Caribbean for 'a white man'.
29 Andrews, p. 49.

10

The Lot of the Rich: The Lot of the Poor

The Nature of Society

Emancipation found Grenadian society rigidly stratified. The society had three major sectors: the white, the freed coloured and the slave. Each of these major sectors had further internal differentiations between groups of people who set themselves off from one another for reasons of perceived differences, usually based on gradations of colour and wealth. Each sector had distinctive lifestyles and social expectations.

This social structure had been created by the demands of a society based on the ownership of many slaves by a small élite. Although there were several instances of slave resistance, this powerful élite had been able to instil a conviction in most people of the superiority of everything white and European, and the shamefulness and depravity of everything black and African. This social hierarchy was thus held together by both fear and power, and a belief that one could improve one's social position by becoming more European in any way possible. Social control was also exercised by encouraging individualism. Thus slaves, who expected to be rewarded for the information they gave to their white masters, often exposed the secrets of other slaves who were planning revolts.

The social structure was almost caste-like, with a virtual impossibility of escaping from one section to a higher one. The élite were white and, after the Fédon Revolution, of British stock. They visited Britain as often as they could, and sent their children to school there. It was in Britain that they sought their spouses, although they were quite happy to romance the brown-skinned or black local girls and add to the free coloured population. The white élite, believing that they were inherently superior by virtue of their colour, despised the coloured population, regarding it as a spurious race, even though they added to it through liaisons made by white males with coloured or black women.

The free people of colour, neither white nor black, acted as a buffer between the élite and the majority of the population. They tried to raise their status in the eyes of the white élite by copying the lifestyles of the white population, within the means that they had. They nevertheless maintained some of their African and French heritage. Some were well educated, wealthy and well mannered. For example, at least one free coloured family in Carriacou held considerable land, and were quite wealthy. Judith Phillip of Carriacou owned 119 slaves in 1829. Her estate was managed by John Dallas, a white man, who was a Major in the Carriacou regiment, and with whom Judith Phillip had children.[1]

The Africans imported as slaves were acculturated to European ways, and to the unique culture of the plantation society, as part of the process of 'seasoning', which was the process of fitting them for their new status. The slaves were Christianized by the French and became devout Roman Catholics, and the humblest section of the population became the most religious. After the British consolidated their position in Grenada, many slaves learnt English, but all spoke a French patois, which contained many African words and phrases. Just before full Emancipation, some would become members of the Church of England, or Methodist Church, but eventually all in Grenada would espouse one Christian religion or the other. Nevertheless, the lowest section in the hierarchy of stratification remained the most African in culture, and was the keeper and caretaker for the African traditions that would later become recognized as an important part of Grenadian culture. The lowest segment, made up of ex-slaves, retained so much of Africa in their behaviour that in the 1950s a debate began as to whether Grenada and societies like Grenada were one society with enough commonalities for a single culture to be recognized, or a plural society with parallel cultures – one culture based on European culture and practised by the upper class, and the other based on the culture of Africa and practised by the lower class.[2]

This rigidly stratified society persisted after Emancipation. Gradually, however, the rigidity of the system was replaced by subtler prejudice, and the stratification based strictly on ascription gradually softened to allow a degree of social prestige based on achievement. This change was very, very gradual – the social divisions among Grenadians would persist for many decades and the remnants can still be noticed in social behaviour in modern Grenada. The value of being as British as possible and expressing loyalty to the British Crown also became an important element in the formation of the Grenadian society, and a common thread binding all the people together. This element of unity would remain until Britain declared Grenada an independent territory.

Stratification in Grenadian society according to colour, financial status and cultural heritage meant differing life chances for the population. The élite had a better chance of living to adulthood, receiving a good education, getting a good job, and becoming financially independent. The life chances declined as the person ranked less and less high in the social hierarchy. In spite of the difference in lifestyles, however, Grenadian society held together because most people accepted their lot, and overall there was the belief that they all belonged to the same system – everyone was a citizen of Great Britain.

Differing Lifestyles

Because of the vast differences in wealth among the people of Grenada, there were glaring contradictions in the way the whites and the coloureds lived in Grenada as compared to the ex-slaves. Lifestyle was so important to maintain that, even after the plantations started to fail, the lifestyle of the élite remained lavish often beyond that which they could match in England. Many families sold all they had, spent their fortunes, and ran into debt just to maintain their standard of living. Many planters opened businesses to supplement the income from the estates, and to allow their lifestyles to continue. The white élite lived mostly on their estates scattered over the island. Some of the whites were lawyers, doctors and businessmen but were landowners as well. Some lived on their estates in the country, but also had town residences to provide for their comfort when their business brought them into the capital. Eventually, some families faced financial disgrace, and had to live the life of 'respectable poor'.

They were anomalies in a society where whiteness of skin meant money in the purse. There were whites who were sailors, soldiers and bookkeepers and other clerks, schoolteachers and other tradesmen. They lived a life of the 'respectable poor', and were disparaged and ill-treated by the élite. The details of a case of frightful advantage taken of a poor white artisan by the Chief Justice of Grenada survives in a 1830 pamphlet published to try to raise funds for the support of John Laurence, a painter and Venetian-blind maker. John Laurence was a German by birth, who had been recruited to serve in the British Army in 1795. His regiment – the 60th Regiment – had been sent to Grenada, and when it was withdrawn in 1802 Laurence requested a discharge and set himself up in business as a painter and Venetian-blind maker. Twenty years later he got into an altercation with the Honourable Jeffrey Hart Bent, the Chief Justice, who refused to pay him the agreed amount for some blinds he made for him. However he tried, he could get no redress for the wrongs done him as he pursued payment for the work done. From 1821 he was blacklisted, and no one gave him any further work. Laurence ended his life blind, penniless and victimized by a government officer who felt that 'I am Chief Justice of this island, and any person must do what I order him'.[3]

Some widows and spinster women without means ended their lives in the Victoria Almshouse for indigent white women. Later the white migrants from Barbados joined the longer established group of poor whites and Maltese who came in as farmers, and later drifted into other low-level jobs. These shared the disparagement of the small community of poor whites that were a part of the society they met.

The houses of the élite were large and furnished with the best of English furniture, or with excellent copies of such furniture made out of the best West Indian wood. Each household had a retinue of servants to attend to every need and comfort. Eileen Gentle, whose father and uncle started the firm of McIntyre Brothers, recalls that

> At the beginning of the twentieth century, most households employed a cook, one or two housemaids (depending on the size of the house), a nurse for the young children, yard boys, a gardener, a butler and a chauffeur. (A laundress would usually be hired on a daily basis.) They worked long hours for low wages and their meals, and had very little free time … the maids and butlers who waited at the table were trained in a rigid set of rules, as any negligence on their part would reflect badly on their employers.[4]

The grounds of the houses were tastefully landscaped, with manicured lawns, artificial rivulets, bowers and footpaths. The food eaten was the best quality Grenada could provide, and the best European wines and spirits, along with the best Grenadian rum, graced the tables. The clothes they wore were mostly imported from Britain, although local seamstresses and tailors were employed to make clothes for the élite where clothes suitable for the tropics could not be had in England. Each house had a livery stable where the horses and buggies were kept for transportation.

Except for deciding what the meals should be, and managing the household servants, the women of the élite lived a life of comfort, pleasure-seeking, and indolence. Again from Eileen Gentle we have an account of the elaborate entertainment the élite put on for each other. There were formal dinner parties, tennis parties, and tea parties, at which the best that money could buy were provided. At the tea parties, for example:

> The best silver tea services and cutlery were used, the cups and saucers were of the finest porcelain, and a dainty embroidered linen tea napkin was at each place setting. The large dining tables

groaned under the weight of numerous dishes ... The maids wore black dresses with pretty lace-trimmed white aprons and caps while serving at tea parties.[5]

Many wives entrusted the care of their children to nursemaids, some from the moment of birth. The men played a more active role on the plantation, overseeing the works and the clerical employees, and networking with other members of the élite to discuss market trends for Grenada in produce, the government of the country, and the financing of the plantation. The plantation owner was like a prince, and often served as legislator, negotiator, jury and judge for minor disputes among those who worked on the plantation, as well an interpreter of the laws of the country that governed them. Concerning the latter, he often interpreted the laws to suit himself. However, where the planter had a social conscience, there were benefits for those working with that particular estate. The training that the servants received in their employment would be of benefit to them throughout their life. Not only would their jobs be secure, but also if for any reason they were in need of a job, evidence of their training would be their best reference. In addition, they were assured of food, clothes and shelter of a quality not assured to agricultural worker or peasant. The servants were socialized into a British colonial way of life, and by exhibiting correct behaviour and better speech patterns, they were regarded by the élites and by the rest of society as being more 'cultured'. Because of the status thus gained, the servants tried to instil the 'manners' they had learned in the great house into their children. Thus were the values of the élites passed down, and thus was the society unified.

Good masters and mistresses also insisted that the children of the household respect the servants. In many cases, the servants were allowed to correct the children if they misbehaved, and their word was accepted by the parent against the child. When servants grew old and could no longer work, they were kept on as 'retainers' in the household, and assumed a special status.

Some estate owners also had commercial establishments that bought cocoa and nutmegs from farmers and sold groceries and other goods. If they had the trust of the people they dealt with, the businesses owned by the planters also acted as bankers for the community:

The small landowners who took their produce to McIntyre Brothers for sale would use the money they received to purchase groceries and other merchandise from the store. Sometimes they received more money than they needed to use at the time and as the only banks in Grenada were in St George's, they would ask for the surplus to be kept for them in the safe at McIntyre Brothers. On other occasions, they would need more money than their produce had been sold for and would get an advance against future deliveries. Very careful accounts had to be kept for each client and a sort of mini-bank was established ... Not only did my father and uncle seem to be the 'keepers of the purse' for all the people of the area, but they seemed to be the main source of advice and help for the poorer members of the community who would come to discuss their problems. They would ask about their rights regarding trespassing on land, molestation by neighbours, and problems concerning livestock, taxes and boundaries. If my father or uncle did not know the answers, they would enquire from the appropriate authorities and advise those who had enquired.[6]

This relationship between the agriculturalists and gentry worked when the member of the élite concern was honest. Unfortunately, many were not honest, and many small landowners or peasants would become victims of the unscrupulous.

The coloured population lived mainly in the towns. Their houses and furniture were modest, and they dressed as finely as they could afford. The better-off could afford to employ a domestic servant or two, or to buy services, such as those of washerwomen. Free coloureds were a part of the Grenadian population very soon after the settlement of Grenada, and their numbers increased, until the group established its own identity, *raison d'etre*, respectability and endogamy,[7] although sexual encounters between this group and the white élite men never ceased.

It had been a tradition among white fathers to give their coloured offspring some education, sending them to Britain to school in some instances. This gave their coloured sons and daughters a jump-start in society, because of their lighter skin-tone and their superior education. For education was the key to social mobility among the free coloured, as it opened up the possibility of becoming professional, respected and respectable. Education was therefore highly prized by this group, and as a result, some of Grenada's coloured population were well educated and highly literate, and had been so for decades. The demand for educational opportunities in Grenada would come from this group.

Other coloureds were less literate, but highly skilled artisans, hucksters and tradesmen. Most had to work hard to earn a living, and were always on the edge of poverty, as they were a proud people, vying with each other to possess every material thing that would enable them to live in a manner close to the lifestyle of the élite.

Although there were some ex-slaves in the town making a living as servants and manual workers, most of the ex-slaves lived the lives of independent subsistence farmers in the rural areas. Their standard of living was very low. They did not have access to health care or education, and their farms did not permit much money to be earned for the provision of essentials, much less luxuries.

For many years, the lower classes were subjected to harsh punishment for the slightest infraction of the laws. The treadmill kept in the yard of the gaol continued to operate. Conditions in the gaol were terrible. Prisoners were locked up for twelve hours without any light during the night. In 1867 Governor Mundy had to intervene, and request that the legislature remedy the 'pernicious' defects in the prison system, so that 'the responsibility for any continued neglect may not rest with the Government'.[8]

Everyone suffered from the lack of cleanliness in Grenada. The risk that Grenada took with the health of its citizens had to be brought to the attention of the legislature by Lieutenant-Governor Freeling. He deplored the continuing practice of dumping excreta on the beach on the Market Square side of town, creating: '[a] reeking mass of decomposing matter emanating day and night poisonous odours, and which is occasionally removed by the prisoners, the process being to haul it into the sea, but soon to be washed up again.'[9] Although he recommended the construction of two jetties into the sea beyond the low water mark to permit the 'night soil', as the excreta was euphemistically called, into deep water, and better sanitary conditions in both the towns and rural areas, better conditions were slow in coming.

Eileen Gentle describes some of the conditions under which the lower classes lived around 1928.

> The poorer people did not have pipe-borne water in their homes, and would get the water for drinking and cooking from public taps in the town, but for all other purposes they used the rivers. They bathed in the rivers, washed their clothes in them and used both the riverbanks and seashores for disposal of their waste of all sorts. The rivers and seas were undoubtedly highly polluted ....[10]

They were the last to be educated, as they did not seek it even when it was first made available to them, because the type of education offered did not lend itself immediately to financial self-improvement.

In many cases it was evident that the British government and its civil servants were much more interested in the poor Grenadian than was the Grenadian of some means. The Grenadian of means also cared little for the sanitation of town and country. The combination of the lack of interest of those who controlled the government, the unhealthy living conditions of the poor, and the lack of sanitation were to culminate in the worst epidemic Grenada has ever experienced. The latter half of the nineteenth century would bring a gradual opening-up of opportunities for the free coloureds in Grenada, and to a lesser extent the population referred to as black, as social services were provided for the poorer people of Grenada by their government, but at the insistence of Britain.

Education for All

At Emancipation the seventeen British colonies in the West Indies were granted £18,200 by the British government for the education of the ex-slaves. Of this, Grenada was allocated £800.[11] This amount was divided between the Anglican and Methodist Churches and used for the erection of schools in the capitals of the parishes and in the most populated areas of Grenada. Although the intention of Britain was that the ex-slaves were to be taught trades and other skills to help them earn a living and become useful to society, this intention was subverted locally. The schools set up for the ex-slaves concentrated on religious instruction, and taught little else that would have bettered the lot of the children who attended them. Suspecting that education in the colonies was far from progressive, and much less than what had been intended under the Negro Education Act, the British government appointed Charles Latrobe to visit the Caribbean, observe the system of education and to provide a report.

Charles Latrobe's report was delivered in 1838. He reported that education in Grenada was designed to provide the estates with a better labour force, and no effort at all was being made to educate the minds of the pupils. He blamed the government for denying the children the chance for a real education that would improve their minds as well as to fit them for industrial as well as agricultural tasks. Little notice was taken of his very valid criticism.

The funds from the Negro Education Act were discontinued in 1845, as these funds had been provided only for a limited time. The British government had expected that the legislatures of the various territories would vote funds to continue to provide for the education of the people. In the six years after the cessation of funds from the Negro Education Act, the Grenada legislature provided some funds to the already existing schools, but these funds were inadequate to keep the schools functioning. Shortfalls were made up by voluntary contributions from church members. As the years went on, the contributions of the government were only marginally increased, and the provision of expanded educational services was virtually taken over by the churches. For example, in 1851 funds were granted to construct a schoolhouse in Carriacou to house eighty-five children, but in 1879 it was Father Aquart, the parish priest of Carriacou and Petit Martinique, who founded the school on Petit Martinique.

In 1857 Lieutenant-Governor Robert Keate caused an Education Act to be passed, in reaction to the ineffectiveness of the school system. Under the provisions of the Act, a Board of Education was established to oversee matters pertaining to education in Grenada. The Lieutenant-Governor chaired the Board himself, and ensured that both Protestant and Catholic members served on it, in recognition of the fact that the majority of the population was Catholic, and of the increasing role of the Roman Catholic Church in providing education for the people of Grenada.

The Education Act prescribed the establishment of a Boys' Grammar School, and a Girls' Grammar School, both for the education of middle and upper class children. It also prescribed the establishment of a Model[12] School for the training of teachers, and a Normal[13] School for children of the lower classes whose parents wished to educate them. The Board was responsible for the appointment of the Principals of these schools. The Board would also apportion the distribution of the vote made for education by the legislature, which was increased to £2000. Each parish priest was to serve as the patron of the school attached to his parish, and he was immediately to select a teacher to be trained in the Model School. Arrangements were to be made by the Board for the inspection of schools, backed by bylaws if necessary. The Principal of the Grammar School was to provide an annual report on the educational system.

The first Principal of the Boys' Grammar School was J. Noble. In his first annual report, he stated that even children in the most advanced classes did not know the common arithmetic tables, could not count up to twenty, nor could they name the days of the week or months of the year. Many schools lacked books, and, when available, these were not standardized, thus making teaching very difficult. Also lacking were maps and desks. He also found that the syllabus hardly differed for children of all ages, abilities and levels of attainment.

Noble's report is important not only because it surveyed the conditions in the schools, but also because it captured the attitudes of the middle and upper classes to education and to teachers. Noble was of the opinion that the elementary school teacher was an agent of social change and an instrument of progress, but that teachers were not regarded in this way by the leaders in society. The middle and upper classes saw the role of the teacher as simply to instil in their pupils a respect for authority and for the status quo. They regarded it as a mistake to educate the lower classes, as they thought that this would make them averse to estate labour, and make them ambitious to improve themselves. It was also thought that, if some of the lower classes became educated, they would regard their fellow labourers as beneath them and withdraw themselves from the class to which they properly belonged. Noble wondered why the teachers persisted in turning up to teach, given the conditions in the school and the prevailing attitudes in society against teachers and popular education. He sympathized with the members of the lower classes who saw no value in sending their children to school when the system of education in Grenada was meaningless, chaotic and futile.

The Assembly accepted Noble's report, and the Board of Education was given the responsibility of putting the recommendations he had made in his report into effect. However, changes were made so slowly that in 1862 Governor Kortwright was able to write that the Education Act of 1857 as well as two subsequent Acts had not produced a satisfactory system of education.

Noble himself was a victim of the society of the day. He valiantly tried to improve the rural schools, because he regarded primary education to be more important than secondary education, as it involved the mass of people. However, his workload as Supervisor of Schools as well as Principal of the Grammar School was simply too heavy. As a consequence, the Grammar School was neglected, and Noble was accused of inefficiency. Noble resigned, but his successor could not manage the workload any better. The Grammar School was closed in 1862.

In 1862, also, the legislature did not provide the usual education grant, causing great hardship to the schools. The churches continued to support the schools the best they could. The next year the legislature granted £500 for the schools that continued to operate in 1862, and £900 for the schools that were operating in 1863. The Grammar School reopened in 1865, but did not prosper. The attendance fell from twenty-three to sixteen.

A Commission of Enquiry was set up in 1866 to look into the operation of not only the Grammar School, but also all schools, and the functioning of education in Grenada. The Commission found that the tuition of the Grammar School was adequate for its purpose, but that parents of prospective students could not meet the fees. For this and other reasons, the Grammar School was to reopen and close several times during the next sixteen years. The Commission recorded that there were twenty-six primary schools and one secondary school (the Boys' Grammar School) catering to the young population of Grenada. Of the primary schools, eight were run by the Church of England, seven by the Roman Catholic Church, five were Methodist primary schools, and six were government primary schools. All schools receiving government grants were later to become known as grant-aided schools. Some schools received no government support at all and were funded entirely by the churches or by private donations.

By 1878 the number of primary schools in the island had increased to thirty-one, with an attendance of 3421, or about 30 per cent of the school-age population. The Grammar School continued to run with only eight pupils, and in contrast to the average grant of £37 per child per year in a primary school, the government granted £57 per child per year for attendance at the Grammar School: such was the influence of the upper classes.

In 1878 Roman Catholic nuns of the order of St Joseph of Cluny opened a secondary school for girls in St George's. This school was called the St Joseph's Convent. The opening enrolment was 145 pupils. The school was funded by the fees from the students and by funds obtained through the Roman Catholic Church. This was the first chance for many coloured girls of the Roman Catholic faith to get a first-class secondary education.

The opening of the Convent School heralded the close of the Grenada Girls' School. So many girls were withdrawn from the government school to be sent to the Convent that there were insufficient numbers to make the effort at maintaining the school worthwhile. There was the added problem of replacing the headmistress with a suitable person, as the English headmistress of the Grenada Girls' School had resigned, and a replacement could not be found. In addition, the school was not supported as envisioned by the previous government, and the number of pupils was decreasing instead of increasing. The Governor pointed out that there were three other schools catering for girls: the St Joseph's Convent, Miss Allen's School and Miss Bertrand's School. The government exhibitioners enrolled in the Grenada Girls' School would be transferred to whichever of the three schools their parents chose.

On learning that the Grenada Girls' School would be closed, the Archdeacon of the Church of England drew up a proposal to start a girls' school at once. It was acknowledged that a grammar school education could only be had at the St Joseph's Convent, the other two schools being more in the line of 'finishing schools', but the Archdeacon felt that the closing of the Grenada Girls' School would put the parents of his congregation in a quandary, because they wanted a good education for their children, but would not want them to attend a Catholic school. The Archdeacon requested and obtained permission to rent from the government the building known as 'Bachelors Hall' on Simmonds Street, that then held the Grenada Girls' School. The government had intended that this property should be renovated for the Chief Justice, but nevertheless gave the Church of England a temporary lease. The government also agreed to an initial grant for the school, as a grant had been made to the

St Joseph's Convent. However, the continuance of the grant would depend on whether the school could maintain an enrolment of fifty pupils: £2 per head would be deducted if the enrolment fell short of this.[14] Thus was the St George's High School for Girls, run by the Anglican Church, started on 26 January 1891. Later it became the Victoria Girls' High School, then the Church of England High School, and much later the Anglican High School.

In 1882 Governor Harley was instrumental in introducing and passing 'the 1882 Education Code of Rules and Ordinance' which was to effect some major changes in the educational system. This piece of legislation provided for the extension of primary education and the provision of adequate standard grants to all church schools where the Christian religion was taught. The Anglican Church had been disestablished in 1874, and under this Ordinance all church schools would benefit equally. This put an end to the greater share of the government grant going the way of the Church of England schools. Schools were now to be divided into classes or standards, and better arrangements made for the training of teachers. This Act also separated the duty of Inspector of Schools from the Principal of the Boy's Grammar School. The Inspector would not only be responsible for school inspection and an annual report on education in Grenada, but he would also be responsible for controlling and administering the education grant of £3000, which was placed at the disposal of the Education Board. It was felt that this would be a more effective means of getting value for money. Finally, the Ordinance called for measures for the better training of teachers. The Inspector would also be responsible for administering the pupil-teacher examinations.

Over the years, the number of primary schools was increased, and the percentage of children attending school rose. During the administration of Governor Sendall six new government primary schools were built at Concord, Birchgrove, Grand Roy, River Sallee, Belvidere and Hillsborough in Carriacou. In addition to building new schools, money was also provided to the older government schools and the grant-aided schools for repair, enlargement and rebuilding. In 1888 an Ordinance made attendance at primary school compulsory for children, although this Ordinance was to be honoured 'in the breach' for a long time.

Realizing that education is more than the number of schools, Governor Sendall sent for Horace Deighton, the headmaster of Harrison College, Barbados, to carry out a comprehensive study of Grenada's education system, and report on his findings. Among the defects uncovered by Deighton was that the Board for Education had not drawn up the rules and regulations for the governance of grant-aided schools as they had been asked to do. There was no understanding of the concept of school organization, and learning was mainly by rote or memorization. There were no infant schools, and insufficient numbers of children attended school, most of these irregularly. However, little heed was taken of Deighton's report, and further educational reform would have to wait for the next century.

The Health of the Nation

This was the era during which the source of infections (bacteria and viruses) had just been discovered by Louis Pasteur (1822–1895). However, before the discovery of penicillin in 1929, doctors had little with which to fight disease but the resilience of the human body and its ability to fight off infection. Hospitals were usually places of isolation for persons expected to die, and death was no respecter of persons. The white population of Grenada and the soldiers stationed in Grenada died just as easily as did the Grenadian at the bottom of the social strata. However, the difference between the percentage of each group that died came with exposure to infection, sanitation measures, nutrition, and the maintenance of general health.

Before the abolition of the slave trade, the slave owner followed a policy of working the slave to death. Little was done to maintain the health of the slave, to provide proper housing, or to pass on to the slave whatever was known about health education. Although there were hospitals on the estate, they were ineffective as treatment centres. Much more could have been done to ease the suffering of the ill and infirm, although little could have been done in this age to cure them. Whatever little use the estate hospitals were, they ceased functioning in 1838.

The slave often relied for alleviation of sickness on the herbal medicines brought from Africa and administered by the knowledgeable medicine men and women who developed a wide knowledge of plants and their uses. The ex-slave continued to have recourse to 'bush' medicine. The belief in the effectiveness of 'bush' or herbal medicine has never disappeared from the Grenadian population, and folk remedies are used instead of or concurrently with modern pharmacology.

Not knowing any better, the ex-slaves often lived and worked in unsanitary conditions. They possessed no latrines, and the river often served as latrine, washbasin, and to provide water for drinking and cooking. Faeces were also passed anywhere – in the vicinity of the huts, in the yards, gardens or in the bush. Stagnant water was allowed to settle around dwellings, and there was a belief that at night living quarters should be shut tightly, cutting off any ventilation.

The same neglect of public health measures was to be seen in the provision of hospitals. The military always maintained a hospital for its exclusive use. This was originally located in Fort George but was later removed to the fort at Richmond Hill. The only hospital for the public was the one originally established in 1734 during French rule. The public hospital was located on the southern and lower part of a hill near the town which ever after was called 'Hospital Hill'. This institution was named the Colony Hospital under the British, and from 1798 was made a Corporation with a Board of Governors, headed by the Governor, and a Board of Directors. The Hospital was supported by private donations, revenue from the lands owned by the Corporation, and by government grants. Among the directors of the hospital were the Anglican Rector, the Chief Justice, the Speaker of the Assembly and the Attorney General.

In 1850 the Colony Hospital stood on five acres of land, which was planted with provisions, and also provided a garden for the Surgeon-General who managed and lived at the institution. The hospital fees were twenty-one shillings on admittance, and the fees and the government grant of £200 were managed by the Surgeon-General and a Secretary-Treasurer, who were both paid £40 per annum to ensure that the hospital was properly maintained and provided the necessary services.

However, conditions at the hospital were appalling and a testament to how little the élite cared about the welfare of the other classes. The hospital was a filthy place, which emitted a stench. It was also badly in need of repair. Its management was disorganized, and it was without the simplest amenities such as bedding, bedclothes or medicine. In 1858 the hospital had accommodation of sorts for forty-eight persons, but the average occupancy was eighteen. Unless you could do no better, you simply did not go there. A Commission of Enquiry, set up in 1850 to investigate the conditions of the hospital, found that both the Surgeon-General and the Secretary-Treasurer were drunkards. They ignored the unkind treatment meted out to inmates by hospital workers, and effected a dreadful waste of hospital funds. They were both fired, and conditions marginally improved.

An Act established Boards of Health for each parish. Inspectors were empowered to tour the parishes, and give instructions for the cleaning-up of garbage, the cleaning of drains, and the inspection of houses to ensure that these met a minimum standard of cleanliness. It became illegal to throw dead animals into the street, and also to keep pigs in the town. Anyone who obstructed the work of the Inspector from the Boards of Health could be fined £5, with lesser fines for violations. For some violations, the informants of the violation would receive a reward. Water works, which included the building of a reservoir and the laying of pipes in St George's, were completed in 1836, the cost being recovered by the levying of water rates on each house and vessel which drew water from the scheme. The water supply was augmented in 1878. However, the Boards of

25 A cocoa plantation owner's house
(Photo: Corbis)

26 A cocoa-drying house
(Photo: Corbis)

27 Cocoa beans drying in the sun (Photo: Eye Ubiquitous)

28 An old waterwheel – a reminder of the days of 'King Sugar' in Grenada (Photo: Jim Rudin)

29 Washerwomen at St John's river, around the end of the nineteenth century. Peasant huts can be seen in the background. (Courtesy Government House)

30 A view of the Carenage and St George's town, *c.*1900
(Courtesy Government House)

31 A basket maker, around the end of the nineteenth century
(Photo courtesy Jim Rudin)

32 Governor Walter Sendall, Governor of Grenada between 1885 and 1889, who was acclaimed by Grenadians as 'the Prince of West Indian Governors'. It was at his direction that the Sendall Tunnel was built to ease the passage of porters going from 'Bay Town' to St George's proper.
(Photo courtesy Government House)

33 Workers collecting nutmegs, around 1880

34 The Didier family, about 1897. The grandparents are surrounded by their grandchildren who were left in their care when their parents – the couple to the right of the picture – emigrated to work on the Panama Canal. They never returned. The senior Mr Didier was a master carpenter who had migrated to Grenada from Barbados. The smallest child, Ruby Didier, later lived a quietly distinguished life on Tyrrel Street, St George's.

(Photo courtesy Ruby Didier)

35 An upper-class Grenadian family poses with their servants and carriage in front of their home in St Andrew's around 1900

36 A Grenadian woman of Indian descent shells nutmegs (Photo: Jim Rudin)

37 A Grenadian from Mount Moritz (Photo: Jim Rudin)

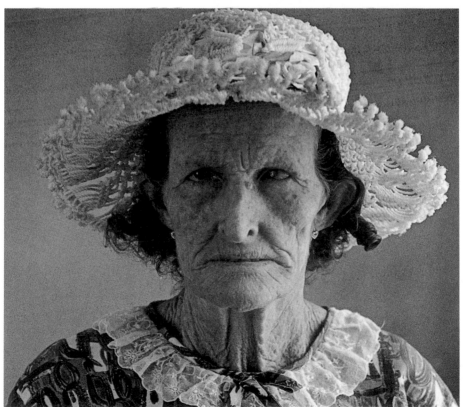

38 William Galwey 'The Lion' Donovan, who was the foremost activist for representative government in Grenada and equal rights for all Grenadians

(Photo courtesy Government House)

39 Theophilus Albert Marryshow, 'the Old Bulldog', Grenadian politician, statesman, journalist, champion of the creative arts. Liked by all who knew him, he advanced the cause of West Indian unity and co-operative ventures.

(UWI Centre Library)

40 Portrait of Dr William Wells, the only dissenting voice in the debate over the surrender of Grenada's representative government in 1877

(Courtesy of the Grenada National Museum)

41 Grenadian soldiers depart for Europe to serve in the First World War

(Courtesy of the Grenada National Museum)

42 Major David Slinger (sitting), who was largely responsible for training the Grenadian troops for service in the First World War, pictured with a colleague from Barbados (Courtesy of Paul Slinger)

43 The National Demonstration against the Customs bill,
led by T.A. Marryshow in 1931

44 Second World War barracks occupy the hill which was levelled
to accommodate the building of the Grenada Boys' Secondary School
(Photo courtesy Leo Cromwell)

45 T.A. Marryshow with his son Julian and his grandson.
Julian Marryshow saw service as a pilot in the RAF during
the Second World War. (UWI Centre Library)

46 An officer of the Southern Defence Force, Herbert Payne,
and a young soldier at the force's headquarters at Ross Point,
St George's (Courtesy of Nellie Payne)

47 The *Island Queen* was lost with 67 people on 5 August 1944, somewhere between Grenada and St Vincent. Grenadians still mourn those who died when this vessel mysteriously disappeared. This picture of the owner and captain, Chykra Salhab (in the dark suit) with Louis Salhab, his brother, was taken on board the *Island Queen* about a year before the disaster.
(Courtesy of Elinor Lashley)

48 Lucy DeRiggs was one of the young people who were lost on board the *Island Queen*
(Courtesy Joan Sylvester)

49 Iri Francis, a Grenadian who served overseas during the Second World War (Courtesy of the Francis family)

50 Rita Kerr, another of the many Grenadians who served during the Second World War (Courtesy of the Grenada National Museum)

51 War memorial to the Grenadians who lost their lives
in the two World Wars (Photo: Jim Rudin)

52 Downtown St George's, *c.*1950 (Courtesy of Leo Cromwell)

53 Buses in the Market Square, c.1950 (Courtesy of Leo Cromwell)

Health were not as effective as they should have been. The towns and habitations in Grenada were absolutely filthy, as the population had no idea at all that cleanliness was essential to their health.

The Cholera Epidemic of 1854

By any definition, the provisions for heath care in Grenada were sadly lacking. The dirty and unsanitary conditions which prevailed and the lack of knowledge of diseases and how they were transmitted, both in town and in the country, made Grenada an ideal place for the rapid spread of any disease transmitted by contaminated water and contaminated food. Grenada also had insufficient medical practitioners, and not every parish had a doctor assigned to it. In retrospect, it is not a surprise that when cholera was introduced into the region the death toll in Grenada was massive.

Cholera was new to the region. It is an infection of the small intestine caused by a bacteria, which produces a toxin that acts on the body to cause the large and small intestine to withdraw large quantities of fluid from the bloodstream. The manifestations of the disease are profuse watery diarrhoea, accompanied by vomiting. Over a pint of fluid may be lost each hour, and if the affected person is not immediately supplied with sufficient fluids and salts to replace those lost, death results within a few hours from severe dehydration. If the affected person drinks infected water in an attempt to replace lost body fluids, the constant re-infection negates any chance of recovery. The onset of the disease is sudden with the symptoms starting one to five days after infection. Cholera was endemic to northeast India, but with the opening-up of trade routes it spread throughout the world.[15]

Cholera first made its appearance in the Caribbean in Jamaica in 1850, and swept in turn through the Bahamas, Barbados, Trinidad and the Eastern Caribbean. It is almost certain that it came to this region carried by the Indian indentured workers, thus the disease was called Asiatic cholera. In Jamaica 32,000 people died, in Barbados 20,000 died, and in three short months from June to August 1884 cholera took the lives of 12 per cent of Grenada's population – 3778 Grenadian people out of a total population of 32,000.

Learning that cholera was devastating the populations of the Caribbean islands, a frenzied clean-up campaign was begun in Grenada, especially in St George's, which was filthy. Dwellings were painted with lime (whitewash), which had proved to be an effective disinfectant in yellow fever epidemics. However, it was impossible to eradicate in such a short time the longstanding habits of neglecting sanitation measures and the lack of public knowledge about the importance of sanitation. There was also the abysmal ignorance of all concerned. For example, people carefully whitewashed their houses outside, leaving the more important insides untreated. Dwellings also needed to be well ventilated, free of dirt and other rubbish in and around the dwelling. Stagnant pools of water near to where people lived needed to be drained. Nor was it only the dwelling places of the poor that were filthy. The buildings where the soldiers were quartered at Fort George were also found to be filthy.

Besides a clean-up campaign, quarantine measures were put in place to try to prevent the entry of infected persons into Grenada. Four vessels arriving in Grenada from Barbados were quarantined for seven days. However, the quarantine could not be effective unless it was universally applied. A detachment of soldiers who had previously been stationed in Barbados was not quarantined, and it is almost certain that some of these soldiers brought the disease into Grenada.

The cholera epidemic broke out in Grenada on 10 June 1854, among artillery soldiers quartered at the barracks in St George's. The troops were moved to Richmond Hill, where the barracks were cleaner and airier. This did nothing to suppress the spread of the disease, which soon spread to the 69th Regiment quartered there. The first civilian cases were recorded on 4 July, the first to be affected being residents of the Morne Jaloux ridge, which is contiguous with Richmond Hill. Once the disease got into the civilian population, there was no stopping it. Soon cholera cases were reported in several places in St George's town and parish.

Dr W. Huggins, a visitor from Trinidad, had some knowledge of epidemiology and the handling of cholera. He volunteered to stay in Grenada to assist in managing the epidemic, and worked assiduously to stem the tide of the epidemic, and to save the lives of the afflicted. A few months later he was joined by another doctor from Trinidad, Dr Mercer, whose services were also invaluable for as long as he could stay, as he was called back to Trinidad when cholera reached that island.

In an effort to contain the outbreak of cholera to St George's, health visitors and doctors immediately visited the houses where the sick were, distributing medicines. If treatment was received early, the virulence of the disease was less. House-to-house visits soon ceased as the disease spread rapidly through the town, and it became clear that there were insufficient doctors and resources to continue the house visits. Instead, Huggins set up a cholera hospital in the abandoned barracks at Fort George, so that the limited resources could serve the greatest number.

When the epidemic reached Calivigny Estate in St George's Parish, the manager and the overseer fled the estate, leaving their workers to their fate.

When a medical team reached the estate, they found that, although cholera had killed many, some had died from starvation, as they had either not gone in search of food after having been abandoned by their employers, or had simply been too weak to do so. The Lieutenant-Governor reported that, at the outbreak of the disease on the estate, and with the panicked departure of the manager and overseer, many of the workers, being abandoned, 'fled and the remainder had huddled themselves together in the huts with every breath of air excluded, awaiting death with apathy and despair.'[16] Police were sent for to bury the dead and burn the surrounding bush and some huts. Doctor Huggins, and another doctor, Aquart, were also sent for to help manage the situation. They managed to commandeer the great house to be used as a hospital for the survivors, and to get the attorney for the estate to provide meat for the sick. All these measures combined eventually brought the epidemic under control on that estate.

By the middle of July St George's was in the grip of a disastrous epidemic. The Colony Hospital had no way of coping with the bodies of the persons who had been admitted only to die. A piece of land was acquired for the purpose of burying the dead. This is the present St George's Cemetery, and the hill on which it is situated became known as Cemetery Hill. In the end, 379[17] persons would die in St George's town alone, and 425 in the other areas of St George's Parish.

The disease spread rapidly to the rural parishes. Few people escaped infection, the disease killing both young and old, those living in clean, neat houses as well as those living in unsanitary conditions. St Patrick's was the hardest hit. By the time the epidemic wore itself out, St Patrick's had lost 25 per cent of its population – 1250 persons out of a population of 5160. Thanks to the tireless activities of Dr Mercer and those working with him, the recovery rate for the parishes of St Andrew's, St John's and St Mark's were good, but the death toll was bad enough. In the rural areas, bodies were buried in the churchyards, on the estates, and on peasants' farms. The fact that, in the haste to bury the cholera victims, the regulatory depth of six feet was not always followed for burials, and some bodies were not sufficiently covered, did not help in disease control. Churches and other available buildings were converted for use as temporary hospitals, and the clergy and many managers and overseers joined the doctors in intense efforts to try to save lives, and prevent the spread of the disease.

Carriacou did not escape. The disease was brought to Carriacou by passengers from St George's travelling to the island by sloops. Within twenty-four hours of arrival in Carriacou, the captain and crew of the *Rose Ann*, apparently healthy when they arrived, were dead. Two of the passengers from another other sloop, the *Recovery*, also died within a day. The people from these boats quickly infected the healthy population of Carriacou. The disease appeared first in Hillsborough, the capital, and then in all other areas. Bogles was particularly devastated, losing 20 per cent of its population. Petit Martinique was also badly hit, and most of the survivors abandoned their homes and took up temporary residence in Carriacou. There were 1000 cases reported in Carriacou and Petit Martinique. Out of these, 386 died. At this time these islands had a combined population of only 4000.

The lack of modern medicine, the reliance on folk remedies, and the reluctance to be treated, all contributed to the spread of the disease. The doctors differed on treatment. One accepted practice treated the patient with large doses of calomel and opium, quinine and chloroform. Another accepted practice was a warm bath, a dressing put over the area of the stomach and liver, and a pill comprising calomel, camphor and a compound known as Dover's powder administered every fifteen minutes until the vomiting stopped and the tongue became moist. 'Bitter Bush', used in Carriacou, was a folk remedy that proved most effective, but other folk remedies were less efficacious, and some were extremely harmful. For example, one of the folk remedies was to place the sick person on the cold earthen floor as the first step in treating the disease, and to keep the bedroom dark and unventilated. This was a recipe for making the patient worse. Other folk remedies included drinking a mixture of brandy and pepper, and another was applying hot stones to the sick person's body.

The villain causing the epidemic, however, was the lack of cleanliness. If only those with the power in Grenada had ensured proper sanitation and fresh water supplies for town and country. This, and the quarantine of the soldiers arriving from Barbados, would have prevented needless suffering and death. That these measures were sufficient is illustrated by the fact that the only group of persons untouched by the disease were the 30 prisoners in St George's gaol, who lived in an institution that insisted on cleanliness, and which provided the inmates with a plain, healthy diet.

Improvements in Public Health

Huggins returned to Trinidad when the epidemic had spent itself in Grenada. Before leaving Grenada, he made several recommendations to the Board of Health, which included a listing of the sanitation measures that were necessary to prevent an epidemic of cholera or any other disease breaking out in the future. These measures were mainly concerned with the proper disposal of household rubbish in the towns, keeping vacant lots and streets free of grass and bush, and preventing the accumulation of stagnant water in drains or anywhere else. These recommendations were followed, and Grenada's standard of sanitation improved.

The government also took other measures to strengthen the health sector. A doctor was appointed for each parish, and he was to see to it that all children received vaccinations, and to attend to the health needs of the poor. A dispensary was set up in Carriacou. The military barracks at Fort George, left vacant after the withdrawal of the garrison, were renovated to house the Colony Hospital, and the hospital was transferred there in 1858. As this was the only hospital on the island, it accepted cases from every parish. The sum of £96 was made available for repairing and altering the barracks so that they could be suitably transformed into a hospital.

The almshouses and the mental hospital, already established in St George's, were also transferred to vacant officers' quarters serving the Fort at Richmond Hill. These also accepted cases from all the parishes. A government officer, assisted by a matron, superintended both these institutions. The almshouse received an annual government grant of £500, and £300 was granted for the running of the mental hospital.

There were other pressing health concerns in Grenada at this time, namely the presence in the population of hookworm infection, yaws and leprosy. The latter two had been brought to the island by the slaves, and all three were endemic to the population. Measures to counteract them, and to rid the population of these scourges, would, however, have to wait three decades. Lepers or diseased persons were taken to Kick 'em Jenny (also called Diamond) rock and left to fend for themselves. Only minor improvements in the health sector would be made with the entry of large numbers of indentured immigrants from India into society. These adjustments were made because they were conditions of the immigration scheme. Even so, the provision of hospitals and health care for the Indian immigrants was not effected with much care and concern. Abuses and negligence were common.

Repercussions on Society

The thinning-out of the labouring population was a cause of great concern to the planters and the managers of the estates. Labour was needed not only for the sugar estates, but also for the conversion of the sugar estates into cocoa and nutmegs, as experimentation in these new crops began around this time. Between 1856 and 1866, in St Mark's, St John's, St George's and St Andrew's, twelve estates were put into cocoa cultivation, which proved to be a very profitable investment.

In a response to the shortage of labour, and also to the hard times affecting both the estates and the labouring population, there was a resurgence of child labour. Child labour, which had decreased after

Emancipation until it reached a low of 271 children in 1861, rose to a new height by 1878 when 3050 were employed.[18]

Notes

1 McDaniel, pp. 181–2.
2 Smith (1965) and Smith (1984).
3 *Case of John Laurence, Painter, and Venetian-blind Maker as Tried in the Supreme Court of Judicature on 10 October 1823*, printed by W.E. Hales, Grenada, 1830, p. 7.
4 Gentle, p. 40.
5 *Ibid.* pp. 40–1.
6 Gentle, p. 34.
7 Marriage confined within one's own social group.
8 Minutes of the Board of the Legislative Council, 1868, British Library (BL).
9 Freeling to Board of Health, St George's, 18 Oct. 1871, in Minutes of the Board of the Legislative Council, 1871, BL.
10 Gentle, p. 50.
11 Brizan, p. 159.
12 A Model School was a school that was built as a pattern, or ideal school, and it was hoped that all providers of education would copy the facilities and functioning of this school.
13 A Normal School was the average school one might expect to see in Grenada.
14 CO 321/288, Minutes for the Board of Education, 18 Aug. 1916, enclosed in a letter by the Governor to the Secretary of State, 30 Aug. 1916, Colonial Office Dispatches, Grenada, 1916, Public Record Office (PRO), London.
15 American Medical Association, p. 274.
16 Dispatch no. 89 of 1854, Lieutenant-Governor Keate to Governor Colebroke, 'Report on the Appearance and Progress of Cholera in Grenada', 6 October, quoted in Brizan, p.181.
17 The mortality statistics and the population figures in this section were taken from Dispatch no. 89, 1854, Keate to Colebroke, 'Report on the Appearance and Progress of Cholera', quoted in Brizan, p. 185.
18 Census returns for 1861 and 1881, quoted by Brizan, p. 141.

11

A Restive Population

In the last quarter of the nineteenth century, most Grenadians were not only very poor citizens in rural areas but they were almost completely alienated from the political arena in Grenada. Participation in the government of the country was still the exclusive domain of the élite. Before Emancipation all the laws passed were for the benefit of the slave owners and élite. Very little was to change in the rest of the nineteenth century. The years between Emancipation and 1876 were to witness how irresponsibly the élite managed the country, and how little they appreciated that Grenada had any sort of representative government. These years were also to witness the struggle of the coloured middle class to have a say in the government of the country, and to restore the empowerment of the people, when this was carelessly given away by the governing élite.

Representative Government Abandoned

The 1763 Grenada Constitution had given Grenada a degree of internal self-government. Except for the suspension of the Constitution between 1779 and 1783, this Constitution had remained virtually unchanged. The legislature mirrored the bi-cameral legislature of Britain, consisting of a Legislative Council of nine members, with the Lieutenant-Governor and the Governor-in-Chief being ex-officio members and a House of Assembly with twenty-six members.

Just as the House of Lords in Britain had veto power over legislation proposed by the House of Commons, so did the Council of the Grenada government have to approve of all Acts passed by the Assembly. Except between 1856 and 1859, eligible citizens were nominated by the Governor to serve on the Council, and these were then appointed by the Secretary of State for the Colonies acting for the British monarch. The Council included top civil servants and individuals of high standing in the community. It was the responsibility of the House of Assembly to raise the money for the running of the country and for public works. They therefore had the power to levy taxes, but could not alter the duties decreed by the Crown. Acts for the governance of the island were introduced, read, debated and passed through the two houses, and then sent to Britain for approval. Unless there was very serious reason, the Act was approved and became law.

To stand for election to the Assembly, one had to be a male, and either to own or jointly own 50 acres (about 20 hectares) of land on which was built a house with a rental value of £40 per year, or be the lessee of a plantation of at least 100 acres (about 40 ha) of which at least 30 had to be under cultivation, or a person who earned at least £200 per annum from a profession or trade. To be eligible to vote to elect a member in the Assembly, a person had to be a male over 21 years of age, who either owned 10 acres (about 4 ha) of land, half of which was in cultivation, or own, or have one's wife own, a property with a dwelling house that could bring in a rent of £10 annually. Also eligible were persons who rented or leased estates or who were creditors with an income of not less than £20 per annum. Even though qualified under these requirements, after 1792[1] to be eligible to vote or sit in either House of the legislature persons also had to take both an oath of allegiance and an oath denying belief in transubstantiation. The disenfranchisement of the French Grenadians otherwise eligible to vote and sit on the Assembly was one of the main causes of disaffection that led to the French Grenadians' support of Fédon.

The restrictions on enfranchisement meant that both the membership of the legislature and the voters were drawn from the same small group of people. Sometimes a person was the only one nominated, and was elected unchallenged. The same person often managed to serve indefinitely, by being re-elected over and over again, in different constituencies.

An illustration of how incestuous the electoral system was can be seen from the results of the 1850 general elections. In that election, the twenty-six members of the House of Assembly were elected by ninety-nine voters, including the twenty-six candidates themselves.[2] Although there was a slight increase in the numbers eligible to vote after this, the actual percentage of the people they represented fell, due to the overall increase in population. Another undesirable phenomenon of the small number of persons eligible to hold public office was that members of the Assembly sometimes held multiple positions. For example, Benjamin Webster was Speaker of the Assembly, Registrar of the High Court, and a Justice of the Peace. Of course, he was also a planter! In addition to the limited franchise, no salaries were paid to members of the legislature. If a member held another post, such as Attorney General, then, of course, he received his salary for that post. This further narrowed those who would offer themselves for election, as they had to be sufficiently well off to devote their time to service without recompense.

Therefore, the only participants in the electoral process in the last quarter of the nineteenth century were the white élite together with a sprinkling of some coloured merchants and professionals who were becoming an important part of society, and tolerated by the whites. These professional people of colour had adopted white attitudes and ways, shared the same interest as the whites and therefore strengthened the white élites, who were slowly declining in number.

It was obvious that the élite of Grenada was interested in monopolizing the places in the Assembly without being interested in the governance of the country. Secure in their power, the élite did not deem it necessary to attend the meetings of the legislature, delegating to colleagues the responsibility to see that their common interest was protected through any legislation proposed or passed. Acts passed by the Assembly were all Acts to secure the power and property of the upper classes, and to maintain the status quo as long as possible. There was also an urban bias in the concerns the members of the legislature did have. They looked after the town better and had little concern for conditions in the rural areas, so much so that they let the rural courthouses and rectories fall into ruin. They were concerned for the future and productivity of the estates, rather than for the building of the country as a whole. Thus after immigrant labour came into Grenada, the legislature let the immigration fund run down.

It was the Governors and Lieutenant-Governors who tried to prod the élite into action to ameliorate social conditions such as education, health, and conditions in the prisons. Even so, the committees formed to study the proposals laid before them took a long time before initiating action on them. For example, on 17 October 1865 the Secretary of State for the Colonies requested the legislature to remedy the condition of the prisons. More than two years later the Governor reminded them that the matter was still outstanding. The legislators were not interested in change, even if the change would eventually improve their own lot. Several Governors upbraided members for their absenteeism and sloth.

So, although the Constitution of Grenada looked good on paper, it had long ceased to be in the best interest of the majority of Grenadians. To many thinking people, it was obvious that those serving in the legislature were unfit to govern. In 1869 a prominent concerned citizen, called Dr Paulin Orgias, described the Assembly as composed of ignorant people who used the sittings of the Assembly to engage for the most part in personal abuse.[3] The Governors had to plead with the members to effect changes of utmost importance. Promises to look into the matter, and to set up subcommittees, were devices used to postpone action as long as possible. Yet when the Assembly wanted to give gratuities to friends, immediate action resulted from such proposals. For example, there was the case of William Lucas, Judge of the High Court and President of the Assembly, who had his Mount George Estate appropriated by the French between 1779 and 1783 for the construction of a fort. When British rule was restored in 1783, Lucas bided his time until he became Acting Governor, then presided over the passage of an Act to compensate himself in the amount of £20,000 for the French appropriation. The Act became law by Lucas giving his approval to it! This fort was subsequently called Fort Lucas. A decade earlier he had bought this estate for only £3000.

The British government was not blind to the abuse of power in Grenada and in other British colonies in the Caribbean. The same wave of humanitarianism that had forced the abolition of slavery and the end of apprenticeship on unwilling planters and their managers also affected British thinking on the matter of governance. The British government was uncomfortable with the situation where a small minority made laws for the majority, these groups having widely divergent interests and agendas.

Britain was also uncomfortable with the idea of placing the government into the hands of the rising educated coloured people, and began to look for a way to take back the reins of government from the unworthy and to exercise direct government of the colonies. St Lucia and Trinidad were already Crown Colonies by 1815. In 1839 an attempt was made to force Jamaica into Crown Colony government, but this was resisted until 1866. Jamaica had just experienced a popular uprising, the Morant Bay uprising in 1865, when George William Gordon and Paul Bogle had led the Jamaican people in protest against Governor Eyre and a colonial system of white minority rule that was excessively oppressive and unjust with respect to the welfare of the general population. Both Gordon and Bogle were tried and executed for their idealism. As a result of this uprising and the subsequent social unrest, Jamaica lost its representative government and was made a Crown Colony.

The Old Representative system, although decaying in Grenada, took some time to finally die. An early move was made in 1833 to tighten administration and to curb independent action when the Constitution of Grenada was changed to make it part of a common administration with St Vincent, Tobago and Barbados. Under this common administration, Grenada shared a Governor-in-Chief with the other islands. The Governor-in-Chief was stationed in Barbados, and a Lieutenant-Governor resided in Grenada. The Lieutenant-Governor was answerable to the Governor-in-Chief. But it was not until four decades later that the government of Grenada was handed over to the Crown.

Despite resistance among the intelligentsia in Grenada to the idea of Crown Colony government, the views of this group still had insufficient sympathizers among those in the government. Therefore, when on

15 September 1875 an Act to create a single legislative chamber in Grenada to replace the House of Assembly and the Legislative Council was introduced, it passed with very little opposition. On 7 January 1876 the Governor-in-Chief, at that time John Pope-Hennessy, dissolved Grenada's 112-year-old legislative bodies.

The petition for Crown Colony status followed quickly. At the first meeting of the new legislature, on 9 February 1876, one of its members, Charles Simmons, introduced the motion that Grenada should petition Queen Victoria to make Grenada a Crown Colony. This motion was passed by a vote of twelve to three. The only voice raised in opposition was that of Dr William Wells, Speaker of the House, and a prominent St David's physician. Wells said that Crown Colony government would cast aside the rights of the people to have a voice in the making of the laws by which they were governed. Grenada should not give up these rights to the British government. His nationalism and progressive political thought found no support, and the élite of Grenada surrendered to Britain the right of all Grenadians to govern themselves. An Imperial Order in Council proclaimed Grenada a Crown Colony on 3 December 1877.

Crown Colony government[4] meant that Britain controlled the affairs of the islands directly and the implementation of the laws passed in Britain was the responsibility of the Governor-in-Chief and his Lieutenant-Governor. A modicum of local participation was provided for through a local Executive Council and Legislative Council. These had no power in their own right, but the Governor relied on the members of these Councils for advice, especially where knowledge of the local situation or culture was an important element in making a wise decision.

The Crown appointed both the Councils, although in practice the Governor nominated the members. It was up to the Governor to choose these sets of advisers carefully, selecting them for their wisdom, knowledge and social conscience, and not solely because they were prominent in Grenadian society. The seven-man Legislative Council had the function of ratifying the decisions taken by the Governor and assisting him in framing laws. It had no other powers. The Executive Council was simply a smaller committee of the members of the Legislative Council, and was made up of those persons whom the Lieutenant-Governor chose as his closest advisers.

When the deposed élite came to the realization that they had deprived themselves of power when they gave up self-government, and that the Governor had chosen other advisers for his Council than themselves, some of them reacted by attacking Lieutenant-Governor Harley. In July 1878 Henry Boyles Beckwith, a former member of the House of Assembly and a druggist and merchant, wrote complaining to the Secretary of State that the Governor had upset the peace and quiet of the community by his high-handed and illegal method of operating the Constitution. Beckwith, with William Simmons, began a newspaper called the *New Era* to provide a forum for the further criticism and harassment of the Governor. Between 1878 and 1880, Beckwith also called several public meetings to rouse up opinion and protest against several government measures, and to solicit support for further attacks against Crown Colony government. Although well advertised, only sixteen persons attended Beckwith's first meeting. He was more successful in getting signatures to a petition to the Secretary of State against a series of fiscal measures proposed by the Governor, and requesting that taxpayers be allowed to elect representatives to the Legislative Council. This petition was signed by 467 merchants, planters, shopkeepers, small proprietors and artisans.

Governor Harley was of the opinion that the criticisms stemmed from Beckwith and Simmons being aggrieved that they had not been included in the Councils of the new government. The Governor was also of the opinion that it was the aim of Beckwith to subvert his attempt to govern. Although Beckwith and his supporters had acquiesced to the change to Crown Colony government, they saw that they could get political mileage out of championing the cause of the small proprietors and new peasantry. For a more genuine and less opportunistic protest against Crown Colony government and the lack of popular representation in government, Grenada would have to wait ten more years.

William Galwey[5] Donovan

William Galwey Donovan was a well-educated coloured Grenadian of Irish and African descent. By the age of 27, he was already known as the foremost intellectual rebel in Grenada, vigorously campaigning against the social and political ills in society. His disposition to erupt in anger at social injustice, combined with his impassioned writing, earned him the nickname 'Lion'.[6]

In 1883 Donovan began to agitate for the removal of Crown Colony government. In that year, along with eighteen others, he submitted to the Crossman Commission a memorandum that expressed the strongest objections to Crown Colony government. He drew the attention of the Commissioners to the 'strong feeling, which pervades the entire community' against Crown Colony government, which was termed 'simply odious'.[7] The memorandum outlined the various instances of neglect and extravagance of the government, and while thanking Britain for being solicitous in seeking the welfare of Grenada, assured Britain, through the Commission, that:

No one can be more solicitous for our well being than ourselves. We know that the people of England entertain very crude notions respecting our condition. Because we are Negroes or mulattoes must we be ignorant? Does God give intellectual power and reasoning faculties only to Whites? We cannot submit to be ruled like serfs when we consider ourselves to be freeborn Britons. We therefore ask you to make such representations as will secure us a share in the management of our own affairs.[8]

Donovan and his colleagues agitated against Crown Colony government in other ways. Donovan was the owner and editor of a newspaper called *Grenada People*, which had the slogan 'A naked freedman is better than a gilded slave'. In this newspaper, Donovan kept up a continuous attack on Crown Colony government in every way he could. His influence over opinion was so strong that, by 1885, an intelligentsia that eleven years previously had welcomed Crown Colony government was totally against it.

In 1885 Donovan criticized a judge of the Circuit Court in the *Grenada People,* and was brought up for libel under an old law that made it a crime to publish any material that was unfavourable to a government official. Although he had printed the truth, he was convicted and imprisoned, and his paper was shut down. In the meantime, the *St George's Chronicle*, a rival newspaper, mourned the closure of the *Grenada People* in these words:

Notwithstanding the violent and objectionable tone ... adopted sometimes, it nevertheless by its fearless demeanour did much to expose the rottenness of Crown Colony government and to educate the British people on our affairs.[9]

Later that year, an Act called 'Lord Campbell's Act' which had been passed in Britain was introduced into Grenada. This Act made it impossible to bring a libel action against a person who published the truth. Donovan was released as soon as this Act was adopted. As soon as he was out of custody, on 9 May 1885, he gave notice of his intention to recommence the publication of the *Grenada People.* He promised that he would continue to advocate the right of the Grenadian people to representative government. He wrote:

I shall criticize freely men and measures, believing as I do that the people of the Colony are qualified to manage through their representatives all local affairs and that until this functional right is restored to the people neither the prosperity of the Colony nor the contentment of the people will be ensured. I shall most strenuously advocate the abolition of Crown Colony and the restoration of self-government. I seek to make the people thoroughly dissatisfied with any system of government, which virtually denies their existence and defiantly and insolently tramples their right. Without representation political liberty is destroyed. No intelligent people, nor people possessed of self-respect and not having surrendered the dignity of their manhood would consent to be branded as political slaves – tamely submitting to see their money expended without regard to their wants and in wanton and insolent defiance of their wishes.[10]

The Bonfire Riots

A manifestation of the growing discontent over a government in which the people had no say, one in which was influenced by the élite and middle class, and one which rode rough-shod over the traditions of the humble people, was the so-called Bonfire Riots that took place in St George's around Guy Fawkes' Day 1885.

The people of St George's had been accustomed to celebrate Guy Fawkes' Day (5 November) with great enthusiasm, the festivities including fireworks and bonfires. In 1885 several of the leading merchants of St George's approached Governor Sendall asking him to ban the annual celebration of Guy Fawkes and the Gunpowder Plot, because of the likelihood of fire when the people indulged in: 'flinging burning, pitch soaked fireballs about the market square (which was surrounded by aging, wooden-frame buildings)'.[11] The Governor agreed to what seemed to him to be a reasonable request and concern. His mistake was to fail to get any viewpoint except from the merchants, and was therefore unaware of the importance this celebration held for the majority of the people in St George's.

On 4 November 1885, without warning, a law was passed forbidding the lighting of all bonfires or the discharging of fireworks in the Market Square or any other public place. The ban infuriated both the lower classes as well as frustrated and rebellious members of the disenfranchised but educated middle class. They were determined that one of the few rights and privileges enjoyed under Crown Colony government was not going to be withdrawn. During the night of 4 November inhabitants of the town lit a bonfire at the foot of Halifax Street, so close to the house of a Mr Gould that it caused Gould's wife inside to utter 'loud and distressing screams', which, Bonham Richardson says 'must have delighted those who had set the fire in the alley next to the house'.[12]

The following night persons unknown ignited tar barrels around St George's and hid nearby. When the police came to try to douse these, they were pelted with various missiles. The next day handwritten leaflets were circulated in St George's stating that it was the intention of the people of St George's to stand up to the Governor's ban on the Guy Fawkes celebration, and that the organizers of the demonstrations against the ban had:

> Taken the precaution in securing a small number of 500 mightly strong and well-armed men, in opposition of any order Mr — may enforce in the market square ... For at least 30 years the 5th of November has always been celebrated by a display of Fireworks in the Town, and if we have to fight against the ... police, it's our intention to lash and go.[13]

On the afternoon of the 5th summonses were issued to 'about one hundred respectable inhabitants of the town'[14] to appear before the Acting Magistrate of St George's by 6 p.m. to be sworn in as special constables to keep the peace that night. As they were assembling at the police station, a man was brought under arrest and was set upon by at least two police who commenced to rain blows on him. Galwey Donovan, who was either observing the preparations for the dispatch of the special constables or who had been the recipient of a summons himself, seeing what was happening, placed himself between the man and the police. The police then began to rain blows on him as well. Two other onlookers, Livingstone Payne and George Otway, went to Donovan's rescue, but were also struck by the police, and seriously injured. Payne received a serious injury to his hand, and Otway was knocked unconscious by a blow to his head from a police truncheon.

The police, reserve police and police aides began patrolling the town from early evening on 5 November. From about 8.30 p.m. until about midnight persons hidden in houses, alleys and vacant lots began throwing stones and missiles of every description, aiming to hit the police and anyone else on the streets who was perceived to be part of the establishment. Several police and civilians were injured, some of them seriously. Among the civilians injured was E.W. Begrie, the Inspector of Schools. In addition to using people as targets, the rioters also took aim at the street lamps in the town, breaking them all, and plunging the town into total darkness. Many of the windows of businesses in the town were also smashed. The activity was greatest on St John, St Juille, Hillsborough,

Melville, Grenville and Halifax Streets, and in and around the Market Square.

Eventually, the situation was brought under control with the help of further reinforcements of police. The police aides had proved to be no help at all, as they had hid themselves in the face of the bombardment, leaving people to their fate, and the injured to fend for themselves. The activities had subsided by 11 p.m., and all was quiet by midnight.

During the night of the disturbance, the police themselves threw stones at the crowd and used their truncheons freely. The next day, the Governor blamed the policemen for a lot of the violent behaviour that had occurred. He asked how a society could expect certain behaviour from the lower classes if the police officers set a bad example. He went on to say that the police, in trying to enforce the law, had not handled the people with tact. This lack of tact was within the police tradition of rough and uncivil manners towards the public. Undoubtedly the Governor knew the details of the incident that had occurred on the afternoon of the 5th.

That night, the town was patrolled by eight groups of fifty police, including special constables sworn in for the occasion. When the police and the special constables reassembled at the police station, Governor Sendall was there to thank them. 'The absurd disturbances of the night previous had been caused by idle and foolish people', he said. He was happy 'to see so large a number of respectable portion of the community prepared to come forward and loyally assist in the preservation of peace'.[15]

This disturbance was entirely confined to the town. It was fuelled by the frustration and discontent of the population at the restraints of Crown Colony government, which did not provide opportunities for the self-determination of the population, or an opportunity for the population to mould and express its culture. Many felt that the time had come for the government of the country to reflect the voices, culture, rights and privileges of the majority, and not the small white minority. The feelings of the majority were vocalized by members of the emerging educated coloured middle class, who were also alleged to have played a major role in organizing the riots. Donovan's newspaper and his own utterances were particularly instrumental both in the formation of public opinion as well as providing a forum for the expression of the *vox populi*.

Parochial Boards and Local Government

Galwey Donovan never ceased to campaign against Crown Colony government. As a means of involving the population in the running of the country, and for better management of the parishes, Governor Sendall had established Parochial Boards in each parish and in Carriacou. Half the members of each board were appointed by the Governor, and the other half were elected by males in the parish who paid rates of at least ten shillings on freehold or leasehold properties, rented property valued at £20 per annum, or had a salary of more than £140 per annum. The boards had the authority and responsibility of levying local rates and spending the income so derived in controlling and managing the town, maintaining the byways, and other local matters. The community had shown a great interest in the boards and had actively participated in them. In 1891 these boards had ceased to have members appointed by the Governor, and were made up totally of members elected by the eligible population.

In 1893 Donovan wrote two memoranda to the Secretary of State, explaining that Crown Colony government was repugnant to the educated Grenadian, who regarded the system as one would regard a public enemy. The purpose of these memoranda was to seek a measure of self-government, by asking that the seven Parochial Boards, one in each parish, and one in Carriacou, which had been set up under Sendall, be converted to Parish Councils. Donovan campaigned for councils with much more power. He advocated that Parish Councils should be responsible for the repair and maintenance of roads, public buildings and public places within the parishes, for water, sanitation, lighting and poor relief, and for the establishment of secondary schools where this was necessary. The councils should also be allowed to raise revenue by property tax and licences on such things as wheeled vehicles, porters, jobbers and dogs.

The reforms that Donovan sought were never introduced in their entirety. However, a Commission was appointed to recommend on the functioning of the Parochial Boards, and their report in 1896 recommended that the parishes be made units of local administration. This took effect in 1900. Also in 1900, Town Boards, the membership of which were partially nominated and partially elected, replaced the elected Parochial Boards. The boards, subject to the Governor's approval, could frame bylaws and carry them into effect.

The boards were designed as a means to give Grenadians a measure of self-government, and to ensure that the needs of the parishes got the attention they deserved. However, the élite held on to power and the control of society by seeking election to the boards. They were largely successful, as many who sought office were on the Legislative Council. Due to the prestige of this position, and the deference offered by the general population to people in such positions, this élite were not only successful in their bid to serve on the boards, but were also prevailed upon to chair the boards. Thus the wealthy upper and middle classes still governed, almost without opposition.

An Eclipse of the Sun

Some excitement occurred in 1886 when there was a total eclipse of the sun, and astronomers came to Green Island, near Grenada, to observe this event. Unfortunately for them, the day was heavily overcast, and their travel was in vain. Father Joseph Perry, an English Jesuit priest, and other priests who had come to observe the eclipse, stayed in Carriacou and got a wonderful view of the eclipse through the telescopes they erected there. Devas records that older heads in Carriacou in 1950 remembered that there was a famine in Carriacou in that year, and associated it with the eclipse, which they called 'the darkness'.[16]

The Visit of King Ja Ja of Opobo

The disenfranchised middle-class intelligentsia had another occasion to let their dissatisfaction at official policy be known when they heard the details of the exile of King Ja Ja of Opobo, a province in Africa.

King Ja Ja had become a thorn in the side of the British government as he opposed some of the operations of Britain in the lands under his control. To enable British enterprises to do as they wished, King Ja Ja was arrested on a trumped-up charge and was sentenced to be exiled. However, finding a suitable place to be King Ja Ja's exiled home proved to be difficult. On 8 May 1885 he was put on a ship called the *Icarus*, and sent to the West Indies. He arrived in Grenada on 8 June, but by the time he arrived it had been decided to send him to St Vincent.

King Ja Ja's exile was a problem to Governor Sendall. As an African king, he had to be treated with respect, and be given quarters and privileges equal to any wealthy European. This would be a source of great scandal in the highly stratified colonial society. No European wanted to have their house used to accommodate an African, even if he were a king. Sendall had hoped to lodge King Ja Ja on Baliseau, a small island off the southern coast of St Vincent, but the owner of the house withdrew his offer to let as soon as he found out who his tenant was to be. Next Sendall tried to find accommodation in Grenada, without success. Eventually, Sendall arranged with the Administrator Llewelyn in St Vincent to accommodate King Ja Ja in a house that the government had recently bought to be converted to a police station. The Grenadian newspapers had taken a great interest in the arrangements to be made for the king. When the Governor claimed that no accommodation could be found for him, one newspaper expressed the view that there was accommodation to be had, but the Governor did not want Ja Ja in Grenada because he would have to invite him to the receptions at Government House. Another newspaper had given a full account of the case of King Ja Ja the day before his arrival. The militant middle class thought that the British government had unfairly dealt with King Ja Ja and that he ought to be permanently located in Grenada. The newspapers called the general mood of Grenadians 'mad', because the government would not offer King Ja Ja a home in Grenada.

When the *Icarus* docked in St George's, the advance publicity ensured that he was greeted by an enthusiastic and curious crowd. Boats filled with the curious went out and surrounded the *Icarus* to see if they could catch a glimpse of the king. They were rewarded with a view of him '[o]n the quarterdeck clad in a light flannel suit, with his son near him, who was also garbed in civilized attire'.[17]

The people were hoping that the king would be allowed to disembark, so that they could get a close-up view of him, and perhaps meet him and engage him in conversation, but the authorities were nervous at the amount of interest all sectors of the population had shown in King Ja Ja, and tried to keep him apart from the people as much as they could. Without landing in Grenada, King Ja Ja sailed away to St Vincent, where he lived for about three years, until he was transferred to lodgings in Barbados.[18]

A Shooting

At this time, the educated middle class were very frustrated at the lack of opportunity and discrimination they experienced due to their skin colour. There was considerable repressed hostility in the civil service in particular, produced by a situation when competent black civil servants were treated with disdain by their white and sometimes not-so-bright and sometimes lazy superior officers. Frederick McDermott Coard described

> the years when the phrase 'superior office' suggested immediate 'kow-towing', tale-bearing or instant dismissal; when individual merit meant nothing; when inefficiency and dull-wittedness, if backed by colour or family prestige, were all powerful factors in determining the fate of darker unfortunates.[19]

It is a tribute to the patience of Grenadians that more incidents like the following did not happen.

On 19 October 1907 Bob Benjamin shot the Honourable Norman Lockhart, the Colonial Treasurer, in St George's. Benjamin was a competent black civil servant who was a native of Gouyave. He is described by Clyne as 'an intelligent man, [who] spoke fluently and well; but was quick tempered'.[20] Every fortnight, on a Friday, he came to St George's to collect money to pay the roadworkers in St John's Parish. On this Friday, the Colonial Treasurer, a white Englishman called Lockhart, gave him an order, which Benjamin told Lockhart he would not carry out, either because the order itself was out of place, or because the manner in which it was given was disrespectful. Tempers flared, and Benjamin pulled out the gun that he always carried, and fired three shots at Lockhart, wounding him in the arm. He then stabbed him in the chest with a butcher's knife. McKie, the Chief Clerk in the Treasury, went to the assistance of Lockhart, and was also wounded.

Benjamin was subsequently tried, and was sentenced to twelve years in prison. However, the people of Grenada identified with Benjamin, and followed the case closely. The *Grenada Handbook* records that a 'riotous demonstration by the common people occurred on the sentence becoming known'.[21]

Who Cared?

The people who held power in Grenada failed to use the Constitution of Grenada for the benefit of all the Grenadian people. In their decadence, those sitting in the House of Assembly gave up representative government with hardly a whisper. Those denied the privilege of sitting in the Assembly agitated for its return for decades. Some of the main agitators like Donovan would never see the restoration of a democratic government in their lifetime. It was by default, therefore, that the British government and its representatives, the Governors and Lieutenant-Governors, were the ones responsible for bringing a modicum of modernity and social reform to Grenada. This was especially true in the case of Governor Sendall. Governor Walter Sendall was an exemplary Governor. Although found to be taciturn and abrupt, and too much inclined to rely on the counsel of a close circle of advisers, by the end of his period as Governor, even the highly critical *Chronicle* newspaper sang Sendall's praises. One writer said that compared to the terms of the other Governors it was hard to believe that all had operated under the same Crown Colony government.

Governor Sendall accomplished much by way of public works and social improvement. He had repealed the unpopular excise laws, extended pipe-borne water to 10 square miles of St George's, enlarged and revamped the Hospital Board, the Botanical Gardens Committee and the Educational Committee, and had, through them, effected many changes for the better. In spite of his earlier misjudgement in the matter of banning the Guy Fawkes celebrations, his handling of the affair and public remonstrance of public officials over their conduct endeared him to the population. Within the four years of his office he did much to neutralize the fears and frustrations built up against the Crown Colony form of government, and found a way to involve more people in governance through the establishment of the Parish Boards. The tunnel he built to assist porters who had to carry heavy loads over 'Canash Hill' from one part of St George's to the other is a lasting and silent testament to Sendall's excellent, caring administration despite his difficult personality. At the end of his term of office the entire population united to try to have his term extended, but to no avail. Despite all efforts, Grenada bade farewell to an English Governor who cared more about the condition of the average Grenadians than did many of the Grenadian élite and coloured middle class. Sendall did not seek approval, but was everywhere called the 'Prince of West Indian Governors'.

Sendall had shown that Crown Colony government could work for the benefit of the people. However, the full import of disenfranchisement and a hunger for empowerment was spreading into the general population already bristling at the blatant discrimination of a society based on colour. It is not surprising that some took matters into their own hands, like Benjamin, or the rioters on Guy Fawkes' Night. But the struggle would have to go on for several decades.

Notes

1 The discrepancy between the date on which the requirements for electoral franchise were provided (1789) and the date it was implemented (1792) is the result of the ruling by the King's Law Offices to revoke the 1768 Hillsborough Royal Order, and reinstate it at the end of 1791. The Election Act, meanwhile, had passed the Assembly by 1787, but had somehow managed to reach the Council only after the Revocation of the Hillsborough Order had come into effect.

2 Brizan, p. 215.

3 Brizan, p. 220.

4 This was a new form of government for Grenada, but it had been introduced in Trinidad, British Guiana and Ceylon (today's Sri Lanka) since the early nineteenth century. It was brought into being to take the power out of the hands of subject peoples who were not of British origin. An antecedent of the Crown Colony system was the 1774 Quebec Act, and the 'Counseil Souverain' that had ruled Grenada before 1763.

5 Some sources spell this name Galway, but all official documentation on William Galwey Donovan, including his death certificate, spells his middle name with an 'e'.

6 Personal communication, Mrs Nellie Donovan-Payne.

7 Quoted in Brizan, p. 225.

8 *Report of the Royal Commission* (Crossman Commission), Part II, 1884, p. 58.

9 *St George's Chronicle and Grenada Gazette*, 8 Feb. 1885, quoted in Brizan, p. 225.

10 *Ibid.*, 9 May 1885, quoted in Brizan, pp. 226–7.

11 Richardson, p. 25.

12 *Ibid.*

13 CO 321/86, Colonial Office papers, no. 125, quoted by Richardson, p. 26.

14 Richardson, p. 26.

15 Richardson, p. 27.

16 Devas (1974), p. 188.

17 Cox (1998), p. 7.

18 By the time he got to Barbados, the king had started to ail, and permission was granted for him to return home to Opobo. A long and unexpected delay at Tenerife resulted in the king's death, without him ever seeing his homeland again. See Cox (1998), p. 28.

19 Coard, p. 9.

20 Clyne, p. 22.

21 Govt of Grenada, *Grenada Handbook*, p. 69.

12

Grenada Enters the Twentieth Century

During the time that the mainstay of Grenada's economy was shifting from sugar to nutmeg and cocoa, and while some Grenadians were establishing themselves as peasant proprietors, or making a new life for themselves in other countries, the face of Grenada was being changed by the advent of new technology and the introduction of a modern infrastructure.

Motor Traffic

In 1904 Leonard Kent brought the first motor vehicle to the island. This was a Triumph motorcycle. Shortly after this George Kent imported the first motorcar. This was a Stanley steam car. It was powered by steam generated by a boiler under the hood. To start the car, you had to light a burner under the boiler, and wait thirty minutes for enough steam to be generated to get the car to move. This car had no gears, only a throttle which you opened to get more steam to enable the car to get over hills. In 1907 George Kent also brought in one of the first cars with a gasoline engine, and two other vehicles were imported shortly after, one by Arnold Williamson who ran his vehicle partially for hire. His was therefore the first motor taxi in Grenada.

Reginald Clyne describes the sensation these first motorcars caused in the population:

> One morning in January 1907, while preparing for school, a sound as of thunder in the far distance, fell on my ears … The sound drew closer and louder. Louder and louder it grew. Everybody within hearing ran out of his or her homes, gazing excitedly in the direction from which it came. What was this mechanical 'monster' belching billows of thick blue-black smoke from its rear; its inside filled with white, pink-faced ladies with hats from which hung fascinators?[1] And who was this white uniformed and gloved driver with cap and visor, steering this horseless vehicle along the macadamised roadway? … Women ran

and screamed, horses neighed frighteningly and shied, unseating their riders. My father fell heavily on his knees, heedless of the sharp edged stones, and lifting his eyes towards heaven exclaimed, 'My eyes hath seen the glory of the Lord. Now let his servant depart in peace!'[2]

This was not Kent's car but an automobile belonging to James Gordon Bennett, owner of the *New York Herald*, who had brought it to Grenada on his private yacht. He took it away when he sailed that afternoon, but not before causing several incidents of bodily harm, and making those little boys who had actually seen the car, famous and popular among their mates.

In 1914 there were five motor vehicles in Grenada,[3] and by 1917 there were 150 motor vehicles on the road. Motorcars soon evolved from being a novelty to becoming a necessity. This form of transport demanded improvement in the roads. The roads in Grenada were historically lacking in quality and maintenance. In 1871 Lieutenant-Governor Freeling said of road maintenance that:

> I sincerely hope that what I myself witnessed of the mode of road making, is not common throughout the island, viz., taking the mud from the ditches at the side and heaping upon a road already deep in mud: such a proceeding can only be a useless waste of public money.[4]

He suggested that the legislature adopt the suggestion of the Surveyor of Public Works that Thompson's traction road engines and Blake's stone breaking machines be imported for the improvement of the roads.

Governor Sendall also tried to improve the roads, and Governor Sadler built on the accomplishments of his predecessors. Many of the roads were tarmacked, or, as the local people said, 'oiled', using pitch from the pitch lake in Trinidad.

Motor vehicles were not only imported for the convenience and pleasure of the élite. Governor Sadler recommended that two officials from the Public Works Department be given cars as 'on these hilly roads [a horse] is only capable of certain amount of work'.[5] He needed the supervisory staff of the Public Works Department to be able to cover more territory, as:

> I have taken a special interest in roadwork since my arrival in Grenada ... the waste of public funds through want of proper supervision ... the native overseers cannot be relied upon unless they are made to feel that the European Officials will be on their tracks unawares and constantly.[6]

In 1916 Governor Sadler reported that a fair road existed from St George's to Sauteurs via St David's and Grenville, but the road to Sauteurs via Woodford, Gouyave, St Mark's and Samaritan was not suitable, even for carriages.[7] The traditional way of moving between these areas and other parts of Grenada by small coasting vessels and large rowboats had to continue.

The Main Road and Byway Ordinance was passed in 1916 to prohibit the planting of coconut trees within certain distance of the public road, and also to regulate the proximity of new houses and buildings to such roads.[8] This was necessary because coconuts falling from the trees were a danger to traffic, and people began to build right up to the road, and in some cases encroach upon it. Compensation was paid to those persons whose trees, which had been planted before the Ordinance, had to be cut down.

Prosperous Times

The private citizens of Grenada and the government were both able to import motor vehicles because Grenada was experiencing a wave of prosperity. In his Annual Report on Grenada for 1913, Governor Sadler wrote to the Secretary of State for the Colonies that the economy had never been better. Revenue for 1911 to 1913 had exceeded that of all preceding years.[9] The wealth of Grenada came from the sale of cocoa, nutmegs, mace, cotton and cottonseed, and the government shared in this wealth through export taxes on these goods, import taxes on luxury and other goods, as well as land and other taxes.

Unfortunately, this wealth was not spread evenly through society, and most of the population remained at subsistence level, earning or producing just enough to keep on living. Although some of the wealth was used to improve all aspects of public works and public amenities in the Colony, these public works did not alleviate the everyday burden of poverty under which the majority of the people laboured. Nevertheless, Grenada was a law-abiding population. For the most part, in spite of the poverty in which most Grenadians lived, Grenada at this time had very little crime and the prison was too large for Grenada alone. Up to 1908 the prison in Grenada housed prisoners from St Vincent as well.

This prosperity was not shared by Carriacou. The lack of water, the over-grazing of land by small stock, the clearing of land for agricultural purposes and to provide timber for houses, boats and fuel had over time impoverished the soil, and caused soil erosion. The fertility of the soil in Carriacou was vastly depleted. There is a sad little vignette painted in 1897 by Sydney Oliver. He visited Grenada first, and found it a 'beautiful place, and quite what a tropical island ought to be'. Then, he says:

> We went on a little further and landed at a little decaying island called Carriacou, where all the people were wretchedly poor. It is all owned by a few absentee proprietors in England and the people cannot get land of their own or rent any except by the year at exorbitant terms. I think the experiment of land national-ization without compensation might very well be inaugurated at Carriacou.[10]

Carriacou had never been without water problems. The report of the police for 1903 related that:

> The want of water was severely felt, especially during the months of April and May: some relief was afforded by the government supplying two loads of water per week by the Revenue Cruiser, but numbers of stock died during that period, for the want of water principally, and on the whole it was a trying time for everything and everybody.[11]

However, better days were ahead for Grenada's sister island. The British government did acquire several large estates from the absentee owners in Carriacou, but instead of confiscating them without compensa-tion, a fair price was paid for them, and the people of Carriacou settled on lands of their own from 1903. This took place under the Land Settlement Scheme introduced in 1903.

The Land Settlement Scheme

In 1897 the Royal West Indian Commission visited Grenada and the other West Indian colonies to investigate social and economic conditions in these countries. Among its recommendations was the compulsory acquisition of uncultivated estates to facilitate the establishment of agricultural workers on their own land as peasant farmers. In accordance with this recommen-dation the Governor of Grenada decided that some of the surplus funds that were in the Grenada Treasury were to be used to help the poor acquire land. In 1901 a law was enacted that enabled the government to acquire and pay a just price for abandoned estates. These estates would be subdivided and sold in small plots to any who could afford the price. The act of acquiring land was made even easier because the land was to be purchased in easy instalments, and the government did all the legal work with regard to the land titles.

The Land Settlement Scheme began in Carriacou where the need was greatest. For thirty years most of the large sugar estates remained uncultivated after the collapse of the sugar industry. No land had been sold to the people from these estates, as had happened in Grenada, because the owners wanted to keep the estates intact. Now the government bought them, and sold the land to the people. The first two estates bought and subdivided in Carriacou were the Harvey Vale and Beausejour Estates.

The allotment of land in Carriacou from the subdivision of these two estates began in 1903. There were 244 lots and 51 building sites available for the development of small farms and for the development of a town. Carriacouans quickly bought the lots, so that by 1913 the Governor could report that the scheme was an immense success because of the 'sterling qualities of its hardy peasants'.[12] The total value of the lots was £8450, and at the end of the payment period £7976 had been paid, with only £474 in arrears, and £692 still to be collected. In 1913 three more estates in Carriacou were purchased – Belair, Bellevue and Mount Pleasant Estates. The Governor reported that the prosperity of all the peasants who purchased land was remarkable, and they had much success in the cultivation of limes and coconuts.[13] The Land Settlement Scheme did so well that by 1920

> Carriacou…is a great deal better off on the whole than its big sister Grenada. There are no signs of poverty in the little island, no rags and tatters to say nothing of nakedness … this is largely due to the Land Settlement Scheme.[14]

The Land Settlement Scheme was introduced into Grenada in 1910. The first lands made available for purchase were Crown Lands in Morne Rouge and True Blue. Sections of the Calivigny and Westerhall Estates were purchased with surplus funds from the Treasury, and these also were made available to the people. The scheme in Grenada was successful, but not quite as successful as in Carriacou. In 1912, of the 453 acres to be allocated, 247 were taken up. Later 62 acres were added to the acreage earmarked for this scheme, and in 1913 another 344 acres[15] were made available. It was expected that the people returning from Panama where they had worked on the Canal would look to invest their money in land,[16] and some of the acreage was brought under the scheme to accommodate the returning workers. In 1915 the St Cyr Estate was bought and subdivided under the scheme.

Grenada was the only Windward or Leeward Island which heeded the recommendation of the Royal West Indian Commission and afforded agricultural labourers widespread opportunities to acquire smallholdings.[17] In 1911, before the scheme was complete, Grenada had 6332 owners of land of less than two and a half acres, 1454 persons who owned between two and a half and five acres, 344 who owned between five and seven acres, and 219 persons who owned between seven to ten acres (an acre being less than half a hectare).

Migration

Whereas some Grenadians put their hopes in land, others looked to better themselves through migration. Historically Grenada had always experienced an outflow of people to neighbouring countries, especially to Trinidad. When Grenada became a colony of Great Britain for the second and last time, there was a massive migration of Grenada's French creoles and their slaves to Trinidad. Then soon after slave emancipation, for example, there was such a rush to migrate to Trinidad that the planters had to resort to propaganda as deterrence. There is, in the *St George's Chronicle and Grenada Gazette* of 4 August 1838, an advertisement by Richard N. Watts, which warned the labourers against those who had been paid money to entice them to Trinidad. He elaborated on the difficulties of cane cultivation in Trinidad, the distance of the fields from the mills, the bad roads, the unhealthy climate, and the high incidence of fever which had caused many deaths.

> 'You live in a healthy island' he exhorted them, 'and are happy. Do not for the value of a few more dogs, more wages, barter that happiness. I assure you I would rather work for an estate in Grenada for two bits a day than one in Trinidad for eight.'[18]

Regardless of Watts' advice, between 1839 and 1845 there were a total of 2239 official migrants to Trinidad from Grenada including Carriacou, and a considerable number more who migrated unofficially.[19] Some of the migration was seasonal, but some people remained permanently in that country.

In the twentieth century, migration took place for reasons similar to previous migrations, but was propelled by a different cause. Both in the previous periods and in the period under discussion, the migrants were seeking a better life. In the earlier period, however, they were driven from Grenada because of religious and cultural oppression. Now people were driven by economic motives and were seeking to better themselves in lands that seemed to offer them more opportunity to do this.

Every year, the amount of migrants increased. Between 1891 and 1901 2575 persons migrated. In the next decade, between 1901 and 1911, the figures rose to 8780. For the period 1911–21 an enormous migration of 12,041 persons took place. Migration was so heavy in the last period that not only was the natural increase of the population wiped out, but there was 'a further draft on the population of 1911 to the extent of 458'.[20] The *Report on the Census* for 1901[21] attributed the emigrations to low wages, as compared to the wages obtainable in the neighbouring colony of Trinidad and in South and Central America, increased difficulty in getting land for making gardens, and the enhanced value of land. Added to this, the people of Carriacou were also under increasing economic pressure due to the steady decrease in the value of cotton. Migrants from the sister isle were well represented in the exodus. Approximately twice as many men as women migrated.

Some Grenadians migrated to the United States, and a few, like the pianist Leslie Hutchinson, were to use the opportunities in America to launch careers that would make them world famous.[22] A total of 1984 Grenadians sought employment in the Panama Canal Zone,[23] working on the construction of the Panama Canal. Farm workers were recruited for Cuba to work on the sugar plantations owned by American companies there, and for Brazil where they were recruited to work on coffee plantations. Brizan reports that some time after 1871 some young men from St David's went to Venezuela to dig for gold, and many were successful, returning home with cash to invest in homes and land.[24] But the greatest proportion of migrants went to Trinidad.

As soon as people became aware that recruiters were busy in Grenada signing up labourers to work abroad, legislation for the protection of workers overseas was passed. In 1899 the Government of Grenada passed the Emigration Regulation Ordinance limiting the recruitment of Grenadian labour to authorized persons. This Ordinance was replaced in 1911 by the Emigrants Protection Ordinance (no. 16 of 1911), and covered emigration to Brazil, Panama, Costa Rica, Nicaragua and Surinam. It was necessary to replace this Ordinance in 1927 by an updated version that made it compulsory for everyone recruiting labour in Grenada to obtain a permit annually. This Ordinance, and the amendment to it passed in 1930, contained several clauses for the protection of emigrants. Among these was the regulation that the recruiters must not deduct anything from the wages quoted to the recruitees, that a fee of ten shillings was to be paid by the agent to the government for every recruit, and that every recruit was to pay the government a fee of two shillings. Both agent and recruited worker had also to pay into the Treasury a sum of 25 shillings to assist the government repatriate workers who were in distress.

Some migrants died on foreign soil, especially those who went to Panama, due to the unhealthy conditions under which they worked. Some of the migrants returned home, often with considerable savings with which they bought land, or set themselves up in business. Most of the migrants did not return, settling permanently in the United States, Panama, Cuba, Trinidad and other foreign countries. Those who stayed abroad did not forget their families at home. The money they sent back to their families was so significant that it was counted as a part of the national income. In 1913 the remittances from Grenadians in the Panama Canal Zone totalled £6407.[25] Remittances in this and other years helped to support those left behind, and to purchase land, construct houses or set up shops or small businesses.

During the period 1926–28, annual net migration fell to 700 persons, compared to the annual net migration of 2000 for 1923.[26] After the opening of the Panama Canal in 1914 there was no more migration to that country. The possibility of migration to the United States decreased with the quota restrictions placed on West Indian immigration to the United States after 1921. Immigration to Cuba was also curtailed around the same time. However, migration to the United States continued despite the quota, reaching a peak in 1923, just before the passing of the United States Immigration Act in 1924, which even more tightly controlled immigration from the Caribbean to the United States. The safety valve of migration to counter economic pressures at home would be kept open by the migration to Trinidad, which continued to welcome an uninterrupted stream of Grenadians until after the mid-century, and by migration to the Netherlands Antilles in response to the expansion of the oil industry there, and the consequent need for workers. In 1929 and 1930 the net migration from Grenada was approximately 1000 persons and 1500 persons respectively.[27]

The Peasant Proprietor

As a result of the Land Settlement Scheme, the numbers of peasant farmers rapidly increased. In 1915 dogs had to be licensed.[28] The significance of this Ordinance was not the effort to keep the dog population under control, or the income earned for the government. The importance for posterity was that it provided Grenada with a definition of 'Peasant'. Under this Ordinance, the owners of all dogs had to license them at four shillings a year for male dogs, and six shillings annually for bitches. Peasant proprietors were allowed a free licence for one dog, peasants being defined as any person who was the owner or occupier of not more than 10 acres of land, and who was an agriculturalist, labourer, domestic or menial servant, artificer, handicraftsman, or otherwise engaged in manual labour.

All did not go well for the peasant proprietor. Many of the new landowners were naive, and were easy prey to unscrupulous moneylenders, who were often merchants and large landowners. Many peasants simply spent too much in the various shops that had opened in St George's and the other parish capitals as well as in some of the districts. They were allowed to take goods against the coming crop, and soon fell into debt. At the first sign of the peasant defaulting on debt payments, the moneylenders would secure a writ of execution from the court on the peasant's land and either sell or acquire the land. Even if the peasant managed to pay the debt instalments, many seemed to be working to pay off a debt that never came to an end. In 1908 a Commission of Enquiry headed by Frank Gurney, was set up to look into the encumbrances of the peasants and other matters. The peasants most affected were those in the Concord, Grand Roy and Mon Plaisair areas, where two moneylenders had been active in attempting to ruin farmers either by acquiring their land if they were freeholders, or by depriving them of the value of the improvements they had made to land that they had leased if they were tenant farmers.

The moneylenders and proprietors complained that the tenant farmers, when they were given the land, had pledged to deliver a specified amount of produce and had agreed that, if the amount fell short of what was agreed, they would pay the renter the difference in cash. If they could not pay, interest would accrue on the debts. The tenant farmers said that they had never agreed to specified amounts of produce, only a percentage of what was produced, and certainly had not agreed that interest would be charged on shortfalls. The interest was oppressive – between 8 and 10 per cent compound interest quarterly or half-yearly. The peasants also expressed dissatisfaction at the price the moneylenders or proprietors gave them for their produce.

The findings of the Commission were that the accusations of the peasants against the moneylenders and proprietors could not be proved. The Commission noted that the peasants were delivering smaller and smaller amounts of produce to their creditors every year. It was also evident that the peasant needed assistance with soil preparation for planting and fertilization, access to more land, and education on how not to be enticed into debt by shopkeepers. The Commission recommended that more plots be made available to the peasants, that depots be established where cocoa could be brought and sold at public auction, and that a Government Land Bank should be established to assist the peasants in the cultivation and improvement of their holdings.

Apart from some initial problems, possession of these small farms would enable the peasant proprietors who worked them to share in the wealth Grenada offered at this time, through diligent agricultural pursuits. Because of the spread of prosperity, Grenada would become more stable. Grenada also became more able to feed itself. The ability to produce food for the nation would be extremely important when Grenada, as a British Colony, along with most of the world, became engulfed in the First World War or, as it was known at the time, 'The Great War'.

Improvements in Public Works and other Infrastructure

In 1915 the Queen's Park Ordinance was passed.[29] This provided for the raising by public subscription of £1000 that would be matched by £1500 raised by the government for the draining and improvement of Queen's Park for use as a public recreational ground. A body known as the Queen's Park Trustees would supervise the park, and the Governor would appoint these for three years. The Trustees would be empowered to charge fees for the use of the park, but they could not mortgage or otherwise encumber the park. [30]

Another major improvement was the lighting of St George's. In a letter to the Secretary of State the Governor had observed:

> To say that the town of St George is lighted is a misnomer. The town is supplied with a few worn out oil lamps, which, when they are supposed to be lighted are more often out than not. The lighting of the public institutions is very unsatisfactory, and, for what is obtained, expensive. A visit to the hospital after sundown is depressing in the extreme. Owing to the darkness and consequent difficulty of detection, excreta is often thrown in the public streets at night, therefore from a health point of view, and the detection of crime, better lighting is absolutely essential.[31]

The Governor's proposal that an electric plant be set up by a private company was accepted. An attempt was also made to establish pipe-borne water across Grenada.

Telephones were becoming more and more common. A telephone switchboard was installed in 1911, and replaced with a better one in 1913. In approximately a quarter of a century, telephone subscribers increased from 120 phones to 410 phones. The police operated a heliograph with which they communicated to Carriacou. At this time a soap factory was established in Tempe. An ice factory began operations, and supplied not only Grenada but also St Lucia and St Vincent with ice.

Fishing and Whaling

Although whaling had been an industry in the Windward Islands since the nineteenth century, Grenada did not have a commercial whaling operation. In 1924, Captain Otto Sverdrup, a well-known Arctic explorer and whaler, visited Grenada to ascertain the feasibility of setting up whaling operations in Grenada. Satisfied that there were sufficient whales to warrant the outlay, Glover Island was purchased by a company set up for the purpose, and a modern whaling factory set up. Whaling operations began in January 1925. During that year 100 'Humpback' whales were caught, and two 'Bryde' whales, one of which was a pregnant female. The project exported 112,963 gallons of whale oil valued at £16,070. In 1926, a total of 72 whales were killed, but none were caught in the next year, and the factory ceased operations. In 1928 the factory was dismantled, but enough was left behind to become scars on the once-pristine islet, and to be a reminder that Captain Sverdrup was the first, but not the last, foreign national to set up a company in Grenada that would add nothing to the general welfare but would deplete the island's natural resources. In years to come, other foreign companies would fish in or near Grenada's territorial limits, depleting the fish stocks and reaping a handsome profit at the expense of the country and the environment. Whales would become a rarity around Grenada and the Grenadines due to the global depletion of this species through over-fishing by selfish nations.

No attention to an organized fishing industry in Grenada was made until 1938. Before this date, fishermen operated with seine nets and small boats that hugged the coast, and therefore had to be content with small catches, and the small income this brought. In Carriacou and the Grenadines, the fishermen fared better, as they were brave and skilful boatmen, not afraid to go far from shore to seek out the better fishing grounds.

The Post Office

In view of the advent of motor traffic, the Governor made a request to the Secretary of State for the Colonies asking that the horse and mule mail coach that ran between St George's and Grenville be replaced by a motor coach, which not only took mail, but also offered a passenger service. The Governor said that this service would not only be profitable, but also be a great convenience to the public. This request was granted.

The roads on the leeward side of the island were not good, and these continued to have their mail cargo and passengers brought to them by two small steamers that called weekly at different points on the leeward coast and bi-weekly at parts of the windward coast that the mail coach could not reach. There was also a weekly service to Carriacou.

Mail between Grenada and the rest of the world had been carried by the Royal Mail Steam Packet Company. The service was irregular, and when the contract came to an end in December 1915 mail to the rest of the world was sent out on regular steamers, and the mail for the Caribbean carried by Canadian Steamers. This arrangement proved quite satisfactory for the receipt and delivery of mail.

In April 1916 penny postage (2 cents) was introduced for all letters between the Windward Islands and the United States of America. This was the domestic rate within the United States of America.

Currency

Up to the end of the nineteenth century, Grenada used two types of money. British pounds, shillings and pence (£ s. d.) were used in commercial transactions, but other currency was in circulation – Joes (or Johannes), dollars and bits being the most commonly used. A diary printed in Grenada in 1787 for the use of a gentleman gives the following advice on conversion: 'To bring currency to sterling – 50 × 2 divided by 3.'[32] In 1835 the following table was given by the Commissioners of Compensation for Slaves being emancipated:

> Doubloon –180 shillings
> Johannes – 60 shillings
> Guineas – 52 shillings and 6 pence
> Sovereigns – 50 shillings
> Dollar –10 shillings[33]

As the twentieth century began, some attempt was made to standardize the currency and all financial accounting in Grenada was to be kept in sterling. However, it was difficult to control the various other coins and notes that were still in circulation. Silver coins were used for smaller transactions, and notes for larger. Although gold coin had never been plentiful in Grenada, it was still legal tender. Some gold and foreign currency came into the island through the tourist trade. However, gold coin was getting scarcer and scarcer as it had become a practice by some private persons to collect and export it. Silver groats, worth four pence, had been a part of the currency in Grenada for decades, and were also now scarce, although they were still legal tender in 1914. By 1915 gold currency was almost non-existent, and no more came into the island due to the cessation of the tourist trade caused by the outbreak of war in 1914. The older currency was gradually replaced with British currency, the most common note in circulation being the £5 note, and the commonest coin the farthing.

In the 1940s a new currency, the British West Indies dollar, was introduced in all the British Caribbean islands. Instead of pounds, shillings and pence, the medium of exchange was dollars and cents. Randolph Mark recalls that: 'The transition period was long and painful, especially among the older folks who had extreme difficulty in relating the value of the dollar to the pound sterling.'[34]

The Eastern Caribbean dollar was introduced in 1951, and remained pegged to the British pound until July 1976, when it was pegged to the United States dollar. The present currency authority is the Eastern Caribbean Central Bank in which Grenada and the other members of the Organization of Eastern Caribbean States have membership.

Improvements in Health

Grenada at this time was really not very healthy. An American physician working in Grenada was distressed at the number of children between one and fifteen years old who died, remarking that over 60 per cent of the island's mortality was due to diseases that were readily preventable. He found that in the first batch of 206 recruits for military service with the British West Indies Regiment,[35] 144 had hookworm and 53 had malaria. In the third batch of 121 examined in 1917 by his successor, twenty-two had a venereal disease, ten had bad hearts, nine had kidney trouble, one had bad teeth, two were 'underdeveloped', four had diseases of the bones, and eleven had various other diseases. These recruits were not a good sample, as they were presumed to be able-bodied. The incidence of disease in the working population was even greater. Dr Angus McDonald, the Chief Medical Officer in Grenada at this time, estimated that 80 per cent of the inhabitants of St Andrew's were infected with hookworm.[36]

Carriacou was deemed to be far healthier than Grenada. The Colonial Surgeon observed that statistics showed an: '[u]nbroken record of lower death rates in Carriacou, but the water supply [is] deemed the worst in the Colony. The water in the ponds is the colour of pea soup and that of the wells is brackish.'[37]

During this era great strides were taken to rid the colony of malaria, hookworm, yaws and other endemic diseases. The key to this was through public works and public health.

Ankylostomiasis or hookworm

Ankylostomiasis, or hookworm, had been identified as a health problem since 1896. Hookworm was a problem for all ages, but was less common in children under ten. This infestation did not kill, but robbed the individual of energy. In 1915 a massive campaign was launched to rid the population of hookworm. The campaign was under the direction of Dr Angus MacDonald, and for two years he worked with indefatigable energy on this project. Leaflets were distributed explaining how to prevent infection, and 'Lantern Lectures' illustrating the causes, prevention and treatment were given, including instruction in general sanitation. As a preventative measure against hookworm, yaws and other diseases spread by contact with bodily fluids and contaminated water, pit latrines were introduced to replace pan latrines. Excreta from the pan latrines had been buried in trenches or dumped in the sea. The pit latrines were a measure to curtail disease spread from contact with excreta or water contaminated by the same. In 1917 pit latrines were provided for all government public schools.

Eradication of yaws

Another major improvement in health was the attention directed towards the treatment and eradication of the disease called yaws. Yaws is a highly infectious, unpleasant and sometimes disfiguring disease. At this time in history, it was rampant in most tropical and sub-tropical areas of the world. Yaws is caused by bacterial infection. If blood or bodily fluids from infested persons come into contact with an abrasion on the skin of a susceptible individual, the disease can be contracted. Yaws can also be spread by flies, or contact with the clothes, rags or towels of an infected person, or from surfaces where the infected person has sat or otherwise touched.

Where it is endemic, the disease is acquired in childhood. Three or four weeks after infection, a highly infectious itchy lumpy growth appears on the site of the infection. Scratching spreads the infection, and leads to the development of more growths elsewhere on the body. Without treatment the growths heal slowly in about six months, but in about 10 per cent of the cases there is disfigurement. Large areas of skin are destroyed, and there can be widespread tissue loss, destruction of the bone, joints, nose, palate and upper jaw.[38]

Yaws was not a new disease in Grenada. It had been introduced into Grenada by the slaves brought from West Africa where yaws was endemic. The historian Brian Edwards mentions that yaws and leprosy were introduced into the West Indies from Africa, and some of the older writers of medical affairs in the West Indies mention the landing of slaves suffering from yaws. The Colonial Surgeon for Grenada remarks that:

The disease was very prevalent in Grenada up to the date of the abolition of slavery. Nearly every estate had its Yaws House for the segregation of slaves suffering from this disease … During the period of apprenticeship … the Yaws Houses were kept up. In 1838 this system expired and the slaves were scattered all over the colony, many of them taking up gardens in the hills. Yaws Houses were done away with and little attention was given to the complaint for many years.[39]

Yaws can be cured by a single large dose of penicillin, but the discovery of this drug was still in the future. Without an effective cure, the best strategy was to mount a campaign to encourage cleanliness and good sanitation. This would not be easy, as they were not yet ingrained habits of the Grenadian people, and the overcrowded and impoverished conditions under which the majority of people had to live militated against the raising of standards of this kind. The Governor of Grenada wrote to the Secretary of State that:

Yaws was particularly widespread in the Parishes of St Andrew's, St David's and St George's. It was limited to the labouring classes, although the occasional case did occur among members of the upper classes. Lacking an effective cure for the disease, all sort of quack remedies were prescribed. One of these was to feed the patient exclusively for months on armadillo, which was first cooked with secret spices, and then suspended and steamed over pots of secret infusions.[40]

Nevertheless, a concerted effort was begun by the last quarter of the nineteenth century. One strategy to eradicate the disease was to isolate the patient. In 1875 the Colony Hospital treated thirty-three cases of yaws. In 1876 a hospital devoted to the treatment and cure of yaws was opened in a building known as Marine Villa in the shadow of Fort George. The hospital remained opened for seven years, and the number offering themselves for treatment steadily grew. In 1881, when the numbers grew so large that the patients could no longer be accommodated at Marine Villa, the hospital closed and a ward at the Colony Hospital known as 'The War Ward' was prepared to accommodate seventy patients.

In 1882 it was estimated that there were 800 hundred cases of yaws in Grenada, which amounted to 2 per cent of the population. Only a small percentage would offer themselves for treatment, as individuals would hide the fact that they had yaws. The treatment demanded residence in hospital, and the days spent there represented lost earnings to the peasant proprietor. Every year until 1885 the number of people treated for yaws at the Colony Hospital declined until 1910, when a more effective cure was found, and people began again to offer themselves for treatment. The largest number of patients treated in this period was in 1915 when 605 patients were treated.[41] It is interesting to note that Carriacou was practically exempt from yaws.

Yaws remained prevalent in Grenada both because the treatment offered prior to 1910 was ineffective and because there was also no concerted effort to improve the poor housing and unsanitary conditions under which people lived. In 1916 the Colonial Surgeon recommended drastic measures in the war against yaws. He said that isolation of the patients had been ineffective by itself, and, along with isolation, preventative measures should be enforced. He recommended that yaws should become a notifiable disease, which meant that a physician was bound to report every case he diagnosed. Key to the control of yaws was public education. The Colonial Surgeon emphasized that it was necessary to instruct the public in the ways in which yaws was contracted and spread, and to try to effect general improvements in domestic sanitation, including proper ventilation of houses, less overcrowding, more use of glass to let the sunlight in, the use of flooring and of beds, especially for the children. Sanitary Inspectors should go from house to house to locate cases. Added to this, new treatments using salvarsan and potassium iodide as a cure for yaws meant that persons would only have to stay in hospital four days, and then attend at the Government Dispensary every week until certified cured. To ensure that the infected were kept track of, a system of cards was strictly maintained at the Office of the Colonial Surgeon.[42]

The International Health Commission of the Rockefeller Foundation offered assistance to Grenada to help control yaws, and this was accepted. Most of these measures necessary to eradicate the disease were carried out, and gradually the incidence of yaws declined.

Leprosy

Leprosy was another disease that had so far gone virtually untreated, and was now to receive attention from the health officials. Leprosy had come to Grenada with the slaves, and the Slave Registers that were compiled from 1812 noted several slaves with the disease. Leprosy is a chronic bacterial infection. It has a long incubation period of about three to five years. If untreated, it leads to blindness and disfigurement. The bacteria attack the nerves, beginning with the nerves of the skin and muscle. Early manifestations of the disease are a darkening or lightening of patches of skin, reduced sensation, increased tenderness and decreased sweating in affected areas. As the disease progresses, the hands, feet and face become numb, and the muscles become paralysed. Although not infectious or highly contagious, and only passed on to others during the first stages of the disease, others living in close quarters are in danger of catching the disease as it is spread in droplets of nasal mucus.[43]

Leprosy has been feared since the beginning of recorded times, because of the complications of the disease. Increasing muscle paralysis leads to deformity. The cartilage and bones of the nose are eroded, as well as bones elsewhere in the body, leading to the loss of fingers, toes, and other body parts. The eyelids cannot close, due to the loss of facial muscle, and the eyes dry out and ulcerate. The eye may also be attacked by bacteria, leading to an inflammation of the eyeball. In either case, blindness results.

Housing conditions during slavery and the crowded living conditions of the ex-slaves after Emancipation were ideal for the spread of this disease. The higher incidence of leprosy in Grenada was only prevented by the nature of the disease. Only 3 per cent of people are susceptible to the disease, and continuing to live in close quarters with a leper will not automatically pass on the disease to the whole household. Nevertheless, the public learned to shun the leper, and persons afflicted with the disease were ostracized, turned off the plantations, and abandoned by their families.

A hospital to care for lepers was established by the end of the nineteenth century, and remained in operation until 1927, when it was dissolved into the leper settlement. This had accommodation for twenty people, and was established near Quarantine Station in Morne Rouge.[44] Although the drugs that are really effective against leprosy were yet to be discovered, physicians had at their disposal medications that did mitigate the disease. However, damage already done to the person was irreversible. Quick diagnosis is important for the prevention of disfigurement, and people at this time did not practise routine examination of workers. People who thought they might be infected also were more liable to try folk medicine, because of the natural distrust they had developed for the white man and his ways. By the time it was obvious that that disease was progressing, and there were no more folk remedies to try, the afflicted person was noticeable, and was driven to seek refuge in the hospital.

Malaria

This era saw the draining of swamps, in an effort to eradicate malaria. The cause of malaria had been traced to the organism carried by the *Aedes Aegypti* mosquito, and transmitted to man through the mosquito bite. Prevention was thought to be the most effective way of ridding the population of this disease. Therefore the habitat of the mosquito – the swamp – was attacked.

The draining of swamps continued after the First World War. In 1930 Grenada received an appreciable grant from the Colonial Development Fund to effect the draining of swamps for malaria control. There was an extensive swamp in the Belmont area, and a little was drained every year. Concrete gutters were constructed to take off water, and low-lying areas were filled in. Of greatest importance, however, was the inauguration of the anti-malarial campaign, funded by the Rockefeller Foundation

Venereal disease

Venereal disease, commonly referred to as 'VD', generally meant syphilis or gonorrhoea, although these were not the only two sexually transmitted diseases. Both of these venereal diseases were prevalent, and there was a relatively high death rate from syphilis.[45] A VD Ordinance was passed in 1917,[46] which provided free treatment for all whose income was less that £400. It was also made a criminal offence to have the disease and not report it, and also criminal to inflict another with the disease. All doctors, whether Government Medical Officers or private practitioners, had to report the number of cases they treated each month. The Governor said that: 'VD is eating into the systems of the people, playing havoc with the economic conditions of the Island, and thereby seriously affecting labour'.[47] He requested a public information campaign on the disease, and asked the help of all doctors and the clergy in getting the people to understand the importance of heeding the provisions of the Ordinance.

Other health concerns

Grenada was not exempt from other diseases, which swept through the population on several occasions, causing many deaths. An epidemic of dysentery affected Grenada in 1914–15, killing 297 people. Tuberculosis was also rampant, and between 1914 and 1950 this disease killed 64, and 107 succumbed to malaria. There were numerous cases of diarrhoea, gastro-enteritis and other diseases of the gastro-intestinal tract. A case of bubonic plague was introduced from Trinidad, but was successfully identified on the ship, and the victim sent to the Quarantine Station, where the person died. Pellagra, although not usually a cause of death, had been identified as a health problem in Grenada since about 1910.

Hospitals

Key to the treatment of disease was effective hospitals. The barracks at Fort George, and at the forts on Richmond Hill, were handed to the government when the garrison of British soldiers was withdrawn in 1853 at the beginning of the Crimean War. The Colony Hospital was moved in 1857 into the barracks at Fort George. The hospital functioned much better in its new location. The wards were later extended, and work had begun on a maternity wing. District hospitals in St John's, St Patrick's and St Andrew's, originally opened to care for the Indian indentured labourers, were opened to the public in 1882. A hospital was built for Carriacou. All these hospitals were supported by the government.

The Mental Hospital, also sited in the old military buildings at Richmond Hill, at first suffered from over-capacity, and solved the problem by offering to take funded mental patients from other islands, such as St Lucia, not as fortunate as Grenada in being provided with an institution for the care of the mentally ill. Taking funded patients from other islands also provided some revenue for the hospital. The Mental Hospital stopped admitting patients from St Lucia in 1914 when St Lucia got its own facility.

An institution called 'the Poor Asylum' or almshouse was now also relocated to vacated army buildings at Richmond Hill. A hospital for patients deemed incurable of tuberculosis was situated at Richmond Hill. This institution was called the Princess Marie Louise Hospital for Consumptives, after the member of the British Royal Family who had opened the building in 1914. An Anti TB Association was also formed in this period.

Public Health

More important than the cure of ill patients are measures to prevent persons from contracting disease in the first place. Public health matters were of great concern to the Royal Commission that was constituted in 1883 to investigate the welfare of the population in the British Caribbean. One of its recommendations was that a Chief Medical Officer be appointed to supervise the health of the country, with a staff of 17 District Medical Officers in the towns and districts. Throughout Grenada there should also be a set of government dispensaries, staffed by qualified drug-gists. There should also be a Board of Visitors for each District Hospital to ensure that standards were maintained, and to note any problems which they might need help and support in solving.

In 1930 the Colonial Development Fund provided, along with the funds for draining swamps for malaria control, money for the construction of and improvements to Visiting Stations, which were clinics staffed by nurses and which medical officers 'visited' on a scheduled basis. From this fund Petit Martinique was provided with its first Visiting Station, and equipment and improvements provided for the General Hospital and the St Andrew's Hospital, including a bacteriological laboratory, an incinerator and steam disinfector. Funds were also provided for the setting up of a dental clinic to treat children in primary school and paupers. This was opened in 1931.

'Tolerably good' health

In spite of the prevalence of yaws, leprosy, venereal disease and other illnesses, the general health of the island was described as 'tolerably good', because these conditions existed elsewhere in the Caribbean, with as much pain and suffering as in Grenada. Medicine was not yet sufficiently advanced to provide all the cures necessary. At this time the death rate in Grenada was 3 per cent, with a high infant mortality rate of 19 per cent. However, relief was soon to come.

Education

At the turn of the century there were three secondary schools – The St Joseph's Convent, the St George's High School and the Grammar or Grenada Secondary School. The total enrolment of 140 children in 1896[48] was mainly white or coloured children of moderate means, as the wealthier classes sent their children away to England or to Barbados to school as soon as they were old enough. There were 37 primary schools – ten run by the government, seven run by the Anglican Church, 14 run by the Roman Catholic Church, four run by the Methodist Church and two run by the Presbyterian Church. In 1896 there was a total enrolment of 7128 children, representing about one-quarter of the school-age population. The average school attendance was 49 per cent of the enrolment. The government grant for the upkeep of these schools was £5792, while the total cost of running the schools was £6134.[49] The churches therefore had to find enough financial support for their schools to make up the shortfall. Of the thirty-seven schools, thirty were deemed by the Inspector of Schools to be good in academic achievement, pedagogy, discipline and keeping of adequate records.

However, attendance was unsatisfactory in all the schools. This was a legacy of the perception among the majority of people that education was of no practical value. Children learnt nothing in schools to help them earn a living or improve themselves. Children were better employed doing household tasks, working on the estates or on the family lands, called 'gardens'. Low attendance was also undoubtedly partially due to the schools being too far away for some children to access, the bad conditions of the footpaths and byways that the children had to use to get from where they lived to the school, which included the need for some children to ford rivers that had no bridges. There were also epidemics of mumps, measles and other diseases, which kept children away for lengthy periods. More schools, sweeping reforms that would drastically change the content of education, and the changed perception of education as an avenue to social mobility would, in the next century, see the percentage of school-aged children receiving education gradually rise to almost 100 per cent. Although the genesis of the educational system had been laid down in the nineteenth century, an informed look at the system showed that there was a dire need to improve the performance of both teachers and pupils in schools. Although the enrolment of children was rising, the percentage of children who regularly attended school was no better than it ever was. One measure to try to cope with this was to get the teachers involved in effecting a more regular attendance of children in school. Teachers were each offered a bonus of six shillings for every child in the preliminary standard who attended school 200 days in the school year. They were also offered a grant of two shillings per pass per child for each subject passed in Standards I to VII.

All the laws and regulations pertaining to primary school education were combined into one Ordinance, which was passed in 1906, and the flaws which were noted in it corrected by a revised Ordinance passed in 1907. Under the new Ordinance, schools were reclassified as Infant, Lower Division or Combined Schools. The salaries of Principals were related to the type of school they supervised. They continued to receive a housing allowance, or free quarters. Bonuses were given to the Principals who successfully trained pupil-teachers for their examinations. Pensions were provided for all teachers including those in the church schools, but not including teachers in infant schools. In 1913 there were fifty-one primary schools: twenty-two of these were Roman Catholic, eleven were Church of England, five Methodist and two Presbyterian. The enrolment was 10,372 pupils and the average attendance was 5261.[50] A 'Ragged School' was opened in St George's in 1913 to provide education for a number of children of the poorest class who could not attend normal school for want of decent clothing. It was a great success, and it was suggested that another one be opened.[51]

The best-paid teachers were those in the secondary schools, who were better off than the best-paid teachers in the primary system, although they often had fewer pupils. The Principals of the high schools continued to be recruited from England or Europe, as were many of the class teachers. The Boys' Secondary School, which had opened in 1911, with thirty-eight pupils, now had eighty-two pupils. The Victoria High School for Girls run by the Church of England was closed in 1911, and reopened in 1912 with thirty-two pupils as the Girls' Secondary School. It closed again in 1916, but was soon opened again as the Church of England High School for Girls. From 1946 this school was called the Anglican High School. The grant of £100 given to St Joseph's Convent was increased to £150 in recognition of its usefulness to the community. It now had seventy-two pupils.

One of the most popular things the Governor did was to propose an Island Scholarship. He had the support of all the sectors of the community for this, including the local press. He was particularly pleased at this, because the local press, as the Governor had remarked, 'is often antagonistic to the Head of the Executive'.[52]

The Scholarship Ordinance was passed in 1916, and provided for an annual scholarship valued at £175 per annum, and an amount to cover travel might be added as well. The scholarship would be for three to four years, tenable at any university or college in Europe or Canada, or any agricultural, scientific or technological institute in Europe, Canada or the United States approved by the Governor in Council. It was based on the Senior Cambridge Examination, and the winner had to pass with honours, and pass those subjects that would exempt him from the London Matriculation. The editorial in *The West Indian* for 2 April 1916 expressed the view that:

> The greatest benefits of the Island Scholarship will be derived not from the few successful lads who shall be educated abroad, but rather from the many who shall earnestly strive to be worthy of the honour. Apart from the success or failure in winning the scholarship, the benefits will best be seen in the dominating incentive given to make school life a serious affair all round, thus serving to build up for Grenada a studentry worthy of the colony, and ensuring for us men better qualified to take up positions in various spheres of local activity.[53]

Domingo Sebastian de Freitas had been a member of the Legislative Council since 1895. He was a planter from St John's, but his behaviour was not typical of others of his class. He was a social reformer and a constant critic of the government. Nevertheless, his gentlemanly behaviour earned him his seat regardless of his critical thinking and outspoken behaviour. De Freitas praised the Governor for the move, but suggested that the scholarship be open to girls as well. He said he was a strong advocate of higher education for women. Not only would they, through education, be placed on the same footing as men, but also the more cultured women were, the wiser and better would be the generations that followed. He felt certain that the future welfare of Grenada depended more on the education of women than of men.[54]

The other newspaper, the *Federalist*, took the opportunity to regret that an Island Scholarship Ordinance had not been passed earlier. The editorial of 1 April 1916 recalled:

> We think in the early Sixties such a scheme was then seriously entertained by the government. It would have materialized, but for one fact. The scholarship winner was a dark lad. The late Julius De Pradines having qualified by being first in everything at the then Grammar School, the House of Assembly threw a cold douche on the idea of the scholarship. He was too dark to be so intelligent. The Legislature of Grenada sought to correct the error of the Creator for having given brains to a dark boy and punished the Colony thereafter. His father, however, sent the brilliant lad to Scotland where he pursued the studies and science of engineering, but returned to Grenada almost only to die.[55]

The Scholarship was suspended in 1924, but revived in 1926 on a biennial basis.

All grants to teachers including results grants were abolished in 1917, and replaced with better, regular salaries. However, the schools were expected to demonstrate a satisfactory level of performance, and certain standards were set. The teachers complained, however, that the performance targets set for them by the government assumed that they had control over the circumstances that determined success or failure. These, however, were outside of their control.

In 1925 a Director of Education was appointed. In 1926 an amendment to the Primary Education Ordinance provided for the establishment of Pupil Teachers' Centres in several districts, and an increase in the salaries for assistant teachers. In 1928 the Governor set up an Education Committee to consider the reorganization of education in Grenada. Although the proposals were rejected by the Board of Education, they sparked off discussion amongst members, which produced a more acceptable set of proposals.

The new set of proposals was passed by the Legislative Council in 1931 and provided for a reclassification of schools. Manual training centres in the main population areas would offer training in handicraft, agriculture and other industrial occupations. Senior schools catered for older pupils who successfully passed a qualifying examination after Standard III. Combined schools conducted classes for junior pupils as well as senior pupils beyond Standard III, while junior schools catered for pupils from ages six to fourteen, and taught the basis of reading, writing and arithmetic up to Standard III. Advanced junior schools offered instruction prescribed for a junior school, and, in addition, further instruction approved by the Director of Education. Assisted schools were those that had received a grant in the previous year, but in which attendance, although exceeding thirty pupils, was below what was required for a full junior school. The type of instruction was similar to that of the junior schools. Infant schools provided instruction for children between the ages of four and nine.

As a result of the reclassification, the churches had to give and take, but in the end the churches took responsibility for running fifty-two of the sixty-one schools in Grenada, not including the secondary schools. The Roman Catholic Church was responsible for twenty-nine schools and accounted for half the number of children enrolled, the Anglican Church ran fourteen, and the government sixteen. There were 250 teachers employed in these schools, but school attendance had not improved much over the past decades. Out of a total enrolment of 13,343, only 62 per cent was in school on any one day.

There were three secondary schools catering for 478 pupils. Poor children had limited access to secondary education through the twenty scholarships given annually for the secondary schools by the government. Eight were for boys tenable at the Grenada Boys' Secondary School, and twelve for girls, six each tenable at the Church of England High School and the St Joseph's Convent. During the period 1930 to 1951, poor children won 50 per cent of the scholarships to the secondary schools.

The children in the secondary schools sat the Junior Cambridge, Senior Cambridge and London Matriculation External Examinations. The pass rate for these examinations was between 37.5 per cent and 56 per cent and would improve steadily. The Island Scholarship continued to give access to higher education to children of the not so well-to-do.

Teachers were sent to be trained at the Rawle Training College in Barbados, and, after 1940, to the Government Training College in Trinidad. In 1936 the government built two large schools, one in St Paul's and the other in Hillsborough, Carriacou. These schools were built, equipped and staffed as ideal structures, on which all other schools should be modelled. They therefore became known as 'Model' Schools, and are called this to this day.

Despite these new Model Schools, other additions and expansions to the education infrastructure, and the improvement in the quality of teaching, the school system was hampered in its effectiveness in preparing the young population for life because the curriculum used in the schools was hardly relevant to Grenada. The children followed a curriculum set out in England for English or, at best, colonial children. The textbooks were standard throughout the Empire, and the result was an alienation of the child from the environment, at the same time the fostering of a mistaken cultural identity.

The benefit of improvements in health and education and the development of the peasantry were felt mainly by the poorer people, although there were benefits to the whole society for having a better-educated and healthier workforce. Other developments were not as salutary for the poor, or of little interest to them. Trade arrangements, for example, did not benefit the poor person directly, although times might have been a little easier when the general economy improved during an upturn in trade.

Reciprocal Trade Arrangements with Canada

A flourishing trade had grown up between Grenada and the United States from as far back as the seventeenth century. Over the years, a preference had been developed for American goods. A quantity of crackers was imported from the United States, which was an important source of carbohydrate in the diet of the poor. The poor also preferred American boots and shoes because they were smart and cheap. Everyone preferred the American buggy, as it was not only cheap, but also light, and suited to Grenada's hilly terrain. Cattle and animal feed were also imported from the United States, as was some butter and cheese. Britain thought that the trade that went in the direction of the United States, with a minor portion going to Germany, should be diverted to Britain, or at least to countries within the British Empire. In 1912 Britain engineered a Reciprocal Trade Agreement between Grenada and Canada, which gave preference to Canadian goods for import. The Governor knew that the curtailment of imports from the United States would be a hardship for Grenadians, especially poor Grenadians. The better-off tried to access British goods, as a matter of preference. The Blue Book[56] noted that:

> It will be a real sacrifice, however, to some of the islands to live up to the agreement, and a true imperial spirit has been shown by them in taking the risk of endangering their trade with the United States. The agreement will be the commencement and development, it is hoped, among the islands of a stronger patriotism, a larger outlook and a truer Imperialism.[57]

In 1915 Governor Haddon-Smith had to point out to the Secretary of State for the Colonies that the preferential agreement with Canada had proved to be totally in favour of Canada. The cost of living, especially for the poor, went up immediately.

The importing firms have benefited by reduced duty, but this has not...reduced the prices to the consumer, thus the very small minority gains the advantage. The bulk of the people are the losers by the arrangement inasmuch as the revenue is reduced and consequently less money is available for general improvements.[58]

Later on, when Grenada was suffering curtailment of imports and exports during the war, the arrangement ceased to be so lop-sided. Canada began to import spices and cocoa from Grenada, and Grenada benefited from the regular Canadian Steamship Service.

Agitation to Change Grenada's Crown Colony Constitution

Agitation for constitutional change really began as a concern of the urban educated, but the political system was gradually reaching out to embrace the poor and the rural peasant proprietors. Some peasant proprietors had qualified for franchise before 1876, and many followed the affairs of the country with interest, even though they may not have had much political power.

Donovan had objected to Crown Colony government immediately on its introduction, and his agitation never ceased. In 1915 he would begin to share his mission for the return of representative government with his protégé, T.A. Marryshow. In this year, Marryshow established a newspaper of his own, *The West Indian.* From its establishment the paper devoted itself to forwarding two causes, that of self-government and that of creating a Federation of the British West Indies. The paper was financially backed by a coloured lawyer, Charles 'Jab Neg' Renwick who was popular and influential in several circles. The quality of Marryshow's paper and the respectability it got from the association with Renwick was instrumental in getting support for these two causes from the Grenadian middle class, who were now the best-educated of all classes.

Two events showed the measure of the support Marryshow was receiving from the general public. One was a resolution of the St George's District Board in August 1917 to support *The West Indian*'s challenge that the Board play a role in demanding a measure of representation of the Grenadian people in the government of the country. As a result of the challenge, the St George's District Board called a meeting of all the other District Boards the next month for the purpose of discussing the issue of representation in the government. This general meeting agreed that a petition would be drawn up to be sent to Great Britain requesting self-government.

The other measure of support was the formation in that same year of the Grenada Representative Association. The first President of the Association was Domingo de Freitas, the well-respected but outspoken member of the Legislative Council, but his moderation was constantly under challenge from Donovan, A.A. Richards and Fleming, who demanded the institution of a fully elected Legislative Council instead of the partly elected legislature proposed by the more cautious reformers such as de Freitas. T.A. Marryshow often performed the role of referee between the two factions in the Association, attempting to reconcile their differing views.

By 1919 the Association was holding public meetings in the main towns of the island, informing people of the issue, and asking for support for constitutional reform. On most of these occasions, the lead speaker was T.A. Marryshow, who quickly became known as a powerful and gripping speaker. In 1920 the Association drew up and sent a petition, moderate in its demands, asking for a partly elected house, and sent it to the Secretary of State for the Colonies, who at that time was Lord Milner. It was signed by twenty-five planters, nineteen merchants, all the elected members of the District Boards, two newspaper editors, members of the Board of Education, and Justices of the Peace. In response, the Governor, George Haddon-Smith, suggested a change in the Legislative Council so that it would be composed of the Governor, six officials, three non-officials and four elected members. This proposal was a great disappointment to Marryshow and Renwick, and more so to Donovan and the other radicals. Agitation began anew for greater reform. Marryshow, like Donovan, devoted his life to the betterment of Grenada and Grenadians, and the cause of West Indian unity. So tenacious were his beliefs, and so vociferous and demanding were his speeches, that he earned the appellation 'The Old Bulldog'. He liked this nickname, and soon adopted it with reference to himself.

The Colour Question

Many Grenadians at this time believed that they were British in exile, regardless of their ancestral origins. They enjoyed, but were embarrassed about, the indigenous culture that was slowly working its way towards recognition. A Grenadian folk culture was already in evidence by the late nineteenth century. Hesketh Bell[59] provided, albeit disparagingly, a record of this culture at the turn of the twentieth century, including a description of the unique music, dances, folklore and beliefs. Grenadian folk culture, a blend of African cultural retentions, French

Grenadian heritage, and experiences unique to Grenadian everyday life, would become 'respectable', after much suppression and ridicule, halfway through the twentieth century, largely through the efforts of Pansy Rowley. Early in the twentieth century the aim of the aspiring middle classes was to be as British as possible. Whereas many of them were successful in imitating the West Indian version of British culture, one thing they could not change was the colour of their skin.

As coloured Grenadians took advantage of opportunities to receive education, the ugly question of colour raised its head. A number of coloured young men who had gone to the United Kingdom had returned to Grenada having qualified as medical practitioners. They were now desirous of working in the Government Service as Medical Officers, posts previously held exclusively by whites. It was not proving easy to recruit white doctors. American and Canadian medical qualifications were not accepted in Grenada, and the salary was smaller than in Britain. The shortage of white doctors became worse during the war. On the Governor's request, the Colonial Office appointed some of the coloured doctors to these posts, but the Governor recommended this with misgivings. He had written that he:

> Viewed with apprehension the number of coloured Medical Officers who are being appointed to Grenada, and it is my opinion that the time has arrived when we must endeavour to obtain a proportion of the Medical Officers from men of European parents.[60]

But the people of Grenada knew nothing of this letter to the Secretary of State for the Colonies. When the Governor's term of office came to an end shortly after he wrote on his reluctance to appoint coloured Medical Officers, loud were the accolades he received. It was said of him that he had administered the Colony in the best interest of the people, and in doing so had made a name for himself that few other Governors had made before him. Haddon-Smith's achievements included the establishment of Queen's Park, the Esplanade, and the introduction of the Island Scholarship, and he had won the whole-hearted support of all classes of the community.

Under the succeeding Governor, the question of letting a coloured Grenadian act as headmaster of the Grenada Boys' School illustrated current attitudes. The post of headmaster fell vacant, and there were no immediate applicants for the job. In a quandary, the Governor wrote to the Secretary of State for the Colonies, hoping that he could help recruit a suitable replacement. He explained:

Mr Hughes, the Second Master, is a good teacher and successful with boys. He is a coloured man, and therefore cannot be left in charge of a school for long; otherwise a certain class of parents will remove their sons.[61]

Nevertheless, Hughes had to act for a while, and during this period three boys were removed from the school, because the parents would not have a coloured man even as Acting Headmaster.

Even more shocking was unwelcome news from Canada. The British government had long hoped that Canada and the British West Indies could be coaxed into a Federation. The Reciprocal Trade Agreement between the West Indies and Canada was seen as a forerunner to the commencement of talks. But in 1918 Queens University in Canada indicated to the West Indian students that Queens would no longer be admitting coloured students. The President of the student club was very bitter, because, he said, West Indians were at that moment 'shedding their red blood for the cause of justice and freedom by the side of Canadians' in the war. Moreover, West Indians had just sent contributions to Canada after the disaster in Halifax on 6 December 1917 when a French ammunition carrier laden with hundreds of tons of high explosives hit a Norwegian freighter, caught fire, and blew up. The explosion and a wave resembling a tidal wave damaged every building in Halifax, especially those on the waterfront. Over 1600 people were killed, and thousands more were injured. In forwarding the letter from the students to the Secretary of State, the Governor's wry comment was 'So much for Advocates of Canadian and West Indian Confederation'. The Governor said that the only solution he could see was, in time, the establishment of a West Indian university.[62]

Another sign that Grenada's institutions would not yet be democratized was that in 1916 the Jury Amendment Ordinance was passed. This Ordinance increased the amount of real property a person had to have to be eligible to sit on a jury from £200 to £800, or alternatively to be qualified by a salary of £80 per annum instead of £50. Jury duty was still a male prerogative. The rationale for this Ordinance was that it was necessary to prevent 'almost illiterate' peasants who owned two to three acres of cocoa land from trying 'cases of the most grave character'. It was the Governor's opinion that 'numerous cases of miscarriage of justice has been the result' of letting peasant proprietors serve, and that jury duty should be reserved for clerks and others of intelligence.[63]

The élite of society in Grenada made slow progress in areas such as attitudes towards the liberalizing of society and the establishment of a meritocracy. In spite of this, much was done to pull Grenada out of a very backward state, and prepare it to enter the modern world. While these changes were taking place in health, education, areas of government administration, the Constitution and civic life, the rest of the world, and particularly Europe, was embroiled in a war, the like of which had never been fought on so many fronts at one time.

Notes

 1 These were decorative veils attached to hats, which were worn on the forehead, sometimes pulled down almost to the level of the eyes. Fascinators on hats were very fashionable at this time. The author's special mention of the fascinators highlights his impression of the *haute couture* of these particular ladies.
 2 Clyne, p. 18.
 3 CO 321/276, no. 6072, Sadler to Harcourt, 1914, Colonial Office papers, Public Record Office (PRO), London.
 4 Minutes of the Board of the Legislative Council, 1871, British Library (BL), London.
 5 *Ibid.*
 6 CO 321/287, Colonial Office Dispatches, Grenada, Governor to Secretary of State, 9 Feb. 1916, PRO, London.
 7 CO 321/287, Colonial Office Dispatches, Grenada, Governor to Secretary of State, 28 June 1916, PRO, London.
 8 Ordinance no. 2 of 1916, *Laws of Grenada*, Sir Archibald Nedd Law Library, St George's.
 9 CO 321/276 no. 2569, Blue Book Report for 1913, PRO, London. See Note 55 below for a description of the Blue Books.
10 *Sydney Oliver, Letters and Selected Writings, Edited with a Memoir by Margaret Oliver*, Allen & Unwin, 1848, quoted in Devas (1974), p. 189.
11 McDaniel, p. 47.
12 CO 321/276, no. 2559, Blue Book Report for 1913, Colonial Office Dispatches, Grenada, 1914, PRO.
13 *Ibid.*
14 Devas (1926), p. 61.
15 *Ibid.*
16 *Ibid.*
17 Shepard, p. 211.
18 Marshall, Woodville (thesis), p. 150.
19 *Ibid.*, p. 151.
20 *Report and General Abstract on the Census of 1921*, St George's, p. 8.
21 *Report and General Abstract on the Census of 1901*, St George's.
22 See Charlotte Breese, *Hutch*, London, 2001.
23 Administrative Reports, *Report and General Abstract of the Registrar General*, St George's, *1910–23*.
24 Brizan, p. 237.
25 CO 321/276, no. 2559, Blue Book Report for 1913, Colonial Office Dispatches, Grenada, 1914, PRO.
26 Harewood, p. 65.
27 *Ibid.*
28 The Licensing of Dogs Ordinance, no. 17 of 1915, *Laws of Grenada*, Sir Archibald Nedd Law Library, St George's.
29 Ordinance no. 3 of 1915, *Laws of Grenada*, Sir Archibald Nedd Law Library, St George's.
30 CO 321/281, no. 1609, Sadler to Harcourt, 1915, PRO.
31 CO 321/287, Governor to Secretary of State, 17 April 1916, Colonial Office Dispatches, Grenada, 1916, PRO.

32 *An Almanac Calculated for the Island of Grenada and the Grenadines for the year of Our Lord MDCCLXXXVII, Being the Third after the Bisextile or Leap Year and of the Julian Period 6500*, printed by George Burnett [1786] St George's.
33 T71/1616, 'Answers to Queries Submitted by the Commissioners of Compensation to the Assistant Commissioner of Grenada on 8 May 1834', PRO.
34 Mark, p 13.
35 See p. 286, and Note 10, for a short discussion on regiments of soldiers from the West Indies serving under Great Britain.
36 CO 321/288, Final Report of Dr Angus McDonald, enclosed in letter of Governor to the Secretary of State dated 12 July 1916, Colonial Office Dispatches, Grenada, 1916, PRO.
37 CO 321/288, End note from the Colonial Surgeon in a dispatch from the Governor to the Secretary of State dated 9 Oct. 1916, Colonial Office Dispatches, Grenada, 1916, PRO.
38 American Medical Association, p. 1086.
39 *Report by the Colonial Surgeon on the Control of Yaws in Grenada*, Government Printing Office, St George's, 1916.
40 Governor to Secretary of State, 'Dr. Nicholls Mission to the Windward Islands', SS 390/91, 18 August 1891, quoted in Brizan, p. 188.
41 CO 321/288, Final Report of Dr Angus McDonald, enclosed in letter of Governor to the Secretary of State, dated 12 July 1916, Colonial Office Dispatches, Grenada, 1916, PRO.
42 *Ibid.*
43 American Medical Association, p. 634.
44 Due to the effectiveness of new drugs for the treatment of this disease, the leper settlement was closed in 1958. The remaining nine cases, four of which were non-infectious, were transferred to the Colony Hospital, or were treated as outpatients. Although some new cases were sent to Trinidad for treatment, the advances in the treatment of the disease now allow outpatient treatment. There were a few remaining persons in the leper settlement who, though cured, did not want to return to their families, or could not because their disfigurement made them an object of superstition and fear. These were quartered in a new building near the almshouse at Richmond Hill, and a few still remain in residence today. See Clyde, pp. 294–6.
45 *Ibid.*
46 Ordinance no. 16 of 1917, *Laws of Grenada*, Sir Archibald Nedd Law Library, St George's.
47 CO 321/299, Governor to Secretary of State, covering letter to the Blue Book for 1917–18, dated 20 July 1918, Colonial Office Dispatches, Grenada, 1918, PRO.
48 See Brizan, p. 173.
49 See Brizan, p. 172.
50 CO 321/276, no. 2569, Blue Book Report for 1913, Colonial Office papers, PRO.
51 CO 321/282, no. 36581, Blue Book Report for 1914–15, Colonial Office papers, PRO.
52 CO 321/287, Governor to Secretary of State, dated 19 April 1916, Colonial Office Dispatches, Grenada, 1916, PRO.
53 *The West Indian*, 2 April 1916.
54 Minutes of the Legislative Council, March 1916, BL.
55 Editorial in the *Federalist* of 1 April 1916.
56 The Blue Book was a report to the Colonial Office on everything that happened in the colony for that year. They were meticulously written, and now provide us with an invaluable, if somewhat dry, historical record. The name referred to the usual blue cover.
57 CO 321/281, no. 11209, Governor to Harcourt, 13 Feb. 1913, containing Blue Book report 1913.

58 *Ibid.*
59 Bell, 1889 (republished 1970).
60 CO 321/287, Governor to Secretary of State, dated 4 April 1916, Colonial Office Dispatches, Grenada, 1916, PRO.
61 CO 321/288, Confidential dispatch from Governor to Secretary of State, dated 31 Aug. 1916, Colonial Office Dispatches, Grenada, 1916, PRO.
62 CO 321/299, Confidential dispatch from Governor to Secretary of State, dated 22 May 1918, Colonial Office Dispatches, Grenada, 1918, PRO.
63 CO 321/288, Governor to Secretary of State, dated 30 Aug. 1918, Colonial Office Dispatches, Grenada, 1918, PRO.

13

The First World War

The Great War was fully expected. Europe was in turmoil after the assassination of the Grand Duke of Austria, and it was only a matter of time before Great Britain involved herself and her Empire, fearing an upset of the balance of power which might endanger the status quo. In advance of the war several measures were taken for the protection of Grenada in the event of invasion. In 1912 the Governor was provided with a 'Defence Scheme' for Grenada. The Grenada Volunteer Corps, formed since 1911, was augmented with a mounted section of twenty-five members from St Andrew's. Rifle ranges were laid out at Queen's Park and Telescope Point, and training provided for members. Twelve Ordinances were passed in 1913 to ensure the protection of Grenada. Ordinance No. 2 was 'To Render the Police Force Liable to Military Duty in Case of Invasion'. In response to this Ordinance, the members of the police force underwent a training course based on one that was prescribed for the Territorial Army in Great Britain. At this time, the police force consisted of 150 rural constables and 81 regular police.

When Great Britain eventually joined the war, communiqués were sent immediately to the Governors of all the colonies advising them of the changed state of affairs. Shortly after the commencement of war was announced to the Executive Council, the Council met to study the implications of war for Grenada.

How Shall We Eat?

A primary concern was that the price of food had immediately started to rise when merchants realized that the importation of goods might be restricted or curtailed. An unfortunate heritage of the plantation era and the present preoccupation with cocoa and nutmeg production was that self-sufficiency in foodstuffs had never been a priority for those directing agricultural policy. Staples of the poor Grenadians' diet included crackers from the United States, made from cheap white flour, and other crackers called 'Pilot Bread', which was almost the same, but larger and made in Trinidad and Barbados. There was now the threat of severe unrest among the population. The Governor, in consultation with the members of the Executive Council, used funds from the Treasury to order 2000 barrels of flour from Canada through the intervention of the Governor of Halifax,[1] as the merchants did not have the resources to bring in more than was their normal practice. Arrangements were made at a later dater to import a small amount of saltfish.[2] The Governor was also given the power to regulate prices.[3] This early move proved to be an effective protective buffer for the poorer people against exploitation by the merchants in a time of shortage. The necessity for price control would be reported on by the Governor in the Blue Books throughout the war. On one occasion he observed that:

> The Schedule of Prices which was enforced through the Colony (was) ... a great boon conferred on the poorer people, who in this island are dependent to a surprising extent on imported foodstuff.[4]

Grenada – the Loyal and Supporting Colony

The second concern of the government was to assure the Crown of the loyalty and support of the people of Grenada. In a meeting on 11 September 1915, the full Legislative Council agreed that a sum of £6000 should be set aside for the purchase of Grenada cocoa as a gift from the people of Grenada to the 'Mother Country' for the use of His Majesty's forces engaged in the war. The Governor received an acknowledgement of this gift in July the next year:

> Will you kindly convey to the donors the sincere thanks of the ship's company of the *HMS Antrim* for the magnificent gift of chocolate presented by the islands of Trinidad, Grenada and St Lucia. A memento of the kindness of these West Indian Colonies.[5]

A sum of £4000 was also donated to the Prince of Wales Relief Fund. In addition, an address to the British government expressing the devoted loyalty of the people of Grenada to Great Britain was composed and despatched. It read:

> AN ADDRESS TO HIS MAJESTY THE KING
> To His Most Excellent Majesty, GEORGE THE FIFTH by the Grace of God, of the United Kingdom of Great Britain and Ireland, and of the British Dominions beyond the Seas, King, Defender of the Faith, Emperor of India:
> May it please Your Majesty

The Legislative Council of Your Majesty's colony of Grenada, moved by deep feelings of duty, respect and affection, desire on behalf of the people of Grenada, at this time of anxiety and danger in the life history of the British Empire, dutifully to tender to Your Majesty's Throne and Person;

Your Majesty's faithful and loyal subjects in Grenada earnestly pray that it may please Divine Providence to protect our Majesty's Naval and Military Forces engaged with conspicuous courage and gallantry in righteous cause, and grant to them an early victory, memorable to all time in the defence of Honour, Freedom and Peace.

DATED AT THE COUNCIL CHAMBER IN ST GEORGE'S, GRENADA, this 11th day of September 1914.

This document was signed by the Acting Governor, the Colonial Secretary and the most important members of the Legislative Council.

War Measures in Grenada

During the rest of 1914, the government began to put other war measures in place. Some of these measures were in response to requests by the Colonial Office; others originated with the Legislative Council, and were approved by the Colonial Office. One of the measures suggested by the Legislative Council related to the availability of money. It was agreed that notes of the Royal Bank of Canada and the Colonial (now Barclays) Bank would be legal tender and the government treasury notes of small denominations (five and ten shillings) would be legal tender should this become necessary due to the hoarding of money by the population. Two of the Directives from the Colonial Office were that all German businesses were to be shut down (there were none in Grenada), and all persons born in Germany, Turkey and Austria resident in the Colony had to be reported, put under surveillance and made to report to the police daily.

Censorship

The problem of leakage of information to the enemy arose early in the war. In a letter dated 7 November 1914, the Acting Governor had written denying the culpability of any of the Windward Islands in inadvertently giving information to the enemy about the movements of His Majesty's ships in the Caribbean. Careful postal and telegraph censorship was effected. To this end, Herbert Ferguson, the Colonial Treasurer and Acting Colonial Secretary, was appointed the Chief Censor for the Colony. Ferguson became the Colonial Secretary in July 1945. The Postmaster, under the direction of the Chief Censor, conducted censorship on both incoming and outgoing letters and telegrams. No mail was permitted other than that which passed through the Post Office. Throughout the war special attention was given to mail coming and going to the Panama Canal Zone and the United States of America, to neutral countries via the United States and the United Kingdom, and to correspondence that suggested suspicious activities by foreign nationals, regardless of origin. Grenada was made a transmittal station for cables, and the Cable Office remained opened around the clock.

The Effect on the Economy

As the First World War progressed, the economy suffered. Both imports and exports were curtailed due to the lack of ships for commerce. Increased prices resulted from the Preferential Agreement with Canada. There was also an increase in insurance due to war, and the scarcity of goods due to the unavailability of shipping for commerce. Although the Governor took measures to curtail the price of essential items, the general cost of living skyrocketed. At the same time, the revenue of the government fell, due to the decrease in both imports and exports, and the resulting decrease in the tax collected. The Blue Book of 1914–15 states that the falling government revenue was made up by increased import taxes, especially for alcohol, tobacco, cigarettes and American flour, and increased export duty on cocoa.[6]

An end of year report from Acting Governor Young to Harcourt, the Secretary of State for the Colonies, on 29 December 1914, summarized the measures taken at the beginning of the war.

1. The Defence Force, the Police Force and the Volunteer Force were brought together to ready them for immediate service in the event of attack by the enemy. They were instructed in the lines of defence as laid down by the Defence Scheme, and some of these were manned round the clock, such as lookout points at Fort George and the Point Salines Lighthouse. Every ship sighted was to be reported by the lookouts and the police at the police stations throughout the island. Arrangements were made for the detention of any enemy ships that might arrive.

2. A guard was placed at the hut where the cable of the West Indies and Panama Telegraph Company came ashore. This hut was connected by telephone to police headquarters. The police also maintained a guard at the Cable Office and the Governor required 24-hour opening of this office.
3. Effective censorship of mail, telegraphs and all forms of public communication was established.
4. The importation of foodstuffs from Canada and the knowledge that the Governor had the power to regulate prices had turned the anxieties of the people in this regard into confidence.
5. At the outbreak of the war the commercial banks had restricted business, and instituted a higher rate of exchange on drafts. The Governor had addressed the managers of these banks, and the banks had responded by reverting to business on almost normal lines.
6. The plantations and the peasants were asked to plant ground provisions to establish a domestic food supply. An agricultural officer was appointed to advise and encourage. The response was good, and food was now plentiful and cheap. In addition, the production of cocoa was maintained, and the price remained high. The Governor reported that there would be no need for relief work, as the people in Grenada had not suffered much deprivation from the circumstances of war. A decrease in revenue of about 10 per cent was expected.
7. A public meeting was called to initiate private subscriptions to the Prince of Wales Funds and the Red Cross.[7]

The Sinking of the SMS *Karlsruhe*

The first real excitement of the war for Grenada was the news that wreckage and lifebuoys marked with the name SMS *Karlsruhe*, had washed up on the Grenadine islands of Mayreau, Canouan and Carriacou, and on the north coast of Grenada. Stores marked with the names of German manufacturers were also found. It was rumoured that this German vessel had been torpedoed off Petit Martinique on 23 November 1914. The inhabitants on Mayreau and Canouan found stores, a sailor's cap and a khaki helmet 'of foreign shape', and a small door marked with the name of the ship. A felt-lined wooden box and candles were picked up in Carriacou. Rumours spread that dead bodies had also been found, but this proved to be false sensationalism.[8]

Another troubling problem was that public servants began to request permission to resign to allow them to return to Britain to enlist. At this time, the highest posts in the government, including the Medical Officers, were mainly held by Britons. A notice was sent to all public servants saying that no more resignations would be accepted. If the officer was determined to leave, thus abandoning his post, his appointment would be terminated, and government would enforce the relevant clauses, including that of refusing to pay the return passage to Britain. In a letter to the Colonial Secretary, the Governor Haddon-Smith remarked that 'If officials are to be allowed to act in this way the civil administration is bound to become dislocated'.[9]

Soon the population began to feel the pinch, and had to curtail their spending, particularly on non-essentials like clothes and shoes. Savings declined as the cost of living rose, and people dipped into their 'nest-eggs'.

Fighting for the Motherland

The socialization of the population of Grenada as members of the British Empire had been very thorough. Many Grenadians wished to go and fight for the 'Mother Country', and began to agitate to offer their services. However, the War Office was consistently adamant that no West Indian who was of mixed blood would be allowed to serve in the British Army. This put the Secretary of State and the Governor in an embarrassing position. The 'colour bar' that had been created in the social relations between Britain and its African, Caribbean and Asian colonies during the long period of British colonialism had not posed a problem up to now, as the relationships had been of white people in superior positions of power to non-white subject peoples. Now the colonials who had been made to think of themselves as 'British', as a result of indoctrination, reacted to the war as loyal subjects would naturally do. They wanted a chance to serve as 'Englishmen'. This could not be countenanced, as war would bring coloured people into contact with white people of the same status, if they were enlisted in the same services. This would happen not only in the rank and file, but also in the command, if the many West Indians and other colonials who were highly qualified were enlisted as officers.

The constant agitation of colonial people to fight in the war continued. After the Secretary of State for the Colonies and the king himself intervened, it was agreed that persons wishing to serve as soldiers in the war would be recruited into the British West Indies Regiment,[10] which would be exclusively for the black soldiers from the Caribbean. This regiment would be subject to the Imperial Army Act, but the soldiers would not be a part of the British Armed Services. No one who was not of pure European blood would be accepted as an officer, even in this regiment.

Although this was not known in the West Indies, the soldiers from the West Indies would receive lower rates of pay and allowances than the British soldiers. The black soldiers would not be used in combat against European troops, and the troops would be used in the same manner as 'labour' details. They would dig trenches, clean latrines and wash linen. Not aware of the attitudes or plans of the British War Office, West Indians embraced the opportunity to serve their king and country. The Governor wrote to the Secretary of State for the Colonies:

> Men of these islands are very keen to enlist and take their share in the present war, and although the financial condition in all these islands is at present exceptionally low and I can see no prospect of improvement, the Legislative Councils are quite prepared to vote the necessary funds to cover the cost of their part of the West Indian Contingent, even if it is necessary to borrow money for the purpose. As regards Grenada, the numbers of men enlisted up to date are 150, but I quite anticipate that half this number will be found unsuitable under Medical examination.[11]

The refusal of the War Office to accept coloured West Indians as officers became a very sensitive matter, as it exposed the hypocrisy of Great Britain towards the subject peoples who had accepted that they were one with the rest of the Empire, and that Britain was their mother country. The case that caused the Governor of Grenada the most pain was the application in 1915 of Dr William Steele Mitchell, a Government Medical Officer in Grenada, for service in the Royal Army Medical Corps. The Governor, in supporting this application, pointed out that he was 'slightly coloured having the African woolly hair'[12] and that Mitchell 'was educated in England and passed his medical examinations very satisfactorily. As regards his ways and feelings, he is thoroughly English'.[13] In reply to his application, Mitchell received a letter from the War Office that said:

> I am to acquaint you that, as Commissions in the Royal Medical Corps can only be granted to those who are of pure European blood, it is regretted that you are ineligible for such an appointment.[14]

On being informed of the reply, the Governor wrote the Secretary of State for the Colonies, stating that the letter of refusal of a Commission in the Medical Corps to Mitchell had caused quite a stir in the Colony, and had been discussed in the newspapers. The Governor was worried that officials in Britain were not sensitive enough to the 'colour question', and that the reply to Mitchell was tactless and heavy-handed. The Governor suggested that at least the rejections to coloured colonials should be reworded so as not to inflict pain.

The Governor's protests got some action. The standard reply to colonial applicants rejected on the basis of their colour changed. Dr Mitchell was also appointed a Surgeon Lieutenant with the West Indian Detachment of enlisted men from the West Indies. The War Office refused, however, to budge on the question of appointing coloured persons to officer status in the armed services of Great Britain.[15]

Recruitment for Service Overseas

It was decided that the first contingent from the Windward Islands for the British West Indies Regiment should consist of 300 men: 150 from Grenada, 100 from St Lucia and 50 from St Vincent. In Grenada, volunteers were called for by an insertion in one of the local papers. On 12 July 1915 people were invited to begin submitting their names as those who would like to serve in the contingent. On the first day of registration, fifty-four men registered, and by 31 July a total of 374 had registered. The men who responded were then screened. Of the applicants, 25 per cent failed the medical. Another thirty were rejected for other reasons, but their names were noted as reinforcements. In the end, the names of the candidates selected were published in the local press. They were given rudimentary training, and enlisted from 7 August 1915. The enlistment consisted of taking an Oath of Allegiance as members of the Grenada Volunteer Force, and also taking an Oath of Attestation for service in His Majesty's Regular Army. A course of instruction including drill was given to 108 of the men who had enlisted.

The enlisted men were paid two shillings and sixpence per day, from which they had to feed themselves. Upon embarkation, they would be paid British rates of pay by the British government. A separation allowance would be paid to the dependants of both married and unmarried soldiers by the Grenada government, also upon departure. The island governments would pay the cost of the transportation to England, and the British government would pay for their uniforms and equipment when the men landed. In a dispatch to the Secretary of State for the Colonies, Governor Haddon-Smith reported that, before they left, each man was:

[p]rovided with a blue serge suit, pair of boots, an overcoat and a cap. The ladies of Grenada have most generously supplied

them with different articles of warm clothing. I am informed that a large sum has been subscribed privately with the idea of providing the men with comforts.[16]

The communication ended with these words:

I cannot close this dispatch without expressing my gratification at the loyal manner in which the sons of the Windward Islands have come forward to take their share in the burdens of Empire to which they are privileged to belong, and to serve their King to whom they are proud to owe allegiance.[17]

The endorsements from members of the Legislative Council of the proposals to fund a contingent of soldiers to fight in the 'Great War' are also of interest. Terrence B. Commissiong, the Colonial Treasurer,[18] remarked that:

There were times in the past when it was thought that these colonies were not treated as they should be by the Mother Country, but when one remembered the security in which one lived here at the present time, there were good reasons to be thankful, and the proposal before the council would enable the people of Grenada to express in a tangible way their gratitude to the Mother Country.[19]

The Legislative Council minutes reported de Freitas as saying that:

He wished it to be felt that Grenadians were loyal sons of the Empire – England was prepared to pledge her last shilling in this war, and Grenada would do its utmost in helping forward the proposals submitted to the Council that day. He laid stress on the fact that the Council had the support of the whole Colony in the matter.[20]

Farewell to the Men of the First Contingent

A special committee appointed on 13 August 1915, called the Windward Islands Contingent Committee, planned a splendid send-off for the departure of the First Contingent of the British West Indies Regiment. The Council felt that it would like to show the men beyond any doubt how much the Colony appreciated their loyalty to the Empire. All the members of the Legislative Council were asked to be present. The send-off included a public meeting in the Market Square to bid farewell to the men, a church service and parade at which the Volunteers and police marched, a parade at Queen's Park, a parade of local forces at York House, and the inspection of the Mounted Infantry Corps of the Grenada Volunteers at Grenville.

The First Contingent of 150 soldiers from Grenada for the British West Indies Regiment departed from Grenada on 21 August 1915 on board the SS *Verdala*. Dr Mitchell sailed with them as their Medical Officer. This ship called at St Vincent where another 50 men joined the contingent, making a total of 200 men. Another 100 men from St Lucia travelled to Trinidad to join a transport there as the *Veralda* had insufficient accommodation to allow all the men from the Windward Islands to travel together. The Contingent was under the command of Major G.J.L. Golding of the St Lucia Police, supported by Lieutenant D. Kerr of the Grenada Volunteers, and Second Lieutenant A.J.K. Ferguson from St Lucia. News was received on 4 October 1915 of the safe arrival of the first detachment in England.

Another detachment of men from the Windward Islands was selected for service overseas later that year. A detachment of fifty-two men from Grenada left for England via Trinidad on 14 November 1915. This time the farewell was more low-key. The men assembled at the Drill Yard where they were inspected by His Excellency the Governor, and listened to speeches by the Governor and others. Captain Slinger was promoted to the rank of Major, and the detachment was put under his command.

War Tax on Cocoa

In December 1915 the Governor discussed with the Legislative Council how the costs involved with the Grenada Contingent would continue to be met. He had intended that the costs would be met through curtailment of expenditure, but had not foreseen the fall in revenue. The Legislative Council, mainly made up of planters, suggested that the money be raised though an export tax on cocoa. The price of cocoa was very high, and they were willing to make the sacrifice 'so that they might feel that they were contributing in a practical way to the needs of the Empire'.[21] The Act to allow the War Tax of one shilling a bag on cocoa was passed on 10 December 1915, as Ordinance no. 29. The Governor reported to the Secretary of State for the Colonies that:

> Words of mine would be inadequate to express fully my appreciation of this further evidence of patriotism from a loyal

class of His Majesty's subjects. It is but a further indication of the feeling which exists in the colonies toward the Crown. I would say it was almost unique for a section of a community to come forward and appeal to be taxed.[22]

The war tax on cocoa allowed the Governor to write to the Secretary of State at a later date that:

Not withstanding the continuance of the war ... it has been possible to provide for all necessary expenditure without increasing any of the duties ... and to avoid increasing the cost of foodstuffs or in any way disturbing taxation ... the present financial condition of the Colony is satisfactory ... I have kept a strict check on expenditure during 1915–16 and my task has been made easy by the loyal and willing assistance received from the Heads of Departments.[23]

Continuation of the War

Everyone hoped that the war would be short, and that all would be over in 1916. Instead the war dragged on for two more years. Some early initiatives could not be sustained until then. The Mounted Section of the Grenada Volunteer Force in St Andrew's was disbanded in December of 1915. Several separate causes were cited for its failure. The Mounted Corps was made up of nineteen young men from the various cocoa estates, but seldom was there half of this number in attendance at drills due to the exigencies of the cocoa crop. Others could not afford to keep up the expenditure of hiring a horse. In any case, it was difficult to recruit members. The introduction of motor vehicles into Grenada made the Corps less important in the Defence Scheme. When the Commander of the Corps, Captain Duncan, decided to leave the island, he recommended that the Corps be disbanded, as he felt that continued expenditure on it was not warranted.

Grenada was also beginning to feel the effects of a decline in economic circumstances due to the high cost of war insurance, the interruption of normal trading, a related decrease in port fees, and the cessation of tourism, which had begun to become important to the island. The cost of living had also risen but wages had not. The town of St George's had been the hardest hit, because unemployment in the town was worse than in the cocoa producing areas of the country. In June 1916 the Governor wrote to the Secretary of State that because of the altered circumstances:

I have been compelled to relax the compulsory attendance clause of the Education Act, as it has been proved to me that in so many instances children cannot attend school because their parents are not able to supply them with garments. If matters do not improve at an early date Government will be compelled to start public works with a view to finding employment.[24]

In this letter the Governor asked Secretary of State for a grant to the St George's District Board to avoid an increase in taxes on 'the people who are suffering through the war owing to the rise in price of foodstuffs and the lack of employment'.[25] A grant of £300 was approved, and could be renewed every year if necessary.

By 1917 the population would evidence malnutrition and a higher death rate. The death rate in 1916 was 17.5, and this rose to 20.6 in 1917. The rise was attributable to the prevailing economic conditions.

The high cost of food has resulted in great hardship to the labourers, and the results of deficient and improper food are particularly noticeable in the case of children and those of advanced age.[26]

Nevertheless, the Blue Book for 1915 stated that:

The general wealth of the planting community has increased on account of a long continued period of high prices for cocoa and spices ... adequate freight facilities and a prolific crop of cocoa was safely brought to market in London and New York.[27]

There was almost no importation of machinery into Grenada, due to the lack of ships, many having been requisitioned for the war for use as transports and supply ships. One of the pieces of machinery needed in Grenada that could not come in was the new switchboard for the telephone company. No orders for stationery and supplies from the Crown Agents could be filled. In June 1917 the Governor was asked to prohibit the import of anything not deemed to be absolutely essential. This applied not only to the United Kingdom and Europe, but also to Canada and the United States due to the need to free shipping for the transport of foodstuffs and war material. Merchants stocks were soon depleted. Restrictions were also put on the export of cocoa.

To help raise money for the war, a set of stamps were overprinted, and an amount added for a War Tax. To the delight of stamp collectors, some of the stamps were printed missing the 'x' in 'Tax', making them rare and perhaps valuable. By the end of 1917, a bonus, which would not be added to the salary for purposes of pension benefits, had to be paid to the subordinate officers in the Government Service to relieve the hardship caused by the high cost of living arising from the war.[28]

Very unpopular income tax measures were also put in place. The Governor was asked by de Freitas to remove the export tax on cocoa if he wanted to institute income tax measures. The Governor said that the export tax could not be removed until the income tax measures had been in effect long enough to prove that the money collected as income tax would be sufficient to make up for the loss of revenue from the export tax. At this, Marryshow took up his pen, and launched a scathing attack on the Governor, saying that he had misled the people. Marryshow then collected signatures on a petition, which he forwarded to the Secretary of State.

More Evidence of the Operation of the Colour Bar

The difference in treatment of soldiers of the Empire because of their colour was demonstrated in all sorts of ways. One of the saddest reflections on the attitudes of Britons towards the West Indian troops was the difference made when it came to compensating the dependants of the soldiers killed in action. It was Governor Haddon-Smith who wrote to the Secretary of State enquiring who should bear the expense of pensions for the dependants of the casualities in the West Indies Regiment. The Secretary of State replied that the War Office did not contemplate granting pensions to dependants, only gratuities, 'except in special cases of married men of pure European parentage'.[29] He suggested that each island bear the cost of pensions, gratuities and separation allowances up to a maximum amount to be fixed at 3 per cent of revenues. He promised, however, that if this maximum were exceeded, Imperial Funds would make up the difference.

There was also another case of a West Indian, otherwise qualified to be a commissioned officer, stumbling over the colour bar. In February 1916 Governor Haddon-Smith wrote to the Secretary of State asking that Major Slinger, who was only 'slightly coloured' be allowed to accompany the next set of Grenada troops to England, as he had good rapport with them and had been instrumental in recruiting and training them. Slinger was prepared to relinquish the command of the Grenadian Contingent on arrival in England. Attitudes had softened since the case of Dr Mitchell. The Secretary of State minuted the request that:

> The War Office won't have coloured officers with the Regiment, but I see no objection to Major Slinger being put in charge of the Windward Island Company for the voyage only ... The other

officers nominated will be subalterns and some of them will very likely resent being of subordinate rank to a man of colour. I don't suppose, however, that any serious friction is likely to arise if Major Slinger is careful to confine the exercise of his authority to the Windward Island Contingent, subject to any extension that Col. Swain may subsequently consider justifiable.[30]

While living in the training camp with recruits for the British West Indies Regiment, Major Slinger became ill, and died on 4 September 1916. He was later honoured posthumously. The Governor's recommendation for the honour made particular mention of the personal sacrifice he made in giving up his business in town to devote himself entirely to the work of training recruits.[31]

All the volunteers in Grenada who were in training for service with the Imperial Army were brought under the Imperial Army Act by an Ordinance passed in 1916. This would facilitate discipline, and allow those in serious breach of the regulations to face a court martial. A preliminary selection of 220 men had been made to form the Third Contingent from Grenada for the British West Indies Regiment. They encamped at Quarantine Station in February 1916. Of these, sixty were let go as unfit or unworthy. The balance should have left Grenada in June, but the arrangement to transport them to Britain was cancelled three or four times. The constant delays had a demoralizing effect on the men, and prevented their removal to healthier quarters, as they were always awaiting a call to depart. Between August and November, many of the men fell ill with malaria, and twenty more men had to be let go as unfit. After Major Slinger died, Lieutenant Bush, the Trinidadian officer who replaced Major Slinger, also got ill, and had to be sent back to Trinidad. A British officer, Lieutenant Chalker, was also sent home after a serious bout of malaria. The original recruits were joined by twenty more selected at the end of 1916, but of the combined recruits, thirty had to be dismissed. Eventually the group sailed in March 1917.

It was becoming more and more difficult to recruit volunteers for service, and in June 1917 the Executive Council in Grenada suggested conscription. Conscription was never resorted to, and during 1917 two more detachments of recruits left Grenada, bringing the total number recruited from Grenada to 446.

Submarines Arrive in Caribbean Waters

Between June and July 1916 six drums of gasoline bearing no marks of identification washed up on the Grenadines. It was believed that these came from a German submarine, the *Bremen*. This and other incidents were at the root of a request made at the end of 1916 for increased vigilance and reporting of any enemy activity at sea. The Governor was asked to provide patrol boats, which were to be armed, if possible, and equipped with the means of signalling. The Governor sent a telegram to the Secretary of State for the Colonies suggesting that the two coastal steamers belonging to the Royal Mail Steam Packet Company, manned by native captains, be used for the purpose of lookout, as there were no Europeans available for service as a coastguard, neither were there any vessels. He considered the native captains quite capable of bringing in reliable information as they cruised about the Windward Islands. The vessels in question were capable of carrying small guns as a protection against submarines but, if these vessels were to be armed, they would have to be manned by military men. In addition, there were three other motor launches that could be used for cruising around the Grenadines.

The people in Grenada were also becoming concerned at the number of steamships and inter-island schooners that were sunk. There is some evidence that agents of anti-war propaganda used the fear of the people to try to rouse up anti-war sentiments in the population, as the Governor suggested to the Secretary of State that news of sinkings should be censored. The Secretary of State was of the opinion that censoring such information would make the situation worse.[32]

Armistice

None too soon, the war ended. When news of the armistice of 11 November 1918 arrived in Grenada, the public rejoiced, and a carnival atmosphere prevailed in St George's. The population was glad that the time of additional privation had come to an end, but they were also proud that Grenada in a small way had contributed to the downfall of the enemies of the Empire. The official thanksgiving took place in July of the next year. Ceremonies were held in different parts of Grenada, and separate public holidays given to allow the population to attend.

The men of the Grenada Contingent of the British West Indies Regiment returned home during 1919. Although there were casualties among Grenadians, all Grenadians killed in action were from the white section of the population, who had chosen to serve in other regiments than the British West Indies Regiment. However, some men serving in the British West Indies Regiment had died from disease during the war, or had been disabled.

The demobilization instructions were that, on returning to Grenada, the men were to be retained and paid for thirty days. They were allowed to wear their uniforms for twenty-eight days. During this month, special officers called Dispersal Officers had the duty of re-settling the men, and trying to find employment for them.

The government made arrangements to celebrate the participation of Grenadian soldiers in the Great War by providing a welcome for the troops that returned on board the troop carrier *Ajax*. The streets of St George's were to be decorated for the day, with particular emphasis on the streets along which the troops would parade. Householders and merchants who had premises along the route were asked to join in the preparations by decorating their houses and business places. After the *Ajax* docked at the wharf of Messrs Martin, Dean and Company, a reception committee would go on board to greet the returnees, and to inform them of the programme that had been planned to celebrate their return. The Contingent would then be drawn up in marching order, and be received and welcomed home by the Governor. After the Governor's address, the men, preceded by the government band, would parade along the wharf, up Young Street, down Halifax Street, up Hillsborough Street, along Grenville Street, down Granby Street, along Melville Street, through the Sendall Tunnel, along Monckton Street and Young Street to the Drill Hall. At the Drill Hall the parade would disband, and the soldiers would be able to greet their relatives and friends, and enjoy refreshments. They would be allowed to go home, if they wished, until a date to be set by the Dispersal Officer. Free transportation home was provided, and sleeping quarters would be provided for whoever needed them at Fort George.

Silver War Badges were given to the men who had been injured or disabled overseas as a result of war service. They were also given pensions. The unharmed soldiers received gratuities. Eight officers and non-commissioned officers were offered the honour of becoming Justices of the Peace, and all accepted, except W.E. Julien, who declined the honour. Several Grenadians soldiers were awarded medals, including Sergeant Wilfred Julien who received a Distinguished Conduct Medal, Company Sergeant-Major Terrence B. Commissiong who was awarded the Meritorious Service Medal, and Sergeant L.O. Taylor who received the Royal Humane Society's Bronze Medal and Certificate.[33]

Unfortunately, the romantic notions held by those who had stayed at home did not match the terrible experiences of the soldiers in the West Indies Regiment. Most of the British West Indies Regiment spent the war in Egypt performing menial services. Some of the troops did take part in the action against Turkish troops in Palestine, but even here they were used to carry ammunition and dig ditches. On several occasions they were humiliated and degraded by the military authorities. One Trinidadian soldier wrote back to his family that the authorities treated the black soldiers neither as Christians not as British citizens, but as West Indian 'niggers' in whom no one was interested, and who had no one to look after their interests.[34]

The soldiers also did not return to the prosperous Colony that they had left. Before the war 'Cocoa was King'. The planters were wealthy, and there was a trickle-down effect of this wealth into the rest of society. During and after the war, no one in Europe had money to buy luxuries such as cocoa. The bottom fell out of the cocoa market, causing widespread unemployment and hardship.

It must be recognized that the government did its best to resettle the servicemen. In March 1919 the Central Contingent Committee issued an appeal to all employers of labour in the Colony, asking their assistance to find employment for the returning servicemen. It read in part:

> Both our duty to the men and the interests of the Colony require that employment should be found for them on their arrival with as little delay as possible.[35]

In a few instances jobs and appointments had been held for the men while they were in the army, but in most instances, the men had no jobs to come back to. The government opened an Employment Bureau in each district of Grenada to locate jobs, and to match these with the returnees who needed them. Employers were asked to let these bureaux know of any vacant position, and reminded that the soldiers were returning with new skills that might be of use to them.

In spite of the appeal, and other efforts made, some of the returning ex-servicemen faced unemployment. Some soldiers were late migrants to Panama, Costa Rica and Cuba, but the migration to these countries was virtually at an end. Some took advantage of the Land Settlement Schemes and bought land, establishing themselves as peasant proprietors. Some migrated to Trinidad. Enough disaffected soldiers were left at a loose end to be organized for protest. Rising food prices put the match to the tinder of discontent. Riots and unrest followed.

Butler, the Ex-servicemen Protests, Fire and the TT Gang

One of the leaders of the protest movement was a returned soldier by the name of Tubal Uriah 'Buzz' Butler. Butler was born in Grenada in 1897, of working-class parents, and was trained as a blacksmith. He was one of the first volunteers for the British West Indies Regiment, and was one of the few West Indians to actually experience combat. During his term with the regiment he had also come under the influence of Captain Andrew Cipriani. Cipriani had been stationed in Italy, where the West Indian troops had been especially badly treated. They were segregated and provided with inferior canteens, cinemas and hospitals. They were given jobs to do that were properly the jobs of labour units, not soldiers. Cipriani led a protest, alleging discrimination, but he was told by the South African Camp Commander that 'niggers' had no right to expect to be treated like British troops, and that there were no grounds for charges of discrimination. After this, a secret Caribbean league among sergeants of the British West Indies Regiment was formed, and although the league was disbanded as soon as it was discovered, it lasted long enough for the ideas of social and labour reform in the West Indies to influence several potential leaders. One of these persons was Buzz Butler. As soon as he returned to Grenada, he joined the Grenada Representative Movement, and founded the Grenada Union of Returned Soldiers, which was an organization designed to lobby for justice, pensions and employment opportunities for returned soldiers.

Unfortunately, there was more than one group protesting conditions in Grenada at this time, and it was difficult for the public to determine which group was responsible for what type of protest action, especially as not all the protests were peaceful. In early January 1920 there were several acts of arson in St George's and the surrounding areas. The abandoned barracks at Richmond Hill were among the buildings to be torched. On 13 January there was an attempt to burn the whole town of St George's. During this period, several persons received threatening letters signed by 'the TT Gang'.[36] At the scene of acts of arson, signs reading 'The TT Gang' were marked on the walls or where they were sure to be noticed. There were also a rash of burglaries and a general feeling of insecurity throughout society, but especially in St George's among the élite.

The government took immediate measures to stem the unrest. In May the government passed the Seditious Publications Ordinance in an attempt to stem public expression of discontent among the people. A copy of this Ordinance was burnt at a mass rally organized by T.A. Marryshow who, since his 'young days', shared Donovan's championing of the causes of the underprivileged in society and of representative government.

Practical measures taken by the government to counter the unrest were more effective than the laws aimed at controlling freedom of expression. The government established a Food Control Committee to come up with ways to lower and control the price of food consumed by the working class. Rewards were offered for information regarding the persons responsible for setting the fires, both by the government and the Associated Insurance Company. A voluntary corps of special constables was also enrolled by the government, and measures taken to bring the police force up to its former numbers, as it was then understaffed by about fifty men. These measures were effective in curtailing the outbreaks.

Things got worse for needy and destitute ex-servicemen. In December 1920 the Governor dissolved the Central Contingent Committee, which had been established in 1918 to assist ex-servicemen, as no provision had been made in the Budget for the continuance of its work. Butler left Grenada in 1921 for Trinidad, to work in the oilfields. His organizing ability and militant spirit would be an important factor in the labour demonstrations and disturbances and strikes in Trinidad during the 1930s, and in the formation of the powerful Oilfields Workers Trade Union. Butler would not forget his homeland, however, and he would later be an important adviser to Eric Matthew Gairy and the Trade Union Movement in Grenada. Butler served as an elected member of the Legislative Council of Trinidad and Tobago from 1950 to 1956. Butler died in Trinidad in 1977. The former Princess Margaret Highway in Trinidad and Tobago was renamed in his honour. The day on which the riots and strikes in Trinidad with which Butler was associated, 19 June,[37] was chosen as Labour (Butler) Day in Trinidad and Tobago.

War Experiences and Social Change

The war had implications for Grenada that no one could have anticipated. The experiences Grenadians had of colour prejudice in the military service of Britain and simultaneous exposure to literature and alternative ways of living in societies relatively free of racial prejudice, such as France, was to stimulate a profound desire for change not only among the soldiers, but all in the society with whom they shared their experiences. Soldiers were stationed in Africa, where their ancestors had been captured and forced into slavery. In Egypt and other places they were able to see the glories of Africa with their own eyes, and for the first time realized that they were not second-class human beings as they had been taught under the rubric of British colonialism. Many soldiers who had served in Africa developed identification with Africa as a result of their war experiences. They were, therefore, very receptive to the doctrines of Marcus Garvey when these came along in a decade or two.

The soldiers and other workers returning from abroad came back educated both by experience and knowledge. They desired self-expression and self-determination, and this craving for self-assertion collided with the rigid colour/class system, which was a heritage of plantation society. Moreover, in 1917, while the soldiers had been in Europe and Africa, the

Bolshevik Revolution had occurred in Russia. West Indian soldiers, including the influential Cipriani, were inspired by the revolution and its ideals. They returned home with socialist ideas, and the belief that it was possible to create in their homeland a social system featuring greater economic equality, mutual respect and meritocracy. The struggle to create a society based on equality and justice would occupy Grenadians for the rest of the twentieth century, taking different forms in different eras under different leaders.

Even though the disturbances had been occasioned by the lack of employment and opportunity for the returned soldiers, these men were often in a far better position than the bulk of the population. Living isolated from the goings-on in the urban sector, the rural population was also isolated from its increasing modernity. Life for the rural peasant was wretched, but life was lived with a fatalism that provided no room for discontent or political action. Both these would have to wait until the 1950s, and the consciousness-raising by Eric Matthew Gairy of the rural poor. In the meantime, daily suffering was borne with unimaginable fortitude.

Notes

1 CO 321/276, no. 35459, Letter from Young to the Colonial Secretary, dated 31 Aug. Colonial Office Dispatches, Windword Islands, Grenada, 1914, Public Record Office (PRO), London.

2 CO 321/276, no. 2996, Governor to Harcourt, dated 29 Dec., Colonial Office Dispatches, Grenada, 1914, PRO.

3 CO 321/276, no. 2996, Governor to Harcourt, dated 29 Dec., Colonial Office Dispatches, Grenada, 1914, PRO.

4 Blue Book Report, 1914–15, PRO.

5 CO 321/282, Copy of letter from Captain V.B. Moltino of the *Antrim* to the Governor, dated 24 July 1915, Colonial Office papers, PRO.

6 CO 321/282, no. 36581, Blue Book Report, Colonial Office Dispatches, Grenada, 1915, PRO.

7 CO 321/276, no. 46694, Governor to Harcourt, dated 7 Nov. 1914, Colonial Office Dispatches, Grenada, 1914, PRO.

8 CO 321/276, no. 51517, Governor to Harcourt, dated 5 Dec. 1914, Colonial Office Dispatches, Grenada, 1914, PRO.

9 CO 321/281, no. 3948, Governor to Harcourt, dated 5 Jan. 1915, Colonial Office Dispatches, Grenada, 1914, PRO.

10 Black regiments had existed in the British Empire since 1779. The necessity had arisen from the devastation caused by tropical diseases among white European troops in tropical areas. Slaves had also been drafted as troops in British North America during 1776 to 1783 to fight on the British side. They were promised and had been given freedom as a reward. Some of these troops were later deployed in the West Indies. On the eve of the French Revolution 300 troops, former members of the Black Carolina Corps, were quartered in Grenada. Among the troops that accompanied Abercromby to Grenada during the Fédon Revolution were black troops of the First West India Regiment. They met the Loyal Black Rangers in Grenada that been formed using slaves from the estates of Governor Ninian Home, Alexander Campbell and others. See Buckley, *Slaves in Red Coats*.

11 CO 321/282, no. 3894, Governor to Bonar Law dated 26 July 1915, Colonial Office Dispatches, Grenada, 1915, PRO.

12 CO 321/282, Governor to Bonar Law dated 7 Aug. 1915, Colonial Office Dispatches, Grenada, 1915, PRO.

13 *Ibid.*

14 CO 321/282, Copies of correspondence including Director General, Army Medical Services to W.S. Marshall, dated 8 July 1915; Haddon-Smith to Bonar Law, dated 7 Aug 1915, Colonial Office Dispatches, Grenada, 1915, PRO.

15 *Ibid.*

16 CO 321/282, no. 45816, Haddon-Smith to Bonar Law, 15 Sept. 1915, Colonial Office Dispatches, Grenada, 1915, PRO.

17 *Ibid.*

18 Terrence (Terry) Commissiong was subsequently to enlist and serve as a Company Sergeant-Major during the war, for which he was decorated. He was later promoted to Colonial Secretary in 1942, the highest post in the civil service at that time.

19 Minutes of the Legislative Council, 23 July 1915, Supreme Court Registry, St George's.

20 *Ibid.*

21 CO 321/282, no. 1226, Haddon-Smith to Bonar Law, 14 Dec. 1915, Colonial Office Dispatches, Grenada, 1915, PRO.

22 *Ibid.*

23 CO 321/287, Haddon-Smith to Bonar Law, 24 March 1916, Colonial Office Dispatches, Grenada, 1916, PRO.

24 CO 321/287, Haddon-Smith to Bonar Law, 29 June 1916, Colonial Office Dispatches, Grenada, 1916, PRO.

25 *Ibid.*

26 CO 321/299, Dispatch from Governor to Secretary of State forwarding Report on the Blue Book for 1917–18, dated 20 Jul. 1918, Colonial Office Dispatches, Grenada, 1918, PRO.

27 Blue Book for 1915.

28 Minutes of the Legislative Council for 23 November 1917, Supreme Court Registry, St George's.

29 CO 321/287, Haddon-Smith to Bonar Law, 15 Feb. 1916, Colonial Office Dispatches, Grenada, 1916, PRO.

30 CO 321/287, Minute to letter, Haddon-Smith to Bonar Law, 22 Feb. 1916, Colonial Office Dispatches, Grenada, 1916, PRO.

31 CO 321/294, no. 1, Haddon-Smith to Walter Lang, Colonial Office Dispatches, Grenada, 1917, PRO.

32 CO 321/294, Telegram dated 9 Jan. 1917, Haddon-Smith to Bonar Law, Colonial Office Dispatches, Grenada, 1917, PRO.

33 Govt of Grenada, *Grenada Handbook*, p. 75.

34 Brereton, p. 158.

35 *Ibid.* p. 360.

36 The meaning of the name of this gang is lost. It is possible that only the gang members knew what it meant. Marjorie McLeish recalls that gang members spoke French Creole among themselves and suggests that 'TT' may stand for words in French Creole. Some sources add a third 'T' to the gang's name, making it the 'TTT Gang'.

37 19 June 1937.

14

Between the World Wars

The prosperity that Grenada had enjoyed just before and during the First World War ended in 1920, shortly after the war. Although nutmegs were doing well, cocoa production decreased due to unfavourable weather. The cotton crops from Carriacou were of poor quality. Attempts were made to introduce limes and coconuts, and to this end a government lime grove was established behind the Botanical Gardens, and the public was invited to visit and inspect with a view to establishing plantings of their own. The attempt to introduce limes was not a success except in Carriacou, as in Grenada they were often planted on unsuitable and marginal lands. However, cane cultivation was stimulated, and there was an increase in the production of sugar and rum.[1]

Even before the war, the Governor had expressed the worry that Grenada's economy was too dependent on cocoa, and was very keen on 'substantial additional industry'[2] established as a guard against a fall in cocoa prices. The Governor's concern for the growing dependence on cocoa was shared by F.H. Watkins, the Colonial Secretary, who warned that Grenada was placing too much stock into cocoa:

> Grenada depends for its prosperity and almost for its entire existence at present, upon cocoa and spices, and the highly remunerative prices obtained for these staples has resulted in the neglect of other industries … Were the price of cocoa to fall below remunerative production, the Colony would be in sore straights.[3]

He foresaw disaster if the bottom ever fell out of the cocoa market. A further warning came from the Imperial Commissioner on Agriculture who visited in 1915. He observed that the best lands were given up to cocoa, and new crops would have little success if they were not given a chance by having some of the best land earmarked for their production.[4] Perhaps by that time it was already too late to diversify and thus prevent yet another episode of very hard times for Grenada. The obsession with the new export crop was so great that cocoa was planted on land not suited to the crop, and was only profitable when the price for cocoa was high.

Cocoa was also depleting the soil, as the farmers failed to replace the nutrients by adding fertilizers. Despite all warnings, planters and peasants alike continued to expand cocoa production. The prices for cocoa dropped dramatically at the end of 1920,[5] and Grenada faced three years of continued low prices for its major export. This had a profound effect on both the resources of the government and of the people. Added to this, all the surpluses in the Government Treasury had been used for the improvements undertaken during the war, and the war effort. The government was now in deficit. Steps were taken for a retrenchment of government programmes, and a revision of the tax structure.

Fortunately, this slump in the economy was short-lived. The price for cocoa and nutmegs recovered, and by 1925 the economy had regained much of its prosperity. Unfortunately, very little of this prosperity trickled down to the workers of the colony, who remained desperately poor, and lived at bare subsistence level.

Agricultural Organization

Grenada's export crops were marketed through the commercial houses on a commission basis, or sold through produce-buying houses. Smallholders disposed of their produce through licensed dealers in the districts, who in turn sold the crops to the commercial dealers.

The Grenada Department of Agriculture was amalgamated with Trinidad in 1925. Under this scheme, eight leading officials from Trinidad would pay frequent visits to Grenada, and Grenada would have access to the Director, Mycologist, Entomologist, Chemist, Cocoa Agronomist and other technical officers based in Trinidad. This greatly enhanced the services provided to farmers, and the health of their crops and animals.

Bananas were introduced as an additional export crop in about 1929, and a banana shed was constructed on the pier. The Canadian Banana Company purchased bananas at the quayside. A sugar factory was established in Woodlands to produce high-quality muscovado sugar for home consumption, and smaller sugar mills produced the crude muscovado sugar preferred by the labouring population. In 1937 the sugar factory distilled 51,329 gallons of rum for home consumption.

Trade Agreement with Canada

In 1920 a Trade Agreement was signed between Canada and the British West Indies. This was later revised with no changes except that the ships on the route were exchanged for modern ships with cold storage facilities for shipping bananas. Increased preferential agreements were made for goods coming into Canada from the islands, and this was reciprocated by preferential agreements in some islands for Canadian goods.

The Conditions of the Peasantry

Approximately 100 years earlier, the peasants had come out of a system of slavery where they had lived under the very worst physical conditions. Before the abolition of the slave trade, the owners were not particularly concerned with keeping slaves healthy; the philosophy was to work the slaves to death, as they could be replaced by purchasing new ones from the incoming batches. After slavery ended, the ex-slaves were only infrequently exposed to higher lifestyles than their own. There was no mechanism whereby the ex-slave could learn of higher standards, and thereby aspire to them. The middle and upper classes in society did set standards for their house servants, and expect that these would be scrupulously observed in the household. These rules did effect a change in the way house servants lived, and new ideas were taken back to their community when on visits. However, even if the ex-slave wished for a better life, he or she was constrained by colour and physical features in a society that despised African looks. Placed in a position where most could only earn a living in agriculture, the economic condition of the majority of Grenadians was controlled because earning power was limited by what they could produce, by the price paid for produce, or by the price of their labour.

Nevertheless, peasant society was an alternative existence for the ex-slave, which also gradually changed the nature of society, and its social geography. Villages and markets evolved throughout the island, the spread of the population was greater, and schools and health centres were built in the rural areas to meet the needs of the communities of peasant farmers and their families. The peasant population was a growing and identifiable sector of the population that had to be catered for in any plan. Politically unrepresented and living at subsistence level though they were, peasants did live a free and independent existence, and a certain amount of contentment was a feature of these people who chose to eke out a living working for themselves on small landholdings.

Europeans and Americans who visited Grenada at this time were either scandalized or amused, depending on their own humanitarian values, at how the majority of people lived and at the disparity between the standards of living of the social classes in Grenada. The standards of living were of particular concern to health professionals like Dr Howard

S. Coleman, Director of the Ankylostomiasis Campaign in 1917. Coleman, without understanding the constraints on the peasant, wrote that the peasants were:

> [p]eople with little responsibility, few desires, and practically no wants, they get along quite contentedly in a small thatched house with a minimum of household furniture. Breadfruit and plantains are too easily obtainable to make real hunger possible. There is no home life. Scant obedience to parents by children; a variable interest in cleanliness; no conception of sanitation.[6]

The condition of the peasant and his household was a reflection on the failure of the people who had power in the society to lift the standard of living of the peasant up to minimum standards. The 1938 Commission appointed to investigate the economic conditions among wage-earners in Grenada with special reference to agriculture found that, in addition to the poor housing of the peasants, their clothing was wretched, and many were emaciated from hookworm, venereal disease and tuberculosis. Peasant children were ravaged by yaws and gastro-enteritis. Many were found to be deficient in Vitamin B, calcium and iron, and also to suffer from protein-calorie malnutrition.

Brizan describes the living conditions of the majority of people at this time:

> houses built of imported deal boards or shingles, on small sup-porting piles to compensate for the uneven foundation and ground on which they stood. They were small with one bedroom and one living room – each about ten feet by eight feet. Their roofs were either thatched or shingled. The houses of labourers and poorer peasants were made of mud and wattle, with cane straw thatched roofs; poorly ventilated ... It was common at the time to find as many as fifteen people living in a two-roomed house; as is evidenced by medical officers' reports. One referred to the houses in his district as ramshackle or dilapidated straw, mud or wooden structures between 12 and 15 feet square ....[7]

The lack of sanitation was not only almost indescribable but also led to severe health problems. Dr Barugh Spearman, reporting in 1938, said:

> It is doubtful if one peasant's house in a hundred is provided with latrine accommodation. Soil pollution was therefore gross and the struggle against flies, flyborne and intestinal infections, such as

the enteric and dysenteric group of diseases and helminthic infections such as Ankylostomiasis and round worms, is rendered
infinitely more difficult.[8]

Josephine Davis, now a respectable senior citizen, remembers that in
her childhood her house in St David's had no latrine. To defecate, all
members of the family went into the bushes that surrounded the house.[9]

Another heritage of the plantation experience was the innate lack of
responsibility exhibited by men for their offspring. Because the plantation
provided economically for all children, men had not fostered the habit of
parental responsibility. The children remained with their mothers, or with
designated females, until they were old enough to be part of the children's
work gang. The bond between women and children therefore remained
intact. However, out of the necessity of the mother having to go to work, a
tradition of family and community support for child-rearing arose, and the
affirmation that all children belong to the village remains as part of the
Grenadian cultural heritage, although it is contra-indicated by the modern
ideals of individual living and independence from the community.

Although the church urged marriage on the population, it was seldom
contracted. The rates of illegitimacy were high, averaging 66 per cent of all
babies born. These babies were the responsibility of the mother, the father
giving meagre or no support to the mother or child. Because of the lack of
family structure, mothers had to leave their babies in the huts while they
went out to the fields or to work. The infants often remained hungry all day,
or managed for food as best they could. There was also little knowledge of
how to care for newborns. There were numerous cases of babies who had
been born healthy and well, being carried to the hospital or clinics several
months later suffering from malnutrition caused by ignorance as to the type
and quantity of food necessary to keep them healthy.

In 1940 the infant mortality rate was an unacceptable 155 per thousand. Generally children were fed too much starch and insufficient
protein. After a child was weaned, the mother often gave the child no more
milk, as it was believed that milk gave the child worms. Not uncommonly,
children had 'bush tea' sweetened with 'wet-sugar' for breakfast, and
breadfruit for their main meal. Many children went hungry for a whole
day, or days at a time. Children were often dressed in rags, or went naked,
and were kept from school for want of clothes to wear. This problem had
been addressed in St George's before the war by the establishment of the
Ragged School.

In 1930 there were 15,319 peasants in Grenada, 84.4 per cent owning
plots of less than two and a half acres.[10] A significant portion of these proprietors were the persons who had received land under the Government

Land Settlement Scheme when lands from five estates in Carriacou and six in Grenada were subdivided. The last subdivision was of Calivigny Estate in Grenada in 1921. In an effort to improve the condition of the poor, the scheme was revived. By 1940 there were 20 Land Settlement Schemes in Grenada, in every parish but St Patrick's. The acreage in land settlement was 3836 acres involving fourteen parcels of land in Grenada comprising 1965 acres and six in Carriacou comprising 2309 acres. The estates or portions of estates that were made available to the peasant were at Limlair in Carriacou, and at Frazé, Mount Cassell, St Cloud, Point Salines, Mount Nesbit, Plaisance, Belair and River Sallee in Grenada.

Owning land did not automatically mean a higher standard of living for the peasant. It may have improved his mental well-being, but many peasants had to continue to live in villages or on the estates where they worked part-time because they could not afford to build a new house, or to move their house to the new location.[11] Land settlement, salutary as it was, was not backed at this time with the structures and policies that would have enabled the peasant to make the best of his opportunities. Credit facilities, subsidy schemes, marketing organizations and other elements of economic and social infrastructure would eventually come into existence, but not during the decade of the 1930s.

In addition to the growth of small proprietors, there was also a growth in tenant farmers and metayers. Fewer and fewer peasants were choosing to work as wage labourers on the remaining estates. In 1921 there were 17,717 agricultural wage labourers. This amount had dwindled to 15,000 in 1930, or 20 per cent of the labour force. By 1949 this number would be reduced to 5323[12] but even so, only 1549 were employed continuously. This reduction was the result of the fact that the wages for labour paid by the estates were below subsistence level. The daily wage for estate labour in 1935 had not changed for almost one hundred years. There was also less work available, owing to a temporary slump in the economy during the 1930s. At this time the world economy was in depression, prices for cocoa fell, and the estates could not afford to employ labour for five days per week, even at the going low wage. Many more tenant farmers and metayers were created by the downturn of the economy as estates tried to survive by renting land to former employees to grow food, thus keeping the loyalty of the workers for when times improved, and doing their part to alleviate social conditions.

The metayage system worked best in Carriacou, but even there metayage and tenant farming were insecure forms of tenure, and had drawbacks for both peasant and landowner. These forms of farming did not encourage proper use or care of the land, and resulted in low production both in terms of productivity per acre, and per man-hours devoted to farming. As in past decades, metayage(or sharecropping) and rental of lands lent itself to many disputes between the peasant and the landlord.

As a result of the 1938 Commission, which looked into the economic conditions of wage earners in Grenada, a Labour Department was set up in 1938 with a Labour Commissioner/Land Settlement Officer. This officer had the duty of advising the government on all matters connected with the labouring classes, including peasants and smallholders, of liasing between the government and labour organizations, of ensuring that the provisions of the labour legislation were observed, especially with regard to the payment of the minimum wage and the employment of women, young persons and children, of examining the conditions of estates and factories, of finding ways of employing the unemployed, and of supervising land settlements. The Commission recommended that the wages for agricultural labour, which were now below subsistence level, be raised. Other results of the work of the Commission were that a Workman's Compensation Ordinance was passed and regulations were put in force governing the opening of shops and stores, and the employment of shop assistants.

The Tenants Compensation Ordinance of 1939 was passed to regulate the conditions and provisions of land tenancy as well as measures to reconcile disputes between landlord and tenant. A significant improvement in wages and conditions would not be enjoyed again for another decade.

The Moyne Commission

The standard of living of the majority of the people in Grenada and the West Indies was becoming a blot on the imperial slate. Not only this, but massive poverty juxtaposed with the high lifestyle of the middle and upper classes created a situation that, under the right conditions, could breed discontent, disturbances and civil commotion. The West Indies at this time had had several riots. In many cases certain members of the middle class exploited the political potential unleashed by these riots, and rose to fame through the leadership role they took to themselves. Their skills in crowd handling, and the prevailing discontent, allowed them to rouse sufficient support from the usually quiescent poor. How much these middle-class instigators cared for the poor and how much they were using the poor to bring themselves into prominence is a moot question for debate and for reflection.

The Colonial Office's reaction to the disquieting news of poverty and unrest was to appoint a committee and charge it with a full-scale investigation of the problems. In 1938 a Royal Commission under the chairmanship of the Right Honourable Lord Moyne, DSO, was appointed to carry out the investigation. Its mandate was to investigate the social and economic conditions of several British West Indian islands, including Grenada. The Moyne Commission visited Grenada from 6 January until 12 January 1939. The Commission met with sixteen groups or individuals representing a cross-section of the community, from whom they took evidence. They also took field trips into the country, and saw first hand the conditions under which people lived.

The Commission was particularly impressed by the peasantry of Grenada, not only remarking on its size, but on 'its ability to alleviate distress' caused by slumps in the international market for Grenada's cocoa and other staples. The Commission wrote:

> It may be noted that the adverse effect of the slump of cocoa on the ordinary worker is somewhat mitigated by the prevalence of peasant proprietorship and the consequent opportunity for a large proportion of the population to supplement their cash earnings by home grown foodstuffs.[13]

The recommendations of the Commission were sweeping, and included reforms and recommendations for the formulation of policies in every sector including agriculture and land settlement, constitution, public administration, public finance, the civil service – including the operation of colour prejudice and colour discrimination within the service – education, public health, housing, labour – including the operation of any trade unions, – and other social needs and services of the population. The Commission also recommended a 'closer union' between the islands of the British West Indies, including an amalgamation of the Windward and Leeward Islands, and a unification of some services.

Whereas Grenada shared many of the problems detailed in the report, Grenada's water supply was singled out as the key to further development, especially on the west coast. The report said that 'Any further land settlement or rural regeneration schemes depends to a considerable extent on adequate and hygienic water-supply'.[14] The Commission thought that the task of collecting, storing and bringing water to the villages was outside the financial powers of Grenada, and promised to recommend help in this regard to the Colonial Development Fund, or to another source of imperial funds. Unfortunately, all improvements recommended by the Moyne Commission, as well as those planned by the Grenada government, had to be shelved when Britain got involved in the Second World War, which in terms of scale and horror put the First World War in the shade.

Visit of the Labour Adviser to the Colonial Office

In February 1939 Major G.M. Orde, the Labour Adviser to the Secretary of State for the Colonies, visited Grenada to continue examining the plight of the labouring population. Grenada was again in an economic slump, due to low prices for cocoa, a poor cocoa harvest, and 'wither-tip' disease in the lime groves. Unemployment was high, and the avenue of migration to Trinidad was shut as Trinidad had curtailed immigration due to its own economic problems. The report written after his visit was bleak:

> A large proportion of the estate labour consists of people who habitually earn three or four shillings a week, on which they contrive to live with the help of produce from their gardens. Within the next two months this meagre wage will largely disappear, while garden produce will also become scarce. A considerable section of the population will therefore be faced with several months of real privation.[15]

He spoke of the need for considerable relief works:

> [Which] might usefully take the form of drainage of several swamps at present unhealthy and malarious, which could thus be rendered fit for occupation and agriculturally valuable ... Expenditure on these lines thus promises to be definitely beneficial and remunerative and not merely unproductive relief work ... The people affected are conspicuously orderly and patient in their misfortunes. A satisfactory and helpful feature of the situation is the good understanding and mutual esteem prevailing between employers and workers; on both sides credible efforts for the general welfare of the whole industry are being made.[16]

A Committee appointed by the Government of Grenada to drain certain swamps and ravines followed up the report. In the midst of an argument between the Secretary of State and the government over the payment for this relief work, everything was put on hold owing to the outbreak of war.

The Genesis of a Trade Union Movement

In the meantime, workers had begun to organize themselves into trade unions. A Trades Union Ordinance had been passed in 1934, and by 1940 there were three unions in Grenada: the Grenada Trades Union, the General Workers Union, and the St John's Labour Party. All of these Unions followed a policy of co-operating with the employers of labour in trying to effect palliatives for the workers' grievances. They also functioned as benefit societies. In 1939 a report on labour said that the relationships between labour and employers were of a friendly nature. A Department of Labour was set up by another Ordinance in 1940.[17] Trade unions continued to operate in a non-confrontational manner until the 1950s and the advent of a more modern type of trade union, featuring worker demands, negotiation and conflict resolution.

Constitutional Development and Movements towards Federation

Since 1763 the British government had tried to group its different possessions in the West Indies into larger administrative units both to govern these islands more effectively and at the same time cut the cost of administration. The 1763 government that was put in place when the British acquired the Windward Islands was termed the Government of Grenada, consisting of Grenada and the Grenadines, Dominica, St Vincent, and Tobago. This government had been bitterly opposed by Dominica, which had been British longer than Grenada, and, beginning with that island, all the islands were eventually given a separate government, so that the unitary Grenada government had all but been abandoned by 1776.

Other attempts were made to amalgamate the government of the Windward Islands and also to bring the Leeward Islands under a unitary government. Once again Britain would use its influence to attempt the unification of the governments of several territories, creating one government for all, even though at this period it was clear that some politicians wanted self-government and not necessarily a Federation.

In 1922 the Honourable E.F.L. Wood, J.P. Ormsby Gore, MP, and W.A. Wiseman, the Parliamentary Under Secretary of State for the Colonies, visited Grenada as part of a tour through the West Indies to enquire into the feasibility of an Association of the Windward Islands and Trinidad as a nucleus of a larger Federation of the British West Indies, and of the introduction of a part-elected Legislative Council. Wood's enquiry lasted just over a year. As was to be expected, foremost among those presenting memoranda was Marryshow, as spokesman for the Grenada Representative Association, who presented proposals for constitutional reform and supported the idea of a Federation.

As a result of Wood's visit, an Order-in-Council setting out the new constitutional provisions for Grenada was received in Grenada in 1924.

The amendments to the Constitution were a disappointment to Marryshow and many others who hungered for a government by the people. The Governor retained his position of President, along with considerable powers, including control over all financial matters. He also had the power to approve or reject any bill passed by the Legislative Council, or to refer to the Secretary of State for the ruling of the imperial government. Although the new Constitution provided for elected members, these were in the minority. Besides the Governor, the new Legislative Council would be composed of three nominated members, and five elected members on the unofficial side, and seven members on the official side, including the Attorney General, Colonial Secretary and Treasurer. The franchise allowed only 7.08 per cent of the adult population to vote.[18]

Marryshow and his fellow Grenadians had to be content with a small victory. The Constitution had been fundamentally revised, and the new provisions marked the end of pure Crown Colony government on 30 November 1924.

Grenada was now divided into five electoral districts, and elections were held for the first time in fifty years. The only contested seats were in the Electoral Districts of St Andrew's and St Patrick's/Carriacou. In the electoral districts of St George's, St David's and St Mark's/St John's, a single candidate was nominated, and was elected unopposed. Two of the persons who had been active in the Grenada Representative Association were elected in 1925 to serve on the first government under the new Constitution. The first five elected members were T.A. Marryshow, C.F.P. Renwick, D.A. McIntyre, Charles H.W.G. Lucas and Fitz Henry Copeland. All five were re-elected in 1927. Between 1924 and 1933 three elections took place under the 1924 Constitution. Carriacou and Petit Martinique became an electoral district in 1936. When Grenada got a measure of representative government in 1925 these islands were linked to St Patrick's. Women were at last enfranchised, although they were barred from being elected to serve on the Legislative Council. In 1937 the privilege of service on juries was extended to women who owned property to the value of £400 or whose salary or income was not less than £40 per annum.

The movement towards Federation continued. In 1932 a conference was held in Dominica to consider West Indies Federation and self-government. Grenada's representative was the Honourable John F. Fleming. In 1939 another conference was held in St Lucia, in which Dominica was foremost in pressing for closer union. Twenty-seven resolutions were passed calling for the uniformity of the civil services and unification of the judiciary and police, exchange of public officers, joint services, the sharing of specialists, joint certification of schoolteachers, and improved sea transport. In January of the next year the Colonial Office sent out to the West Indies 'Closer Union Commissioners' in the persons of General Sir Charles Ferguson, Sir Charles Orr and S. McNeil Campbell. Their report was issued in April, and in October the Governor received instructions to extend the life of the existing Legislative Councils and put on hold the next general elections.

Frustration at Political Impotence

His Excellency Sir Frederick Seton James became Governor-in-Chief of Grenada and the Windward Islands on 26 July 1924. One of his priorities had been to meet with the District Boards to discuss the needs of the parishes, and to make these findings the basis for a working plan. The main points of this working plan were: closer association with the Windward Islands and Trinidad as suggested by the Wood Report, diversification of agricultural export crops through the introduction of bananas, pineapples and citrus fruits, the formation of an adequate agricultural department in conjunction with that of Trinidad, the improvement of education, health measures and sanitation, the extension and purification of water supplies and electric lighting. By the end of his tenure, he had been largely successful in keeping his promises. Seton-James was not popular with Marryshow, but others felt that: 'The successful introduction of most of these measures within the short space of two years is a testimony to the Governor's ability and interest in the colony's affairs.'[19]

Seton James was succeeded in 1930 by Sir Thomas Alexander Vans Best, who arrived just in time to witness the result of keeping an educated and restive population under too much restraint as regards their governance. Not having proper representation in the legislature, Grenadians felt that the only way to have their displeasure at legislation noted was to 'talk with their feet'. Thus the political peace of Grenada was interrupted in October 1931 by a massive demonstration of over 10,000 people led by T.A. Marryshow and the Grenada Workingmen's Association against the Customs Amendment Order of 1931–32. This action so displeased the Governor that he revoked Marryshow's appointment as Justice of the Peace.

In 1932, also, all the elected members of the Legislative Council resigned in protest over the Governor's disregard of their recommendations on the Budget Bill for that year. The resignations were mainly to make a point, as all who resigned offered themselves for re-election in the by-election made necessary by the resignations. They were returned unopposed. However, the new Council decided to send a two-member delegation of T.A. Marryshow and G.E. Edwards to Britain to put forward proposals for a greater say in the government of the island. The delegation's negotiations did not meet with the hoped-for success.

New proposals were sent from Britain for an amended Constitution for Grenada. This Constitution was for a government of elected members. The Governor would retain his veto power and the power to pass laws without the consent of the legislature. T.A. Marryshow violently opposed the proposals, using his newspaper as an effective forum for condemning the recommendation, and airing counter-proposals. After months of wrangling, on 15 May 1935, the members of the Legislative Council accepted the revised position of the British government, which removed the Governor's official majority in the Legislative Council, creating an unofficial majority of nominated and elected members. The new legislature would comprise the Governor, the Colonial Secretary, the Attorney General and the Colonial Treasurer as three ex-officio members, four nominated members and seven elected members. The Governor was given the power to pass any measure in the interest of the good government of the Colony. Elections under the new Constitution were held in March 1937, and the new legislature sat for the first time a few days after the election.

Demands for further constitutional development continued to be made, but the responses to the demands were increasingly couched in terms of a Federation of the West Indies, both from the British government and from T.A. Marryshow and his supporters. Britain's attempt to draw its Caribbean possessions into a unitary state in the 1930s and 1940s was enthusiastically espoused by the Windward Islands and Barbados and was supported to a lesser extent by the Leeward Islands. Powerful support came from Marryshow, as well as from other notable politicians in the smaller islands. These advocates of Federation saw an independent Federation as the destiny of the British Caribbean.

The plan proposed for closer union by Britain was for the unification of the Windward and Leeward Islands and Trinidad and Tobago. It did not include Jamaica or British Guiana. If this plan had been adhered to, and if all movement toward closer union or a Federation had not been cut off by the outbreak of war, the political and economic history of the Caribbean might have been vastly different.

The Modernization of Grenada

Between the wars, there were many developments that ensured that Grenada was not left behind in the general developmental changes taking place in the world. Essential to creating a modern society out of Grenada was the facility of travel within the island. The 'Green' bridge over the St John's River at Queen's Park was constructed in 1927, but in October 1938 a violent rainstorm lashed Grenada, resulting in the loss of five lives, and damaging cultivation. The new bridge was completely destroyed and had to be rebuilt.

To facilitate the sale of agricultural produce, a Covered Market in Grenville was opened. The government took over Queen's Park in 1926, and began work on a pavilion, which was completed in 1928.

The telephone system was modernized in 1927, and underwent a period of rapid expansion. By 1938 there were 516 telephone subscribers in the island. Grenada was connected to the rest of the world by wireless in 1925 when a wireless station worked by the Pacific Cable Board was built at Old Fort. The population of Grenada was thus supplied by an improved news service, which included advice on the movement of steamers. The same year the government installed a wireless station in Carriacou, to the great delight of business and the community, as messages could now pass with efficiency and speed between Grenada and its sister isle.

In 1930 the old female prison was transformed into a Government Residence, and a house built at Mount Royal for the Colonial Secretary. In 1928 a Central Water Authority was established to assume control of the water supply for the whole of Grenada. In 1930 the Colonial Development Fund made available the money to improve and extend the existing water supply, and to establish new supplies. By 1939 pipe-borne water was being distributed throughout the island. In 1938 a passenger bus service linked all the towns in Grenada. There were now 461 miles of road suitable for motor transport. The town of St George's was electrified in 1928, from a hydroelectric scheme using water from the Annandale River. Electricity was extended to the Woodlands Sugar Factory and to Grand Anse in 1937.

As in the past decades, mail was sent abroad by ships, which generally also took passengers and transported goods to and from Grenada. The Canadian National Steamship Company provided a fortnightly service between Grenada, the United States of America and Canada, while the ships of Furness Withy Line provided a fortnightly service between Grenada and the United Kingdom, and the Harrison Line provided a monthly service to that country. Travel between the Caribbean islands was by auxiliary and sailing vessels. A passenger service between Martinique and Cayenne also called at Grenada.

The first aircraft, a United States Flying Boat, paid a visit to Grenada on 10 March 1924. It was used to carry the Acting Governor, Lieutenant-Colonel Davidson Houston, on a visit to Grenada, St Lucia and St

Vincent, all in the space of one day. The visit was looked upon as an experiment in increased communication between the islands, but it foreshadowed the presence of the United States military in the Caribbean during the war to come, and thereafter. The growing American military presence in the Caribbean was again highlighted in 1927 when a squadron of amphibian planes belonging to the United States Army beached at Queen's Park, proceeding to St Vincent the next day.

The biggest civil engineering project was the preparation of the site for the new Grenada Boys' Secondary School. The *Annual Report* conveys some of the excitement and magnitude of the work entailed:

> The top of a hill which forms a promontory in the inner harbour is being levelled off and the excavated material used for the reclamation of a shallow bay which will be used for a playing field. The work of levelling and reclamation of the site is expected to be finished by the middle of 1939.[20]

In 1938 a committee was appointed to investigate housing conditions. The standard and the overcrowding of housing had been cited by health officials as being the main cause of the spread of infections and contagious diseases. The committee began to prepare legislation to make loans available for the improvement of the housing of peasants and agricultural labourers.

New construction and improvements extended to the hospitals. A private ward with six private rooms was added to the hospital buildings in 1921, and a nurses' hostel in 1924. A mortuary and laundry, funded by the British Red Cross, were built in 1915. The British Red Cross also funded the reconstruction of the sanatorium at Grand Etang in 1925. Eleven years later, in 1936, a tuberculosis hospital was erected at Cherry Hill. In 1934 the Poor House was enlarged to accommodate eighty-six inmates, and its name was changed to the House of Refuge. A New Health Ordinance was passed in 1925, uniting the Board of Health and several local sanitary authorities under one body, on which the District Boards were represented.

Social Welfare

Lady Seton James, wife of the Governor, had started a Baby Welfare Movement in 1924. One of the first activities of the Movement was to open a crèche for babies of working mothers in St George's, to avoid babies being left untended for most of the day when the mothers were at work. In 1934 the government provided a house near the Botanical Gardens for the St George's District Board to use for the establishment of a home for destitute children. The home accommodated fourteen children.

Tourism and Sport

A nucleus of the tourist industry had been in existence before the First World War. Tourism as an income earner grew in importance during the years between the wars. A Tourist Committee was appointed by Governor Seton-James in 1928 to encourage tourism in Grenada. This Governor introduced golf to Grenada, and was instrumental in the opening of the Golf Club of Grenada. The Golf Club was formed in 1925 and a nine-hole golf course was laid out at Queen's Park. Governor Seton-James was the first President of the Golf Club, and was also instrumental in starting a second golf club in St Andrews, which used the pasture at Pearls for links. Later, the St George's Golf Club would be moved to its present site at 'Golf Lands' and be an important attraction for tourists, as well as a favourite sport of the Grenadian business and professional class.

The Coronation of King George VI and Queen Elizabeth

That Grenadian children were being brought up to believe that they were British was highlighted by the importance given to the coronation of the new King and Queen in 1937. The *Annual Report* for 1937–38 reports:

> The Coronation of His Majesty the King and Her Majesty Queen Elizabeth was celebrated with the greatest enthusiasm by the children of the schools of the Colony. Three days holiday were given. On Coronation Day the children attended divine services in their respective churches, and those in St George's witnessed a fireworks display in the evening. Next day over four thousand children assembled at Queen's Park from the schools in St George's and listened to a speech from the Governor. They then marched past His Excellency and saluted the Flag, and returned to their respective schools where treats were prepared for them. On the following day His Excellency drove round the island and addressed thousands of school children assembled at seven points along the route.[21]

This loyalty to the British Crown would be tested during the period 1939–45 when Grenadians, along with the rest of the colonial people of the British West Indies had to call on all their survival skills and fortitude in order to survive the Second World War.

Notes

1 Colonial Reports no. 1078 for 1920, HMSO, London, 1921.
2 See letter from Governor to Earle of Crewe, CO 8522, 22 Feb. 1910, Public Record Office (PRO), London.
3 Remarks in Blue Book 1913, contained in CO 44123, PRO.
4 CO 321/282, no. 36581, Blue Book Report, Colonial Office Dispatches, Grenada, 1915, PRO.
5 At this time there was a glut of cocoa on the market. Other large producers, such as the Gold Coast (Ghana) were now producing and exporting large amounts of cocoa, and as levels of consumption had reached saturation point, the demand for cocoa levelled off.
6 Dr Howard S. Coleman, 'Report of the Grenada Ankylostomiasis Commission', 1916, enclosed with dispatch no. 25 to the Secretary of State from the Governor, 29 Jan. 1917, CO 321/294, Colonial Office papers, PRO.
7 Brizan, p. 263.
8 Dr B. Spearman, 'Economic Conditions of the Grenada Peasantry', 1938, quoted by Brizan, p. 265.
9 Josephine Davis, interview with B. Steele, 21 Dec. 2000.
10 Brizan, p. 251.
11 See the 'Report on Land Settlement in Grenada and Carriacou for 1938', Council Paper no. 18 of 1939, dated 10 Nov., Mona Campus, University of the West Indies.
12 *Ibid*, p. 256.
13 *Report of the West India Royal Commission* (the Moyne Commission Report), HMSO, London, 1945.
14 *Ibid*.
15 'Report of the Visit of Major G.M. Orde Browne to Grenada, 16–21 Feb. 1939, to the Secretary of State for the Colonies', 2 March 1939, PRO.
16 *Ibid*.
17 Department of Labour Ordinance no. 6 of 1940, *Laws of Grenada*, Sir Archibald Nedd Law Library, St George's.
18 See Brizan, p. 351, and Govt of Grenada, *Grenada Handbook*, p. 81.
19 Govt of Grenada, *Grenada Handbook*, p. 80.
20 *Annual Report on the Social and Economic Progress of the People of Grenada, 1937 and 1938*, HMSO, London, 1939, p. 22.
21 *Annual Report on the Social and Economic Progress of the People of Grenada, 1937 and 1938*, HMSO, London 1939. p. 17.

15

How Grenada Won the Second World War

The ringing of church bells announced the beginning of the Second World War in Grenada. All day long on 3 September 1939 the bells of the parish churches tolled for sorrows to come. Cosmos Cape, who was later to see active service in the war, remembers that he was paid six shilling and nine pence for ringing the bell at the St Andrew's Roman Catholic Church in Grenville.[1]

Part of Britain's strategy to maintain social stability in its colonial empire was a thorough socialization of the colonial peoples in the belief that Britain was powerful, paternal and just, and that it was their good fortune to be a part of the realm, to be 'His Majesty's Subjects'. Most colonial people were loyal to the Crown, and respected its officers and laws. This inculcated loyalty had just been given a boost in Grenada, and elsewhere, as a new King and Queen had been crowned, and Grenada had been treated to appropriate celebrations, along with the other countries of the British Empire.

Grenada was also on the brink of several developments, and hope had been kindled for the amelioration of some of the abysmal social and economic conditions to be found in the Colony. The Royal Commission, called the Moyne Commission after its head, was appointed in 1937 to collect evidence on every aspect of Grenadian life, and the Commission had not only taken evidence but also visited several places to get a 'feel' of the prevailing circumstances for themselves. Crown Colony government, which had long been protested, had been replaced in 1924 with a Constitution that allowed some popular representation. There had also been major reforms in education and health, and developments in communications.

Although progress towards modernization would now have to be shelved while Britain fought for its very existence, nearly every Grenadian was filled with patriotic feelings when the bells of Grenada pealed out the news of war. Any disagreements and grievances previously expressed about the neglect of Grenada or the limited say Grenadians had in government were put aside. Apart from traditional loyalty to Great Britain, the thought of the institution of totalitarian government with its attendant philosophy, which included the superiority of the Aryan race, was anathema to those who had come to appreciate democracy as practised in Britain, which they hoped would one day be practised in the Colony.

Grenadian patriotism, however, was flavoured with anxiety and certain knowledge that there would be profound changes in the lifestyle of Grenadians. Nothing was manufactured in Grenada, and Grenada depended entirely on sea transport for food and other supplies.

Unlike the previous war, Britain did not enter into the hostilities solely to maintain the balance of power in Europe. After Hitler invaded Poland, Britons feared that this too might be their fate. As soon as Britain entered the war, all of her colonies were similarly involved. Two years later, in December 1941, Britain and her colonies would also be at war with Finland, Hungary, Romania and Japan.

The Governors during the war years were Sir Henry Bradshaw Popham and Sir Arthur Francis Grimble, who replaced Popham on 18 May 1942. It was the job of these two Governors, particularly Grimble, to attend to everyday matters in Grenada, and also to do what was necessary to protect Grenada not only from the enemy attack by sea or air, but also from enemy who might attack from within through espionage.

Immediate Reactions to the Declaration of War

As soon as the Declaration of War was announced, the unofficial members of the Legislative Council felt the urge to send a message of loyalty and fealty to the Secretary of State for the Colonies using the following words:

> At this momentous hour when the Armed Forces of the Empire have once again been called upon to uphold the cause of righteousness, the people of the Colony of Grenada, through their chosen representatives on the Legislative Council, with their humble duty to Your Majesty desire to affirm their dutiful and abiding loyalty to Your Majesty's Throne and Person and unreservedly to offer Your Majesty their services in any capacity which may appear to Your Majesty's Ministers in the United Kingdom helpful to our common cause.[2]

The actual announcement of the war had been preceded by an urgent dispatch, dated 26 August 1939, to the Governor containing an Imperial Order-in-Council extending the provisions of the Imperial Emergency Powers Act to Grenada. The Government immediately instituted price controls to prevent an upward revision in the price of goods by merchants inflating prices and causing distress in the population as had happened with the outbreak of the First World War. This avoiding action could not prevent a rise in the cost of living, but the rise was not as steep as it would have been without the imposed price restrictions.

An office known as the Competent Authority was quickly set up to manage all trade matters and whatever was necessary to stabilize the economy and to manage the available resources at the beginning of and during the war. Its immediate concern was to exercise control over all imports, and the price of everything that was offered for sale. The government, however, had no control over the commercial banks, which dropped the interest rate to 1 per cent on saving accounts from 1 October 1939.

Urgent steps were also taken to pass Colonial Defence Regulations for Grenada, and to establish postal and telegraph censorship. One after another, Ordinances similar to those issued during the First World War were drafted for the colonies, and were passed by the Legislative Council for Grenada. Many of these Ordinances had little relevance in Grenada, such as the Trading with the Enemy Ordinance.[3] Some others[4] would be the cause of shameful incidents in some of the other islands, like Jamaica, where a boatload of Jews fleeing from certain extermination in Germany was not permitted to land.

The war meant additional expenditure to Grenada. The Censorship Service, the Competent Authority, relief to government employees on military duty, first aid, and medical emergency supplies and blackout material for government institutions, all cost money. This extra expense and the fall in government revenue attributable to the restrictions of imports during wartime were met with export tax on nutmegs, mace and cocoa, which could stand the levy as the prices of these commodities had risen during the war, and affected only the planters and exporters.

Voluntary Service

Apart from the money raised for war expenditures in Grenada, Grenadians gave generously to the war effort. A War Purposes Committee was set up to collect funds and decide on their disbursement. A total of £20,069 18s. 3d. was collected. Among the items purchased with the funds from Grenada were one fighter plane and half of a mobile canteen, and donations were made to the British Red Cross and to the local Red Cross for the purpose of providing hampers for Grenadians in active service, and to various other charities that helped people hurt by the war. Among the recipients of financial aid from Grenada was the West Indian War Services Fund.

Once again, as during the First World War, the middle-class housewives not only knitted balaclavas, scarves, gloves and socks for the troops overseas, but taught their maids to do the same. Many of these women were given certificates from the Red Cross at the end of the war in appreciation of their quiet contribution in providing warm clothing for the troops on the European front. Many Grenadians also invested in War Bonds.

Grenadians in Military Service

Early in 1939, in anticipation of war, the Grenada Volunteer Force and Reserve, which had remained active in the years between the wars, was amalgamated with the Police Force and put under one commanding officer as the Grenada Defence Force. As soon as war was declared, it was the immediate job of the Grenada Defence Force to man vulnerable points in accordance with the Defence Scheme for the island.

The Grenada Volunteer Reserve was also formed, and the men were given some military training and equipped with uniforms and rifles. In 1944 the Southern Caribbean Force was formed, under the command of both English and Caribbean officers. The Grenada Detachment of the Windward Islands Garrison of the Southern Caribbean Force comprised 139 recruits. The Grenadians who served in the Southern Caribbean Force served not only in Grenada, but also in several islands in the Caribbean. Although it was not with the same pride and glory as in the First World War that some people volunteered for service, enlistment meant for many Grenadians steady pay and a chance to see somewhere else besides Grenada. Among the Grenadians who served in the Southern Caribbean Force were Allan Gentle, Ben Jones, Derek Knight and Claude Bartholomew.

An arm of the infantry and an arm of the artillery were stationed near St George's. The infantry were housed in barracks built on the site that had been prepared for the Grenada Boys' School at Tanteen. Training facilities were also located at Tanteen. Some of the Grenadians who were trained there were Cosmos Cape, Lawrence Fletcher, Jerry Fletcher, Al James, Byron Steele, Joy Beggs, Millington Bain, George Pierre and Lowhar George.[5] The training facilities and barracks at Tanteen later became classrooms when the school was relocated to that site after the war. The artillery was barracked on Ross Point.

There were two major gun emplacements. One battery was at Ross Point, and the other at Richmond Hill on the site of the present Lions' Den and office block of the Richmond Hill Prison. The presence of the Southern Caribbean Force and the two batteries served to make the island believe it was protected, and gave Grenadians a measure of psychological comfort, although for a period Germany could have taken Grenada and any of the islands if it had chosen to do this. A British Commander, Commander Castle, was appointed to oversee military operations in Grenada during the war. He also served as the Chief Censor in Grenada. His wife, together with Laurie Harbin, Estelle Garraway, Betty Whiteman and Mollie McIntyre, assisted him in his censorship function. Subsequently, H.H. Pilgrim was assigned the censorship duties. Censorship for the Grenadian public meant that persons had to acquire the habit of putting a return address on their letters. Each letter was read, and Grenadians occasionally received letters with pieces cut out.

The United States (US) also had a presence in Grenada. There was an American Consulate on the Carenage, upstairs in the building on the corner of the right side of Young Street and the Carenage. The American Consul, Charles H. Whitaker, was in residence, and maintained a powerful motor vessel in a state of readiness.

Personnel of the United States military frequently visited Grenada, sometimes without warning. On one occasion, a vessel brought in several ten-wheeled trucks. When they were offloaded, heavy artillery was loaded onto them. US military officers then drove off through St George's, ending up at various sites at Richmond Hill, returning later to sail away without setting up the artillery they had brought. The Administrator,[6] Terrence B. Commissiong, knew nothing about the intended visit and, after lodging a complaint, was told that there was no need for concern, as the site at Richmond Hill proved unsuitable for the envisioned purpose!

Some Grenadians chose to enlist in the British armed forces. Due to a change in the attitude of the War Office, West Indians who volunteered for service were recruited directly into the British Army, unlike the situation in the First World War. Grenadians also served in the Canadian armed forces. Among the prominent Grenadians who served outside the Caribbean was Leo de Gale, who would become the second local Governor of Grenada, and who was at this time a qualified land surveyor and public accountant. He joined the Canadian Army and spent the war surveying in Italy, France, Belgium, Holland, Canada and Britain. Colin Ross, John Ferris and Julian Marryshow, the son of T.A. Marryshow, served in the Royal Air Force. Irie Francis and Julian Mitchell served in the British Army, and Mike Bain served in the Canadian Army. Several Grenadians also served in the Trinidad Volunteer Naval Reserves. In 1942 the War Office in Britain sent out a call for women to join the ranks of the military for service in the Auxiliary Territorial Service (ATS). Several Grenadian women joined, including Betty Kent-Mascoll of St Patrick's. Betty Mascoll was awarded the Defence Medal and Overseas Service Medal for her service in Britain from 1943 to 1946. Other Grenadians who served abroad acquitted themselves well, although they faced some incidents of race prejudice from the British military officers, the British government and from the British public.

German Agents in Grenada

German agents present in Grenada sought to collect sensitive information on ship movements, and to spread anti-British and anti-war propaganda, using effectively the mistrust and antagonisms generated as a result of the treatment of black soldiers during the earlier war. They were effective in that some recruits for the armed services were persuaded to withdraw, sometimes at the last moment. Grenadians loyal to the Crown tried to counter this as best they could. In a speech to the St Andrew's Detachment of the Grenada Contingent, C.H. Lucas, a respected coloured lawyer and politician, expressed the following sentiments:

> In spite of the mischievous activities of a few, happily very few; in spite of the ignorance of some; in spite of the arrant cowardice of others; over fifty of our fellow parishioners are here today to attest their patriotism and their loyalty. I would remind those who would be seditious that their freedom of lying pro-German talk is only possible under the generous rule of Britain. The malevolent talk about being 'windbreaks' for the British troops is meant to injure recruiting, but only deserves the ridicule of those who know the conditions of modern warfare ... As to the cowards who first signed on, then were medically examined, and at last turned tail and ran away from the oaths – well, I will not parley with cowards.[7]

There is also the tale told of two spies who came to Grenada saying they were American wrestlers. They called themselves Joe 'Whiskers' Blake and Joe Gotch. Later, when these were checked, there indeed had been American wrestlers by these names but they were long deceased. Blake and Gotch gave several demonstrations in Grenada, and then one day they disappeared completely. 'Whiskers' Blake is alleged to have been arrested later as a spy in Trinidad and escorted to Great Britain.

The Caribbean as a Theatre of War

Unlike the Great War, the Second World War was truly global, with the advent of faster ships, modern aircraft and better submarines. The

Caribbean and Southern North Atlantic regions, which saw little action in the Great War, were to be major theatres of naval warfare during the Second World War because the oil and bauxite that the region produced and refined were essential to keep a motorized war moving.

In 1941 Winston Churchill, Prime Minister of Great Britain, signed an agreement with the United States which granted them permission to acquire land for bases in Trinidad, St Lucia, Antigua and elsewhere in the Caribbean in exchange for fifty destroyers. This agreement is popularly known as the 'Bases for Destroyers' agreement. Airfields and other stations in support of the war strategy were set up throughout the Caribbean.

Under this agreement, an airfield was opened in Grenada at Pearls, St Andrew's. The first plane landed there in 1942, and the airfield was officially opened in 1943 to serve both military and civilian aircraft. More important than the airfield was the navigational beam established at the Pearls airfield with the call letters ZGT. This beam was much more powerful than those in some of the other islands, because it was designed to be picked up by military aircraft leaving Puerto Rico bound for the airfield at Wallerfield in Trinidad. The Northern Range in Trinidad blocked the beam from that airfield, and the beam from Grenada was designed to guide aircraft into Trinidad. The navigational beam at Pearls was also of use to air traffic in the Caribbean bound for points in South America and West Africa.[8]

The Point Salines Lighthouse was also an important navigational aid to shipping transiting the southern entrance to the Caribbean. Thus, although not as important as Trinidad, Grenada had a crucial role as a strategically placed island, near to Trinidad.

However, the most important role for a Caribbean island in the war was played by Trinidad. Under the same agreement Churchill had negotiated with the United State, two huge American bases – a naval base at Chaguaramas, and the air force base at Wallerfield – were set up. Trinidad was made the convoy assembly point for oil tankers going from the Caribbean oil refineries to North Africa and Europe, and the Gulf of Paria was used for the final exercise of US carriers and planes before they were dispatched to the Pacific theatre, via the Panama Canal. Planes for the Eighth Army in North Africa were ferried through Trinidad. Vessels and planes from South America had to be cleared at Trinidad before they were allowed to proceed to their North American or European destinations. A large censorship department served as a cover for British and US agents searching for Latin Americans who used the neutrality of Spain and Portugal to engage in smuggling or espionage for Germany.

U-boat Activity in the Caribbean

Because of the oil and other materials the Caribbean supplied to Britain, and because of the uses to which the Caribbean islands were put in the war effort, the Germans directed much of their attention to countering the benefits Britain could derive from this part of the world. Germany used U-boats[9] as its most important weapon in the Caribbean theatre. U-boats swarmed westward into the Caribbean as soon as the United States of America joined the war. Up until then, the Germans had honoured the Declaration of Panama signed on 3 October 1939, by twenty-one American republics, which mapped out a Pan American Neutrality Zone. Now, their objective was to disrupt marine traffic travelling through the Panama Canal between the Atlantic and Pacific Oceans, to and from the American and Asian theatres of war, and to cut off communication between Europe and the Americas. They also sought to destroy oil installations and oil tankers.

The U-boats were extremely successful. They sank many tankers and cargo ships travelling from Aruba, Curacao, Venezuela and Trinidad to Britain carrying oil, gas, bauxite and sugar desperately needed in Britain. The U-boats also attacked shipping coming to the Caribbean carrying food and other necessities for the colonies, intending to gradually starve the peoples in the colonies, and make them disaffected with the war.

The Allies were powerless against the U-boats. In March 1941 the average loss on merchant shipping in the area was one ship per day[10] and until the middle of 1943 the Gulf of Mexico and the Caribbean frontier was the most dangerous theatre in the world for Allied shipping of any sort. Most shocking and devastating was a twenty-day period in March 1943 when 97 Allied ships were sunk within a twenty-day period. The ubiquitous U-boat menace caused Winston Churchill, Prime Minister of Great Britain, to send a cable to Franklin Roosevelt, the American President, saying that: 'I am most deeply concerned at the immense sinking of tankers west of the 40th meridian and in the Caribbean Sea. The situation is so serious that drastic action of some kind is necessary.'[11]

The U-boats came very close to disrupting communications between Europe and the Caribbean. From time to time they surfaced in Caribbean waters and showed themselves to those on land. There were many sightings of these vessels off Ross Point and other locations in Grenada, but the Southern Caribbean Force was instructed not to fire on them, as each submarine was powerfully armed, and Grenada was not equipped with anything resembling shore batteries.

In 1943 a British destroyer, HMS *Petard*, captured a German U-boat in the Mediterranean. Rather than let the submarine fall into the hands of the British, with all its secrets, the German crew scuttled the vessel, before accepting the rescue offered by the crew of the destroyer. While the rescue of the German sailors was in progress, however, two crewmen of the destroyer dived into the water, and entered the rapidly sinking vessel. From it they recovered the German coding machines and code-books, and managed to hand them to other members of the crew before being pulled under and drowned as the submarine sank. This was an invaluable prize for the British. The Germans never knew that the coding equipment had come into the possession of the British, and they had only to wonder how the British were now able to pinpoint the position of every U-boat and German vessel. The heroic action of the two British sailors was one of the factors responsible for turning the tide of the war in Britain's favour.

Until the U-boat menace was brought to an end, foreign shipping to the Caribbean was severely curtailed. Although Grenada was not directly attacked, the attacks on the oil tankers and oil installations at Aruba and Curacao, and Maracibo in Venezuela, were near enough to home to cause concern. Two ships were also torpedoed in Port of Spain Harbour, which was practically on Grenada's doorstep. A large ship was torpedoed in Bridgetown Harbour, and two in the Castries Harbour in St Lucia. One of these was *Lady Nelson*, one of the four 'Lady Boats' that plied between Canada and the Caribbean providing much-appreciated transport between the islands. These boats, which were very fondly regarded by the population of Grenada and the other islands, were soon temporarily withdrawn due to the danger from submarines.

Local boats filled the gap for Grenada and other smaller islands by transporting passengers and ferrying goods from Barbados or Trinidad. Schooners and small steamers carried identification letters and numerals that had to be displayed prominently on the sails, bow and stern of the vessel. All the boats from the Windward Islands carried the letter 'W', and the boats from the Leeward Islands the letter 'L'. Thus the *Harriet Whittacker* had the identification code W257, and that of the *Emmanuel Florence* was W256.

When local vessels put out to sea there was always uncertainty if they would return. Local schooners and steamers were sometimes challenged by the U-boats. On most of the occasions, the U-boats would surface and hail the local vessel, giving the crew and passengers a few minutes to get into the lifeboats before the boat was torpedoed, or sunk by the submarine's gunfire. Larger vessels of the merchant marine were torpedoed with impunity. People watched fearfully for the return of mariners when they heard that a boat had been struck. One of the most talked-about losses was that of the SS *Davidson* that was bringing bank notes to Grenada from Trinidad. This boat was reported lost in the *Grenada Gazette* of 24 August 1940. Grenadians maintained a coastal watch, and rescued any survivors that drifted into shore. In Carriacou there is the grave of an unknown soldier or sailor whose body was washed ashore. The grave is still a focus for Remembrance Day celebrations on that island.

Locals who met this type of misfortune on the sea, as well as several members of the armed forces and other civilians, arrived in Grenada in lifeboats, some badly burned. These included several German sailors, often declaring that they were civilian survivors of merchant shipping, because the war on the sea did not always go the way of Germany. All unidentified shipwreck survivors were taken to the Colony Hospital for any treatment necessary and then held for further 'observation' until they could be handed over to British authorities.

Grenada, however, did not share Dominica's grisly experience of having corpses of German and Allied seamen, both military and civilian, wash up on the beaches half-eaten by fish.[12] Once sixteen bodies were washed up on the beaches of the Carib Reserve there. These were sailors from a Spanish ship blown up by mistake by a German submarine sixty miles east of Dominica. The German captain, in apologizing for the sinking of a neutral ship said that he had thought that the Spanish ship was a British merchant ship that had been disguised. That this captain shot first and looked after has implications for a later incident near Grenada.

It was also possibly true, and certainly believed by Grenadians, that German sailors from submarines landed on Grenadine islands to take exercise, get some sun and help themselves to coconuts. Bridget Brereton corroborates this. She says that the waters around Trinidad: '[w]ere infested with German submarines and they sometimes surfaced and shelled reconnaissance planes based on the island; occasionally they landed at lonely beaches in the eastern Caribbean to exercise their crews.'[13]

Eileen Gentle records that: 'It was also believed that U-boats used the small unprotected and often uninhabited islands of the Grenadines between Grenada and St Vincent for refuelling.'[14] It is perhaps less likely that German sailors from submarines were allowed to come into St George's to go to the cinema,[15] although one respondent told me that two Germans were arrested at the Roxy Cinema in Port of Spain.[16]

'Blackouts' were practised regularly in St George's, and volunteer blackout wardens walked the dark streets, knocking at the doors of anyone who let a chink of light escape though the thick, black curtains that hung over the windows. People were discouraged from using lights in their homes after dark. Everyone was asked to travel at night only in emergencies. Vehicles were required to partially cover their headlights, or to direct the beams downwards.

News of the War

Radio had been introduced in the 1930s, and radio broadcasting was still in its infancy. The Second World War spurred the development of radio broadcasting in the British Caribbean as the British government felt the need to relay war news and to present programmes designed to boost the morale of the people. The news bulletins from the British Broadcasting Corporation (BBC) provided news of the progress of the war. These were relayed by local stations. In Grenada people also gathered around the occasional radio, or stood within earshot of one to hear daily bulletins coming from the BBC. Thus Grenadians and other Caribbean people had access to exactly the same news as was available to the British public. Grenadian newspapers were also a source of news. Information on the war was posted on boards in the police stations. Those who could read did so aloud for the others to listen. Since the official news dealt mainly with the progress of the war in Europe, the majority of Grenadians would have been unaware of the enormity of enemy action in the waters around them. However, tales of torpedoed ships and sightings of U-boats circulated among the population, almost exclusively among the men, who chivalrously chose not to alarm the women with this type of news.

The rum shop played a role in news dissemination. This was important because some of the Grenadians who took boats out into the dangerous waters surrounding Grenada had no other source of news of hazards and ships lost but 'each one tell one'. No one expected the news of the loss of a West Indian schooner to make the next BBC news bulletin.

Grenada Adjusts to War Conditions

It must be appreciated that, as the financial strain of prolonged war on Empire resources is likely to be great, all expenditure by Government (and indeed by the general public) should, as far as possible, be avoided which (a) involves use of foreign exchange ... (b) creates demand for unessential goods and so deflects men, material and shipping from war purposes. In this connection you will appreciate that it will be very desirable to replace imported goods of all kinds, especially foodstuffs, by local produce wherever possible ...

I am anxious to see existing social services and development activities disturbed as little as possible both because retrenchment and serious curtailment of services at present juncture might have very unfortunate effect on Colonial people and also because on grounds of policy it is important to maintain our reputation for enlightened Colonial Administration. In particular I am anxious to avoid any retrenchment of personnel.[17]

The above is a part of the text of a circular telegram to all Governors from the Secretary of State for the Colonies at the beginning of the war. The message that imports would have to be restricted, and many completely barred due to exigencies of the war, was conveyed to a meeting of the Legislative Council called on 29 September 1939.[18]

As predicted, shortages of everything very quickly appeared: petrol, wheat flour, salt, fats, kerosene, matches, imported butter, cloth and a number of other items. For years wheat flour would not be sold except to licensed bakers, and even then, there was a severe shortage. Frederick McDermott Coard, in his autobiography written many years after the war, thought it important to mention that an invitation to tea by the Chief Revenue Officer during the war was remarkable because: 'I saw some welcome slices of bread on the table, a sight I had not beheld for several weeks'.[19] Biscuits made in Trinidad were brought over by schooners and were highly prized.

Here was where the war made the biggest difference to the average Grenadian. To survive the war would mean that they had to find a counter to the shortages and deprivation. For a start, they went back to the land to produce more food. They also used their ingenuity to create substitutes for imported food by treating the local food with appropriate technology. The urban/rural flow of commerce was now reversed, as town dwellers travelled to the rural areas to buy food such as sweet potatoes, yam, dasheen and plantains, breadfruit. To alleviate the acute shortage of wheat flour, breadfruit flour was made by first sun-drying and then pounding the breadfruit. Farine, and cassava made from the root of the manioc since the time of the Kalinago,[20] and cassava cakes made from this, were other locally processed foods used extensively during the war as substitutes for the preferred imported rice and potatoes. Bananas dried in the sun were also used as a substitute for prunes. 'Dressed up,' they made a delightful dessert for the elegant table.

The cooks of Grenada also excelled in making one type of food resemble another. They provided for the elegant table pigeon peas cooked to resemble the canned *petit pois*. Butter was made by creaming off the cow's milk, and shaking or churning this with salt and other ingredients.

Some people found the butter produced in this way too white. Soon it was discovered that a drop of annatto was all that was required to give the butter the usual yellow hue.

The Grenadian people also had to resume the abandoned habit of getting where they wanted to go by walking, or to plan in advance. Gasoline was short, and motor vehicles were immobilized for the duration of the war. However, essential services were supplied with petrol, but one had to book a seat on the mail bus two weeks in advance if one needed to travel from the country to town.

Migration to Trinidad

In spite of the dangers to local shipping posed by the submarines, the war years saw the peak of Grenadian migration to Trinidad. Crowds would gather outside the shipping offices waiting for the opening hour when they could buy tickets. Three of the boats that plied regularly between Grenada and Trinidad carrying migrants were the *Enterprise*, the *May I Pick*, and the *Rosemarie*. So many manual workers went to Trinidad at this time, seeking jobs on the American bases at Chaguaramas and Wallerfield, to build the Churchill Roosevelt Highway, to work on the docks, to get work in the oilfields, or to fill the positions left by the Trinidadians who vacated them to work in the new areas as above, that Ordinances were passed in Trinidad in 1942 and 1944 to prohibit immigration to Trinidad except for persons under contract to perform agricultural labour. It was not only the working class who went to Trinidad to seek their fortune. Several educated young men of the coloured middle class were willing to engage in manual work in such jobs as stevedores, as the pay was higher than anything they could hope to earn in Grenada as clerks and junior white-collar workers. Among the migrants to Trinidad was Elton George Griffith. He left Grenada around 20 June 1941, with plans to leave from there for Syria. Before departing for Syria, he met with his brothers and sisters who had migrated to Trinidad before him, and decided to stay in Trinidad. He later involved himself in the struggle to restore the Shouter Baptists'[21] rights to their form of worship.[22]

Grenadians also migrated to the Dutch islands of Curaçao and Aruba to work in jobs aligned to the oil-refining industry. Two such migrants were Eric Matthew Gairy, an intelligent and ambitious teacher who migrated to Aruba and worked there as a clerk in an oil refinery, and Rupert Bishop, whose wife was a descendant of Louis La Grenade, who also went to make his fortune in Aruba, and started his family there, giving Maurice Bishop, his famous son, an Aruban birth certificate in 1944.

During 1941 to 1944 the net loss of the population of Grenada to migration was 8300 persons.[23]

Grenadians were winning the war at home through their indomitable spirit. There were inconveniences, but the economy was not too badly off, as the price for nutmegs and cocoa, which had slumped in 1938, rose again during the war. When Pearl Harbor was bombed on 7 December 1941 it was quickly understood that there would be no more shipments of nutmegs from the Far East to Europe or America. This meant that the price of Grenadian nutmegs would rise. Those who could afford it quickly bought up as much nutmegs as they could, and the price offered to farmers rose with each passing hour. Dealers who had nutmeg stocks were to make fortunes.

Shopkeepers in Grenada were hard hit by import restrictions. They managed to survive by retailing local food. It helped that often the shopkeeper was also a small farmer, and might in addition be the local middleman in the process of buying and reselling Grenada's export crops.

The people of Carriacou and Petit Martinique, being self-sufficient, were not unduly deprived by the shortages of the Second World War. Captains of vessels and fishermen had to be more vigilant to ensure their safety, and that of their boat and cargo, from being sunk by German U-boats. Otherwise it was life as usual.

The *Island Queen* Disaster, and the Carriacou Mine Tragedy

The greatest pain during the war for Grenadians was the disappearance with all on board of the auxiliary schooner, the *Island Queen,* on 5 August 1944. An excursion had been arranged to St Vincent over the Emancipation Holiday, and the passengers distributed between two boats: the *Providence Mark* and the *Island Queen,* the latter a larger boat that regularly plied between Grenada and Trinidad. Among the excursionists were almost the entire membership of the All Blacks Club, a football team made up of young educated coloured men, many of whom were later to enter the ranks of the professional class. There were also a number of young people going to attend the wedding of a popular Vincentian whose two sisters had married into prominent families in Grenada. Among the passengers were some of the most beautiful middle-class girls in Grenada, and some of the most promising and good-looking young men.

The St George's pier was filled with holiday atmosphere as families waved goodbye to the young people, whose future seemed as bright as that Saturday afternoon. Most of the young people wanted to travel on the

Island Queen, as there was every possibility of gaiety and fêting on the boat during the entire journey. Several thought themselves fortunate to be able to exchange their places on the *Providence Mark* with older or quieter folks on the *Island Queen* who were not keen 'to party'. The members of the All Blacks travelled together on the *Providence Mark*, chivalrously giving up their places to the young ladies who preferred to travel on the *Island Queen*. Up to the last minute, people were exchanging places, and one young man hopped from the *Providence Mark* to the *Island Queen* while the boats were moving, almost falling into the water.

Both vessels were of the same power and speed, but the *Island Queen* had the edge. The boats pulled out almost together, and stayed on a parallel course for a long time, the *Island Queen* travelling out further than the *Providence Mark*, which hugged the coastline. Night fell and then the weather became blustery. An eyewitness[24] on the *Providence Mark* recalls seeing the lights of the *Island Queen* as the boats passed Duquesne, between 8 and 8.30 p.m. After that, the lights disappeared as the boats separated.

When the *Providence Mark* reached the harbour in St Vincent, the passengers were slightly surprised but a little delighted that they had beaten the *Island Queen*. One of the little excitements of travel with another boat was to see which boat could reach its destination first. All the passengers were cleared by customs by 8 a.m. After that, most of the passengers waited around for their friends on the *Island Queen*, fully expecting that it could not be far behind. They waited in vain, because the *Island Queen* would never dock.

By 10 a.m. worry started to make itself felt. Telephone calls were made to Carriacou to see if the *Island Queen* had had engine trouble and had put in there. By midday on Sunday, the Grenadians in St Vincent began calling Trinidad, Grenada and wherever else they could think that the boat could be. Searches by air and sea included planes from the Fleet Air Arm based in Trinidad, and motor torpedo vessels based in the Grenadines. The search continued for weeks, but it was never publicly admitted that any wreckage from the *Island Queen* was ever found. However, there were rumours that hats, shoes and other clothing were found on the north coast of Grenada, and on the Venezuelan coast.[25]

The *Providence Mark*'s passengers returned to Grenada on Tuesday. The crowd at the harbour was anxious and sombre, because some parents were unsure as to who had travelled on which boat, as there were last minute 'swaps'. Soon parents were joyously embracing the children they had never expected to see again, while the sorrow of those whose children were never to return was immeasurable. Nearly every middle-class family had a son or a daughter on board the vessel. T.A. Marryshow himself lost three children. Dr Evelyn Slinger, a well-respected physician in Grenada, and his Vincentian wife lost their two little daughters whom they sent on the *Island Queen* in the care of an older lady to visit their grandmother in St Vincent. A few days before they had been brought by their father to see Eileen Gentle, who had just had her first baby at the Private Block of the General Hospital. She remembers that the two Slinger children 'waved to me as they passed the hospital on the *Island Queen*'. [26] The entire population of Grenada mourned in unison for the loss of these bright and beautiful young people, and the crew of this proud vessel. The total number of persons lost on the *Island Queen* was fifty-six passengers and eleven crew.

Parents and friends of the lost kept hoping. There were many theories as to what had happened. Among the quite fantastic was the tale that a German submarine had captured the ship and embarked some of her own crew and passengers. Hitler, it was said, had been among the passengers. The *Island Queen* had then been re-directed to South America, Patagonia perhaps, where all the passengers had been put ashore. The expectation was that at the end of the war the young people would be released and allowed home. Many people recalled that the *Island Queen* was painted black, befitting a boat that was to be the funerary barge carrying the young people across the River Styx to parts unknown, whereas the *Island Queen* was in fact painted red.

After a lengthy search, the *Island Queen* was presumed sunk with all on board. An official enquiry was set up by the government, headed by Magistrate Henry Steele. The conclusion reached after all the evidence had been examined was that the *Island Queen* had caught fire and burnt. Persons at the hospital in Carriacou reported having seen a plume of smoke out to sea around the time when the *Island Queen* should have been passing in the vicinity.

This official closure to the incident was not universally accepted. There was a commonly held plausible suspicion that an Allied submarine had torpedoed the *Island Queen*. The vessel had a relatively new German engine, which could have made the vessel a target for a torpedo from a submarine that did not care to use its periscope to look, or to surface, as was common practice before destroying shipping, even enemy shipping. It was suspicious that no wreckage had been admitted to, even though there were rumours of hats, shoes and clothes found on the beaches. And a fire on board would have left survivors to tell the tale, and bits of wreckage such as was common from vessels wrecked between St Vincent and Grenada, notwithstanding the sharks that were common in the sea between the islands. If the suspicions were correct, US boats of various kinds, including the very fast motor launch belonging to the American

Consul stationed in Grenada, allegedly dispatched to direct the search for the *Island Queen*, were really sent out to effect a hasty but fairly thorough clean-up operation before the arrival of the local population in their boats. Every bit of evidence of a terrible and tragic mistake may have been collected, and then the truth suppressed to prevent a major scandal erupting in the middle of the war.

Then again, a German submarine may have sunk the *Island Queen* without warning, not allowing the passengers to get into the lifeboats as was usually the custom. Recall that a German submarine had sunk a Spanish ship by accident earlier in the war. Another possibility was that the *Island Queen* had been struck by a floating mine, and exploded with everybody and everything on the boat being blown to smithereens, with debris too fine to be recognized. The harbours at St Lucia and Martinique were heavily mined during the war and it is not impossible that one of these mines worked itself loose and floated into the Grenadines. This theory was supported by another tragic incident in Carriacou shortly after the war ended when a floating mine washed up on the beach at Windward. Recently Dr Jan Lindsay of the Seismic Unit of the University of the West Indies[28] has put forward a theory that the *Island Queen* passed over the Kick 'em Jenny submarine volcano at a time when the volcano was producing methane gas. The bubbles of methane gas changed the water density, and the *Island Queen*, with all its passengers, was sucked down into a watery grave at the foot of the volcano, with no hope of escape. But then what of the supposed wreckage and clothes found on the beaches of the north coast of Grenada?

Perhaps the truth about the *Island Queen*'s disappearance will never be known. If the evidence is still in the official Second World War records, it might soon be revealed, as these records are slowly being released for public scrutiny sixty years after the end of the war.

The greatest tragedy of the war for Carriacou came after the hostilities ended. Throughout the war, barrels of oil, tins of milk, lumber, barrels of flour and other canned goods had washed up on the shores of Carriacou from vessels torpedoed in nearby waters. At the height of submarine activity, people would get up early to see what the sea would yield. On 6 July 1945 a different looking 'barrel', which was really a floating mine, washed up on the beach at Windward. They could not discover any easy way to open it, and so left it on the beach to be a plaything for the children. One afternoon, a few villagers decided to open the 'barrel' by attacking it with axes and crowbars. It exploded, killing nine and injuring two people. Among the dead were Clarence McLawrence, Smith Martineau and his two daughters, 'Sankey' Patrice and his son Clarence, Hyacinth Patrice, Ronald Patrice, John Rolk and Nicholas Roberts. Two of the dead were the persons trying to open the 'barrel' and two were nearby working on a boat. The others were on the road ten yards from the beach. Many others narrowly missed being injured or killed by shrapnel flying through the air. Everything around the disaster site was completely flattened. A big crater was left in the sand by the explosion. If the main force of the blast had not been directed downwards, the damage would have been much greater.

After this incident fishermen were warned to look out for floating mines, and four more were spotted. One was washed up on a reef. All were exploded safely by gunfire from British naval vessels.

The War Ends

As in the rest of the Allied countries, 8 May 1945 was 'VE Day' (Victory in Europe) for Grenada. The news was celebrated with spontaneous rejoicing, and the streets were filled with music, dancing and carnival-like parades and celebration. More rejoicing took place on 'VJ Day', on 14 August, marking the Allied victory over Japan. The government set about dismantling the arrangements put in place for the war, and soon the soldiers came home. Many were offered positions in the police force, prisons or civil service. Some had had their positions kept open for them. Others went away to study, or were otherwise absorbed into the workforce.

Grenada Won the War!

Grenada had won the war as it pertained to Grenada. Grenadians had not starved, or nearly starved, as the people of Barbados almost did. Even though they might not have had as much to eat as they were accustomed to, they had enough. They had risen to the occasion by producing what food they needed for home consumption, and being thankful for it, even if it was not the food of their choice. They had patiently restrained their desire for improvements in the various sectors of Grenadian life. They had gone about their lives in as normal a way as possible, coping with the alarms and frights of the war with courage and fortitude. Despite how they felt about Britain, many volunteered for service at home and abroad, and contributed to the war effort. They had stoically borne the loss of fifty-six young people on board the *Island Queen*, and other Grenadians and those from neighbouring islands lost in marine disasters in the Caribbean Sea and the Atlantic. Now they were ready to resume with vigour the battle for improvements to their condition and way of life, including the right of every man to vote, and the right to self-government.

Grenada was fortunate that only three Grenadian soldiers did not return from the war. The names of Flight Officer Colin P. Ross, Sergeant J.D. 'Jack' Arthur and Sergeant John Ferris, all members of the Royal Air Force who lost their lives in the skies of Europe, were added to the new war memorial that stands in the Botanical Gardens and Ministerial Complex in Tanteen. A few people still remember and respect that these young men gave up their lives for country, empire, and a philosophy of life precious to all Grenadians.

Notes

1　Notes from the Grenada National Museum.
2　This telegram is reprinted in Govt of Grenada, *Grenada Handbook*, p. 363.
3　Ordinance no. 19 of 1939, *Laws of Grenada*, Sir Archibald Nedd Law Library, St George's.
4　Ordinance no. 1 of 1939, *Laws of Grenada*, Sir Archibald Nedd Law Library, St George's.
5　Information from the Grenada National Museum.
6　At various times during Grenada's history it was governed as a unit with other islands, usually called 'the Windward Islands'. This unit would have one Governor-in-Chief. When the Governor was in another island, or absent, the island was overseen by an Administrator or, in an earlier period, Lieutenant-Governor, who answered to the Governor or Governor-in-Chief.
7　Lucas, C.H., 'An Address to the St Andrew's Detachment of the Grenada Contingent', n.p., n.d., *c.* 1939, Grenada Centre, University of the West Indies (UWI).
8　Ray Smith, of Belmont, St George's, supplied this information.
9　Short for the German *Unterseeboote*.
10　Gentle, p. 66.
11　From Gentle, p. 67.
12　Honychurch, p. 171.
13　Brereton, p. 191.
14　Gentle, p. 66.
15　This was told to me by several people interviewed to complete this section of the book.
16　Information provided by Ray Smith.
17　CO 321/386, Circular telegram from Secretary of State for the Colonies to all colonial dependencies except Palestine and Trans Jordan, dated 15 Sept., Colonial Office Dispatches, Grenada, 1939, Public Record Office (PRO), London.
18　Minutes of the Legislative Council, 29 September 1939, Supreme Court Registry, St George's.
19　Coard, p. 90.
20　See Chapters 1 and 2.
21　Although the Shouter Baptists are found in Trinidad and Tobago, similar groups exist throughout the Caribbean. These are grouped together by sociologists as revivalist cults. See Simpson, *Religious Cults of the Caribbean*.
22　See Jacobs, C.M. (1996).
23　Harewood, p. 66.
24　See 'The *Island Queen* Disaster' by Cosmo St Bernard, in the *Grenadian Voice* newspaper, Friday 30 July 1999.
25　Corroborative evidence was obtained from Ray Smith of Belmont, St George's, and the late Ruby Didier of Tyrrel (H.A. Blaize) Street, St George's. I am indebted

to Basil Bonaparte of Archibald Avenue for the information that clothing and other wreckage were found on the beaches of Venezuela as well.

26 Gentle, p. 93.
27 Story attributed to Gittens-Knight, see Steele (1974), p. 15.
28 Lindsay, Shepherd and Lynch, 'Kick 'em Jenny Submarine Volcano',

16

Events to Remember

Although the Second World War had cut off quite abruptly several projects for improvement in Grenada, the war years were not devoid of development. After the war ended, while Grenada rushed to complete all the unfinished business that had been put on hold, it became embroiled in other developments that were to change the social structure of Grenada for ever. This chapter will attempt an account of the major developments in the economy, health and education of the people. It will also deal with the West Indian Federation and the subsequent alternative federal endeavours as well as the events surrounding 'Hurricane Janet' which devastated Grenada in 1955. The events necessarily overlap those to which the next chapter is dedicated, that of the evolution of the trade union movement, the constitutional development of the island, and the rise to power of Eric Matthew Gairy. Although the politics of a country pervades everything that happens in it, yet some things seem to have their own life, although political will can make for faster happening and greater success.

Eradication of Some Endemic Diseases

Grenadians had been plagued by several diseases over their history, and had no effective weapons with which to fight them until the twentieth century. With the discovery of bacteria and viruses, together with the understanding of proper sanitation, clean water, and isolation of infected patients, doctors were better able to control disease. Real medical progress came, however, in the second half of the twentieth century with improved medicines and treatments, plus the use of insecticides for the elimination of mosquitoes. Soon the incidence of certain diseases was reduced until they were no longer major problems in society.

Malnutrition
The nutrition of the population had been a cause for concern for half a century. The health of both children and adults greatly improved with the eradication of hookworm, but people still had not learnt to make the best

325

use of the food available, and to eat what they produced, instead of selling it to buy less nutritious biscuits, macaroni and imported food.

The health of babies and children remained a particular concern. It was the special target of Child Welfare and Well-Baby Clinics, generally operated from the Health Centres, and of public education campaigns promoted by the health authorities, together with elements of health and nutrition introduced into the syllabus of the schools.

Tuberculosis

Tuberculosis is spread by infection by the *Mycobacterium tuberculosis* through the spittle of an infected person, or through water contaminated with bacteria from an infected person. The eradication, then, entails isolation of the person, treatment, and public health. Before the advent of new treatments, tuberculosis was treated by isolation, improved diet and letting nature take its course.

Tuberculosis patients were treated at the Princess Louise Hospital at Richmond Hill until the hospital was relocated to Cherry Hill. Because patients were kept isolated, few offered themselves for treatment, and when they did, the disease was so advanced, they were admitted to hospital to die. A new treatment of collapse therapy was a major advance in the treatment of tuberculosis. The infected lung was collapsed temporarily, to let it heal. A new class of drugs introduced after the war was highly effective against this disease. This, and an inoculation campaign, regular examinations for food handlers and teachers, and the tracing of all contacts, with treatment if necessary, reduced the incidence of the disease to a point where it no longer was a major threat to health.

Typhoid

Typhoid is spread by water infected with the *Salmonella typhi* bacteria. An outbreak in Carriacou in 1940 was stemmed when two contaminated wells were cleaned, and a guard positioned at both to prevent people using the same water for consumption, bathing and washing clothes. The persons who had contracted typhoid were treated, and all contacts with the cases were inoculated. People were instructed to boil all drinking water.

The disease reached Grenada during the war, and the incidence of cases became high enough to warrant the setting-up of a specialist hospital at the tuberculosis hospital at Cherry Hill, sending the remaining tuberculosis patients back to the old hospital at Richmond Hill. One in six patients at the hospital died, until antibiotics were introduced between 1947 and 1956.

Antibiotics made the treatment so effective that the recovery rate was rapid and the mortality reduced to minimal levels. As a preventative

measure against the disease, schoolchildren, and then the entire population, were inoculated against typhoid from 1947. Inoculation and public
health measures have virtually eradicated this disease from Grenada,
although there have been incidental recurrences. These are treated by
identifying the source of the infection and by the inoculation of contacts.

Malaria
Malaria is spread through the bite of the *Aedes Aegypti* mosquito. This had
been known for some time, and through the decades great efforts had been
made to drain and fill in the swamps in Grenada. A highly effective insecticide called DDT was now used to kill the mosquito. Several campaigns of
spraying were carried out, during which all houses were sprayed. Oil was
also spread on the remaining swamps. New drugs also got rid of the
malarial parasite in infected people.

These measures proved effective in Carriacou when there was an outbreak in 1951. Altogether 1612 cases were identified, and there were eight
deaths. By isolating and treating every case, and every past case, to remove
the malarial parasite from the blood of Grenadians, the malaria cycle was
broken and malaria eradicated, even though there seems to be no way to
get rid of the mosquito on a permanent basis.

A Malaria Eradication Campaign including spraying continues
because, although the incidence of malaria is minimal, it can so easily be
reintroduced into the island from other countries. Efforts at mosquito
control continue, although the insecticide DDT is no longer used, as it has
proved harmful to man and to wildlife. A Public Education Campaign
urges each person to play a part in decreasing the number of breeding
places available to the mosquito, by treating all standing water with chem-
icals, and by properly disposing of rubbish. Mosquito control was stepped
up in 1953 when the dengue virus was discovered in Trinidad.

Dengue
Dengue, less virulent than malaria, but nevertheless a nuisance and the
occasional cause of death, was introduced into Grenada, possibly from
Trinidad, in the 1950s. It is carried by the *Anopheles* mosquito, and
succumbs to the same types of eradication campaigns levelled at the *Aedes
Aegypti.*

Venereal disease and yaws
The incidence of these diseases remained very high in the population,
despite the best efforts of the medical personnel to identify and treat
people. Of the people examined by medical personnel in 1947 yaws was
found in 16.4 per cent of the patients.[1] With the advent of penicillin and

other antibiotics, both of these diseases became easily cured. Yaws was completely eradicated through a campaign, beginning in 1947, which involved the inspection of schoolchildren and the examination of all houses where yaws cases were identified. Instructions in sanitation were given to the families of persons affected, and also made a part of school curriculum. Penicillin was reserved for the most serious cases, as microbes can build up a resistance to it. But, in most cases, the less powerful drugs proved effective.

Venereal disease was not as easy to eradicate, as there is a natural reluctance to admit to the infection and to name contacts. The yaws campaign was amalgamated with a campaign to eradicate venereal diseases in 1948. Clinics were instituted at the Health Centres throughout the island. When the word spread that treatment was now fast and confidential, many more people offered themselves for treatment, and were cured.

Rabies

The mongoose had been introduced into Grenada from Jamaica in 1870 as a measure against rats. In the 1950s it was discovered that mongoose were carriers of rabies, which could be passed to both animals and humans. Hurricane Janet brought on an increase in rabies cases, as starving dogs attacked the mongoose that came into town in search of food. In 1956 a full-scale anti-rabies programme was launched which involved the compulsory inoculation of all dogs, the capture and destruction of stray dogs, and the eradication of the mongoose. In two years, 10,000 mongoose were poisoned.

The campaign was only partly successful, as the baiting of mongoose had to be discontinued because of the prevalence of accidental poisoning of domestic and farm animals. During the period 1952–67, 358 cases of rabies infection were identified, involving 3 people, 1 bat, 88 dogs, 3 cats, 70 cattle, 142 mongoose and 51 other animals. As soon as there was a cessation of the programme, the incidence of rabies increased, but the vaccination programme proved to be a more effective way of controlling the disease in humans than efforts to eradicate the mongoose.

New health concerns

Grenada was spared diseases such as the plague and smallpox by quarantine regulations and vigilance. For many years there was a Rat Gang, hired to exterminate rats, which are carriers of plague, from the storehouses and harbour of St George's. At one point, the public were offered one penny for every rat presented to the health authorities, dead or alive, and some individuals took up this offer enthusiastically, especially during the depression of the 1930s.

It was when quarantine regulations were not applied universally that Grenada paid the price and epidemics occurred, as in the case of the cholera epidemic of 1854. With the advent of air travel after the Second World War, therefore, Grenada had to be more careful as diseases not endemic to the island could be brought in before infected persons even knew they were sick. Recognizing this, the public heath authorities suggested that the quarantine regulations be enlarged to include the incidence of quarantine of any unidentified fever or ailment.

Some diseases remained outside the realm of quarantine. These were cancer, diabetes, hypertension and, since the 1980s, HIV/AIDS. As with all the diseases that Grenada has fought against and conquered, public education, better diet and improved lifestyle are most effective measures of prevention.

Enduring Poverty

In 1942 the Secretary of State for the Colonies arranged for Sir Cosmo Parkinson to visit Grenada to inquire into Grenada's needs. Once again, the views of the Churches, businessmen, public services, and other citizens were sought, but this time the intelligentsia of Grenada was not mollified. They thought that the fact-finders ought to go out in the field and see the conditions for themselves instead of having the truth filtered though the eyes and attitudes of others. The editorial of *The West Indian* on New Year's Day 1943 made this sentiment quite clear: 'The business of the Colonial Development and Welfare would receive a decided stimulus were M.P.'s privileged to get a clearer insight of conditions in these parts.'[2]

Exploitation by Britain was also blamed for the state of Grenada. Dudley Slinger, a respected citizen, wrote angrily to the newspapers:

Tell her [England] that on account of the uneconomic prices paid by her manufacturers for our products we are too impoverished to build the necessary schools, to house and educate our children properly, that under present conditions hundreds of children are crammed into small buildings...[where] it is impossible to teach them even discipline and we are faced with an unruly mob of illiterates for the future. Tell her that the majority of the estate labourers in this island exist on a wage of two shillings and one pence a day for men and one shilling, eight pence for women...[an] annual income of £45. In England workers in the cocoa industry are paid handsomely and everything is done for them so that their lives should be pleasant, their incomes secure, their children provided for. How? Is there any need to give the

answer? We know it, and so does the Colonial Office. What a
pity the British public cannot be told![3]

Unfortunately, the Grenadian middle class failed to realize that there
was also exploitation at home of Grenadians by Grenadians. The
Governor, however, had sensed disquiet in the population, evidenced by
lassitude. He complained to the Under Secretary of State that the workers
would not work anything but a very short week, and that they lacked
motivation and discipline. Failing to recognize the root cause, he suggested
the introduction of 4-H Clubs, YMCAs and YWCAs, child welfare
centres and trade unions that might help to change the attitudes of the
workers and give them incentives towards a higher lifestyle.

However, the workers felt powerless to change their situation. They
knew that they would never achieve any reasonable standard of living
regardless of how hard they worked. They tried the best with what
resources they had, maintaining a bare subsistence, and trying to take
comfort and enjoyment in things that did not cost money, like story-
telling, music played on self-made instruments, dancing, church services,
and association with each other.

The report of the Moyne Commission, which visited just before the
war, was released in 1945, and once more highlighted the extreme poverty
and plight of the majority of the population. The response to the report by
those who held the power in Grenada was to determine that the problems
reported were for Britain to solve by sending Development and Welfare
Funds to Grenada for the alleviation of these conditions. It never occurred
to them that a better long-term solution was to effect a radical economic
transformation by paying the workers a reasonable return on their labour.
Instead, the planters were allowed to siphon off almost all of the profits
from agricultural exports, which were the mainstay of the economy,
paying the workers just enough to keep body and soul together.

Expansion of Education

Although the Report of the Moyne Commission was not made public
until after the war, reaction to the report preceded its publication. In 1942
Grenada was included in the duty tour to the British West Indies of S.A.
Hammond. Hammond was commissioned to examine the educational
system and make recommendations both for changes and for funding
through the Colonial Development and Welfare Fund.

Most of Hammond's recommendations concerned the structure of the
primary school system. He suggested that schools in this educational

sector be divided into three types. The infant schools would cater for children under the age of six. Junior schools would admit children between the ages of six and twelve, and education at the junior school level should be compulsory. Senior schools would cater for children who were aged 12–16, where the attendance would be voluntary. He further recommended that there should be secondary school courses for prospective teachers from ages 15–18, the initiation of a student-teacher system, and a considerable increase in the number of pupil-teachers to reduce the size of the classes, and to allow the pupil-teachers to study for half of the working day. He also recommended that the pupil-teachers[4] not be left to cope on their own, but that they should be supervised by experienced teachers.

As a result of these recommendations and subsequent funding or subsidization, the Grenada Boys' Secondary School, the St Joseph's Convent and the Anglican High School began to offer a three-year teacher-training course, and scholarships were provided to fund students. This scheme ceased in 1952 when it was deemed that a sufficient number of new teachers had been trained. After the end of the scheme, and until 1963, an average of four teachers per year were sent annually to the Erdison Teachers' Training College in Barbados. A sixth pupil-teachers' centre was opened, and 100 extra pupil-teachers were being trained by 1945. Seven adult education centres were opened and partly subsidized by the Colonial Welfare and Development Fund, schools were built and repaired, providing 2270 more places, and a scholarship in medicine provided. A model school and farm was built at Grand Roy, which was to be the prototype for five others.

During the first five years of the operation of the Colonial Welfare and Development Scheme, the sum of £300,000 was spent in Grenada to strengthen the education system.[5] Unfortunately, very little was done to change the curriculum or its content.

The places available for secondary education were also increased with the opening in 1945 of the co-educational St Andrew's Anglican Secondary School, the Presentation Brothers College by a congregation of Roman Catholic Religious Brothers from Ireland in 1947, and a second Convent School run by the Sisters of St Joseph of Cluny in St Andrew's in 1952. The Grenada Boys' Secondary School finally got to use the spot in Tanteen prepared for them at the beginning of the century, when their school was transferred into the barracks vacated by the Southern Caribbean Force in 1946. Around this time, the Grenada Boys' Secondary School started preparing pupils for the Cambridge Higher Schools Certificate.

In 1963 the Teachers' Training College was opened, funded by the Colonial Welfare and Development Fund. Dr R.O. Staples, a Canadian, was the first Principal. The education of teachers at this college was in special relationship with the University College of the West Indies, which had opened its doors in 1948, and began to play a crucial role in moulding West Indian education to suit the needs of West Indians. From 1963 to date, the University has monitored both the curriculum and the standards of teacher training in Grenada, and has underwritten the qualifications.

The West Indies Federation

Although negotiations towards a closer union between the Windward and Leeward Islands had been going on apace right up to the war, hostilities and the preoccupation with the war put an end to any further developments in this area. The release of the Moyne Commission Report in 1945 gave new impetus to the federal movement. It strongly supported a Federation of the Windward and Leeward Islands, with wide powers, and the amalgamation of all services. A conference of representatives of the islands concerned was held in 1945 in Grenada to work on the stated proposals.

A new twist to the federal talks took place in 1947, when a conference was held in Jamaica, with delegations from all British Caribbean territories, including Jamaica and Trinidad. During the conference, Jamaica and Trinidad both signalled their intention of joining the Federation, and were party to the resolutions of the conference. These resolutions were that there would be a federation of ten islands, Antigua, Barbados, Dominica, Grenada, Jamaica, Montserrat, St Kitts, St Lucia, St Vincent and Trinidad and Tobago. The central government of the Federation would have sweeping powers, controlling the destiny of the islands in the Federation.

Based on these resolutions, long and complex negotiations took place, thrashing out the details. During these negotiations a difference of opinion between Jamaica and the other territories arose. Jamaica had agreed to a strong centre with a unicameral legislature that had powers over all forms of taxation including income tax, customs and the post office. The Federal legislature would also have the right to review the budgets of the Island Councils, and the direction of agriculture, fisheries, marketing, immigration and emigration, federal loans, labour and trade unions. Elections of unofficial members to this legislature would be on an island basis. The terms as set out were supported strongly by Eric Williams, even before he became Chief Minister of Trinidad and Tobago in 1956, but were now resisted by Norman Manley, then Chief Minister of Jamaica. This difference in opinion became a rift, and an impediment to the harmony of all the following talks.

As the federal talks progressed, the proposals for a strong central government were watered down on the insistence of Manley, to the dismay of many. The feeling that the Leeward and Windward Islands should simultaneously pursue unification among themselves and join the Federation as a single unit was dissuaded. Eventually a Federation with virtually no powers was agreed at a conference in London in 1956.

Where to Put the Federal Capital?

No sooner was the Federation agreed to than a terrible wrangling began among members as to the site of the Federal capital. A Commission chaired by Sir Francis Mudie was appointed to go into this issue. The Mudie Commission suggested that Barbados, Jamaica and Trinidad were the most suitable, in that order. Immediately the decision met with unthinkable northerly attacks from Jamaica. The opinion was expressed that Barbados did not belong to the West Indies in spirit, that it was riddled by class and colour prejudice, that 'it was the world's largest naturally occurring septic tank'.[6]

The matter was reconsidered by another Commission in 1957, and this time it was decided to go with the third choice. Trinidad was particularly happy at being selected as the site, as this meant that Trinidad could pressure the Americans out of the Naval Base at Chaguaramas, using the excuse that it was needed for the Federal capital.

Federal elections were held in all the territories in February 1958. Grantley Adams of Barbados became the Prime Minister of the Federation of the West Indies; Lord Hailes was appointed Governor-General. Grenada was represented in the 45-member Federal House of Representatives by T.J. Gibbs and Dr Alban Radix (who was elected the Deputy Speaker of the House). T.A. Marryshow and John B. Renwick served as Grenada's Senators. When Marryshow died on 19 October 1958, A. Norris Hughes filled his place in the Senate.

The Federation was a partnership of unequal players, and it did not have equal commitment from all the people. The people of the Windward and Leeward Islands were fully behind the Federation and had been for decades. They were the initiators of the present project. The Federation was supported fully by Eric Williams, but not with as much enthusiasm by Manley, and none at all by the opposition leader in Jamaica, Alexander Bustamante.

There were also fundamental differences of opinion between Eric Williams and Norman Manley on the nature of the Federation. Williams had always maintained that the Federal government should be independent and strong, with powers of taxation in all areas, and the final word on matters affecting planning and development in all fields, with the larger territories supporting the smaller. A period of boom in Jamaica's economy based on bauxite mining, tourism and agricultural production made Manley, who had previously been supportive of Federation, begin to change his mind about Federation. He did not want to share the wealth of Jamaica with the smaller islands, and chafed under the idea of Jamaica being controlled from the Federal centre in Trinidad. He insisted that the powers of the Federation should be so limited as to leave Jamaica free to do as it pleased.[7]

Although Manley and Williams agreed to abandon their extreme positions at a secret meeting in 1960 with Vere Bird, Chief Minister of Antigua, the fact that the contents of this meeting remained secret roused the suspicions of the other eight territories. Tensions increased to the point where all the leaders seemed to be at loggerheads. This was not a good atmosphere for the meeting at Lancaster House in England in June 1960, where it was observed that none of the principal leaders seemed to be on speaking terms with the others. Manley and Williams were once more in disagreement, and the leaders of the Windwards and Leewards thought that they were being used as pawns in the struggle between Jamaica and Trinidad. At the end of this conference, the powers of the Federal legislature had been so diminished that it was virtually impotent and the Federation was a loose grouping of territories rather than a strong unitary state, as had been preferred by the smaller islands.

Jamaica Pulls Out

Then came a disastrous blow from Jamaica. The Jamaica Labour Party led by Sir Alexander Bustamante began to disseminate anti-Federal propaganda, making the Jamaican population, who knew little of the rest of the Caribbean, afraid that a Federation would be a drain on Jamaican coffers towards the less developed islands. A referendum was held, and the people of Jamaica voted against Federation. Jamaica's continued membership in the Federation was a major platform issue during first general elections in Jamaica after the Federation. Campaigning against continued membership, Alexander Bustamante and the Jamaican Labour Party won the next general election. Jamaica pulled out of the Federation in September 1961.

Eric Williams, the Prime Minister of Trinidad and Tobago, who had been the strongest advocate of the Federation, demonstrated his famous mathematical equation that 'one from ten leaves nought'. Trinidad seceded in January of 1962. The First West Indian Federation, created on 2 August 1958, was dissolved in 1962.

The Federation originally envisioned for the Windward and Leeward Islands was sabotaged by Jamaica, which was never intended to be a part of it. The collapse was a devastating blow to the political activists of the Windwards and Leewards, and an unfitting legacy for West Indian patriots such as Marryshow of Grenada, C.E.A. Rawle[8] of Dominica and George McIntosh of St Vincent, who had devoted much of their lives to this dream, investing in the federal idea their hopes for political, social and economic advancement of the entire set of islands.

A Federation of the 'Little Eight'?

Salvage efforts to revert to a Federation of the 'Little Eight' were pursued, and all looked hopeful for a little while. Britain, Canada and the US seemed willing to give financial assistance to the 'Little Eight', and at the end of 1962, in response to a request from Britain, Sir Arthur Lewis of St Lucia drafted and submitted a thorough plan for a new Federation in an amazingly short time.

The Federation of the 'Little Eight' stumbled on the question of finance, and delays by Britain. Britain insisted that the Little Eight Federation should be financially independent. An inordinately long time was taken by Britain to respond to proposals sent to them from the negotiators in the Caribbean, and these long delays produced tensions, and allowed frustrations, petty jealousies and disagreements to surface among the West Indian negotiators. When Eric Williams of Trinidad offered the smaller territories of the former Federation unitary statehood with Trinidad, Grenada accepted the offer, and thereby was accused of betraying the cause.

Unitary Statehood with Trinidad

Although Grenada's decision to go with Trinidad seemed selfish, Trinidad's offer appeared too good to turn down. Since the eighteenth century, Grenada had had close links with Trinidad. Migration, beginning in the 1700s, had never stopped, binding Grenada to Trinidad through social, cultural and economic ties. The idea that the future of Grenada would become one with Trinidad, that Grenada would be able to take advantage of Trinidad's economic wealth and natural resources, and that there would now be free movement of people had almost unanimous support in the population. An election was fought with unitary statehood as one of the main platforms. So powerful was Grenadian desire for unification with Trinidad, that Herbert Blaize and his Grenada National Party won the election without any difficulty (see Chapter 17), even in spite of Eric Gairy's mass appeal. After the election, several feasibility studies were carried out towards effecting unification.

Grenadians had believed that voting for unitary statehood would have meant immediate citizenship of Trinidad and Tobago. The day after the 1962 election, the editor of *The West Indian* had written, 'Grenada will be part of Trinidad and 88,000 Grenadians will be calling themselves "Trinidadians"'.[9] The Chief Minister had also declared that within one year Grenada would be a part of Trinidad.

However, it soon became clear that Trinidad was having second thoughts. Not only would unification be an expensive proposition, but also the Trinidadian people were against it. Trinidadians were concerned that Grenadians would flood into Trinidad, swamping the job market. The East Indian population was additionally concerned that Grenadians would all become supporters of the People's National Movement and an important factor in politics. In his best interest, Eric Williams withdrew the offer about two years after it had been made, to the chagrin of Grenada's Chief Minister and to the grave disillusionment of Grenadians.

Sorely disappointed by the failure of the plan for a unitary state with Trinidad and Tobago, the majority of voters turned against Blaize and would never give him popular support again. Gairy's party gained the majority, and Gairy became Grenada's first Premier.

An Ignominious End to a Dream

In the meantime, Antigua and Montserrat withdrew from the federal talks over Vere Bird's insistence that Antigua retain control of the post office, and Montserrat's unwillingness to join a Federation without Antigua. All hope was shattered when John Compton, Chief Minister of St Lucia, questioned the *bona fides* of the Barbados Cabinet in relation to the Federal negotiations. Errol Barrow, Chief Minister of Barbados, very angry at Compton's remarks, walked out of the meeting, which was adjourned on 19 April 1965, *sine die*, never to be resumed. Barbados decided at this point to pursue independence following the examples of Jamaica and Trinidad.

Associated Statehood

Grenada and the rest of the Windward and Leeward Islands were eventually given a great measure of self-government under a political device called Associated Statehood. Grenada was granted Associated Statehood with Britain in 1967. Later, all of these islands, originally deemed to be too small to be viable independent states, would become independent nations, as Britain tired of the financial and other responsibilities of her West Indian colonies, colonies that had brought much wealth to Britain, but which had so declined in status as to be now deemed a financial liability to the mother country.

The Creation of Co-operative Societies

The economy of Grenada had for some time now been dependent on the cash crops of nutmegs, cocoa and, since the 1930s, bananas. The establishment of co-operatives to monitor the production of these cash crops and to maintain standards was a feature of the post-war years. In 1951, the Colonial Welfare and Development Fund provided the money for a massive rehabilitation scheme for cocoa and, as part of the project, set up the Cocoa Rehabilitation Board to advise the Ministry of Agriculture on all matters concerning the improvement of cocoa. It was superseded by the Grenada Cocoa Industry Board in 1964.

The functions of the Board were mainly marketing, but it also encouraged the improvement in the quality of cocoa. To ensure that cocoa was at its best, the most favourable conditions for the purchase of wet cocoa from the farmers had to be maintained, the fermentation and drying process had to be carefully monitored, the handling and grading of the cocoa had to be carefully supervised, and the conditions under which it was exported had to be dictated. The Board did what it could to instruct farmers in how to produce and deliver the best quality cocoa, which helped both the Board and the farmer, as the farmer would benefit by slightly higher prices if the Board were able to fetch the best price for cocoa on the market.

The Cocoa Board became the sole entity licensed to export Grenadian cocoa, but the Board could issue licences under its name for other people to export the product, when this was deemed necessary. As the Board became established, it also took on the functions of farmers' co-operative.

Similar Boards were set up for the other major cash crops. In 1947 the Grenada Co-operative Nutmeg Association (GCNA) was established by a special provision in the Nutmeg Ordinance. A major benefit of membership in the Association was that farmers who were members received a higher price for the nutmegs they had produced themselves than did the dealers, who bought nutmegs and sold them on to the Association. This arrangement cut out middlemen, and encouraged the nutmeg farmers to become members of the Association. The Association's monopoly on export nutmegs was challenged on several occasions by persons accustomed to dealing in nutmegs, but to no avail.

The GCNA set up several nutmeg collecting and processing stations around Grenada for the convenience of farmers. Still in operation today, the GCNA maintains a reserve fund to cushion farmers against a sudden fall in the price of nutmegs, and distributes earnings to farmers on a regular basis, with any excess funds converted into a nutmeg bonus, paid to farmers at the end of the year, generally just before Christmas.

The first contract for Grenadian bananas was with the Canadian Banana Company, but in 1953 negotiations for a long-term contract with Geest resulted in the importation of suckers of the *Lacatan* and *Gros Michel* variety into Grenada from Jamaica and Dominica respectively. The Banana Ordinance established the Co-operative Society in 1954. This gave the Society similar exclusive rights to the export of bananas as the other Ordinances had provided for cocoa and nutmegs.

Each of these co-operatives had a Board, the membership of which was elected by the members of the co-operative. This gave the farmers, large and small, a voice in determining the affairs of the co-operative, and was an important freedom that they eventually would have to fight to retain.

Hurricane Janet

Because Grenada lies south of the hurricane belt, in the 400 years of Grenada's recorded history, up to 1955 no 'real' hurricane had hit Grenada,[10] although severe storms such as the 'hurricane' of 1921 had inflicted considerable damage. Hurricane Janet, which ravaged Grenada on 22 and 23 September 1955, was therefore exceptional and broke all the rules.

Weather forecasting was not as sophisticated then as it is today. Nevertheless in good time the Weather Bureau of the Caribbean prepared bulletins of a dangerous hurricane called 'Janet' and sent them to the Windward Islands Broadcasting Service (WIBS), which served all the islands, but was located in Grenada. The bulletins clearly indicated that Grenada was in the direct path of the hurricane, and the hurricane warnings were broadcast by WIBS from noon on 22 September, and with increased frequency and urgency thereafter.

Unfortunately, people took insufficient notice of the warnings. Although they knew that Grenada was in the path, hurricanes always swung to the north sooner or later. They assumed that Janet would do the same thing. But Janet was a freak hurricane that would lash out at

Barbados, and then turn south for a direct hit on Grenada and Carriacou, on a path that would take the eye over Happy Hill, St George's.

Shortly after midday, thick heavy clouds began to gather, and the sea became extremely turbulent. Two volleys were fired from the cannon at Fort George, and the red hurricane flag was hoisted. Still the population of Grenada did not take the warnings seriously and made little preparation. Instead, Grenadians were out and about, sightseeing. Crowds gathered on the Esplanade to watch the rising waves, which threatened to carry away parked cars. The water in the usually placid Carenage also became extremely rough, with waves washing into the street. The swells along the east coast rose to frightening heights. Still people ignored the signs of nature.

Sympathy messages were sent to Barbados and St Vincent, as it was generally believed that one or other of these islands would be the likely target of this powerful storm, which they fully expected to swing north of Grenada. At last the population's blasé attitude vanished with the arrival of hurricane force winds and torrential rains at 6.30 p.m. From this hour and until 6 a.m. the next morning, Hurricane Janet, packing winds up to 130 miles per hour, punched, trod on, ripped up and otherwise laid waste Grenada, Carriacou and Petit Martinique.

Within two hours the roofs of most people's houses were blown off. Many small wooden houses disintegrated in the wind, leaving the occupants to wait out the storm in the open, soaked by the driving rain and surrounded by the howling wind. The hammering rain caused the rivers and streams to become torrents. The water courses in spate ate away the banks of the rivers, causing houses and trees nearby to collapse and slide down the banks. The water then took away the houses and trees, people and animals, earth and boulders, all churned up into an unholy soup, not stopping until the water ran out its force far out to sea.

The La Fortune river in St Patrick's carried away eleven people when Raeburn's shop in which they were sheltering collapsed into the river. Only two of the thirteen people sheltering in the shop survived. One was Mathura, a descendant of the indentured Indians. Bruised, battered and half-drowned, he managed to get a grip on a branch from a downed bread-fruit tree that was now half-buried in the sand, and crawled onto it. The other, Raeburn, was dumped by the river in a bluggoe stool.[11] Both were found in a pitiable state the next morning. In the Parish of St Andrew, the Paradise river carried away a house with two women in it. They escaped drowning by clinging to the rafters of the house until dawn of the next day. In La Sagesse, another house was carried away with a family inside. The woman and children were drowned, but the father was thrown out against a coconut tree, which he climbed, and so did not share the same fate as his family. Also in St Andrew's the Post Royal river claimed the lives of Jimmy Peters and his granddaughter's husband when their house washed away. In Gouyave, Leonard Peters, his wife and child lived close to a river. All three were swept away in their house when the river burst its banks. Victor Jones, his wife and six children were buried alive as their hillside home was buried in a gigantic landslide. Their bodies were discovered five days later. Some of the bodies of victims swept out to sea were never recovered. The ferocious winds tore off the sign from Pearls Airport, carrying it to Carriacou, 23 miles away.

The people of Grenada woke up to a very changed land and, as the death toll began to be known, mourned both lives and a vastly changed land. There were 120 lives lost, and many more people were injured. Some of these were incapacitated for life. Over 50 per cent of the housing was lost or severely damaged, and the telephone and electricity services disrupted for months. The supply of piped water was similarly disrupted, and the water in the reservoirs polluted. Coastal roads and bridges collapsed, and there were many landslides. Communication between parts of the island was severely disrupted and, as in the days of old, people had to resort to travelling from one part of Grenada to another by boat until the roads were cleared and repaired. The pier and its warehouses were both victims of the hurricane's furious waves, sinking into the Carenage, carrying with it millions of dollars of merchandise.

Grenada's forests were denuded, and the economy was in shambles. The island lost 70 per cent of all the nutmeg trees, the significance of which becomes clear when it is understood that it takes five to seven years for a nutmeg tree to bear, and twelve to fifteen for it to come to full bearing. In addition, it was estimated that only 2 per cent of the cocoa trees survived the storm intact. In one day, Grenada's main cash crops were severely depleted, and this reduction in income and the revenue based on the exports of cocoa and nutmegs did not reach its former level for years. The total physical damage was estimated at US$20 million dollars: this sum did not include the recurrent losses of estimated earnings from treecrops. The total loss would be, of course, in today's terms considerably more. Grenadians did not know how they would ever recover from this blow, but gradually they did.

Carriacou and Petit Martinique were also completely devastated. Not only were almost all the population left homeless, but there were twenty-seven deaths, and 500 injured, several who would remain crippled for the rest of their lives. The Carriacou District Hospital and all the schools were also demolished. The beautiful Beausejour Great House that had become the Anglican Rectory lost its top storey. Residents who lived abroad owned much of the housing destroyed in the hurricane. Several chose not

54 The sea pounding the damaged Esplanade after Hurricane Janet
had hit Grenada on 22-23 September 1955 (Courtesy Government Information Service)

55 The Roman Catholic Church in Carriacou after Hurricane Janet
took away the roof (Courtesy Government Information Service)

56 A coconut plantation devasted by Hurricane Janet
(Courtesy Government Information Service)

57 Prefabricated dwellings called 'Janet Houses' were made available
for those left homeless after the hurricane (Photo: Jim Rudin)

58 The *Bianca C*, a tourist liner calling at Grenada in October 1961, caught fire and burnt in the harbour of St George's (Courtesy of the Grenada National Museum)

59 Rosa and Curtis Hughes (the tallest man) and three crew members of the *Bianca C* whom they welcomed to their home until arrangements were made for their passage out of Grenada (Courtesy of Rosa Hughes)

60 The 'Christ of the Deep' statue which was given to Grenada by the owners of the Costa Line, in gratitude for the hospitality shown to the passengers and crew of the *Bianca C* (Photo: Jim Rudin)

61 The GMMWU rally reaches the Market Square, 1951
(Courtesy of Leo Cromwell)

62 Uniformed members of the GMMWU march up
Young Street in 1951 (Courtesy of Leo Cromwell)

63 Eric Matthew Gairy,
trade unionist, leading a
1951 rally in St George's
(Courtesy of Leo Cromwell)

64 A later portrait of Gairy,
first Premier and First Prime
Minister of Grenada
(Photo: Jim Rudin)

65 Jimmy Lloyd, the Administrator of Grenada, who had responsibility for Grenada during the rise to prominence of E.M. Gairy
(Courtesy Government House)

66 Lord Hailes, the Governor General of the short-lived West Indies Federation, with T.A. Marryshow on his right, and other dignitaries during the Governor General's only visit to Grenada
(UWI Centre Library)

67 The hoisting of the Grenada flag on Independence Night, 7 February 1974

(Photo: Jim Rudin)

68 The airport at Point Salines under construction – a major project of the People's Revolutionary Government

(Courtesy Government Information Office)

69 Members of the Young Pioneer Movement with rifles (UWI Centre Library)

70 Maurice Bishop addresses a rally during the People's Revolutionary Government (Photo: Jim Rudin)

71 Female members of the Grand Roy Militia
(Courtesy Government Information Service)

72 The People's Revolutionary Army march through Gouyave
(Courtesy Government Information Service)

73 Maurice Bishop inspects the St Andrew's Militia
(Courtesy Government Information Service)

74 The attack on Fort George on 19 October 1983 when
Maurice Bishop and most of the Ministers loyal to him were killed

(Photo: Wayne Carter)

75 Crowd in the Market Square on 19 October 1983, awaiting the arrival of Maurice Bishop – an arrival that never took place (Photo: Wayne Carter)

76 The memorial erected in St George's Cemetery by friends of Maurice Bishop. The remains of Maurice Bishop and those killed with him at Fort George have never been recovered. (Photo: Jim Rudin)

77 An armed soldier of the US Army on guard over some of the ammunition discovered at Frequente after the fall of the People's Revolutionary Government (Courtesy US Embassy, Grenada)

78 A US Army tank travels around Lagoon Road, St George's
(Courtesy US Embassy, Grenada)

79 Herbert Blaize, the first Prime Minister of Grenada after the People's Revolution, greets Queen Elizabeth II and Prince Philip during their visit to Grenada in 1986 (Photo: Jim Rudin)

80 Sir Paul Scoon remained the Governor General and representative of the Queen throughout the revolution. He retired from the post in 1992. He is seen here with George Bush, Vice President of the United States, on his visit to Grenada in March 1985. (Photo: Jim Rudin)

81 Keith Mitchell, Prime Minister of Grenada since 1995, and the Vice Chancellor of the University of the West Indies, the Hon. Rex Nettleford, at the Grenada Campus, UWI, during the university's Fiftieth Anniversary celebrations in 1998 (Photo: Harold Quash)

to rebuild, and skeletons of the concrete structures remain a silent testimony to the cruelty which nature occasionally wreaks on the inhabitants of the planet. Fifty years after the event, awestruck tones are still used to tell the tales of that night of terror.

A state of emergency was declared and generous aid poured into Grenada from the Caribbean, the United Nations, Britain, the United States, and other countries. To avoid the outbreak of disease, 80 per cent of the population was vaccinated against typhoid. Food blankets, tents and medicines poured in, the first supplies arriving on two destroyers from the US Naval Base at San Juan, Puerto Rico. Sailors and soldiers came in to help with the rebuilding. A number of prefabricated houses came from Surinam as part of the aid, and were used to house the homeless. Referred to as 'Janet Houses', they proved to be very durable, and, until recently, could be seen all over Grenada. Carriacou and Petit Martinique shared in the foreign aid that helped to alleviate the initial distress, and helped the islanders get back on their feet again.

Grenadians were particularly thrilled by a visit in October 1955 from Colonel Hubert F. Julian. Julian was a Grenadian who had migrated to Trinidad many years before, and then went to the United States. In 1935 Ethiopia (Abyssinia) was invaded by Italy. The invasion was sanctioned by Britain and this support brought a howl of protest from many groups in the West Indies. Many West Indians would have gone to fight for Ethiopia, had not the British government passed a Foreign Enlistment Act to prevent this. Britain was sufficiently concerned about the reactions of Caribbean peoples to Britain's role in Ethiopia that a propaganda campaign was mounted aimed at convincing West Indians that Britain was playing a peace-keeping role in Ethiopia, and was making superlative efforts to end the war there. The British also monitored every meeting called to discuss the situation in Ethiopia, and certain meetings were banned altogether.

It was against this background that Julian, in the United States, volunteered his services as a trained airman to the Government of Ethiopia to assist in building up the Ethiopian air force. His offer was accepted and he served for some years in the armed services there, rising to the rank of Colonel. He eventually went back to the United States where he made a fortune. Popularly known as 'The Black Eagle' or 'Tango King', he was regarded as a Grenadian hero.[12]

Large crowds gathered to greet him, and cheered lustily as he arrived in a rowboat from the *Canadian Constructor* accompanied by the impressive set of people who had gone on board to welcome him. He was dressed in 'a light grey tweed suit, white tie, helmet and sun glasses'.[13] He then left for a visit to the Governor, C.M. Deverell, at Government House in the

Governor's car. That afternoon at the wharf, he handed over a personal donation of 'a lighter laden with supplies'[14] to the Governor, in front of an even more impressive group of Grenada's top civil servants and members of the legislature. He promised to send further assistance, including a complete field kitchen, and whatever else Grenada needed to help alleviate distress.

During his visit, a public meeting was arranged for Colonel Julian in the market square. He was introduced by an ageing Marryshow, whom he referred to as his 'Uncle Albert',[15] and Marryshow referred to Julian as 'one of the miracle men of the age'.[16] Again Julian promised a wealth of assistance, including 200 beds and mattresses, equipment, an ambulance and a station wagon for the Colony Hospital, and a further $100,000 in aid for Grenada, Barbados and the other Windward Islands damaged by Hurricane Janet. The visit did a lot to distract people from their plight, and hearts were warmed by the donations of one of Grenada's extremely popular and flamboyant figures.

Gradually Grenada began to rise like a phoenix from the ashes after the devastation of the hurricane. Farmers were urged to replant their tree crops with new and improved varieties, and to plant bananas as an interim money earner, until the treecrops came to full bearing. Pine trees were planted in the Forest Reserve as they grew quickly and would give the normal more slow-growing vegetation time to regenerate. Estate owners and smallholders could apply for Hurricane Relief Aid. A £2 million Hurricane Rehabilitation Fund was made available from Britain. Some of the foreigners who owned estates decided not to replant, and put their estates up for sale. Members of the middle class and the descendants of the Indian workers who had made good bought these properties. Within ten years, the Grenadian economy had recovered to its pre-Janet level.

Grenada and Grenadians learnt many things from Hurricane Janet. Perhaps the finest was the realization that Grenadians could work together to do the practical things necessary to get Grenada back on its feet. Estate managers and workers, middle class and the 'Small Man' were seen using shovels, axes, saws and other implements to clear roads, and to restore a semblance of normalcy during the first hours after the storm. The second was to respect every hurricane warning, as no one could predict which one would choose to behave like Janet.

Trinidad and England, Here We Come!

In the light of the heartbreak, desolation and destruction left by Hurricane Janet, many Grenadians took full advantage of the possibility of migration to Trinidad, which had just relaxed its immigration restrictions in preparation for free movement of member states prior to the Federation. Grenadians also left for England, which was another avenue of escape still open to them. In 1955, persons migrating to Trinidad and the United Kingdom numbered 1100. In 1958 these were joined by 2500 more Grenadians, and between 1958 and 1960 the emigration figure for Grenada was 6600 persons.[17] In 1959 alone, 2.6 per cent of the entire population of Grenada migrated. In addition to the 'pull factors' of the promise of employment at relatively high wages, Hurricane Janet was a very strong 'push factor' at this time.

The attractions of Trinidad and the United Kingdom were almost equal to the Grenadian. We hear Trinidadians voicing their anxieties through V.S. Naipaul, as he describes in one of his novels the scene when ships with Grenadians on board called at Port of Spain before setting off across the Atlantic:

> 'I hope Immigration keep a eye on these fellows,' Mr Mackay said. 'Trinidad is a second paradise to them, you know. Give them half a chance and half of them jump ship right here' ... We docked. The emigrants massed on deck and chocked their way down the gangplank to get a glimpse of Trinidad (and a few, according to Mr Mackay, to stay).[18]

There were many scenes of human drama when the ships bound for the United Kingdom docked and took on their passengers for the United Kingdom. With last messages being shouted at them by their relatives and friends who had come down from the country in buses and trucks, and to the accompaniment of loud cries of grief, the emigrants got into lighters usually used to transport produce to and from the ships. With all on board, the lighters were towed to the waiting ships, and the people with their bags and parcels were hustled aboard.

The ships maintained a reasonable standard of service for the emigrants, and the trip across the Atlantic must have been, in the beginning, like a fairytale to many, especially the meals with white table linen, shining cutlery, abundant food and white stewards. Reality began to dawn as they reached colder latitudes, and the full realization hit as soon as they landed in England. Many migrants were totally unprepared for the weather or the hardship they would have to face until they acclimatized, got a job and a comfortable place to live. In the later years of immigration, Britain placed a social worker on every immigrant ship to speak to the immigrants about some of the adjustments they would have to make in Britain.

Immigration to Britain was short-lived. Britain passed the Commonwealth Immigrants Act in 1961, which put an end to mass migration of Commonwealth citizens into Britain. By the 1960s, not only would the possibility of migrating to Britain be no more but all the countries that had been the escape routes for Grenadians would close their doors to further immigration. The only avenues left were immigration to the United States and Canada through a restrictive quota system. Grenada would never again be able to rid itself of its excess population through migration. The new challenge was, then, as it continues to be, for Grenada to seek new ways to curb its population growth, and to develop itself so as to provide a reasonable living standard for its entire people.

The Creation of the Tourist Industry and the Unexpected Fate of *Bianca C*

Visitors, ordinary and of note, had come to Grenada from very early in its history. Grenada was on the itinerary of James Anthony Froude to the West Indies in 1887. Grenada was covered in many a Victorian travel book, including *Stark's Guide and History of Trinidad including Tobago, Grenada and St Vincent etc.* in 1897.[19] Books were also written exclusively on Grenada, with the object of attracting travellers, residents and investment. These included, *Obeah: Witchcraft in the West Indies* by Hesketh Bell in 1889, written to paint delightful highlights of the island, as was Septimus Wells's *Historical and Descriptive Sketch of the Island of Grenada* in 1890. By the outbreak of the First World War, tourism was of enough importance for complaints to be made about the loss of income during this period. *The Grenada Handbook, Directory and Almanac for 1914* (published by the Government of Grenada) contains a section written especially for the tourist, and lists eight hotels and guest houses. Despite these early attempts, tourism became a pillar of the Grenadian economy only after the introduction of air travel to Grenada in 1948, and the inclusion of Grenada on the itinerary of luxury cruise liners. The first luxury hotel, the Santa Maria Hotel (later to be renamed the Islander Hotel) was constructed in 1949, and 'Tikal', the first shop especially for tourists, was opened in December 1959.

A catastrophe involving one of these luxury liners was to show to the world how hospitable Grenadians were to strangers. The *Bianca C* was a large tourist liner belonging to the Italian Costa Line, which frequently visited Grenada; it was so large that it had to anchor in the outer harbour at St George's. On 22 October 1961, a bright Sunday morning, the *Bianca C* was making preparations for departure from Grenada, having taken on board a few emigrants destined for Britain and some tourists who had spent a day on the island. Before it could pull up anchor, however, there was a terrific explosion in the engine room, and the fire from those quarters quickly spread. Immediately the ship began a continuous sounding of its horn and displayed a flag recognizable to all sailors, informing them that the ship was on fire. The ship's horn eventually got the attention of Grenadians. Members of the Grenada Yacht Club assembled at the Club saw the ship's flag of distress, and soon it was clear to everyone that the ship was in serious trouble, as clouds of black smoke began issuing from it.

The members of the Yacht Club alerted the harbour authorities without delay. In turn, the harbour authorities asked every boat in harbour to go to the aid of the *Bianca C*. The members of the Yacht Club set out themselves in their pleasure craft. In the meantime, fishermen from Gouyave noticed the boat in distress, and set out in their fishing craft. Thus, those rushing to the assistance of the liner included:

> ocean going yachts, some small day-sailors, and rough-an-ready fishing boats in all sizes. There were powerboats, sailing boats, tiny dinghies, and fifty-ton inter-island trading schooners. Even a few rowing boats were there.[20]

It was fortunate that the reaction was immediate because, by the time the boats arrived, the liner was almost all engulfed in flames. Further powerful explosions tore the ship open from its bowels to its superstructure, catapulting debris into the air. The fire was raging in the bow of the ship, and the passengers and crew were now huddled at the stern. Some of the ship's lifeboats had been launched, and passengers were already being evacuated, guided down swaying ladders by the crew. The Grenadian boats took some of the passengers, and the lifeboats were towed to the shore by the more powerful speedboats. As soon as the wet, dazed and traumatized passengers were put ashore, the boats headed out again for another load. The sense of urgency was increased by further explosions. Perhaps the whole liner would be blown apart the next minute.

All the passengers and crew were eventually saved, except one crewman who had lost his life in an early explosion. Another died later at the General Hospital from burns. A special camp was hastily set up by the government to receive the passengers, and volunteers, including taxis, transported them there. There was insufficient accommodation for the nearly 400 passengers and 300 crew, as at this time Grenada's tourist plant was very small. The small number of hotels and guest houses took some people, but the rest were assisted by Grenadians who opened their houses free of charge to the unfortunate travellers, clothing and feeding them until the Costa Line made arrangements for their transport out of Grenada.

The *Bianca C* burnt all Sunday, and was still burning on Monday morning, watched the entire time in fascinated horror by the captain of the liner, Captain Francisco Crevaco, and some of his officers. When the fire had nearly burnt itself out and the boat cooled sufficiently, two members of the crew made an inspection of what was left of the liner for the purpose of assessing the damage. It surprised no one that the damage was total. HMS *Londonderry* had been asked by the Governor to tow the liner out of the harbour. The plan was to sink her on a reef off Point Salines Reef. Just before the *Bianca C* reached her designated resting place, she chose another for herself. The towing chain broke and, before another could be affixed, the *Bianca C* sank in 160 feet of water, about one and a quarter miles off Point Salines.

In gratitude for the assistance the Grenadian public offered so readily to the passengers, the Costa Line presented Grenada with the large bronze statue called 'Christ of the Deep' which now stands on the Carenage, but which was originally placed at the entrance to the inner harbour. W.E. Julien, the managing director of the company which was the agent for the Costa Line, and who had played a central role in the arrangements for the passengers and crew in Grenada, was awarded the Cavalier of the Order of Merit by the Italian government. The *Bianca C* is now an attraction for experienced scuba divers, its scars covered with a plethora of coral and other forms of marine life.

The Loss of the *City of St George*

Ten years after the loss of the *Bianca C,* a tragedy of the sea far worse in terms of the loss of life took place between Trinidad and Grenada. On 19 June 1971, a motor schooner called the *City of St George* was on its way from Trinidad to Grenada with a boatload of passengers and some cargo. The boat left Trinidad shortly before evening fell, and all was well until fire broke out in the hold, and the vessel quickly became engulfed in flames. Some of the passengers and crew managed to get into the only lifeboat, leaving the rest of the people to fend for themselves. Twenty-two of the passengers and crew drowned. Of the twenty-two who died, thirteen people were from Carriacou, most of them from Windward. One person from Petit Martinique was also among the dead. Many in Grenada but all in Carriacou were in mourning, and nearly every person in Windward was bereaved.

Since the event took place while the vessel was still in Trinidad's territorial waters, and since the Laws of Grenada did not permit an inquest into matters not occurring within the State of Grenada, an Act was passed seventeen months later, on 16 December 1972,[21] to declare the victims of the tragedy dead, so as to assist the surviving relatives. The only memorial to this disaster is in the Grand Anse Roman Catholic Church.

Modern Trade Unionism

During the Second World War Grenadians had been exposed, through various means, to new and modern ideas. They had also seen what many already suspected during their military service or while working on the construction of the bases in Trinidad or the oil refineries in the Dutch A-B-C Islands.[22] This was that white people were the same under the skin as black people: white people were not only plantation owners and élite, but they were also manual labourers, who sweated and swore, got drunk and womanized, were killed by bullets and drowned, like their darker colleagues.

Although some of the Grenadian servicemen had been faced with racial prejudice in Europe, many had enjoyed an equality they had not experienced at home. Although few Grenadians had served overseas, there were enough who, with those who had been maintaining a fight for equal rights at home, were no longer daunted by the paler-skinned élite, or no longer thought themselves inferior to them. Through the trade union movement they would begin a process that would blow away the old plantation social structure for ever.

During the 1920s trade unions had been encouraged as a means to institute discipline among the workers, to act as mutual benefit societies, and to contain conflict between the employers and workers. After the war, the field was wide open for the formation of modern trade unions which would aggressively bargain for better salaries and working conditions for their members.

The first workers to be part of a modern trade union were the longshoremen. In 1950 Eric Gairy and George Otway formed the Grenada Workers Union (GWU). The Union had one branch in St George's and another branch in Gouyave. Soon the Union would open its membership to agricultural labour. In 1952 the GWU broke apart. The longshoremen formed a separate union, the Seamen and Waterfront Workers Union. Gairy mustered what was left, renaming the Union the Grenada Manual and Mental Workers' Union.

Other unions with particular appeal to sectors of the working public were formed in the years to follow. The Commercial and Industrial Workers Union was registered in 1956, the Technical and Allied Workers

Union in 1958, the Grenada Civil Service Association in 1959, and the Grenada Teachers Union in 1960. By 1969 there were thirteen trade unions in Grenada. The trade union movement was a means by which the working class in consort acquired a great degree of power over its own destiny. The unions were helped by older unions to acquire knowledge as to union responsibilities to members, including that of being guardians of the rights and freedoms of the individual member. Unions took this particular responsibility very seriously and fiercely guarded and protected these rights. Therefore, trade unions became an effective deterrent to any leader who dreamed that dictatorship would be the answer to the management of the people. It was to be through the trade union movement, as well as through a fully representative government with universal adult suffrage that Grenadians would at last enjoy the self-government and freedom that had been denied them since the French annihilation of the Grenadian aboriginal peoples. The return to self-rule had taken three hundred years.

Notes

1 Clyde, p. 337.
2 Editorial of *The West Indian* for 1 January 1943.
3 Letter in *The West Indian* 14 February 1943 by Dudley Slinger.
4 The student teachers were those in the secondary schools training to be teachers. The pupil-teachers were students in the senior classes of the primary schools who were identified as having ability to teach, and were trained as teachers through mentoring, and who qualified themselves by taking the examinations of the College of Preceptors.
5 Brizan, p. 326.
6 Morris Cargill in the *Advocate* of 23 January 1957, quoted in Hoyos, p. 229.
7 Springer, pp. 18–19.
8 C.E.A. Rawle, a lawyer, was born in Trinidad but adopted Dominica as his country. He worked assiduously for constitutional reform in Dominica, and towards the formation of the West Indies Federation.
9 *The West Indian*, 14 Sept. 1962.
10 Devas (1974), p. 193.
11 Bluggoes are a variety of bananas, usually used as a vegetable, rather than as a fruit. All banana trees grow in clumps, known as stools.
12 Colonel Julian's autobiography (*The Black Eagle*, London, 1964) recounts some of his experiences in Ethiopia.
13 McIntosh, p. 16.
14 *Ibid.*
15 *Ibid.*, p. 18.
16 *Ibid.*
17 Harewood, p. 66.
18 Naipaul, p. 40.
19 For details of the following publications, see Bibliography.
20 Hughes, p..21.
21 Act no. 41 of 1972, *Laws of Grenada*, Sir Archibald Nedd Law Library, St George's.
22 Aruba, Curaçao and Bonaire.

17

The Revolution that Lost its Way

One of the most successful trade union leaders in Grenada, especially up to 1967, was Eric Matthew Gairy. Although the wages of the agricultural workers in Grenada had improved marginally after the Report of the Committee to Inquire into the Wages and Conditions of Workers in Grenada, it was not until Gairy established a strong union which had the power to force estate owners and other employers to pay an equitable wage to their employees that the wealth of the island began to be shared more universally. Gairy was from the beginning a flamboyant and controversial figure who carried within his personality many contrary tendencies. His methods were often 'strong-arm', and many people got badly hurt by some of the things he thought it necessary to do. Gairy's command of public oratory allowed him to use words as a weapon against those whom he perceived as impeding the progress of the working class. Towards the end of his career, his methods to stem the tide of opposition tarnished his reputation. Nevertheless, it was Gairy who taught people to fight for their rights and to be fearless in the face of oppression, even if he was to later become the source of such oppression.

A Humble Beginning

Gairy was born in 1922 in Moyah, a small village in St Andrew's. He was born poor, but bright. His pleasing personality and his diligence made him both a favourite of his teachers and of the Roman Catholic priest for whom he was regularly the altar boy at Mass in the parish church. When he completed his studies at the LaFilette Roman Catholic primary school, he became a pupil-teacher there. Realizing that teaching would not get him where he wanted to go, Gairy set out for Trinidad where he worked briefly on the American base, then travelled to Aruba, where he worked in the offices of an oil company as a clerk, at the same time learning all he could about trade union activities, an experience that was completely new to him, and which fascinated him. He returned to Grenada in 1949, full of ideas as to how a trade union movement could uplift an oppressed population. The timing of his return was just right: the prosperity Grenada had enjoyed during the war had all vanished, the cost of living had skyrocketed, and workers in every sector of the economy were experiencing severe hardship.

Realizing that the poor people in his home parish of St Andrew's had no one to champion their cause or to be their voice, Gairy began to help them in ways that seemed insignificant, but were very important to the individual. He wrote letters to the government for individuals with concerns, or who had run afoul of some regulation. He composed letters of application for utilities or assistance on behalf of those who could not write, or who had insufficient literary skills to deal with officialdom, or cope with Government 'red-tape'. He quickly became both known and beloved. As he gained confidence in himself, he began to take on greater challenges. In 1950, when a dispute between some tenant farmers and the new English owner of one of the estates ended in the eviction of the tenants, Gairy fought for and got compensation for the tenants under the Tenants Compensation Ordinance. Gairy made his reputation on this incident, becoming a mediator between the peasants and the world of officialdom in St George's, and writing petitions on behalf of the peasants to the government.

Gairy was respected in his own community but not by the élite who held power in society. He realized that, in order to get a measure of respect and to make an impact on the status quo so that he could effect the changes in society needed to better the lot of the poor peasants, he needed to harness the power of the people. To do this, he would have to organize them. Archie Singham, a political scientist from the University of the West Indies, speaking of Gairy's thoughts at this time says:

> It soon became apparent to him that if he were to make any real impact in Grenada he would have to have an organization. He says his Aruban experience had taught him that the one institution that both government and employers respected was the trade union.[1]

Gairy's union would not be like those already operating in Grenada. His aim in getting involved in trade unionism was to transform the fledgling ameliorative movement he found in Grenada into a modern movement where the workers would be militant and be able to bargain with employers for as much pay and privileges as they could get.

Gairy, with George Otway, had formed the Grenada Workers Union in 1950. From the beginning, he made himself personally accessible to his followers and encouraged them to call him 'Uncle'. He instituted the practice of 'holding court' once a week, where he met his clients, and fed whoever was around at lunchtime. This practice was to continue throughout his career as a trade unionist and political leader.

The Sugar Workers' Strike

In July 1950 Gairy tested his strength. The Grenada Sugar Factory was owned and operated by members of the type of middle and upper class Grenadians that Gairy totally despised. Gairy submitted a claim on the workers' behalf for a pay rise of 50 per cent, paid vacation leave, an eight-hour day, with time-and-a-half paid for hours worked in excess of eight hours, and other improvements in working conditions. When the Board of Directors of the factory did not reply after three weeks, Gairy asked the labourers to stop work. He also called on the workers on twelve other estates to stop work. The workers who had withdrawn their labour went back to work only when the dispute went to arbitration.

In the meantime, Gairy made a claim for a 20 per cent rise in wages for all agricultural labourers to the Grenada Agricultural Employers' Society. The Society ignored Gairy and negotiated instead with the Grenada Trades Union Council. A September agreement between these two linked the wages of cocoa estate workers to the price of cocoa. As far as the agreement with the sugar workers was concerned, the arbitration tribunal granted the sugar workers half of what Gairy had asked, as well as holiday pay for some categories of workers, and double pay for workers who had to turn out on holidays.

Gairy's Struggle for Recognition

In October Gairy put in a new demand to the Employers' Society, although they had just ignored him and negotiated with the Grenada Trades Union Council (GTUC). Most of his demands were brushed aside, although the workers were granted minor concessions on vacation pay. When the price of cocoa fell shortly after this, the GTUC begged the employers not to cut the wages of the workers, which were now tied to the price of cocoa, as they feared the reaction of the cocoa workers. The Employers' Society failed to heed the pleas of the GTUC, and did not reply to Gairy's claim for higher wages.

On 29 January 1951, Gairy called a strike of cocoa workers starting on the same estate where he had successfully got compensation for some of the evicted tenants. The next day the workers on the adjoining estate went on strike. Two weeks later another estate was shut down by strike action. Gairy charged the Employers' Society with bad faith, and the Society replied that they had an agreement with the GTUC. Isolated acts of violence occurred, and tension began to mount in society, especially among the middle class. A number of St George's merchants thought that Gairy had fallen under the influence of the communists in Trinidad and was executing a well-designed plan to overthrow the government. It did not help that Gairy was in contact with and advised by Uriah 'Buzz' Butler in Trinidad and Alexander Bustamante of Jamaica. Both of these trade union leaders had been branded communists by many members of the élite in the West Indies.

'Sky Red'

On 21 February 1951 Gairy brought his rural supporters into St George's and staged a massive all-day demonstration outside the Legislative Council at York House. Throughout the day, he sent messages to Acting Governor George Green that he would like to meet with him. The next day more supporters flocked into St George's and assembled in the Market Square. An account in *The West Indian* newspaper says that:

> Shouts went up when Mr Gairy arrived on the scene, dressed in a mixture of sports and eveningwear, bareheaded and carrying his walking stick. The big crowd followed him from the Market Square to the top of St John's Street where they were halted by a cordon of police guarding the entrance to Church Street.[2]

Although frustrated in his intent to head for York House again, he told the workers that their fight was not with the police, but with the employers. They were therefore not to try to force themselves through the police cordon. He told them that the Legislative Council was then meeting to pass laws that would bring them back to slavery but 'We shall stand together, and we shall die together.'[3]

The Acting Governor never did meet with Gairy on that occasion. To do so would have given legitimacy to a man who was challenging the whole social order, and who had greatly upset the island's élite. Yet Green did not want to deal harshly with Gairy because of his massive popularity. He solved the dilemma by detaining but not arresting Gairy and his associate Gascoigne Blaize, and putting them aboard HMS *Devonshire*, which sailed up to Carriacou. Gairy enjoyed himself. The naval officers on this British gunboat were very civil to him and to Gascoigne Blaize, and Gairy claimed later that they showed him more respect than had the brown employers of Grenada.⁴ More than that, 'The armed might of the British Empire had to be used to curtail a young trade union leader in a small West Indian Island'.⁵

In the meantime, while Gairy was in Carriacou, rioting, violence, civil disorder and general uproar broke out among Gairy's supporters as well among anyone who wanted to take advantage of the situation to loot, burn and destroy. The Labour Adviser described what happened in his report on the unrest:

> Grenada experienced a strike of agricultural workers that caused an upheaval such as has not been known within living memory. Workers who showed a disinclination to go on strike were intimidated by their co-workers, by the unemployed and by the unemployables; estates were looted in broad daylight, while the management stood by unable to interfere; valuable produce trees were deliberately damaged; estate buildings, medical health centres, schools and privately owned residences were burnt; rioting and bloodshed occurred; the small police force appeared totally inadequate to deal with the situation, and it became necessary to seek assistance from ... St Lucia and Trinidad. Units of the British Navy were hastily summoned, and a small garrison of British Troops⁶ was stationed here for months afterwards.⁷

With looting, acts of violence, intimidation and larceny widespread throughout Grenada, the government had to ask for outside help in keeping the peace and protecting the citizens. This was the legendary 'Sky Red'.

During the two months of the General Strike with the attendant rioting and looting, damage to livestock and crops amounting to £195,000 were carried out by workers and troublemakers joining the mayhem. The government buildings burnt included the Belmont Government School, the Roman Catholic School in Grenville, and the Governor's private beach house. Agatha Fraser, her brother Snell Fraser, and John Duncan were killed at La Tante when the police fired into a hostile crowd of rioters who obstructed the police as they went to the assistance of a shopkeeper who had just been looted. The destination of this crowd was the St David's Courthouse where the objective was to demand the release of eight workers who had been arrested the previous day for stealing cocoa from Marlemount Estate, belonging to John Renwick. A fourth person, Allick Andrews, was shot when he attacked the watchman on Mount Pleasant Estate with a cutlass.

During 'Sky Red', the estate managers, large landowners and middle class armed themselves if they could. The strikers, demonstrating a long held hostility against the élite of the country, were egged on by Gairy's rhetoric, which included statements that the land in Grenada had been taken away from them one hundred years ago, and the time had come to take it back. The police force dealt with a number of incidents but was ineffective to stop the widespread disorder.

Gairy was the recipient of regional support during his exile. On 28 February 1951 Alexander Bustamante of Jamaica, deemed to be the Dean of the West Indian Trade Union Movement, sent the Acting Governor a telegram, condemning what he interpreted as victimization of the trade union movement. In Trinidad, a meeting at Woodford Square condemned the government's handling of the whole affair.

The strike came to an end with the return to Grenada of the Governor from Britain. The Governor returned on 5 March, accompanied by the Labour Adviser to the Secretary of State for the Colonies. As soon as he returned, he called a meeting of his Executive Council and told them that he was going to release Gairy and Gascoigne Blaize. On his release, Gairy promised the Governor peace, saying that the unrest had been the result of his detention.

However, Gairy had to make several appeals to the workers before things calmed down. Between 8 and 22 March, Gairy addressed several public meetings, calling for a cessation of hostile actions by the workers, and setting out a plan of action whereby the ills in the society were to be eradicated. His island-wide broadcast on 15 March carried a note of panic, indicating that he, also, may have wondered if the situation had escalated beyond his control:

> I told His Excellency the Governor that I have gained your respect and your implicit confidence and you will obey me without fail. Now don't let me down. I ERIC MATTHEW GAIRY, am now making this serious appeal to you to start living your normal peaceful life, take my example and be a respectful, decent citizen, as I say, starting now. Let me make this point, however, everyone knows that I am a serious young man and when I say 'No' I mean 'No'; and when I say 'Yes' I mean 'Yes'. Now listen to this: I am now in search for gangsters and hooligans, I ask every one of my people to help me, and if anyone is found setting fire to any place, breaking open or robbing in any way, interfering with people who are working, there will be nothing to save you, because the law will deal with you most severely, and 'Uncle Gairy' will turn you down completely. So

join me now in saying no more violence. Come on now those of you listening, let's say no more violence three times together, 'No more violence', 'No more violence', 'No more violence'; thank you.[8]

In this speech he also asked the workers to return to their jobs the following Monday morning, 19 March 1951, telling them that this was an instruction coming from 'their Leader' and he expected it to be carried out without fail. Most of the workers did return, and the island settled down into its everyday routine. Gairy was pleased. The island had been brought to a standstill for a whole month, and he was the only person capable of re-establishing law and order.

Several people at the time gave their views on the cause of the unrest. The Governor said that the unrest was a confrontation between organized labour and the employers of labour. He condemned the planters for acting as if this was the first strike that had ever occurred anywhere before. W.E. Julien, a leading merchant, and somewhat of a maverick in his class, said:

I am one of the men in Grenada who feel that there would never have been a Gairy if what I call 'the plantocracy' and other employers of labour in Grenada had forgotten their selfishness and had got down to making some arrangements whereby the labourers would have received some benefits which war and the aftermath of war have brought to the owners of land. Some of them have definitely brought it on themselves.[9]

A retired British Brigadier, P.J.T. Pickthall, who had been brought in from Barbados to head the police, said in his report on this period that the employers of labour were not ready to accept trade unionism, and the unions did not understand the mechanics of collective bargaining. When the Governor had returned hastily to Grenada in the face of the unrest, he was accompanied by a Labour Adviser, E.W. Barltrop, who had been asked by the Secretary of State to come back with the Governor to help him mediate and restore order. Barltrop considered the unrest not simply a labour dispute, but a social revolution. The black agricultural workers had overturned the social structure by revolting against a virtual state of peonage.

Michael Smith, a noted Jamaican sociologist, observed that Gairy's success was the basis for a further rift in society between the élite and the rest of the population. The population was already divided culturally, with the élite imbued with British traditions, and the population following a culture with African and French creole roots. Now the élite would not accept Gairy. Many resented his methods and disapproved of his leadership, but Smith says, 'Workers endowed him with the awe of charisma.'[10]

The 'Sky Red' events of 1951 are still discussed with awe by all sections of the population, especially by the middle class, who had been traumatized by the events. Gairy would later be able to use this terror and insecurity as a tool to get his way. 'Sky Red' was the delayed version of the labour revolt that swept most of the Caribbean region in the 1930s, except that Grenada's episode was about twenty years delayed. The period was remembered by the working class who, while they were under his leadership, would be unafraid to challenge authority.

The improvements that were forthcoming as a result of the strikes and the subsequent settlements purchased for Gairy everlasting loyalty and devotion from almost every member of the working class. In response to the strike, the lot of the average worker was considerably improved. Wages increased sometimes as much as 35 per cent, and for the first time workers were given paid leave.

The 'Upper Brackets'

Throughout the strike and the events leading up to it, Gairy made it clear that it was not the colonial government itself that was the major cause of oppression in Grenada. He told his supporters that the major oppressors in Grenada were those in the 'upper brackets' who continued to display a haughty attitude to the people of the working class and showed no interest in their welfare. 'Grenada', Gairy declared, 'is a nice little island, but there is a certain class that lives in Grenada that makes Grenada a "Hell"'.[11]

Gairy accused the 'upper brackets' of passing any legislation they wanted, and of controlling the mainstays of Grenada's economy – the nutmeg, cocoa and sugar industries. He said they were responsible for colour prejudice in society, and continued to employ persons in business and the civil service according to their colour and connections. Workers, on the other hand, had always been exploited, overworked and underpaid by the 'upper brackets'. It was time that workers fought for their rights, because there was no one else to do it for them.

Gairy Consolidates his Reputation as a Trade Union Leader

Gairy had proved himself a fearless union leader and a great showman, attributes greatly appreciated by the populace. Within three months of its formation, Gairy's union, the Grenada Manual and Mental Workers Union

(GMMWU) reached a membership of over 2000, mainly agricultural workers and daily paid government workers.

Gairy targeted the 'upper brackets' rather than singling out the fair-skinned or preaching race hatred because he was well aware that colour did not have a one-to-one relationship with wealth. Many of his supporters were the poor white people from Mount Moritz. On the other hand, many of those in the 'upper brackets' were not white or even clear-skinned. Many wealthy professionals were coloured, and so were the new 'plantocracy'. Estates had been bought by black professionals, especially lawyers, who had slipped without much trouble into the role of the old plantocracy. Descendants of Indian indentured labourers, who, through the frugal living of their fathers and grandfathers, were the heirs to considerable wealth, also bought estates. The skin colour of the estate owners and managers did not dictate their attitude towards the workers. Black Grenadians displayed some of the very worst anti-worker attitudes, and some of the fairer-skinned practised humanitarian management of workers. The myth that light skin equated with being 'bourgeoisie' would be spun in the decades of the 1970s and 80s by those who misunderstood the relevance of Black Power to Grenada, and did not have Gairy's practical understanding of class and class-consciousness.

Gairy's reputation as an astute trade union leader spread and earned him accolades not only from Alexander Bustamante, who had sent a message of support after his detention, but also from Robert Bradshaw of St Kitts, another veteran in the trade union movement. On 22 March 1951 Bradshaw addressed a meeting in Grenada, welcoming Gairy into the ranks of West Indian leaders. In this address there is an interesting hint to Gairy that he should look to older persons for advice in shaping his career.

> This island is fortunate in having the youngest Labour Leader in the West Indies and the eldest Statesman in the West Indies in the persons of Gairy and Marryshow. What one lacks in experience the other one has in a storehouse. I wish I had somebody like Marryshow with whom I could join forces. I say Grenada is fortunate in having two such extremes.[12]

Gairy, however, would take advice from nobody. His trade union and, later, his party, were his virtual army, complete with uniforms for the rank and file. He took to himself the role of commander, the President-General for life. And he always dressed the part, sometimes in top hat and tails, sometimes in the regalia of a general, sometimes in pure white. The Grenadian worker loved it. They created anthems and set them to the tunes of rousing marches to sing in his support:

We shall never let our leader fall
We love him best of all.
We don't want to show our might,
But when we start we'll fight, fight, fight.

In peace or war you hear us sing,
God save our leader,
God save our king.
Gairy to the end of the world,
The flag unfurled, we'll never let our leader fall.

Nothing could stand in the way of their loyalty and adoration.

The years following 1951 were marked with further demands of the GMMWU on behalf of agricultural workers. There were several work stoppages and threatened strikes. A few more buildings were set on fire. The government was able to prevent further looting by placing heavy penalties on the possession, receiving or purchase of stolen goods and by strengthening the police force, raising its morale and increasing efficiency. A volunteer militia of 200 was formed, and British cruisers were never far from Grenada.

A measure of peace and stability returned to society through the interplay of education and compromise. A new Labour Adviser educated the trade union leaders in the trade union techniques of negotiation and conflict management, and legislation revising the labour laws was passed. Labour relations improved so much that when the GMMWU called a general strike in 1953, it was resolved quickly through negotiation. Labour relations had progressed from a semi-feudal symbiotic and paternalistic relationship between the worker and the plantation owner and/or manager to a modern one in which the worker was tied to the estate by negotiated contract.

Party Politics

In 1951 Grenada was given universal adult suffrage, with the removal of all barriers to enfranchisement, including illiteracy. A new Constitution replaced the modified Crown Colony government. The Legislative Council comprised three nominated members, and eight elected members, providing for an elected majority in the Council. Drawing on the tremendous support Gairy had garnered for his trade union, Gairy formed the Grenada United Labour Party (GULP) in preparation for elections in 1951. He was elected President-General in perpetuity. Gairy's GULP won a resounding victory in the elections, receiving 71 per cent of the votes, and six of the eight elected seats. In the next election, in 1954, the GULP also took a majority of the elected seats.

In 1957 the GULP did not do as well, and managed to capture only two seats. Many reasons are given for the GULP's poor showing at the polls. One was that Gairy's trade union membership was flagging because he failed to sustain trade union organizational efforts in times of relative industrial calm. Another was that many of his supporters migrated during this period. A further reason was that there were new work opportunities after the passage of Hurricane Janet, and this distracted the workers from militancy. There were also rumours that all of the funds received for hurricane rehabilitation were not properly administered.[13] Moreover, in 1957, Gairy had to face competition from a new political party.

In 1954 Dr John Watts, a dentist who had trained in the United States of America, together with some like-minded educated citizens, formed the Grenada National Party (GNP). This party prepared a comprehensive plan for Grenada's development that stressed logical approaches to organizing every sector of Grenada, and advocated modernization and constitutional reform. The GNP's platform was that the party wanted a better Grenada for all its citizens. The GNP felt that the only way to achieve lasting improvement for the working class was through the slow process of education. One of their stated goals was 'the Development of the Rich and Poor in Grenada'.

Watts chose for himself the role of party chairman, and retained this position until the GNP merged with others in 1976 to form the People's Alliance. He preferred to remain as chairman and to let others head election campaigns and take the political posts. This is why it was Herbert Blaize who led the government on the few occasions when the party was asked to form the government.

Herbert A. Blaize was a soft-spoken lawyer from Carriacou. In spite of his lack of flamboyance, his gentle manner and quiet humour, and above all his logical approach to the business of government, earned him continuing trust, respect and loyalty, not only in Carriacou where he was regarded as a hero, but also to a wide cross-section of the Grenadian public.

In 1957 Herbert Blaize was asked to form the Government of Grenada, as the independent members who had won their seats threw in their lot with the GNP to form a coalition government. During this period, a committee system[14] was introduced into the legislature. This change was designed to prepare Grenadians for independence under the West Indian Federation.

A new Constitution in 1959 gave the real authority for governing the country to a Chief Minister and those from the majority party in the Legislative Council. The representative of the Queen was to be an Administrator, with reduced powers. The legislature would consist of ten elected members, and two nominated members. A ministerial system was introduced, and changes made in the public service mandated by the new Constitution. James 'Jimmy' Lloyd, a Jamaican, became Grenada's first and only Administrator.

The Eric Gairy/Administrator Lloyd Tug-of-War

As soon as Lloyd arrived in Grenada, antagonisms developed between himself and Gairy. Jimmy Lloyd was intelligent and handsome with a complexion which was as deep a brown as Gairy's. Lloyd's authority was higher than Gairy's, and thus Lloyd was outside his control. The conflicts between Gairy and Lloyd were not only conflicts over the limits of power and procedures but a struggle for primacy of authority and status.

The first conflict Gairy had with Administrator Lloyd was over a five-year ban on political activity imposed on Gairy. This ban was imposed on Gairy for disrupting an opponent's political meeting by leading a steel band through it. Consequently, when the date for elections was set for 1961, Gairy was still not eligible to be a candidate, as the ban had ten months to run at the time the election procedures began. He asked Lloyd to forgive the rest of the term. Gairy's situation produced a great debate among several of the politically conscious members of society, including the two Federal Senators, J.B. Renwick and A. Norris Hughes. They thought that Gairy should be allowed to run for election, that Gairy's offence had not warranted such a severe punishment as it had been little more than a prank. Others pointed out that in other colonies the British government had commuted or dismissed more serious infringements of the law; in any case, the ban was nearly up and Gairy had suffered enough. On the other side were those who supported the Administrator and the Attorney General in their respect for the due process of the law. In the end, the decision stood that Gairy could not offer himself as a candidate for the election.

Gairy turned the ban to advantage. He told his followers that the 'upper brackets' were again trying to suppress him, but he would be vindicated by the actions of the people. Gairy continued to challenge the Administrator on a number of constitutional issues concerning his temporary ban from the legislature, with Administrator Lloyd always upholding the Constitution and disallowing every request. Gairy was never to forgive

Lloyd for what he considered a lack of flexibility, and was determined to get rid of the Administrator as he regarded him as a stumbling block to his plans.

Gairy's party won the 1961 election. In this election, Cynthia Gairy, Gairy's wife, became the first woman to be elected to the legislature. It was rumoured that she would be Grenada's next Chief Minister. The public was surprised when George E.D. Clyne, a lawyer, was asked by the Administrator to form the government. Joshua Thorne, Gairy's friend and supporter, had contested and won in Gairy's constituency. Thorne 'held' Gairy's place for him until the ban on Gairy's political activity expired.

During the months Gairy spent outside the legislature, he behaved as if he was still the Chief Minister. He held virtual cabinet meetings at his home, and announced policy in public meetings in the Market Square. Three months after the election, the British government suggested that the Grenada legislature should decide the matter of lifting Gairy's disenfranchisement. In record time, the bill to restore Gairy's franchise was passed though the legislature, and Gairy was able to resume his seat through a by-election provided by Thorne's resignation. Clyne resigned as Chief Minister, leaving the way clear for Gairy to be later sworn into this position.

'Squandermania'

On 18 June 1962, fifteen months after the election, Administrator Lloyd suspended the Constitution and appointed a Commission to inquire into the spending of public funds since the GULP had been in power. There were really three issues. The first was the belief that Gairy had failed to respect the rules and regulations regarding the operation of the civil service, and that the power of the politician was circumscribed by the rules under which the civil servants operated. The second one was that it was alleged that Gairy had operated outside the boundaries of proper financial controls and administration in the Ministry of Finance, which was his own Ministry. The third issue was that the Administrator felt that Gairy had not stayed within the guidelines of the previously approved budget.

Thirty-seven people gave evidence before the Commission. The Report of the Commission said that Gairy, as the Minister of Finance, and others under his instructions, had approved expenditures in excess of the budget, sometimes without a warrant. Warrants, when they were issued, were often issued in excess of what was permitted by law. Expenditures had been incurred by people who were not in control of the votes, and without the knowledge of those who were in control. There was other evidence of disregard for financial controls, possible misappropriation of funds, and instances that were regarded as wasteful extravagance.

In spite of the evidence, some people thought that the punishment did not fit the crime, and it would have been better to put Gairy in a situation where he would have to learn good governance, rather than humiliating him by suspending the Constitution. There was no school where the new breed of politicians like Gairy could learn how to manage a country without transgressing the rules and regulations that had been set, without the functions explained. Those in authority could have helped Gairy see that the checks and balances were there not to frustrate and confine the leader, but for his eventual good, and the good governance of the country. Some feel that Gairy's downfall should be blamed on those who were too anxious to discipline him and not perceptive enough to see the benefits of helping such an able and popular politician develop a political conscience. The moot question is: Would Gairy have submitted himself to guided discipline?

After the Commission concluded its work, the Administrator was given wider reserve powers, including that of appointing the Minister of Finance. New elections were held later in 1962. Riding high on the promise of unitary statehood with Trinidad, and profiting from the financial disgrace of Gairy and the GULP, Herbert Blaize led the GNP to an election victory. During the five-year term of office, the GNP government effected developments in the areas of education, agriculture, health and communications, in addition to pursuing their stated goal of unification with Trinidad and Tobago. Gairy took the loss of the 1961 elections badly, but put his time to good use building up his support. His growing support was demonstrated by the action of the workers who responded to his many calls for strikes during this period.

When Grenada became a State in Association with Great Britain in 1967, this amounted to virtual self-government, with Britain keeping control of defence and foreign affairs. The power of the Governor was greatly reduced by the new Constitution. Helped by the disappointment of the population over unitary statehood with Trinidad, Gairy won the first election under the new Constitution. In the new regime there would be no more Jimmy Lloyd to try to balance Gairy's power with the checks and balances of the Constitution.

The New Regime

Gairy had effectively used the power of his union to attain political power, and now he used his political power to keep the loyalty of his union members, and to consolidate his control over society. Using his considerable political and people-handling skills, Gairy now neutralized the influence of anyone who differed with him on any matter, governmental or otherwise. In addition he created a superstitious aura about his person. Gairy was reputed to have the ability to walk on water and have the power of bi-location. He began promoting his belief in the occult. He also developed a reputation for dabbling in obeah and participating in Spiritual Baptist ceremonies[15] that were rooted in African religion but tainted with sorcery and magic. To cater to more modern myth, he became widely known as a promoter of the belief in alien visitations and the surveillance of earth by unidentified flying objects.[16]

None of this would have mattered if he had at the same time continued the transformation of society including better services for the working class and a more equitable distribution of wealth. But building his image as a mystic, organizing the settling of personal vendettas and playing out his obsession with controlling everything and everybody distracted him from the task of governance. Gairy's promised social revolution had lost its way. His revolution finally aborted in 1968 when he began to infringe on the constitutional rights of the population.

One of the first indications of tightening controls on the population was the passing of the Firearms Act in 1968. By this act, all firearms on the island had to be presented and registered. Nothing was essentially wrong with the law, but there was discrimination in the way the law was applied. Anyone whom Gairy assessed to be opposed to him was denied a firearms licence, and any firearms they possessed were confiscated and stored in the police armoury. Gairy then gave his approval for the formation of special gangs referred to as 'Police Aides' but more popularly called the 'Mongoose Gang', the 'Secret Police' or the 'Ton Ton Macoutes'.

> He also recruited into the police force men with criminal records – by his own declaration 'some of the roughest and toughest roughnecks'...Gairy stated that, 'We are going to fight fire with fire', and used the Mongoose gang and police force as weapons to intimidate opponents.[17]

Members of the 'Mongoose Gang' also spied and reported on the activities and movements of designated members of the public, so that Gairy always knew everything that could be of the slightest importance about them, and their public and private lives. On the other hand, Gairy would use patronage to strengthen his position and his support. Gairy prospered and his friends prospered. The rest, especially if they were non-Grenadians, were cautious of

what they said and where they said it, as any words which could
be regarded as derogatory to Gairy and his Government were
reported to him, and could result in their deportation and their
property expropriated.[18]

Because Gairy put too much effort into consolidating his control over
society and insufficient energy into maintaining the country's infrastructure, things began to fall apart. The road system in Grenada deteriorated
for lack of maintenance, and all the public buildings, including the schools,
hospitals and clinics fell into serious disrepair. The education system which
had been gradually developing for the last hundred years, and which was
almost at the point of offering the working class full access to all levels of
education, was left to decay. Not only were the eighty-two schools in
ruins, but also efforts made to maintain a percentage of trained teachers in
the system were abandoned, and the percentage slipped. During the period
1967 to 1979 only 36 per cent of the primary school teachers had any
training, and only 7 per cent of the secondary school teachers had professional training. Only 15 per cent of the children from primary schools got
places in the secondary schools. Class size was now well above the
optimum, with up to eighty children in some classes. The situation regarding textbooks and other equipment for the primary schools was abysmal.
The government owed US$1.5 million to the University of the West
Indies,[19] and that institution, funded as it was by the financial support of
its member territories, was becoming reluctant to grant entry to additional
students at any of its campuses, unless either the government paid its debt
or the student paid the full rather than subsidized cost.

In the health field, neglect was also apparent. The General Hospital
lacked the most basic equipment and supplies. Dental clinics ceased operating in the rural areas, and many Health Centres were left without the
services of a Medical Officer. In November 1970 nurses from the General
Hospital demonstrated against the appalling conditions there. Those
nurses identified by Gairy as the ringleaders of the protest were charged or
transferred to Carriacou or the most remote health stations on the island.
Demonstrations by the nurses resumed in December, and this time the
demonstration was broken up with clubs and tear-gas, and twenty-two
nurses were gaoled.

Under a scheme Gairy called 'Land for the Landless' prosperous
working estates were acquired. Some were subdivided into small plots and
distributed to his supporters, others were just left to 'go to seed', demonstrating that the real reason behind the acquisition was not to revive the
Land Settlement Scheme, but simply to deprive the owners of the means of
their livelihood.

Gairy began acquiring whole estates – usually the property of those he considered to be political enemies or nonsupporters of his party. By 1971 he had acquired fourteen estates…We were dismayed and shocked – but hardly surprised – when, one Thursday in February 1972, the Land Acquisition Officer visited our cousin Mollie, the owner of half of our estate, Loretto. He told her that the government would buy the estate at half the price we had formerly asked, demanded an immediate answer, and stated that failure to comply would result in acquisition. The price offered was obviously ridiculous, so we knew they meant to acquire. This is how it was done: the notice of acquisition was published in the Government Gazette two days later and again a week later, at which date the estate passed from us to the Government. No compensation was paid. In only nine days we had to vacate all the buildings on the estate, including the house, which the manager had occupied for several years. Luckily, he had some land of his own and a small house, so was not destitute. In this brief space of time we had to find alternative accommodation for all the agricultural implements and hardware as well as for the animals on the estate.[20]

Gairy acquired thirty estates in this manner by 1978.

The consequence of this ill-conceived policy was that the economy as a whole, and the estate workers in particular, were hurt more than were the landowners. Unlike the Land Settlement Scheme, under which unworked estates were bought, the estates acquired without payment were those in full production. 'The newly acquired estates were often put in the care of very incompetent managers, usually staunch party members with no knowledge of agriculture, with the result that production dropped to unbelievably low levels'.[21]

In some cases the people mistakenly thought that they would be given land free of charge, and immediately squatted on the estate and reaped the produce. After that the people who occupied the lands did not farm them, and no institutions were put in place to encourage them to do this so that they could earn a livelihood or at least support themselves by subsistence farming. The former estate workers soon became destitute for want of a regular wage.

Gairy now turned his attention to the agricultural co-operatives that had been established in the 1940s to assure the greatest profits to the farmers for their produce and to ensure the quality of the agricultural produce sold. Control over these Boards would put the livelihood of approximately 1000 farmers into Gairy's direct control, and ruin the independence they enjoyed through the Boards. Between 1972 and 1975 he abolished the membership-elected Boards of all the co-operatives, and replaced them with government-nominated interim Boards. With respect to the largest and wealthiest Board, the Grenada Co-operative Nutmeg Association, Gairy appointed a Commission to look into the financial affairs of the Board from 1969 to 1975. Members of the elected Board took legal action to stop the Commission until certain conditions were met. This and all subsequent appeals were disallowed, and the Commission began to meet. This was not the end of the legal battle, however. While the Commission was in progress, a motion was filed in the High Court in the names of the elected Board members. The motion declared that the dismissal of the Board was *ultra vires* by the government, that the Interim Board was both unconstitutional and *ultra vires*, and restrained the Commission from meeting. The motion was successful, but was appealed, and the Appeal Court upset the original ruling. The matter then went to the Privy Council in Britain, as was allowed under the Grenada Constitution.

During this period, Gairy finished the erosion of the functions of the Public Service Commission that he had started in 1961. Since 1961, Gairy had tried to establish that the Ministers, not the civil servant heads of departments, were in charge of the government. The heads of departments had only an administrative function. Constitutional change had allowed Gairy to complete his control of the Public Service Commission and the civil service and he could hire, fire, or send on indefinite leave whomever he chose.

Additionally, Gairy established his control over all governmental matters. Gairy, in the presence of his Cabinet, made all the decisions of government, from the minor to those of major importance. Laws to enforce these decisions were then taken to Parliament, and other matters directed to the agencies that, under the Constitution, needed to give their stamp of approval. There was little that anyone could do constitutionally to stem Gairy's power and control of the political machinery.

The Birth of the New Jewel Movement

When nurses marched against conditions at the hospital in 1970, two young lawyers and fast friends, who had just returned from England, defended those facing legal charges. The Nurses' Strike and its repercussions catapulted these two able and promising young men onto the national stage in the role of defenders of the wronged, and challengers to Gairy's title of hero of the working class. These two lawyers had espoused the Marxist ideology then popular in the various black students' clubs in England. They returned to Grenada imbued with rosy ideas about Marxist society and the possibility of radical social transformation, equality and the elimination of class, only to face Gairy's increasing totalitarianism. If they did not already have a blueprint for revolution mapped out for them by Marxist friends in London, they soon developed one. In the meantime, they set about using their skills to become heroes to those dissatisfied with Gairy.

The two lawyers were Maurice Bishop and Kendrick Radix. Maurice Bishop, the son of Rupert and Alimenta Bishop, was born in 1944. His mother's roots in the middle class could be traced in a direct line to Louis La Grenade, the coloured Grenadian who had remained loyal to the British during the Fédon Revolution. His father was no less respectable, but was of humbler origin. He had migrated to Aruba, where he saved enough money to set up a small business in St George's on his return. The entire Bishop and La Grenade families were staunch members of the Roman Catholic Church. Kendrick Radix, although much darker in complexion, came from the professional middle class. His father was a dentist, and his brother, Michael, was a doctor, as were several cousins.

Shortly after the Nurses' Strike, Bishop and Radix began to recruit like-minded persons for the formation of a study group, and to work out a political ideology that would set Grenada on a new path to popular government. Unfortunately, this group absorbed the fledgling Black Power movement in Grenada, and elements of the group remained tainted with the tenets of Black Power. These tenets were reinforced through connections with the National Joint Action Committee in Trinidad. Marxist principles would now be in an unholy marriage with race hatred, and the enemy of the working class was for the first time in Grenada identified with light-skinned people. This was unfortunate as it blinded members of the group to the fact that enemies could come in differing skin colours. Bishop, by reason of his personal charm and considerable charisma, soon emerged as the leader of the group, while Radix, completely without jealousy, remained his lieutenant, loyal supporter and closest personal friend. Bishop's group, which attracted a mainly urban following, took the name 'Movement for the Assemblies of the People' (MAP). In the meantime, another group emerged almost simultaneously in St David's, headed by Unison Whiteman.

Whiteman was, like Bishop and Radix, from a staunch Roman Catholic background. He had imbibed the ideals of social justice preached by the brothers of the Presentation College where he received his secondary education, and also by his church. His sympathies were with those who longed for rural development. Whiteman was determined to use the

Masters Degree in Economics he had obtained in the United States to somehow effect the transformation of the economy so that it would serve the needs of all the people of Grenada. Of unassuming personality, he was nevertheless a commanding speaker. He called his group the JEWEL, an acronym for Joint Endeavour for Welfare, Education and Liberation. In time, Whiteman also joined the MAP.

On 21 January 1973 members of the JEWEL and the MAP organized a joint protest on the La Sagesse Estate in St David's that had recently been purchased by an Englishman, Lord Brownlow. Lord Brownlow may or may not have understood local customs. Whether he did or not, he had erected a gate and a fence blocking a commonly used access to the beach. Now the people of the area were urged by the JEWEL and MAP to take action. Membership of both groups, together with a number of supporters and residents of the area, marched to the gates and took them down. Then Lord Brownlow was 'tried' in a 'Peoples Court', *in absentia,* the charge being denying the people of St David's access to the beach, which they used as a base for fishing and for recreation. The people claimed that they had been allowed the use of these facilities for over a hundred years by the various owners, all of them Grenadians. They had been able to use the grounds freely for fairs, sporting and other community activities. The new owner had no right to take from them their traditionally held rights.

Although there was a police presence at this demonstration, the police did not break up the proceedings. The event was allowed to continue to its end under the watchful eyes of the Inspector Innocent Belmar, a top officer in the Royal Grenada Police Force. Later, the forty people whom Belmar had observed playing an active part in the proceedings were charged with disorderly conduct and destruction of property. These charges were subsequently defeated in court.

On 11 March 1973 the New Jewel Movement (NJM) was formed. The JEWEL and the MAP were combined by mutual consent, and the leadership of the new organization was drawn from the two movements. Unison Whiteman, Teddy Victor and Sebastian Thomas, former members of the JEWEL, entered the inner circle of the NJM together with Maurice Bishop and Franklyn Harvey from MAP. Unison Whiteman and Bishop would be joint co-ordinating secretaries of the amalgamated movement. It did not take Teddy Victor too long to become disenchanted with the NJM. He left the organization in 1976, and was subsequently detained by his former political colleagues when they came to power.

From the moment of amalgamation, the members of the NJM began the work of building the movement and attracting support. Cells were formed everywhere, and larger groups were infiltrated by supporters of the NJM. This infiltration took place in places of employment, within church groups, unions, and in the secondary schools. A manifesto was prepared and widely circulated. Entitled *Power to the People*, it dealt with the whole range of activities and put forward their plans for development as well as for new initiatives. The manifesto also called for an end to party politics and the replacement of the present democratic structures with Assemblies of the People in which participatory democracy would ensure the involvement of the people in the decision-making of the country. Very few recognized the Marxist rhetoric and ideas contained in this manifesto. If they did, they might not have cared, as the compelling and initial popular reason for the support of the NJM was getting rid of Gairy.

The Politics of Violence

As the NJM grew in strength, Gairy tried to scare people away from associating with them. Members of the NJM were harassed, intimidated, beaten and shot by the Mongoose Gang and members of the regular police. When the police shot Jeremiah Richardson, a youth of St Andrew's Parish on 22 April 1973, the NJM organized a massive protest demonstration in St Andrew's, which culminated in the closure of the airport, which was then at Pearls, St Andrew's. During the demonstration, police fired on the demonstrators, wounding at least ten.

The NJM decided to rally popular support around the issue of independence, due to be granted to Grenada on 7 February 1974. Independence talks were proceeding with the involvement of the opposition leader Herbert Blaize. Blaize chose as his advisers Wellington Friday, a veteran politician and member of the GNP, and Bernard Coard, a young Canadian-trained intellectual who was a staff member of the University of the West Indies. Bernard Coard was the son of a respected civil servant, Frederick McDermott Coard and his wife, Flora. Bernard's wife, Phyllis, was from an upper middle class Jamaican family. Her uncle was the inventor of the Jamaican liqueur, Tia Maria. Phyllis Coard had been educated in England. Regardless of opposition's representation at the independence talks, many in society did not welcome the granting of independence under Gairy, as they feared what the complete severance from Britain might mean under Gairy's continued rule. The NJM were therefore assured of a sympathetic hearing.

A People's Convention on Independence was scheduled for 6 May 1973 at the Seamoon Pavilion in St Andrew's. A massive crowd of all ages and walks of life attended the convention. The substance of the message presented to the people was that independence was a good thing, but only if the people had a say in the independence constitution, and only if with political independence came efforts to right the ills in society, and only if mechanisms were put in place to make Grenadians truly socially and economically independent. The only organization that could help Grenada achieve this type of independence was the New Jewel Movement. The New Jewel Movement would demand at independence that Britain repatriate some of the money that had been exported from Grenada during three centuries of British rule.

Despite the repercussions of the earlier protest action at the airport, supporters of the NJM again went to Pearls Airport to heckle Gairy when he returned on 27 May 1973 from independence talks in Britain. The Mongoose Gang beat several demonstrators. Several other incidents where bodily harm was inflicted on members of the NJM followed in quick succession. On 1 June, Alston Williams was 'chopped' by the Mongoose Gang for selling the mimeographed newspaper of the NJM popularly called the *Jewel*. On 9 June, a well-known farmer of St John's Parish, Clarence Ferguson, was set on and beaten so badly by the Mongoose Gang that he had to be hospitalized. The men stripped off all the clothes from his teen-aged daughter who was with him. After this incident, the floodgates of mounting discontent threatened to burst and a popular uprising was only prevented by Gairy agreeing to set up a Commission of Inquiry. The Commission of Inquiry into the Breakdown of Law and Order, and Police Brutality in Grenada was set up in 1975 under the chairmanship of the Honourable Herbert Duffus, retired Chief Justice of Jamaica.

Before the Commission of Enquiry could finish its work, things came to a head after the People's Congress in Seamoon in November 1973. Eight thousand people attended, unfazed by police searches and a show of force by armed police at the site. At this Congress, a prepared list of Gairy's commissions, omissions, bad administration and fraudulent activities was circulated, and the crowd brought to fever pitch through the skilful use of rhetoric. The 'People's Indictment', as the list was called, was subsequently sent by the NJM to Gairy and other members of government. They were all asked to resign from 18 November 1973. The NJM leadership informed the government that, if they did not resign, a general strike would result, and the country would be shut down until they did. So far, although the harassment and intimidation of the NJM members and supporters was constant, Gairy had not challenged the movement publicly. Now, sensing that the NJM was a real danger and seemed to have enough public support at their disposal to interfere with the upcoming independence celebrations, Gairy decided to react.

'Bloody Sunday'

A public meeting was called by Gairy at the Grenville Market Square, St Andrew's, on 4 November 1973. Government supporters beat some

NJM members who were present. The next Thursday, Gairy went on the radio to announce that he was bringing fifty-four charges including sedition against members of the NJM. Then, on Sunday 18 November, select members of the NJM planned a private meeting in Grenville to discuss with members of the Grenville business community their participation in the planned general strike. Gairy found out, and sent Inspector Innocent Belmar to apprehend them and have them beaten by the Mongoose Gang.

The six members of the NJM were severely beaten with axe handles, clubs and pistol butts. They were then thrown into jail and denied medical attention. So savage was this beating that one member, Unison Whiteman, almost lost the sight of one eye, and suffered permanent disfigurement of the face. Maurice Bishop's face was also so smashed that it took all the skill of the best plastic surgeons to reconstruct his jaw and facial bones to permit him to eat and speak. He never completely recovered from the effects of his shattered jaw and damaged back. Kendrick Radix was also beaten beyond recognition and his face left scarred in spite of plastic surgery. The other three, Selwyn Strachan, Simon Daniel and Hudson Austin, fared only slightly better.

The savagery displayed was the proverbial last straw for the people, who had been chafing under Gairy's rule. Besides, these young men were not 'rabble' but were most of them the educated sons of respected middle-class families. Hudson Austin, although not in the social class of Bishop and Radix, was a well-respected lay preacher in the Methodist Church. The day of the beatings in St Andrew's was to be thereafter called Bloody Sunday by members of the NJM, by those who supported the movement, by those who were anti-Gairy, and by those who were simply sorry for 'the boys'. Later the arrest and beating of the six would be justified by testimony, all of it false, that the meeting was being held for subversive purposes, that the six were in possession of a rifle and ammunition, and that their intention was the capture of the Grenville Police Station.

'Bloody Monday'

The day after Bloody Sunday, the 'Committee of 22' was formed. This was a group of businessmen, professionals and religious leaders of note, and represented the most conservative section of society. The amount of support the NJM had at this time from every sector was manifested in the fact that it was this Committee of 22 and not the NJM that called for an island-wide strike until Gairy disciplined the men who had beaten the six members of the NJM, instituted an inquiry into the whole event, and also inquired into the practices of law enforcement in the country.

The medical progress of the six near-martyrs was followed closely by a wide cross-section of society. They determined to come out and march in support of 'the boys' as soon as they healed sufficiently to resume their activities. Gairy, by ordering the beating of the six NJM members, had 'cooked his own goose' because, if he had not beaten the six so badly, or beaten them at all, the next set of demonstrations would not have brought out on the street all but the closest of Gairy's supporters.

In January 1974 a series of marches began that attracted participation from the young and the old, the middle class and the poor worker, young Marxists and ultra-conservatives, men, women and children. The phenomenon of the marches was so traumatizing for the Governor, Dame Hilda Bynoe, that she resigned and left immediately for Trinidad, where she had a home. The marches escalated until 21 January 1974, when 'Gairy summoned the police aides/Mongoose Gang to his home, and instructed them to break up a meeting then taking place on the Carenage, where a large crowd was listening to addresses by various leaders.'[22]

The police aides/Mongoose Gang, armed with orange bottled drinks to use as missiles, were sent running down Lucas Street and along Tyrrel (now H.A. Blaize) Street to the Carenage[23] to break up the demonstration then in progress. On the Carenage, armed regular police joined the Secret Police in throwing missiles and beating the marchers. In the mêlée, hundreds were hurt. A policeman shot Rupert Bishop, the father of Maurice Bishop, while he was trying to protect women and schoolchildren huddled for protection in a room in Otway House, the headquarters of the Seamen and Waterfront Workers Union.

Looting of businesses in St George's followed, first by the police aides/Mongoose Gang and then by others following their horrible example. Members of the Royal Grenada Police Force looked on and did nothing. The country was completely shut down, but the plans for independence went through amidst the social turmoil. The general shutdown of the island, which began on 21 January, ended two weeks after independence.

Independence for Grenada – Myth or Reality?

The British government was well aware that the country was in turmoil. A very minor member of the Royal Family replaced the member originally selected to be present on the night of 6 February 1974 to witness Grenada's birth as a new nation. Special lighting had to be arranged for the ceremony on the Fort, as there was no electricity, due to the general strike in progress. In a show of military might, trucks of soldiers belonging to the Grenada Defence Force, called in derision the 'Green Beasts', roared up and down the streets of the town, shooting their weapons in the air. The disgust and betrayal many Grenadians felt with Britain for allowing independence to take place amidst this confusion was symbolically signified by Vivie Lucas and Ivy Smith, two senior citizens living near the town. Marshalling all their courage during the commotion, they got out of their beds when the trucks of soldiers passed their house, took the pictures of the Queen and the Duke of Edinburgh from the pride of place on their living room wall, and shoved them under their bed until they could dispose of them in the morning.[24] Not only was independence under these conditions a myth, but also this was the end to the hopes and dreams many had had for Grenada and its prosperity.

Many Grenadians fled the country for the duration of the strike. Among the 'refugees' in Carriacou were Bernard and Phyllis Coard. They had visited Grenada from time to time ostensibly to see Coard's mother and father. From now on, their visits would become more and more frequent and they were to be seen more and more with Bishop and involved in the affairs of the NJM.

The Duffus Commission Report

To compound Gairy's public relations problems at this time, the Report of the Duffus Commission, which had started meeting in December 1973, was completed in May 1975, and the findings released to the public. The mandate of this Commission had been extended twice: to cover the arrest and beatings of the six NJM members in Grenville on Bloody Sunday, and secondly to look into the events of Bloody Monday, when Rupert Bishop had been shot and so many other citizens hurt. The Report[25] was hardly complimentary to Gairy. It found that there had indeed been a breakdown in law and order, and that the evidence showed that there had been infringements of the constitutional rights of citizens both by the regular police and police aides who acted on behalf of the government.

On the matter of the arrest and beating of the six NJM members, the Commission found that Gairy was not justified in arresting and beating them, that there was no evidence to support allegations that any of the six was armed, that the meeting was not subversive, or threatening to the security of the state. The actions of the NJM might have threatened the progress of Grenada towards political independence, but this in itself was not subversion, and therefore the constitutional rights of the six had been violated. Similarly, the events of Bloody Monday were designed as a protest against independence at this time, and the measures ordered by

Gairy were designed to break up this demonstration, and to demonstrate the futility of mounting any further protest against independence.

The general recommendations of the Commission were that the Police Aides were to be disbanded and the police force thoroughly reorganized. The Commission called for the removal of Innocent Belmar, who had been promoted to the rank of Assistant Superintendent of Police, and that he be banned from holding any other office in the public services. It also called for the removal of certain magistrates because they had failed to discharge their duties with impartiality and competence, and for an inquiry into the conduct of the Solicitor General, who was responsible for civil matters, with a view of removing him from office. The Commission advised that all criminal charges before the court involving violent incidents in the periods under the mandate of the Commission should be dealt with without delay.

Gairy literally thumbed his nose at all the recommendations of the Commission's Report. The most blatant example of his disrespect for the Commission was that, although removing Innocent Belmar from his post in the police service, in the next election he let him run on the GULP ticket in the constituency of St Andrew's North West, which was a strong GULP constituency. Since it was Gairy the people voted for and not the incumbent, Belmar won this seat and eventually became a member of the Grenada Parliament and Minister of Agriculture.

State Control of the Media

Then Gairy set about trying to control the press. In 1961 he had replaced the Government Information Officer, a position created in 1956, which answered to the Administrator, with a Public Relations Officer responsible to the Chief Minister. He changed the name of the government newsletter to *The Star*, which was his party symbol. In 1969 he had acquired *The West Indian* newspaper, which had been so instrumental in providing public information and forming public opinion since its inception in 1915. His concern now was with the remaining newspaper *The Torchlight*, and with the popular *Jewel.*

In 1975 Gairy introduced an Act to Amend the Newspaper Ordinance, which passed without a problem, as Gairy was in almost total control of both Houses in the Parliament. This Act increased the deposit that each newspaper had to leave with the government from $900 to $20,000. In the end, the Act only illustrated the increasing totalitarianism of the government. *The Torchlight* managed to raise the deposit, and kept publishing. The *Jewel* went underground. As a hedge against possible future prosecution, and also to make Gairy and his Newspaper Act look ridiculous, each issue of the *Jewel* came out as Volume 1 Number 1, and with a new name. The testing of the semantics of the *Jewel* editors was the only real difference made to the publication of this paper, which was now reputed to have a readership of over 10,000.

The 1976 Elections

In 1975 Bernard Coard resigned his position at the University of the West Indies and moved to Grenada, accompanied by Phyllis. Coard told people he had come to Grenada to do research, and Phyllis to teach at the Anglican High School. However, the real reason for their relocation was to begin to play a stronger role in the NJM, of which he had been made a member prior to 1974, even though resident in Jamaica. The Coards also assisted Maurice Bishop organize the NJM, working especially in the area of political education of the youth. The cells in the schools, particularly the Anglican High School and Grenada Boys' Secondary School became the special task of Phyllis Coard, who gained the admiration, devotion and loyalty of the younger cohort of the NJM through an amazing ability to organize, influence thought, inspire and mentor. Soon Bernard Coard became second in command to Bishop, edging out the gentler Whiteman.

Bernard had timed his return to Grenada to allow him to participate in the 1976 elections. In the first elections after independence, a united opposition called the People's Alliance opposed Gairy's very strong GULP. This was an amalgamation of the NJM, the GNP and a smaller party called the United People's Party (UPP). In the run-up to the election, the Alliance faced a situation of unequal opportunity. The use of public address systems by the Alliance was restricted, and sometimes denied altogether. The government was accused of massive rigging and for the intimidation of voters. The result of the election was disappointing for the Alliance in that they won six seats and the GULP nine. However, Gairy thought he would have achieved a much wider margin. Since the Alliance had polled 48.5 per cent of the votes, Gairy realized that he now faced a formidable opposition for the first time since 1967.

Gairy's solution to facing a formidable opposition was to keep the meetings of Parliament to a minimum. Parliament seldom met, and when it did, the opposition did not receive copies of the proposed bills in time for any in-depth debate on them. When the opposition was in a position to say something on one of them, little time if any was permitted for this purpose. No contributions by the opposition were rebroadcast on the radio. Bills were often railroaded through Parliament. On some occasions, the opposition walked out in protest. The way Gairy dealt with this unexpected situation was by using his Cabinet and a carefully moulded civil service to govern, instead of using Parliament.

Struggle for Control

The danger that the NJM might seize power in a manner other than through the Constitution was now one that Gairy had to face. In order to be prepared for such an eventuality, Gairy set about increasing his military capability. He cultivated friendship with Augusto Pinochet of Chile, visiting him in 1976. An agreement subsequently signed between the two governments provided for training of some of the officers of the Defence Force in Chile and for donations of arms and ammunition.

By this time, Gairy had lost the support of the leaders of the Caribbean, many of whom had been his stalwart supporters in 1951. Schoenhals reports that:

> The Trinidadian Prime Minister, Eric Williams, gave orders that he must never be seen in public with Gairy. The Barbadian head of State, Errol Barrow, labelled Gairy a 'political bandit'.[26]

Queen Elizabeth II knighted Gairy in June 1977.

Gairy also had to struggle against the trade unions. The NJM had gradually made their influence felt within this movement and Gairy responded to the growing influence of the NJM within the unions by trying to curb the power of all other unions but the GMMWU.

Legislative action to curb the power of the Seamen and Waterfront Workers Trade Union resulted in the Port Authority (Amendment) Act of 1978. This established a Port Authority to provide and maintain efficient port services. Not only did this Act change the relationship between the Seamens Union and the Grenada Shipping Agents, but it also weakened the position of the Union. If the Union called a strike or 'go slow' the Authority could now, under the Act, step in and hire independent stevedores to perform the duties of the workers on strike. Another Act – the Essential Services Act – decreed that the essential services could only settle disputes through arbitration. From then on, any strike of essential workers would be illegal.

In this year, also, the Civil Service Association, the Grenada Union of Teachers and the Technical and Allied Workers Union, trade unions that represented civil servants, came out in protest over government's salary revision. This time the partial ban on the use of loudspeakers by the People's Alliance was made complete for all groups. Nevertheless, meetings continued at which the issues were discussed and debated, and the civil servants informed of their rights. The negotiations between the government and the workers came to an impasse when Gairy decided that the government would pay what the government was prepared to grant and no more. The civil service, teachers and allied workers went on strike. The leaders of the churches tried to mediate between the workers and the government, but were unsuccessful.

In 1977 Innocent Belmar was shot and killed in suspicious circumstances while relaxing at a rum shop in his constituency. Two members of the NJM, the Budhlall brothers, were arrested and charged with the crime.

Then, on 26 January 1978, Gairy addressed the nation by radio, and called a rally of supporters on 28 January 1978. At this rally, the names of the union leaders were displayed, and they were castigated for their part in stirring up trouble. Gairy associated the militancy of the civil servants with the shooting of Belmar, and repeatedly said that he was well prepared to deal with strike action, that this would be the last strike that the named union leaders would ever call. The unions, convinced that further strike action would put the welfare of their union leaders in serious jeopardy, decided to accept the increases that the government had decided upon, and called off the strike. In November of that year, a NJM rally was called off in the face of similar threats against the leadership.

The Curtain Comes Down

All chances of a constitutional settlement of the conflict for power in Grenada were negated by the control the government had over the election machinery and the police. All the safety valves of freedom of speech, freedom to assemble, freedom of the press, and freedom to choose a union had been closed. Gairy had not chosen to counter the threats to his power with a better performance and improvements in society. This tactic might have worked, as workers are so often lulled into inaction by becoming comfortable. Instead, Gairy chose repression, neutralizing the avenues of democracy that would have provided the people a chance to voice their concerns, and ruling by terror, without mitigating this terror by any sign of concern for the population or mitigation of the hardships attendant in society. Grenadians, prizing their freedom, bristled under a regime of fear, anxiety and terror. Far from being cowed, they put their faith in the NJM, encouraging them to stand up to the regime and to continue the struggle against the destruction of democracy. Grenadians continued to buy *Jewels* despite the risk, and quietly slipped money to the Movement to help in the cause. No one, except the executive of the NJM, knew that democracy, as Grenadians understood it, was not on the agenda of the NJM.

Gairy planned a trip to the United States for 12 March 1979. Although this trip was announced as a business trip, supporters of the NJM in the police and army warned the executive of the NJM that the trip was to effect his absence while his orders to arrest them were carried out. Although this could have been another scare tactic in the hope that the leadership would flee, the leadership had no intention of leaving Grenada. In fact, they had been carefully laying plans for an armed takeover. In one of the amazing parallels to the Fédon Revolution, the revolution began shortly after midnight on 13 March 1979. Within a few hours the NJM would quickly consolidate its control of Grenada.

After the coup, every effort was made by the Maurice Bishop government to discredit Gairy's private life and public activities. The trappings of his practice of obeah were first open to viewing at his residence, Mount Royal, to a select number of people, and then put on display in the Grenada National Museum,[27] which had been founded by his supporters, and under his patronage. Scandalous stories of his own immorality and seduction of key civil servants by hostesses at Therese, one of Gairy's personally owned nightclubs, or his own seduction of female civil servants and police officers and the taking of compromising secret pictures used thereafter for blackmail, were met with reactions of disbelief and disgust by the general public. No evidence to prove any of these tales was ever produced, but the ridicule was so virulent, putrid and sustained, that many of his former followers distanced themselves from the remainders of the party and union.

Maurice Bishop and his Revolutionary Government hardly needed to blacken Gairy any further, for Gairy had done a good job of disappointing many of the people who had put him into power, and kept him there for thirty years. The hurt and disillusion at Gairy's social revolution that lost its way allowed Grenadians, almost in total unison, to place their hope in another charismatic leader, in the hope that this would be the native son who would lead them to the promised land.

Although the People's Revolutionary Government requested the extradition of Gairy from the United States, this request was not granted, and Gairy lived in exile until the People's Revolutionary Government itself fell in 1983.

Notes

1 Singham, p. 155.
2 *The West Indian*, 22 Feb. 1951, quoted in Singham, p. 159.
3 *Ibid.*
4 See Singham, p. 161.

5　*Ibid.*
6　The British troops were the Royal Welsh Fusiliers, and they occupied the barracks recently vacated by the Southern Defence Force on the site later to become the Grenada Boys' Secondary School.
7　'Report of the Labour Department 1951', Grenada Council Paper, 1954, p. 4, St George's.
8　Singham, p. 166.
9　'Grenada Disturbances: Report of the Governor to the Colonial Office', no. 117, 5 April 1951, quoted in Brizan, p. 275.
10　Smith (1963), p. 6.
11　See Singham, p. 167.
12　Singham, p. 168.
13　Singham, p. 176.
14　The committe system was the precursor and preparatory step to the formation of government Ministries. Like the Ministries, the committees were assigned responsibilities for policies and action of designated sectors of the economy and society.
15　The Spiritual Baptist 'Bishop' was prominent in Gairy's funeral ceremonies held at the Grenada Trade Centre on 31 August 1997.
16　See the *Address of Sir Eric Matthew Gairy, Prime Minister of Grenada to the Thirty-Second Session of the General Assembly of the United Nations*, 7 October 1977, Grenada Centre, University of the West Indies.
17　Gentle, p. 126.
18　Gentle, p. 127.
19　Schoenhals, p. xxi.
20　Gentle, p. 128.
21　Gentle, p. 128.
22　Gentle, p. 130.
23　I stood at the windows of the Marryshow House, University Centre, University of the West Indies, and watched as these men came along this route. It was only as they turned down Hughes Street that I was able to make out that the orange objects they had in their hands were sweet drink bottles. I was an eyewitness to whatever transpired in view from the windows of the building. I was trapped in the building until the disturbance died down.
24　Personal communication.
25　Duffus, Herbert, H. Aubrey Fraser and Archbishop Samuel Carter, *Report of the Duffus Commission of Enquiry into the Breakdown of Law and Order, and Police Brutality in Grenada*, St George's, 1975.
26　Schoenhals, p. xxiii.
27　Gairy denied the ownership of these: see Zwerneman, p. 23.

18

No Bishop, No Revolution!

When Grenadians woke up on 13 March 1979, and turned on their radios, they were amazed to hear very different broadcasting to the usual morning music and news. They heard different voices announcing that Radio Grenada was now Radio Free Grenada and that the country was in the hands of the People's Revolutionary Government, headed by Maurice Bishop. Throughout the day, members of the New Jewel Movement, including Maurice Bishop and Bernard Coard, manned the microphones, asking named supporters in the rural areas to go the police stations and take them over in the name of the Revolution. There was an announcement requesting a well-respected doctor to attend at the radio station, and the ladies of the nation were called upon to make sandwiches to feed the comrades. Later on, Ministers of the Gairy government were called on to tell the people that they would not oppose the new regime. One Minister went as far as to offer his services to the new government in any way that they could be used. An announcement was made that Derek Knight, a close associate of Gairy, had escaped, possibly by boat, and comrades and friends were to see if they could effect his capture. In his first broadcast, Maurice Bishop asked the people to: '[g]ather at all central places all over the country, and prepare to welcome and assist the people's armed forces when they come into your area.'[1]

'Revolution by Radio' was the succinct phrase used to refer to the People's Revolutionary Government's extensive use of the radio to take control of the country.

The Events of March Thirteenth

Slowly the events that had transpired during the dark hours of the morning of 13 March were brought to light. Just after midnight, forty-six armed comrades had made an assault on the Grenada Defence Force Barracks at True Blue, St George's. They caught the 230 soldiers by complete surprise and, after a brief skirmish, they were all rounded up

380

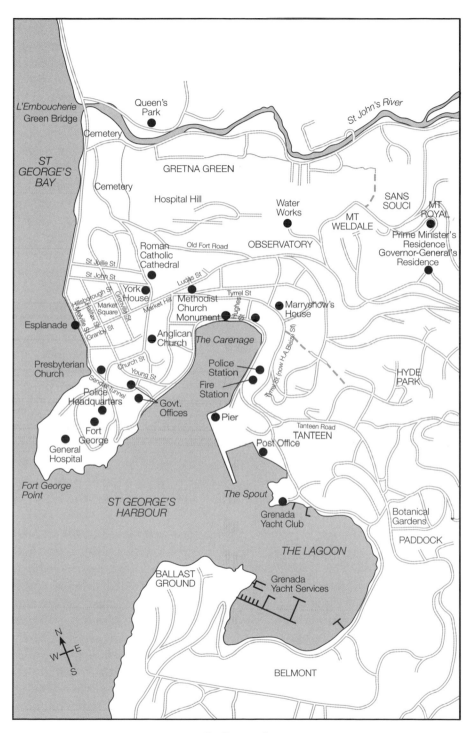

St George's

and put under guard. Until recently, it was a secret that the soldiers were transported to the Richmond Hill Prisons where they were interrogated, some of them undergoing painful 'encouragement' before being released over a number of months.[2] Some soldiers were detained over three years, and some were not freed until the collapse of the Revolution. The only confirmed death among the soldiers was that of an officer, Hyacinth Brizan, but it is widely believed that there were more.

After neutralizing the Defence Force, the National Liberation Army, as armed comrades were briefly called, then stormed the Radio Station, and was able to take it without much problem. The coup d'état was complete by 4.30 a.m. Maurice Bishop's first broadcast to the people of Grenada appealed for their support:

> People of Grenada, this revolution is for work, for food, for decent housing and health services and for a bright future for our children and great-grandchildren. The benefits of the revolution will be given to everyone regardless of political opinion or which political party they support. Let us all unite as one.

> Let me assure the people of Grenada that all democratic freedoms, including freedom of elections, religious and political opinion, will be fully restored to the people. The personal safety and property of individuals will be protected …

> Long live the people of Grenada. Long live freedom and democracy. Let us together build a just Grenada. [3]

His words were like honey, and the excitement of most of the population was palpable, especially in the youth, who had ceased to believe in the possibility of a brighter future.

Before the sun was very high, jubilant crowds danced in the streets, singing 'Freedom Come, Gairy Go, Gairy gone with UFO'. Some had already copied the flag of the Revolution, which was a red dot centred in a background of white, and waved it around as they paraded, or wore it as a head-tie. Men, including bearded members of the Ras Tafari sect,[4] stood vigilant at the roundabouts and street corners, armed with Soviet-made AK rifles and strung with garlands of bullets in case of any show of resistance; but there was none. The euphoria lasted for days, shared by almost the entire population, excepting only those who would maintain an unconditional love of Gairy until his death, and those whose critical ability had alerted them to the Marxist leanings of the NJM, and who now worried about the implications of this for the type of regime that would be set up in Grenada.

Nevertheless, Grenadians were willing to work with the People's Revolutionary Government (PRG). They saw numbered among the Ministers members of the middle class, not only Maurice Bishop himself, but also Bernard Coard, Phyllis Coard and Jacqueline Creft, Dr Bernard Gittens, Palm Buxo, a small hotel owner, and Lyden Ramdhanny, the son of a well-off merchant in Grenville. The fact that Bishop included conservatives in his inner circle allayed many people's fears. Maurice Bishop was named Prime Minister, and Bernard Coard, Deputy Prime Minister. Unison Whiteman was assigned the Ministry of Agriculture, and Jacqueline Creft the Ministry of Education.

The Consolidation of 'The Revo'

The leaders of the Revolution used a Victory Rally on 23 March 1979 to announce the declaration of People's Law No. 1, which suspended the Constitution of Grenada retroactively to be effective from 12.01 a.m. on 13 March 1979, thereby making 'All acts or deeds by or under the authority of the People's Revolutionary Government...deemed and declared to have been legally done'.[5] The same law also promised to observe the rights and freedoms of Grenadians 'subject to certain measures necessary to the maintenance of stability, peace, order and good government; the final eradication of Gairyism; and the protection of the People's Revolution'.[6]

People's Law No. 7 established the People's Revolutionary Army (PRA). Members of the PRA were given the same powers of arrest and search as enjoyed traditionally by the Royal Grenada Police Force. Recruitment for the PRA began, starting with those who had been trained in secret to effect the armed takeover. The members of the Ras Tafari sect who were members of the initial People's Liberation Army and who were so prominent in the first days of the Revolution were told that they would have to cut their dreadlocks to be eligible for entry into the army. Some of the younger members abandoned the tenets of their religion for participation in the PRA, but many others turned sadly away. Bishop had courted their friendship during the days of the struggle against Gairy, and the NJM had championed the cause of the Ras Tafari in Grenada and in the Caribbean. Bishop had convinced Ras Tafari that, instead of looking to go back to Africa, they should stay in Grenada and participate in the falling of 'Babylon'.[7] Bishop had defended a Ras Tafari, Ras Kabinda, in Dominica and had defended many members who had been arrested for possession of weed.[8] The Ras Tafari was the first group in Grenada to suffer disillusionment.

Support for the 'Revo'

As Bishop wanted to stay within the Organization of Eastern Caribbean States (OECS) and the Caribbean Common Market (CARICOM), he invited all the leaders of neighbouring countries to visit, and many of them did come within two or three weeks to investigate conditions and the popular support for the Revolution. A mechanism was found to allow the Caribbean countries to accept Maurice Bishop as Prime Minister and the People's Revolutionary Government as the legal government when it was obvious that the country was peaceful and that the people were accepting of the Revolutionary Government. Bishop also made a promise to hold a general election in six months.

Soon support flowed into Grenada from several sources. In the early months of the PRG, a contingent of intellectuals from the University of the West Indies visited Grenada, to offer their expertise to the PRG on the setting up of their new programmes, such as the National In-Service Teacher Training Programme (NISTEP). Some of these intellectuals who were 'ideologically pure' Marxists, along with Marxists from elsewhere in the Caribbean and wider world, would be later seconded to fill key posts in the government.

The PRG were also able to mobilize the population to accomplish a great deal of self-help. The schools were repaired through community effort, and volunteerism was at its height for very many projects of the Revolution, including the literacy programme. Many of the volunteers were drawn from the membership of the mass organizations of the PRG that were launched around this time.

The tangible benefits of the Revolution did not only come from the co-operative effort of the Grenadian people and the people of the Caribbean. Goodwill and gifts for Grenada came also from the Soviet Bloc and from Venezuela, which donated petroleum products, equipment for the dental clinics, and school equipment. The European Economic Community and Libya sent monetary aid. Grenada was also the recipient of volunteer work from a host of 'internationalist' workers, who worked without salary on projects of the PRG.

Most of the aid that came to Grenada was, however, through Cuba. On 11 April 1979, one month after it seized power in Grenada, the PRG established diplomatic relations with Cuba. A great deal of aid from Cuba was developmental. Cuban teachers came to teach Spanish, both in the schools and to anyone who wished to learn. The Sandino Plant, donated by Cuba, produced all the building blocks necessary for the PRG's housing programme as well as for the construction of farm buildings and storage facilities. Cuba also donated an asphalt plant and stone-crushing equipment to provide material for road repair, and a fleet of fishing vessels to be used for the instruction of fishermen in modern fishing methods.

But most of the aid from Cuba would be arms and ammunition. As soon as the Cuban Embassy was set up at Morne Jaloux and the Ambassador installed, arms and ammunition from Cuba, along with military instructors, and up to 800 Cuban troops began to arrive in Grenada. Most of the ammunition was stored at Camp Calivigny, but there was also a stockpile at St Paul's. Military Camps were established all over the island. There were camps at Grand Etang, the Villa, Fort George, Fort Frederick, Butler House, Hillsborough on Carriacou, and in many other locations.

Arms did not only come from Cuba but also from the Soviet Union, East Germany, North Korea, Czechoslovakia, Bulgaria and other Communist countries.[9] These weapons would be unloaded after dark under cover of an electrical blackout. Vehicles were stopped or sent on a detour before they reached the part of the road where the convoys transporting the arms would pass. Arms would be taken for storage to several large warehouses originally built as factory shells. Some were also stored in the armed camps around the island. The PRG hid the massive arms build-up in Grenada from Grenadians and, as much as possible, from the rest of the world, but could not completely hide the fact that Grenada was rapidly becoming an arms depot.[10] 'Even policemen were ordered off the streets during the curfews imposed to cover the arrival of Cuban arms shipments and other secret business.'[11]

US Reaction

The United States was very upset at the establishment of diplomatic ties between the PRG and Cuba. The United States government sent a stern message to the PRG though the US Ambassador to the Eastern Caribbean, Frank Ortiz. The United States would also refuse to accept the diplomatic credentials of the person designated as Ambassador to Washington, Dessima Williams, a Grenadian lecturer at the State University of New York. When the new Ambassador to the Eastern Caribbean, Sally Shelton, took over from Ortiz, she was instructed to have no further talks with the Grenadian Prime Minister.

The warnings to Grenada from the United States were transmitted to the population, who were told that, if they stood fast, they could overcome any 'imperialist threats'. The population was warned through radio messages, slogans, literature, posters and any other means available that everyone had to be vigilant against the 'counters' who wanted to turn back the Grenada Revolution. Very soon, the PRG began to imprison without trial anyone who opposed them, or who they thought were a threat to the Revolution.[12] Still the population offered the PRG its trust and goodwill.

A New Type of Governance

The Revolutionary Government was run by a circle of Ministers and party officials called the Central Committee, but not all Ministers were members of the Central Committee. At the beginning, several non-Marxist supporters like Lyden Ramdhanny, Palm Buxo and Bernard Gittens were made Ministers, in an effort to win the confidence of those who might have suspected that the NJM was communist. This strategy was revealed in a speech Bishop made later, called the 'Line of March' speech, which Bishop delivered on 13 September 1982.[13]

The People's Laws were passed by decree, after being drafted and discussed by the Central Committee. The Central Committee was itself controlled by the Politburo, which was the highest level of the party, the card-carrying members of the NJM. The NJM recruited its members from loyal supporters, most of whom had been inducted before the Revolution, including those who had been members of the Youth Arm of the Party, the Organization for Revolution, Education and Liberation (OREL).

It was not easy to become a member of either the NJM or OREL, which was the youth arm of the NJM. The application process was similar. First you had to apply for membership. Then your behaviour, revolutionary commitment and ideological development would be scrutinized thoroughly by members in several levels of the party. If your application was not weeded out, it was again scrutinized by the top membership of the party, who would vote on it. If it was approved, you were admitted as a candidate member. Candidate members had to undergo classes in political education that included the principles and practices of Marxism. When the leadership was satisfied at the candidate's performance, full membership was considered. The classes for candidates to the party had been the prerogative since 1975 of the Coards and their protégés, who were very effective as teachers and mentors.

The PRG's Early Achievements

Grenadians knew that the PRG inherited a severely debilitated society, with neglected infrastructure. Several worthy projects were started by the PRG and enthusiastically embraced for a time by the population. For the first year of the Revolution, Bishop was given *carte blanche* to make any changes he wanted in any sector of society, and Grenadians would embrace the projects and work assiduously to make them a success.

Worthy of note were the several endeavours in education. Education at all levels was made free. Places at the secondary schools were increased from 302 to 1032 in 1980. A book and uniform assistance programme was instituted for children who could not afford these. Community Educational Councils were established to keep the schools in good running order and to help plan the school curriculum. Fridays in each week were to be devoted to teaching work-related skills to the students so that when they left school they would be ready for the world of work. Volunteers, including carpenters, basket makers, farmers, calypsonians and other creative artists who offered their services, were sent to the schools on schedules drawn up by the Community School Day Programme.

While the students were engaged in the Community Day Programme on Fridays, the untrained teachers at each school would attend NISTEP, designed to train all those working in the school system in a three-year period. The PRG engaged the University of the West Indies in dialogue towards getting the same sort of recognition for graduates of this programme as was previously given to the graduates of the now phased-out teachers' training college. These negotiations were never completed. Finally, the PRG set up a literacy programme. The Centre for Popular Education (CPE) aimed at 100 per cent literacy for Grenada. At its peak, 3000 persons were registered in the CPE.

The immense debt that the Gairy government had run up with the University of the West Indies was amortized by the PRG, and the PRG handpicked young supporters to study at the University. In addition, a very generous scholarship programme to Cuban universities began, and later this was augmented by offer of university places in the Soviet Union and East Germany. A total of 223 university scholarships were provided during the PRG regime. The range of subjects studied included Medicine, Food Technology, Accounting, Engineering, Physical Education and Political Education. Members of the PRA received training in Cuba, Russia, and East Germany.

Health care was made free in both the hospitals and the clinics, and the health care delivery system improved. Milk, butter fat and rice were distributed to all pregnant women in the low-income brackets throughout the island. Twelve Cuban doctors gave free medical aid to Grenadians through the health system. Cuban dentists also arrived, and were stationed in Carriacou and the rural health centres, as any oral care of the Grenadians in the rural areas had been non-existent for years.

The PRG also tried to revive agriculture, and mounted a campaign to make farming attractive to the young population. The Mirabeau Farm

School, which had been closed under the Gairy government, was reopened, and several other training centres established, including one in Carriacou. Through the National Cooperative Development Agency, aspiring young farmers were provided with training, loans, land, and the use of equipment to establish farms. Many of the estates seized by Gairy and left fallow were used for this purpose. Others became farm co-operatives, and a few were maintained as model farms. The marketing of the produce became the task of the Marketing and National Import Board, which, in addition to managing the sale of farm produce, also imported and set the price for cement, fertilizers, sugar and milk.

The PRG also experimented with food-processing factories, which used Grenadian fruit to make jams, jellies, tomato products and other items that could substitute for imports, as well as find a market overseas. The Grenada National Institute of Handicraft was established to encourage artists, sculptors, and handicraft workers to improve, and to provide a sales outlet for these items. Two of the country's banks were nationalized, the Royal Bank of Canada becoming the Grenada Bank of Commerce, and the Canadian Imperial Bank of Commerce becoming the National Commercial Bank.

Perhaps the achievement that was the most appreciated and lasting was the PRG's Housing Programme. In 1981 the first thirty-two houses were completed, and in 1982 the PRG embarked on the first phase of a grander scheme for 289 low-cost houses. Over $1.3 million Eastern Caribbean (EC) dollars were used to give grants or 'soft' loans through the National House Repair Programme to low-income earners.

The International Airport

The most impressive project of the PRG was the construction of the international airport. This project, which was accomplished with the aid of Cuba, began in January 1980, and had a completion deadline of 13 March 1984, the fifth anniversary of the Revolution. A large part of the Point Salines Estate had been under covenant since the 1950s for the construction of a modern airport that could accommodate large jetliners. Now this land was acquired, but not paid for, along with all the houses belonging to the Julien family who owned the land. Three hundred Cuban engineers and construction workers were brought into Grenada to work on the project.

It was a mammoth task. Hills had to be flattened and the old salt ponds that gave Point Salines its name had to be filled up. The engineers were faced with the problems created by of the soft rock called 'Tiff' (tufa) of which the hills were composed. This type of rock absorbed the shocks of the dynamite rather than shattering as a result of the explosion. Another challenge for the engineers was to find a way to build the runway across Hardy Bay. Regardless of how Grenadians felt about the PRG, there was unqualified admiration for the skill of the Cuban engineers who designed the airport, and for the industry of the Cuban workers who worked on it.

Although the airport project was funded mainly by Cuba, substantial financial aid for it also came from Venezuela, Nigeria, Algeria, Syria, Iraq and Libya. The Grenadian taxpayer also contributed substantially to meeting the cost. The cost of the airport was estimated at EC$191 million.[14] During the construction and the equipping of the airport, specific sub-projects were contracted out to companies based in England, Finland and the United States.

The rapid build-up of arms and the construction of the airport were viewed with alarm by the United States, who saw both as a security threat to the region and to regimes in South and Central America. Ronald Reagan, President of the United States, was convinced that the airport was really a Cuban–Soviet military installation, which was to be used for the trans-shipment of troops to South and Central America. In June 1980 the United States issued a statement detailing their concern about happenings in Grenada.[15] The statement pointed out that 30 per cent of the oil that the United States consumed was transported to the United States through the Caribbean Sea. Grenada sat on the northern edge of the Tobago Passage through which the tankers from Aruba and Africa moved. A Communist state in Grenada would therefore be a threat to the United States' oil supplies.

The balance of power in the region was also threatened if, through Grenada, revolution was to spread through the English-speaking Caribbean, and revolutionary causes supplied with arms from Grenada's weapons stockpiles. Cuban soldiers could be sent to assist Caribbean revolutionaries through Grenada. The Revolution in Grenada and its links to the Soviet Union, Cuba, and other Communist countries was interpreted by President Ronald Reagan as a threat to the United States, and he ordered military manoeuvres in the Caribbean to prepare the United States for possible military intervention in Grenada. These manoeuvres created a tension in Grenada, and elicited a barrage of rhetoric from the PRG aimed at the United States.

The PRA was increased in size, and held fortnightly manoeuvres of its own. A People's Militia was established for the training of part-time soldiers. Among the ranks of the militia were several hundred school-children. In the primary schools, the Young Pioneer Movement[16] was introduced. One seven-year-old expressed the reasons why he liked to be a

Pioneer: 'They said we would play games after school and we would hold real guns.'[17].

Economic Matters

The PRG ran a tight ship with regards to government expenditure. The PRG boasted that gross national product showed a steady rise from 1978 to 1982, but most of this activity concerned the construction of infrastructure. This growth, however, did not affect people's living standards, which were threatened by factors largely outside the control of the PRG.

For almost the entire duration of the PRG, the prices for nutmegs and cocoa were the lowest they had been for many years. The health of Grenada's economy had in the past reflected a direct relationship with the prices of these two staples, and now the economy was in trouble, just at a time when the PRG needed to show some returns for the effort it was exerting to make Grenada's agriculture one of the main pillars of the economy.

Tourism, another industry proclaimed to be a pillar of the economy, was also in shambles. The tourist industry had been ruined from inside and outside. United States citizens were warned of the dangers of coming to Grenada. Those who ignored the ban and came to Grenada, or tourists from other countries who chose Grenada as their tourist destination, were frightened by the common practice of the PRA practising manoeuvres in the hotel district, even between blocks of hotel rooms. Armed members of the PRA also held up buses taking tourists on sightseeing trips, to inspect the passengers, purportedly to find spies among them. Many of the tourist attractions, for example the area surrounding Grand Etang Lake, including the Rest House, Fort Frederick and Fort George, were taken over as camps for the PRG and were off-limits to tourists and locals alike. The cost of building the international airport took all the government's available revenue, and once more the roads and other infrastructure fell into great disrepair. The engines that supplied the country with electricity began to fail, and power cuts were constant.

Worse, the cost of living rose steeply. The purchasing power of the dollar in 1982 was 56 per cent of what it was in January 1979, and although it was pointed out[18] that wages also rose to the extent that the increase in wages was 11 per cent more than prices during the period, not everyone felt the impact, especially the self-employed.

The PRG did make a real effort to widen the economic base of the country by initiating several export industries that would allow Grenada to export non-traditional products. These included establishing a clothing industry and a furniture industry. A flourmill started operations, and Grenada exported flour and animal feed to other Caribbean islands. Perhaps the most important endeavour was the establishment of Grenada Agro Industries. The operation of this factory depended on the production of the required fruit and vegetables by the farmers. In so far as they were able to grow these, they were able to supplement their income from the traditional export crops. In terms of the whole economy, however, this fledgling manufacturing sector was small, and the size of the plants were too large for the amount of the product for which there was a market.

By 1983, the PRG had to face up to the fact that the economic package meant to provide Grenada with a measure of prosperity had failed, and now they could not generate enough income to service their debts. In 1983 they had no choice but to go to the International Monetary Fund (IMF) for a structural adjustment programme.

Disillusionment Sets In

When the economic squeeze began to make itself felt among the farmers and other members of the working class, the enthusiasm of the population began to wane. The programmes designed to alleviate unemployment were not as effective as they should have been, and things went from bad to worse. The population began to withdraw its support from the regime. The early support and energy applied to the projects of the PRG began to fizzle out. No one would turn up to the rallies; all the mass organizations were in the doldrums. Even the soldiers in the PRA began to grumble about their small pay in the face of a rapidly rising cost of living.

In 1980 public workers, represented by three trade unions, began a dispute with the PRG over wages. The government took a hard stand, and so did the unions. Eventually the workers went on strike. The government then accused the workers of sabotaging the second anniversary celebrations of the PRG. The union membership was livid and, although the wage negotiations were completed satisfactorily, the arrogance and hostility of the PRG towards the unions embittered both the civil servants and the unions, costing the PRG the support of the Public Workers Union that they had enjoyed until this impasse.

The NJM had controlled several unions prior to the Revolution. Now they tried to control the rest. One of their principal targets was the very strong and very independent Seamen and Waterfront Workers

Trade Union, led by Eric Pierre. In an interview in 1984, Pierre said that at the beginning Bishop courted the friendship of the workers. When he thought he had majority support, he tried to run the unions along communist lines.

> The PRG would put up a slate of candidates and then ask us to accept them. What kind of election is that? Not one at all. When I spoke out against this Selwyn Strachan, the Minister of National Mobilization, came to me and said, 'So I understand that you are trying to overthrow the Government.' Every move you made was perceived as an attempt to overthrow the PRG.[19]

The civil servants were submitted to constant indoctrination, but many were not deemed sufficiently 'ideologically pure' to head the government ministries and departments. Marxist intellectuals from abroad were brought in to fill the top civil service posts. As part of this process towards staffing the civil service with those who shared the political ideology of the government, the promotion, increments and advancement of civil servants in all departments became based on the incumbent's political activity. To each ministry and department a 'foreign adviser' was attached. The head of the department or ministry was sent to a Communist country to learn the Marxist way of running government departments, and under an 'adviser' he or she was asked to prepare a manual for the future operation of the ministry or department. Values other than Marxist values and contrary to the traditional value system of Grenadians were also promoted by the 'foreign advisers', and caused conflict and dissatisfaction in a population not ready to accept such 'modern' ideas as the acceptability of having illegitimate children, or that religion was backwardness and superstition.

Indoctrination in the Schools

The schools were targeted as institutions for the germination of a new and untainted generation of Marxists. Principals who were religious, or with whom the PRG did not want to work were removed into a 'Research Unit' of the Ministry of Education. Others chose to resign. In the church schools, both Catholic and non-Catholic, religious instruction was relegated to once a week, and only held during the first period, the time of day when many children were absent, and when the classes were constantly disrupted by late arrivals. Teachers were encouraged to take the religious choruses and put Revolutionary themes to them. A musically gifted 'internationalist' worker from Jamaica spent a great deal of energy teaching the children in primary school to sing the Grenadian version of the Communist *Internationale* that he had composed especially for this purpose.

In the secondary schools, pupils were encouraged to join the Militia and were taught to handle and fire weapons. Parents were alarmed when their school-aged children were called out on manoeuvres, and could not tell them where they would be for the entire weekend. Discipline began to crack in the schools, because the children in the Militia seemed to have more authority than the teachers, and, on occasion, brandished weapons brought to school to intimidate the teachers. A primary school teacher was stoned by his revolutionary pupils.

A Quantity of Repressive Laws

By 1980 as many as 63 People's Laws had been passed, many of them contrary to the promises made in People's Law No. 1, to uphold the freedom of the individual. People's Laws Nos 17 and 23 allowed the PRG and its agents to arrest and hold indefinitely without bail or trial anyone whom the Minister of National Security thought could act in a manner detrimental either to public safety, public order, the defence of Grenada, or with a view to subverting or sabotaging the PRG. Under this law, the person detained had no recourse whatever. They could not have recourse to the time-honoured writ of *habeas corpus*, nor to the Supreme Court, nor to any other court. During the time of the PRG, it is estimated that over 1000 persons[20] were arbitrarily arrested and sent 'up the hill'.[21]

In addition to the laws that were actually passed, others were planned, but the PRG had to stay their hand at implementing them because of the disquiet they generated in the public. Aspects of the PRG's land reform policy had to be abandoned. Grenadians had acquired houses and land though hard work and sacrifice. They did not like the sound of any laws that would take away their right to leave to their children that for which they had worked so hard.[22]

Torture

The darkest side of the PRG was perhaps the torture inflicted on new prisoners and on the inmates in prison. Citizens of Grenada who had not been officially charged with any crime, and not convicted in a court of law, and not able to defend themselves by any means whatever, were beaten, stuck with ice picks, subjected to electric shocks, had lighted cigarettes pushed up their noses, and most horribly, male prisoners were held down, while their genitals were cut with razor blades and pepper rubbed into them. Sometimes immobilized prisoners were placed naked near wasp nests, and had helmets filled with bees or wasps fixed to their heads.[23] The former home of the Prime Minister, Mount Royal, was the main torture centre of the PRG, and top members of the PRG often watched the torture of detainees.

Inmates in the Richmond Hill Prisons were constantly subjected to a variety of imaginative indignities.[24] Sometimes detainees went for days without being allowed to bathe. Access to toilets was given at the whim of the prison guards. Food was sometimes adequate but at other times old and unfit for consumption. Several of the detainees were forced to live in an overcrowded concrete cell with a barred ceiling, exposed to the elements. One man was left to urinate in his pants, forced to mop the floor with the pants and then required to wear them again unwashed.[25]

A Sense of Betrayal

Along with the disappointments over the non-appearance of 'the land of milk and honey' came popular anger that every promise Bishop had made to the population on 13 March 1979 had been broken. The PRG rapidly brought back all the agents of oppression that had turned the Grenadian people against Gairy. There was, by 1983, no freedom of the press. Free speech was virtually impossible without the danger of severe reprisal. Private property was acquired, the most celebrated case being that of the CocaCola Factory, owned by the firm of W.E. Julian and Co., and managed by Sandy Taylor, who had demonstrated his support for the NJM by suffering a beating during a pro-NJM demonstration prior to the Revolution. The people realized too late that they had exchanged one repressive totalitarian state for another.

Moreover, the habits and demeanour of members of the PRG and PRA left a lot to be desired. Many were arrogant and threatening. An example of their disrespect for the ordinary citizen was that they would go into restaurants and order the most expensive meals, refusing to pay for them, or charging the meal to the government. Some restaurants faced bankruptcy. The first elected government after the Revolution honoured these debts. A similar type of behaviour was foisted on small shopkeepers. Goods would be 'trusted'[26] and never paid for. When payment was requested, the owners would be insulted and threatened with 'up the hill'.

A lasting cause of disenchantment for many was that Bishop never kept his promise to have elections. Instead, when Herbert Blaize attempted to hold a political meeting, the meeting was terminated immediately by the PRA. Clearly, party politics had no place in the PRG.

Moves against the Church

The Roman Catholic Church had been the church of most Grenadians since the days of French colonization. It was a grassroots church, as it came to represent the poor descendants of the slaves rather than the scions of the British élite, who were members of the Church of England or Scots Kirk. During the latter half of the Gairy era, the NJM worked closely with the Roman Catholic Church in its efforts to re-institute a measure of social justice, or so the church thought. Under the cover of membership in church organizations, the NJM gradually infiltrated the church, especially the Youth Groups. When the church held 'Assembly 78',[27] the strongest contingent was that of the youth. The NJM's strategy was to use the occasion to portray an image of itself as a party interested in justice and Christianity, and to prepare the minds of the youth to accept Marxism. As Zwerneman says:

> By using Assembly 78 as a means to voice its opposition to Gairy's policies and to pose as a leader in promoting human rights in Grenada, the NJM captured the attention, admiration and loyalty of many Catholics – especially the youth[28]

Within a year, the church realized that it, along with the Grenadian people, had been duped. The Anglican Youth Group as well as the Catholic had been infiltrated by young supporters of the NJM. Now all the members transferred their support to the PRG, leaving the Youth Groups deprived of leadership, decimated of membership, demoralized and floundering. Religious education in the schools was limited, and the principals and teachers of church schools were timid about passing on religious values to the children. Religious broadcasting was limited to Sundays. Priests and ministers were kept under surveillance, and their sermons and public utterances listened to by agents of the PRG who would report on them to a special committee. A minister in one of the 'fundamentalist' churches said that he and his family were: 'Scared, between life and death all the time. We couldn't talk to anyone about politics, even to our best friends. And there were spies in the church every time I preached.'[29]

Bishop Charles of the Roman Catholic Church believed his telephone was tapped, for every time he picked up the phone he could hear a 'strange mechanical device go on'.[30]

This was not all. Work permits were withheld for some missionaries. A Methodist minister was deported after he refused to bury an NJM supporter on Sunday, a day on which the Council of Churches had decided not to hold funerals. A smear campaign reduced two very popular priests recruited from Africa to tears. People who wanted to be good Catholics and good revolutionaries soon understood that they had to choose one or the other. Community work, such as repairing schools and roads, was scheduled for Sundays, so that the young people had to choose between involvement in this salutary aspect of the Revolution and their religious obligations. Youths who remained faithful to the church were ridiculed, derisively called 'church girl' or 'church boy' and asked mockingly why 'After all these years, you are still in that thing?' Churchgoers were sometimes accused of destabilization. Others were warned that: 'It is not good to be seen too often up by the Church.'[31]

In order to utilize the devotion to the church, the PRG invited the revolutionary cleric from Nicaragua, Ernesto Cardenal, to visit Grenada. A huge rally was organized in conjunction with the visit to showcase Cardenal with all his charisma and appeal. The rally had the intended effect. The Catholic youth invariably compared the revolutionary priest with the ageing, conservative clerics who administered their churches. They longed for a revolutionary church, full of life and vigour. One young person described the visit of Cardenal in these words: 'He praised the Revolution and said we must fight. People looked at him and said, "Why can't our priests be like that? Look at our priests. They're bourgeois!"'[32]

Although the church lost some young supporters, most church members remained steadfast in their faith, to the disappointment of the regime. The Corpus Christi procession in 1983 was the largest ever observed. It was observed closely, and with chagrin, by disappointed members of the PRG, as well as by their comrades from abroad.[33]

All churches were under stress from the Revolution, but they took comfort in mutual support. The Archdeacon of the Anglican Church, the Reverend Hoskins Huggins, the Methodist Minister, the Reverend Philip Poncé, and the Roman Catholic Bishop, Bishop Sydney Charles, formed a formidable threesome – one from which members of all churches took delight and drew strength.[34]

Suppression and Tyranny

The PRG, from the first moments of the Revolution, were awake to the possibility of a US invasion of Grenada. But they also used the threat of invasion as an excuse to construct phantom plots, on the basis of which they would arrest and detain innocent people. Even when the threat was real, they used the opportunity to get rid of whoever had fallen out of favour with them.

On 19 June 1980 thousands of supporters gathered at Queen's Park at a rally to honour two Grenadians who had been named among the Heroes of the Revolution. These were Tubal Uriah 'Buzz' Butler, who had died in 1978, and Alister Strachan, a youth who had died during the anti-Gairy struggle in 1973. While the rally went on, a bomb was in place unnoticed under the grandstand. The bomb subsequently exploded, hurting none of the leadership, but killing three young women and injuring scores of others.

When the remains of the bomb were examined, it was found to be constructed with a sophistication and technology previously unknown in Grenada. The immediate verdict without investigation or trial was that this was the work of former PRA officer Strachan Phillip. Phillip had been entrusted with building up the fighting force of NJM supporters, and had commanded these forces in the storming of the Defence Force's barracks on 13 March 1979. He had later become disillusioned with the direction the PRG had taken, and resigned from the PRA. Troops were immediately dispatched to his home in Mount Airy, and his home was riddled with gunfire and rockets. The description Maurice Paterson gives of Phillips' last minutes is easily believable:

> When the shooting ceased Strachan Phillip lay riddled by AK bullets where he had run out into the yard shouting at the soldiers. He would lie there for a long-time (before he died), cussing Pump Head[35] with his last breath: 'Why you do this to me, Pump Head? Why?' he asked. [36]

The coroner's report counted nineteen bullet wounds in Phillip's body.[37] The execution of Strachan Phillip was carried out without a shred of evidence linking him to the bombing. But such were the times that the leadership could order the PRA to shoot a man without tangible proof of guilt. Tales circulated that the bombing at Queen's Park was the work of the PRG itself, to provide 'proof' of subversion in society. Another supposition was that it was the work of disaffected supporters of the NJM. Whoever planted the bomb at Queen's Park, it was not Strachan Phillip. On 26 June 1980, a week after the Queen's Park bomb blast, seven days after Phillip was dead, another bomb of similar design exploded in St Patrick's. It killed a Ras Tafarian linked to a disaffected group led by the Budhlall Brothers.

War Against the Ras Tafari

Around this time the PRA shot three youths, two Stanislaus brothers and Stephen Lalsee, in St Patrick's. Lalsee was a student at the Institute for Further Education in St George's. The PRG tried to cover up the incident, and when they failed they said it was a terrible mistake, and that their car had been mistaken for another. They then sent the PRA into the hills around Mount Rich to hunt down Ras Tafarians. Three Ras Tafarians were killed during this exercise. Unbelievably, the PRG hoped by this exercise to placate the anger of the citizens of St Patrick's engendered by the shooting of the three youths!

The Ras Tafari brethren, once stalwart supporters of the Revolution, were now targeted for brutal suppression. The PRG began to suspect that the sect was growing restive, as the PRG clamped down on the growing of marijuana and the smoking of it. The PRG feared subversion through the spreading of discontent. They also feared that the Ras Tafari would be used by persons in the drug trade to subvert the government because of its Marxist stance against illegal drugs.

In October 1979 two young Ras Tafari, Ras Nna Nna and Ras Ersto Jo Jo, went to *The Torchlight* newspaper, and gave a long interview to the editor. The issue of the newspaper for 19 October reported on the interview, in which the PRG was condemned for being anti-Rasta and for delaying elections. In part, the interview said:

> We are not supporters of Cuba and Russia, we see [these countries] as enemies of Rasta, since they do not acknowledge Rastafarian doctrine. The Twelve Tribes of Israel congratulate *Torchlight* for its brave stand in this time.[38]

Immediately, demonstrations were organized against these two Ras Tafari, and a statement signed by six brethren from La Digue was circulated. This incident was a demonstration of the growing tensions between the PRG and the Ras Tafari. The Ras Tafari had hoped that the PRG would legalize weed when it came to power. Instead, the PRG sought to stamp out the increasing cultivation of weed for sale to international dealers. Since this trade, and the sale of weed for domestic use, was a large part of the bread and butter of the Ras Tafari brethren, as well as being sacred to their religion, the Ras Tafari looked on the suppression of the cultivation, sale and use of weed as a betrayal of them by Bishop.

In May 1980 the weed-growers organized a demonstration in Grenville to show their opposition to the suppression by the PRG of the large-scale planting of weed. They met up with a counter-demonstration of PRG supporters promoting greater productivity in the field of agriculture and food production. After the bomb blast in Queen's Park, and the second bomb, which exploded killing the Ras Tafari brother who was carrying it, the PRG decided to round up approximately 300 members of the Ras Tafari sect who might pose further problems, and confine them to a camp.

The camp, referred to as a 're-orientation' camp, was established at Hope Vale, near Vincennes, St David's. It not only accommodated members of the Ras Tafari sect, but also others who were to be singled out for special humiliation. The conditions at this camp were insanitary, and the detainees were subject to long and arduous hours of work. The detainees spent many nights and days in the open air. When they were given shelter, the shelters leaked, and they were given discarded mattresses from the mental hospital, contaminated with faeces and blood, to sleep on.

Here those confined would grow food to feed the PRA, and be persuaded to accept the Revolution through non-stop indoctrination. The heads of the Ras Tafari Brethren were shaved with broken glass bottles, leaving deep wounds that left visible scars. They were also force-fed pork, which their religion forbade, and made to compromise their religious beliefs and practices in other ways. They were beaten for the slightest infringement of camp codes. Ras Nna Nna, who was one of those interned there, said of Hope Vale: 'It was the most wicked thing in the world.'[39]

Curtailment of Press Freedom

The second act of the Revolution on 13 March 1979 had been the seizure of Grenada's only radio station, Radio Grenada. Referred to as 'Radio Lie-o-Nel' by the NJM prior to 13 March 1979, the station now became Radio Free Grenada. As soon as arrangements could be made, Radio Free Grenada and the only television station, now dubbed Grenada Free Television, were put in the hands of communication 'experts' who were brought in from Jamaica through the connection Phyllis Coard had with the Workers Party of Jamaica, headed by Trevor Munroe. These 'ideologically pure' managers worked under the supervision of Phyllis Coard. Many of the existing workers at the station were transferred and replaced by others who were handpicked for their loyalty to the Revolution. A huge transmitter was built at Beausejour[40] not only to broadcast Radio Free Grenada to the entire Eastern and Southern Caribbean, but also to block out the reception of all radio signals from outside Grenada.

The West Indian newspaper, started by Marryshow and Renwick in 1915 to stimulate debate on issues important to Grenada and Grenadians, and which Gairy had acquired, became in turn the mouthpiece of the PRG under a new banner: the *Free West Indian.* The only other newspaper was *The Torchlight*, which was regarded as a conservative paper, reflecting, if anything, an ideology close to that of Herbert Blaize. *The Torchlight* was allowed to publish until October 1979. The PRG used the excuse of *The Torchlight's* publication of the interview with Ras Nna Nna and Ras Ersto Jo Jo to move against the newspaper. In dramatic fashion, the PRG declared that *The Torchlight* and the printshop attached to it were to be given to the workers to own and operate. *The Torchlight* never appeared again, although the printshop continued a desultory operation under the management of the workers.

On the virtual closure of the *The Torchlight*, an amendment to the Newspaper Act[41] was passed requiring a deposit that was sufficiently large to prevent most companies in Grenada from attempting activity in the publications field. Notwithstanding, twenty-six business people got together and subscribed the funds to meet the deposit and to put out a mimeographed sheet called *The Grenadian Voice*. This newsletter ran to only one issue. Immediately on its publication, some of members of 'The Gang of 26', as they were called by the PRG, were imprisoned in the Richmond Hill Prisons, some until they were freed by US soldiers after the US invasion. In a wry comment on the arrest of these middle-class supporters of democracy, Paterson says: 'This was a revolution, and it would soon make jail a more democratic and less class-oriented place.'[42]

There were members of the Gang of 26 that the PRG could not touch for various reasons. Some were elderly, and could not withstand prison conditions. The PRG would rather not have the embarrassment of them dying in gaol. Some were leaders of the business community in Grenada and the Caribbean. Their detention would have sparked off protests in the other islands that would have cut into the solidarity the NJM was trying to establish in those territories. Detention of too many middle-class people would also have precipitated a flight of capital from the island. The PRG also could not detain Alister Hughes. Hughes was a giant among West Indian journalists, and had become immensely popular for his stance against Gairy and his impartial reporting of the measures taken against the NJM by Gairy. He had risked his life to cover the events of 'Bloody Monday'. Embassies and international organizations inside and outside

Grenada subscribed to his *Monthly Bulletin*. In 1990 the University of the West Indies would honour him for his outstanding performance in the field of journalism by awarding him an Honorary Doctor of Laws.

Those members of the Gang of 26 who could not be touched for various reasons were mocked and threatened. Signs were painted in large letters on the roads leading to the houses of each member of the Gang to the effect that 'Heavy Manners' would be the fate of all 'Counters'.[43]

The Roman Catholic Diocesan newspaper was also a victim of the clampdown on the free press. The only news organ other than the *Free West Indian* and other publications of the PRG allowed to operate was Alister Hughes' *Monthly Bulletin*. To counter any negative writing about the PRG, Grenada was flooded by publications that glorified the Revolution, its supporting institutions, and its outstanding supporters.

The Leadership Split

With total control of the island and the continued support of Cuba and the Soviet Union, no amount of disaffection could have brought down the regime. The end of the PRG started when, at the beginning of 1983, the leadership turned on itself, and quarrels broke out over differences of opinion as to the path of the Revolution and the management of the country. The PRG was split into two camps: those who were ideological hardliners, and those who were accused by the 'hardliners' of being 'soft-liners' or 'social democrats'. The hardliners, headed by the Coards, were very impatient at the time it was taking to transform Grenada into Marxist state. Bishop himself thought that the revolutionary process could not be rushed. Frustrated at Bishop's determined belief that the Revolution had to take time, Bernard Coard resigned from the Central Committee, although his wife remained.

The rift between the supporters of the Coards and the supporters of Bishop within the Central Committee widened at a meeting held between 16 and 24 September 1983. Bishop's agenda for this meeting was rejected, and replaced by one drawn up by 'Chalkie' Ventour, a supporter of the Coards. What is described as 'a scathing, cold-blooded and calculated attack' was made on Bishop by most members of the Central Committee 'who spoke as if programmed and rehearsed'.[44] Bishop was charged with the responsibility for the evident public despondency, public dissatisfaction, low morale among the party members and the danger of the Revolution's disintegration, the 'timidity' of the leadership, and the poor quality of the leadership of the mass organizations.

In reply to these charges, Bishop pointed out that the members of the Central Committee were not pulling together as they should. He pointed out as an example that they were often absent from zonal and parish councils. Neither the analysis of the Coard faction nor that of Bishop entertained the thesis that 'The Revo' was failing because the hardline Marxist/Leninist ideology and practice had been rejected by the people, and that they had demonstrated this rejection by withdrawing their support and participation from a Revolution that had turned out to be far from what they had hoped for and had been promised.

Bishop was further accused of 'petit bourgeoisie trends' and 'right opportunism', and leading the Revolution down the path to social democracy. Liam James expressed the view that what the Revolution needed was a Leninist level of organization and discipline, great depth in ideological clarity and brilliance in strategy and tactics.[45] He lobbied for Bernard Coard to move up to 'joint leadership' with Bishop. In this, Phyllis Coard, Selwyn Strachan, 'Chalkie' Ventour, Ewart Layne, 'Bogo' Cornwall, 'Kamu' McBarnette, Christopher DeRiggs and Tan Bartholomew supported Liam James. Whiteman and George Louison supported Bishop as best they could, but their support was unequal to the vicious criticism of the young hardliners who were the protégés of Phyllis and Bernard Coard. Phyllis Coard also harshly criticized Bishop. She told Bishop that he was disorganized, avoided responsibility, and was hostile to criticism. He had opposed both the closing of *The Torchlight* and the persecution of the Gang of 26 who had resisted the suppression of press freedom.[46]

The turmoil facing Bishop at this point in time seems not to have been any hesitancy on his part about the concept of joint leadership, but his deep concern that joint leadership could be a device to cast him in the role of figurehead, while the real power would lie with the Coards and their supporters. Bishop understood the Grenadian people, and worried for the future of the Revolution if they were forced to go where they did not want to, because they were simply not ready for major ideological change and the structures that went with it. He therefore told the Central Committee that he did not have a problem with sharing power, but he was concerned as to how it would operate, how it would be explained to the people, and whether or not they would see it as a power struggle. Bishop undoubtedly knew that he still had the goodwill and affection of the people of Grenada, and probably suspected that the legitimacy of the Revolution rested in his persona and not in the ideology. Without him the Revolution would collapse. The Coards were not so wise or so perceptive. A much-quoted saying of Bernard highlights his approach to popular_opposition: 'If the people do not like it, they will have to learn to like it.' Bishop asked the Central Committee to give him time to think.

The Central Committee now decided on a strategy to put the question of joint leadership to the party. Remembering that party members were handpicked ideologues, trained mainly by the Coards, a vote putting the Coards in a power position and espousing hardline Marxist-Leninist policies in place of the gentler and more palatable democratic socialism was certain. On 22 September 1983 the issue of joint leadership was put to the 300-strong membership of the NJM. Bishop did not want to attend the meeting, and initially refused to go. On learning that Bishop had refused to attend, Bernard Coard also stayed away. The members of the party summoned both.

When he was asked to explain his refusal to attend the meeting, Bishop confessed that he was very confused and upset. He said that the actions of the Central Committee seemed to point to a desire of the Committee to transform the party into a Marxist-Leninist party, and the Revolution into a Marxist-Leninist revolution. Bishop had always supported the ideal of democratic socialism. Liam James delivered a scathing attack against Bishop. He accused Bishop of disrespecting the Leninist principles of democratic centralism by questioning the decision of the Central Committee and of suspecting a conspiracy to unseat him.

After a very difficult and contentious meeting, the membership of the NJM voted in favour of joint leadership. Bishop accepted the decision, embracing Bernard Coard as a sign that there were no hard feelings. All reports of the meeting indicate, however, that Whiteman and George Louison were very uncomfortable with the proceedings of the meeting and did not fully accept the decision that Maurice Bishop and Bernard Coard should become joint leaders.

The Coup

Soon after this meeting, Bishop, accompanied by Whiteman and George Louison, left to pay state visits to Czechoslovakia and Hungary. While in Hungary, Bishop changed his mind on the joint leadership issue, and George Louison addressed a group of Grenadians telling them that Bishop had rejected the suggestion of joint leadership. Word got back to the Central Committee, and the faction supporting the idea became incensed. Whiteman and Louison did not return with Bishop, both having a longer itinerary. When Bishop returned to the island on 8 October, he got an icy welcome from the solitary Minister, Selwyn Strachan, who came to meet him. Sensing danger, Bishop gave orders that this driver was to travel by the longer route through St David's rather than the mountain route across the Grand Etang. On his arrival in St George's, Bishop was immediately put under guard.

On 12 October, Bishop was summoned before the Central Committee to answer to his change of mind. Bishop told the Central Committee that he had reconsidered the matter and was now firmly against the sharing of leadership, giving the reasons for his decision. Apart from any other considerations, it seemed to him that the Coards and their supporters were using the concept of joint leadership as a scheme to displace him.

While the meeting was in progress, it was disrupted by reports of rumours circulating in St George's that the Coards were planning to kill Bishop. There was a very strong rumour that Bishop had escaped assassination on the Grand Etang Road. By using the St David's Road to St George's on his return from Europe, he had escaped the planned scenario whereby he would have been ambushed, killed, and his death hailed as martyrdom by 'imperialist forces'. Bernard Coard would assume leadership immediately and supervise the national mourning.

The presence of the rumours worried the Central Committee because the rumours made sense to a population startled by the news that Bishop had been placed under house arrest as soon as he had arrived in St George's on 8 October. On 14 October, Cletus St Paul, Bishop's bodyguard, and Bishop himself, were questioned as to the origin of the rumours. Both Bishop and St Paul denied starting these rumours. St Paul was arrested and sent to Camp Calivigny, and later to Fort Frederick. Bishop was told that he had to make a public denial by radio. This he refused to do.

The next morning, 15 October, there was a meeting of some of the members of the Central Committee at the Coards' home. Coard defended the decision to keep Bishop under house arrest and – since 14 October – completely incommunicado, saying that Bishop was the cause of all the problems the Revolution was facing and of the present crisis. He deserved to be punished. Another meeting of the entire Central Committee was called for that evening. Bishop was brought forcibly to the meeting, and asked to answer charges that he had spread the rumours against the Coards. Again Bishop denied the charges. He was then confronted by his security officer, who testified that Bishop had given him instructions to spread the rumours. Denouncement of Bishop as a 'disgrace to the party and a man beyond redemption'[47] followed, and Bishop was expelled from the Central Committee, along with George Louison and Fitzroy Bain who supported him.

All doubt about whether Bishop was under house arrest, expelled from the Central Committee, and had been replaced by Coard as Prime

Minister were removed when, later that afternoon, Selwyn Strachan made a public announcement to this effect outside of the offices of the *Free West Indian* in St George's. As soon as the words were out of his mouth and their meaning had sunk in, he had to move swiftly off the scene to prevent damage to his person due to the ugly mood of the crowd that gathered spontaneously. Shouts were heard: 'No Bishop, No Revolution!' 'Revolution Yes! Communism No!' 'Coard stands for Communism'. Disbelief, fear, horror and anxiety for the future were unmistakable common public reactions. The Coard supporters in the Central Committee had not remembered that the Revolution was essentially a People's Revolution. Bishop was the hero of the Revolution and, even if things had not been going as they had hoped with the Revolution, no one but the people had the right to dismiss their leader.

Hearing and understanding for the first time that the Grenadian people wanted Bishop and only Bishop, Bernard and Phyllis Coard resigned from the Central Committee. Whiteman, Louison and Creft, who had never faltered in their loyalty to Bishop, also resigned.

Whiteman, returning to Grenada through Barbados, was advised of the dangerous situation in Grenada by the Barbadian Prime Minister, Tom Adams, who went to intercept him at Barbados Airport as he made his connections to Grenada on his way home after his tour of duty abroad. Tom Adams was no friend of the Revolution. Bishop had constantly berated him for a pro-American stance, calling him Reagan's 'Yard Fowl'. Nevertheless, Adams was concerned for Whiteman's personal safety, and offered him political asylum in Barbados. Whiteman was touched by the offer but told Adams that he had to go home to see what he could do to resolve the grave problems facing the country. On his arrival in Grenada, Whiteman met with George Louison and jointly negotiated with Bernard Coard and Strachan for some measure of conciliation. Michael Als of the People's Popular Movement in Trinidad and Tobago and Rupert Roopnarine of the Working People's Alliance in Guyana intervened in the crisis, and tried to work with the key players in Grenada to effect a compromise. After many tries, a compromise was reached that might work. Austin was delegated to make a radio broadcast on 16 October, designed to allay fears, and Bishop was to address the nation on 18 October.

These conciliatory measures were too late. Pro-Bishop demonstrations had already started in Grenville, and the schools there were closed. Children from the secondary schools in St Andrew's invaded Pearls Airport and sat on the tarmac to protest the situation, putting the airport out of service for many hours. Louison was arrested for agitating the people. His incarceration and the subsequent incarceration of Radix saved their lives. Whiteman eluded the agents seeking his arrest.

That evening, Bishop made his last broadcast. In the broadcast, Bishop said that the rumours that were circulating about the rift in the Central Committee were false and were spread by imperialist agents. He warned the people not to be taken in by the rumours spread by counter-revolutionaries. He told them that the security forces were vigorously searching for the persons who had started the rumours and that one person had so far been arrested. He reaffirmed that the New Jewel Movement remained as firm as ever, and was committed to bringing greater benefits to the working people of Grenada. This time the general population did not believe a word their leader said. They decided to take whatever action was necessary to free him.

The End Day

Early the next morning, 19 October, people started to stream into St George's by car, buses, trucks, and any vehicle that could be pressed into service for transportation. The schoolchildren from Grenville came down in droves. Many had made their protest posters and banners overnight. One child had a placard marked 'Only monster have two heads'. By 8.00 a.m. Whiteman was in St George's gathering Bishop supporters for a march on the Prime Minister's residence at Mount Wheldale, where Bishop was being held. By the time the demonstration got to the gates of Mount Wheldale, it was massive. People of all walks of life were represented, and schoolchildren were much in evidence in their uniforms, as they had joined the demonstration in town instead of going to school, or had left school when they heard about the demonstration. The guards at the gate fired into the air in an attempt to stop the crowd from reaching the house, but the crowd surged through. The leaders of the demonstration went into the house and found Bishop, half-naked, tied to his bed with his arms tied over his head. He looked very weak. Jacqueline Creft, Bishop's close comrade and adviser, was found in another room in a similar condition. Jacqueline Creft was the mother of Bishop's child Vladimir, and was several months pregnant with another child for him. Clothes were found for them, and Bishop and Creft were brought outside. One witness said that Bishop was weak and was crying: '"The masses. The masses. The masses." It was all he was saying. Tears wash down his face.'[48]

Bishop and Creft were both seated in a vehicle, as the plan was that Bishop would be taken to the Market Square where he would address the people. Some of the crowd went ahead of the vehicle, while about one-third followed behind. As the procession passed her mother's house,

Jacqueline Creft called out to her mother, Lynn, that she should come to the Fort with refreshments for Bishop. Lynn Creft busied herself with the task, and went with a young neighbour to the Fort to deliver the refreshments. As the procession reached the confluence of Church Street and Market Hill, Bishop asked that he be taken to the Fort instead, as he was too weak to stand before a crowd. He knew that there was recording equipment at the Fort, and he planned to record a message to be played to the people at the Market Square. This is why most of the crowd went down the hill to the Market Square and only a portion accompanied Bishop to the Fort.

On reaching the Fort, the soldiers were asked by Bishop to surrender their arms to the base commander, Captain Christopher Stroude, which they did, even though they were privy to the fact that Bishop had been deposed. Bishop, Creft, Vincent Noel, a member of the PRG in charge of the unions, and about forty other persons crowded into the Operations Room at the Fort, where Bishop and Whiteman began to compose the address that Bishop would later deliver. Bishop also asked that the police canteen be opened, so that the crowd could refresh themselves. Nurses in the demonstration went to the General Hospital situated next to the Fort, to get oxygen to assist in reviving Bishop sufficiently for him to make his tape-recorded speech.

A desperate attempt at negotiation took place between Coard's supporters among the PRA personnel at Fort George[49] and at Fort Frederick in the hills overlooking St George's, and Bishop and his supporters. Bishop wanted all the members of the Coard faction arrested, but Stroude's deputy, Lester Redhead, asked him to try negotiation first. Bishop, backed by Whiteman, refused to negotiate. He announced that he was removing Hudson Austin as commander of the PRA, and that Einstein Louison, the brother of George Louison, his loyal supporter, should take command. Einstein Louison was given the keys to the armoury, and told to distribute arms to those civilians among the crowd at the Fort who had been trained in weapon use. The members of the defunct Central Committee at Fort Frederick were kept fully informed of events at Fort George through telephone calls made for that purpose by Stroude, who was sympathetic to the Coards.

Amazed at the strength of popular support for Bishop, and that Bishop's supporters now had arms, the Coard side of the defunct Central Committee, who were ensconced at Fort Frederick, ordered an assault on Fort George by armed personnel carriers dispatched from the PRA at Camp Calivigny. The assault was led by Captain Conrad Mayers, a Grenadian who had been in the US Army, and who had come back to support the Revolution. Thundering down Lucas Street, the armed personnel carriers entered Church Street and charged up the short hill to the Fort, blocking the only entrance. The time was approximately 1.10 p.m.

In the confusion of the circumstances, there are differences of opinion as to who fired the first shot. One version is that a person yet to be identified shot and killed Captain Mayers and two other officers, Dorset Peters and Raphael Mason, who were riding exposed on top of the armed personnel carriers. The other version is that, as soon as they arrived, personnel in the carriers began to fire heavy artillery mounted on the carriers into the building where Bishop, Noel, Creft and some civilians were sitting, and this was answered by shooting from the people who were now armed. In any event, shells and a hail of bullets fired from the armed personnel carriers raked though the building killed several in the room where Bishop was, including Gemma Belmar, a schoolgirl. Maurice Bishop's anguished cry was: 'Oh God! Oh God! They have turned their guns on the People!'

The firing went on for between seven to ten minutes. People at the Fort scattered screaming. They ran in all directions. The Reverend Philip Poncé, the Methodist minister, had a clear view of what was happening from a window on the second floor of his residence, Wesley House. He saw: 'Bodies jumping from the impact of the bullets; bodies lying dead; people were screaming and scrambling for the walls of the Fort'.[50]

The PRA were merciless in the ensuing slaughter. Many who jumped over the 40-foot-high walls of the Fort fell to their death, but provided a cushion for those falling after them, which enabled those to escape. Some people hid in the tunnels for which the Fort was famous, only to be rounded up later by the PRA and shot. One of those killed was Lynn Creft's young neighbour, while she herself got away unharmed.

The shooting began again, and then stopped. When the shooting stopped for the second time, Bishop, Creft, Fitzroy Bain, and supporters Norris Bain, 'Brat' Bullen, Evelyn Maitland and 'Pumphead' Hayling, as well as others who were in the room, went outside. Two were allowed to carry away the lifeless body of Gemma Belmar, while the others surrendered to what must now be called Coard's forces. Bishop said he would not have any more people killed on account of him.

At about 1.30 p.m. another burst of firing was heard. Later people realized that this burst of fire signalled the execution of their Revolutionary Prime Minister, two Ministers and five others. Bishop, Creft, Whiteman, Fitzroy Bain, Norris Bain and others had been taken to the basketball court within the Fort, lined up, read a sentence purportedly composed by the Central Committee, and told to face the wall. Allegedly, Lester Redhead was in charge of the execution squad.[51] Payne, Sutton and Thorndyke report that:

Jacqueline Creft screamed, 'Comrades, you mean to say you're going to shoot us? To kill us?' Redhead's alleged reply was to the point. 'You ... bitch ... who are you calling comrades? You're one of those who was going to let the imperialist in'.[52]

It is said that Bishop refused to face the wall saying: 'They shot my father in his back; if they are going to shoot me, I want to look at my executioners in their eyes'.[53] An eyewitness reported that Bishop then: 'Gave a deep sigh, folded his arms, and turned to face his executioners, who shot him in the head.'[54]

Bishop and his colleagues were shot over and over with ammunition so powerful that their bodies were torn apart.[55] It is alleged that later someone split Bishop's skull,[56] that his throat was slashed, and that his finger was cut off to get the ring that he had been given by his friend and leader of Libya, Mustafa Gadaffi.[57] When the execution of Bishop, Creft, Whiteman and the others was completed, a white flare was fired by Coard's forces at Fort George to inform Coard and his colleagues at Fort Frederick that the job they had been sent to do was completed.[58]

The crowd at the Market Square awaiting Bishop is estimated to have numbered approximately 10,000. They were thrown into confusion when they heard the firing at the Fort, and eventually persons escaping from Fort George told them what had happened. Still, some people remained until members of Coard's forces were sent to disperse them, and everyone scattered in terror, and took to the roads to go home, as all available transport preceded them out of town, not waiting for any passengers.

In spite of several efforts to collect the names of those who died on the Fort, the people of Grenada saw no point in this exercise. Years later, a monument was placed at the Fort, listing all the known dead, and indicating that so many more were killed, but remain nameless. How many people were among the nameless killed is not known. One count puts the number killed at nineteen.[59] Most estimates put the number at 200–300, but some go as high as 400. *The Times* newspaper reported that one soldier counted 60 bodies outside the Fort's walls alone.[60] What is known is that it took several trips made by the large trucks to remove all the dead bodies and dispose of them in ways that are still only whispered about.

Many people whose houses on the hills around faced the Fort watched the frenzied attempts during the next few days to get rid of the evidence of the massacre. The bodies of Maurice Bishop, Jacqueline Creft, Unison Whiteman and those executed with them were taken to Camp Calivigny. The bodies were placed in a pit, and gasoline poured over them.

The gasoline was then lit, and the bodies were left to burn overnight. The next day the pit was covered.[61]

The Aftermath

At 9.00 p.m. on the evening of 19 October 1983, General Hudson Austin came on the radio announcing that the events at the Fort were to be blamed on Bishop and his colleagues. Bishop and seven others had been killed in crossfire at the Fort, and a curfew was now in effect. Anyone seen outside would be shot. Anyone who sought to demonstrate or disturb the peace would be shot. He announced that a Revolutionary Military Council (RMC) had been formed that day, and that this Council would govern Grenada until normalcy was restored. Except for a brief respite to allow animals to be fed and for people to buy food in the 'corner shops', the curfew was not lifted for four days.

When Grenadians were allowed out of their houses and instructed to return to work by the RMC, they were traumatized and dazed. Their anxiety as to their future and the future of Grenada was enormous. Grocery shelves were denuded, as people bought as much food as they could afford, as a hedge against the unknown.

Invasion, Intervention and Rescue Mission

On the morning of 25 October, the United States invaded Grenada. While the population was kept under house arrest, Eugenia Charles, Prime Minister of Dominica and at the time chairman of the OECS, the Prime Ministers of all the OECS countries and Barbados, and President Ronald Reagan and his staff had been meeting. Eugenia Charles led the negotiations that ended in the armed intervention in Grenada by the United States, supported by military and police personnel from Barbados and the OECS. A battle lasting four days ensued between the forces of the PRA joined by Cuban soldiers, and the US forces, conducted first from the air and then on the ground. Although the PRA and Cuban forces had no air cover, several helicopters were shot down, one landing in the middle of the cricket pitch at Tanteen. The US used its latest military technology to destroy key targets such as the radio station and the PRA barracks. In order to draw fire away from the PRA Camp at Richmond Hill, the PRA soldiers dressed the inmates in the neighbouring mental hospital in uniforms, and ran up the PRG flag on the flagpole. Unfortunately, the bait was taken, and the mental hospital shelled. The mental patients constituted most of the casualties of this war.

The United States government gave three reasons for their invasion. The first was to ensure the safety of approximately 1000 United States citizens living in Grenada at the time. Most of these were students at the American offshore medical school, the St George's University School of Medicine in True Blue and Grand Anse. The medical school had been set up with the permission of Gairy, and now catered for approximately 500 students. These were removed with great drama from Grand Anse Beach by helicopters, which flew them to battleships that hovered just offshore.

The second reason given was to respond to the formal request for assistance from the OECS. This request for assistance from the US had been made on 23 October, citing:

> The current anarchic conditions, the serious violations of human rights and bloodshed that had occurred and the consequent unprecedented threat to peace and security of the region created by the vacuum of authority in Grenada.[62]

The third reason given was: 'To respond to a confidential appeal from the Governor-General, Sir Paul Scoon, to the OECS and other regional states to restore order on the island'.[63] The Governor-General could do this as, with the Prime Minister dead, he was the sole remaining source of governmental legitimacy in Grenada. During the four days of battle, all the detainees at Richmond Hill were freed. Some had been held for the entire duration of the PRG.

During the four days of battle some pigs got loose in the Point Salines area. They had not been fed for several days, and were hungry. In another startling parallel to events in the Fédon Revolution, where pigs are said to have fed on the slain hostages killed by Fédon, pigs ate at least a few of the corpses that lay unattended on the main battlefields around Calliste, Frequente, L'Ance aux Epines, Mount Hartman and Point Salines.

Not since the defeat of Fédon had the Grenadian people been in so much anguish. Centuries had been spent trying to shake off oppression and subjugation. The older folks had put their trust in Gairy, who promised them a different society to the one controlled by the people of the 'upper brackets'. Then there was the Federation and the ideal of Caribbean brotherhood that had been torpedoed by the Jamaican brothers and sisters who preferred to 'Go it Alone'. Next came Blaize and Eric Williams with the promise of unitary statehood, which was wrecked by the selfishness of Trinidadians and their lack of faith in Grenada. Now, even before the first US Black Hawk helicopter flew over St George's, Prime Minister George Chambers had slapped Grenadians in their collective face by banning Grenadians from entering Trinidad without a visa.

At home, both young and old had seen the Gairy regime become unbearably repressive. It would have to be another native son who would lead them out of the shambles of their dreams, and this time, to guide them into the Promised Land. Maurice Bishop had emerged as this saviour. Now he, too, was gone. Like Fédon, Maurice Bishop's remains were never found. [64]

Both Maurice Bishop and Julien Fédon had been approximately the same age when they took control of Grenada by armed revolution. Both were motivated to free the oppressed people of Grenada from injustice. Both leaders had made fatal mistakes. The first mistake was seek and accept the help of foreign countries, accept a foreign ideology, and engage hemispheric animosities in what was a local struggle against oppression. The other mistake was that of condoning unnecessary measures of suppression and brutality against their own Grenadian people.

Notes

1 Bishop, p. 4.
2 See Zwerneman, ch. 3.
3 *Ibid.*
4 The Ras Tafari are a social and religious group with origins in the protest group associated with Marcus Garvey. Ras Tafarianism quickly spread from Jamaica to other islands in the Caribbean, and to West Indian groups in North America and the United Kingdom. Ras Tafarianism was brought to the attention of the world by the famous Jamaican singer and musician Bob Marley who was a member of this group. Horace Campbell (p. 50) states that over 400 members of the Ras Tafari sect were members of the National Liberation Army, and participated in the overthrow of the Gairy regime.
5 People's Law no. 1, *Laws of Grenada*, Sir Archibald Nedd Law Library, St George's.
6 *Ibid.*
7 Campbell, Horace, p. 50.
8 Weed, herb, marijuana or ganja – same thing!
9 Sandford and Vigilante, p. 93. Also Seabury and McDougall, pp. 17–53.
10 See Seabury and McDougall, p. 17.
11 Sandford and Vigilante, p. 133.
12 Zwerneman, p. 63.
13 See US Department of State (1984), Document 1.
14 Approximately US$71 million.
15 National Security Record, *Report on the Congress and National Security Affairs*, Washington, June 1980.
16 The Young Pioneer Movement in Grenada was an extension of the movement in Cuba. Children of primary school age engaged in a militarized version of a movement otherwise similar to the Cubs and Brownies popular in Grenada since the late 1940s.
17 Zwerneman, p. 7.
18 Brizan, p. 412.

19 Zwerneman, p. 7.
20 Sandford and Vigilante, p. 30.
21 A euphemism for the Richmond Hill Prisons.
22 Sandford and Vigilante, p.70.
23 See Brizan, p. 422, Zwerneman, pp. 64–75, and Sandford and Vigilante, p. 30.
24 See Brizan, p. 422 and Zwerneman, pp. 64–75.
25 Zwerneman, pp. 63–4.
26 'To trust' is a West Indian institution simply meaning to have an account at a shop or establishment, where the goods or services are paid for periodically, usually on payday.
27 'Assembly 78' was an intensive self-evaluation by the Roman Catholic Church of its social action programmes in Grenada as these related to the ills and abuses in Grenadian society. It involved both the laity and the clergy, and was attended by concerned non-Catholic laity and clergy.
28 Zwerneman, p. 29.
29 Zwerneman, p. 56.
30 *Ibid.*
31 This was a personal warning given to me by an avid supporter of Maurice Bishop.
32 Zwerneman, p. 43.
33 Corpus Christi is one of the most celebrated of the feast days of the Catholic Church. It is marked in the formerly French islands of the OECS and in Trinidad by a street procession, in which the Sacrament is carried. The procession in Grenada follows a route from the Cathedral on Church Street, through the town of St George's to the Market Square, and then by a circuitous route back to the Cathedral.
34 See also US Dept of State and Dept of Defense, *Grenada Documents*, Documents 4 and 5, for the review of the churches in Grenada, complete with recommendations made by Michael Roberts and Keith Roberts, both officers of the PRG with special assignment to monitor the churches.
35 'Pumphead' or 'Pomphead' was the nickname for Keith Hayling. Hayling lost his life at the Fort on 19 October 1983.
36 Paterson, Maurice (1991), p. 32.
37 Sandford and Vigilante, p. 131.
38 *The Torchlight*, 19 Oct. 1979.
39 See Zwerneman, p. 75. Also personal communication with Ras Nna Nna.
40 Gentle, p. 138.
41 Peoples Law no. 81, *Laws of Grenada*, Sir Archibald Nedd Law Library, St George's.
42 Paterson, Maurice (1996), p. 54.
43 Counter-revolutionaries.
44 Brizan, p. 431.
45 US Dept of State and Dept of Defense, *Grenada Documents*, Extraordinary Meeting of the Central Committee of the NJM, 14–16 Sept., p. 10.
46 See Payne, Sutton and Thorndyke, p. 119.
47 Payne, Sutton and Thorndyke, p. 156.
48 Payne, Sutton and Thorndyke, p. 134.
49 I have generally refused to name the Fort. When the PRG came to power, Maurice renamed the historic Fort George 'Fort Rupert' in honour of his slain father. The Fort reverted to its earlier name of Fort George immediately after the end of the Revolution. With the passage of time, the name 'Fort Rupert' is almost forgotten, and its use might confuse contemporary readers.
50 Zwerneman, p. 83.
51 Payne, Sutton and Thorndyke, p. 136.
52 *Ibid.*

53 Brizan, p. 441.
54 Payne, Sutton and Thorndyke, p. 136.
55 *Ibid.*
56 These were persistent rumours at the time. I heard them from several different sources. It was also part of the general folklore that someone had cut off Bishop's head, and taken it home as a trophy. It was hidden under earth in a flowerpot, and a plant put in so that the pot would escape notice.
57 Gentle, p. 140.
58 Sandford and Vigilante, p. 165.
59 Young Leaders of Presentation College, *Under Cover of Darkness.*
60 Payne, Sutton and Thorndyke, p. 136.
61 See Lewis, p. 59.
62 US Department of State, p. 3.
63 *Ibid.*
64 See the booklet by the Young Leaders of Presentation College for an investigative discussion as to what happened to the bodies of Maurice Bishop and his colleagues after they were taken to Camp Calivigny following the events on the Fort.

The End of the Beginning

'If God can't come, he does send' is a Grenadian expression. The American Invasion was an answer to the prayers of beleaguered Grenadians. Almost the entire population welcomed the United States Marines and Airborne Divisions that arrived in Grenada. The advent of the Americans saved the lives of many, including George Louison and Kendrick Radix who would have faced a fate similar to Bishop had the Revolutionary Military Council been recognized as a legitimate government. Whatever were the stated or unstated motives of President Ronald Reagan, the immediate effect of the invasion on Grenada was to cut short the suffering and the trauma of the people of Grenada.

Why was it so difficult for some intellectuals outside Grenada to understand that? The barrage of protests from the Caribbean and wider world at the American invasion further traumatized the Grenadian people. Didn't the Grenadian people have the right to be thankful that the invasion by the United States on behalf of the OECS nations had prevented further Grenadian blood being spilt, and the institution of draconian regulations and restrictions on a dazed people? Didn't those who picked up their pens to protest realize that without the American invasion there would have been no end to the regime that had killed most of the leadership of the Grenadian Revolution, and no punishment for the perpetrators of this unprecedented atrocity? Was it possible that these intellectuals, comfortable in their own environments could be so callous as to put their own agenda and ideological arguments ahead of the feelings and safety of the Grenadian people? Had they forgotten that 'Stone a' river bottom no know what is sun hot'?[1]

After the American invasion, Grenada was ostracized by intellectual communities in Trinidad, Jamaica, Guyana, Britain and the British Commonwealth, the Black Caucus in the United States, and a host of leftist intellectuals who would for years after bombard the reading public with statements, pamphlets and books all lauding the Revolution, but never understanding nor telling the absolute truth about its darker side. Grenadians are still put on the defensive when intellectuals of a certain ilk try to tell them how they ought to think and ought to feel. Quite unlike the collapse of the Gairy regime, when Gairy's sins were detailed and repeated until the public knew them all, only a few were brave enough to detail some of the sins of the PRG. The denial of free speech and the fear of future reprisal froze the pens of many who would otherwise would have written to correct the skewed views published by supporters of the Revolution outside Grenada. Many secrets still lie unknown, buried in the memory of the perpetrators and also of the victims who survived.

Reversing the Revolution

Mirroring the events which took place immediately after the end of the Fédon Revolution, most of the persons involved in the attempted coup of the Maurice Bishop Government were caught within days. As soon as most of the fighting was over, roadblocks were established by the US forces to search for members of the Central Committee, officers of the PRA and any Cubans who had not reported as instructed to the Cuban Embassy, where they were given asylum until their departure could be arranged. Before the week was out, Bernard Coard, his wife Phyllis, and all of his supporters were captured and detained. Not one of the members of the Central Committee had joined the PRA and the Cubans in defending the Revolution. They were captured hiding in the homes of supporters.

Within a week, Grenadians could go back to work. A facility was established at Queen's Park and members of the PRA and Militia invited to turn themselves in with their guns and ammunition. After a brief questioning, most were allowed to go. Rewards were offered for information leading to the discovery of hidden ammunition. Daily detonations of the stockpiles of ammunition were carried out at Camp Calivigny. On one occasion, an extremely powerful bomb was discovered and detonated which was so powerful that a temporary evacuation order was in effect for all within a three-mile radius of Camp Calivigny. Grenadians and the world were absolutely amazed when the United States forces opened some of the factory shells at Frequente. They had no idea that so many weapons had been brought into the island. Acute embarrassment followed revelation after revelation. The Revolution had kept many of its secrets very well.

Gradually a measure of peace and order was restored under the supervision of the US forces and police from the OECS and Barbados, but there were several frightening incidents of young Militia members terrorizing people living from Belmont to Grand Anse stretch, principally, it appears, for the simple enjoyment of creating fear and panic, and to attempt the abduction and rape of young women.

By the time Grenadians began to move around their country freely, an Embassy of the United States had been established in the Ross Point Hotel near St George's, and a branch of the United States Information Service, which was first temporarily set up in classrooms of the University of the West Indies Centre loaned for the purpose, was established at the Charles of Grenada building in the heart of St George's. Both agencies would oversee the political and economic rehabilitation of Grenada.

The United States immediately allocated funds for the rehabilitation of Grenada. During the first two years after the Revolution, the United States spent US$37 million on construction projects, the bulk of the money (US$21.1 million) being earmarked for the completion of the airport at Point Salines. Aid money was also used to repair the road system that had deteriorated to a condition worse than it had been when the PRG seized power, to build a new sewer system, and to repair schools. Compensation was also paid to any person whose property had been damaged during the invasion. As soon as possible after the invasion, anyone who had been inadvertently injured, whether by US forces or by the Grenadian/Cuban forces, was flown to military hospitals for treatment.

The United States sent an offer to all Grenadian students in Cuba to abandon their studies and to accept instead scholarships in the United States. Most took up this offer, but a few remained in Cuba, especially if they were near to graduation. The first doctors trained in Cuba were allowed to register as medical practitioners in Grenada after they completed a two-year internship. Dentists were registered after a one-year internship. Unfortunately, students who had studied law could not fit back into the legal system, due to the different systems of law practised in the British Commonwealth and in Cuba. Those who had studied politics were similarly disadvantaged, due to the emphasis on Marxism and the political structures of a Marxist state.

The damage to the infrastructure of Grenada during the invasion was also repaired. The Richmond Hill Mental Hospital that had been bombed during the invasion was rebuilt. The former detainees, especially the long-term ones, were provided with the tools of their trade or seed money to start them on their way to economic recovery.

Experts from the United States visited Grenada and advised on every aspect of the economy. American businessmen were personally invited by President Reagan to consider setting up factories in Grenada. The first of these, a toy factory, became a source of acute embarrassment to the President, as the funds allocated to it were embezzled and the factory abandoned.

The United States Embassy contained within it several advisers whose job it was to strengthen the police force and guide the country in matters of security and international relations. One such officer was a young, handsome, well-educated black officer named John Butler. On 28 June 1989 a curious incident occurred at the Central Police Station in St George's. John Butler was shot and killed, along with the Acting Commissioner of Police, Cosmos Raymond. The alleged assassin was the Deputy Commissioner of Police, Grafton Bascombe, an officer on loan from the St Vincent government, who then shot himself. The investigations that followed left many questions unanswered and provided no real explanation to the public for the death of this promising young man and two senior police officers, one from their island neighbour.

The Interim Government

The United States, as always, tried to avoid being seen in the role of a colonizer. They urged the Governor-General, Sir Paul Scoon, to find a mechanism by which Grenada could be governed until elections could be held. In November 1983 Sir Paul Scoon appointed a twelve-person Advisory Council to assist him in the task of governance until arrangements could be made for elections. The members of the Advisory Council were chosen for their expertise in various fields and from across the spectrum of political opinion. The first choice for Chairman was Alister McIntyre, who was by this time a recognized name in the field of Caribbean and world economics. Unfortunately, he had to decline the invitation, but Sir Paul Scoon's second candidate, Nicholas Brathwaite, proved an excellent choice.

Brathwaite, a career civil servant, was born in Carriacou, one of many children of a large family. Like Marryshow before him, his early promise was noticed by a family friend, who persuaded his father to allow him to mentor Nicholas, to bring him to Grenada to attend school in St George's, having him live as a member of his own family. When Brathwaite graduated from secondary school, he chose teaching as his profession, was promoted and eventually transferred to an administrative position in the Ministry of Education. He was already educated in the soundest sense when he was sent to the University of the West Indies to read for a Bachelor's Degree in Education, which he achieved without difficulty. After early retirement from the civil service in Grenada, Brathwaite was appointed to serve as the head of the Commonwealth Youth Programme in Guyana. His leadership was known to be fair, sensitive and thoughtful. He proved to be the ideal person to help Grenada begin to heal.

The other members of the Council comprised Dr Alan Kirton, an economist; Arnold Cruickshank, an expert in agriculture and development; Patrick Emmanuel, an academic from the University of the West Indies with expertise in political science and trade union matters; James deVere Pitt, with a wide-ranging field of interest including education, the environment, science and technology; Joan Purcell, with both an academic background and a practitioner's experience in social welfare, social development and women's affairs; Ray Smith, a telecommunications engineer; Christopher Williams, with an interest in rural development and voluntary services; and Randolph Mark, a successful small farmer from St Andrew's, a philosopher and commentator on Grenadian affairs, and a firm advocate of nation-building through self-help and self-reliance. Tony Rushford was appointed Legal Adviser, but decided to resign after two weeks.

Every single member of the Advisory Council had been born in Grenada, although some were now serving in other Caribbean countries. Most were graduates of the University of the West Indies. They were among the best and most independent-minded of Grenada's sons and daughters, and went about their mandate of effecting their own demise by ensuring that all was in place for the restoration of the Westminster style of parliamentary democracy that had been chosen as the mode of government and was enshrined in the 1974 Independence Constitution of Grenada.

All but two members of the Advisory Council were given portfolios, and had offices in the major Ministries. Their mandate was to survey what needed to be done, leaving the major decisions and changes to an elected government. The Interim Government repealed only those People's Laws that would hinder the return to democracy. The holding of elections as soon as possible was a major priority. They also had to balance continued threats to national security with the need to effect the restoration of Grenada's sovereignty, as well as to attend to the everyday matters of the nation, which included the winding-up of the projects left incomplete at the fall of the People's Revolutionary Government. The Advisory Council became a focus for the invective of the unrealistic and unsympathetic foreign commentators who were against the American invasion. The Advisory Council was called a 'Puppet of the US Government', and the members were generally belittled for their agreement to participate in the Interim Government for their bruised and torn country.

The major project that had to be finished was the international airport. The United States was initially against the completion of the airport, but was persuaded that this project that would have major implications for the expansion of the tourist industry and the shipping of agricultural and horticultural products to overseas markets. In addition to the grants from the United States government, loans and grants enabled

Grenada to see the airport through to completion, and Sir Paul Scoon opened the Point Salines International Airport on 25 October 1984.

Elections

Voter registration for the general elections was held between April and June 1984. It was decided that the voters' lists should be constructed from scratch. The last elections were in 1976, and it was felt that having new lists would inspire the confidence of the voting population in the determination of the Governor-General and his Advisory Committee to restore the democratic process in Grenada. For the first time, each voter would be issued with a national identity card with a photograph, which they would have to present on Election Day.

For over twenty years Grenada had had government without there being a viable opposition. In preparation for the elections, political parties now mushroomed. The plethora of political parties reflected the various interferences with the democratic tradition that usually produced two strong parties under the Westminster model of government, traditional in Grenada and in the Commonwealth Caribbean. This unfortunate legacy would be carried forward into the short-term future of Grenadian politics.

In preparation for elections, Gairy returned to Grenada from the United States, where he had lived for the entire duration of the PRG. A surprise to many was that Gairy still commanded a loyal following both among the grassroots of the country and among the middle class. There were speculations that the GULP would win the elections, ushering in another dictatorial government. In the interest of defeating Gairy, the leadership of the parties led by Francis Alexis, Herbert Blaize, George Brizan and Winston Whyte agreed to work together and to form a single party to provide Grenada with the political leadership and a viable opposition to Gairy. The merger produced the National Party, and it was agreed that the veteran politician, Herbert Blaize, would lead it.

The Advisory Council was dissolved on 30 November 1984, and Grenada went to the polls on 3 December 1984. The National Party was chosen by the Grenadian voters to be the first post-revolutionary elected government. The GULP received 37 per cent of the votes cast, demonstrating that popular support for 'Uncle' Gairy was by no means dead.

Under the Blaize Government, structures that the PRG had put in place were either dismantled or given new names. The CPE became ACE (Agency for Continuing Education). The NISTEP programme was phased out, and the Grenada Teachers' College reopened. Civil servants who had espoused the Revolution were transferred into non-influential positions. A new organization for women replaced the National Organization for Women. Under the auspices of the Roman Catholic Church, the New Life Organization was founded, initially to retrain the members of the PRA and later for all school drop-outs, and sited at Pope Paul's Camp, which had become during the PRG a facility for indoctrination of the youth of the nation.

The new government instituted measures they deemed necessary to stabilize the country. One was a ban on all Communist literature. Another was declaring some former international supporters of the PRG *persona non grata*, and denying them entry to the country. The passports of a few members of the PRG and PRA were confiscated for a short while, to ensure that they remained in Grenada while investigation into the events of 19 October 1983 were completed.

As a climax to the US presence in Grenada, both the man who was later to become US President, George Bush Sr, and President Ronald Reagan visited Grenada. Vice-President Bush visited in March 1985. His visit was brief, and was a public relations gesture. Grenadians came out in their numbers to a rally in Tanteen to give him a rousing welcome, and to demonstrate their gratitude for the help the United States had given Grenada in its troubles. During his visit, Bush unveiled a memorial to US soldiers who had lost their lives during the American intervention. Later, Grenada would construct a national memorial located near the airport to these soldiers of the United States. The following year, in February 1986, President Ronald Reagan visited. A crowd of about 15,000 people gave him a vociferous welcome at a rally at Queen's Park. This contrasted sharply to the polite greeting given to Her Majesty Queen Elizabeth II when she visited in October of the same year.

The Trial of the Nineteen

The trial of Phyllis and Bernard Coard and others for the murder of Maurice Bishop and others began in April 1986. The courthouse in which the trial was held had to be specially commissioned for the trial, as an angry mob attacked the bus in which the accused were being taken to the normal courthouse at York House. Subsequently, the government decided not to risk putting the prisoners in harm's way by transporting them again. The accused were given the expensive lawyers they demanded for their defence, for they all pleaded 'Not Guilty'. After a trial that lasted nine months, and which was disrupted at every sitting by the accused, a verdict of 'Guilty' was brought in. Fourteen of the seventeen accused were sentenced to death by hanging, including the Coards, Strachan and Austin. The verdict was appealed, but the appeal was not successful.[2]

Herbert Blaize Dies

Prime Minister Herbert Blaize had been ailing for most of his term in office. He had received treatment at the some of the best military hospitals in the United States, but to no avail. He died just before Christmas on 19 December 1989. His body lay in state at York House on the day of his state funeral at the Anglican Church, St George's. His body was viewed by hundreds of Grenadians from all walks of life who passed in a sombre and orderly procession before his casket. After a state funeral his body was taken to Carriacou for burial. Apart from fighting cancer that was the cause of his physical decline, Blaize was heartbroken that his united party broke apart in 1987 when George Brizan, Francis Alexis and Tillman Thomas resigned their ministerial posts and formed the New National Party because of conflicts on policy matters. Nevertheless, Blaize struggled to hold the government together until the date of the next elections. His body gave up before he was ready, and for the six-month remainder of the National Party's term in office, the government was led by Ben Jones, a veteran politician from Grenville and a gentleman *par excellence*.

The Brathwaite Government

General elections were held on 13 March 1990, but the results were inconclusive. An agreement by the National Party, led by Ben Jones, to merge with the National Democratic Party (NDC), led by Nicholas Brathwaite, put that party in power, with Brathwaite at the helm. Grenada had high hopes of this government. During his term as Prime Minister, Nicholas Brathwaite once more demonstrated a leadership characterized by fairness, sensitivity and thoughtfulness. His first priority was the re-establishment of peace, stability, confidence and prosperity in Grenada. His success in doing so can be measured in the attitudes of people before and after his term of office. At the beginning of his term in office as Prime Minister, people were still timid and demoralized. By the end of his term, people were again confident of their right to free speech, and once again engaged in their favourite pastime of political discussion and criticism of the government.

Two important events during the Brathwaite Government will stand as memorials to Brathwaite's belief in justice, tolerance and freedom. The first one was the lifting of the ban on leftist literature and the easing of other restrictive measures such as the deportation of certain Marxists and the confiscation of the passports of former members of the Revolutionary Military Council which were instituted just after the invasion, and which had stayed in effect during the Blaize administration. Secondly, and more importantly, Brathwaite commuted the death sentences passed on fourteen of the nineteen prisoners 'On the Hill' to life imprisonment without the possibility of parole.

Brathwaite's efforts to re-create confidence in the stability of the country led to the establishment of a good investment climate. Although his single term as Prime Minister was only four years long, it was during this short period, and not before, that Grenadians regained their spirit and their sense of being free. Brathwaite was already beyond the usual retirement age for civil servants and private sector workers when he became Prime Minister. However, his job of leading his Cabinet was not easy. The strain of making so many strong personalities work as a team took a great toll of his health, and six months before elections were due he resigned, leaving George Brizan to lead the party into the election campaign.

The Mitchell Administration

When the results of the 1995 elections were announced, the New National Party led by Keith Mitchell had won eight seats, the NDC led by George Brizan won five, and the GULP led by Eric Gairy won two. Keith Mitchell, the new Prime Minister, immediately strengthened his government by forming a 'strategic cooperation agreement' with the GULP. This meant that the two members of the GULP who had won seats agreed to join the NNP for the purpose of forming the government. The government was sorely embarrassed at the end of 1998 when two of the Ministers, Raphael Fletcher and Grace Duncan, resigned from the party. Instead of trying to continue to govern under threat of a motion of no confidence, Mitchell called a 'snap' election. The new elections were held on 18 January 1998, and the results vindicated Mitchell, as his NNP won every seat, obtaining 90 per cent of the votes.

The Passing of an Era

In August 1997 Sir Eric Matthew Gairy, former Prime Minister and trade union leader, died after a long slow decline. His funeral service was held at the Trade Centre located in the electoral district that had been his 'sure seat' for so many years. The service was conducted by the Roman Catholic Bishop of St George's, Bishop Sydney Charles, who was assisted by Monsignor Cyril La Montagne. All the major churches in Grenada were represented. Archbishop Noel of the Spiritual Baptist Church was particularly resplendently attired for the occasion. Representatives of Caribbean governments and governments of nations friendly to Grenada were among the specially invited guests. The huge building and the grounds outside were filled with thousands of distressed mourners.

Before the service commenced, the casket containing Sir Eric's body lay in state, and thousands of mourners joined the long lines queuing to take a last look at 'The Leader' and to pay their last respects. Jerry Seales and Clarence Rapier, two younger members of the GULP, acted as an unofficial guard of honour. While functioning to control the more unrestrained of the mourners who might upset the casket, they nevertheless warmly invited all to 'Say goodbye to Uncle'. After the service, the crowd followed Sir Eric's casket to the place of burial in St George's Cemetery. The crowd was so huge that, before some of the vehicles carrying mourners could exit the precincts of the Trade Centre, the interment proceedings had already begun.

If one stands at Sir Eric's last resting place, the new twin national stadia for cricket and athletics can be seen. The Mount St Eloi/Cherry Hill point where Jacques Chadeau was hanged in 1808 is also plainly visible. The cemetery is on the slopes of Hospital Hill, which was fortified by Governor Macartney, and on which he was forced to surrender Grenada in 1779. Fort George (known as Fort Royale and Fort Rupert in differing times) is visible from the crest of Cemetery Hill, just a few yards up the road. From this crest also, the magnificent town of St George's can be seen, as well as the extensive renovation project to enlarge the port facilities, and therefore to support commerce in the island. Also visible is the Lagoon and Tanteen, the sites of the first European settlement and tobacco plantations. Beyond the mountains to the north, east and west lie the more rural parts of Grenada, with their own stories to tell.

Further down the hill, in the same cemetery where Gairy's mortal remains were laid, is Donovan's grave. Above, in the 'Portuguese' Cemetery, Marryshow lies with his mentors, the Franco family. Bishop, Creft, Whiteman and the victims of the massacres of 19 October most likely lie in this cemetery in a grave yet to be discovered. And lest we forget, ordinary people in their scores lie buried here. Less distinguished, but no less important, Grenada's greatness resulted from their imagination, innovation and hard work. The cemetery itself was donated to provide a place in which the cholera victims of the 1854 epidemic could be buried. And so in death and this place of monuments, the people of the past are remembered, and the future is glimpsed on the horizon.

Sir Eric's death marked the closing of an era. Once foreign-owned and governed from Europe, Grenada is now owned by the people, and governed by its own people. Gairy was the first Chief Minister to preside over a government elected by universal adult suffrage, a privilege won for Grenadians at that particular point in time by the constant clamouring of people like Donovan, Marryshow and C.F.P. Renwick. The baton of power has not always been handed over smoothly, often being dropped and needing to be picked up again. After decades of trial and error and three failed revolutions, Grenadians, resilient as ever, have their energy back, a little behind some of their Caribbean neighbours in terms of economic development, but fast catching up.

Sir Eric's funeral might well be regarded as the 'End of the Beginning'. The achievement of true independence for Grenada might well be in the future. Beset with all the problems of a small state with a dependent economy, surrounded by a new world order exemplified by shifting paradigms and changing alliances, Grenada has to find a way not only to survive but also to survive with pride.

Notes

1 This is a West Indian proverb meaning that those who had never experienced trouble could not know what trouble was.

2 Phyllis Coard was granted six months' leave from prison and released into the custody of her daughter in 2001 to seek medical attention abroad. She travelled to Jamaica, where she received treatment for colon cancer. She is still alive, and still on leave.

Bibliography

Books, Articles and Dissertations

Alleyne, Warren, *Barbados at War, 1939–1945*, Cole's Printery, Barbados, 1998.

Allsopp, Richard, *A Dictionary of Caribbean English Usage*, Oxford University Press, 1996.

American Medical Association, *The Encyclopedia of Medicine*, Random House, New York, 1989.

Andrews, H. Gordon, 'White Trash in the Antilles', in *Negro Anthology*, ed. Nancy Cunard, first published in 1934, reprinted by Negro Universities Press, New York, 1969.

Ashby, Timothy, 'Fédon's Rebellion', *Journal of the Society for Army Historical Research*, vol. 62, no. 251, pp. 155–68, and no. 252, pp. 227–35.

[Baillie, James] *A Few Remarks on Colonial Legislation as Connected with the Late Communications for the Noble Secretary of State for the Colonies by a Member of the Assembly of Grenada*, John Sphan, 1823.

Barome, Joseph, 'Spain and Dominica, 1493–1647', *Caribbean Quarterly*, vol. 12, no. 4 (1966).

Bayley, F.W.N. *Five Years' Residence in the West Indies*, William Kidd, London, 1830.

Bell, Hesketh J. *Obeah: Witchcraft in the West Indies*, first published in 1889, reprinted by Negro Universities Press, Connecticut, 1970.

Besson, Gerard and Bridget Brereton, *The Book of Trinidad*, Paria, Port of Spain, 1991.

Bishop, Maurice, *Selected Speeches, 1979–81,* Casas de las Americas, Havana, 1982.

Bracey, R. *Eighteenth-Century Studies and Other Papers*, Blackwell, Oxford, 1925.

Breese, Charlotte, *Hutch*, Bloomsbury, London, 2001.

Brereton, Bridget, *A History of Modern Trinidad, 1783–1962*, Heinemann, 1981.

Brinkley, Frances, *This is Carriacou*, 2nd edn, Carenage Press, St George's, 1971.

Brinkley, Frances, 'An Analysis of the 1750 Carriacou Census', *Caribbean Quarterly*, vol. 24, nos. 1&2 (1978).

Brizan, George, *Grenada – Island of Conflict*, 2nd edn, Macmillan Education, London and Basingstoke, 1998.

Buckley, Roger Norman, *Slaves in Red Coats: The British West India Regiments 1775–1815*, Yale University Press, New Haven and London, 1979.

Buckley, Roger Norman, *The British Army in the British West Indies, 1775–1815*, University of Florida Press and Press UWI, Jamaica, Trinidad and Barbados, 1998.

Buisseret David, 'The Elusive Deodand: A Study of Fortified Refuges of the Lesser Antilles', *Journal of Caribbean History*, vols 6 & 7 (1973).

Bullbrook, J.A. 'Aboriginal Remains of Trinidad and the West Indies', *Caribbean Quarterly*, vol. 1, no. 1 (1949).

Bullen, Ripley P. *The Archaeology of Grenada, West Indies*, University of Florida Press, Gainesville, 1964.

Burn, W.L. *The British West Indies*, reprinted by Greenwood Press, Westport, Connecticut, 1975.

Burn, W.L. *Emancipation and Apprenticeship*, Johnson's Reprint Corporation, New York, 1970.

[Campbell, John] *Candid and Impartial Considerations in the Nature of the Sugar Trade, the Comparative Importance of the British and French Islands in the West Indies with the Value and Consequence of St Lucia and Grenada, Truly Stated*, printed for R. Baldwin, London, 1763.

Campbell, Horace, 'The Rastafarians in the Eastern Caribbean', *Caribbean Quarterly*, vol. 20, no. 4. December 1980.

Caribbean Conservation Association, *Grenada Environmental Profile*, Caribbean Conservation Association, Barbados, 1991.

Clement, Paul C. *Petite Martinique: Traditions and Social Change*, Carib Books, New York, 1999.

Clyde, David F. *Health in Grenada*, Vade Mecum, London, 1985.

Clyne, Reginald H. *Against the Currents*, Grenada, 1996.

Coard, Frederick McDermott, *Bittersweet and Spice – These Things I Remember*, Arthur H. Stockwell, Ilfracombe, Devon, 1970.

Cody, Ann, 'From the Site of Pearls, Grenada: Exotic Lithics and Radiocarbon Dates', in *Proceedings of the Thirteenth Congress for Caribbean Archaeology*, Curacao, 1989.

Cody, Ann, 'Faces and Figures on Grenada: Their Historical and Cultural Relations', in *Rock Art Papers*, vol. 7, San Diego Museum Papers, no. 26, San Diego Museum of Man, 1990.

Cody Holdren, Ann, 'Raiders and Traders: Caraibe Social and Political Networks at the Time of the European Contact and Colonization in the Eastern Caribbean', a dissertation submitted for the partial satisfaction of the requirements for the degree of Doctor of Philosophy in Anthropology, University of California, Los Angeles, 1998.

Cox, Edward, *Free Coloureds in the Slave Societies of St Kitts and Grenada, 1763–1833*, University of Tennessee Press, Knoxville, 1984.

Cox, Edward, *Rekindling the Ancestral Memory: King Ja Ja of Opobo in St Vincent and Barbados, 1888–1891*, Department of History, University of the West Indies, Cave Hill, and the Barbados Museum and Historical Society, St Ann's Garrison, Barbados, 1998.

Crouse, Nellis M. *French Pioneers in the West Indies*, Octagon, New York, 1977.

Cunard, Nancy (ed.) *Negro Anthology*, first published in 1934, reprinted by Negro Universities Press, New York, 1969.

David, Christine, *The Folklore of Carriacou*, Coles Printery, Barbados, 1985.

Davis, Dave D. and R. Christopher Goodwin, 'Island Carib Origins: Evidence and Nonevidence', *American Antiquity*, vol. 55, no. 1 (1990).

Devas, Raymond P. *Up Hill and Down Dale in Grenada*, Sands, London, Edinburgh and Glasgow, 1926.

Devas, Raymond P. *Conception Island. Or The Troubled Story of the Catholic Church in Grenada, B.W.I.*, Sands, London, 1932.

Devas, Raymond P. 'The Caribs', n.p., *circa* 1952.

Devas, Raymond P. *History of the Island of Grenada, 1498–1796*, Carenage Press, St George's, 1974.

Duffus, Herbert, H. Aubrey Fraser and Archbishop Samuel Carter, *Report of the Duffus Commission of Enquiry into the Breakdown of Law and Order, and Police Brutality in Grenada*, St George's, 1975.

Eaden, John (ed.) *The Memoirs of Père Labat, 1693–1705*, Frank Cass, 1970.

Edwards, Brian, *History Civil and Commercial of the British West Indies*, T. Miller, Cheapside, 1815.

Emmanuel, Patrick, *Crown Colony Politics in Grenada 1917–1951*, Institute of Social and Economic Studies, University of the West Indies, 1978.

Ferguson, James, *Grenada – Revolution in Reverse*, Latin American Bureau (Research and Action), UK, *circa* 1990.

Fortesque, J.W. 'The West Indian Rebellion', in *Macmillan's Magazine*, vol. 70, October (1894).

Franklyn, Omawale Dave, *Morne Sauteurs (Leapers Hill): Encounter Between Two Worlds in Grenada, 1650–1654*, Talented House, St George's, 1992.

Franklyn, Omawale Dave, *Bridging the Two Grenadas*, Talented House, St George's, 1999.

Garraway, D.G. *A Short Account of the Insurrection that Broke out in Grenada*, St George's, 1823.

Gentle, Eileen, *Before the Sunset*, Shoreline, Quebec, 1989.

Gomes, Sue-Anne, 'Phillipe-Rose Roumé de Saint-Laurent – The Coloniser of Trinidad', in *The Book of Trinidad*, ed. Bridget Brereton, Paria, Port of Spain, 1991.

Goveia, Elsa V. *A Study on the Historiography of the British West Indies to the end of the Nineteenth Century*, Mexico, 1956.

Government of Grenada, *The Grenada Handbook and Directory, 1946*, compiled by E.Gittens-Knight, St George's, 1946.

Grant, Kenneth James, *My Missionary Memories*, Imperial, Halifax, Nova Scotia, *circa* 1923.

Grenada Planter, A [Gordon Turnbull] *A Brief Enquiry into the Causes of the Insurrection*, London, 1796.

Groome, John R. *A Natural History of the Island of Grenada*, Grenada, 1970.

Hall, Douglas, 'Incalculability as a Feature of Sugar Production during the Eighteenth Century', *Social and Economic Studies*, vol. 10, no. 3 (1961).

Harewood, Jack, 'Population Growth in Grenada in the Twentieth Century', *Social and Economic Studies*, vol. 15, no. 2 (1960).

Hay, John, *Narrative of the Insurrection in the Island of Grenada*, J. Ridgeway, London, 1823.

Honychurch, Lennox, *The Dominica Story – A History of the Island*, Macmillan Education, London and Basingstoke, 1995.

Hoyos, F. Alexander, *Barbados – A History from Amerindians to Independence*, Macmillan Education, 1978.

Hughes, Alister, 'The Saga of the *Bianca C*', *Greeting Magazine*, Winter 1993/94.

Jacobs, C.M. *Joy Comes in the Morning: Elton Griffith and the Shouter Baptists*, Caribbean Historical Society, Port of Spain, 1996.

Jacobs, Curtis, 'African Symbolisms in Fédon's Rebellion', History Forum paper, Department of History, University of the West Indies, 28 February 2000.

Jessamy, Michael, *Forts and Coastal Batteries of Grenada*, Roland's Image, Grenada, 1998.

Jesse, C. 'Sold for a Song', *Caribbean Quarterly*, vol. 13, no. 4 (1967).

Keens-Douglas, Paul, *Tell Me Again*, Keensdee, Trinidad, 1979.

Latin America Bureau, *Grenada – Whose Freedom?* Latin America Bureau (Research and Action), UK, 1984.

Laurence, K.O. *Immigration into the West Indies in the 19th Century*, Caribbean Universities Press, Barbados, 1971.

Lewis, Gordon K. *Grenada: The Jewel Despoiled*, Johns Hopkins University Press, Baltimore and London, 1987.

Lindsay, Jan, John Shepherd and Lloyd Lynch, 'Kick 'em Jenny Submarine Volcano: A Discussion of Hazards and the New Alert Level System', paper given at the Grenada Country Conference, University of the West Indies, University Centre, Grenada, 7–9 January 2002.

Lucas, C.H. *An Address to the St Andrew's Detachment of the Grenada Contingent*, n.p., *circa* 1939.

McDaniel, Lorna, 'Memory Songs: Community Fight and Conflict in the Big Drum Ceremony of Carriacou, Grenada', PhD thesis, University of Maryland, UMI Dissertation Service, Ann Arbor, Michigan, 1986.

McIntosh, Norma, *'Hurricane Janet' in Grenada and Carriacou*, Advocate, Bridgetown, *circa* 1955.

McMahon, Francis, *A Narrative of the Insurrection of Grenada*, St George's, 1823.

Mark, Randolph, *The History and Development of the Royal Mt Carmel Waterfalls, Grenada, West Indies*, St Andrew's Development Organisation, 1995.

Marshall, Bernard, 'Attempts at Windward/Leeward Federation', *Caribbean Quarterly*, vol. 18, no. 2 (1972).

Marshall, Bernard, *Society and Economy in the British Windward Islands, 1763–1823*, PhD thesis, University of the West Indies, Mona, Jamaica, 1972.

Marshall, Woodville K. *The Social and Economic Development of the Windward Islands, 1838–1865*, PhD thesis, University of the West Indies, Mona, Jamaica, 1963.

Marshall, Woodville K., 'Metayage in the Sugar Industry of the British Windward Islands, 1838–1965', *Jamaican Historical Review*, May (1965).

Marshall, Woodville K. 'Notes on Peasant Development in the West Indies since 1938', *Social and Economic Studies*, vol. 17, no. 3, Sept. (1968).

Marshall, Woodville K., 'Provision Ground and Plantation Labour in Four Windward Islands', in *Cultivation and Culture: The Shaping of Slave Life in the Americas*, ed. Ira Berlin and Philip D. Morgan, University Press of Virginia, Charlottesville, 1993.

[Moyne Commission Report] 1938–39, *Report of the West India Royal Commission*, HMSO, London, 1945.

Naipaul, V.S. *The Middle Passage*, Penguin, Harmondsworth, 1969.

Narrative of the Proceedings upon the Complaint Against Governor Melvill, A, printed for T. Beckett and P.A. de Hondt in the Strand, London, 1770.

National Geographic Society, 'Crossroads Cultures' in *Lost Empires, Living Tribes*, National Geographic Society, Washington, 1982.

National Security Record, *Report on the Congress and National Security Affairs*, Washington, June 1980.

Ober, Frederick A. *Camps in the Caribbees*, Lee & Shepard, Boston, 1886.

Olsen, Fred, *Indian Creek: Amerindian Site in Antigua, West Indies*, University of Oklahoma Press, Norman, 1974.

Olsen, Fred, *On the Trail of the Arawaks*, University of Oklahoma Press, Norman, 1974.

Paterson, Lieutenant Daniel (Assistant to the Quartermaster General), *A Topographical Description of the Island of Grenada surveyed by Monsier*

Pinel in 1763 by Order of the Government with the Addition of English Names, Alternations of Property and other Improvements To Present Time, W. Faden Baldwin, London [1780].

Paterson, Maurice, *The Future of the Past*, Carenage Press, St George's, 1991.

Paterson, Maurice, *Big Sky, Little Bullet*, rev. edn, published by arrangement with the St George's Bookshop, Grenada, 1996.

Payne, Anthony, Paul Sutton and Tony Thorndyke, *Grenada – Revolution and Invasion*, St Martin's Press, New York, 1984.

Peters, Cecelia and Derek Penny, *Our Country – Grenada* (Caribbean Social Studies Series 4), Macmillan, London and Basingstoke, 1994.

Ragatz, Lowell J. *The Fall of the Planter Class in the British Caribbean, 1763–1833*, Octagon, New York, 1963.

Raynal, Abbé Guiallamme T.F. *A Philosophical and Political History of the Settlements and Trade of the Europeans in the East and West Indies. Translated from the French by J.O. Justamond, FRS with a New Set of Maps adapted to the Work, and a copious Index*, originally published in 1798 by J. Mundell, reprinted by Negro Universities Press, New York, 1969.

Richardson, Bonham C. 'A Respectable Riot: Guy Fawkes Night in St George's, Grenada', *Journal of Caribbean History*, vol. 27, no. 1 (1992).

Roberts, George W. 'Immigration from the Island of Barbados', *Social and Economic Studies*, Institute of Social and Economic Research, UWI, vol. 4, no. 3, Sept. (1955).

Roberts, G.W. and J. Byrne, 'Summary Statistics on Indenture and Associated Migration Affecting the West Indies, 1834–1918', reprinted from *Population Studies* in *CSO Papers, Trinidad and Tobago*, no. 4, Dec. (1967).

Roget, Jacques Petitjean (ed.) *Historie de l'Isle de Grenade*, Les Presses de l'Université de Montréal, 1975.

Roux, Phillipe de, *Le Marquis de Casaux, un Planteur des Antilles, Inspirator de Mirabeau*, Societe de l'Historie des Colonies Francaises, Librair Larose, Paris, 1951.

St Bernard, Cosmo, 'The *Island Queen* Disaster', in *Grenadian Voice*, Friday 30 July 1999.

Sandford, Gregory, and Richard Vigilante, *Grenada: The Untold Story*, Madison, Lanham, New York, and London, 1984.

Schoenhals, Kai, *Grenada* (World Bibliographic Series vol. 119), Clio, Oxford, California and Colorado, 1990.

Scott, David, *To the West Indies and Back: One Hundred Days*, Motherwell, Scotland, *circa* 1908.

Seabury, Paul and Walter A. McDougall (eds) *The Grenada Papers*, ICS Press, Institute for Contemporary Studies, San Francisco, 1984.

Searle, Chris (ed.) *Carriacou and Petit Martinique in the Mainstream of the Revolution*, Fedon, St George's, 1982.

Shepard, C.Y. *Peasant Agriculture in the Leeward and Windward Islands*, Imperial College of Tropical Agriculture, St Augustine, Trinidad, 1945.

Sheppard, Jill, *The 'Redlegs' of Barbados*, KTO, New York, 1977.

Sheppard, Jill, *Marryshow of Grenada: An Introduction*, Lechworth, Barbados, 1987.

Sheridan, Richard, *Sugar and Slavery*, Johns Hopkins University Press, Baltimore, 1974.

Sheridan, Richard, 'The Condition of Slaves in the Settlement and Economic Development of the British Windward Islands, 1763–1775', *Journal of Caribbean History*, vol. 24, no. 2 (1990).

Simpson, George Eaton, *Relgious Cults of the Caribbean: Trinidad, Jamaica and Haiti*, 3rd edn, Institute of Caribbean Studies, University of Puerto Rico, Rio Piedras, 1980.

Sinclair, Norma, 'A Wedding in Petit Martinique', *The Greeting*, vol. 12, (2000).

Singham, Archie, *The Hero and the Crowd in a Colonial Polity*, Yale University Press, New Haven and London, 1968.

Smith, Michael G. *Kinship and Community in Carriacou*, Yale University Press, New Haven and London, 1962.

Smith, Michael G. *The Dark Puritan*, Department of Extra Mural Studies, University of the West Indies, Jamaica, 1963.

Smith, Michael G. *The Plural Society in the British West Indies*, University of California Press, Berkeley and Los Angeles, 1965.

Smith, Michael G. *Culture, Race and Class in the Commonwealth Caribbean*, Department of Extra Mural Studies, University of the West Indies, Jamaica, 1984.

Springer, Hugh, *Reflections on the Failure of the First West Indian Federation*, Harvard, 1963.

Stark, James H. *Stark's Guide and History of Trinidad: Including Tobago, Grenada and St Vincent; also a Trip up the Orinoco and a Description of the Great Venezuelan Pitch Lake; Containing a Description of Everything Relating to These Places that Would be of Interest to Tourists and Residents*, James H. Stark, Boston, 1897.

Steele, Beverley A. 'Grenada, an Island State: Its History and its People', *Caribbean Quarterly*, vol. 20, no. 1 (1974).

Steele, Beverley A., 'The East Indian Indenture and the Work of the Presbyterian Church among the Indians in Grenada', *Caribbean Quarterly*, vol. 22, no. 1 (1976).

Sutty, Lesley Ann, 'A Preliminary Inventory and Short Essay on Ceramic and Stone Artifacts from Recent Excavations on Grenada and in the Southern Grenadines', unpublished paper held at the Grenada Centre, University of the West Indies, n.d., *c.* 1980s.

[Turnbull, Gordon] *A Narrative of the Revolt and Insurrection of the French Inhabitants of the Island of Grenada*, by an Eyewitness, Edinburgh, 1795.

US Department of State, *Grenada: A Preliminary Report*, Washington, DC, 1983.

US Department of State and Department of Defence, *The Grenada Documents: An Overview and Selection*, Washington DC, 1984.

University of the West Indies Conference Committee (eds) *Independence for Grenada – Myth or Reality?* Institute of International Relations, UWI, St Augustine, Trinidad, 1974.

Wells, Septimus, *Historical and Descriptive Sketch of the Island of Grenada*, Aston W. Gardener, Kingston, Jamaica, 1890.

Williams, Eric, *From Columbus to Castro*, Andre Deutsch, London, 1970.

Wise, Thomas Turner, *A Review of Events Which have Happened in Grenada*, Grenada, 1795.

Wood, Donald, *Trinidad in Transition*, Oxford University Press for the Institute of Race Relations, London and New York, 1968.

Young Leaders of Presentation College, *Under Cover of Darkness*, Young Leaders of Presentation College, Grenada, 2002.

Zwerneman, Anthony J. *In Bloody Terms*, Greenlawn, Indiana, *circa* 1984.

Reports, letters and other documents

Under each archive, these are listed chronologically, as far as possible.

Public Library, St George's, Grenada

Blue Books, 1913, 1915.

Report and General Abstract on the Census of 1901, St George's.

Report and General Abstract on the Census of 1921, St George's.

Report and General Abstract of the Registrar General, St George's, 1901–23.

The West Indian, 2 April 1916; 14 Feb. 1943; 14 Sept. 1962.

'Report of the Labour Department, 1951', Grenada Council Paper, 1954.

University of the West Indies

Grenada Centre

Cary Papers (copies of letters held by the Massachusetts Historical Society, Boston): 6, 10, 12, 14 May; 16 June; 12 Aug; 15 Sept. 1795.

Address of Sir Eric Matthew Gairy, Prime Minister of Grenada, to the Thirty-Second Session of the General Assembly of the United Nations, 7 Oct. 1977, Grenada.

The Torchlight newspaper, 1979.

Mona Campus, Kingston, Jamaica
'Report on Land Settlement in Grenada and Carriacou for 1938', Council Paper
  no.18, 10 Nov. 1939.

St Augustine Campus, Trinidad
British Parliamentary Papers, Sessions 1856–58, General Reports of the
  Emigration Commission.

The Registry of the Supreme Court, York House, St George's

Old French Records: 'Births, Deaths and Record of Property', vol. July
  1772–Aug. 1809.
'Presentation on the Propriety of Permitting the French Inhabitants to Remain in
  Grenada', 1784.
Minutes of the Legislative Council, 23 July 1915; 30 March 1916; 23 Nov. 1917;
  29 Sept. 1939.

Sir Archibald Nedd Law Library, Supreme Court, York House, St George's

Government of Grenada, *Laws of Grenada*, 1915–40.

British Library, London

Third Annual Report of the Society for the Education of the Poor, W.E. Baker, 1827.
St Andrew's Journal and La Baye Miscellany, edited by Alexander McCombie,
  Free Press, 1828, 1829.
*Reports made for the year 1863 to the Secretary of State from the Governor of.the
  British Colonies, Transmitted with the Blue Book for 1863, Part 1*, HMSO,
  London, 1865.
*Annual Report on the Social and Economic Progress of the People of Grenada,
  1937 and 1938*, HMSO, London, 1939.
Minutes of the Board of the Grenada Legislative Council, various years.

Public Records Office, London

Colonial Office papers.
Blue Book Reports, 1913–1915.
Slave Registers for St George's, St Andrew's, St David's and Carriacou, Grenada,
  1817: T71/267.
'Answers to Queries Submitted by the Commissioners of Compensation to the
  Assistant Commissioner of Grenada on 8 May 1834'.
Dr Howard S. Colwell, 'Report of the Grenada Ankylostomiasis Commission',
  1916, enclosed with Dispatch no.25 to the Secretary of State for the Colonies
  from the Governor, 29 Jan. 1917: CO 321/294.

'Report of the Visit of Major G.M. Orde-Browne to Grenada, 16–21 Feb. 1939 to the Secretary of State for the Colonies', 2 March 1939.

Scottish Record Office, Edinburgh

George Home papers, GD 267/5/19/1.

Index